American Social Leaders and Activists

NEIL A. HAMILTON

☑® Facts On File, Inc.

American Social Leaders and Activists

Facts On File, Inc.
132 West 31st Street
New York NY 10001

Library of Congress Cataloging-in-Publication Data

Hamilton, Neil A., 1949–
    American social leaders and activists / by Neil A. Hamilton.
        p. cm. — (American biographies)
    Includes bibliographical references and index.
    ISBN 0-8160-4535-6
    1. Social reformers—United States—Biography—Dictionaries. I. Title. II. Series.
    HV27 .H345 2002
    303.48'4'092273—dc21

Facts On File books are available at special discounts when purchased in bulk quantities for businesses, associations, institutions, or sales promotions. Please call our Special Sales Department in New York at (212) 967-8800 or (800) 322-8755.

You can find Facts On File on the World Wide Web at http://www.factsonfile.com

Text design by Joan M. Toro

c.1

Cover design by Cathy Rincon

Printed in the United States of America

VB Hermitage 10 9 8 7 6 5 4 3 2 1

This book is printed on acid-free paper.

CONTENTS

Note on Photos

Many of the illustrations and photographs used in this book are old, historical images. The quality of the prints is not always up to modern standards, as in some cases the originals are from glass negatives or are damaged. The content of the illustrations, however, made their inclusion important despite problems in reproduction.

LIST OF ENTRIES

v

ACKNOWLEDGMENTS

I would like to thank Bret Heim, the government documents and reference librarian at Thomas Byrne Memorial Library in Mobile, Alabama, for his help in tracking down sources, and Phyllis Compretta, public service assistant, for her invaluable assistance in acquiring numerous books and articles through interlibrary loan in her usual prompt and courteous manner.

I owe a special debt of thanks to Nicole Bowen, executive editor for American history at Facts On File. She originated the idea for this book and provided invaluable guidance in seeing it through to publication. My thanks goes also to her assistant Gene Springs for helping to acquire photographs.

Finally, I would like to thank my brother for his words of encouragement and my mother for the time she took in reading the profiles and offering suggestions that made them clearer and more succinct.

My hope is that the reader will find as much enjoyment in reading the entries as I had in researching and writing them. The leaders and activists herein described are but a sampling, but they attest to the diversity of individual influence that worked largely from outside the mainstream political structure to shape and reshape American society.

INTRODUCTION

The words *social leaders and activists* in this book's title refer to those men and women who have been at the forefront of social reform and, to a lesser extent, those who have directed reactionary movements. America owes its birth to social reform. When the Puritans arrived at Massachusetts Bay in 1619 they carried with them their Bibles and their goal to improve the individual and society. They intended to build a City upon a Hill, a settlement purged of corruption, sin, and profanity—one where all would be joined in a harmonious community filled with brotherly love. In that way each settler would be morally and spiritually uplifted (though still deprived of the certainty of salvation, a bestowal made by an inscrutable God). They intended their settlement to be a model for the rest of the world to emulate.

In short order, other societies appeared with their own lofty goals: William Penn in 1681 with his "holy experiment" of Pennsylvania; the Labadists in 1684 with their commune dedicated to Christ; Johanne Conrad Beissel in 1732 with his pietist commune; and so on. Each was driven by ideas generated in Europe and by the beckoning American frontier that allowed a seemingly unfettered pursuit of innovative plans. But inherent in each society were forces that opposed it—those who wanted a corrective and reformers ready to point people in a totally different direction. Such has been the nature of society that it incubates its own seeds of change.

Social reform has ranged all the way from the peaceful to the violent and from those who have sought minor adjustments to those who have sought radically altered systems. Such diversity has made it difficult to define *reformer* with precision and to distinguish among moderate and radical reformers. Ronald G. Walters recognized this problem in *American Reformers: 1815–1860* (1978): "It is time to face up to a serious difficulty in terminology. It concerns the words *radical* and *reformer*." In struggling with a definition, he concluded:

> By radicals I mean those who wish to change the structure of society. By reformers I mean those who wish to improve individuals or existing social, economic, and political arrangements. . . . Radicals seek to overturn the present order while successful reformers may actually strengthen it by making it work better.

That distinction, however, remained murky, as Walters himself noted when he said that it "frequently breaks down." It can be argued, for example, that in seeking to gain independence from a monarchical government, American revolutionaries in 1776 wanted to change the structure of society; it can just as easily be argued that they sought independence to maintain and improve the existing social, economic, and political order (minus the imperial government and its regulations).

In writing *American Social Leaders and Activists*, I have found Walters's distinction useful in measuring the degree of reform, but I have subsumed radicals under the broader term *reformers*. In addition, Walters stated: "Some scholars try to draw a line between genuine reformers . . . and reactionaries, whom they see as wanting change to move backward, toward old ways of doing things."

Under the rubric *activists,* I have endeavored to survey a handful of reactionaries, such as white supremacists.

Obviously, I have made no attempt to include all of America's reformers, a narrative that would take many volumes. Herein the reader will find a sampling encompassing prominent categories such as abolitionists, socialists, communists, temperance crusaders, communards, women's suffragists, peace advocates, civil rights workers, labor organizers, and antiwar protesters. I have arbitrarily chosen those people I consider to be the most prominent, most controversial or interesting, most useful to study, and most representative in the given categories. Admittedly, this approach allows wide latitude for disagreement about who should have been included and who should have been left out of this dictionary.

I have also worked within guidelines set down by the publisher for the series that encompasses this book, meaning that I have tried to exclude reformers whose work was primarily political, religious, literary, artistic, athletic, entrepreneurial, technological, or scientific and so are covered in other books in the series. Here again, though, my decision was subject to close calls. For example, despite Martin Luther King, Jr.'s, status as a minister, I decided to include him because his secular impact outweighed his religious one and because to discuss civil rights reformers without him would leave the category devoid of its most dynamic leader. I have also included Upton Sinclair, whose run for public office as a socialist took him beyond his literary career, and Rachel Louise Carson, whose scientifically based book *Silent Spring* is central to understanding the modern environmental movement. Finally, I have focused on post-Revolutionary America, particularly picking up the story with abolitionism.

In fact, abolitionism emerged after the Revolution as a vanguard in the antebellum reform movement, expressing the ideals found in the Declaration of Independence. Over the ensuing years, other reforms would reflect the country's changing political, economic, and social environment.

Abolitionism reacted to more than the existence of slavery; it reacted to its spread into the western territories. To a certain extent, it reflected

the values of evangelical Christianity, whose adherents suggested that by eliminating slavery, Americans would uplift society morally. Such evangelical enthusiasm carried over to the temperance movement. Many abolitionists teethed on temperance works that called for a more righteous society.

The women's rights movement was also a part of the abolitionist connection. Whereas some abolitionists thought women should remain in the background, others such as William Lloyd Garrison thought that women should have a central role in the movement, and they insisted that the fight for black rights march hand in hand with that for women's rights.

Several reformers in the antebellum period established communes. These ranged from the religious to the secular, from those that allowed private property to those that forbade it. Because antebellum reform occurred amid a changing economy—whose overall growth provided the wherewithal for reformers to experiment and whose changing social practices produced a dissonance that encouraged reformers to seek a better way of life—it has been said that the communes confronted "for the first time . . . the effects of the modern industrial world."

Industrial development accelerated so rapidly after the Civil War and produced so many problems—urban slums, child labor, corrupt politics, to name a few—that it gave birth to Progressive reform. Diverse and dynamic, Progressivism tried to cure industrial and urban ills. Largely middle-class in sensibility and background, Progressives established settlement houses to help immigrants, peace groups to end war, suffrage organizations to secure women's right to vote, birth control clinics to protect women's health, children's bureaus to protect youths from abuse and families from disintegration, and conservation programs to protect the natural environment from destruction. Within the spirit of the era, white and black reformers formed civil rights groups to challenge Jim Crow segregation, while black nationalists organized to separate African Americans from white society.

The civil rights movement did much to shape reform after World War II by exposing injustice during a decade—the 1950s—when, in general, conformity and complacency prevailed. In the 1960s it splintered into the black power movement and provided the training ground for white college students who organized campus protests for free speech and against the Vietnam War.

During the 1960s and 1970s reform entered a dynamic and diverse stage as part of a countercultural protest. The black power and antiwar activists were joined by women's liberation advocates, the Chicano movement, the environmental crusade, violent revolutionary groups, and many others. By the late 1970s, the counterculture had weakened, exhausted by its own spent energy, by factional fights, by a conservative reaction, and by government efforts to repress it. Yet there appeared new reformers and activists who advocated militias and antiabortion crusades, fought to protect civil liberties, and grappled again with civil rights and women's rights issues while trying to correct numerous other social injustices.

As surely as society remained imperfect, social leaders and activists, reformers and reactionaries, continued their work, forming a dynamic that was crucial to propelling America in untested directions. Whatever their own time, reformers who sought to improve the individual and society often emulated the 1960s vision of Senator Robert Kennedy: "Some people see things as they are and say why. I dream things that never were and say why not?"

Abbott, Grace
(1878–1939) *social worker, child labor reformer*

As director of the Immigrants' Protective League and head of the federal Children's Bureau, Grace Abbott was an important force in social reform. She was born on November 17, 1878, in Grand Island, Nebraska, the daughter of Othman Abbott, a lawyer and businessman, and Elizabeth Griffin Abbott.

Othman Abbott influenced Grace through the value he put on reading and discussing political ideas. So, too, did Elizabeth Abbott, with her participation in the women's suffrage movement. Grace later remembered that her mother used to tell her and her sister, the reformer Edith Abbott, "I was always a suffragist, and . . . you can be suffragists too because it is right and just." In 1882, Grace met SUSAN BROWNELL ANTHONY, who stayed at the Abbott house during a lecture tour.

Grace Abbott graduated from Grand Island College in 1898, and she began teaching school in the small town of Broken Bow. A bout with typhoid fever caused her to quit, however, and she spent the next several years recuperating and teaching at Grand Island. She interrupted that routine when she took graduate courses at the University of Nebraska from 1902 to 1903. In 1907 she left Grand Island to enroll at the University of Chicago (where she had already taken a few courses). She primarily studied economics, political science, and law, which were traditionally male

bastions. In 1909 Abbott obtained her doctorate in political science.

While enrolled at the university, Abbott lived at Hull-House, the settlement house founded by JANE ADDAMS to help immigrants. In *Two Sisters for Social Justice: A Biography of Grace and Edith Abbott* (1983), Lela B. Costin writes that Hull-House and Chicago allowed Abbott to "find a creative solution to the restrictive status of women" and to meet her "strong personal needs for work and achievement, and contribute to social reform."

By 1909 Abbott had joined the Immigrants' Protective League, formed just two years earlier, and soon thereafter became its director. Unlike other charitable organizations, the league rejected the notion that the problems suffered by immigrants stemmed from personal limitations; instead, they believed that these problems arose from environmental conditions, such as slums or oppressive jobs. Also, Abbot opposed the eradication of immigrant culture; to her the cultures added diversity and richness to society.

Many Americans, though, disagreed with Abbott and thought the immigrant culture a threat to traditional American values. They pressured Congress to pass legislation restricting immigration, especially from southern and eastern Europe. Abbott fought hard against such a law but eventually lost.

To those who argued that the immigrants depressed wages for workers, Abbott said that rather than restrict the influx of immigrants, Congress should pass measures to protect immigrants in the

Grace Abbott fought for social reform on behalf of the urban working classes and is shown here as chief of the Children's Bureau of the Department of Labor. *(Library of Congress)*

workplace. To those who argued that when fully a third of the immigrants returned home, they took with them the wealth they had accumulated in the United States, Abbott answered that those who returned "had never been known to take back with [them] the railroads, canals, and subways" that they had built "or the great industries" in which they had worked.

Abbott especially sympathized with young peasant women, who as newcomers to America often felt lost. She reported to the league:

> Most of them are, at first, homesick and disappointed. The streets of the city are not always broad and beautiful, and life not always gay and bright as they had hoped it would be. . . . Sometimes it seems to the peasant girls as if they had exchanged green fields and woods and the long, quiet winters for a hideous round of noise, heat, and bitter cold.

Abbott worked with the Cook County Bar Association to see that immigrants in Chicago had access to interpreters who could help them in court. She convinced the city government to investigate employment agencies that found work for immigrants but sometimes cheated them out of money, and she persuaded the Illinois legislature to pass a law stating that work contracts for immigrants must be written in a language they understood. She was also instrumental in getting Congress to pass legislation in 1913 that required inspectors and matrons to be posted on trains so that immigrants could be provided with directions and help as they traveled from, for example, New York City to Chicago.

At about the same time, Abbott joined other women in lobbying the Illinois legislature for a law that would grant women's suffrage. In 1913 their effort resulted in legislation that allowed women to vote in state and local elections, thus making Illinois the first state east of the Mississippi River to pass a women's suffrage bill.

Still at Hull-House in 1915, Abbott served as a delegate to an international conference of pacifist women at the Hague. With World War I under way, the women tried to convince the belligerent countries to engage in continuous mediation. The following year, Abbott organized a Conference of Oppressed or Dependent Nationalities held in Washington, D.C. The conference stressed the right of people everywhere to determine their own future without interference from outside countries.

In 1917, the same year that Abbott published her book *The Immigrant and the Community,* she became director of the child labor division of the U.S. Children's Bureau in Washington, D.C. The bureau had been created in 1912 to investigate all matters concerning the welfare of children, including infant mortality, childhood diseases, juvenile courts, and child labor.

In 1919 Abbott returned to Illinois as director of the state's Immigrants' Commission; in 1921 JULIA CLIFFORD LATHROP stepped down as head of the federal Children's Bureau, and on her recommendation, President Warren G. Harding appointed Abbott to the post. To her fell the responsibility of administering the Sheppard-Towner Act, passed by Congress just two months after she had returned to Washington, which provided federal aid to the states for programs in maternal and infant health care. Congress had been motivated to act by the nation's unacceptably high infant mortality rate. To Abbott, passage of the act showed the clout that could be wielded by women. She said the act not only "constituted a demonstration . . . of the political power of American women now that they have the ballot," but also furnished "a concrete example of why this power is valuable to them as women."

To administer the act, Abbott traveled extensively, observing state programs and consulting program directors, nurses, and other professionals. Nevertheless, Congress ended the aid program in 1929.

As head of the Children's Bureau, Abbott in the 1920s advocated the passage of a constitutional amendment that would prohibit child labor. At that time, child labor in factories, which had declined around 1910, was expanding substantially. The Children's Bureau reported increases as high as 167 percent in Toledo, Ohio; 92 percent in Boston; and 63 percent in Indianapolis.

Congress passed an amendment in 1924, but it encountered substantial opposition in the states, especially from the National Association of Manufacturers and the Catholic Church. The manufacturers fought it because it would eliminate a cheap form of labor. The Catholic Church argued that it would require children to go to school and that the federal government would then stipulate the types of schools children would attend—and in so doing, the church feared, erode parochial schools.

The opponents to the amendment, though, sometimes cast the fight in extremist tones. One magazine called Abbott and her "gang" a bunch of radicals "under direct order of the Communist International" who wanted to "nationalize" education. The publication asked, "[Will] American mothers and fathers . . . tamely submit to turning over their sons and daughters to Miss Grace Abbott as an overparent?"

The states failed to ratify the amendment, but on Abbott's advice, President Franklin D. Roosevelt included provisions governing child labor in the 1937 Fair Labor Standards Act. Abbott, who had resigned form the Children's Bureau in 1934,

was appointed professor of public welfare at the University of Chicago's School of Social Service Administration. In 1938 she published her two-volume work, *The Child and the State.*

Grace Abbott died on June 19, 1939, in Chicago. She had never married but had considered the nation's children her special welfare case, linked to the plight of immigrants and workers in general. To reduce child labor would, she believed, improve working conditions for adults. She observed: "The child labor movement has in every country supplied the shock troops in the struggle for decent working conditions."

Further Reading

Costin, Lela B. *Two Sisters for Social Justice: A Biography of Grace and Edith Abbott.* Urbana: University of Illinois Press, 1983.

Lindenmeyer, Kriste. *A Right to Childhood: The U.S. Children's Bureau and Child Welfare, 1912–46.* Urbana: University of Illinois Press, 1997.

Abernathy, Ralph David
(1926–1990) *civil rights leader*

Ralph David Abernathy was a successor to MARTIN LUTHER KING, JR., as head of the Southern Christian Leadership Conference (SCLC) and one of the most important African-American civil rights leaders in post–World War II America. He was born on March 11, 1926, in Marengo County, Alabama, where his father, William L. Abernathy, and mother, Louivery Valentine Bell Abernathy, worked a 500-acre farm.

As a child, Ralph Abernathy enjoyed a middle-class existence; he wrote in his autobiography, "We never wanted for any of life's necessities. Everything I learned about the Great Depression was from a textbook." Abernathy served in the U.S. Army during World War II and fought in France and Germany. Soon after returning home, he took classes and earned a general equivalency diploma; shortly after that he was ordained a Baptist minister. In 1950 he received a B.S. in mathematics from Alabama State University and in 1951 an M.A. in sociology from Atlanta University. It was in Atlanta that Abernathy attended a lecture given by Martin Luther King, Jr., and afterward met him.

Later in 1951 Abernathy began his work as pastor of the First Baptist Church in Montgomery, Alabama. The following year he married Juanita Odessa Jones; they had five children. Abernathy rose to prominence in the civil rights movement during the Montgomery bus boycott that began in December 1955 after ROSA PARKS refused to relinquish her seat on a city bus to a white passenger. While King led the boycott, Abernathy was his chief assistant, taking care of details but also mobilizing support with stirring speeches.

The relationship between Abernathy and King had its difficulties. Although Abernathy admired King's leadership and intelligence, he was jealous of the adulation that King received from fellow blacks. Yet he applied King's ideas with precision. "As Martin expounded philosophy," he recalled, "I saw its practical application at the local level."

King's main tenet was nonviolent protest, which entailed street demonstrations and boycotts. He insisted that civil rights protesters march without weapons and, if attacked, turn the other cheek. But he wanted to provoke the oppressors, in this case the white segregationists, into a violent reaction to expose their wrongdoing. Abernathy and King well knew that nothing could raise support for the civil rights movement as effectively as vivid pictures on television showing African Americans being jeered at and beaten by racist whites. About Bull Connor, the black-hating sheriff in Birmingham, Alabama, Abernathy recalled, "Dogs and [water] hoses had proven invaluable to us in mustering national support for our demands."

In January 1957 Abernathy joined King in forming the SCLC, a group dedicated to nonviolent protest based on Christian principles. King served as president, and Abernathy as secretary-treasurer. With the SCLC protesting the laws of racial segregation in the South, they spent many days in jail together, locked up because of their civil disobedience.

In 1961 Abernathy moved to Atlanta on King's suggestion that he live near the SCLC headquarters. He served as vice president of the SCLC and as pastor of the West Hunter Baptist Church. Six years later he began planning a new tactic in the civil rights movement: a march of poor people on Washington, D.C.

Before he could launch the protest, however, in April 1968 King was assassinated in Memphis, Tennessee, where he had been supporting a strike by the city's sanitation workers. (Abernathy always doubted that the convicted assassin, James Earl Ray, had really murdered King; he believed that King was killed as part of a conspiracy.) With King's death, Abernathy became the president of the SCLC, and he continued King's plan to support the strikers.

Wearing bib overalls, Abernathy led the Poor People's Campaign in May 1968. He did so despite the chaotic atmosphere: race riots in the country's cities in response to King's assassination and confusion besetting the SCLC. About 50,000 protesters, much fewer than expected, marched on Washington to demand congressional action to help poor people—a goal that went well beyond the SCLC's previous civil rights program to promote racial integration. Now economic demands were being made with the intention that society had to be radically restructured to promote a more equitable distribution of wealth. The *New York Times* said the protest "was planned to probe the essence of the American system, to see whether it could make a massive material and spiritual readjustment to change the lives of its poverty-stricken millions and construct a rational future where base poverty would not coexist with stupendous wealth."

The Poor People's Campaign failed miserably. The marchers set up a shantytown, called Resurrection City, near the Lincoln Memorial, but it turned into a muddy mess, complete with roving gangs; the government arrested Abernathy—he spent 20 days in jail—and forced the demonstrators out.

As the SCLC shifted its focus from racism in the South to racism in the North and economic injustice across the nation—a shift begun under King—Abernathy seemed unable to grasp the change in strategy. Coworkers within the SCLC complained about his ineffective leadership and, compared to King, his lack of charisma. In 1971 one of King's former aides, JESSE LOUIS JACKSON, and his supporters bolted from the SCLC. An angry Abernathy accused Jackson of robbing the SCLC treasury. Over the next several years, differences erupted between Abernathy and King's widow, CORETTA SCOTT KING, and the two vied for power within the SCLC.

By 1977 the SCLC had declined in members and money, and Abernathy quit the organization. Most accounts attribute his departure to being forced out by the board of directors, though Abernathy said he left so he could run for Congress. In the same year, he entered the Democratic primary for the congressional seat that encompassed Atlanta, but he polled only 3,614 votes of more than 200,000 cast.

Abernathy shifted to the right politically and in 1980 stunned many civil rights activists when he supported the conservative Republican Ronald Reagan for president. Abernathy said he made the endorsement so he could have influence within the administration. Others claim he did so because he was angry with Democratic leaders. Reverend Darneau V. Stewart, vice president of the Detroit Board of Education and pastor of Peoples Community Church, expressed the feeling of many blacks when he said about Abernathy's endorsement, "My gut reaction when I . . . heard what he had to say was that he was a traitor." Traitor or not, Abernathy wielded no power with Reagan. In 1987, Abernathy joined the right-wing American Freedom Coalition as its vice president.

In 1989 he published his autobiography, *And the Walls Came Tumbling Down*. Many African Americans condemned it and called him disloyal to King for revealing King's adulterous affairs with several women. (Abernathy himself had at least one affair in the 1950s but failed to divulge it in his book.) Abernathy insisted, however, "I have written nothing in malice and omitted nothing out of cowardice."

Abernathy, who had suffered a severe stroke in 1983, died of heart failure on April 17, 1990. Andrew Young, the former black mayor of Atlanta, remembered him as a silent laborer "very much needed" in the civil rights movement.

Further Reading

Abernathy, Ralph. *And the Walls Came Tumbling Down: An Autobiography*. New York: Harper & Row, 1989.

Reef, Catherine. *Ralph David Abernathy*. Parsippany, N.J.: Dillon Press, 1995.

Addams, Jane

(1860–1935) *Progressive reformer, peace activist*

One of the most prominent and influential Progressive reformers, Jane Addams was the founder of Hull-House as well as an advocate of peace. She was born on September 6, 1860, in Cedarville, Illinois, to John Huy Addams, a businessman, and Sarah Weber Addams.

According to Daniel Levine in *Jane Addams and the Liberal Tradition* (1971), the stronger parental influence on Jane Addams was her father's. He made for an impressive role model. John Addams owned a prosperous mill, invested profitably in a railroad, and engaged in numerous projects to help his community, while adhering to his principles regardless of what anyone else said or did. He opposed slavery and fought against its expansion into the western territories by helping to found the Republican Party. Jane Addams revered his ambition, his community service, and his moral values.

After Jane completed her secondary school education, she wanted to head east to Smith College, but her father insisted that she stay closer to home, so she enrolled at Rockford Female Seminary and in 1881 graduated at the top of her class. Just a few months later her father died.

That fall, Addams entered the Women's Medical College of Pennsylvania, but her declining health forced her to withdraw. Some historians believe that her illness owed less to physical ailments than to psychosomatic ones, perhaps stirred by trauma caused by her father's death.

For the next few years, Addams groped for direction in her life. She traveled to Europe, learned foreign languages, returned to the United States, and helped her brother, George, as he sank into insanity and his life faded away.

In 1887 she took a second trip to Europe in a continuing search for direction. Some of her drifting was the result of her personal experiences, but a good deal of it was a reaction to the restrictions society placed on women. The ideal woman was expected to stay at home and take care of her husband and children. This meant that intelligent and ambitious young women, such as Addams, were largely prevented from applying their talents to politics or the professions.

In the past, women who chafed under such constraints found an outlet in social reform—in abolitionism, the women's rights movement, and the temperance movement. Jane Addams followed a similar route. While in Europe in 1888 she began to take note of the poor, and she and her friend, Ellen Gates Starr, agreed that when they returned home they would do something to help poor people in America.

Here photographed during World War I, Jane Addams was at the forefront of women's social activism and founded the first Chicago settlement house to help immigrants, called Hull-House. *(National Archives and Records Administration)*

By that time a reform movement, called Progressivism, had emerged in the United States with the goal of correcting the worst industrial abuses, such as corrupt politics, abusive child labor, and slum housing. Progressive reformers challenged the prevailing social Darwinist ideology, which held that life was survival of the fittest and anything that interfered with that process would do more harm than good. The Progressives countered with reform Darwinism, the belief that changing the environment in which people lived could improve their lives. Reform Darwinism encouraged an active approach to social problems, and in that Jane Addams agreed.

Addams insisted that cities could be improved by encouraging community—in effect reaching back to the era of the close-knit village. In England, she had seen what community could do in the urban environment when she visited Toynbee Hall, a settlement house founded to help the poor. In 1886 Stanton Coit applied the Toynbee concept to a settlement house he began in New York City. Three years later, two of Coit's colleagues opened a second settlement house in New York.

In September 1889 Jane Addams and Ellen Gates Starr opened Hull-House in Chicago. A city of contrasts, Chicago was known for its new technology and explosive business growth, represented by its motto, "I will," but it was also an immigrant city—more than half the population consisted of immigrants or the children of immigrants—and a city of large poverty-stricken neighborhoods.

Addams and Starr applied their own brand of "I will" to social reform when they located Hull-House in an immigrant neighborhood. They decided that they, and those who worked with them, would live in the house, among the immigrants, so they could grasp the problems facing the neighborhood and deal with them directly. Hull-House provided immigrants with hot lunches, child care, classes on speaking English, lectures on art and history, and rooms for union meetings. Addams built Hull-House into a political center, too, from which she could launch reform campaigns.

She attracted to Hull-House men and women who became leading Progressive reformers. These included JOHN DEWEY, FLORENCE

KELLEY, CLARENCE SEWARD DARROW, UPTON SIN-CLAIR, and ALICE HAMILTON. At Hull-House Addams put together a minicommunity to build a large community; years later she recalled, "More gratifying than any understanding or response from without could possibly be, was the consciousness that a growing group of residents was gathering at Hull-House, held together in that soundest of all social bonds, the companionship of mutual interests." Hull-House was so successful, and Addams so forceful in publicizing her work, that it inspired other Progressives to establish settlement houses elsewhere.

In line with prevailing Progressive thought, Addams articulated ever more strongly the view that poverty resulted not from innate shortcomings of the poor but from problems in industrial society at large, such as low wages and inadequate public services. She believed that women should take the lead in correcting abuses. Addams said women had a special talent and an instinct for nurturing that made them more effective reformers than men—an assessment similar to one she would make years later when she became a leader in the peace movement and insisted that women could do more for peace than men because they were less warlike.

Addams wrote several books during this time, including *The Spirit of Youth and the City Streets* (1909), which looked into conflicts among different generations of immigrants; *Twenty Years at Hull-House* (1910), which described her experiences at the settlement house; and *Ancient Evil* (1912), which discussed prostitution.

Addams's settlement work made her keenly aware of how industries exploited child labor. More than anything else, she said, the factory harmed children by making them work long hours at routine, monotonous tasks that either dulled them or made them rebellious. "By premature factory work, for which youth is unprepared," Addams said, "society perpetually extinguishes that variety and promise, that bloom of life which is the unique possession of the young." She added:

> The discovery of the labor power of youth was to our age like the discovery of a new natural resource, although it was merely incidental to the invention of modern machinery and the

consequent subdivision of labor. In utilizing it thus ruthlessly we are not only in danger of quenching the divine fire of youth, but we are imperiling industry itself when we venture to ignore those very sources of beauty, of variety, and of suggestion.

Addams also campaigned for prohibition and women's suffrage. In 1912 she supported the Progressive Party and its presidential candidate, Theodore Roosevelt, whose nomination she seconded at the national convention, and who lost to the Democrat Woodrow Wilson. Addams's decision to back him was especially interesting given his bellicosity in foreign affairs and her own pacifism. Addams and Roosevelt parted ways when World War I began, as her pacifist views led her to become chair of the Women's Peace Party and president of the International Congress of Women.

In 1915 Addams traveled to Europe in a futile effort to negotiate a settlement of the war. After the United States entered the conflict in 1917, she cofounded the Women's Peace Party (WPP) and served as its chairwoman. She explained that she formed the party because "in this case the demand has been so universal and spontaneous over the country that it seemed to me best to take it up." In its platform, the WPP demanded that neutral nations meet to mediate the war; that arms be limited; that women be consulted on all issues of war and peace; that a world court be established; and that the economic causes of war be eliminated.

The party's stand against military preparedness found support among many Americans who, though not pacifists, wanted the country to stay out of the war; isolationists, for example, sided with the WPP. But once the United States entered the war, the WPP was labeled as extremist, and even un-American, when it opposed the Conscription Act. As criticism of the WPP escalated, Addams endured considerable strain. In 1917 she complained that she was weary of being a social outcast.

When the war ended, Addams worked for Herbert Hoover's war relief staff in Europe. A strong internationalist, she was elected president of the Women's International League for Peace and Freedom in 1919. She supported American entry into the League of Nations—which never came about—and argued that political internationalism, which the league would foster, would lead to humanitarian internationalism.

In the 1920s Addams came under attack from conservatives who accused her of being a socialist, even a Bolshevik. They were angered by her pacifism during the war and by her support for the League of Nations, and many conservatives disliked her support for unions. Indeed, in conflicts between capital and labor, Addams had long sided with labor and had supported strikes. But ideally she wanted a society devoid of class consciousness and, toward that end, saw unions as only a stopgap to counterbalance corporate power; in the long run, she believed, unions would foster class consciousness rather than erase it.

Addams stopped short of advocating a socialist system. In a letter to a newspaper she protested:

> I am not in any sense a Socialist, have never belonged to the party and have never especially affiliated with them. I am certainly not a communist or bolshevik. I am, of course, president of the Women's International League for Peace and Freedom and we have advocated recognition of soviet Russia, not because we have been in favor of the government any more than we were with that of the czars. . . .
>
> I do not know why I am called a bolshevik except as a term of opprobrium that is easily flung about.

Whereas Addams wanted the government to regulate business to make society more just, according to the historian Victoria Bissell Brown, the reformer favored compromise too much ever to be an ideological socialist.

In 1931 Jane Addams received the Nobel Peace Prize. She died on May 21, 1935, of cancer. "I am not so sure that we succeeded in our endeavors," she wrote in *Twenty Years at Hull-House.* "But Hull-House was soberly opened on the theory that the dependence of classes on each other is reciprocal."

Further Reading
Brown, Victoria Bissell, ed. *Twenty Years at Hull-House, with Autobiographical Notes.* Boston: Bedford Books, 1999.
Davis, Allen Freeman. *American Heroine: The Life and Legend of Jane Addams.* Chicago: Ivan R. Dee, 2000.
Linn, James Weber. *Jane Addams: A Biography.* Urbana: University of Illinois Press, 2000.

Adler, Felix
(1851–1933) *ethical reformer*

Felix Adler founded the ethical culture movement, which was intended to provide moral direction without religious dogma or a reliance on the supernatural. "In order to find a common basis whereon good men, whether believers or unbelievers, can unite," Adler wrote, "we look to the moral law itself, whose certainty rests in the universal experience of civilized humanity."

Felix Adler was born in Alzey, Germany, on August 13, 1851, to Samuel Adler and Henrietta Frankfurter Adler. He left Germany in 1857 when his father accepted a rabbinical appointment to Temple Emanuel in New York City. Felix attended public and private schools and then entered Columbia College. Soon after his graduation in 1870, he headed back to Europe with the goal of following his father as a rabbi. At the same time that he studied theology, philosophy, and linguistics at a Judaic school in Berlin, he studied ethics, along with labor and social reform, at the University of Berlin. Continuing his studies, in 1873 he graduated from the University of Heidelberg with a doctorate.

At that point, he returned to New York to begin his service as a rabbi but lost faith in his religious teachings, rejected theism, and in 1874 moved upstate to Ithaca. There he began lecturing at Cornell University as a professor of Hebrew and Oriental literature.

Two years later, Adler resigned from Cornell and returned to New York City, and on May 15, 1876, while the United States prepared to celebrate the centennial of its independence, he presented to a group of about 100 people what he called "the sketch of a religious society imbued with the spirit of religion without its dogmas." This began the New York Society for Ethical Culture.

Adler claimed that disputes over the Scriptures and "so-called duties toward God" had placed obstacles in the way of the moral relations that human beings owed to each other as fonts of divine power. He advocated that people live "not by the creed but by the deed" and sought to evoke a moral commitment to social problems.

In order to sanctify the Society for Ethical Culture, Adler held Sunday services without prayer or ritual, but nevertheless with a speaker, often him, "steeped in the religious and ethical thought of the past" with the object "to communicate light and heat to . . . hearers, . . . quicken their spiritual aspirations, and . . . help them in the struggle toward spiritual freedom." His ethical movement spread to Chicago in 1882, Philadelphia in 1885, and Saint Louis in 1886, at a time when rapid industrial growth, an emerging corporate capitalist economy, and the popularity of Darwinian evolutionary ideas disrupted social relations and challenged traditional thought. Adler saw his effort as akin to the Social Gospel movement—though minus the religion—that tackled modern slum conditions and industrial abuses. Both he and the Social Gospel leaders believed in the general goodness of human beings and in their ability to be shaped by moral persuasion.

True to his call for social action, in the late 1870s Adler founded America's first free kindergarten and promoted a program for low-income housing. Later, he advocated racial integration and supported President Woodrow Wilson's proposal for a League of Nations. He wanted to abolish child labor, and he called for using surplus income to improve conditions for the working classes.

Adler criticized religious fundamentalists, who claimed morality required the acceptance of the Bible, and disagreed with voluntarists who said the individual was more important than any "binding ties" to other people. Such a view, he insisted, eroded marriage and the family—an issue that concerned him all the more after he married Helen Goldmark in 1880 and had five children.

Felix Adler wrote several books, including *Creed and Deed* (1877), *The Essentials of Spirituality* (1905), *An Ethical Philosophy of Life* (1918), and *The Reconstruction of the Spiritual Ideal* (1924). Beginning in 1902, he held a professorship in political and social ethics at Columbia University. He died

in New York City on April 24, 1933, as his ethical movement continued to expand.

Further Reading
Freiss, Horace L. *Felix Adler and Ethical Culture: Memories and Studies.* New York: Columbia University Press, 1981.

Guttchen, Robert S. *Felix Adler.* New York: Twayne, 1974.

Radest, Howard B. *Felix Adler: An Ethical Culture.* New York: Peter Lang, 1998.

Agassiz, Elizabeth Cary
(1822–1907) *education reformer*

Elizabeth Cary Agassiz was known for her scientific writings and her efforts to expand education for women. She was born Elizabeth Cary on December 5, 1822, in Boston, Massachusetts, to Thomas Graves Cary and Mary Perkins Cary.

Because of illness, Elizabeth was educated at home. In 1849, she moved to Cambridge, Massachusetts, where she lived with her older sister, who was married to a Harvard professor. The move turned out to be fortuitous, for her sister introduced Elizabeth to Louis Agassiz, a Swiss scientist and a widower who had recently immigrated to the United States and was teaching at Harvard.

They married in 1850, and Elizabeth assisted her husband by editing his scientific articles in geology, zoology, and paleontology. At the same time, she learned natural history and became a scientist in her own right. Elizabeth and Louis founded a marine laboratory on Sullivan's Island, South Carolina, and in 1859 she published *Actaea, a First Lesson in Natural History.*

Back in Cambridge, Elizabeth founded a high school for girls, which drew criticism from conservatives who thought advanced education proper only for boys. In addition, she helped Louis Agassiz found the Museum of Comparative Zoology at Harvard and the Anderson Natural History School on Pekinese Island near Cape Cod, which was the first school to introduce women who were high school teachers to laboratory biology.

Elizabeth and Louis Agassiz published *Seaside Studies in Natural History* in 1866 as part of their effort to popularize science. The following year she published *A Journey in Brazil*, which recounted their journey to that land, and the book sold widely.

After her husband died in 1873, Elizabeth Agassiz focused her career on education. In 1879 she joined the president of Harvard and several other educators in founding the Society for the Collegiate Instruction of Women. More popularly called Harvard Annex, its courses for women were taught by Harvard professors. In 1893, Harvard Annex became Radcliffe College and Agassiz, who had been president of the Annex since 1882, became president of the new institution.

Under Agassiz's leadership, Radcliffe provided scientific laboratories for its female students, and those who graduated from the college received Harvard degrees. Agassiz retired from Radcliffe in 1903 and the following year suffered a severe stroke. She died on June 27, 1907.

Further Reading

Bergman, Linda S. "A Troubled Marriage of Discourses: Science Writing and Travel Narrative in Louis and Elizabeth Agassiz's 'A Journey in Brazil.'" *Journal of American Culture* 18 (Summer 1995): 83+.

Tharp, Louise Hall. *Adventurous Alliance: The Story of the Agassiz Family of Boston.* Boston: Little, Brown, 1959.

Alcott, Amos Bronson

(1799–1888) *education reformer, transcendentalist*

Amos Bronson Alcott was a transcendentalist who advocated educational reform, vegetarianism, and the end of slavery. He was born on November 29, 1799, in Wolcott, Connecticut, to Joseph Chatfield Alcox and Anna Bronson Alcox, and he joined his cousin, the reformer WILLIAM ANDRUS ALCOTT in changing the spelling of their last name.

Alcott possessed a visionary and largely impractical mind. He obtained a rudimentary education and then, while still in his teens, journeyed to Virginia to become a teacher. Failing at that endeavor, he took up selling dry goods as a peddler, a job that required him to travel throughout Virginia and North Carolina.

He next returned to the North to teach and moved frequently as the various schools he founded in Connecticut, Massachusetts, and at Germantown, Pennsylvania, survived for only short periods. By this time, he had developed radical educational and religious ideas and applied them to his students. He believed that education placed too much emphasis on rote memorization and discipline. Alcott wanted learning to be enjoyed for its intrinsic value rather than treated as a means to accumulate knowledge.

He wanted students also to free their imagination. His daughter, Louisa May Alcott, later said, "My father taught in the wise way which unfolds what lies in the child's nature, as a flower blooms, rather than crammed it, like a Strasbourg goose, with more than it could digest." A believer in developing the body as well as the mind, Alcott employed gymnastics and organized play, all highly innovative for the early 19th century.

At Germantown, Alcott read Plato and concluded that the spirit within each person could be freed from its imprisonment in a world of matter by the development of intuitive self-knowledge. His questioning of traditional religious practices raised a storm of controversy and caused many parents to shun his schools.

In 1830 he married Abigail May, and they raised a large family, whom he had difficulty supporting. That same year he published *Observations on the Principles and Methods of Infant Instruction*. In 1834 he opened his Temple School in Boston, where he tried to integrate the mental, physical, and spiritual development of his students. He applied a Socratic question-and-answer method to elicit ethical ideas, but when he encouraged his pupils to think independently about religion, he raised the ire of the community. On top of that, he allowed an African-American girl to enroll, whereupon many parents withdrew their children from the school, causing it to collapse in 1839. Meanwhile, three years earlier he had published *The Doctrine and Discipline of Human Culture*.

Alcott moved to Concord, Massachusetts, in 1840. There he farmed and contributed his "Orphic Sayings" to the *Dial*, a transcendentalist periodical he helped establish. Many observers ridiculed his writing as incomprehensible nonsense, and the *Boston Transcript* called them "Gastric Sayings." The "Orphic Sayings" were meant to provide readers with transcendentalist advice. Alcott wrote:

> Solitude is Wisdom's school. Attend then the lessons of your own soul; become a pupil of the wise God within you, for by his tuitions alone shall you grow into the knowledge and stature of the deities. The seraphs descend from heaven, in the solitudes of meditation, in the stillness of prayer.
>
> He who marvels at nothing, who feels nothing to be mysterious, but must needs bare all things to sense, lacks both wisdom and piety.
>
> All life is eternal; there is none other; and all unrest is but the struggle of the soul to reassure herself of all her inborn immortality.

In 1842 Alcott journeyed to England to visit a school founded on his ideas. There he made contact with English mystics, including Henry Wright and Charles and William Lane. In 1844 they joined Alcott in forming Fruitlands, a commune south of Boston. Alcott dedicated the commune to an extreme form of vegetarianism, according to which the 11 settlers made no use of horses or even of animal manure and planted and ate only "aspiring vegetables," meaning those that grew upward, as opposed to those that grew downward into the earth.

Unfortunately for the fate of Fruitlands, Alcott and the other settlers were more interested in holding meetings than in tending and harvesting their crops, and in 1845 the commune collapsed. Alcott returned to Concord, on several occasions visited the author and transcendentalist Henry David Thoreau at his cabin on Walden Pond, and for the next two decades lived in poverty. While he lectured for meager sums and refused regular employment, saying it would interfere with the liberty of his soul, only a small amount of money inherited by his wife, along with the jobs she and their daughter held as maids, kept the family afloat. Yet as a fighter against oppression he advocated black civil rights and made his home a stop-

ping point for runaway slaves along the Underground Railroad.

In 1859 Alcott was appointed superintendent of the Concord schools; during his six years in that position he introduced calisthenics, physiology, and dancing into the curriculum, along with reading aloud. The publication in 1868 of *Little Women* by his daughter Louisa May Alcott finally freed him from financial hardship.

Amos Bronson Alcott suffered a paralyzing stroke in 1882 and died on March 4, 1888. He was remembered as a leader in the transcendentalist "flowering of New England."

Further Reading

Alcott, Amos Bronson. *How Like an Angel Came I Down: Conversations with Children on the Gospels.* Edited by Alice O. Howell. Hudson, N.Y.: Lindisfarne Press, 1991.

Barton, Cynthia H. *Transcendental Wife: The Life of Abigail May Alcott.* Lanham, Md.: University Press of America, 1996.

Dahlstrand, Frederick C. *Amos Bronson Alcott: An Intellectual Biography.* Rutherford, N.J.: Farleigh Dickinson University Press, 1982.

McCuskey, Dorothy. *Bronson Alcott, Teacher.* New York: Macmillan, 1940.

Shepard, Odell. *Pedlar's Progress: The Life of Bronson Alcott.* Boston: Little, Brown, 1937.

Alcott, William Andrus
(1798–1859) *education and health reformer*

Throughout his life, William Andrus Alcott was a tireless promoter of improving schools and an advocate of bettering public health. He was born on August 6, 1798, in Wolcott, Connecticut. His parents were John Alcox and Anna Alcox; like his cousin, the reformer AMOS BRONSON ALCOTT, William changed the spelling of his last name.

William Alcott showed an interest in public education while still a child when, at age 14, he and several other boys formed a library for the neighborhood children. At age 18, Alcott began teaching school in Wolcott and Hartford. After a two-year hiatus from teaching, he returned to the job in 1822 and pushed for reforms, such as improved ventilation in school houses, that displayed his linking of education to public health.

Alcott's long hours teaching and working for reform cost him his own health, however, and he suffered recurring episodes of tuberculosis. His experience with the disease resulted in his decision to study medicine, and in 1826 he received a diploma from Yale Medical School.

Returning to Wolcott, he took charge of the town's Central School and applied several reforms. He added grammar and geography to the curriculum and set up his classroom with such innovative devices as maps, flowers, and plants to provide a more cultured and healthy environment for his students.

Alcott's illness felled him in the late 1820s, and he subsequently devoted most of his time to writing. Through these works and several lectures he promoted his ideas about education and public health. From 1831 until 1833 he edited *Juvenile Rambler*, probably the first children's magazine ever published in the United States. In 1836 he married Phebe Bronson, with whom he had two children.

Alcott's many magazine and journal articles showed the depth of his knowledge of education and the strength of his commitment to reform. His book *The Mother's Assistant* (1845) questioned the publishing of pictures books because they exposed children to immoral practices. "One of the best books for children and families with which I am acquainted . . . ," he wrote,

> has for its first picture, a scene whose morality is slightly questionable. I allude to the representation of a venerable old gentleman with a pipe in his mouth, smoking. . . . Here, in the foreground of the first picture of one of the best books of one of our first writers for families and schools, we find this vulgar presentation of a tobacco-pipe.

Directly addressing that issue, in 1883 Alcott published *Tobacco, Its Effects on the Human System,* in which he outlined some of the damage to health caused by tobacco:

> The soundness of teeth will always bear an exact proportion to the soundness and firm-
ness of the gums, and of the lining membrane of the mouth, and the whole alimentary canal. But, that tobacco makes the gums loose and spongy, and injures the lining membrane of the alimentary canal, especially that part of it called the stomach, is as well attested as any fact in physiology.
>
> A substance so powerful, whether in its more solid form, or in that of powder or smoke, cannot be applied to membranes in the region of the eyes, ears, nose and brain, day after day, and year after year, without seriously affecting them.
>
> Tobacco not only leads to intemperance—of itself a disease—it both originates and aggravates a great many more of the complaints to which flesh in its fallen estate is heir. . . . Tobacco is not only an irritant but a poison.

Alcott wrote dozens of books dedicated to reform. He spent his last years in Newton, Massachusetts, and died on March 29, 1859.

Further Reading

Alcott, William A. *Tobacco: Its Effects On the Human System.* New York: Fowler and Wells, 1883. Available online. URL: http://www.nimbus.org/ElectronicTexts/Tobacco.Effects.1883.html. Downloaded on March 25, 2002.

Bedell, Madelon. *The Alcotts: Biography of a Family.* New York: C. N. Potter, 1980.

Alinsky, Saul
(1909–1972) *community activist*

Saul Alinsky was a community organizer known not only for his radical neighborhood activism, but also for his refusal to engage in violence. He was born in Chicago on January 30, 1909, to Benjamin Alinsky and Sarah Tannenbaum Alinsky.

Alinsky graduated from Marshall High School in Chicago and then attended the University of Chicago as an undergraduate from 1926 until 1930, when he received a bachelor's degree in sociology. He continued his work in sociology and criminology when he entered the university's graduate program, and in 1930 he worked with renowned sociologist Clifford Shaw and his Institute for Juvenile Research. Alinsky agreed with Shaw's position that juvenile delinquency owed more to social conditions than to individual makeup.

By 1934 Alinsky had dropped out of the graduate program, and he became a staff sociologist at Illinois State Penitentiary. He and Shaw then began the Chicago Area Project to fight juvenile delinquency, but they parted ways when Alinsky disagreed with Shaw's emphasis on inducing delinquents to adopt middle-class practices and values.

Alinsky's different approach to urban problems appeared evident in 1936, when, through the Area Project, he organized the Back-of-the-Yards Neighborhood Council (BYNC). Alinsky, by now a political radical who had embraced socialism, though he never joined the Socialist Party, wanted to help residents of the poor Back-of-the-Yards Neighborhood, the same district written about in UPTON SINCLAIR's reformist novel *The Jungle*, not by forcing them to accept middle-class values, but by encouraging them to build on their existing family, social, and religious ties to form organizations that could challenge the city power structure and obtain benefits for the community. He convinced the residents to pressure the city council for programs, and after the BYNC succeeded so well that it gained national attention, he expanded it to other cities, though with only limited results.

In the 1940s Alinsky drifted away from community activism to work for the War Manpower Board and to write. His *Reveille for Radicals* (1946) served as a guidebook to democratic radicalism. In 1947 the death of his wife, Helen Simon, with whom he had two children, shocked him and sent him into a depression.

In 1952 Alinsky married Jean Graham, and in 1961 he organized the Temporary Woodlawn Association (TWA), after the University of Chicago announced plans to uproot thousands of poor blacks and whites in the Woodlawn neighborhood so it could expand its campus. The TWA spread throughout Chicago's South Side, and as it broadened its protests, it used marches, pickets, and boycotts, along with rent strikes against slum landlords, to fight racial segregation and poverty.

When President Lyndon Johnson began his War on Poverty in 1964, Alinsky criticized it. Although he accepted some funding from the federal government for various projects, he believed that little of the money Johnson proposed to spend on the war would actually reach poor people. Bureaucrats and politicians, he said, would consume it. At one point Alinsky called the War on Poverty "a prize piece of political pornography."

The upheavals of the 1960s moved Alinsky's brand of activism to the fore. Yet he disagreed with those countercultural radicals who wanted to use violence to overthrow the political system. He thought such a stand foolish when those in authority held nearly all of the weapons. At the same time, he objected to those 1960s reformers who wanted to show the poor how to live. He continued to insist that those who resided in the neighborhoods to be changed must direct the change.

In the mid-1960s Alinsky organized protesters in Rochester, New York, to pressure the city's two largest employers, Xerox and Eastman Kodak, to hire more African-American workers. In 1969 he divorced Jean Graham, and in 1971 he married Irene McGinnis.

That same year, he published *Rules for Radicals*, a call for a second American Revolution. "In the world of give and take," Alinsky wrote, "tactics is the art of how to take and how to give. Here our concern is with the tactic of taking; how the have-nots can take power from the Haves." The book outlined a bold tactic called proxy voting, whereby activists would purchase stock in a corporation so they could gain entry to the annual meeting of the board of directors.

Alinsky opposed using proxies to elect members to the board, for he considered that a useless effort. Rather, he wanted to use proxies to publicize harmful practices and activate those demoralized by the barriers to social protest. In 1970, for example, following Alinsky's tactic, proxies attended the annual board meeting of Commonwealth Edison, the giant Chicago utility that had been polluting the air with its soft-coal plant. At that meeting 800 protesting proxies chanted, "Let us breathe!" These and other pressures led to concessions by the utility.

Alinsky said in *Rules for Radicals*, "The vast majority of Americans, who feel helpless in the huge corporate economy, who don't know which way to turn, have begun to turn *away* from America, to abdicate as citizens. . . . Proxies can be the mechanism by which these people can organize, and once they are organized they will re-enter politics."

Alinsky died on June 12, 1972, of a heart attack. Over the ensuing years the organizations he founded have either collapsed or changed so much they bear little resemblance to what he expected them to be. The BYNC, for example, has become a homeowners association.

Writing in 1989, the historian Sean Wilentz evaluated Alinsky's contribution. He said it "was to reverse the logic of Progressive-style reform, by wrestling control away from the professional do-gooders and handing it over to the people that they were supposed to help. He did not invent neighborhood organizing. He changed it from the liberal, elite-led endeavor it had become around 1900 into something he hoped would be more hardheaded and democratic."

Further Reading

Doering, Bernard. *The Philosopher and the Provocateur: The Correspondence of Jacques Maritain and Saul Alinsky.* Notre Dame, Ind. University of Notre Dame Press, 1994.

Horwitt, Sanford D. *Let Them Call Me Rebel: Saul Alinsky, His Life and Legacy.* New York: Knopf, 1989.

Reitzes, Donald Charles. *The Alinsky Legacy: Alive and Kicking.* Greenwich, Conn.: JAI Press, 1987.

Allen, Richard

(1760–1831) *African-American activist, abolitionist*

Richard Allen began his life as a slave, but once free, he devoted himself to the abolition of slavery and the creation of African-American churches. He was born on February 14, 1760, in Philadelphia and was owned by Benjamin Chew, a prominent lawyer, who later served as chief justice of Pennsylvania. Soon after Richard's birth, Chew sold Richard, his parents, and his three siblings to Stokeley Sturgis, a planter in Delaware. As was often the case with slaves, Richard's family was soon broken up when Sturgis sold the boy's mother to another planter.

Sturgis turned out to be a benevolent master. After Richard Allen experienced a religious conversion and joined the Methodist Society in 1777, Sturgis allowed him to attend church meetings. Allen then began proselytizing and converted several friends and neighbors to the faith. Some whites, however, complained about the slave's behavior; they thought him disruptive and too independent. At that point, Allen applied himself to his chores more dutifully, determined to show that his faith would not endanger slave society. Allen later said, "We frequently went to meeting on every other Thursday; but if we were likely to be backward with our crops we would refrain from going."

Yet he disliked the limitations imposed by slavery. He recalled: "I had it often impressed upon my mind that I should one day enjoy my freedom. For slavery is a bitter pill notwithstanding we had a good master."

Allen convinced Sturgis to listen to a Methodist preacher, whose preaching caused Sturgis to foreswear slavery and allow Allen to buy his freedom and that of his brother for $2,000. To earn the money he needed, Allen worked at various odd jobs, chopping wood and making bricks. During the Revolutionary War he drove a wagon for American troops.

A free man, Allen settled in Philadelphia and began preaching to the black congregants at Saint George's Methodist Episcopal Church. But as the number of black worshippers increased, the white congregants at the church restricted their use of the facilities, whereupon Allen and several other African Americans rebelled and walked out. Allen later stated, "I established prayer meetings; I raised a society . . . of forty-two members. I saw the necessity of erecting a place of worship for the colored people. I proposed it to the most respectable people of color in this City, but here I met with opposition."

Allen's Free African Society, established with the help of Reverend Absalom Jones, was a black mutual aid society that evolved into the African Church of Philadelphia. At first the congregants met in a storeroom, but in 1794 construction of a church building was completed. Soon afterward, the Philadelphia Episcopal Diocese admitted the church into membership as the Saint Thomas African Episcopal Church.

As a Methodist, however, Allen disagreed with the move and left Saint Thomas to begin the Bethel African Church. It joined other churches in 1816 to form the African Methodist Episcopal Church, and Allen was named its bishop and was consecrated in that position by Bishop Francis Asbury of the white Methodist Episcopal Church. The African Methodist Episcopal Church existed only in the North prior to the Civil War, but it later spread rapidly through the South.

When some whites and African Americans promoted a program to liberate slaves by settling them in Liberia, Allen opposed the move. While denouncing slavery and stating "We were stolen from our mother country and brought here," he said of American, "This land which we have watered with our tears and our blood, is now our mother country, and we are well satisfied to stay where wisdom abounds and the gospel is free." He added that blacks were unfit to be the rulers of a country in Africa because slavery had degraded them and denied them the education and expertise they needed for such a responsibility. In 1817 he organized some 3,000 African Americans to protest the Liberian colonization scheme. Yet in 1830 he supported a plan to resettle numerous blacks in Canada.

In addition to his formation of the African Methodist Episcopal Church and his position against slavery, over the years Allen organized black Philadelphians in a number of community service projects. Most notably, in 1793 he led an effort to fight the city's yellow fever epidemic, and during the War of 1812 he enlisted African Americans to build the defenses needed to protect the city from an attack by the British. Allen, who had married and had children, died on March 26, 1831, in Philadelphia.

Further Reading

George, Carol V. R. *Segregated Sabbaths: Richard Allen and the Emergence of Independent Black Churches, 1760–1840.* New York: Oxford University Press, 1973.

Knots, Steve. *Richard Allen.* New York: Chelsea House Publishers, 1991.

Mathews, Marcia M. *Richard Allen.* Baltimore: Helcion, 1963.

Wesley, Charles H. *Richard Allen: Apostle of Freedom.* Washington, D.C.: Associated Publishers, 1935.

Ameringer, Oscar
(1870–1943) *socialist, labor activist*

Oscar Ameringer was a German who immigrant to the United States and became a leader in the Socialist Party. He was born in Achstetten, near Ulm, in the German kingdom of Wurttemberg on August 4, 1870.

Ameringer's father, August Ameringer, was a musician and cabinetmaker, and Oscar Ameringer trained for that craft. He was, however, by his own description, "unruly." He left school early and while in his teens rebelled against the military service he was expected to perform in duty to the state. Ameringer recalled: "I had heard . . . ex-soldiers discuss, as if the words were sweet on their tongues, how they had abused, insulted, and browbeaten underlings, or how they themselves had been abused, mauled, and browbeaten by their superiors."

To avoid military service, and to escape the criticism of townspeople who thought him a troublemaker, at age 16 Ameringer left his homeland to join his brother, who lived in Cincinnati, Ohio. Soon after his arrival, he found work in a furniture factory, but his union activities for the Knights of Labor resulted in his being fired.

For a while he played the coronet in a traveling band; for the most part, though, he spent the winter of 1887–88 reading in the Cincinnati public library and educating himself in English and U.S. history. After earning money as a portrait painter and obtaining his American citizenship, he returned to Germany and studied art in Munich for five years.

Ameringer returned to the United States in 1896 and played in the Canton, Ohio, band that promoted William McKinley's presidential campaign—an odd development since Ameringer's political views were opposite McKinley's Republican conservatism. Shortly after marrying Lulu Wood, Ameringer settled in Columbus, Ohio, and sold insurance. Through his reading, he was influenced by the socialist ideas of the novelist EDWARD BELLAMY and the radical economic theories of HENRY GEORGE. In 1903 he ran unsuccessfully for the state legislature as a socialist.

Four years later, after publishing a newspaper called *Labor World,* which collapsed, Ameringer moved to Oklahoma City, where he worked as a field organizer for the Socialist Party. He also began writing socialist tracts and founded another newspaper, the *Industrial Democrat.* After that failed, he founded the *Oklahoma Pioneer.*

Ameringer journeyed north in 1910 to help in the congressional campaign of Victor Berger, a Milwaukee, Wisconsin, socialist. In crafting an appeal, Ameringer applied his knowledge of German language and culture to the city's large number of German voters, and with his effective writing style, he was instrumental in helping Berger to win the office. He then was appointed state coordinator for the Socialist Party.

Back in Oklahoma City, Ameringer founded the *Oklahoma Leader* in 1914 and ran for mayor as a socialist, losing by a narrow margin. Four years later he returned to Milwaukee and ran unsuccessfully for Congress.

After World War I, he again returned to Oklahoma City and helped organize the Farmer-Labor Reconstruction League, a coalition of Progressives, socialists, factory workers, and farmers. The league was able to help Jack C. Walton, a union official, be elected governor, but he was impeached and removed from office in 1923. Ameringer struggled to keep the *Oklahoma Leader* going, and from 1922 to 1931 he edited and published the *Illinois Miner,* which earned him some extra income.

For that publication he wrote a humorous column, "Adam Coaldigger," that poet Carl Sandburg later praised for its wit. Ameringer changed the name *Oklahoma Leader* to *American Guardian* and the paper gained a wide circulation among industrial workers. Today, Ameringer is best known for a statement of his that appears in his 1940 autobiography, *If You Don't Weaken,* where he defined politics as "the art by which politicians obtain campaign contributions from the rich and votes from the poor on the pretext of protecting each from the other."

Ameringer died on November 5, 1943. He was survived by three sons, and by a daughter born to his second wife, Freda Hogan, whom he had married in 1930 after his first marriage had ended in divorce.

Further Reading

Ameringer, Oscar. *If You Don't Weaken: The Autobiography of Oscar Ameringer.* New York: Holt, 1940.

Ames, Jessie Daniel
(Jessie Harriet Daniel)
(1883–1972) *women's suffragist, civil rights activist*

Jessie Daniel Ames is remembered for being a crusader for women's suffrage and a strong voice against the lynching of African Americans. She was born Jessie Harriet Daniel on November 2, 1883, in Palestine, Texas, to James Malcolm Daniel, a train dispatcher and telegraph operator, and Laura Maria Leonard Daniel, a schoolteacher.

Jessie Daniel grew up in a strongly religious family. When she was four, they moved to Georgetown, Texas, and she attended the public schools before enrolling at Southwestern University, a local college founded by the Methodist Church just 20 years earlier. In 1905 she married Roger Post Ames, an army surgeon, to avoid the spinsterhood she greatly feared. The marriage turned out to be a disaster; although they decided against divorce for the sake of their three children, they lived apart, Roger engaging in medical research in South America and Jessie living with her wealthy married sister in Tennessee.

Roger died in 1914, and Jessie Ames returned to Texas. There she and her mother ran a local telephone company, and she worked as the bookkeeper and later the manager. With her new status as a businesswoman, Ames determined that she should be allowed to vote and exert greater political influence. Her biographer, Jacquelyn Dowd Hall, states that "she became a 'new woman,' no longer a dependent, humiliated wife but an aggressive and effective leader."

Ames was elected treasurer of the Texas Equal Suffrage Association in 1918, and soon after the Nineteenth Amendment to the U.S. Constitution guaranteed women the right to vote in 1919, she became founding president of the Texas League of Women Voters. She also served as a delegate to the Democratic National Convention in the 1920s.

As Ames awakened to social injustice, she decided to oppose racial discrimination and in 1922 became director of the women's division of the Commission on Interracial Cooperation, located in Atlanta, Georgia. In 1930 she founded the Association of Southern Women for the Prevention of Lynching (ASWPL). Lynchings of blacks by whites in the South had long been a part of the racist society; the hangings struck at the accused but also at the entire black community as whites attempted to control African Americans through fear. Whites argued that the lynchings almost always resulted from African-American rapes of white women. They claimed that black men were innately predatory toward white women, who had to be protected.

Ames fought that attitude by encouraging white women to reject the stereotypical view of their vulnerability to black aggression and by educating whites about the shortcomings in their argument. Through her own research she showed that of 204 lynchings in an eight-year period only 29 percent of those blacks hanged had been accused of crimes against white women.

To organize chapters of the ASWPL, Ames traveled throughout the South. She found considerable support from those who wanted to attract capital into the region for economic development but believed that their efforts were being hindered by the negative publicity surrounding the lynchings. Ames admitted the importance of economics when in 1939 she said to an audience:

> We have managed to reduce lynchings not because we've grown more law-abiding or respectable but because lynchings became such bad advertising. The South is going after big industry at the moment, and a lawless, lynch-mob population isn't going to attract very much outside capital. And this is the type of attitude which can be turned to advantage

much more speedily than the abstract appeal to brotherly love.

But the ASWPL suffered from Ames's iron hand administration and her failure to recruit blacks into the organization or build a close alliance with the National Association for the Advancement of Colored People (NAACP), which under WALTER FRANCIS WHITE had also started a campaign against lynching. In short, her efforts smacked of a paternalistic attitude toward blacks. For a variety of reasons lynchings declined in the South, and in 1942 the ASWPL was disbanded.

Ames moved to North Carolina in the 1940s and participated in Democratic politics. Crippled by arthritis, she returned to Texas to be near her daughter. She died on February 21, 1972, in Austin. Jacquelyn Down Hall writes that Jessie Ames had, through her work, "asserted control over her own destiny and over the definition of women in southern society."

Further Reading

Alpern, Sarah, ed. *The Challenge of Feminist Biography: Writing the Lives of Modern American Women.* Urbana: University of Illinois Press, 1992.

Hall, Jacquelyn Dowd. *Revolt against Chivalry: Jessie Daniel Ames and the Women's Campaign against Lynching.* New York: Columbia University Press, 1979.

Andrews, Fannie Fern
(1867–1950) *peace activist*

Fannie Fern Andrews devoted her life to the promotion of peace studies through education. She was born in Lynn, Massachusetts, in 1867 to William Wallace Andrews, a shoemaker, and Anna Maria Brown Andrews, an activist in the temperance movement.

At the age of three, according to her own account, Fannie decided she wanted to be a teacher. She attended Salem (Massachusetts) Normal School, after which she taught for six years. She then enrolled at Radcliffe College, from which she received a degree in psychology and education in 1902.

In 1908 Andrews founded the American School Peace League, dedicated to promoting peace by teaching international justice in public schools, and served as its executive director. She accomplished this during a time of increased interest in peace; more than 45 peace organizations were founded in the United States between 1900 and 1914. Internationalist in outlook, these groups feared what might happen as a result of the large-scale buildup of armaments. As it turned out, the worst occurred, when World War I began in June 1914.

By 1915 Andrews had promoted the league so effectively that it had become a national organization with branches in at least 40 states, and the group had been able to convince many public schools to observe a "Peace Day." That year she attended the International Congress of Women at the Hague, which sought to arrange an end to the war.

As part of the league's activities, Andrews and four other women wrote a 400-page curriculum guide based on the premise that children could be shaped to practice justice by teaching them to avoid conflicts and to treat their peers with respect. The guide also encouraged the study of "peace heroes," whom Andrews called "patriots in higher spheres and with higher tools than the man with the gun." Because the peace heroes included women, Andrews was also promoting a change in education from its male-dominant content. At the same time, she counteracted the virulent nativism then sweeping America in a time of substantial immigration by advancing the concept of respect for all people. She states in the curriculum guide that "American life is made rich and fruitful by the gifts and service of many nationalities."

Nevertheless, America's entry into World War I made the entire peace movement suspect as unpatriotic, and to blunt political attacks against her organization, she changed its name in 1918 to the American School Citizenship League. She broke with more pacifistic peace activists when, having campaigned for neutrality, she supported President Woodrow Wilson's decision to enter the war. She subsequently revised the curriculum guide to tone down its pacifist passages.

Unlike other women who were peace activists, and perhaps influenced by her own ASPL's inclu-

sion of men as members, Andrews moved away from working for peace through primarily female organizations. Thus while JANE ADDAMS helped lead the Women's International League for Peace and Freedom, Andrews preferred to work within the traditionally male political system.

Through her work before the war to create an international bureau of education, Andrews gained the attention of President Woodrow Wilson; consequently, in 1918 he chose her to serve as a delegate to the Paris Peace Conference. There she lobbied, unsuccessfully as it turned out, for the proposed League of Nations to include an international bureau of education that would promote peace. "Although no action was taken by this body on the proposal," Andrews recalled, "there was no doubt of its general approval." She said President Woodrow Wilson told her at the time that the failure to adopt the proposal "does not signify hostility to the subject . . . but that we think it wise to confine ourselves merely to the setting up of the framework of the League of Nations, leaving the complete organization for future development." In other words, Wilson wanted nothing done that would risk gaining approval for his beloved League of Nations.

In 1923 Andrews earned a doctorate in diplomacy and international law from Radcliffe. Her other peace activities included serving in the International Law Association, the World Peace Foundation, and the International Guild. She worked for peace right up to her death in 1950.

Further Reading
Andrews, Fannie Fern. *Memory: Pages of My Life.* Boston: Talisman Press, 1948.

Stomfay-Stitz, Aline M. *Peace Education in America, 1828–1990: A Sourcebook for Education and Research.* Metuchen, N.J.: Scarecrow Press, 1993.

Andrews, John Bertram
(1880–1943) *labor reformer*

John Bertram Andrews was a promoter of labor reform, particularly health insurance and unemployment benefits. He was born on August 2, 1880, in South Wayne, Wisconsin, the son of Philo Edmund Andrews, a farmer, and Sara Jane Maddrell Andrews.

While a boy, John Andrews worked on his family's farm and attended the local schools before entering the University of Wisconsin at Madison. He obtained a B.A. in 1904 and the following year earned an M.A. from Dartmouth College in New Hampshire. He then returned to the University of Wisconsin to pursue a doctorate in history and economics, which he received in 1908.

At Wisconsin, Andrews studied under John R. Commons, who was associated with the American Bureau of Industrial Research, and the two men formed a close working relationship and collaborated in the writing of several books. In December 1908 Commons obtained an appointment for Andrews as executive secretary of the recently organized American Association for Labor Legislation (AALL). While working for that group he met Irene Osgood; they married in 1910 and eventually had one child.

The AALL was formed as the Progressive reform movement was under way, a time when highly trained experts, many of them academics, were trying to solve social problems through rational analysis. With Andrews as its leader, the AALL promoted laws that would provide workers with compensation for industrial accidents along with insurance for health expenses and unemployment. Writing in the *Journal of Economic Issues* (September 1991), John Dennis Chasse claims that "between 1910 and World War II, the AALL was the major influence on state and federal labor legislation."

A report written by Andrews caused the federal government to broaden its definition of industrial accidents to include occupational disease, and as a result in 1912 Congress passed a law that prohibited the use of poisonous white phosphorus in the making of matches. About that time, Andrews began publishing and editing the *American Labor Legislation Review.*

In 1915 the AALL called for compulsory health insurance that would provide medical and cash benefits to workers. Andrews lobbied the legislatures in California and New York to pass such a bill, but employers and doctors called it socialistic and it went down to defeat.

Chastened by the experience, Andrews retreated from proposing required programs to emphasizing voluntary ones. Working with John R. Commons he developed a plan for fighting unemployment through market analysis, public works programs, and production planning. In addition to those measures, he and Commons proposed that each employer set aside funds in individual company reserves to compensate unemployed workers.

Their proposal caused a rift among labor reformers, two of whom, Abraham Epstein and Isaac Rubinow, attacked the plan as overly conservative and unworkable. They wanted a government-controlled program under which unemployment moneys contributed by companies would be pooled and placed into a trust fund. In 1935 the state of New York adopted their plan.

When Congress passed the Social Security Act of 1935, it included a provision for unemployment insurance that would be financed by a federal tax on payrolls but would allow each state to administer the system to give it flexibility. In so doing, Congress sided with Andrews over Epstein, who wanted a more uniform system that he believed would better serve the country's highly mobile population.

"I want to say with particular reference to the unemployment compensation feature of this bill," Andrews testified before Congress in February 1935, "that on the whole, as the result of all of the study and all of the conferences that have been held, that with a few perfecting amendments, it is the kind of a measure that ought to be passed and ought to be passed as promptly as possible." He said that as a cooperative venture between the federal government and the states, "this plan gives to the good employer his opportunity to go ahead with the assurance that he will not be undercut unfairly in competition with his competitors in States that otherwise might not take the legislative action."

John Andrews died on January 4, 1943, in New York City, leaving a legacy, according to John Dennis Chasse, that "justice and reasonableness are not likely in a society that ignores the voices of its own citizens."

Further Reading

Chasse, John Dennis. "The American Association for Labor Legislation: An Episode in Institutionalist Policy Analysis." *Journal of Economic Issues* 25, no. 3 (September 1991): 799+.

Harter, Lafayette G. *John R. Commons: His Assault on Laissez-Faire.* Corvallis: Oregon State University Press, 1962.

Andrews, Stephen Pearl

(1812–1886) *abolitionist*

Throughout his life Stephen Andrews pursued a variety of reforms, most notably abolitionism. He was born on March 22, 1812, in Templeton, Massachusetts, to Reverend Elisha Andrews and Wealthy Ann Lathrop Andrews.

Andrews attended a village school, was taught at home by his father, and then studied in the classical department of Amherst Academy in Amherst, Massachusetts, from 1828 to 1829. In 1830 he moved to Jackson, Louisiana, where he taught at the Jackson Female Seminary. He subsequently studied law and in 1833 was admitted to the Louisiana bar. Two years later he moved to New Orleans, where he began his legal practice and married Mary Ann Gordon. The couple had three sons.

With the slave trading blocks practically at his doorstep, Andrews advocated the ending of slavery. In 1839 he moved to the Republic of Texas and practiced law in Houston. Because he continued to condemn slavery, in 1843 a mob attacked his house, and he barely escaped with his life. Soon afterward, he traveled to Britain, where he tried to arrange a loan from the government to finance a plan to free the slaves in Texas.

He failed and returned to the United States where he settled in Boston with the goal of making popular a phonetic writing system called phonography. He believed the system could especially help educate illiterate black children. In 1845 he published *The Comprehensive Phonographic Class-Book* and *The Phonographic Reader*, both of which sold widely. He also developed an international language that was the forerunner to Esperanto.

In 1848 he moved to New York City and dropped his involvement in phonography to promote the Equitable Commerce Plan. Developed by Josiah Warren, the plan sought to minimize government and place trade under the control of the workers. Warren had opened a time store in 1827 in Cincinnati, Ohio, and it prospered under a peculiar system: Shoppers paid cash for items whose prices were set to cover their cost and that of some basic overhead, such as store rent. But the prices did not reflect the amount of time Warren had to spend in helping the shopper; to cover that cost, the shopper would agree to "pay" Warren by providing him with a service. A watchmaker, for example, might agree to work on one of Warren's watches without charge for a set number of minutes.

Andrews and Warren founded in 1851 the Modern Times community in Islip, Long Island, New York, complete with a time store and with stipulations that the economy be run through a barter system and that none of the land or buildings ever be sold for a profit (though the settlers could own their property). The founders gushed: "The settlers on the ground at the opening of this spring, all comfortably housed, and beginning to establish various trades and branches of business, are about 70. . . . There are great facilities for building here. . . . The climate is salubrious and delightful." But Modern Times soon disbanded after nearby residents complained about its free love principles and after the settlers violated the economic strictures and started selling land for a profit and ignoring the barter system.

Andrews's wife died in 1855, and the following year he married Esther Hussey Bartlet Jones. In 1860 he formulated Pantarchy, which he called "a new spiritual Government for the world." In his later years, he developed Universology, a deductive science of the universe, and in 1872 he published *The Basic Outline of Universology*, a ponderous attempt to bring together the sciences, arts, and philosophies.

Andrews died in New York City on May 21, 1886. Though nearly all of his reform efforts failed, he had drawn attention to problems facing society, most particularly slavery, and in that way encouraged others to fight for change.

Further Reading

Stern, Madeleine B. *The Pantarch: A Biography of Stephen Pearl Andrews.* Austin: University of Texas Press 1968.

Fisher, David. "Stephen Pearl Andrews." Available online. URL: http://www.tsha.utexas.edu/handbook/online/articles/view/AA/fan25.html. Downloaded on March 25, 2002.

Anthony, Susan Brownell
(1820–1906) *women's suffragist*

Susan B. Anthony was a temperance reformer, abolitionist, and tireless worker for women's right to vote. She was born on February 15, 1820, in Adams, Massachusetts, to Daniel Anthony, a manufacturer and farmer, and Lucy Read Anthony.

Susan B. Anthony grew up in a reform-minded family. Her parents, both Quakers, were dedicated to social causes. At age six, Susan relocated with them to Battensville, New York.

She attended public schools and a school run by her father for neighborhood children, and then she became a teacher; in that job she first encountered sex discrimination. In the 1840s Susan began teaching school in upstate New York and discovered that she was being paid about one-fifth the salary paid to her male colleagues. When she complained, the district school board fired her. Nevertheless, in 1846 she became principal at Canjoharie Academy in Rochester, New York, a position she held until 1850, when she left education.

While living with her parents in Rochester, Anthony met some of the leading reformers of the day, including the abolitionists WILLIAM LLOYD GARRISON, WENDELL PHILLIPS, and FREDERICK DOUGLASS. In 1851 she met AMELIA JENKS BLOOMER and ELIZABETH CADY STANTON at a temperance convention in Seneca Falls, New York. From that meeting she and Stanton developed a lasting friendship and began a close collaboration.

Anthony was drawn to the temperance movement by the stories she had heard of drunken husbands beating their wives. In 1852 she served as a delegate to the Sons of Temperance meeting in Albany. When the group's leaders prevented her from speaking because of her sex, she formed the Woman's State Temperance Society of New York. As she continued to speak out against the evils of alcohol and encountered more hostility toward women participating in public debates, she gravitated toward the women's rights movement. Like many other women reformers who began as temperance advocates, she also joined the abolitionist cause and supported William Lloyd Garrison's demands for the immediate end to slavery.

Anthony traveled and lectured almost constantly. Elizabeth Cady Stanton, who had a husband and children and could not tour as extensively, saw her as the great proselytizer for women's rights. Stanton said, "I forged the thunderbolts and she fired them."

Several months after the Civil War began in 1861, Anthony and Stanton formed the National Woman's Loyal League, which sent to Congress a petition bearing 400,000 signatures calling for a constitutional amendment to abolish slavery. Congress indeed approved such a change, ratified by the states in December 1863 as the Thirteenth Amendment. Three years later, as Congress debated sending the Fourteenth Amendment to the states—with its provisions that defined national citizenship and prohibited any state from denying individuals their life, liberty, or property without due process of the law—Anthony urged that its wording be changed so that it would specifically guarantee women's right to vote.

Congress refused, and a schism split the suffrage movement when some women insisted that the issue of their gaining the ballot should take priority over blacks' gaining the right to vote. Others believed that extending the vote to blacks could be used as a foundation for extending it to women.

Anthony thought blacks should wait for suffrage. She criticized the push for the Fifteenth Amendment, which would prohibit denying a person the right to vote on the basis of race, and said that as voters, black men would join white men in oppressing women. Many of her comments included bigoted remarks, and in 1868 she began publishing *The Revolution*, a women's rights journal financed by George Francis Train, a racist. In it, Anthony dealt with such issues as divorce,

A tireless crusader for women's suffrage, Susan B. Anthony was honored by the federal government in 1979 when it coined a dollar that bore her likeness. *(Library of Congress)*

prostitution, and the plight of women workers in an exploitive industrial environment.

In 1869 she and Stanton organized the National Woman Suffrage Association (NWSA), which advocated working through the federal government to secure women's right to vote. At various times Anthony demanded a sixteenth amendment that would guarantee women's suffrage; at other times the NWSA pursued congressional laws to implement what it saw as the voting rights already guaranteed in the Fourteenth Amendment. A rival organization, the American Woman Suffrage Association (AWSA), led by LUCY STONE, advocated obtaining voting rights for women by working through the individual state legislatures. Unlike the NWSA, the AWSA supported the Fifteenth Amendment and the drive for black suffrage.

On November 1, 1872, in Rochester, Anthony and several other women entered a barbershop, a traditional male bastion, where voters were registering. There she demanded that she be allowed to sign up to vote. Taken aback, the male registrars, or inspectors, did not know what to do; as they hesitated, Anthony told them she had voting rights under the New York constitution and the Fourteenth Amendment. She warned that if she were refused, she would sue the inspectors. They debated among themselves for an hour, before finally agreeing to let her register. Newspapers then vilified them for that action. The *Rochester Union and Advertiser* said, "Citizenship no more carries the right to vote than it carries the power to fly to the moon. . . . If these women in the Eighth Ward offer to vote, they should be challenged, and if they take the oaths and the Inspectors receive and deposit their ballots, they should all be prosecuted to the full extent of the law."

On November 5 Anthony cast her vote for president (as did about 50 other women). She wrote to Stanton, "Well I have been & gone & done it!!—positively voted the Republican ticket—strait this a.m. at 7 Oclock. . . . If only now—all the . . . suffrage women would work to this end of enforcing the existing constitution—supremacy of national law over state law—what strides we might make this winter—But I'm awful tired—for five days I have been on the constant run—but to splendid purpose—So all right—I hope you voted too."

Two weeks later marshals arrested her for voting illegally in a federal election. She told a friend, "I never dreamed the U.S. officers [would prosecute] me for voting." In the months before her trial she lectured extensively around Rochester, arguing that women had the right to vote, which was based on the Civil War amendments to the U.S. Constitution, natural law, "and yet one more authority," she said, "THOMAS PAINE . . . [who] more ably vindicated the principles upon which government is founded: 'The right of voting for representatives is the primary right by which other rights are protected. To take away this right is to reduce man to a state of slavery.'"

Trying to influence potential jurors in her trial, Anthony called on juries "to fail to return verdicts of 'guilty' against honest, law-abiding, tax paying United States citizens for offering their votes at our elections." She swayed so many people that Judge Ward Hunt agreed to a change of venue from Monroe County to Ontario County, whereupon Anthony began speaking there.

At Anthony's trial, which began on June 17, 1873, Hunt stunned the jury when he announced he was ending the proceedings and handing down a verdict of guilty. He actually had written the verdict before the trial had even begun. "The Fourteenth Amendment gives no right to a woman to vote," Hunt said, "and the voting by Miss Anthony was in violation of the law." That night, Anthony wrote in her diary that the trial was "the greatest judicial outrage history has ever recorded!"

Anthony remained defiant. At her sentencing, when Judge Hunt asked her whether she had anything to say, she launched into a long statement. The judge interrupted her several times, ordering her to sit down, but she refused. "Robbed of the fundamental privilege of citizenship," she said, "I am degraded from the status of a citizen to that of a subject; and not only myself individually, but all of my sex, are, by your honor's verdict, doomed to political subjection under this, so-called, form of government." Judge Hunt fined Anthony $100. She said she would never pay it, and she never did.

Anthony continued to fight for women's rights, and from 1892 until 1900 she served as president of the National American Woman Suffrage Association, formed after the NWSA and AWSA merged. She died on March 13, 1906. This was before the Nineteenth Amendment finally guaranteed women's right to vote, but her strenuous efforts for suffrage in the face of hostile audiences did much to advance the cause, and her trial in 1873 motivated those who supported the movement by showing the extent to which authority would be used to prevent women from voting.

According to Kathleen Barry, writing in *Susan B. Anthony: A Biography of a Singular Feminist* (1988), "More than anything Anthony believed in women's ability to assume their moral imperative and bring about a greater good in society." Toward that goal, while speaking about temperance, Anthony once said:

> How is this great change to be wrought, who are to urge on this vast work of reform? Shall it not be women, who are most aggrieved by the foul destroyer's inroads? Most certainly. Then arises the question, how are we to accomplish the end desired? I answer not by confining our influence to our own home circle, not by centering all our benevolent feelings upon our own kindred, not by caring naught for the culture of our minds, save those of our own darlings. No, no; the gratification of the *selfish* impulses *alone,* can never produce a desirable change in the Moral aspect of Society.

In 1979 the federal government honored Susan B. Anthony by coining a dollar that bore her likeness. The government hoped that Americans would take to the coin and reduce their reliance on paper dollars, which wear out quickly. But the coin's size, which made it look like a quarter, and the public's force of habit doomed the Anthony dollar to obscurity. The U.S. Mint ended its production in 1981. Interestingly, the Anthony dollar enjoyed a resurgence in the 1990s for use in vending machines; only a few of the coins, however, are now in circulation.

Further Reading

Barry, Kathleen. *Susan B. Anthony: A Biography of a Singular Feminist.* New York: New York University Press, 1988.

Harper, Ida Husted. *Life and Work of Susan B. Anthony.* New York: Arno Press, 1969.

Sherr, Lynn. *Failure Is Impossible: Susan B. Anthony in Her Own Words.* New York: Times Books, 1995.

Venet, Wendy Hamand. *Neither Ballots nor Bullets: Women Abolitionists and the Civil War.* Charlottesville: University of Virginia Press, 1991.

Aquash, Anna Mae Pictou

(1945–1976) *Indian rights activist*

Raised in dire poverty, Anna Mae Pictou Aquash struggled throughout her short life to find a purpose and discovered it in her devotion to traditional Indian culture, which led to her involvement in the American Indian Movement as a recruiter, organizer, and advocate. She was born Anna Mae Pictou on March 27, 1945, on the Micmac Indian Reservation near Shubenacadie, Nova Scotia, Canada, to Mary Ellen Pictou and Francis Thomas Levi.

Pictou's birthplace, the Micmac reservation, was a hardscrabble settlement of 1,000 acres and a few hundred people, devoid of electricity or even running water. When Anna Mae was a young child, her father left the reservation to find a job and never returned. In 1949 her mother married Noel Sapier, from the nearby Pictou Landing Reservation. He died in 1956. Mary Ellen Pictou deserted her daughter later that year, and the child was then cared for by her sister and brother-in-law.

In 1962, having received only a limited education at a reservation school, Pictou joined the annual migration of Indians to pick blueberries for farmers in Maine. She stayed there into the fall so she could harvest potatoes, a job that required backbreaking work. There she met Jake Maloney, a fellow Micmac.

A short time later Pictou began working at a small sewing factory in Boston, Massachusetts, while living with Maloney. She gave birth to two daughters, one in 1964 and the other in 1965. Her relationship with Jake Maloney, however, began deteriorating, and she grew uneasy about her detachment from Indian culture. After Maloney left her, she began drinking heavily. That problem led her in 1969 to help found the Boston Indian Council, dedicated to providing the city's Native Americans with drug and alcohol education, job placement, and housing referrals.

The following year Pictou joined a protest organized by the American Indian Movement (AIM) at the *Mayflower II*, a replica of the original *Mayflower*, which had carried the Pilgrims to Plymouth Bay. AIM, founded in 1968 to fight for Native American rights, wanted to expose injustices toward Indians, including the biased stories in history books that ignored the depredations committed by white settlers against tribes in early America.

Also in 1970, Pictou joined Teaching and Research in Bicultural Education (TRIBE) at Acadia National Park in Maine, where she instructed Indians in arts, crafts, and music. By 1972 she was embracing traditional Indian culture and turning against the white ways she thought had weakened and hurt her people. That year she again joined AIM activists, this time in the "Trail of Broken Treaties" protest, when about 2,000 Indians from 100 reservations rallied in Washington, D.C., to publicize the failure of the federal government to adhere to its agreements with the tribes; in addition, the protesters wanted government officials to meet with them and discuss unemployment and other problems on their tribal lands.

Then in 1973 she heard about a desperate AIM showdown with the government on the Pine Ridge Reservation in South Dakota. AIM activists had been called onto the reservation by Oglala Sioux (Lakota) Indians who wanted to protect their traditional rights from violations by Richard Wilson, the tribal president, who was working with the federal government to sell Indian landholdings. Wilson's police confronted AIM, and the protesters barricaded themselves at Wounded Knee, a site important to the Sioux (Dakota, Nakota, Lakota) as the place where, in 1890, white soldiers had massacred unarmed Indians.

In March Pictou left her job on the assembly line at the General Motors plant in Framingham, Massachusetts, and rushed to Wounded Knee. As gunfire erupted between the activists and federal marshals, she gathered food, used a golf club to dig bunkers, and patrolled the village. While at Wounded Knee, she married Nogeeshik Aquash, a traditional Chippewa artist with whom she had been involved back east.

Anna Mae and Nogeeshik Aquash left Wounded Knee before the siege ended and settled in Ottawa, Canada, where they made Indian beadwork and jewelry. By 1974 she and Nogeeshik had separated, and that year she taught Indian students about their heritage at the AIM-run Red Schoolhouse in Saint Paul, Minnesota. From there she went to Los Angeles and helped AIM organize that city's chapter. A Sioux leader recalled, "Anna Mae was an operator and a real go-getter; she didn't let no grass grow under her feet."

Then in June 1975 Anna Mae Aquash returned to Pine Ridge. She called together Indian women, who were as a rule nonpolitical, explained to them how the federal government had violated Sioux treaty rights, and convinced them to speak out against the unhealthy government food rations on the reservation. "I wouldn't feed that canned meat to my dog," she told them. "You're so brainwashed you just let everything go. That's how come you end up like this."

But by 1975 Pine Ridge had become an even more dangerous place than it had been during the Wounded Knee showdown. AIM supporters and their opponents were engaging in violence; most of the attacks were perpetrated by Wilson's supporters against AIM. Eighteen murders and 67 assaults on persons and property in the first half of the year spread fear and anger. When a shootout between AIM members and FBI agents in June left two agents dead, the government sought Aquash for questioning, though she had been nowhere near the scene. In September she was arrested during a raid at the nearby Rosebud Reservation and charged with the illegal possession of a firearm. Aquash said about the FBI: "I think they most definitely want to destroy the Indian nation if it will not submit to the living conditions of a so-called reservation. They definitely are out to destroy our concept of freedom." She later said to a friend that an FBI agent who questioned her told her that if she failed to cooperate, she would be dead within a year.

Aquash jumped bail and in November was arrested while traveling in a motor home with AIM fugitives DENNIS JAMES BANKS and LEONARD PELTIER. Banks and Peltier fled, but the police captured Aquash and extradited her to South Dakota. When a judge released her into the custody of her attorney, several AIM members suspected she had received favorable treatment because, they believed, she was an FBI informant.

Nonetheless, Aquash continued to work for AIM, which was by that time beset with factional fighting. On February 24, 1976, a rancher reported finding the body of a woman near Wanblee, on the Pine Ridge Reservation. Teams of FBI agents descended on the scene, cut off the woman's hands, and sent them to Washington, so they could be fingerprinted. The agents ordered an autopsy that determined the woman had died of exposure. She was then quickly buried and later identified as Anna Mae Aquash.

AIM suspected a cover-up, demanded a second autopsy, and got it. The new finding revealed Aquash had been shot in the back of the head at close range, execution-style. She was reburied in an Oglala Lakota ceremony on the Pine Ridge Reservation.

To this day, questions surround Aquash's death. Why were so many FBI agents sent to the site where her body was found? Why were her hands removed when her fingerprints could have been taken at the scene? Why was no attempt made to summon anyone to the morgue to identify the body? What was she doing out in the middle of nowhere?

The FBI has long promoted the view that a faction within AIM thought her to be an informant and killed her. Some evidence supports that view. Others believe that persons working for the FBI murdered her at a time when the government was known for infiltrating dissident groups and encouraging them to commit acts of violence. Her death occurred after she had been under surveillance by the FBI for some time and after she had told disbelieving agents that she knew nothing about the June 1975 murders of their two colleagues on the Pine Ridge Reservation. Whatever the final verdict, she knew that with her activism she was risking her life. "They'll execute me," she told a friend in 1973. "That's what they do to Indians who fight for their people."

Further Reading

Brand, Johanna. *The Life and Death of Anna Mae Aquash.* Toronto: James Lorimer & Company, 1993.
Matthiessen, Peter. *In the Spirit of Crazy Horse.* New York: Viking, 1991.

Avery, Rachel Foster
(1858–1919) *women's suffragist*

Rachel Foster Avery, a friend and close associate of the suffragist SUSAN BROWNELL ANTHONY, worked to give women the right to vote. She was born Rachel Foster on December 30, 1858, in Pittsburgh, Pennsylvania, to Quaker parents.

In 1879 Foster attended the National Woman Suffrage Association (NWSA) meeting as a delegate, where she met Anthony. The following year, she was elected the organization's corresponding secretary, and in 1882 she directed the NWSA suffrage campaign in Nebraska. In 1883 she accompanied Anthony on her fellow suffragist's tour of Europe, and shortly thereafter she studied political economy at the University of Zurich.

Foster married Cyrus Avery in 1888, a decision that strained her relations with Anthony, who thought that her friend's commitment to women's suffrage would waver. Relations between the two worsened when Rachel Avery disagreed with Anthony and criticized ELIZABETH CADY STANTON's *The Woman's Bible* (1895), a revised Bible that expunged the original's bias against women.

Avery had previously worked with Anthony, LUCY STONE, and ALICE STONE BLACKWELL to merge the NWSA with the American Woman Suffrage Association, and from 1907 until 1910 she served as the vice president of the resulting organization, the National American Woman Suffrage Association.

In 1908 she revived the women's suffrage movement in Pennsylvania by heading that state's Woman Suffrage Association. With that accomplishment, she once again showed that her greatest talent was in assembling the nuts and bolts that gave the suffrage movement its much-needed organization.

Avery died in Philadelphia on October 26, 1919, shortly before the Nineteenth Amendment, which guaranteed women's right to vote, was ratified.

Further Reading

Kraditor, Aileen S. *The Ideas of the Woman Suffrage Movement.* New York: W. W. Norton, 1981.

Wheeler, Marjorie Spruill, ed. *One Woman, One Vote: Rediscovering the Woman Suffrage Movement.* Troutdale, Ore.: NewSage Press, 1995.

B

Baez, Joan
(1941–) *antiwar and peace activist*

A folk musician, Joan Baez committed herself to participating in protests and movements that would fight injustice through nonviolent means. She was born on January 9, 1941, on Staten Island, New York, to Albert V. Baez, a physicist who had emigrated from Mexico, and Joan Bridge Baez, a Scottish immigrant.

In the 1950s Baez moved to Palo Alto, California, with her family. She graduated from high school in 1958 and relocated to Boston, where her father taught college. She then attended Boston University but soon withdrew because she disliked the rigidity of academics and, in any event, preferred to play her music, which she had been interested in since her teenage years.

Over the next few months she gained a substantial following in the coffeehouses that dotted Cambridge, Massachusetts, and in 1959 garnered national recognition when she played at the Newport Folk Festival. Within two years, she signed a contract with Vanguard Records; released her first album, *Joan Baez;* toured with folk musician Bob Dylan; and increased her major concert appearances to more than 20 annually.

She refused, however, to perform on "Hootenanny," a folk music show on ABC television, when the network banned her fellow musician Pete Seeger from appearing because of his leftist beliefs. Baez grew more popular as a folk music revival attracted young people. Folk music's themes dealt with racial and economic oppression, expressed a longing for a simpler past, and coincided with the expansion of the civil rights movement and the stirrings of the 1960s counterculture. Baez enthusiastically participated in the era's political protests, and while living in California and continuing to develop and record her music, she spent a good part of the 1960s engaged in reform movements.

Beginning in 1964 and continuing for several years thereafter, Baez withheld payment of a portion of her federal income tax as a way to protest the Vietnam War. In 1965 she founded the Institute for the Study of Non-Violence in a former schoolhouse near where she lived in the Carmel Valley.

The following year she joined a silent march in Grenada, Mississippi, to protest the beating of black elementary school children by the parents of white students, and she performed at a benefit to help Chicano farm workers then on strike in Santa Monica, California. In 1967 she was arrested twice, in October and in December, for protesting the draft by engaging in a sit-in outside the Oakland Induction Center. At the same time, she contributed money to The Resistance, a prominent antidraft organization begun by David Harris, a student at Stanford University. She and Harris married in 1968 and divorced three years later. Meanwhile, she released two highly successful albums, *Baptism,* in 1968, and *Any Day Now,* in 1969.

After the 1960s, her social commitment remained fused with her work as an artist, though her records took a more commercial turn. In the late 1970s Baez helped found an international human rights commission, Humanitas.

Shortly after completing a recording session in 1968, Joan Baez stated: "No matter how many good or bad records I make, the important thing is to get people to stop murdering each other." In that spirit she has been able to make her ballads sing with cause of social justice.

Further Reading

Baez, Joan. *And a Voice to Sing With: A Memoir.* New York: Summit, 1987.

Cantwell, Robert. *When We Were Good: The Folk Revival.* Cambridge, Mass.: Harvard University Press, 1996.

Baker, Ella Josephine

(1903–1986) *civil rights leader*

Ella Josephine Baker was an African-American civil rights activist who helped found the Student Non-Violent Coordinating Committee. She was born on December 13, 1903, in Norfolk, Virginia, the daughter of Blake Baker, a steamship waiter, and Georgianna Ross Baker, a schoolteacher and community leader.

Ella Baker grew up in Littleton, North Carolina, and learned from her parents and maternal grandparents, who had been slaves, the importance of resisting oppression and contributing to the larger community. Baker received her secondary education at a boarding school in Raleigh, North Carolina, and in 1923 she attended that city's Shaw University. Four years later she graduated as class valedictorian with a major in sociology.

Baker hoped to go on to graduate school at the University of Chicago, but her finances prevented it, and in 1927 she moved to New York City, where she worked as a waitress and a factory laborer. The onset of the Great Depression in 1929 exposed her to massive poverty in Harlem and to some of the radical political ideas being discussed to alleviate it. She joined the Young Negroes Cooperative League, formed as a consumer cooperative, and in 1931 became its national director.

Writing in *Social Policy* (Winter 1999), Lisa Y. Sullivan, a community activist, states that Baker "believed that cooperatives emphasized the values of interdependency, group decision making, and the sharing of economic resources." She wanted to relate these values to young people. "Most of all," Sullivan writes, "Baker sought to increase the social, political, and economic understanding of Black youth in the 1930s. By using an informational approach to Black youth rather than dogma, she aimed to educate and then lead her peers into self-directed action." She would do the same years later when she guided college students to found the Student Non-Violent Coordinating Committee.

In the 1930s the federal government hired Baker through the Works Progress Administration to begin a consumer education project. In the middle of the decade she worked on the editorial staff of the *American West Indian News* and the *Negro National News.* About 1938 she married T. J. Roberts but kept her own name.

Baker's direct involvement in civil rights began in 1938 when she joined the National Association for the Advancement of Colored People (NAACP) as a field secretary. In that post, she traveled throughout the South, raising money and recruiting members. The job strengthened her organizational skills, made her a better speaker, and broadened her contacts with African-American leaders. At a time when black organizers in the South risked bodily harm, even death, at the hands of racist whites, Baker showed tenacity and courage.

She returned to New York City in 1943 and was named national director of the NAACP branches. Relations between her and the NAACP grew strained, however, when she complained about the organization's excessive reliance on legal challenges to racial segregation. She wanted to reach out and engage African Americans in more direct protest. Baker resigned from her job in the NAACP in 1946, but to maintain harmony within the group, she worked as a volunteer at the New York City branch.

In 1953 Baker ran for the New York State Assembly on the Liberal Party ticket but lost. The following year she healed her rift with the NAACP and became president of the New York City branch and chaired its education committee. She saw to it that local public school boards abided by the Supreme Court's 1954 *Brown v. Board of Education* ruling, which had struck down school segregation.

At the request of advisers to MARTIN LUTHER KING, JR., Baker moved to Atlanta, Georgia, in 1957 to join King's Southern Christian Leadership Conference (SCLC) as coordinator of its Crusade for Citizenship, a drive to register 3 million black voters over two years. The crusade fell far short of its target and enrolled only 160,000 blacks. The failure, however, was less attributable to Baker than to the white resistance to black suffrage in the South, made all the more vicious as the civil rights movement intensified.

In 1959 Baker was named executive director of the SCLC. Under the arrangement, King remained the group's leader, while Baker coordinated programs. With her guidance, SCLC membership increased substantially, but Baker grew dissatisfied and sought changes. For one, she disliked the highly centralized hierarchy within the SCLC. Believing in group decision making, she claimed that the organization relied too heavily on King and his preferences. Second, she thought the SCLC too timid and wanted it to become more aggressive in its fight for civil rights. Third, she recoiled at the sexual discrimination she suffered from the male-dominated leadership. In *Running for Freedom* (1991), historian Steven F. Lawson writes that Baker "suffered from the slights of paternalistic male preachers, who did not view women as equal partners and whose powerful egos made it difficult to impose strict organizational discipline on them."

In February 1960 four black college students in Greensboro, North Carolina, took it upon themselves to begin a sit-in at a Woolworth's lunch counter to protest its segregation policy. Their action ignited a wave of sit-ins by young blacks across the South. Baker saw in the protests an opportunity to mobilize energetic youths for the civil rights movement and to introduce the more aggressive tactics she had long desired. Joanne Grant writes in *Ella Baker: Freedom Bound* (1998), "To Ella Baker it was a dream come true. Here was the beginning of the civil rights revolution which she

had looked forward to since the days of the 1930s when she had ventured from neighborhood to neighborhood listening to speeches that carried the promise of change."

So at age 60 Baker convinced the SCLC to sponsor a conference of the sit-in leaders at her alma mater, Shaw University, and went about organizing it. The SCLC expected some 100 students to attend—but more than 300 showed up, a clear display of the indignation over the slow pace of the civil rights movement and the excitement the students felt to do more.

The students let it be known that although they respected King, they wanted to develop their own organization independently of him. On this point, Baker encouraged them. One of the students, JOHN ROBERT LEWIS, recalled: "She kept daring us to go further. She was much more radical than King, more like [ASA] PHILIP RANDOLPH in his youth, well to the movement's left. She was very creative. She did not want the students used by the SCLC or the NAACP. She left a deep imprint on us."

At her suggestion, the students formed a Temporary Student Non-Violent Coordinating Committee whose structure would be separate from the SCLC. In agreement with Baker's beliefs and their own views, the students kept the organization decentralized to emphasize decision making by the entire group. Here then began what Joanne Grant calls in her book "a new phase of the civil rights movement." She writes: "It was no longer to be controlled by a stodgy ministerial or bureaucratic presence. It was to be led by a new force."

A few weeks later the students formally convened an organizational meeting in Atlanta. They consulted King, the NAACP, and other civil rights leaders and organizations, but they were clearly going their own way. In fall 1960, the SCLC fired Baker for her role in creating the student group, and that October the students formally established the Student Non-Violent Coordinating Committee, or SNCC. Baker remained an adviser to SNCC until 1964. It was, to say the least, an interesting development in which a black matriarch of the civil rights movement had come to be a founder of such a militant, youth-centered group. Yet her role with SNCC drew on her earlier experience with the

Young Negroes Cooperative League; she had from the start of her activism wanted to reach out to black youths.

In 1964 Baker helped found the Mississippi Freedom Democratic Party (MFDP), an alternative to that state's whites-only Democratic Party. The MFDP tried to seat its delegates at the Democratic National Convention, and although they failed, their attempt placed the political spotlight on racial segregation and led to promises by the national Democratic leadership that in the future exclusively white delegations would no longer be allowed.

Baker remained active in the civil rights movement throughout the rest of the 1960s and 1970s. She worked with the Southern Conference Educational Fund, served as vice chair of the Mass Party Organizing Committee in New York City, and sat on the national board of the Puerto Rican Solidarity Committee.

Baker, who had battled all her life with asthma, died at her home in New York City on December 13, 1986. Lisa Y. Sullivan writes, "Not since her death has a leader emerged in the modern 20th century Freedom Movement committed to strengthening the ties that bind social and political action."

Further Reading

Grant, Joanne. *Ella Baker: Freedom Bound.* New York: Wiley, 1998.

Lawson, Steven F. *Running for Freedom: Civil Rights and Black Politics in America since 1941.* Philadelphia: Temple University Press, 1991.

Lerner, Gerda. *Black Women in White America: A Documentary History.* New York: Vintage Books, 1973.

Sullivan, Lisa Y. "Ella Baker." *Social Policy* 30 (Winter 1999): 54.

Balch, Emily Greene

(1867–1961) *peace activist, feminist*

The Nobel Prize winner Emily Greene Balch spent most of her life working for peace and women's rights. The daughter of Francis Vergnies Balch and Maria Noyes Balch, she was born on January 8, 1867, in Jamaica Plain, Massachusetts.

Emily Balch attended Miss Catherine Ireland's School in Boston in 1886 before entering Bryn Mawr, where she studied economics. She graduated in 1889 and received the college's first European Fellowship, allowing her to attend the Sorbonne in France. Balch studied the system of poor relief in Paris and wrote a report on her findings, which was published by the American Economic Association.

Balch returned to the United States in 1891 and joined the settlement house movement, recently begun by JANE ADDAMS, to assist poor immigrants in urban districts. In Boston she helped found Denison House and briefly served as its director.

She then returned to her academic studies, attending the University of Chicago, Harvard Annex (today Radcliffe College), and the University of Berlin. In 1896 she began teaching economics at Wellesley College.

In 1902 Balch became president of the Women's Trade Union League of Boston, and in 1906 she announced her commitment to socialism. She advanced professionally in 1913 through her appointment as chairperson of Wellesley's economics and sociology department.

With World War I under way in Europe, Balch joined the Women's Peace Party, organized in January 1915 in Washington. That spring Balch, JANE ADDAMS, and several other prominent American women attended the International Congress of Women at the Hague, where the delegates talked about ways to end the war. Balch was instrumental in resolving numerous differences among the delegates, and because, in addition to English, she spoke French and German, she served as a translator at discussions. She thought the conference extremely important, as evidenced when she wrote to a friend that "futile as talk seems, the way it is dreaded shows that it does have its effect. Ideas seem so unreal, so powerless, before the vast physical force of the military masses today; it is easy to forget that it is only ideas that created the force and that keep it in action. Let war once be disbelieved in, and that force melts into nothing."

The congress proposed a permanent peace that foreshadowed President Woodrow Wilson's plan for ending the war, his Fourteen Points.

Among its proposals, the women's congress asserted the following:

> No land should be transferred without the consent of the men and women in it, and the right of conquest should not be recognized.
>
> Autonomy and a democratic parliament should not be refused to any people, and women should be granted equal political rights with men. Governments should refer future international disputes to arbitration or conciliation.
>
> [There should be] democratic control of foreign policy with no secret treaties.
>
> [There should be] universal disarmament.

In 1916 Balch took a leave of absence from Wellesley to join the International Committee on Mediation established by Henry Ford. At the same time, she served on the Committee on Constructive Peace and opposed war reparations, while supporting international control over colonies.

Shortly after the United States entered World War I, Balch's affiliation with the American Union against Militarism and the Women's Peace Party, labeled by many as extreme for their antiwar stands, caused Wellesley in 1919 to dismiss her. The federal government's military intelligence bureau described her as someone with "dangerous, destructive and anarchistic sentiments."

Later that year Balch attended another session of the International Congress of Women and was elected secretary-treasurer of the Women's International League for Peace and Freedom (WILPF). In 1921 she joined the London Society of Friends (Quakers) and worked for adequate representation of small countries in the League of Nations.

World War II challenged her pacifist beliefs, and she took a compromise stand. Still active in her late 70s, she opposed U.S. entry into the conflict but urged the federal government to admit refugees from Nazi-occupied countries, and after Japan attacked Pearl Harbor, she supported the American war effort as a necessary evil to defeat totalitarianism. She won the Nobel Prize in peace in 1945.

Balch, who never married, died in Cambridge, Massachusetts, on January 10, 1961. In her work for peace, she had challenged the restrictions placed on women by society and insisted that women could make the ultimate difference in ridding the world of war.

Further Reading

McDonald, Lynn, ed. *Women Theorists on Society and Politics*. Waterloo, Ontario, Canada: Wilfrid Laurier University Press, 1998.

Randall, Mercedes M. *Improper Bostonian: Emily Greene Balch, Nobel Peace Laureate, 1946*. New York: Twayne Publishers, 1964.

Baldwin, Roger Nash
(1884–1981) *civil liberties activist*

Founder of the American Civil Liberties Union, Roger Nash Baldwin was a pacifist who fought to ensure the civil rights of all people. He was born on January 21, 1884, in the Boston suburb of Wellesley Hills to Frank Fenno Baldwin, a leather merchant, and Lucy Cushing Nash Baldwin.

Raised in comfortable surroundings and educated in the best schools, Roger Baldwin was exposed to liberal causes as a child, largely as a result of the work of his mother in the women's movement and that of an uncle, William Baldwin, in civil rights and child reform. Roger Baldwin graduated from Wellesley High School and then entered Harvard. In 1904 he received a bachelor's degree and, the following year, a master's degree in anthropology.

While at Harvard, Baldwin had been profoundly influenced by the Progressive reform movement, and with his degrees in hand, he accepted a position as head of a settlement house organized to help poor immigrants in Saint Louis. He also assisted in founding the sociology department at Washington University. In 1908 he met anarchist EMMA GOLDMAN and counted her as one of the great influences in his life; he particularly embraced her pacifist ideas and belief in individual freedom.

After 1907 Baldwin served as chief probation officer for the Saint Louis Juvenile Court and coauthored *Juvenile Courts and Probation*, the first book to advocate professional standards in courts for young offenders. In 1910 he headed the Saint Louis Civic League, a Progressive urban reform group that tried to democratize city government.

Like many other prominent liberal reformers, Baldwin condemned the outbreak of World War I in 1914 and opposed U.S. entry into the conflict. He declared himself a conscientious objector and relocated to New York City to join the American Union Against Militarism (AUAM) as its secretary. After the United States entered the war and Congress passed the Selective Service Act in May 1917, Baldwin became head of the AUAM's Civil Liberties Bureau, which he had organized. It tried but failed to persuade Congress to include in the Selective Service Act a provision that would permit conscientious objection.

While Baldwin continued to defend conscientious objectors, he assured federal officials that he was loyal to the United States, was not involved in recruiting men to become objectors, and was advocating objector status only for committed pacifists. He stated:

> The principle of liberty of conscience . . . does not admit of propaganda in war time. A man's conscience is too much an individual matter founded upon deep personal conviction to be treated from any such standpoint. Our efforts have been directed solely to insuring those men who hold themselves out as conscientious objectors, of just and humane treatment.

Nevertheless, federal agents began spying on Baldwin.

In October 1917 Baldwin and the AUAM's chair, CRYSTAL EASTMAN, left the AUAM and founded the National Civil Liberties Bureau (NCLB), which they committed to defending freedom of speech and of the press, to pursuing disarmament, and to protecting conscientious objectors from government oppression. In a letter, Baldwin wrote that the bureau was "a national independent organization . . . free . . . for a larger work than some of our conservative friends in the AUAM committee are willing to stand for."

Meanwhile, the government continued to watch Baldwin, and the Office of Naval Intelligence claimed that he favored "extreme radicalism and violence." In August 1918 federal agents raided the offices of the NCLB, looking for evidence that the organization had advised men to resist the draft. One month later Baldwin was himself called up. To his draft board he said:

> I am opposed to the use of force to accomplish any end, however good. I am therefore opposed to participation in this or any other war. My opposition is not only to direct military service, but to any service whatsoever designed to help prosecute the war. I am furthermore opposed to the principle of conscription in time of war or peace, for any purpose whatever. I will decline to perform any service under compulsion regardless of its character.

Baldwin was tried, was sentenced to prison, and served his time from November 1918 to August 1919. On his release he married Madeleine Zabriskie Doty, a social worker. He then returned to the NCLB and in January 1920 reorganized it and changed its name to the American Civil Liberties Union (ACLU). He would serve as its director for the next 25 years. The group's statement of purpose insisted that "all thought on matters of public concern should be freely expressed, without interference. Orderly social progress is promoted by unrestricted freedom of opinion."

Yet at a time when oppression chilled dissent in the United States through the Red Scare of 1919–20, Baldwin expanded the mission of the ACLU beyond the protection of free speech and freedom of the press to include the defense of other First Amendment rights—religious freedom and the right to assemble—and to fight for racial equality. The ACLU gained national prominence and increased support in 1925, when it hired CLARENCE SEWARD DARROW to defend John Scopes in the "Monkey Trial" in Dayton, Tennessee. Scopes had been accused of violating state law by teaching the theory of evolution in a public school. Even though Darrow lost the case, it rallied liberal opinion behind the ACLU.

For all of his commitment to free speech, Baldwin published *Liberty under the Soviets* (1927), which was based on a trip he took to the Soviet Union, in which he described the communist government's repression as necessary to further its revolutionary agenda. But he changed his view in

1940; when the Soviet Union signed a pact with Adolf Hitler, the ACLU, acting under Baldwin's leadership, passed a resolution that prohibited communists from serving on the organization's board, and it expelled one board member, ELIZABETH GURLEY FLYNN, for her communist allegiance. Clearly, Baldwin had compromised his commitment to free speech; ironically, the ACLU resolution served as a model for similar resolutions used by trade unions and government agencies during the nationwide hunt for communists in the late 1940s and 1950s that violated First Amendment freedoms.

During World War II, the ACLU defended the rights of Japanese Americans interred by the government in relocation camps. In 1947, at the request of General Douglas MacArthur, Baldwin served as a consultant on civil liberties in Japan.

Because Baldwin often neglected his duties as head of the ACLU, the organization's board pressured him to retire in 1949. He continued to work for the ACLU, however, and for other groups in which he promoted civil liberties in the United States and overseas.

In 1981 the federal government awarded him the Medal of Freedom. He died that year on August 26.

Further Reading

Cottrell, Robert. *Roger Nash Baldwin and the American Civil Liberties Union.* New York: Columbia University Press, 2000.

Lamson, Peggy. *Roger Baldwin: Founder of the American Civil Liberties Union.* Boston: Houghton Mifflin, 1976.

Walker, Samuel. *In Defense of American Liberties: A History of the ACLU.* New York: Oxford University Press, 1990.

Banks, Dennis James

(ca. 1930–   ) *Indian rights activist*

Dennis James Banks, whose original name was Nowacumig, meaning "Standing Outside," helped found the militant American Indian Movement (AIM) to protect tribal and civil rights. He was born on April 12, 1930 (some sources give the year as 1937), on the Leech Lake Indian Reservation in northern Minnesota, and grew up in poverty while his parents, both Anishinabe Indians, struggled for survival.

At age five Banks was taken from them and sent to boarding schools operated by the Bureau of Indian Affairs (BIA) in North and South Dakota, and then he was sent to a military school at Pipestone, Minnesota. These experiences distanced him from his Native American heritage, particularly since the BIA's policy at the time was to eradicate Indian culture.

In 1953 Banks enlisted in the United States Air Force and trained as an aerial photographer before being sent to Japan and South Korea. Discharged in 1959, he returned to Leech Lake, worked sporadically as a laborer, and sank into alcoholism. He was arrested on a burglary charge in 1966 and was sent to prison. While there, he gave up drinking and read extensively about Indian culture and the black civil rights movement. He committed himself to do for Indians what African Americans had done for their people, namely, to fight white oppression.

Banks was released from prison in 1968, whereupon he cofounded the American Indian Movement to protest the mistreatment by police of Native Americans in Minneapolis, Minnesota. AIM wanted to prevent false arrests, harassment, and brutality—much as the Black Panthers were attempting in African-American neighborhoods—and AIM's efforts succeeded in reducing the number of such incidents. AIM also pledged to fight racial discrimination in housing, health care, and employment, along with violations of Indian treaty rights.

In 1969 AIM began expanding into a national organization, sparked by the Indians of All Tribes (IAT) protest in California. Supported by Banks and other AIM leaders, IAT occupied Alcatraz Island, recently abandoned as a prison site, and demanded that under existing treaty provisions it be turned over to them. IAT failed to accomplish its goal, but the takeover, which lasted two years, highlighted Indian grievances and encouraged younger Indians, such as those active in AIM, to expand their protests.

By 1970 AIM chapters had formed in San Francisco, Los Angeles, Denver, Chicago, Cleveland, and Milwaukee. Their members were from many different tribes, including the Santee Dakota, Oglala Lakota, Ponca, Navajo (Dineh), Oneida, Cherokee, and Winnebago (Ho-Chunn). The diversity of tribes reflected AIM's desire to unite all Indians.

In fall 1972 AIM organized the Trail of Broken Treaties, a motorcade of about 2,000 Native Americans from more than 100 reservations who traveled to Washington, D.C., where Banks and other protesters held rallies and meetings with government officials to discuss Indian grievances. At one point the protesters occupied the BIA building and held it for several days.

In 1973 Banks led an AIM demonstration at Custer, South Dakota, against a biased trial that had resulted in a white man's being found innocent of murdering an Indian. Violence erupted between police and the protesters, and charges were filed against Banks, but he was for the time being set free.

A few weeks later AIM occupied the village of Wounded Knee on South Dakota's Pine Ridge Reservation, where in 1890 the United States. Cavalry had massacred at least 200 Oglala Lakota Sioux men, women, and children. AIM protested corrupt practices by Richard Wilson, the Sioux Nation president, who they believed was colluding with the federal government to allow it to exploit Indian land for its uranium deposits. When Wilson's patrol force interfered with the protest, several hundred AIM members and their supporters, with Banks as their leader, barricaded themselves at Wounded Knee, and a 71-day siege followed as police, U.S. marshals, FBI agents, and vigilantes converged on the scene. The federal government arrayed enormous firepower against AIM, including 130,000 rounds of M-16 ammunition, 41,000 rounds of M-1 ammunition, 12 M-79 grenade launchers, 100 rounds of M-4 explosives, and Phantom jets. Two Indians were killed in the AIM compound.

Banks and the other protesters held out from February 28 until May 7, 1973, when they reached an agreement with federal authorities that ended the siege. Banks was arrested but later acquitted of charges relating to the violence at Wounded Knee.

In August 1973 Banks won election as national director of AIM, and the group announced it would seek to repeal the Indian Reorganization Act of 1934 and end the BIA. Banks was convicted of riot and assault charges related to the protest at Custer, South Dakota, and he and his wife, Kamook, an Oglala Lakota Sioux, fled to California, where Governor Jerry Brown granted him asylum. From 1976 until 1983 Banks studied at the University of California at Davis, where he earned an associate of arts degree; he also served as chancellor of Indian-controlled Deganawida Quetzecoatl University. In 1978 he organized The Longest Walk from Alcatraz in San Francisco to Washington, D.C., a protest that at times numbered more than 30,000 Native Americans and that helped to defeat congressional legislation aimed at abolishing Indian treaties with the government.

In 1983 George Deukmejian succeeded Brown as governor of California and threatened to extradite Banks to South Dakota. At that point Banks received sanctuary from the Onondaga Nation at its reservation near Syracuse, New York. While there, he organized the Great Jim Thorpe Longest Run from New York City to Los Angeles to call attention to life's sacredness.

Banks surrendered to authorities in 1985 and served 18 months in prison. He received parole and moved to Oglala, South Dakota, near Wounded Knee; worked as a drug and alcohol counselor on the Pine Ridge Reservation; and founded Loneman Industries to train and employ Indians. In 1987 Banks worked to halt grave robbers in Uniontown, Kentucky, who were unearthing artifacts at Indian grave sites. He organized the reburial ceremonies for remains that had been exposed, and Kentucky and Indiana subsequently passed laws against grave desecration.

Banks published his autobiography, *Sacred Soul*, in 1988, and in the 1990s continued to organize runs similar to the Jim Thorpe run. One such event covered 7,000 miles from London to Moscow; others traversed Alaska, Japan, Canada, Australia, and New Zealand. During one sacred run, Banks and several volunteers collected more than 700,000 signatures to demand the release of the jailed AIM leader LEONARD PELTIER, who was serving consecutive life terms for the killing of two FBI agents during violence in the 1970s on the Pine Ridge Reservation.

In 1999 Banks, then living on the Anishinabe Reservation in northern Minnesota, offered a mixed review of the casinos being constructed on Indian land. "I've seen new hospitals and new clinics built by my people," he said. "They've improved the infrastructure and been able to keep their tribal governments intact. Because of gaming, there have been a lot of pluses." But he also observed that the benefits from the casinos, and the greater intrusion of white society's materialism, had pulled young Indians away from their heritage.

In June 2000 Banks led a protest by 50 Native Americans at the Wine-E-Mac School in Erskine, Minnesota, where at a pep rally several teachers had dressed up as Indians and cowboys, the cowboys holding toy pistols and telling the Indians they would send them "back to the reservation." At the protest Native Americans played drums, sang, and burned sage. Banks said, "We offer sage to bring an end to racism, to skits, pranks, jokes, mascots, and anything else that causes us pain. The sage is to purify this school and the people inside it who need purification."

Looking back on his activism with AIM, Banks observed:

> What we did in the 1960s and early 1970s was raise the consciousness of white America that this government has a responsibility to Indian people. That there are treaties; that textbooks in every school in America have the responsibility to tell the truth. An awareness reached across America that if Native American people had to resort to arms at Wounded Knee, there must really be something wrong. And Americans realized that native people are still here, that they have a moral standing, a legal standing. From that, our own people began to sense their pride.

In the year 2000 Banks vowed to continue his work for AIM. "If there were only two people left in this world saying that they are AIM, I would be one of them," he said.

Further Reading

Sayer, John William. *Ghost Dancing the Law: The Wounded Knee Trials.* Cambridge, Mass.: Harvard University Press, 1997.

Stern, Kenneth S. *Loud Hawk: The United States Versus the American Indian Movement.* Norman: University of Oklahoma Press, 1994.

Barnard, Henry
(1811–1900) *education reformer*

A crusader for public education, Henry Barnard published the *American Journal of Education* and served at the first U.S. commission of education. He was born on January 24, 1811, in Hartford, Connecticut, to Chauncey Barnard, a prosperous farmer, and Elizabeth Andrus Barnard.

Henry Barnard graduated from Monson Academy in Monson, Massachusetts, and entered Yale College in 1826. As a student he read extensively, took charge of the literary society's library, and developed an interest in public education. He came to believe that public schools should be the place where all Americans were educated, above all else because everyone should be taught the middle-class morals essential to a stable and orderly society.

Yet after graduating from Yale in 1830, Barnard opted for a legal rather than an educational career when he entered Yale Law School. After completing his studies there in 1834, he was admitted to the bar. Politically active as a member of the Whig Party, he was elected to the Connecticut state legislature in 1837 and reelected in 1838 and 1839. During his tenure, as HORACE MANN led a school reform movement in neighboring Massachusetts, he pushed through the Connecticut legislature a bill to establish state supervision of the public schools through a board of commissioners headed by a secretary of education. The first board then appointed him secretary.

Barnard faced a daunting task in rallying support for the public schools. Poorly financed, ill-equipped, and staffed with untrained teachers, they had such a bad reputation that most parents of any reasonable means sent their children to private academies, leaving the public schools largely the refuge of the poor.

Through numerous reports that he wrote, Barnard revealed the conditions in the schools and cultivated public opinion. Yet in 21st-century terms, his view of education was far from enlightened. He supported racial segregation and thought girls should have a less demanding curriculum than the one provided for boys. He thought of schools as moral instructors that, far from expanding democracy, would control the masses, whom he distrusted.

Political opponents abolished Barnard's office in 1842, and he subsequently promoted education reform in Rhode Island. He was made state agent for the schools there in 1843, and in 1845 he established the Rhode Island Institute of Instruction to train teachers.

Barnard married Josephine Desnoyers in 1847, and in their largely unhappy marriage they had five children. Back in Connecticut in 1849, Barnard was made principal of the normal school at New Britain and superintendent of the common schools for the entire state. He issued yet more authoritative reports before resigning in 1855 to publish the *American Journal of Education.* He always preferred work on the journal to anything else, and it was through articles in which he discussed the state of education that he gained his greatest influence.

While publishing the journal, Barnard served as chancellor of the University of Wisconsin from 1858 until 1860 and president of Saint John's College in Annapolis, Maryland, from 1866 until 1867. During the 1860s, according to the historian Ronald Walters, "Americans were becoming committed to free public education, at least through the primary levels," and in 1867 Barnard was appointed the first U.S. commissioner of education. But he accomplished little in the job, and after experiencing its downgrading to an office within the Department of the Interior, he resigned in 1870.

Barnard continued to publish his *American Journal of Education.* He died on July 5, 1900, in relative obscurity, bypassed by current educational developments of the period.

Further Reading

MacMullen, Edith Nye. *In the Cause of True Education: Henry Barnard and Nineteenth-Century School Reform.* New Haven, Conn.: Yale University Press, 1991.

Barton, Clara
(Clarissa Harlowe Barton)
(1821–1912) *health reformer*

Clarissa Harlow Barton, who went by the name Clara, was born on December 25, 1821, in Oxford, Massachusetts, to Stephen Barton, a farmer and state legislator, and Sarah Stone Barton. An independent woman who helped nurse soldiers and get supplies during the Civil War, Clara Barton is best known for founding the American Red Cross.

Although Clara Barton received little formal education, at age 15 she began teaching at a school near her home, in North Oxford. In 1850 she founded a free school at Bordentown, New Jersey, one of the few in that state. She quit, however, when the town officials passed her over and appointed a man as principal.

In 1853 Clara Barton was appointed a copyist in the federal Patent Office in Washington, D.C. With the outbreak of the Civil War in 1861, the diminutive Barton, who stood five feet tall, decided to help the Union troops. She was shocked at the attitude in the military, which held that ambulances, medical supplies, and hospitals were luxuries. When she discovered that a regiment from her home state of Massachusetts lacked beds and other supplies and was being forced to make its quarters in the U.S. Senate chambers, she acted quickly to obtain provisions from donors in Massachusetts and distribute the items to the men.

She then began collecting supplies for other troops and in 1862, with the approval of Union generals, started taking them to the front lines. Despite having no training as a nurse, she ministered to the wounded, and in 1864 she served as superintendent of nurses attached to the Army of the James. Barton, who earned the nickname "Angel of the Battlefield," worked under difficult conditions; writing in her journal, she said about the Battle of Fredericksburg in 1864:

> I saw [the soldiers] lying there early this morning—they had been wounded two and three days previous, had been brought from the front, and after all this lay still another night without care or food or shelter, many doubtless famished. . . . The city is full of houses

and this morning . . . parlors were thrown open and displayed to the view of the rebel occupants the bodies of the dead Union soldiers lying beside the wagons in which they perished. Only those most slightly wounded have been taken to [Washington]. The roads are fearful and it is not worth the life of a wounded man to remove him over them.

Except in one brief period, during the war Barton never served in an official government position, nor was she a member of any organization. She preferred to act independently and in that showed the fortitude that marked her career. Despite her activities as a nurse, her main contribution was in obtaining supplies for the soldiers.

She later identified and marked Union graves at the Confederate prison camp near Andersonville, Georgia. In 1865 she worked to locate missing soldiers from around the country and eventually traced 20,000 names. High-strung and suffering from a nervous disorder, in 1869 Barton traveled to Geneva, Switzerland, to regain her health. But while she was in Europe, the Franco-Prussian War broke out, and with her characteristic commitment to helping others, she organized women in Strasbourg to sew garments for the needy. At the same time, she arranged for the women, who lived in poverty, to be paid for their work.

Barton distributed food in Paris after the war, and in 1873 the German emperor, William I, awarded her the Iron Cross of Merit. She received also the Red Cross of Geneva and the Empress Augusta medal.

Clara Barton returned to the United States in 1876 and settled at Danville, New York. Still suffering from a nervous disorder, she lived for a while in that town's sanitarium. In 1877 she wrote to the International Red Cross and offered to establish an American branch. Over the next few years she worked to convince the U.S. government to sign the Geneva Convention, which had provided for a Red Cross. She incorporated the American Red Cross in 1881 and served as its first president. In 1882 Congress confirmed the Geneva Convention treaty.

Barton attended several international conferences, and at one in Geneva in 1884 she per-

The Civil War photographer Mathew Brady took this photograph of Clara Barton during the sectional conflict. *(National Archives and Records Administration)*

suaded the International Red Cross to accept an amendment that committed the organization to providing relief during disasters unrelated to war. She personally supervised many relief efforts, such as in the wake of fires that swept Michigan in 1882 and an earthquake that same year that devastated Charleston, South Carolina; floods that inundated settlements along the Ohio River in 1884 and Johnstown, Pennsylvania, in 1889; famine that killed thousands in Russia in 1891; and a hurricane that destroyed Galveston, Texas, in 1900. In addition to these activities, she helped Cubans and Americans during the Spanish-American War.

But by running everything herself, Barton did little to attract members to the American Red Cross. And her inept handling of finances generated much criticism. In 1900 Congress reincorporated the Red Cross and required that it make annual financial reports.

Complaints continued, however, and other Red Cross members attacked Barton for her arbitrary rule. Nevertheless, an investigation uncovered no wrongdoing, and some historians have concluded that her critics were primarily motivated by a desire to replace her with a centralized bureaucracy and professional management.

Worn down by the disputes within the Red Cross, Barton quit the organization in 1904 and retired to Glen Echo, Maryland, where she died on April 12, 1912. She was never a reformer in the sense of wanting to remake society, but she was indefatigable in helping those in need through the American Red Cross and through her earlier efforts.

Further Reading

Burton, David Henry. *Clara Barton: In the Service of Humanity.* Westport, Conn.: Greenwood Press, 1995.

Pryor, Elizabeth Brown. *Clara Barton: Professional Angel.* Philadelphia: University of Pennsylvania Press, 1987.

Ross, Ishbel. *Angel of the Battlefield: The Life of Clara Barton.* New York: Harper, 1956.

Beard, Mary Ritter

(1876–1958) *women's rights advocate*

An activist who promoted women's suffrage, Mary Ritter Beard was also a historian who insisted that the role of women in America's past must receive due credit. She was born Mary Ritter on August 5, 1876, in Indianapolis, Indiana, to Eli Foster Ritter and Narcissa Smith Lockwood Ritter.

Three years after graduating from DePauw University in Greencastle, Indiana, Mary Ritter married a college friend, Charles Austin Beard. Shortly afterward, they sailed for England, where Charles studied as an Oxford scholar. While there, Mary Beard participated in the women's trade union and suffrage movements.

The Beards returned to the United States in 1902, and Charles pursued his doctorate at Columbia University in New York City. Mary enrolled at Columbia for a brief period but withdrew to raise the couple's two children. She remained politically active, however, and in the wake of a terrible fire at the Triangle shirtwaist factory, she helped organize a strike by women garment workers. A suffragist, she edited *The Woman Voter,* a journal published by the Woman Suffrage League of New York, and she allied herself with militants who pursued more radical tactics, such as street marches.

Mary Beard began publishing her historical works in 1915, with *Woman's Work in Municipalities.* She collaborated with her husband in writing their most famous work, *The Rise of American Civilization* (1927), which presented a Progressive economic interpretation stating that the dynamic force in American development had been an ongoing struggle between the haves and the have-nots.

Despite her support for the suffragists, her view of women in history differed markedly from that of many feminists. She strongly disagreed with those who said women had always been oppressed by men, or that all evil had emanated from them. Rather, she thought that women had been oppressed in early history along class rather than gender lines.

More than any of her other works, *Woman as a Force in History* (1946) defined her view of women's role in the past. In it she wrote, "What does modern critical scholarship find in the long review of English legal history prior to 1765? It finds men and women . . . on a similar footing with regard to their property holdings under the requirements of a strong feudal state. It finds men and women making powerful efforts, individually and together, to protect their families against the encroachments of that State." She added:

> From modern times running back into and through the medieval ages of Western feudalism and Christian contests with barbarism, the force of woman was a powerful factor in all the infamies, tyrannies, liberties, activities, and aspirations that constituted the history of this stage of humanity's self-expression.

To Beard, oppression based on sex first appeared with the advent of capitalism.

Mary Beard opposed the complete integration of women into a male culture because it would destroy the feminine culture that had and could continue to make valuable contributions to society. But she insisted that if women only understood their powerful role in the past, they could do more than enter existing society on an equal footing with men; they could remake it and in the end advance humanity. After Charles Beard died in 1948, Mary Beard continued to write, and in 1955 she published a survey of her husband's work. She died in Scottsdale, Arizona, on August 14, 1958.

Further Reading

Cott, Nancy F., ed. *A Woman Making History: Mary Ritter Beard through Her Letter.* New Haven, Conn.: Yale University Press, 1991.

Turoff, Barbara K. *Mary Beard as a Social Force.* Dayton, Ohio: Wright State University Press, 1979.

Beecher, Catharine
(1800–1878) *education reformer*

An advocate of expanded schooling and teaching for women as a way to improve society's morals, Catharine Beecher was conservative on the issue of women's rights, stressing the importance of domestic duties and criticizing female activists. She was born on September 6, 1800, in East Hampton, Long Island, New York.

Catharine Beecher was a member of a prominent family allied with the Christian morality that permeated her era's reform movements, ranging from temperance, to abolition, to women's rights. Her mother was Roxana Foote Beecher, and her father was Lyman Beecher, a Congregationalist minister. Two of her brothers, HENRY WARD BEECHER and Edward Beecher, were also ministers, and her sister, Harriet Beecher Stowe, wrote the novel *Uncle Tom's Cabin,* an abolitionist tract.

In 1809 Catharine Beecher attended Miss Pierce's School in Litchfield, Connecticut, the town to which her family had moved, and continued to matriculate there until 1816, when she was forced to help take care of her family after her mother died. In her early 20s, Beecher began teaching at a private school for girls in New London, Connecticut. Personal tragedy struck two years later when her fiancé died in a shipwreck. At that point, she committed herself to projects that would improve society.

In 1823 she founded a small school for girls in Hartford, Connecticut, and created a curriculum that included algebra, chemistry, Latin, history, philosophy, and rhetoric. She believed that "the training of the human mind in the years of *infancy and childhood* . . . is the appropriate and highest vocation of woman." Eventually more than 150 students enrolled at the school, and it gained a favorable reputation for its progressive methods.

Beecher and her family moved to Cincinnati, Ohio, in 1832, where she began the Western Female Institute as a school for women, which she continued to operate until 1837, when health problems forced her to close it. Yet she still worked to found several women's colleges in the West, and she recruited women to teach in various towns in the newly settled region.

Beecher believed that women should be educated so in their role as mothers they could provide their children with a sound moral upbringing. That, in turn, would improve the country's morals. Her reformist activity pressed only slightly against the boundaries of traditional society, for Beecher did not generally look at education as a means for women to enter the professions or to enter endeavors previously reserved for men. There was, however, one exception: She thought women better suited to teaching than men. "In all those states and cities of our country where education prospers the most," she said, "it has flourished exactly in proportion to the extent to which men have forsaken and women have been restored to this employ."

But with that advocacy, Beecher reinforced the role of women in society as motherly. Teaching, after all, was best for women because it was an extension of their domestic talent as guardians of children.

In insisting that women could best reform society by asserting their moral leadership in the home, she opposed social activism. In 1837 she published her essay *Slavery and Abolition with Reference to the Duty of American Females* in which she proclaimed her dislike of slavery but made clear her disagreement with the abolitionists. They antagonized southerners, she wrote, and made them defensive. "The moment a man is publicly rebuked," she said, "shame, anger, and pride of opinion, all combine to make him defend his practice, and refuse wither to own himself wrong, or to cease from his evil ways."

Her argument shows anxiety about black-led violence. She wrote that the defensive-minded southerners would in time crush all critics of slavery in the South, making the slave system harsher and leaving blacks with a greater sense of oppression—a "volcano" that "will burst," resulting in "insurrection and servile wars." She lamented: "Oh the countless horrors of such a day! . . . Will the terrors of insurrection sweep over the South, and no Northern and Western blood be shed?"

In 1841 Beecher published her *Treatise on Domestic Economy,* which sold so widely it went through 15 printings. The *Treatise* offered practical advice on cooking meals, raising children, and providing health care, but it also extolled women's domestic chores as part of an effort to elevate the status of women's work in the home by making them feel better about it and by showing Americans how important it was to society. In that sense she agreed with feminists that women should be neither weak nor perceived as weak.

Beecher opposed the women's suffrage movement and became a leader in the fight against it. After returning to the East, she founded the Women's Education Association of New York in 1852, which lasted for 10 years. In her book *American Woman's Home* (1869), she began exploring alternatives to family domesticity for women but stopped short of breaking completely with her earlier ideas. She died in Elmira, New York, on May 12, 1878.

Beecher never embraced the radicalism championed by feminists of her day, but she did widen the educational opportunities for women, as both students and teachers, and tried to reform attitudes about domestic work. In placing such work on a pedestal, and disdaining to call it mere drudgery, she tried to elevate the status of women.

Further Reading
Barker-Benfield, G. J. *Portraits of American Women.* 2 vols. New York: St. Martin's Press, 1991.
Sklar, Kathryn Kish. *Catharine Beecher: A Study in American Domesticity.* New York: Norton, 1976.

Beecher, Henry Ward
(1813–1887) *abolitionist*

A leading religious figure in the mid-19th century, Henry Ward Beecher embraced numerous reforms, most notably abolitionism. He was born on June 24, 1813, in Litchfield, Connecticut, and was raised in a religious family. His father, Lyman Beecher, was pastor of the Congregationalist church in Litchfield and fully expected his son to enter the ministry. Henry's mother, Roxana Foote Beecher, died when he was only three years old, but his stepmother, Harriet Porter, provided a strong sense of proper behavior. His older sister, CATHARINE BEECHER, was also a reformer; a brother, Edward Beecher, also joined the ministry; and another sister, Harriet Beecher Stowe, wrote the novel *Uncle Tom's Cabin.*

As a young man Henry Ward Beecher doubted he would follow in his father's profession. In 1834 he graduated from Amherst College in Massachusetts and entered Lane Theological Seminary in Cincinnati, Ohio, but he did so mainly at his father's behest and without any strong desire to preach. He had little interest in theology and disliked the harshness of Calvinism, which conflicted with his lighthearted personality. Then he experienced a deep religious conversion that erased all doubts about his future. He graduated from Lane in 1837 (the same year he married Eunice White Bullard) and was ordained in 1838. While preaching in Indiana, he wrote *Seven Lectures to Young Men* (1844), a widely read collection of his sermons, which included " Gamblers and Gambling," "The Strange Woman," and "Twelve Causes of Dishonesty."

At Plymouth Church in Brooklyn, New York, where he preached from 1847 until the end of his life, he attracted audiences exceeding 2,000 each week. His parishioners were attracted to his warmth, humor, and dramatic style; he rejected a lectern and instead stood directly in front of his congregation and spoke without a written text. A recorder usually wrote down his words, and these were distributed in pamphlet form, thus widening his audience even more.

Beecher's antislavery lectures ranked him among the foremost abolitionist leaders. Yet he disagreed with the movement's radical wing; its hatred repulsed him, and he rejected WILLIAM LLOYD GARRISON's calls for no cooperation with the federal government and no union with slaveholders. Beecher believed the Constitution protected slavery where it already existed, but he strenuously opposed its extension into the western territories and urged Northerners to disobey the Fugitive Slave Act.

Beecher's Plymouth ministry occurred as the conflict over slavery intensified: War with Mexico had acquired new lands for the United States, the discovery of gold in California peopled that territory quickly, and Kansas prepared to form a territorial government. In reaction to these developments, Beecher raised money to buy rifles for antislavery settlers in Kansas, weapons called "Beecher's Bibles," with the exhortation that the settlers would "not need to use arms when it is known that you have them."

In a sensational and much publicized incident, Beecher held a reverse "slave auction" at the Plymouth Church in 1856, when he presented a young slave woman to the audience and urged his parishioners to contribute money that would be used to buy her freedom. After the young lady ascended the speaker's platform and sat in a chair, with thousands of eyes affixed to her, Beecher intoned, "And this is a marketable commodity. Such as she are put into one balance and silver into the other."

During the Civil War, Beecher pushed for Lincoln to free the slaves and expressed frustration over the president's delay in issuing the Emancipation Proclamation. With the war over he advocated that the South be rapidly rejoined to the Union. He also campaigned for women's suffrage. In the 1870s he denied charges of adultery that had been made against him in court and a hung jury led to the case being dropped. Beecher died on March 8, 1887, in New York City.

Further Reading

Abbot, Lyman. *Henry Ward Beecher.* New York: Chelsea House, 1980.

Clark, Clifford Edward. *Henry Ward Beecher: Spokesman for a Middle-Class America.* Urbana: University of Illinois Press, 1978.

Fox, Richard Wightman. *Trials of Intimacy: Love and Loss in the Beecher-Tilton Scandal.* Chicago: University of Chicago Press, 1999.

McLoughlin, William Gerald. *The Meaning of Henry Ward Beecher: An Essay on the Shifting Values of*

Henry Ward Beecher's antislavery lectures ranked him among the nation's foremost abolitionist leaders. *(National Archives and Records Administration)*

Mid-Victorian America, 1840–1870. New York: Knopf, 1970.

Ryan, Halford Ross. *Henry Ward Beecher: Peripatetic Preacher.* New York: Greenwood Press, 1990.

Shaplen, Robert. *Free Love and Heavenly Sinners: The Story of the Great Henry Ward Beecher Scandal.* New York: Knopf, 1954.

Bellamy, Edward
(1850–1898) *socialist*

Edward Bellamy promoted socialist reform in his widely popular novel, *Looking Backward, 2000–1887,* and advocated a new society based on cooperation rather than competition. He was born on May 26, 1850, in Chicopee Falls, Massachusetts, to Rufus King Bellamy, a Baptist minister, and Maria Louisa Putnam Bellamy.

Edward Bellamy envisioned the day when Americans would live in a socialist utopia. *(Library of Congress)*

Shy and reticent, Edward Bellamy spent nearly his entire life in New England. He was educated at local schools and then matriculated at Union College in Schenectady, New York. He quit, however, after one year and at age 18 traveled to Germany. There he was stunned by the squalid conditions in which industrial workers lived.

When Bellamy returned to the United States in 1869, he studied law in Springfield, Massachusetts, and soon afterward opened his own legal practice. Disgusted with the profession, however, he left it after trying only one case and instead devoted his time to journalism and writing. In several articles he criticized child labor and the inequality of wealth.

In 1880 he and his brother founded the *Springfield Daily News*. He also wrote short stories for magazines and authored four novels, none of which attracted much attention. But he had mar-

ried Sylvia Bowman in 1882, and with the birth of their second child, he began thinking in earnest about social conditions and how the world could be improved for his children and future generations. He was influenced as well by Laurence Gronlund's *The Cooperative Commonwealth* (1884), a Marxist work.

At that time, America was experiencing substantial upheaval: Rapid industrialization was causing the quick growth of cities and expansion of slums; factory workers were enduring long hours and brutal conditions; and labor strikes were threatening to disrupt the economy and spread disorder. All the while, social inequality was widening, while the rich were flaunting their wealth in an era called the Gilded Age.

With these conditions in mind, Bellamy wrote his novel *Looking Backward* (1888). It sold more copies than any book previously published in the United States, with the exception of Harriet Beecher Stowe's *Uncle Tom's Cabin*. The novel tells of Julian West, who falls asleep in 1887 after being hypnotized and wakes up in the year 2000. Gone are the muddy streets, the poverty, the slums. In their place stands a utopian society—clean, prosperous, and equitable. West describes his surroundings: "Public buildings of a colossal size and architectural grandeur unparalleled in my day raised their stately piles on every side."

Looking Backward presents a socialist society, or what Bellamy called a "Nationalist" society, in which the state controls production and distribution. The result is an enlightened utopia with universal comfort, education, and art bound by cooperation and love. To some readers in the 1880s and 1890s, *Looking Backward* presented a wondrous alternative to existing conditions, and the book led to the formation of Bellamy Clubs, whose members gathered to discuss the virtues of the novel's society. A Nationalist movement promoted Bellamy's ideas in the political arena, though it soon faltered after it sided with the farmer-based Populist movement and lost momentum in the fervor of the Spanish-American War and the economic expansion of the late 1890s.

In 1891 Bellamy began the short-lived *New Nation*, a magazine devoted to utopian ideas. He became much more the promoter and propagandist for Nationalism than the shy writer he had been. Six years later, he published a sequel to *Looking Backward*, titled *Equality*, that clarified his ideas, but it failed to gain widespread readership.

Yet *Looking Backward* continued to generate interest. Many reformers credited the book with changing their life. The socialist leader EUGENE VICTOR DEBS said it helped him "out of darkness into the light," and the socialists NORMAN MATTOON THOMAS and UPTON SINCLAIR credited the novel with a similar influence. So, too, did the novelist Jack London, the historians Charles Beard and Vernon Parrington, and the economist Thorstein Veblen. Even as late as the 1930s some government leaders gave credit to Bellamy's work as an influence on policy; Arthur Ernest Morgan, chairman of Franklin Roosevelt's Tennessee Valley Authority, said, "Striking parallels may be drawn between *Looking Backward* and various important aspects of [the] New Deal."

While Edward Bellamy worked on *Equality*, his health declined. He died on May 22, 1898, in Chicopee Falls, of tuberculosis.

Further Reading

Bowman, Sylvia E. *The Year 2000: A Critical Biography of Edward Bellamy.* New York: Octagon Books, 1979.

Morgan, Arthur Ernest. *Edward Bellamy.* New York: Columbia University Press, 1944.

Simon, Linda. "Writer and Writing: Looking Backward." *World and I* 14 (June 1999): 2897.

Berkman, Alexander
(1870–1936) *anarchist*

A revolutionary anarchist who believed that assassination was an effective way to expose oppression, Alexander Berkman once attempted to kill the general manager of the Carnegie Steel Company. Berkman was born on November 21, 1870, in Vilna, Russia, to Joseph Schmidt Berkman, a wealthy leather wholesaler, and Yetta Natanson Berkman, whose older sister was a member of a terrorist group that assassinated Czar Alexander II in 1881.

After Berkman's father died, the youngster moved with his mother and siblings to Kovno in Russian Lithuania. By age 15, he was already reading revolutionary literature and admiring Russian extremists who in their protests against authority assassinated government leaders.

Berkman immigrated to the United States in 1887, expecting to find freedom but instead finding an oppressive society that he considered equivalent to any found in Europe. Berkman encountered an American economy undergoing a wrenching change from an agricultural and small business structure to one dominated by large corporations and their leaders, the "captains of industry." So tumultuous was the change, marked by two severe economic depressions, one in the mid-1870s and the other in the mid-1880s, that labor protests had erupted on a large scale.

At the time Berkman arrived, seven anarchists were facing trial, accused of planting a bomb that killed several policemen during a labor rally at Chicago's Haymarket Square. The conviction of the anarchists—in a trial notable for the prosecution's use of bribery and tainted evidence, and for the prejudices of the judge and jury, and the subsequent hanging of four of them—convinced Berkman that the wealthy corporate leaders owned America's political system.

The Homestead steel strike of 1892 in Pennsylvania propelled Berkman to national prominence. During the strike, Henry Frick, the general manager of the Carnegie Steel Company, used Pinkerton agents to crush the workers. The violence that ensued resulted in the Pinkertons killing several strikers. In retaliation, Berkman decided to kill Frick, an act that expressed his anarchist belief in assassination as a means to expose oppression. On July 23, 1892, Berkman entered the general manager's office and shot Frick. The wounded businessman lived, despite having three bullets lodged in his body, and Berkman was arrested and sentenced to 22 years in Pennsylvania's Western Penitentiary. He served 14 years of his sentence and was released in 1906.

Over the next five years Berkman wrote his *Prison Memoirs of an Anarchist*, published in 1912. He then edited a revolutionary labor newspaper, the *Blast*, which declared itself against war and for birth control, worker unity, and free speech. When the United States entered World War I, he spoke

Anarchist Alexander Berkman is shown here after his conviction for conspiring with Emma Goldman (left) to violate the draft law during World War I. *(National Archives and Records Administration)*

out against the country's war policies and urged young men to resist the draft. The war, he claimed, had "unmasked the vicious character of capitalist competition." In summer 1917 he and his fellow anarchist EMMA GOLDMAN—he was one of her lovers and the person whom she called "the greatest force in my life"—were arrested and found guilty of conspiring to obstruct the operation of the selective service law.

At the federal penitentiary in Atlanta, Georgia, Berkman tried to organize a protest against the mistreatment of prisoners and was thrown into solitary confinement for seven months. Just a few weeks after his release from the penitentiary on

October 1, 1919, the federal government deported him, Goldman, and 250 other radicals to Russia.

Although Berkman at first supported Russia's Bolshevik Revolution, he soon condemned the communists for creating a state that was oppressive of the workers. He left Russia in 1922, lived briefly in Sweden and then for several years in Germany, before settling in France in 1930. There he published articles and journals intended to help imprisoned anarchists and wrote his best-known book, *The ABC of Communist Anarchism*. In it, he claimed that capitalism, socialism, and Bolshevism had all failed to free the individual. "To the anarchists, there is nothing surprising in all this," he wrote. "They have always claimed that the State is destructive to individual liberty and social harmony, and that only the abolition of coercive authority and material inequality can solve our political, economic, and national problems."

Berkman grew increasingly depressed as his health declined. He committed suicide in Nice, France, on June 28, 1936.

Further Reading

Berkman, Alexander. *Prison Memoirs of an Anarchist.* New York: New York Review of Books, 1999.

Fellner, Gene, ed. *The Alexander Berkman Reader.* New York: Four Walls Eight Windows, 1992.

Berrigan, Daniel (1921–   ) and Philip Berrigan (1923–   )
peace activists, social reformers

Deeply committed to a Christian ideal of peace, Daniel and Philip Berrigan protested the Vietnam War and social injustices so strenuously that they were on occasion arrested and sentenced to prison. Both Berrigans were born in northern Minnesota, Daniel on May 9, 1921, in the town of Virginia, and Philip on October 5, 1923, in the town of Two Harbors, to Thomas and Frida Berrigan. During the Great Depression, Thomas Berrigan, a union activist and socialist, moved the family to Syracuse, New York.

While still a teenager, Daniel Berrigan had become obsessed with the suffering he saw in the world, and when he entered his senior year in high school, he decided to enter the order of Jesuits (Society of Jesus). After graduation in 1939, he began training for the priesthood and was ordained in June 1952. Two years later, Daniel began teaching French and theology at the Jesuit-run Brooklyn Preparatory School in New York. While there, he led students in a project to help impoverished Puerto Ricans and blacks in Brooklyn and the Lower East Side.

Along with his energy and commitment to humanitarian causes, Daniel Berrigan possessed a high degree of intelligence and a keen writing talent, and in 1957 he won the Lamont Prize and was nominated for a National Book Award for his collection of poems, *Time without Number.* That same year, he was appointed professor of New Testament Studies at La Moyne College, a Jesuit school in Syracuse. There he led students in rent strikes and picketing to help ghetto residents, an action that often angered wealthy donors to the college who owned property in the slums.

A critical turning point for Daniel occurred in 1963, when he attended the Christian Peace Conference in Prague, Czechoslovakia, and from there journeyed to Russia and South Africa. At the conference he listened to criticism of the Vietnam War; in Russia he witnessed Catholics bravely maintaining their faith amid government persecution; and in South Africa he saw apartheid in its most brutal form. He later said his trip overseas helped him realize "what it might cost to be a Christian" and "what it might cost even at home, if things continued in the direction I felt events were taking."

Soon after his return to the United States in 1964, he plunged into the civil rights and antiwar movements. He and his brother, Philip, along with THOMAS MERTON, a liberal Trappist monk and writer, founded the Catholic Peace Fellowship, the first Catholic antiwar organization in America. Near the same time, in spring 1965, Daniel joined the civil rights march at Selma, Alabama, and with Philip signed a Declaration of Conscience, sent to the White House, in which they declared their opposition to the Vietnam War.

Daniel Berrigan gained considerable attention when he defended the actions of David Miller, a Catholic who, in October 1965, burned his draft card in front of the armed forces induction center in Manhattan—the first burning since a new law imposing stiff penalties for the offense had gone into effect. Meanwhile, the Catholic Peace Fellowship ran advertisements in several publications, denouncing the war as immoral and calling for its end.

Daniel's antiwar actions raised enormous opposition among church leaders, and they decided to silence the rebellious priest by assigning him to South America, where he reported for *Jesuit Missions,* a magazine he edited. The move, however, stirred Catholic liberals, who demanded Daniel's return, and within three months the leaders relented.

In fall 1967 Daniel Berrigan moved to Ithaca, New York, to help direct the United Religious Work Program at Cornell University. Continuing his outspoken opposition to the war, he participated in a march on the Pentagon that October and was one of several hundred demonstrators who were arrested. The following year he traveled to Hanoi with a leftist professor, Howard Zinn, and helped gain the release of three American prisoners of war. During his stay he had to hide in bomb shelters to escape attacks by American planes. Later that year he published an account of his experience, *Night Flight to Hanoi.*

During this period Philip Berrigan had staged an antiwar protest at the customs house in Baltimore, Maryland, where he and three accomplices entered the Selective Service Office and destroyed its files. While awaiting sentencing for that deed, he approached his brother Daniel about staging another spectacular protest. Daniel agreed, and on May 17, 1968, they and seven fellow protesters walked into the Selective Service Office in Cantonsville, Maryland, and startled workers by grabbing hundreds of files, putting them in trash cans, taking them outside, and burning them with homemade napalm. In a statement, the protesters said:

> We are Catholic Christians who take our faith seriously. We use napalm because it has burned people to death in Vietnam, Guatemala and Peru and because it may be used in American ghettoes. We destroyed these records because they exploit our young men and represent misplaced power concentrated in the hands of the ruling class. . . . We believe some property has no right to exist.

Known as the Cantonsville Nine (and one year later immortalized in *The Trial of the Cantonsville Nine*, a play Daniel Berrigan wrote) the group, faced charges of conspiracy and destruction of government property. A jury found them guilty, and a judge sentenced Daniel Berrigan to three years in prison. But in April 1970, after his appeal failed, Daniel and Philip went underground, convinced they could do the most good as radicals slipping in

and out of towns and spreading the protest message. Much to the embarrassment of the FBI, whose agents were pursuing them, Daniel appeared at a Methodist church on August 2, 1970, and presented a sermon in which he called for courageous actions to win the peace. Nine days later, however, the FBI captured Daniel at Block Island, Rhode Island. His imprisonment lasted until February 24, 1972, after which he led rallies to help his brother, who was on trial for another incident.

Philip Berrigan showed the same religiosity and spirit of rebellion as that of his brother. When he entered Saint Michael's College in Toronto, Canada, World War II was under way, and he was drafted. The war deeply affected Philip. For one, while training in the South he witnessed so much white racism and black poverty that he determined both injustices had to be corrected. For another, his battle experience in Europe, where he rose to the rank of second lieutenant, made him detest war.

Philip returned to the United States in 1945 and studied at Holy Cross University. He graduated in 1950 and to study for the priesthood joined the Society of Saint Joseph, an order dedicated to helping African Americans. He was ordained in 1955 and assigned to New Orleans, where he earned a B.S. in secondary education at Loyola University in 1957 and an M.S. at Xavier University three years later.

Philip Berrigan gained notice in 1963 when he started out for a civil rights march in Jackson, Mississippi, with the intent of getting arrested during the demonstration and becoming the first Catholic priest to be thrown into jail. His superior, though, learned of his plan and ordered him to end his trip. He did so, but only after telling newspaper reporters what had happened, a public revelation disliked by the Catholic leadership.

Consequently the order transferred him from New Orleans to the faculty of the Josephite seminary in Newburgh, New York. By that time, Philip, appalled at the threat of nuclear war, had become a pacifist, and his outspoken views, while earning him criticism from conservative Catholics, made him a sought-after speaker at numerous colleges and seminaries.

In 1965 Philip Berrigan caused yet another stir when he addressed the Newburgh Community Affairs Council and linked the civil rights struggle to the Vietnam War. He said the conflict in Asia was symptomatic of a racist society. Shortly after that he and his brother Daniel signed the Declaration of Conscience.

Because of their action, Philip was again transferred, this time to Saint Peter Claver Church, a black inner-city parish in Baltimore, Maryland, under strict orders that he refrain from discussing the Vietnam War. Neither the move nor the dictate silenced him, and he formed clubs in ghetto neighborhoods through which blacks pressured landlords to repair buildings; held masses during which he called the war racist; and started a new antiwar group, the Baltimore Interfaith Peace Mission.

In 1966 Philip and other clergymen drove to Washington, D.C., and picketed the homes of Secretary of State Dean Rusk and Secretary of Defense Robert McNamara. Philip eventually obtained an audience with Rusk, but the secretary rejected the priest's ideas.

With the Baltimore Interfaith Peace Mission, Philip Berrigan concluded that those who opposed the war must risk arrest and even death to stop it. On October 27, 1967, he and three other protesters entered the Baltimore Selective Service Office carrying containers filled with pig's blood and, as startled workers watched, poured the contents onto hundreds of files.

It was at that point, while Philip was awaiting sentence for the attack, that he and Daniel planned their protest against the Selective Service Office at Cantonsville, Maryland. As part of the Cantonsville Nine, Philip was found guilty of conspiracy and destruction of government property and received a three-and-a-half-year sentence to run concurrently with the six years he had been given for his role in destroying the files at Baltimore. In April 1970, while out on bail after a failed appeal, he joined his brother in going underground. FBI agents captured him on April 21 in New York City and took him to the federal penitentiary at Lewisburg, Pennsylvania.

There he began sending letters to a run, Elizabeth McAlister, whom he had secretly married the previous year. Prison rules forbade him to engage in correspondence, but a fellow inmate smuggled the letters out for him. In one letter, McAlister discussed a plan circulated by a few protesters to blow up some government buildings and kidnap presidential adviser Henry Kissinger to place him on mock trial for war crimes.

Philip opposed the idea, but the FBI obtained copies of his letters from his fellow inmate, and the government indicted him, McAlister, and five others on charges of conspiracy. They also charged him and McAlister with letter smuggling.

Except for the smuggling, the charges had little substance and were part of a larger government effort to discredit antiwar protesters and embroil them in legal battles. The jury found Philip Berrigan and Elizabeth McAlister guilty of the letter smuggling but deadlocked on the other charges. Later, an appeals court overturned the conviction, and the government decided against pursuing a retrial.

Philip Berrigan was granted parole in December 1972 and left the priesthood in 1973, shortly after making his marriage public. The former priest and his wife, along with their daughter, moved to a commune in a black neighborhood in Baltimore.

Both Daniel and Philip Berrigan remained active in social causes, including the peace movement, and they continued their protests for justice into the 1990s. In May 1997 Daniel damaged a U.S. Navy missile cruiser in Portland, Maine, and in March 2000 Philip was sentenced to 30 months in jail for vandalizing two U.S. warplanes at an Air National Guard base in Maryland. He had committed the act the previous year to protest the use of depleted uranium in missiles deployed on the planes.

Further Reading

Curtis, Richard. *The Berrigan Brothers: The Story of Daniel and Philip Berrigan.* New York: Hawthorn Books, 1974.

Dear, John, ed. *Apostle of Peace: Essays in Honor of Daniel Berrigan.* Maryknoll, N.Y.: Orbis Books, 1996.

Polner, Murray. *Disarmed and Dangerous: The Radical Lives and Times of Daniel and Philip Berrigan.* New York: Basic Books, 1997.

Bethune, Mary McLeod
(1875–1955) *civil rights activist*

A college president and government official, Mary McLeod Bethune worked to advance the role of blacks in society. She was born on July 10, 1875, in Mayesville, South Carolina, to Samuel McLeod and Patsy McIntosh McLeod. Her parents were former slaves, freed after the Civil War, who acquired land and raised cotton and rice.

McLeod received an elementary education at a school begun by Presbyterians to teach black children, and in 1887 she entered Scotia Seminary (today Barber-Scotia College), a school for girls in Concord, North Carolina. In 1894 she completed what was called the "normal course," which prepared her to teach. But she wanted to become a missionary in Africa and toward that end enrolled in the Moody Bible Institute, a Presbyterian school, in Chicago. In 1895 she applied to the Presbyterian Mission Board, only to be told that as a black woman she could not serve in Africa.

At that point she found work as a teacher at various schools for blacks, all sponsored by the Presbyterian Church: the mission school in Mayesville, South Carolina, which she had attended (1895–1896); Haines Institute in Augusta, Georgia (1896–1897); and Kindell Institute in Sumter, South Carolina (1897–1898). In May 1898 she married Albertus L. Bethune, a schoolteacher. They had one son, but it was an unhappy marriage, and they soon separated.

From 1899 to 1903 Mary Bethune taught at the Palatka Mission School in Palatka, Florida. In October 1904 she founded the Daytona Normal and Industrial Institute in Daytona Beach, Florida, with her first class consisting of five girls. Starting with practically no resources—"about a dollar and a half and some prayers," she later said—she used her ingenuity to raise money, such as by making and selling sweet potato pies and ice cream, the profits from which she used to buy land.

Gradually, Bethune acquired financial support from whites. At first offering only an elementary education, she expanded her school to include classes at the secondary level. Although some of the courses emphasized developing her students'

intellect, she stressed moral character, religious values, and vocational training as important for finding jobs. Her classes included sewing, laundering, and gardening—an education that many today would dismiss as encouraging subservience to whites but at that time reflected the jobs available to blacks.

In fact, Bethune was anything but subservient. In 1924, one year after her school merged with the all-male Cookman Institute, founded by the Methodist Episcopal Church, she began the first of her two terms as president of the 10,000-member National Association of Colored Women (NACW). Under her leadership the NACW became the first black organization to establish a permanent headquarters in Washington, D.C. In 1929 her school became Bethune-Cookman College and offered a junior college curriculum that would, shortly after World War II, be expanded into a full four-year college program.

In 1935 Bethune founded the National Council of Negro Women, intended to be more centralized than the NACW. She served as president until 1949, a term that overlapped with her service as president of the Association for Negro Life and History, from 1936 until 1951, and as vice president of the National Association for the Advancement of Colored People, from 1940 until 1955.

During the Great Depression of the 1930s, Bethune received one of the highest appointments for a black woman in the federal government when President Franklin Roosevelt named her his administrative assistant in charge of Negro affairs in the National Youth Administration (NYA). As part of the New Deal, the NYA was formed to provide jobs for unemployed young people. Because of Bethune's work, the agency avoided becoming a "white only" program and provided jobs to black youths roughly equivalent to their proportion in the overall population. She also insisted that the NYA practice nondiscrimination in its policies. Bethune believed that the NYA should help develop black leadership, and she saw herself as a liaison between the white and black communities, assisting each to understand the other. At one point NYA chief Aubrey Williams praised Bethune's accomplishments: "No one can do what Mrs. Bethune can do," she said.

In 1936 Bethune organized the Federal Council on Negro Affairs, sometimes called the black cabinet because it consisted of African Americans within the Roosevelt administration. The council coordinated government programs for blacks and advised the president on civil rights. Bethune exhorted, "Let us band together and work together as one big brotherhood and give momentum to the great ball that is starting to roll for Negroes." The group used its influence to end segregation at Virginia's Shenandoah National Park and in government cafeterias.

Within the NYA Bethune established a Special Fund for Higher Education, through which she raised scholarship money so African Americans could attend college. Over seven years she collected more than $600,000 for a black educational fund. At the same time, she supported protests against racial segregation; joined a picket line around a segregated drugstore in Washington, D.C.; and in 1941 endorsed plans for a civil rights march on the nation's capital.

A power within the Democratic Party, Bethune urged it to embrace the cause of civil rights. She gained considerable access to President Roosevelt and developed a friendship with the first lady, ELEANOR ROOSEVELT, who learned much from Bethune about what African Americans wanted.

After Franklin Roosevelt died, Bethune met with President Harry Truman and in 1951 urged him to extend civil rights to blacks, calling the action the most effective weapon against communism. She presented him with a list of six requests:

To use your power and influence to abolish, immediately, racial segregation in the nation's capital.
To appoint qualified Negroes on the administrative and policy making level of our government.
To integrate Negroes in all new agencies that are being established.
To appoint Negroes more widely in the foreign and diplomatic service of our country.
To issue an Executive Order guaranteeing the maximum use of all manpower in all production efforts irrespective of color, race, or national origin in the defense emergency.

To abolish once and for all racial segregation of Negro soldiers in the United States Army.

During the post–World War II Red Scare (when Americans were hunting communists and other radicals), Bethune suffered from the smear tactics then widely in use when the Anti-Communist League of Englewood, New Jersey, and the American Legion branded her a communist. The charge was absurd: In addition to her comments to Truman, in a weekly newspaper column she had repeatedly referred to "the sickness of communism and of totalitarianism in all its forms."

Bethune died on May 18, 1955. A promoter of racial harmony, she had extolled democracy, saying that its weakness resided in its failure to include black Americans on an equal footing with whites,

Mary McLeod Bethune received one of the highest appointments of a black woman in the federal government during the 1930s when President Franklin Roosevelt named her as his administrative assistant in charge of Negro affairs in the National Youth Administration. *(Library of Congress)*

and that this shortcoming could and should be corrected. She said racial isolation was destructive because it "allows the rise of misunderstanding and suspicion, providing rich soil for the seeds of antagonism and conflict," and in revising the words of the black leader BOOKER TALIAFERRO WASHINGTON, she called on whites and blacks to live "not 'one as the hand and separate as the fingers,' but one as the clasped hands of friendly cooperation."

Further Reading

Holt, Rackham. *Mary McLeod Bethune: A Biography.* Garden City, N.Y.: Doubleday, 1964.

McCluskey, Audrey Thomas, and Elaine M. Smith, eds. *Mary McLeod Bethune: Building a Better World.* Bloomington: Indiana University Press, 1999.

Blackwell, Alice Stone

(1857–1950) *women's suffragist*

Alice Stone Blackwell's family heritage was one of social activism, especially in the fight for women's rights. She was the only child of Henry Browne Blackwell and LUCY STONE, and was born on September 14, 1857, in Orange, New Jersey. Her mother was a leader in the movement; an aunt, ELIZABETH BLACKWELL, was the first woman in the United States to graduate from medical school; another aunt, EMILY BLACKWELL, was also a pioneer for women in medicine; and yet a third aunt, ANTOINETTE BLACKWELL, was the first American woman to be ordained a minister.

While Alice Stone Blackwell was still a child, she moved with her parents to Dorchester, Massachusetts. She graduated from Chauncy High School in Boston and attended Boston University, where she received a bachelor's degree in 1881.

Blackwell then joined the *Woman's Journal* as an editor. Founded by Lucy Stone, the *Journal* was the magazine of the American Woman Suffrage Association (AWSA), then in competition with the National Woman Suffrage Association (NWSA). SUSAN BROWNELL ANTHONY and ELIZABETH CADY STANTON were the leaders of the NWSA, and whereas they were willing to ally with radicals in the women's rights movement

and pursue a strategy of lobbying Congress for suffrage legislation, the AWSA favored a more moderate approach and concentrated on influencing the state legislatures to advance the women's cause.

Blackwell was instrumental in healing the rift between the AWSA and NWSA, and after the two groups merged in 1890 to form the National American Woman Suffrage Association, she served as its recording secretary, a post she held until 1918. Blackwell effectively expressed her views about suffrage in her pamphlet "Objections Answered," published in 1915. By that time she was supporting the passage of a constitutional amendment to guarantee women's suffrage. "The reasons why women should vote are the same as the reasons why men should vote . . . ," she wrote. "It is fair and right that the people who must obey the laws should have a voice in choosing the lawmakers, and that those who must pay the taxes should have a voice as to the amount of the tax, and the way in which the money shall be spent." In a series of statements and answers, she responded to those who opposed women's suffrage:

> *It would double the ignorant vote.*
>
> Statistics published by the National Bureau of Education show that the high schools of every state in the Union are graduating more girls than boys—some of them twice and three times as many.
>
> *If women vote, they ought to fight and do police duty.*
>
> If no men were allowed to vote except those who were able and willing to do military and police duty, women might consistently be debarred for that reason. But so long as the old, the infirm, the halt, the lame, and the blind are freely admitted to the ballot box, some better reason must be found for excluding women than the fact that they do not fight.
>
> *It will destroy chivalry.*
>
> Justice would be worth more to women than chivalry, if they could not have both. A working girl put the case in a nutshell when she said, "I would gladly stand for twenty minutes in the street car going home if by doing so I could get the same pay that a man would have had for doing my day's work."

Blackwell edited the *Women's Journal* until 1917 and at the same time wrote articles for it. From 1887 until 1905 she also published "Woman's Column," a report on women's suffrage activities sent to newspapers around the country.

Her social activism encompassed other movements. She participated, for example, in the causes of oppressed people overseas and founded the Friends of Russian Freedom in reaction to czarist persecutions. With these sympathies in mind, she edited works written by authors of other nationalities, such as *Armenian Poems* (1896 and 1916) and *Songs of Russia* (1906).

Blackwell was active in the Woman's Christian Temperance Union, the Women's Trade Union League, the National Association for the Advancement of Colored People, and the American Peace Society. She was a socialist, though not a party member. In the 1920s she supported the defense of Sacco and Vanzetti, two Italian immigrant anarchists charged with murder and robbery in Massachusetts. (Both were found guilty and executed.)

Blackwell helped organize the Massachusetts League of Women Voters and in the 1930s led them in opposing the practice of firing women from municipal jobs so men with families could work. Yet she preferred that women stay at home and raise their children.

Blackwell died of heart disease on March 15, 1950, at Cambridge, Massachusetts.

Further Reading

Merrill, Marlene Deahl, ed. *Growing Up in Boston's Gilded Age: The Journal of Alice Stone.* New Haven Conn.: Yale University Press, 1990.

Blackwell, Antoinette
(Antoinette Louisa Brown)
(1825–1921) *women's rights activist*

Antoinette Blackwell became the first American woman to be ordained a minister and advocated temperance, abolition, and women's rights. She was born Antoinette Louisa Brown on May 20, 1825, in Henrietta, New York, the daughter of Joseph Brown and Abby Morse Brown.

As a child, Antoinette joined the Congregational Church and showed an inclination toward the ministry when she began speaking out at church meetings. She briefly taught school and later entered Oberlin College, the first college in the United States to grant degrees to women. There she formed a lifelong friendship with another future activist in the women's movement, LUCY STONE.

Despite its reputation for liberalism, Oberlin held to many traditional practices, and Antoinette Brown experienced sexual discrimination that encouraged her to speak out for women's rights. Female students at Oberlin cleaned rooms, did the wash, and served men at their meals. Since women were prohibited from engaging with men in public debates, she and several other female students formed the Ladies Literary Society to present their views.

Antoinette Brown obtained her bachelor's degree in 1847 and then shocked Oberlin's faculty by announcing she would enroll in the college's theology program. Several teachers tried to dissuade her, arguing that it was improper for a woman to become a minister. But she rejected their stand. When she completed her theology studies in 1850, the faculty refused to grant her a degree.

In the 1850s Blackwell lectured for temperance and against slavery. Like other public-spirited women, she had the double challenge of not only having to argue her point but also showing that, in a male-dominated society where women were supposed to stay at home, she should be allowed to speak her mind.

In 1853 Blackwell was ordained a minister in the First Congregational Church in South Butler, New York. She quit one year later—and joined the Unitarians—largely because she was moving away from the Bible and gravitating toward a more scientific view of the world. She recalled,

> I was always reading papers—Herbert Spencer, Darwin, etc. I was more or less influenced, perhaps, by people I was with. In four or five months after I was ordained the bottom of my theology suddenly fell out . . . I began to feel I must resign. My health failed under the strain

and I resigned under that plea and went home and studied these questions.

That same year, she served as a delegate to the World's Temperance Convention in New York City and generated controversy when she spent more than three hours trying to be heard above the shouts of men demanding that, as a woman, she be silenced. While in the city she observed slum conditions and wrote about them for the *New York Tribune*. In 1856 she married Samuel Blackwell, the brother of women's rights leaders ELIZABETH BLACKWELL and EMILY BLACKWELL, and the brother-in-law of Lucy Stone. The couple had five daughters who lived past infancy, and Antoinette reduced her public speaking so she could spend more time raising her children.

But she continued to voice her opinions through her writing. She wrote 10 books in all, among them *Studies in General Science* (1869) and *The Sexes throughout Nature* (1875). In *The Sexes* she set out to counter the conservative interpretation of Charles Darwin's theory of evolution. The conservatives had argued that nature intended women to be secondary in society to men because women's brains were smaller than those of men and that, physically, women were more like children than adults. Blackwell accepted the conservative premise of women's mental inferiority, but she argued that it resulted not from nature but from women's restriction by society. If women were allowed a greater intellectual role, she wrote, their mental faculties would improve.

In 1868 Blackwell joined Lucy Stone to petition the New Jersey legislature to enable women to vote and allow married women to have property rights equal to those enjoyed by men. They wrote in part "We pray you Honorable body so to amend the statutes of this State that *Married Women* may make a *valid will* of all property, real, personal and mixed, in the same manner that all other sane adult persons are now free to do."

Blackwell returned to lecturing in the 1870s while she continued to write. She cast her first vote in 1920 at age 95 after the Nineteenth Amendment, guaranteeing women the right to vote, had been ratified. She died on November 5, 1921, in Elizabeth, New Jersey.

Further Reading

Cazden, Elizabeth. *Antoinette Brown Blackwell: A Biography.* Old Westbury, N.Y.: The Feminist Press, 1983.

Lasser, Carol, and Marlene Deahl Merrill, eds. *Friends and Sisters: Letters between Lucy Stone and Antoinette Brown Blackwell, 1846–1893.* Urbana: University of Illinois Press, 1987.

Munson, Elizabeth, and Greg Dickinson. "Hearing Women Speak: Antoinette Brown Blackwell and the Dilemma of Authority." *Journal of Women's History* 10 (Spring 1998): 108+.

Blackwell, Elizabeth (1821–1910) and Emily Blackwell (1826–1910)
medical reformers

Elizabeth and Emily Blackwell challenged male-dominated society by obtaining medical degrees, founding their own hospital and medical school, and advocating that other women become doctors. Elizabeth was born on February 3, 1821, and Emily on October 8, 1826, both in Bristol, England, to Hannah Lane Blackwell and Samuel Blackwell, a sugar refiner.

In 1833 Elizabeth and Emily Blackwell immigrated to New York City when their parents moved there from Bristol. Two years later the family moved again, this time to Cincinnati, Ohio. As a young woman, Elizabeth disliked the prospect of finding a husband, marrying, and raising children. Instead, she stayed single, a decision in part necessitated by the death of her father soon after the family's arrival in Cincinnati and the subsequent economic straits that forced her to teach school for several years.

In 1845 Elizabeth visited a friend who was dying of a uterine disorder. The friend told her about how she had delayed seeing a doctor because she was too embarrassed to talk about her problem with a male physician. She suggested that Elizabeth become a doctor, but Elizabeth at first considered the idea preposterous. After her friend died of the disease, however, she changed her mind and began applying to medical schools for acceptance. Every one of them turned her down, except the Medical College in Geneva, New York, which admitted her in 1847.

Her degree in hand, Elizabeth was nevertheless denied internship in American hospitals because of her sex, so she journeyed to Paris and continued her studies at La Maternité, a prominent hospital in that city. She had planned to practice surgery, but in November 1849 she contracted purulent ophthalmia, which left her blind in one eye and partially blind in the other.

She then returned to the United States in 1851, settled in New York City, and promptly experienced more rejection when hospitals refused to employ her as a doctor, a profession still considered inappropriate for women. Elizabeth lectured and in 1852 published *The Laws of Life,* a book about feminine hygiene.

That same year, Emily Blackwell followed her sister's example and pursued a career in medicine. She entered Rush Medical College in Chicago but the state medical society protested her admission, and she was forced to leave. She completed her studies in 1854 at the Medical College of Western Reserve University in Cleveland.

In 1857 Elizabeth, Emily, and a third doctor, Marie Zakrzewska, expanded a dispensary Elizabeth had opened in 1853 and converted it into a hospital, the New York Infirmary for Women and Children. No other hospital in the country was staffed completely by women to provide medical service to them.

During the Civil War, Elizabeth Blackwell trained nurses to serve in the Union army. In 1868 she founded the Women's Medical College of the New York Infirmary and established rigorous standards to preclude criticism that it offered an education inferior to that of men. The medical college changed the practice of medicine by training hundreds of women physicians before it merged in 1899 with the Cornell University Medical College.

Elizabeth returned to England in 1869, leaving Emily in charge of the Women's Medical College. In 1875 Elizabeth was appointed professor of gynecology at the London School of Medicine for Women. She retired the next year after suffering an illness, and she died on May 31, 1910. Emily Blackwell continued to work at the Medical College until her retirement in 1900. She died a few

months after Elizabeth, on September 7, 1910. Together, Elizabeth and Emily Blackwell challenged the prevailing belief that women should mind their husbands and families and leave more cerebral pursuits to men.

Further Reading

Chambers, Peggy. *A Doctor Alone: The Biography of Elizabeth Blackwell, The First Woman Doctor, 1821–1910.* London: Bodley Head, 1956.

"Elizabeth Blackwell: The First Woman Doctor." *Child Life* 79 (April 2000): 24.

Hays, Elinor Rice. *Those Extraordinary Blackwells: The Story of a Journey to a Better World.* New York: Harcourt, Brace & World, 1967.

Sahli, Nancy Ann. *Elizabeth Blackwell, M.D.: A Biography.* New York: Arno Press, 1974.

Blatch, Harriot Stanton
(1856–1940) *women's suffragist*

A militant women's suffragist, Harriot Stanton Blatch followed the example of her outspoken parents. She was born Harriot Stanton on January 20, 1856, in Seneca Falls, New York, to Henry Brewster Stanton and ELIZABETH CADY STANTON. Her mother was a leader in the women's rights movement, and both of her parents had helped organize the 1848 women's rights convention at Seneca Falls.

With such activists for parents, Harriot Stanton grew up accustomed to discussing social issues. She graduated from Vassar College in 1878 with honors and attended the Boston School of Oratory for one year before traveling to Europe.

In 1882 she involved herself in the women's suffrage movement when she wrote a chapter for *History of Woman Suffrage,* a book being compiled by her mother and by SUSAN BROWNELL ANTHONY. Harriot Stanton's chapter surveyed the activities of the American Woman Suffrage Association and presented a different view from the rest of the book, which looked at developments from the standpoint of a rival group, Anthony's National Woman Suffrage Association (NWSA). Some historians believe that Harriot Stanton's work (along with the effort of ALICE STONE BLACK-WELL) helped reconcile the two organizations, which merged shortly afterward.

Harriot Stanton married William Henry Blatch, an English businessman, late in 1882, and the couple settled near London, where they raised two children. She participated in several women's organizations and in the Fabian Society, a socialist group.

In the 1890s Harriet Stanton Blatch engaged in a debate then intensifying in American suffragist circles that caused her to split philosophically with her mother. Elizabeth Cady Stanton argued that voting rights should be extended only to educated women. Writing to her mother in 1894, Blatch insisted that a diploma in no way assured intelligent thinking and that many college graduates were ignorant. Besides that, she believed that working-class women should be allowed to vote: first, because they knew their plight better than anyone else; and second, because in a republic all adults affected by taxation and other measures should vote for the representatives who determined them.

She later said about elite women: "Whatever merit [their homes] possess, is largely due to the fact that the actress when on the stage, the doctor when by her patient's side, the writer when at her desk, has a Bridget [working woman] to do the homebuilding for her." In an address to the NWSA in Washington, D.C., in February 1898, she said that the women's suffrage movement should recruit working women because by holding jobs they had been changing public attitudes about women's role in society.

The NWSA rejected her argument. In fact, the organization increasingly embraced a conservative stand that strove to prevent immigrants and African Americans from voting. Writing in *The Ideas of the Woman Suffrage Movement* (1981), the historian Aileen S. Kraditor states: "The woman suffrage movement had ceased to be a campaign to *extend the franchise to* all adult Americans. Instead, *one* important part of its rationale had become the proposal to *take the vote away from* some Americans—Negroes in the South and naturalized citizens in the North."

Harriot Stanton Blatch returned to the United States in 1902 and plunged directly into the women's suffrage movement. "There are born politicians just as there are born artists, writers, painters," she said. "I confess that I should be a politician, that I am not interested in machine politics, but that the devotion to the public cause . . . rather than the individual, appeals to me."

She determined to pursue her 1898 address and recruit working women into the suffrage campaign. The times were on her side: The Progressive movement was then under way, and many male reformers believed that social change could advance if women were voters. Harriot Stanton Blatch combined this reform spirit, and an already vibrant appeal to women in America by radicals such as socialists and anarchists, with her experience in Britain as a member of the Women's Trade Union League and the Fabians, groups that had built her faith in appealing to working women and had raised her class consciousness.

In New York in 1907 she organized the Equality League of Self-Supporting Women (later the Women's Political Union) and recruited women from industry and from unions, along with business women and professional women. Believing that the NWSA had grown too sedate and detached from the masses, she advocated militant tactics, such as open-air rallies and marches. She led the first women's suffrage parade down New York City's Fifth Avenue in 1910, a move that generated criticism from more conservative women. She wanted to engage in events that would force the largely complacent press to cover and publicize the suffrage movement. Ultimately these tactics not only drew attention to the voting issue, but also raised the larger question of women's role in society.

The publication *American Suffragette* proclaimed: "We . . . believe in standing on street corners and fighting our way to recognition, forcing the men to think about us. We glory . . . that we are theatrical." Even the word *suffragette*, as opposed to *suffragist*, bespoke a new commitment as American women adopted it from British militants. Yet Blatch was a member of an elite family and maintained her contacts with her peers. In many ways, she served as an important conduit between workers and the upper class, particularly in educating the elite to the conditions faced by working women.

In 1916 Blatch merged the Women's Political Union with the Congressional Union (later the National Woman's Party). During World War I she headed the speakers' bureau of the Food Administration and served as director of the Women's Land Army. In 1918 she wrote *Mobilizing Woman Power*, which told about women's work in Europe on behalf of the war, and in 1920 she wrote *A Woman's Point of View: Some Roads to Peace*, which described the effect of the war on Europe. She supported the formation of the League of Nations and believed that if women participated in it, and in politics in general, there would be fewer wars.

Active in women's labor causes, she also campaigned for the Progressive Party. In 1922 she edited, with her brother Theodore Stanton, *Elizabeth Cady Stanton, as Revealed in Her Letters, Diary, and Reminiscences*. Her memoir, *Challenging Years*, was published in 1940.

Harriot Stanton Blatch died in Greenwich, Connecticut, on November 20, 1940. According to her biographer, Ellen Carol DuBois, Blatch in her suffrage campaign "saw working-class women more as exemplars for women like herself rather than 'victims to be succored.'"

Further Reading

DuBois, Ellen Carol. *Harriot Stanton Blatch and the Winning of Woman Suffrage*. New Haven, Conn.: Yale University Press, 1997.

Wheeler, Marjorie Spruill. *One Woman. One Vote: Rediscovering the Woman Suffrage Movement*. Troutdale, Ore.: NewSage Press, 1998.

Bloomer, Amelia Jenks
(1818–1894) *women's rights activist*

A leading advocate for women's rights, Amelia Bloomer's greatest legacy resulted from a type of clothing she tried to popularize. She was born Amelia Jenks on May 27, 1818, in Homer, New York, to Anania Jenks, a clothier, and Lucy Webb Jenks.

Amelia obtained only a limited education but became a tutor in 1837. Three years later she married Dexter C. Bloomer, a lawyer and part owner of a newspaper. Quaker in background, he encouraged her to write articles on social issues, and she did. In 1848 she attended the Woman's Rights Convention at Seneca Falls, New York. She took no part in the proceedings beyond observing them, but the following year she founded a temperance newspaper, *Lily*, that within a few months carried articles devoted to women's rights. In short order its circulation grew from a few hundred to about 4,000.

It was in an article Bloomer wrote for *Lily* in 1851 that she made her proposal to change women's clothing. At that time, society prescribed outfits that were considered attractive yet protective of a woman's body and morals. Women were to wear tight corsets, several layers of petticoats, and full-length dresses.

Bloomer recognized the problems with this attire. The restrictive corsets made women feel as if they were latter-day Jonahs imprisoned by whalebone (the material used in their construction); the dresses dragged on the ground and collected dirt; and the ensemble weighed some 15 pounds.

As an alternative, Bloomer advocated a loose bodice, along with baggy ankle-length pantaloons and dresses with a hemline at the knee. She did not invent the design—a few other women had been wearing these outfits for years—but she did argue for it so strongly that it was eventually called the "Bloomer Costume" or simply "bloomers." Amelia Bloomer wore bloomers until the late 1850s and was joined in her sartorial revolution by such women's rights leaders as ELIZABETH CADY STANTON and SUSAN BROWNELL ANTHONY.

Mainstream America, though, derided the outfit, calling it odd and indecent. So strong was the outcry (while the curious flocked to see Amelia Bloomer lecture in dress and pantaloons for women's rights), that by 1860 the bloomer costume had been relegated to the storage chest of history.

When Americans criticized bloomers as indecent and strange looking, they may well have been motivated in their attacks by the identification of the ensemble with women's rights. To more traditional Americans, bloomers became the symbol of women undermining social values.

Amelia Bloomer continued her campaign for women's rights long beyond the clothing controversy. In 1855 she and her husband moved to Council Bluffs, Iowa, and although she ceased publishing *Lily,* she lectured and wrote extensively, and from 1871 until 1873 she served as president of the state Woman Suffrage Association. She arranged also for Stanton, Anthony, and LUCY STONE to speak in Iowa on women's issues.

Bloomer was most forceful in her advocacy of women's suffrage. She said, "I hold, not only that the exclusion of woman from the ballot-box is grossly unjust, but that it is her duty . . . to go to it and cast her vote along with her husband and brother; and that, until she shall do so, we can never expect to have a perfectly just and upright government under which the rights of the people—of all the people—are respected and secured." And she insisted:

> If we would have great men, we must first have great women. If we would have great statesmen and great philanthropists, we must have mothers whose thoughts soar above the trifling objects which now engage the attention of the mass of women, and who are capable of impressing those thoughts upon the minds of their offspring.

Women's clothing in the late 1800s adopted some of the bloomer look, but the basic rights of women would await their significant advance until the suffrage ideas of Amelia Bloomer and those like her gained wider acceptance.

Further Reading
Bloomer, Dexter C. *Life and Writings of Amelia Bloomer.* St. Clair Shores, Mich.: Scholarly Press, 1976.
Coone, Anne C., ed. *Hear Me Patiently: The Reform Speeches of Amelia Jenks Bloomer.* Westport, Conn.: Greenwood Press, 1994.

Bond, Julian
(1940–   ) *civil rights leader*

Though a politician criticized for laziness, Julian Bond was a founding member of the Student Non-Violent Coordinating Committee (SNCC) and a director of the National Association for the Advancement of Colored People (NAACP). He was born on January 14, 1940, in Nashville, Tennessee, to Horace Mann Bond and Julia Washington Bond.

Even though Julian Bond earned his reputation as a civil rights worker in the South, he spent most of his childhood in Pennsylvania, where his father served as the first black president of Lincoln University at Oxford. Bond completed his elementary education at a largely white school and then attended a Quaker preparatory school near Philadelphia. More interested in athletics than in academics, he took five years rather than the usual four to complete his education.

Bond subsequently enrolled at all-black Morehouse College in Atlanta, Georgia, in 1957, after his father had accepted the position of dean of the school of education at Atlanta University. Bond went to Atlanta with trepidation, well aware that whites in Georgia were reacting to the civil rights movement with recriminatory violence. Only three years earlier, the U.S. Supreme Court had issued its ruling in *Brown v. Board of Education,* and Georgians detested the order to desegregate their schools. They opposed also the recent black boycott of buses in Montgomery, Alabama, and the nonviolent protests being launched by MARTIN LUTHER KING, JR.

Then on February 1, 1960, black college students at Greensboro, North Carolina, staged a sit-in to desegregate the lunch counter at the local Woolworth's store. Bond joined this youth-based civil rights movement after Lonnie King, a fellow student, recruited him to organize a meeting to discuss the protest. Together they formed the Committee on Appeal for Human Rights, and on March 15, 1960, Bond led the group in a sit-in at the all-white cafeteria inside Atlanta's city hall; he was promptly arrested.

In April 1960 Bond attended a meeting of black college students from around the South at Raleigh, North Carolina. Breaking with the more traditional NAACP and King's Southern Christian Leadership Conference, they founded SNCC, geared to young blacks who wanted to escalate and quicken the civil rights protest. Bond later said in an interview that the NAACP "just seemed so out of touch. . . . They opposed the sit-ins. They didn't like direct action. They didn't like civil disobedience. They believed in law and litigation. And we were tired of that. We didn't want that. It took too long."

Shortly afterward, Bond worked as a reporter for the *Atlanta Inquirer*, a student newspaper supporting the sit-ins, and became its managing editor. He also worked as the communications director for SNCC, a post he held until 1965. His preoccupation with the civil rights movement, and his marriage to Alice Clopton in July 1961, caused him to reduce his course load at Morehouse and then to drop out. (He eventually returned and received a bachelor's degree in 1971).

With more and more blacks in Georgia gaining the right to vote, SNCC asked Julian Bond to run for the state legislature. His activism, good looks, and articulate manner made him a strong candidate, and in 1965 he won election to the House of Representatives from a largely black district that included Atlanta.

Getting seated in the legislature was another problem. Early in 1966 Bond told a newspaper reporter that he supported a recent SNCC statement condemning the Vietnam War. The Georgia house then voted to prevent Bond from taking his seat, claiming that he had committed treason in opposing the war. On Bond's appeal to the courts, the legislature was ordered to let the black leader take office.

Many observers labeled Bond an ineffective legislator, too indifferent and lackadaisical in his job. Yet his problems in leadership arose mainly from the months-long ostracism he suffered from his fellow legislators, who disliked being forced to let him take his seat. Whatever Bond's limitations, he won re-election several times, serving in the house until 1975, and then was elected to the state senate. He relinquished his seat in 1986 to run for the U.S. Congress, but he lost in the Democratic primary to a former SNCC colleague, JOHN ROBERT LEWIS.

At the time of that setback, Bond's marriage began to unravel, and he and his wife divorced in 1989. The following year Bond admitted he had fathered a child with a woman alleged to have been his mistress, and a court ordered him to pay child support.

Bond then turned to writing and public speaking, and he narrated "Eyes on the Prize," a television documentary on the civil rights movement. He also moderated the TV program "America's Black Forum." In the late 1980s and 1990s he taught at various colleges as a visiting professor.

In 1995 Bond was elected to his fourth term as a board member of the NAACP, and in 1998 he was elected its chairman as the venerable civil rights organization turned to new leadership in an attempt to recover from recent scandals. Bond stated, "I want to try to help restore the NAACP to the luster it deserves. It's the biggest civil rights organization in America, the major advocate for the rights of black people." In an interview, he compared his leadership, and that of the group's new president, KWEISI MFUME, to the refurbishing of an old historical mansion:

> We're going to polish up the brass, and we're going to have people come to the mansion and say, "Boy, this is so pretty, but it's livable now, it's worthy of being occupied. Just because it's old, doesn't mean it's unusable. It's utilitarian. We can occupy it now. It's still good.

Amid controversy that the year 2000 national election was being marred in several localities by attempts to prevent blacks from voting, Bond said: "No voter, at any place, at anytime, should smell even the faintest odor of impropriety or irregularity at the polling place." He vowed that the NAACP would end such behavior. Looking back to the past—his and that of so many civil rights workers—he said, "Too much blood has been spilled, too many gains have been made, and too much is at stake . . . for even one person to be kept away from the voting booth."

Further Reading

Bond, Julian. *A Time to Speak, a Time to Act: The Movement in Politics*. New York: Simon & Schuster, 1972.

Chappell, Kevin. "Where Are the Civil Rights Icons of the '60s?" *Ebony*, August 1996, 108+.

Neary, John. *Julian Bond: Black Rebel*. New York: Morrow, 1971.

Bonnin, Gertrude Simmons
(Zitkala-Sa)
(1876–1938) *Indian rights activist*

Gertrude Simmons Bonnin advocated citizenship for Indians. She wanted to assimilate Native Americans into white society, a goal that raised the anger of those Indians who preferred to protect their distinct culture.

Gertrude Simmons experienced the clash of cultures at her birth on February 22, 1876, in Greenwood, Nebraska. Her father, who was her mother's third husband, was a white man named Felker. Her mother, Ellen Simmons, who kept the last name of her second husband, was a Yankton Sioux. Ellen gave the name Simmons to Gertrude.

Gertrude spent her early childhood on the Yankton Reservation in South Dakota before enrolling in 1884 at White's Manual Institute, a Quaker school in Wabash, Indiana. There the teachers told her that her Indian culture was inferior and forced her to treat it as a disease that must be expelled from her body and mind. Many Indians on the Yankton Reservation subsequently criticized her for turning her back on Sioux practices.

After White's Institute, Simmons attended another Quaker school, Earlham College, in Richmond, Indiana. Although illness forced her to leave Earlham before she could graduate, as a student she excelled at public speaking and poetry. In 1898 she began teaching at Carlisle Indian School in Carlisle, Pennsylvania, and later that year returned to her reservation, where she adopted the name Zitkala-Sa, meaning "Red Bird."

Also in 1898 she studied violin at the New England Conservatory of Music in Boston and then wrote articles and short stories that appeared in magazines, including *Atlantic Monthly* and *Harper's*. In one essay she defended the right of Indians to seek revenge. "Is patriotism a virtue only in Saxon hearts?" she wrote. Yet she conceded white society's wisdom when she said, "We come . . . seeking the 'White Man's ways.' Seeking your skill in industry and art, seeking labor and honest independence, seeking the treasures of knowledge and wisdom."

In May 1902 she married a Yankton, Raymond T. Bonnin, and resumed using the name Gertrude. She and her husband lived on the Uintah and Ouray Reservation in Utah, where he worked as a school superintendent for the Bureau of Indian Affairs (BIA), and she spent most of her time raising their son.

In 1916 she won election as secretary of the Society of American Indians (SAI) in Washington, D.C., and from then until 1919 edited its *American Indian Magazine*. As she promoted U.S. citizenship for Indians, she lectured on the topic of Indian rights. When the SAI dissolved in 1920, she joined the General Federation of Women's Clubs and persuaded the group to establish an Indian welfare committee. Her 1923 report, *Oklahoma's Poor Rich Indians*, exposed corruption among federal officials, showing how they had used fraud to steal Indian land.

Congress approved U.S. citizenship for Indians in 1926, and she and her husband founded the National Council of American Indians (NCAI) to help Native American voters organize for their rights. She served as president of the NCAI for 12 years and earned praise for her effective lobbying of the BIA. Gertrude Simmons Bonnin died on January 25, 1938, her assimilationist activities reflective of her own experiences with white and Indian cultures.

Further Reading
Bonnin, Gertrude. *Oklahoma's Poor Rich Indians: An Orgy of Graft and Exploitation of the Five Civilized Tribes—Legalized Robbery.* Philadelphia: Office of the Indian Rights Association, 1924.
Champagne, Duane. *Native America: Portrait of the Peoples.* Detroit: Visible Ink Press, 1994.

Boulding, Kenneth Ewart
(1910–1993) *pacifist*

An economist, social scientist, and poet, Kenneth Ewart Boulding was an impassioned pacifist. He was born on January 18, 1910, in Liverpool, England, to William Boulding and Bessie Rowe Boulding. Both parents were members of blue-collar families, and William worked as a plumber while also operating his own small shop from behind his house.

Kenneth Boulding's biographer, Cynthia Earl Kerman, traces Boulding's pacifism to his boyhood during World War I, when he heard stories about relatives and neighbors who were maimed or killed in the conflict. Once, when Boulding was about eight years of age, his mother took him to see his aunt, who had lost her mind after the death of her son in the war. His mother later remembered: "The incident made a great impression on Kenneth and I think the memory of it, later on, helped to make a Quaker of him. Wars make tragic the private lives of ordinary people." At age 16 Boulding began attending the Liverpool Friends Meeting; he remained a Quaker for the rest of his life and joined several peace protests.

Boulding was the first in his family educated beyond elementary school, eventually winning a scholarship in chemistry to New College at Oxford in England. One year later he left the sciences to study politics, philosophy, and economics. He graduated from Oxford with honors and received a fellowship to study in the United States at the University of Chicago. In 1934 he returned to the British Isles and taught at the University of Edinburgh.

As a professor he made several speeches at peace meetings, and at the request of the Edinburgh Friends Meeting, in 1935 he sent a letter to the prime minister requesting changes in the Treaty of Versailles that had ended World War I so that there could be a "true, just, and generous" peace. From 1936 until 1937 he served on the Northern Friends Peace Board.

Later that year Boulding immigrated to the United States and over the ensuing years taught at several different colleges, including Colgate University in New York. While still at Colgate in 1939 he received his master's degree from Oxford. From 1941 to 1942 he worked as an economist for the League of Nations Economic and Financial Section. During that year he married Elise Biorn-Hansen. They had five children.

A prolific writer, Boulding published articles and books—more than a thousand works in all—that wandered well beyond his training in economics and covered an array of subjects. His first book, *Economic Analysis* (1941), went through four editions. His *Reconstruction of Economics* (1950)

presented new concepts that displayed his brilliance as a seminal thinker. Several of his writings attempted to expand economics into ethical, religious, and sociological considerations. In short, he became a generalist, exploring and incorporating into his work all of the social sciences and philosophy. He recalled: "The study of labor was my undoing as a pure economist, as I became convinced that if one were going to study any particular segment of the real world, like the labor movement, one had to do this with the skills not only of the economist, but of the sociologist, the political scientist, the anthropologist, and even the philosopher and theologian." In addition to his other works, he wrote two books of poetry.

When Boulding applied for his U.S. citizenship in 1948, he stuck by his pacifist principles and refused to make the customary promise to bear arms to defend his adopted country. He obtained citizenship anyway.

In 1958 he organized a vigil at the University of Michigan to protest the testing of nuclear weapons. He later stated, "I conceived the act as (for me) a moral obligation of citizenship in the United States." During the Vietnam War he was at the forefront of the antiwar movement. In March 1965 he helped plan and conduct America's first teach-in on the war, an event in which students at the University of Michigan listened to debates between those who supported and those who opposed the military commitment.

Kenneth Boulding died on March 19, 1993, of cancer. Writing in 1974, Cynthia Earl Kerman said of him:

> If any one article of Kenneth Boulding's faith and practice is completely consistent, utterly undeniable, persistent throughout life, and coloring everything else he does, it is the doctrine of pacifism or nonviolence. This is not something, like socialism, enthusiastically adopted in adolescence and replaced later in a more rational process of examination; it begins much earlier and runs far deeper.

Further Reading

Kerman, Cynthia Earl. *Creative Tension: The Life and Thought of Kenneth Boulding.* Ann Arbor: University of Michigan Press, 1974.

Szenberg, Michael, ed. *Eminent Economists: Their Life Philosophies.* Cambridge: Cambridge University Press, 1992.

Bowditch, Henry Ingersoll
(1808–1892) *abolitionist, health reformer*

Henry Bowditch combined his medical career with a crusade against slavery and after the Civil War led America's public health movement. He was born on August 9, 1808, in Salem, Massachusetts, the son of the famed mathematician Nathaniel Bowditch.

Henry Bowditch lived in Salem until 1823, when his family moved to Boston. He graduated from Boston Public Latin School and entered Harvard in 1825, followed by Harvard Medical School, where he received a degree in 1832. Later that year, after interning at Massachusetts General Hospital in Boston, he sailed across the Atlantic to Paris. There his father's reputation put him into contact with French intellectuals, and he continued his studies in medicine under Pierre Charles Alexander Louis, one of Europe's leading physicians. He stayed briefly in London, where he saw medical practices that he criticized and then returned to Paris and, finally, to Boston in 1834.

Despite Bowditch's disappointment with his experience in London, he was influenced there by the writings of William Wilberforce, a prominent member of Parliament. Wilberforce had worked to end the slave trade within the British Empire and in the early 1800s joined the abolitionist movement. Three days before his death in 1833, the House of Commons emancipated all slaves under the British flag. Bowditch took Wilberforce's ideas and reformist zeal with him to the United States, and after hearing the Massachusetts abolitionist WILLIAM LLOYD GARRISON demand the immediate end to slavery joined the movement, which demanded no compromise with slaveholders.

In 1842 the arrest of runaway slave George Latimer in Boston caused Bowditch and two other leading Bostonians, William F. Channing and Frederick S. Cabot, to form the "Latimer Committee," aimed at securing the slave's freedom and rallying public opinion against slavery. The three abolitionists edited the *Latimer Journal and North Star* from 1842 until 1843 and circulated an antislavery petition signed by hundreds of Bostonians. Congressman John Quincy Adams presented the petition to the House of Representatives, but the gag rule then in effect prevented it from being heard. The episode illustrated that the rule violated the constitutional right to petition the government. Despite the congressional rejection, the Latimer Committee bought Latimer's freedom from his master for $400.

In subsequent years prior to the Civil War, Bowditch helped other runaways. Through his actions, he became a significant figure in the abolitionist movement, and he prized his friendship with the African-American abolitionist FREDERICK DOUGLASS. At the same time, he pioneered innovative surgical techniques.

During the Civil War Bowditch wrote a pamphlet that led to the government's creating an ambulance unit to care for the wounded in the Union army. When the fighting ended, he took the lead in promoting the public health movement. In 1869 he founded the Massachusetts State Board of Health, only the second such board in the entire country, and served as its first chairman. He published his most important book, *Public Hygiene in America,* in 1877, and two years later he served on the National Board of Health and as president of the American Medical Association. Bowditch died on January 14, 1892.

Further Reading
Bowditch, Vincent Yardley. *Life and Correspondence of Henry Ingersoll Bowditch.* 2 vols. Boston: Houghton Mifflin, 1902.

Bridges, Harry
(Alfred Bryant Renton Bridges)
(1901–1990) *labor activist*

A union organizer for longshoremen, Alfred Bryant Renton Bridges, who went by the name of Harry, was a self-professed Marxist. He was born into a comfortable middle-class family in Melbourne, Australia, on July 28, 1901. His father, Alfred Ernest Bridges, was a real estate agent, music composer, and writer of poetry; his mother, Julia Dorgen Bridges, was a devout Catholic.

Restless as a youth, Harry Bridges dropped out of school at age 14, and under the influence of Jack London's book *The Sea Wolf,* two years later he went to sea. For five years he sailed the world, and with his exposure to the injustices he found in other societies, he became a radical. Bridges saw the horrid conditions in Bombay under which many Indians lived, and he witnessed the poor pay and equally poor housing for workers in London— "The filthiest, most unhealthy place I ever had seen," he later stated. He was affected too by the Great Strike in Australia during the summer of 1917, when protesting workers nearly shut down the country's entire economy. "I did not know what it was all about then," Bridges recalled in 1967, "but later on I could look back and I could remember. . . . No [labor movement] since 1917 has ever organized the power to shut down industry as Australian unions shut down this whole country [then]; no nation before 1917 did it, no nation since has managed it. [It] began my real working class education." He revealed his radicalization after his arrival in the United States in 1921, when he briefly joined the Industrial Workers of the World, a militant, anticapitalist union.

The following year Bridges gave up seafaring altogether to work as a cargo loader on the San Francisco waterfront. The dangerous job, known for its high rate of injuries, paid only 85 cents an hour. The work also turned out to be humiliating as longshoremen had to endure the shape-up, meaning they had to wait each morning in long lines while the shipping companies arbitrarily picked the workers of the day. Participation in the shape-up required membership in the Longshoreman's Association of the Port of San Francisco, a union dominated by the companies. Anyone who complained about the union or its procedures would find himself bypassed in the shape-up lines, no matter how often he appeared or how long he waited.

The system made Bridges more radical. He was even blacklisted for several months when he tried to form a rival union and was fired from a job when he tried to help a fellow worker collect back wages.

With the onset of the Great Depression, conditions at the port worsened. In 1934 Bridges led a strike of the dockworkers along the Pacific coast, as they demanded higher wages and recognition for their union, the International Longshoremen's Association (ILA). His victory later that year replaced the shape-up with union hiring halls run independently of the shipping companies.

Beginning in 1935, Bridges went beyond the docks to organize warehouse workers. His attempt to recruit all types of laborers involved in shipping ran afoul of leaders within the American Federation of Labor (AFL), of which the ILA was a part. And in 1937 Bridges withdrew the union from the AFL and united it with the Congress of Industrial Organizations (CIO). He then reorganized the union into the International Longshoremen's and Warehousemen's Union (ILWU) and served as its president until 1977.

Bridge's militancy angered employers, and his enemies, along with a few colleagues within the CIO, began attacking him for his ties to communists. He publicly admitted he was a Marxist, but while working closely with the Communist Party (CP), he denied he had ever officially joined it. Nevertheless, he said that he admired the Soviet Union, and he once called the communists "friends of the working class." His son recalled: "He was pretty blind to problems in the Soviet Union. I remember when he went to [communist] Romania, he had a few complaints about his treatment, but all in all he had nothing but praise for the system." Congress investigated Bridges, and on several occasions the government tried to deport him. According to the historian Robert W. Cherny, "Bridges was . . . the most significant American labor leader to have maintained such close ties to the CP over such a long time." After Bridges's death evidence that confirmed he was a party member was uncovered.

During World War II Bridges pledged that in the spirit of unity the ILWU would refrain from staging any strikes. In 1945 he was naturalized as a U.S. citizen.

Shortly afterward, Bridges led a long strike among the Pacific Coast waterfront workers that in 1948 produced another victory for the ILWU. But as the Red Scare intensified (a hunt by the federal government and by state governments for communists and other radicals in the United States), in 1950 the CIO expelled the ILWU from its ranks for its communist allegiance. Undeterred, Bridges continued to lead the union, and in 1960 he arranged a new contract with the shipping companies that displayed a more moderate stance and made concessions to management that many workers criticized. Under the contract, the union accepted mechanized cargo handling and the use of large prepacked containers that could be easily transported from ships to railroad cars but that required the labor of fewer dockworkers. In exchange for these concessions, Bridges obtained substantial wage increases and higher pensions. Many of the changes in the contract were mandated by technological developments beyond the ILWU's control. Still, the impact of the agreement was massive: By the time Bridges retired as leader in 1977—after having lived on a modest salary of $27,000 a year, a testament to his refusal to pocket union dues for his own luxuries—the ILWU's membership had plummeted.

Bridges died of emphysema on March 30, 1990, with the reputation, as Robert Cherny notes, of having been, from the mid-1930s to the late 1970s, "the leading voice of the left within organized labor."

Further Reading

Cherny, Robert W. "The Making of a Labor Radical: Harry Bridges." *Pacific Historical Review* 64 (August 1995): 363+.

Larrowe, Charles P. *Harry Bridges: The Rise and Fall of Radical Labor in the United States.* New York: L. Hill, 1972.

Nelson, Bruce. *Workers on the Waterfront: Seamen, Longshoremen, and Unionism in the 1930s.* Urbana: University of Illinois Press, 1988.

Brower, David Ross

(1912–2000) *environmentalist*

An environmentalist likened in terms of his fanaticism to the abolitionist JOHN BROWN, David Ross Brower was called by many the "archdruid." He was born on July 1, 1912, in Berkeley, California,

to Ross Brower, a professor of mechanical drawing, and Mary Grace Barlow Brower.

Brower's love for nature developed at an early age when as a child he explored nearby hills and mountains. He became the "eyes" for his blind mother on family camping trips. Taking her on walks, he would describe for her the wondrous Sierra Nevada.

On graduating from high school, Brower entered the University of California at Berkeley—where his father taught—to study entomology, but he dropped out in 1931. Two years later he joined the Sierra Club, founded by JOHN MUIR to preserve the natural environment. While working most of the year in a candy company, Brower spent his summers hiking and climbing in the Sierras. In 1936 he landed a job with the Yosemite Park and Curry Company, operating a printing machine. Through the company he began working with the photographer Ansel Adams, renowned for his nature scenes, on projects to promote the beauty of Yosemite. In an interview with *The Progressive* in May 1994, Brower listed Adams among the people who most influenced him:

> John Muir was one of my role models. . . . I learned a lot from Aldo Leopold, whom I never met. I did meet Ansel Adams, whom I knew for fifty years and learned a lot from. And Howard Zahniser, who was executive secretary of the Wilderness Society. He was the last person I know of in the environmental leadership who had the ability to glue the organizations together instead of them fighting over turf and becoming fragmented.

An avid mountain climber, Brower led more than 70 first ascents in the 1930s and 1940s, and in 1939 he became the first person to reach the summit of Shiprock Peak in New Mexico. That same year, he was hired by the Sierra Club to map and catalog climbing sites around San Francisco Bay and to write the local chapter's newsletter. He also worked on a film, *Ski-Land Trails of the Kings*, whose influence some credit with leading to the establishment of Kings Canyon National Park.

Brower began working as an editor at the University of California Press in 1941, and two years later he married Anne Hus, a coeditor. They had four children. With World War II under way, Brower enlisted in the army and trained the soldiers who formed the U.S. Army's 10th Mountain Division. He himself served in Italy as a battalion intelligence officer.

With the war over, Brower returned to his job at the University of California Press while editing the *Sierra Club Bulletin* and the *Sierra Club Handbook*, published in 1947. In 1952 he left his job at the press to become the Sierra Club's first executive director. An aggressive leader, he took the largely somnolent group, which was more interested in hiking trips than in political lobbying, and mobilized it to fight the destruction of forests and the building of dams, including one proposed for the Green River in Utah that would have flooded parts of Dinosaur National Monument. He was also instrumental in persuading Congress to pass the Wilderness Preservation Act in 1964.

Brower became an untiring "preacher," as he called himself, for the environment. In *Encounters with the Archdruid* (1971), John McPhee presents one of Brower's sermons:

> We're hooked on growth. We're addicted to it. In my lifetime, man has used more resources than in all previous history. Technology has just begun to happen. They are *mining* water under Arizona. Cotton is subsidized by all that water. Why grow cotton in Arizona? There is no point to this. People in Texas want to divert the Yukon and have it flow to Texas. We are going to fill San Francisco Bay so we can have another Los Angeles in a state that deserves only one. Why grow to the point of repugnance? Aren't we repugnant enough already? . . . The United States has six per cent of the world's population and uses sixty per cent of the world's resources, and one per cent of Americans use sixty per cent of that. When one country gets more than its share, it builds tensions. War is waged over resources. Expansion will destroy us.

Over the years Brower's sermon changed in detail but never in tone. To those who called him extreme, he responded, "We're not blindly opposed to progress, we're opposed to blind progress."

From his experience in 1960 in assembling an exhibit of landscape photographs and text to be shown at Yosemite Valley, Brower developed the idea of the Sierra Club's publishing a series of picture books later that decade. These four-pound works combined scenic photos with text from classic writers such as Henry David Thoreau and John Muir. Brower realized these books could win more converts to the environmental movement than any abstract or theoretical propaganda. They ranged in subject and title from *Summer Island—Penobscot Country*, to *Gentle Wilderness—the Sierra Nevada*, to *The Wild Cascades*.

The tactics Brower used to fight two proposed dams in the Grand Canyon caused the Sierra Club to lose its tax-exempt status. But Brower called it the best thing that could happen to the organization, for it freed it to lobby Congress with no strings attached. "If you are tax-deductive," Brower later explained, "you have limitations on your lobbying activity and prohibitions on your political activity."

Although Brower at first supported nuclear power as an alternative to hydroelectric dams, he later changed his mind and opposed it primarily for its pollution, but also for its danger and its cost. Consequently, in the 1960s he led the fight over the building of a nuclear power plant in California's Diablo Canyon. He eventually lost but was vindicated in his analysis when the project cost 17 times more than the original estimate for it.

He failed, too, to save Glen Canyon in 1963 from a dam and flooding. He later considered it his greatest defeat, and it became the source of rumination in John McPhee's *Encounters with the Archdruid*. Glen Canyon had deep rock walls, waterfalls accompanied by quiet pools, and Indian inscriptions: what Bower called "the most beautiful place on earth, no exception."

Many in the Sierra Club disagreed with Brower's stand on the Diablo Canyon nuclear plant, were concerned about the organization's financial deficit, and were uncomfortable with the direction in which Brower was taking them—he was trying to make them realize that to protect the environment they must do more than save trees and must tackle a broad range of threats from nuclear power to air pollution. So after an anti-Brower slate won election to the executive board in 1969, Brower was forced to quit as executive director. Yet under his leadership, the Sierra Club had grown from a membership of 7,000 and a budget of $75,000 to a membership of 77,000 and assets of $3 million.

And he had become the foremost figure in the environmental movement, a status reinforced by John McPhee's book. Writing in *Rolling Stone* in December 2000, Bill McKibben states that after McPhee's work appeared, "Brower came to personify the cause in a way that no one since John Muir had managed, and so he was in constant demand; in Kyrgyzstan one week, Nairobi the next. If you were trying to block a hydroelectric project in northern Canada, if you needed to get out the environmental vote in a last-minute campaign blitz, there he was."

Brower went on to found the John Muir Institute for Environmental Studies and the group Friends of the Earth (FOE), for which he served as president. FOE looked beyond the borders of the United States to work on global environmental issues and was among the first organizations to fight against acid rain and to define nuclear war as an environmental issue. FOE also pushed for countries to end the slaughter of whales and promoted population control. Brower edited the group's 10-volume *The Earth's Wild Places* (1970–77) and its *Celebrating the Earth* (1972–73).

In 1982 Brower founded Earth Island Institute to oversee an array of environmental programs, including the Rainforest Health Alliance, the International Rivers Network, the International Marine Mammal Project, and the Sea Turtle Restoration Project. "One of the main goals of the organization," Brower stated in his interview with *The Progressive*, "is to forward the ideas of creative individuals and to provide an umbrella for a number of innovate projects. . . . The International Marine Mammal Project has been quite successful through its tuna boycott campaign, and recently launched a major campaign against Norway's return to commercial whaling."

Brower healed his rift with the Sierra Club and in 1983 won election to its executive board. But he encountered trouble with FOE when, as the Sierra Club had earlier, it complained about excessive spending. The board reduced the organization's staff, and Brower tried to have the board members recalled, but he failed and in 1984 was dismissed as president. Reinstated a few weeks later, he resigned in 1986.

Brower considered himself to be an optimist, but he often warned about the future of the Earth in dire terms and believed that environmental groups needed to do more. In *The Progressive* interview he pointed out several weaknesses among the groups:

> They are too much indentured to corporate thinking. A lot of the funds come from corporations.
> There is political potential, political clout, but they are not using it. The numbers are there, but we need to inform members more often.
> The activists are too much involved in turf and ego.

Brower published his autobiography, *For Earth's Sake: The Life and Times of David Brower*, in 1990, and *Let the Mountains Talk, Let the Rivers Run: A Call to Those Who Would Save the Earth*, in 1995. In spring 2000 he resigned from the board of the Sierra Club over another dispute, this time involving the refusal of the organization to back restrictions on immigration from Mexico, which he saw as part of a larger worldwide problem of overpopulation and excessive demands on resources. But in a larger sense, Brower thought the Sierra Club too timid. "The world is burning," he said, "and all I hear from them is the music of violins. May the Sierra Club become what John Muir wanted it to be and what I have alleged it was."

In the year 2000 presidential race, Brower supported the Green Party candidate and reformer RALPH NADER. David Brower died on November 5, 2000. In 1971 John McPhee had written about him: "The clamorous concern now being expressed about conservation issues and environmental problems is an amplification—a delayed echo—of what Brower and others have been saying for decades. Brower is a visionary. He wants—literally—to save the world."

Further Reading

Brower, David Ross. *For Earth's Sake: The Life and Times of David Brower*. Salt Lake City, Utah: Peregrine Smith Books, 1990.

———. *Let the Mountains Talk, Let the Rivers Run: A Call to Those Who Would Save the Earth*. San Francisco: HarperCollins West, 1995.

McPhee, John. *Encounters With the Archdruid*. New York: Farrar, Straus & Giroux, 1971.

Brown, John

(1800–1859) *abolitionist*

John Brown was a fervent leader in the abolitionist movement. His murder of proslavery advocates at Pottawatomie Creek in Kansas and his raid on the federal arsenal at Harper's Ferry, Virginia, (today Harpers Ferry, West Virginia) contributed to the violence leading up to the Civil War. He was born on May 4, 1800, in Torrington, Connecticut, to Owen Brown and Ruth Mills Brown.

Contemporaries and historians have debated the question of whether John Brown was a madman. Brown's family history lends credence to those who have portrayed him as unbalanced. His mother, who died when he was eight years old, was insane, as was his maternal grandmother. His mother's sister also died insane, and insanity struck others in the family line.

Owen Brown moved frequently, but John Brown grew up mainly in Hudson, Ohio. Like his father, John was religious and hated slavery. He later told of how he converted to abolitionism at age 12, after seeing a master beat a slave with an iron shovel.

In 1820 John Brown married Dianthe Lusk. They had seven children, two of whom suffered from mental illness. His wife died in 1832 after her own battle with insanity, and the following year he married Mary Ann Day, with whom he had 13 children. Brown, who had once studied for the ministry, held various jobs but mainly plied his father's trade as a tanner. He lived in constant debt and at one point declared bankruptcy.

Brown made his first public abolitionist statement in 1837, when he rose in the back of a church in Ohio and said, "Here before God, in the presence of these witnesses, I consecrate my life to the destruction of slavery." He housed runaways in the Underground Railroad, and while living in Springfield, Massachusetts, he organized blacks to protect themselves from fugitive slave hunters. In the 1850s Brown was drawn deeper into the antislavery battle after five of his sons settled in Kansas, a territory embroiled in an intense fight between proslavery and antislavery groups, as both sides tried to gain control of the government and shape the local constitution to their desires. A letter from John Brown, Jr., to his father in June 1855 depicted the showdown: "The storm every day thickens; its near approach is hourly more clearly seen by all. . . . The great drama will open here, when will be presented the great struggle in arms, of Freedom and Despotism in America. Give us the arms, and we are ready for the contest."

John Brown did just that. He raised money in the East, loaded a wagon with guns and ammunition, and headed for Kansas. On his arrival he

Wild-eyed and stern, John Brown advocated the violent overthrow of slavery. *(National Archives and Records Administration)*

stated with determination, "I am here to promote the killing of slavery." In John Brown's mind that meant death to proslavery advocates. Bloodshed would purge the land of the evil institution; beyond that it would purge the land of sin.

An attack by proslavery forces against antislavery settlers at Lawrence, Kansas, sent Brown into action. In spring 1856 he led four of his sons and two other followers in a massacre of six proslavery settlers at Pottawatomie Creek. Methodically they knocked on the doors of three separate cabins and hauled four men from their families, as their victims' wives and children looked on and trembled in fear. Brown's group hacked the men to death with broadswords; they killed one of the victims by gashing open his head and cutting off his arms, at which point John Brown stood over the dead body and fired a bullet through its head.

Back east in summer 1856, Brown raised money for his crusade in Kansas with the help of several prominent Massachusetts abolitionists, among them Theodore Parker, Samuel Gridley Howe, and THOMAS WENTWORTH HIGGINSON. Some who met him, however, thought him insane. He returned to Kansas and engaged a proslavery force in battle at Osawatomie, during which his son Frederick was killed.

Early in 1857 Brown began putting together his plan for invading the South. He intended to incite a slave uprising and form a free state under his leadership. In April 1858 he sent John, Jr., to Harper's Ferry, where a federal arsenal was located, to reconnoiter the small town tucked away in Virginia's western mountains. At a meeting in Chatham, Canada, his followers endorsed the plan and his proposed state constitution, which called slavery "a most barbarous, unprovoked, unjustifiable war of one portion of [America's] citizens upon another portion."

Before attacking Harper's Ferry, Brown led a raid from Kansas into Missouri in which he captured 11 slaves and took them to freedom in Canada. Another fund-raising tour in the East ensued; then Brown rented a farm five miles north of Harper's Ferry and prepared 16 whites and five blacks to participate in his raid.

On the overcast night of October 16, 1859, Brown and his men descended on Harper's Ferry. They cut the telegraph wires and quickly gained control of the bridges and the armory with its arsenal. As bells tolled in Harper's Ferry and nearby towns, signaling what Virginians thought was a slave uprising, several slaves joined Brown's group. Whites quickly rallied, and a militia trapped Brown and his men in the armory engine house. On the night of October 17, marines under the command of Colonel Robert E. Lee and Lieutenant J. E. B. Stuart arrived. When Brown refused to surrender, they stormed the engine house. A marine thrust a sword into Brown, severely wounding him. Ten of Brown's men died and seven were captured; one marine was killed, along with four civilians, including the black baggage master at the local train station, who was shot accidentally by Brown's men.

Brown was quickly put on trial for treason against Virginia, conspiracy with slaves, and first-degree murder. He offered no defense and on November 2 was found guilty. On December 2 he rode in a wagon, sitting on his coffin as he headed for his hanging. Prior to his execution, Brown had slipped a note to his jailer stating: "I John Brown am now quite certain that the crimes of *this guilty land will never be purged away; but with Blood.*"

Seventeen affidavits attesting to Brown's insanity had been sent to Virginia's governor, but the governor chose to ignore them. The political leader Salmon P. Chase said about Brown: "How sadly misled by his imaginations! How rash—how mad—how criminal." His plan and mode of operation supported the notion of his insanity. Brown had raided a mountain town, distant from the heart of the southern plantations, and he had relied on bloodshed.

Yet Brown's plan had received the endorsement of several abolitionists, and his use of violence differed little from that of others in an era when congressmen were regularly carrying knives into the Capitol. Brown thought himself on a divine mission, "an instrument in the hand of Providence."

Whereas many Northerners considered John Brown a martyr and hailed him as a hero, he was reviled throughout the South. The actor and future Lincoln assassin John Wilkes Booth, who attended Brown's hanging, said, "I looked at the traitor and terrorizer, with unlimited undeniable contempt."

Abraham Lincoln thought little of Brown's raid. "That affair, in its philosophy," he said, "corresponds with the many attempts, related in history, at the assassination of kings and emperors. An enthusiast broods over the oppression of the people till he fancies himself commissioned by Heaven to liberate them. He ventures the attempt, which ends in little else than his own execution." The abolitionist FREDERICK DOUGLASS, though, measured the raid at Harper's Ferry quite differently: "Did John Brown fail? . . . John Brown began the war that ended American slavery and made this a free Republic."

Further Reading

Anderson, Osborne P. *A Voice from Harper's Ferry, 1859.* New York: World View Forum, 2000.

Keller, Allan. *Thunder at Harper's Ferry.* Englewood Cliffs, N.J.: Prentice-Hall, 1958.

Oates, Stephen B. *To Purge This Land with Blood: A Biography of John Brown.* New York: Harper & Row, 1970.

Brown, Lester Russell

(1934–   ) *environmentalist*

Founder of the environmental Worldwatch Institute, Lester Russell Brown is an advocate of international programs to address global warming. He was born on March 28, 1934, in Bridgeton, New Jersey, to Calvin C. Brown and Delia Smith Brown.

Lester Brown developed an interest in the land from an early age. His parents owned a small farm, and at age 14 he and his brother began their own tomato farm. By the time he entered Rutgers University in New Brunswick, New Jersey, he was raising more than 1 million pounds of tomatoes a year, making him one of the largest tomato growers on the East Coast. With that background, and with a bachelor's degree in agricultural science, which he obtained in 1955, Brown expected to continue as a farmer.

But soon after he graduated from Rutgers, he spent six months in India as part of the Farm Youth Exchange Program of the National 4-H Foundation, and the hunger he witnessed made him think more about food problems overseas. He earned a master's degree in agricultural economics from the University of Maryland in 1959 and joined the Foreign Agricultural Service, part of the United States Department of Agriculture (USDA), as an international agricultural analyst. In 1960 he married Shirley Ann Woolington. They had two children and later divorced.

Brown took a leave of absence from the USDA and then earned a second master's degree, this one in public administration, from Harvard University. Returning to the USDA, he completed a study in 1963 that gained coverage in the mainstream press for its conclusion that population growth imperiled food supplies and threatened widespread famine. From that report he published his first book, *Man, Land and Food: Looking Ahead at World Food Needs* (1963).

In 1964 Secretary of Agriculture Orville Freemen made Brown his adviser on foreign agricultural policy and two years later appointed him administrator of the USDA's International Agricultural Development Service. Brown left the federal government in 1969 to help found the Overseas Development Council, a private, nonprofit group that studied the effects of economic and political issues on relations between the United States and developing countries. While working for the council he wrote *Seeds of Change: The Green Revolution and Development in the 1970s* (1970) and *World without Borders* (1972).

Brown wanted to start a think tank that would analyze issues of food supplies, natural resources, and population growth, and in 1973 the Rockefeller Brothers Fund agreed to finance his Worldwatch Institute to the amount of $500,000. As its name implies, Worldwatch approaches its studies from a global perspective. In addition to its Worldwatch papers, it issues its annual *State of the World*, known for its readability and its coverage of topics relating to developing countries, agricultural and economic events, and population changes, with the goal of promoting economic growth through environmentally friendly policies. In 1974

Brown wrote *By Bread Alone,* in which he advocated several measures to improve the world's food supply, such as consuming less meat—thereby decreasing the strain on land needed for grazing animals—and expanding people's access to birth control.

In 1975, while the industrial world worried about oil supplies, Worldwatch issued a report, "The Other Energy Crisis: Firewood." Brown later explained: "Everyone was thinking about the fourfold increase in the price of oil, [but our report discussed] Third World firewood scarcity. It was something that anyone who'd been in Afghanistan or Peru or India knew about, but no one realized how pervasive it was. This was the energy issue for a billion and a half of the world's people."

Brown wrote *The Twenty-ninth Day: Accommodating Human Needs and Numbers to the Earth's Resources* in 1978 and *Building a Sustainable Society* in 1981. As he advocated reforestation, environmental research, birth control, and immunization programs in developing countries, critics accused Worldwatch of failing to consider practical political necessities. They especially pilloried his call for countries to reduce defense spending and employ their armies in such tasks as planting trees.

Brown maintained, however, that he proposed nothing more than had been done in China, where monies previously used for the military had been reduced to fund family planning and agricultural development. In a series of interviews given around 1990, Brown, noted for his refusal to own a car and his preference to bicycle almost everywhere, expressed his concerns about environmental problems:

> We have reached the point of development in places like Africa where we have to recognize that simply applying economic criteria to development projects is no longer viable. When there were 200 million people in Africa in 1950, development agencies could invest money and conditions would improve. But with a population of 580 million humans, demands are exceeding the carrying capacity of local biological systems, leading to the consumption of the systems themselves. That's why Africa's forests are disappearing, its grasslands are deteriorating, and its soils are eroding.

> [If we make needed changes] the "throwaway society" will become obsolete. We will live by what environmentalists call the three R's of the future: reduce, reuse, and recycle.

> If we do things to destabilize the climate, as we are doing now, and set in motion a warming process that raises temperatures several degrees over the next half century, we're in trouble.

In 1991 Brown wrote *Saving the Planet,* and that same year the American Humanist Association named him Humanist of the Year. He has won several other awards and holds honorary degrees from 15 universities. Writing in the year 2001, Brown expressed confidence in environmental reform. He stated, "Once individuals, businesses, and governments become advocates for sustainability, a global transformation as great as the Industrial Revolution could be unleashed."

Further Reading

Brown, Lester. *Building a Sustainable Society.* New York: Norton, 1981.
———. *Saving the Planet.* New York: Norton, 1991.

Brownmiller, Susan
(1935–) *feminist*

A writer and activist, Susan Brownmiller is a strong voice for feminist causes. She was born in Brooklyn, New York, on February 15, 1935.

Brownmiller graduated from Cornell University in Ithaca, New York, in 1955 before working briefly as an actress in New York City and beginning her career as a journalist and writer of several books. She worked as assistant to the managing editor of *Coronet* magazine from 1959 to 1960, as editor of *Albany Report* from 1961 to 1962, as national affairs researcher at *Newsweek* from 1963 to 1964, and as staff writer for the *Village Voice* in 1965. She also participated in the civil rights drive in Mississippi.

In 1968 she cofounded a group called New York Radical Feminists. They believed in mass protests to advance women's rights and condemned men's oppression of women, which they attributed to egotistical motives independent of any class or economic influences. Brownmiller participated in the group's highly publicized sit-in at the offices of the *Ladies' Home Journal*, a magazine they criticized for an attitude that treated women as second-class citizens whose main functions were to do household chores and please men.

Brownmiller continued her feminist critique in her writings, the most controversial of which was *Against Our Will: Men, Women and Rape*, published in 1975. In that book she traced the history of rape and discussed rape victims. She concluded that rape was less motivated by sexual desire than by the desire of men to maintain their domination over women. Rape, she wrote, "is nothing more or less than a conscious process of intimidation by which *all men* keep *all women* in a state of fear." Rape had its origins, she said, in the unequal physical power of men and women and in male physiological attributes—or what she called an "anatomical fiat"—and those conditions were continuing to warp relationships between the sexes.

Some reviewers praised Brownmiller for her thorough research and bold thesis; others ripped her conclusions as misinterpreting facts and seeking to condemn men. Her findings were certainly shaped by the views she held when she began her research. In 1972 Brownmiller said that feminists "are convinced that rape is a political crime and can be eradicated like lynching. We have the power to eradicate it, but that won't be done until it is understood not as deviant behavior but as the logical result of sexism."

Against Our Will reached the best-seller lists and in 1975 resulted in *Time* magazine declaring Brownmiller Woman of the Year. Writing about *Against Our Will* in *The Nation* 25 years later, Linda Gordon said, "The fact that rape has been recognized as a war crime in the year 2000 is owing in part to Brownmiller's contribution."

Brownmiller's book influenced numerous women to join the feminist movement, as Megan Marshall wrote in the *New Republic* in 1984: "Many a feminist of the 1970s was made by a reading of her book." In 1979 Brownmiller led a group she founded, Women Against Pornography, in a protest against the pornography then prevalent in New York City's Times Square. She said that pornography contributed to toleration of rape and

thus stood outside the constitutional protection of free speech and should be banned.

For Brownmiller, the feminist movement gave meaning to her life. She once recalled of New York Radical Feminists, "All of a sudden I knew I was home."

Further Reading

Brownmiller, Susan. *Against Our Will: Men, Women, and Rape.* New York: Simon & Schuster, 1975.
———. *In Our Time: Memoir of a Revolution.* New York: Dial Press, 2000.

Bruner, Joseph
(Tah-Yah-Cho-Chee)
(1872–1957) *Indian rights activist*

Joseph Bruner was an advocate of Native Americans adopting many of the practices of white society. He was born on September 20, 1872, to John Bruner and Lucy Fife, Creek Indians, in what is today Tulsa, Oklahoma, but was then land allotted to Native Americans in the Indian Territory.

John Bruner's Creek name was Tah-Yah-Cho-Chee, meaning "Lightning Bolt of the Deer Clan." Educated at the Creek National School, where he learned English, Bruner briefly attended Bacone College, a Baptist school for Indians, in Muskogee, Oklahoma. In 1893 he married Marguerite Elma Dart, a Shawnee Indian, and moved to Sapulpa, near Tulsa. He sold real estate, began an insurance business, and invested in oil.

In 1905 Bruner emerged as a leader at the Sequoyah Convention, which met at Muskogee. There the "Five Civilized Tribes,"* those Native Americans forcibly relocated from the southeastern United States in the 1830s, tried unsuccessfully to form their own state, carved out of the Indian Territory.

By the 1930s Bruner had become an assimilationist, meaning he wanted to integrate Indians into white society. When Congress passed the Indian Reorganization (Wheeler-Howard) Act of

---

* Cherokee, Creek, Seminole, Choctaw, and Chickasaw.

1934, Bruner protested it. The act rescinded the Dawes Act, which had been passed in 1887 and had ended the autonomy of Indian tribes while distributing reservation land to individual Native Americans. It was an assimilationist law that had led to corrupt land dealings and had failed as a means to assimilate the Indians. The Indian Reorganization Act returned remaining Indian lands to the tribes and encouraged tribal self-government. Bruner believed the Reorganization Act would end individual Indian land titles, hamper oil exploration, and segregate the tribes. As a result, Indian economic development would suffer.

In 1935 he formed the American Indian Federation (AIF) and went to Washington to lobby for the group. Shortly afterward, he testified before Congress against the Reorganization Act and against John Collier, the head of the Bureau of Indian Affairs who had promoted the act. This led to a bitter political battle between Bruner and Collier.

In the late 1930s the AIF was suspected of sympathizing with the Nazi movement. Bruner continued to lead the organization into the 1950s. He died on January 13, 1957.

Further Reading

Philp, Kenneth R. *John Collier's Crusade for Indian Reform, 1920–1954.* Tucson: University of Arizona Press, 1977.

———. *Termination Revisited: American Indians on the Trail to Self-Determination, 1933–1953.* Lincoln: University of Nebraska Press, 1999.

Butler, Nicholas Murray

(1862–1947) *education reformer, peace activist*

Serving for more than 40 years as president of Columbia University, Nicholas Murray Butler advocated educational reform and supported the formation of international peace organizations. He was born on April 2, 1862, to Henry Leny Butler, a manufacturer, and Mary Jones Murray Butler, in Elizabeth, New Jersey.

One of five children, Butler grew up in a comfortable, middle-class family, in which Republican politics ruled. He attended private school in Paterson, New Jersey, and in 1878 entered Columbia in New York City, beginning an association with the college that would last nearly the rest of his life. Graduating with a bachelor's degree in 1882, he stayed at Columbia and earned a master's degree in 1883 and a doctorate in 1884, with his dissertation in philosophy. The following year he traveled to Europe.

Butler returned to the United States in 1885 and began teaching philosophy at Columbia. In 1889 he founded *Educational Review,* a journal that presented articles on education by scholars around the world. To improve the training of teachers, he founded Teacher's College, chartered in 1889; in 1893 it became affiliated with Columbia.

Meanwhile, he had been appointed full professor at Columbia. In the 1890s he completed work that led to the development of a more professional school system in New York City, headed by a superintendent, and this effort earned him a national reputation as an education reformer. As president of the National Education Association from 1894 to 1895, he helped create the Committee of Ten and the Committee on College Entrance Requirements, which developed nationwide standards.

In 1901 Butler began his tenure as president of Columbia, which had become a university and attracted prominent scholars to its already formidable faculty. Under Butler Columbia expanded its buildings and programs and emerged as one of the top universities in the country. Yet controversy embroiled him during World War I when he violated tenets of academic freedom and fired two professors who were critical of the draft.

Active politically, Butler was an adviser to three presidents: Theodore Roosevelt (until he broke with him in 1908 over what he considered to be the administration's increasingly liberal policies), William Howard Taft, and Warren G. Harding. Concerned with developing international peace organizations, Butler was elected president of the Lake Mohonk Conference on International Arbitration in 1907, a group that worked to reconcile differences between France and Germany, and between France and England. Through his influence, the Carnegie Endowment for Peace was established in 1910. He would head the organization from 1925 until 1945.

After World War I he supported the formation of the League of Nations, though he advocated some changes in the treaty that created it. He played an important role in the signing of the Kellogg-Briand Peace Pact in 1928, in which nations renounced war. Butler advised President Calvin Coolidge to pursue such an agreement, and at the invitation of the State Department Butler drafted the pact. His speeches, delivered across the country on its behalf, convinced the Senate to ratify it. In 1931 Butler, along with reformer JANE ADDAMS, won the Nobel Prize in peace. In presenting the award, Halvdan Koht, a member of the Nobel Committee, said about Butler.

> His main concern has always been the gathering of information on all kinds of international conditions and relationships, and his great ambition has been to create an "international mind," [with] the will and the ability to examine every question from an international point of view which never forgets that in any dispute each of the two combatants may have his justification and consequently the right to a fair hearing.

Butler supported the formation of the United Nations after World War II. He died on December 7, 1947. Although not a pacifist, he had advocated reforms that would minimize the risk of war, and his numerous books, such as *The Basis of a Durable Peace* (1917) and *The Family of Nations* (1938), outlined his proposals.

President of Columbia University, Nicholas Murray Butler supported U.S. entry into the League of Nations. *(Library of Congress)*

Further Reading

Marrin, Albert. *Nicholas Murray Butler.* Boston: Twayne Publishers, 1976.

C

Carmichael, Stokely
(Kwame Toure, Kwame Turé)
(1941–1998) *black power leader*

Stokely Carmichael is remembered for his work as a black power advocate in the 1960s counterculture. He was born on June 29, 1941, at Port-of-Spain, Trinidad, to Adolphus Carmichael, a carpenter, and Mable Carmichael. In 1943 his parents moved to Harlem in New York City, leaving Stokely in Trinidad in the care of two aunts and a grandmother. He attended Tranquillity Boys' School, where he obtained an education that he later characterized as flawed by its white biases. In 1962 he joined his parents in the United States.

As a young man Carmichael thought that in America there would be equality, but instead he found racism and discrimination. Uprooted and restless, he joined a gang, yet he had remarkable intelligence and scored well on an exam he took to enter the prestigious Bronx High School of Science. There, he associated with intellectual white students and read extensively, especially the works of Leon Trotsky and Karl Marx. He joined the Young Socialists and hung out at the plush Park Avenue apartments where his friends lived. He later observed, "I was the good little nigger and everybody was nice to me."

That his friends applied socialist ideas to the problems facing white society but ignored black society disturbed him. Within a short time, he gravitated toward the writings of civil rights leader BAYARD RUSTIN, who applied socialist ideas to

conditions facing African Americans. In his senior year Carmichael avidly followed the lunch counter sit-in led by black college students in Greensboro, North Carolina. To him, the protest represented a new era in the fight for African-American freedom.

He joined the activist upsurge when he traveled to Washington, D.C., and helped picket the House Un-American Activities Committee, a zealous congressional body that believed communists had infiltrated and taken over civil rights groups. When Carmichael graduated from high school, he decided to attend predominantly black Howard University in the nation's capital, a college known for its activism.

There he joined a campus organization affiliated with the Student Non-Violent Coordinating Committee (SNCC). Carmichael immersed himself in direct action in 1961 when he participated in the Freedom Rides, a campaign by blacks in the South to ride buses into terminals and desegregate them. Whites attacked the riders, often beating them unmercifully. After the police arrested Carmichael in Jackson, Mississippi, he was sent to Parchman Prison, notorious for its inhuman conditions. At one point he angered the guards by leading his fellow imprisoned riders in spirited singing.

Released from prison, Carmichael joined SNCC and engaged in sit-ins and a voter registration drive. During the 1964 Freedom Summer, he led a campaign to register black voters in the Mississippi Second Congressional District. Again the activists encountered massive white resistance and violent attacks, including beatings and shootings. In this setting Carmichael, who had long distrusted the nonviolent strategy promoted by MARTIN LUTHER KING, JR., said blacks should carry weapons for self-defense.

Carmichael continued his studies at Howard and graduated in 1964 with a bachelor's degree in philosophy. The following year he supervised a successful SNCC voter registration drive in Lowndes County, Alabama. Carmichael convinced 2,000 blacks to register in the face of intimidation that had previously kept the voting rolls all-white. In addition, he founded the Lowndes County Freedom Organization, an African-American party intended to challenge the local Democrats. Although the group failed to get its candidates elected, it stimulated activism around a new symbol, a black panther. From this came its name, the Black Panther Party. (Other Black Panther parties, not linked to Lowndes County, organized later.)

In 1966 Carmichael won election as chairman of SNCC. This organization had pioneered direct action by young people, such as sit-ins. Originally, it embraced King's nonviolent, integrationist ideology, but Carmichael led SNCC in shifting from integration to liberation. In so doing, he represented SNCC's radical urban wing, based in the northern states. He accused the group's white members of trying to control the organization and of knowing little about black oppression and expelled them. He considered voter registration important, not so much to increase the number of African Americans who could cast ballots as to promote courage and pride, which he believed would advance the black cause.

Also in 1966 Carmichael made a much-celebrated speech in which he declared: "We been saying" 'freedom' for six years and we ain't got nothin'! What we gonna start sayin' now is—Black Power!" His words attracted media attention to radical African Americans. Never precise about what black power meant, he nevertheless used it as an effective rallying cry, implying that African Americans needed to reject white assistance and develop their own institutions. Carmichael said that "every Negro is a potential black man." And he wrote: "Black Power . . . is a call for black people in this country to unite, to recognize their heritage, to

build a sense of community. . . . It is a call to reject the racist institutions and values of this society."

Carmichael made this declaration about the same time he journeyed to Havana, Cuba, where he expressed support for liberation movements against imperialists and observed that blacks in the United States were forming urban guerrilla groups. He adopted Pan-Africanism, expressing his belief that blacks in Africa and America should unite to end their oppression. He soon declared his opposition to the Vietnam War and criticized the Selective Service as "white people sending black people to make war on yellow people in order to defend the land they stole from red people."

Carmichael left the SNCC chairmanship in 1967 and joined a new militant Black Panther Party organizing in Oakland, California. But he broke with the Panthers just months later, after they decided to seek alliances with white radicals. In 1968 he married South African singer-activist Miriam Makeba. (The marriage ended in divorce, as did his second marriage, to Marlyatou Barry. He had one son.)

Persecuted in the United States for his racial views and his opposition to the Vietnam War—he once said, "We do not want peace in Vietnam. We want the Vietnamese people to defeat the United States"—and desiring to help Ghanaian ruler Kwame Nkrumah, in 1969 he immigrated to Guinea in West Africa.

There he took the name Kwame Toure (sometimes spelled Kwame Turé), a combination of Kwame Nkrumah's name with that of African socialist Ahmed Seko Toure. Although in the early 1990s Carmichael believed that progress had been made in the United States toward racial equality, on a visit to Michigan State University in 1993 he expressed his continuing revolutionary ideology when he equated capitalism with slavery. In a second edition to his book *Black Power: The Politics of Liberation in America* (1992), which he first published in 1967, Carmichael wrote that for the oppression of blacks to end there had to be "mass political organization on a Pan African scale." He added: "Black Power can only be realized when there exists a unified socialist Africa."

In 1996 Carmichael learned that he had prostate cancer. He received medical treatment in

Cuba, and then with the help of Louis Farrakhan, the leader of the Nation of Islam (Black Muslims), he was admitted to a hospital in New York City. Benefits were held in New York, Denver, and Atlanta to raise money for his medical expenses.

Stokely Carmichael died in Guinea on November 15, 1998, and was buried in the country's capital, Conakry. An advocate of radical change to the very end, he typically answered his phone with the phrase "Ready for the revolution!"

Further Reading

Anderson, Terry H. *The Movement and the Sixties.* New York: Oxford University Press, 1995.

Johnson, Jacqueline. *Stokely Carmichael: The Story of Black Power.* Englewood Cliffs, N.J.: Silver Burdett Press, 1990.

Ture, Kwame, and Charles V. Hamilton. *Black Power: The Politics of Liberation in America.* New York: Random House, 1967. Revised ed. 1992.

Carson, Rachel Louise

(1907–1964) *environmentalist*

An environmentalist and writer, Rachel Louise Carson wrote *Silent Spring,* which alerted the world to the dangers of pesticides and herbicides. She was born on May 27, 1907, in Springdale, Pennsylvania, to Robert Warden Carson and Maria Frazier McLean Carson.

Rachel Carson was raised on a 65-acre farm and from an early age learned about nature, often guided in her lessons by her mother, with whom she was close. She liked to write and in time would combine her interests.

Carson graduated from high school in Parnassus, Pennsylvania, and entered the Pennsylvania College for Women (today Chatham College) in Pittsburgh, where she decided to pursue a career in science. She obtained a B.S. degree in zoology in 1929, joined the zoology department at the University of Maryland, and then entered the master's degree program at Johns Hopkins University, where she received her degree in 1932.

At the same time, she gained experience in appealing to popular audiences when she wrote science articles for the *Baltimore Sunday Sun.* In 1936 she left the University of Maryland to join the federal government's Bureau of Fisheries (later renamed the Fish and Wildlife Service), and in the late 1940s she became editor in chief of the bureau's publications.

Carson continued to write magazine articles, and in 1951 a series she wrote for *New Yorker* resulted in *The Sea around Us,* a book that combined a survey of geological forces that created the oceans with the continuing human attraction to the sea. It stayed on the *New York Times* best-seller list for 86 weeks and won the National Book Award in nonfiction.

With the money from her book sales, Carson left her government job in 1952 to devote her full time to writing. Her *Edge of the Sea* (1956) also reached the best-seller list.

But *Silent Spring,* published in 1962, received the greatest notice and generated an intense reaction from the chemical industry. *Silent Spring* revealed the dangers of pesticides and herbicides, indicated that some of them could be found in nearly all living things, and concluded that they were killing fish and wildlife and endangering human beings.

In the ominously titled chapter "Elixirs of Death," she began:

> For THE FIRST TIME in the history of the world, every human being is now subjected to contact with dangerous chemicals, from the moment of conception until death. In the less than two decades of their use, the synthetic pesticides have been so thoroughly distributed throughout the animate and inanimate world that they occur virtually everywhere. They have been recovered from most of the major river systems and even from streams of groundwater flowing unseen through the earth. . . . They have entered and lodged in the bodies of fish, birds, reptiles, and domestic and wild animals so universally that scientists carrying on animal experiments find it almost impossible to locate subjects free from such contamination.

She added that the chemicals could be found in most human beings: "They occur in the mother's milk, and probably in the tissues of the unborn child."

Spokespeople for the chemical industry and scientists tied to that industry attacked Carson's findings with misleading reports, and they even attacked her personally. (The criticism revealed another hitherto ignored development: the co-opting of many scientists, and scientific objectivity, by corporations.) Yet Carson's work led to the formation of a presidential advisory commission to investigate the problem and, eventually, to laws banning many pesticides, such as dichloro-diphenyl-trichloro-ethane (DDT), or laws restricting their use.

Rachel Carson died on April 14, 1964, in Silver Spring, Maryland, of breast cancer. One writer stated in 1998 that her "skill to penetrate to the roots of biological reality and an eloquence that made her findings heard" led to "the Age of Ecology."

Further Reading

Carson, Rachel. *Silent Spring.* Boston: Houghton Mifflin, 1962. Reprint 1994.

Freeman, Martha, ed. *Always, Rachel: The Letters of Rachel Carson and Dorothy Freeman, 1952–1964.* Boston: Beacon Press, 1995.

Lear, Linda J. *Rachel Carson: Witness for Nature.* New York: Henry Holt, 1997.

Carter, William Hodding, Jr.

(1907–1972) *civil rights leader*

A southern editor, publisher, and writer, William Hodding Carter, Jr., spoke out against his region's racial prejudice. He was born on February 3, 1907, in Hammond, Louisiana, to William Hodding Carter, a farmer and businessman, and Irma Dutartre Carter.

William Hodding Carter, Jr., who went by the name Hodding, was forever haunted by something he stumbled across in the woods while still a child: the burned, hanging body of a black person lynched by a white mob. For him it remained a powerful reminder of the tragedy of injustice, and it helped shape his views about race relations.

He graduated in 1927 from Bowdoin College in Maine and studied journalism at Columbia University in New York City. He then returned to Louisiana and from 1928 to 1929 taught English at Tulane University in New Orleans. There he met Betty Werlein, and they married in October 1931. The couple had three sons.

Carter once said, "I would rather be a small city newspaper editor and publisher than anything I know." In 1932 he returned home to Hammond and founded the *Daily Courier.* He earned a reputation for his attacks on the state's powerful politician Huey Long, whom he vilified as corrupt, and for his support of President Franklin Roosevelt's New Deal.

Repeated threats against him and his newspaper caused Carter to leave Hammond in 1936 and begin another newspaper, the *Delta Star,* in Greenville, Mississippi. While working as editor, he began writing novels set in the area.

In 1938 Carter merged his newspaper with another to form the *Delta Democrat-Times,* which he continued to publish for the rest of his life. In 1940 he took a leave of absence to edit a newspaper in New York City, and during World War II he worked in the War Department's Public Relations Bureau and in military intelligence.

His years in the North, and his recognition that a contradiction existed between America's war goal of fighting Nazi racial oppression and the continuing racial segregation in the South made him critical of the way whites treated blacks. He wrote several articles condemning racial and religious prejudice, and in 1946 won the Pulitzer Prize for his editorials about state and local issues.

Along with criticizing race relations, Carter defended many of the South's cultural traits and opposed liberals who wanted the federal government to force changes on the region. Thus he stood against court-ordered desegregation, and when the Supreme Court issued its *Brown v. Board of Education* decision in 1954, he advised southerners to upgrade black school facilities equal to white ones but said the South must work out its racial problems on its own. On the one hand, he condemned white supremacist groups; on the other, he thought sit-ins and boycotts by blacks ill advised, since they would lead to federal interference.

In the 1960s Carter turned over much of the daily routine of operating the *Delta Democrat-Times* to his son, Hodding Carter III, and concentrated on writing histories and novels, including *So the Heffners Left McComb* (1965), which took racial radicals to task for their intolerance toward moderates. Carter died of a heart attack in Greenville on April 4, 1972.

Further Reading

Waldron, Ann. *Hodding Carter: The Reconstruction of a Racist.* Chapel Hill, N.C.: Algonquin Books of Chapel Hill, 1993.

Catt, Carrie Chapman
(Carrie Lane)
(1859–1947) *women's suffragist, peace activist*

A leader in the women's suffrage movement and an advocate of world peace, Carrie Chapman Catt was born Carrie Lane on January 9, 1859, in Ripon, Wisconsin to Lucius Lane, a farmer, and Maria Clinton Lane.

In 1866 Carrie Lane moved with her family to a farm near Charles City, Iowa. She graduated from Charles City High School and in 1877 entered Iowa State College in Ames. There she earned her bachelor of science degree in 1880 and planned to study law, but in October 1881 she was appointed principal of Mason City High School in Iowa and two years later was made superintendent of the Mason City schools.

Carrie gave up her job in 1885 to marry Leo Chapman, who owned and edited the *Mason City Republican.* She worked as an assistant editor at the newspaper. That same year she attended a meeting of the Iowa Suffrage Association and determined she would join the fight for women's voting rights. According to her biographer, Robert Booth Fowler, no single event caused Chapman to make this commitment; her activism developed over time, stirred by the increasing prominence of the suffrage movement itself and by the influence of the Progressive ideas that sought to reform society.

Carrie Chapman was an evolutionary optimist. She believed that a God-ordained evolution would advance everyone. That idea could have made her conservative or fatalistic, but although she thought evolution was a part of God's plan, she believed that people needed to move it along; she said that "evolution would move faster and avoid pit falls if there were plenty of 'evolutors' who would try and think straight and act accordingly."

Chapman rejected formal religion; she thought it superstitious and disliked the way the churches repressed women. Religion, though, was never high on her list of concerns; she was more focused on "applying her optimistic faith to life." She believed that women would gain the right to vote, and with that done, they would advance in society and make the world a better place in which to live.

Her commitment to the women's movement intensified in 1885. That year her husband died, and while working at a newspaper in San Francisco selling advertising, she experienced sexual harassment. In his biography Fowler says the harassment "fueled her anger over relations between the sexes and strengthened her determination to help fashion a world in which women were accorded the same dignity and respect as men." She never hated men, but she hated what she considered to be their warlike aggressiveness.

Chapman went to Washington in 1890 as a delegate to the National American Woman Suffrage Association (NAWSA), and at the behest of SUSAN BROWNELL ANTHONY, she worked in South Dakota for a suffrage referendum. Later that year she married George William Catt, a supporter of women's suffrage, with the understanding that he would fully support her work. According to her, "[George Catt] said to me: 'I am as earnest a reformer as you are, but we must live. Therefore I will earn the living for two and you will do reform work enough for both.'"

Two years later they moved from Iowa to New York City, where George Catt worked as president of a marine construction business, and with his considerable income she was indeed able to continue her suffrage activities. In 1895, at Carrie Catt's suggestion, the NAWSA formed a national organization committee. Under her direction, it raised money and coordinated activities among state and local auxiliaries. Catt displayed her talent for masterful planning and effective speaking, and when Susan B. Anthony retired from the NAWSA presidency in 1900, she chose Catt to succeed her. With Anthony's backing, Catt won election.

Believing that NAWSA relied too heavily on publications and speeches, Catt worked to make it more activist, but by and large she operated within Anthony's shadow and accomplished little (though she gained valuable experience). At the same time, she engaged in the campaign for women's voting rights overseas when in 1904 she helped establish the International Woman Suffrage Alliance. Catt was forced to quit the NAWSA presidency in 1904 because of her husband's illness. He died in 1905, but she put aside any thoughts of remarrying, for by then she considered marriage oppressive and marveled at older unmarried women whom she met, saying they "had their freedom and were very happy. I thought I had at last found the most perfectly located human being in the world."

Carrie Catt subsequently rejoined the suffrage movement. From 1906 until 1913 she presided over several international suffrage congresses, and from 1911 until 1913 she toured Asia and Africa, organizing women to fight for suffrage in their countries. Beginning in 1915 she devoted most of her energy to persuading New Yorkers to approve a suffrage referendum. Toward that end, she chaired the Empire State Campaign Committee and toured the state. Moreover, she organized the New York State Suffrage Party to coordinate the work of several suffrage groups. Her efforts paid off in 1917, when New York finally approved the referendum.

Meanwhile, in 1916 Catt returned to the NAWSA presidency amid a dispute when ALICE PAUL and her followers quit to form the more militant Women's Party. Paul wanted NAWSA to shift from emphasizing state referendums to lobbying Congress to pass a constitutional amendment. As it turned out, Catt had the same objective—though she advocated less militant tactics—and moved the NAWSA in that direction.

Finally in 1919 Congress passed an amendment, and in 1920 the states ratified it, granting women the right to vote. That same year, at Catt's urging, the League of Women Voters was established to encourage women to use their newly won right.

As a peace activist and women's suffragist, Carrie Chapman Catt presided over several international suffrage congresses. *(Library of Congress)*

With suffrage obtained, Catt turned her attention to peace issues, supporting American entry into the League of Nations—which the Senate rejected—and forming the Conference on the Cause and Cure of War, which met in Washington, D.C., every year from 1925 until 1939, attracting women delegates from many countries.

In her later years Catt spoke against the proposed Equal Rights Amendment, claiming that if it passed, many of the Progressive reforms meant to protect women in the workplace would be voided. She died on March 9, 1947, in New York City. She once observed, "I have spent my life in a sincere endeavor to help God's law of Evolution evolve."

Further Reading

Robert Booth Fowler. *Carrie Catt: Feminist Politician.* Boston: Northeastern University Press, 1986.

"Remarks by Late Women's Rights Crusader Sparks Blacks' Objection to University's Effort to Honor Her." *Jet* 27, May 1996, 22+.

Cervantes, Maggie

(1958–   ) *Chicano and women's rights
activist*

An activist in the Latino community of Los Angeles, Maggie Cervantes has been a strong voice for the rights of Chicanos and women. She was born on October 27, 1958, in Los Angeles County to Albert Cervantes and Dolores Barron Cervantes.

Maggie Cervantes grew up in a family in which both of her parents worked, her father as an upholsterer and her mother as a bank teller and escrow officer. When she was age 12, her father's alcoholism caused her parents to divorce. Maggie lived in East Los Angeles with her mother, and after graduating from high school, she attended East Los Angeles Community College. She obtained an associate of arts degree in 1979 and enrolled at Loyola Marymount University, from which she graduated in 1981 with a bachelor of arts degree in Chicano studies.

While at Loyola, Cervantes founded and served as the first president of the college's student chapter of Comision Femenil Nacional (CFMN). An organization dedicated to expanding opportunities for Hispanic women, CFMN grew out of the Chicano activism of the 1970s. She worked also for Californios for Fair Representation, which tried, with mixed results, to enhance Latino power during state legislative redistricting. Her experience with that group put her in contact with many Latino leaders.

After graduation from Loyola Marymount, Cervantes continued to work for the CFMN while pursuing a career with the city of Los Angeles. Over the next 10 years she moved up the bureaucracy and became an administrative analyst. But in 1992 she decided to leave her job and apply herself full-time to social causes. She was hired that year as executive director of New Economics for Women (NEW), a volunteer organization founded in 1985 in Los Angeles. NEW sought to help Hispanic women financially, especially by assisting them to find affordable housing.

In the wake of the Los Angeles riot of 1992, Cervantes worked through the CFMN, which she then headed as president, to obtain financial support to rebuild Latino neighborhoods damaged by the violence. She was also appointed to the Rebuild LA Housing Committee and collected private donations used to help pay the rent for persons displaced from their homes.

Cervantes continued as executive director of NEW into the year 2001. In the late 1990s the organization won praise from the federal government for its approach to affordable housing; one city leader said, "They don't just rehabilitate a building, they try to revitalize the entire neighborhood." Referring to herself and her colleagues within NEW, Cervantes said, "We all grew up in poor communities and yet became successful. What made us succeed? It was family and community support, and we want to give that to these families."

Further Reading

Schultz, Jeffrey D., et al., eds. *Encyclopedia of Minorities in American Politics.* Vol. II. Phoenix, Ariz.: Oryx Press, 2000.

Chavez, Cesar

(1927–1993) *labor organizer, Chicano rights leader*

Founder of the National Farm Workers Association and the United Farm Workers, Cesar Chavez fought for the rights of laborers and Chicanos. He was born on March 31, 1927, near Yuma, Arizona, to Librado Chavez, the owner of a small grocery store and auto repair shop, and Juana Chavez.

In a reversal for the Chavez family, Librado lost his business during the Great Depression, and Cesar was forced to work with the rest of his family as a migrant farm laborer, picking fruits and vegetables and living in cabins made of tar paper and wood. As a result, he attended school only through the seventh grade and was unable to read and write competently until years later.

While still a youngster, Chavez watched his father join various fledgling farm workers' unions and participate in strikes, only to meet with failure. For two years, beginning in 1944, young Chavez served in the navy. When World War II ended, he returned to migrant farm work, laboring in vineyards, cotton fields, and fruit orchards in Arizona and California, while marrying and raising a family.

In 1952 the Community Service Organization (CSO) recruited Chavez to work among Mexican Americans. Begun by SAUL ALINSKY, a Chicago activist, the CSO sought to draw together poor people so they could win political and economic concessions. Chavez first worked as an unpaid volunteer, and he later received a small monthly salary. As a CSO organizer, he led a successful voter registration drive in San Jose, California, and founded chapters in Oakland and various towns throughout the San Joaquin Valley.

In 1962 Chavez quit the CSO over policy differences, and with his own meager capital he began the National Farm Workers Association (NFWA) as a union for migrant laborers. Organizing, though, proved to be a tough uphill battle. Chavez had to overcome the resistance of not only growers but also farmworkers demoralized by previous failed union efforts.

Nevertheless, by 1965 he had enrolled 1,700 families in the NFWA, and this membership provided enough strength to win pay raises from growers in the country around Delano, California. At the same time he began a credit union for the workers, along with a coop store, newspaper, and insurance club. In fact, Chavez considered his effort more than a unionizing one, and he called it La Causa, or the movement, an attempt to activate and uplift an entire community.

Chavez wanted no more labor battles until he could get better organized, but in September 1965 another union, led by LARRY DULAY ITLIONG and representing migrant Filipino workers, went on strike over low wages, and Chavez decided the NFWA had to join them. This began a long strike against grape growers in California's San Joaquin, Imperial, and Coachella Valleys.

Chavez pursued tactics similar to those used in the civil rights movement: sit-ins, marches, and support from the clergy. He even obtained help from activists sent in by the Congress of Racial Equality, and as the strike continued, he merged the NFWA with Itliong's Agricultural Workers Organizing Committee, creating the United Farm Workers Organizing Committee (UFWOC).

Although the UFWOC won contracts from 11 major wine grape growers, it failed to make headway against the table grape growers, those who provided the fruit sold in grocery stores and supermarkets. At that point Chavez decided in spring 1968 to boycott all table grapes grown in California. About 200 UFWOC members toured the United States and Canada, holding demonstrations to rally consumers and pressure city governments to join the boycott.

Chavez went on a 25-day hunger strike to gain national attention, and Senator Robert Kennedy of New York boosted the protest when he told the labor leader he firmly supported the principles that had led him to begin his fast. In reaction to this strike, the growers labeled Chavez a communist, recruited strike breakers, and pressured the federal government to allow more Mexican immigrants into the United States so they could be used to work the fields.

By the following year, the boycott had taken its economic toll. In July several large growers who produced half the state's table grapes signed agreements with the UFWOC. Chavez followed this triumph with a lettuce boycott that also won concessions.

Chavez's efforts, though not exclusively geared to Mexican Americans, intensified Chicano awareness. Throughout the late 1960s "brown pride" expanded, and in helping Chicanos economically, Chavez furthered this development. Larger dimensions to his movement appeared when, in the early 1970s, he helped organize a Chicano march to oppose the draft and the Vietnam War, and in 1976 he presented the presidential nominating speech for the California governor, Jerry Brown, at the Democratic National Convention.

Chavez continued his work for the UFWOC, by then called the United Farm Workers (UFW), into the 1990s and in 1992 helped organize a large-scale walkout by farm laborers in the Coachella Valley. Chavez had lost considerable strength over the years due to his hunger strikes and on April 23, 1993, he died in his sleep. He was survived by his wife, Helen Favila, and their eight children.

In tribute, the union leader Lane Kirkland said that "the improved lives of millions of farmworkers and their families will endure as a testimonial to

Cesar and his life's work." And a colleague, Luis Valdez, said about Chavez: "You shall never die. The seed of your heart will keep on singing, keep on flowering, for the cause."

Further Reading

Griswold del Castillo, Richard, and Richard A. Garcia. *Cesar Chavez: A Triumph of Spirit.* Norman: University of Oklahoma Press, 1995.

Rodriguez, Consuelo. *Cesar Chavez.* New York: Chelsea House, 1991.

Child, Lydia Maria Francis

(1802–1880) *abolitionist, women's rights leader*

Lydia Maria Francis Child was a prolific writer who wielded her pen against the injustices of her time, particularly slavery and the oppression of women. She was born Lydia Maria Francis on February 11, 1802, in Medford, Massachusetts.

Child received little formal education, but she read extensively, and in 1824, at the age of 22, she published her first novel, *Hobomok.* The novel reflected her liberal sympathies in its portrayal of racial intermarriage, in this case that of an Indian, Hobomok, and a white woman, Mary Conant. About Mary, Child says, "She knew that her own nation looked upon her as lost and degraded." Despite the presentation of Hobomok as a kind and caring person—Child refers to him as a "noble savage"—he was in several ways inferior to Mary and, by extension, white society.

Hobomok sold widely and, along with her second novel, *The Rebels* (1825), earned her a national reputation as a distinguished writer. In 1826 she began *Juvenile Miscellany,* a magazine for children and wrote children's stories. In 1828 she married David Lee Child, a lawyer, state legislator, and editor of the *Massachusetts Journal.* He was an abolitionist and a friend of fellow abolitionist WILLIAM LLOYD GARRISON; together, they converted Child to their cause. About Garrison, Lydia Child said, "He got hold of the strings of my conscience and pulled me into reform. . . . Old dreams vanished, old associates departed, and all things became new."

In 1829 Lydia Child wrote *The Frugal House-wife,* which provided advice about household management and went into 33 editions. Shortly thereafter, she wrote three volumes of biographical essays for young people that won acclaim from the *North American Review,* a prominent literary publication.

Then she stunned many of her readers in 1833 when she published *Appeal in Favor of That Class of Americans Called Africans.* Although several future abolitionists credited the book with convincing them to join the fight against slavery, the *Appeal* caused many of Child's readers to desert her momentarily when she went beyond condemning slavery and attacked racial discrimination, including laws that prohibited miscegenation. In agreement with the Garrison wing of the abolitionist movement, she called for the immediate end to slavery.

As did other women engaged in the abolitionist movement, Child fought for women's rights. She said that differences between men and women meant the sexes would often have different social roles, but she disliked laws that restricted women solely on the basis of gender. She once said, "The word and act of every reflecting woman should show that she considers herself an individual, responsible being—not the passive tool, or sensual plaything, of man."

A woman, she insisted, should be able to apply her talents as an editor, writer, teacher—in whatever occupation she was good at and found rewarding. And she believed that her effort as a reformer against slavery would in the end help women. "It is best not to *talk* about our rights," she said, "but simply go forward and *do* whatsoever we deem a duty. In toiling for the freedom of others, we shall find our own."

Child followed her *Appeal* with other abolitionist works, most notably an anthology, *The Oasis* (1834). She thought it essential to change people's minds about slavery: Political abolitionism, she complained, sought to push change before consciences had been awakened and in so doing would lead to war.

Beginning in 1840 she edited the New York–based *National Anti-Slavery Standard,* a Garrison publication. In 1843, however, she quit the abolitionist crusade and moved to Wayland, Massachusetts. She was, she said, tired of factional disputes within the movement and charged extremists with overzealousness in demanding ideological purity among their followers. Child disagreed with Garrison's complete repudiation of the Constitution and his stand that there should be "no union with slaveholders." She was, she said, "weary, weary of this ever lasting pulling down and no building up."

Child thought she could have much more of an impact as an author, "infusing as I must necessarily do, *principles* in favor of peace, universal freedom, &c into all I write." Her fictional stories typically presented light-skinned women of mixed race as heroines and revealed the cruelties of white masters. They depicted slavery destroying families and encouraging the sexual abuse of women. Her biographer Carolyn L. Karcher states in *The First Woman in the Republic* (1994), that Child's short story "Slavery's Pleasant Homes," published in 1843, revealed how life among the slaveholding elite produced "racial and sexual oppression that turned the home into a harem."

In 1855 Child's *Progress of Religious Ideas through Successive Ages,* a three-volume history of religion in which she urged that all faiths be treated with respect because all together revealed one universal truth, appeared. She predicted that Christianity would fade but that its spirit would remain.

Sympathetic to JOHN BROWN's raid at Harper's Ferry in 1859, she began a correspondence with Brown that was later reprinted as a pamphlet and sold more than 3 million copies. To critics who said she was siding with violence, she replied that the real violence came from those who attacked abolitionists.

After the Civil War she advocated programs to help former slaves. She fought for black suffrage and land redistribution, and she attacked racism and discrimination.

In 1868 she wrote *An Appeal for the Indians,* and in the 1870s she wrote articles promoting civil service reform and the eight-hour day for workers. Lydia Child died on October 20, 1880, remembered for her diverse activities in support of social reform as "the first woman in the republic."

Further Reading

Baer, Helene Gilbert. *The Heart is Like Heaven: The Life of Lydia Maria Child.* Philadelphia: University of Pennsylvania Press, 1964.

Karcher, Carolyn L. *The First Woman in the Republic: A Cultural Biography of Lydia Maria Child.* Durham, N.C.: Duke University Press, 1994.

Meltzer, Milton. *Tongue of Flame: The Life of Lydia Maria Child.* New York: Crowell, 1965.

Chomsky, Noam
(1928–) *antiwar activist*

A world-renowned linguist and political commentator, Noam Chomsky used his pen and his voice in the 1960s to speak out against the Vietnam War. He was born on December 7, 1928, in Philadelphia, Pennsylvania, to William Chomsky, a Hebrew scholar, and Elsie Simonofsky Chomsky.

Noam Chomsky developed his interest in linguistics at the University of Pennsylvania, where he enrolled in 1945. He obtained a bachelor's degree in 1949—the same year he married Carol Doris Schatz (the couple would have three children)—and continued his studies at the university, earning a master's degree in 1951 and a doctorate in 1955. He began his teaching career that year at the Massachusetts Institute of Technology in modern languages and linguistics.

Chomsky began challenging the prevailing linguistic theories while still an undergraduate, and his *Syntactic Structures,* published in 1957, revolutionized the discipline. Chomsky asserted that all human beings have an innate ability to learn language, an ability that explains why they are able to recognize sentence structures they have never seen. His theory had implications for psychology, too, because it undermined the ideas of the behaviorists, who said that human behavior can be explained as a reaction to external stimuli that produces a conditioned response.

In the 1960s Chomsky turned his attention to politics, writing books on American foreign policy. His *American Power and the New Mandarins* (1969) attacked those who insisted that in Vietnam the United States had worthy intentions but had committed too many mistakes. On the contrary,

Chomsky insisted, the United States never meant well in Vietnam; its policy there resulted from arrogance and from a capitalist industrial system that through its aggressive nature created militaristic behavior. He particularly criticized the "New Mandarins," those bureaucrats, intellectuals, and scholars who defended America's right to dominate other countries.

That same year, on October 15, he joined 23 other professors across the United States in signing a statement supporting a student boycott of college classes, called the Moratorium, as a demonstration against the war. In 1970 Chomsky served on a private committee that investigated American war crimes in Vietnam, and he visited Laos and North Vietnam, where he met with scholars in Hanoi.

As the war continued, Chomsky wrote articles against it and presented numerous speeches attacking it. One observer said that he had become "one of the most articulate spokesmen of the resistance against the Vietnam War."

When the war ended, Chomsky continued to attack American policy. His argument remained that the United States acted from self-interest and that any professed attachments to morality, justice, or human rights was linked to the desire to promote business and protect its profits. "This is a long-term process," he noted. "It basically never changes. The United States is more of a business-run society than others. . . . Business is very class-conscious, so it is always fighting a class war. People just won't face that society is run by private tyrannies. Modern corporations are about as totalitarian as any human institution has been in history."

Further Reading

Barsky, Robert F. *Noam Chomsky: A Life of Dissent.* Cambridge, Mass.: MIT Press, 1997.

Lyons, John. *Chomsky.* 3rd ed. London: Fontana Press, 1991.

Cleaver, Eldridge
(1935–1998) *black power leader*

A leader among the Black Panthers, Eldridge Cleaver was a talented writer who led a life full of

controversy. He was born on August 31, 1935, in Wabbaseka, near Little Rock, Arkansas, but grew up in Los Angeles, where his father worked for the railroad and his mother worked as a janitor in a public school.

Before deserting the family in 1948, the elder Cleaver often beat Eldridge. As a youngster, Cleaver got into trouble with the law and spent time in reform schools. Released in 1952 from the Preston School of Industry, he got into trouble again when the police arrested him for drug possession, and he served more than two years at Soledad Prison in California.

Racist conditions at Soledad, along with the intensifying civil rights movement outside the prison, awakened him to the oppression African Americans faced. Cleaver received parole in 1957 and, by his own admission, soon began raping white women. Later in the year, he was arrested for assault with intent to kill and sentenced to San Quentin.

While incarcerated, he began following the Black Muslims and identified strongly with MALCOLM X. Through correspondence he became acquainted with Beverly Axelrod, a lawyer. She knew the editor at *Ramparts* magazine and convinced him to read some essays Cleaver had written. The editor, in turn, asked several prominent writers, including Norman Mailer, Leslie Fiedler, Norman Podhoretz, and Maxwell Geismar, to evaluate the essays. They praised Cleaver's writing, and their influence, along with Axelrod's legal efforts, resulted in his release on parole.

A free man in 1966, Eldridge Cleaver was shaken by the murder of Malcolm X. Searching for a role model, early in 1967 he developed a friendship with HUEY PERCY NEWTON. Newton's bravado attracted Cleaver, especially his willingness to carry a loaded gun and stand up to the police. He soon called Newton the "ideological descendant, heir, and successor of Malcolm X." Cleaver joined the Black Panthers, organized by Newton and BOBBY SEALE, and edited the Panther newspaper while still writing for *Ramparts.* The Panther commitment to black power and militancy, including paramilitary organization, jeopardized Cleaver's already shaky standing with the authorities, though he made it a point to remain unarmed. His appearance at a rally in San Diego on April 15, 1967, where he denounced the Vietnam War, evoked a sharp warning from his parole officer and convinced Cleaver that dissenters faced chilling restriction on their freedom of speech.

After Newton was imprisoned in October, and with Seale already in jail, Cleaver emerged as the chief spokesman for the Panthers. He continued to develop ideas based on several intellectual influences, particularly those of Robert Williams, a black protester in the 1950s who called on African Americans to meet white violence with an armed counterattack; Frantz Fanon, a black psychiatrist who considered violence necessary therapy for oppressed people; and Che Guevara, the Cuban revolutionary who stressed self-sacrifice in fighting imperialism.

In February 1968 Cleaver's *Soul on Ice*, a book that pleased radicals, enraged conservatives, and received glowing reviews for its style, was published. The *New York Times* declared *Soul* the book of the year, and it eventually sold 1 million copies.

In this work, a collection of essays, Cleaver railed against an oppressive white society. He declared: "One tactic by which the rulers of America have kept the bemused millions of Negroes in optimum subjugation has been a conscious, systematic emasculation of Negro leadership." And he proclaimed: "We shall have our manhood. We shall have it or the earth will be leveled by our attempts to gain it." Cleaver's cynicism toward America's leaders and institutions, past and present, corresponded with the cynicism of the 1960s counterculture. Indeed, one essay in *Soul on Ice* praised white youth for their rebellion against an American way of life that Cleaver called "a fossil of history."

Cleaver faced prison again after a 90-minute gun battle on April 6, 1968, between police and the Panthers. The shoot-out resulted in the death of Bob Hutton, the Panther treasurer, and the wounding of four men, including Cleaver (who claimed he was unarmed). The Panthers charged that the police had surrounded them and initiated the fight. Whatever the case, the authorities rescinded Cleaver's parole. He remained in jail until June 12, when a superior court judge released him on bail.

In fall 1968 Cleaver ran for president of the United States as the nominee of the Peace and Freedom Party, which consisted of white and black radicals. He won only 30,000 votes but gained considerable media coverage for his militant views. Meanwhile, a higher court in California overruled the superior court decision to grant Cleaver bail, and his rearrest appeared imminent.

In November Cleaver exhausted all legal avenues and fled the country. Some of his supporters considered his action foolish, because it would isolate him and destroy his political influence, but Cleaver was convinced that if he went to jail, he would be murdered. Carrying $15,000 that he had received in royalties, Cleaver arrived in Canada and then took a freighter to Cuba. He expected a warm reception from Fidel Castro's government

In his book *Soul on Ice,* Eldridge Cleaver railed against an oppressive white society. *(Library of Congress)*

but instead got a cold one and quickly grew disenchanted when the Cubans refused to support his plans to organize a Black Panther center in Havana and begin radio broadcasts to the United States.

In July 1969 the Cuban government decided to expel Cleaver, so he was sent to Algeria. The following year, he made a brief visit to North Korea and established contacts with North Vietnam. Back in the United States, the Federal Bureau of Investigation (FBI) acted to harass and destroy the Panthers. They encouraged police attacks on Panther members and sent forged letters to Cleaver, supposedly from fellow Panthers, warning him about a move by some within the organization to isolate him. At the same time, an undercover agent worked on Newton, convincing him that Cleaver intended to grab absolute power. (Newton had been released from prison and was once again the Panther leader.)

In 1970 the National Guard killed several students at Kent State University in Ohio, and the police killed several more at Jackson State College, a black college in Mississippi, causing Cleaver to write that a revolution—an immediate, armed insurrection—had to be pursued. He claimed, "Pigs are carrying out a genocidal conspiracy of extermination against our people." His stand, however, conflicted with Newton's, a strategy emphasizing community education and self-help. When in early 1971 the FBI sent Newton a phony letter revealing a supposed plot by Cleaver to kill him, Cleaver was expelled from the Panthers.

Cleaver's finances worsened when the U.S. government withheld royalty checks due him for his writing. In order to earn money, he and the small group around him in Algeria turned to trafficking in counterfeit visas and stolen cars from Europe. Cleaver had a falling out with the Algerian government in January 1973 and moved to Paris, where he obtained residency status. He felt isolated, however, as few people in America listened to him and his writing stagnated.

He then underwent a remarkable change. First, he talked about the need for the United States to be the strongest nation in the world militarily; then he returned to American in 1975 and announced his conversion as a born-again Christian. In 1977 he founded Eldridge Cleaver Crusades in California while, curiously, pushing his new design for men's pants: a zipper replaced by a pouch and a tube for the testicles and penis—what he claimed to be the liberation of the male sex organ.

In 1980 Cleaver was given probation for his 1968 shoot-out with the police. His religious ideas continued to change: First he joined the Unification Church of the Reverend Sun Myung Moon; then he claimed that God dwelled not in Mecca but in man's sperm; then he joined the Mormons. In 1984 he ran for Congress as an independent conservative, against California Democrat Ron Dellums, an African American, but lost.

Two years later he entered the Republican Senate primary and called for an end to welfare and abortions and vigorous enforcement of the death penalty. He again lost and was soon arrested for burglary and possession of cocaine, for which he received three years probation. In the 1990s he professed allegiance to the Republican Party.

Cleaver, who was married and divorced, died on May 2, 1998, in a Pomona, California, hospital after battling prostate cancer and diabetes. Critics claimed that he never knew anything more than opportunism. Whatever the case, few people listened to him after he fled the United States—he had his greatest influence in the 1960s through his outspoken black power advocacy and blunt writing.

Further Reading

Rajiv, Sudhi. *Forms of Black Consciousness.* New York: Advent Books, 1992.

Rout, Kathleen. *Eldridge Cleaver.* Boston: Twayne, 1991.

Cloud, Henry Roe
(Wo-Na-Xi-Lay-Hunka)
(1886–1950) *Indian rights leader*

An Indian activist, Henry Roe Cloud believed that Native Americans should assimilate to white culture. He was born on December 28, 1886, into the Winnebago Indian tribe in Nebraska. His father's name was Na-Xi-Lay-Hunk-Kay, and his mother's was "Hard-to-See." Henry's Winnebago name was Wo- Na-Xi-Lay-Hunka.

At about the age of seven, Cloud began his formal education at the Indian school in Genoa, Nebraska. There he learned about white culture and was taught to speak and write English. Shortly thereafter, he attended a school on the Winnebago reservation, where a Presbyterian minister befriended him, and he adopted Christianity. He was then baptized and took the name Henry Cloud.

He attended the Santee Mission School and Mount Hermon, a school in Massachusetts, and in 1906 entered Yale University. To learn more about other Indian cultures, he spent summer 1907 at the Fort Sill Reservation in Oklahoma, where he met Reverend Walter C. Roe, a missionary in the Dutch Reformed Church. They established a close friendship, and before long Walter Roe and his wife adopted Cloud, who then took Roe as his middle name.

Cloud graduated from Yale in 1910—the first Indian ever to do so. He spent one year at Oberlin College in Ohio studying sociology, and in 1913 he earned a bachelor in divinity degree from Auburn Theological Seminary. In 1914 he obtained a master's degree in anthropology from Yale.

The following year Cloud founded the Roe Indian Institute in Wichita, Kansas, to train Indians in leadership and Christian values. Unlike other schools for Native Americans that taught vocational subjects, the institute provided courses geared to intellectual development.

In 1916 Cloud married Elizabeth Georgian Bender, a Minnesota Ojibway. They had four daughters, as well as a son who died in infancy.

In the 1920s Henry Roe Cloud served as a staff member for a survey of Indian affairs being conducted by the Institute for Government Research. He cowrote the resulting Meriam Report presented in 1928 to the secretary of the interior. The report revealed the wretched conditions on Indian reservations—the poverty, health problems, and substandard housing.

Cloud served as special regional representative in the Office of Indian Affairs from 1931 to 1933, and he helped develop the Indian Reorganization Act of 1934, which encouraged tribal self-governmental. President Franklin Roosevelt then named him superintendent of Haskell Institute in Lawrence, Kansas, as the federal government sought to appoint qualified Native Americans to schools and agencies for Indians. While Cloud approached his appointment from the standpoint that Indians needed to adopt white culture, he insisted that they were the ones who should direct the assimilation and that whites should not dictate to them.

Cloud left Haskell Institute in 1936 to accept the post of assistant supervisor of Indian education in the Office of Indian Affairs. He served as superintendent of the Umatilla Indian Agency in Pendleton, Oregon, from 1947 to 1950, and during most of that time he was the regional representative for the Grande Ronde and Siletz Agencies in Oregon. He died of a heart attack in Siletz, Oregon, on February 9, 1950.

Further Reading

Dockstader, Frederick J. *Great North American Indians.* New York: Van Nostrand Reinhold, 1977.

Gridley, Marion E. *Indians of Today.* Chicago: Millar Publishing, 1947.

Coffin, William Sloane, Jr.
(1924–) *antiwar and civil rights leader*

A Presbyterian minister whose liberal activism spanned the decades from the 1960s through the 1990s, William Sloane Coffin, Jr., was involved in protest activities related to civil rights, the Vietnam War, nuclear disarmament, and the Persian Gulf War. He was born on June 1, 1924, in New York City to William Sloane Coffin, Sr., the vice president of a furniture store, and Catherine Butterfield Coffin.

With the sudden death of William, Sr., in 1933, Catherine Coffin moved the family to Carmel, California. There young William attended public school; in 1937 he entered Deerfield Academy in Deerfield, Massachusetts. In 1938 he accompanied his family to Paris, where he studied piano in hopes of becoming a concert pianist. The outbreak of World War II in 1939, however, forced the family to return to the United States, and William completed his high school education at Phillips Academy in Andover, Massachusetts.

In 1942 Coffin entered the Yale University Music School, but the following year he joined the United States Army and became a captain in military intelligence. He remained in the army until 1947, when he returned to Yale. He graduated in 1949 and entered Union Theological Seminary, but with the outbreak of the Korean War, his career took a different turn.

Coffin had long opposed communism; his dislike for it in part was derived from his experience in World War II, when he served as a liaison with the Russian army and learned about Soviet dictator Joseph Stalin's barbarous rule. As a result, in 1950 he joined the Central Intelligence Agency (CIA) and served three years in Europe, training Russian refugees to reenter the Soviet Union as American spies.

Coffin left the CIA in 1953 and enrolled at Yale Divinity School, where he earned a bachelor's degree in 1956. He was ordained a Presbyterian minister later that year and in 1958 became chaplain at Yale.

The beginning of his chaplaincy coincided with the intensification of the civil rights movement, and in 1961 Coffin took part in the Freedom Rides, joining other white and black protesters in riding buses into segregated terminals in the South and challenging the laws that required the races be kept apart. During one such ride in Montgomery, Alabama, in May 1961, he was arrested for disturbing the peace. Several other arrests followed as he continued to protest racial segregation.

As the Vietnam War expanded, Coffin joined John Bennett, president of the Union Theological Seminary, and Abraham Heschel, professor of social ethics at the Jewish Theological Seminary, to form the group Clergy and Laity Concerned about Vietnam. In 1967 its members announced they would provide draft resisters with sanctuary in churches and synagogues.

In August 1967 Coffin, along with Dr. BEN-JAMIN SPOCK and three other protest leaders, issued "A Call to Resist Illegitimate Authority." Their proclamation expressed the anger and defiance at work in the antiwar movement:

> An ever growing number of young American men are finding that the American war in Vietnam so outrages their deepest moral and

religious sense that they cannot contribute to it in any way. We share their moral outrage.

> We further believe that the war is unconstitutional and illegal. . . . Moreover, this war violates international agreements, treaties, and principles of law which the United States government has solemnly endorsed.

> We believe . . . that open resistance to the war and the draft is the course of action most likely to strengthen the moral resolve with which all of us can oppose the war.

> We will continue to lend our support to those who undertake resistance to this war. We will raise funds to organize draft resistance unions, to supply legal defense and bail, to support families and otherwise aid resistance to the war in whatever ways may seen appropriate.

In October they followed their call with a rally in Boston at which they collected draft cards and sent them to the Justice Department. These actions caused a federal grand jury to indict them in January 1968 on charges of conspiring to counsel young men to violate the draft laws. The *New York Times* reported, "The indictment represents the strongest countermove by the Government so far to the antidraft movement." General Lewis B. Hershey, director of Selective Service, said, "I think the Department of Justice has done a fine job in getting them indicted, and it's a job that ought to be done."

Coffin and his colleagues were tried and found guilty later that year, but their convictions were overturned in 1970, and the government dropped the charges. Meanwhile, Coffin spoke at antiwar rallies, and in 1972 he journeyed to North Vietnam to accompany three released prisoners of war as they flew back to the United States.

Coffin's protests made him controversial at Yale, but he continued as chaplain until 1976, when he resigned to become senior minister at Riverside Church in New York City. The church was known for its support of liberal approaches to social problems such as poverty, homelessness, and the accumulation of nuclear weapons.

Coffin continued his work for Clergy and Laity Concerned (the reference to *Vietnam* was dropped after the war), now pursuing arms control. In 1979 he journeyed to Iran, where he met with Americans being held hostage by terrorists. His trip, along with his comment that the United States should recognize its own unjust acts in Iran, raised an outcry as many Americans concluded he was pro-Iranian.

Coffin resigned from the Riverside Church in 1987 to spend more time pursuing nuclear disarmament and toward that end served as president of the group SANE/FREEZE. In 1989 he refuted the argument that nuclear arms were crucial to keeping the United States and the Soviet Union out of war. He said, "Well, no nukes, no peace means nukes on both sides, which doubles the already high risk of miscalculation and accident."

Coffin opposed American involvement in the 1990 Gulf War, but he supported the sending of troops to Bosnia, saying it was necessary to end the ethnic slaughter there. He retired as president of SANE/FREEZE in the early 1990s but continued to speak out against nuclear weapons and to call for global cooperation to attain world peace.

Further Reading

Coffin, William Sloane. *Once to Every Man: A Memoir.* New York: Atheneum, 1977.
"Retired But Untiring." *The Christian Century,* October 10, 2001, 17.

Commoner, Barry
(1917–) *environmentalist*

A scientist and writer, Barry Commoner has contributed much to the cause of environmentalism. He was born in New York City on May 28, 1917, to Isidore Commoner, a Russian immigrant, and Goldie Yarmlinsky Commoner.

Despite the urban setting in which Barry Commoner grew up, in his boyhood he developed an interest in nature, spending much time in Brooklyn's parks, where he collected specimens to study. He graduated from James Madison High School and entered Columbia College in 1933; there he majored in zoology. He graduated with honors in 1937 and enrolled at Harvard, where he received his doctorate in 1941 while teaching in New York at Queens College.

With the outbreak of World War II, Commoner served as a science officer to the Naval Tactical Air Squadron in Patuxent, Maryland. It was in that job that he became aware of the threat to the environment from technology when, in testing the insecticide dichloro-diphenyl-trichloroethane (DDT), he witnessed the killing of millions of fish by the chemical runoff.

From 1946 to 1947 Commoner worked as the associate editor of *Science Illustrated* magazine. He married Gloria C. Gordon, a psychologist, in 1946; they had two children. Commoner began teaching at Washington University in Saint Louis, Missouri, in 1947, and in 1953 he became a full professor of plant physiology. At his insistence, in 1958 the American Association for the Advancement of Science formed a Committee on Science in the Promotion of Human Welfare, which conducted a symposium on nuclear fallout. Beginning in 1963, and continuing for the next 17 years, he served on the board of directors of the Scientists' Institute for Public Information and as its chairman for a portion of that time. The group made scientific findings more available to nonscientists.

Commoner was appointed chairman of the botany department at Washington University in 1965 and the following year established the Center for the Biology of Natural Systems, committed to researching environmental and energy issues. During his academic advancement Commoner published several scholarly and popular articles, and in 1963 he published his first book, *Science and Survival,* in which he discussed the damage to the environment caused by the increased use of nitrogen fertilizers and gas-guzzling, air-polluting automobiles.

Commoner wrote his next book, *The Closing Circle: Nature, Man, and Technology,* in 1971. The *New York Times* called it "the most sober, rigorous, well-organized statement of what our environmental problems are, how we got them, and what we should do about them." *Closing Circle* influenced an entire generation of young people just then being attracted to the environmental movement by such activities as Earth Day.

Commoner wrote: "We are in an environmental crisis because the means by which we use the ecosphere to produce wealth are destructive of the ecosphere itself." He presented his case that in pursuing environmentally friendly development, Americans did not have to sacrifice their high standard of living, but to save the world from destruction they had to follow policies that complemented the environment rather than fight it. Drawing on his knowledge of botany, he said, "The first photosynthetic organisms transformed the rapacious, linear course of life into the earth's first great ecological cycle. By closing the circle they achieved what no living organism, alone, can accomplish—survival." That lesson, he insisted, must be learned by everyone. "Human beings have broken out of the circle of life, driven not by biological need, but by the social organization they have devised to 'conquer' nature . . . the end result is the environmental crisis, a crisis of survival. Once more, to survive, we must close the circle."

Commoner followed *The Closing Circle* with *The Poverty of Power: Energy and the Economic Crisis* (1976) and *The Politics of Energy* (1979). In 1981 he became professor in the department of earth and environmental science at Queen's College of the City University of New York. He continued to write and lecture in the 1990s, and in 1995 he criticized what he called "control strategy," the way in which Americans had chosen to deal with most environmental problems. For example, to reduce carbon dioxide emissions, which contributed to global warming, they had installed improved catalytic converters on cars. Yet the reduction had fallen short of the level needed. Commoner proposed instead that Americans use "preventive strategy," meaning that they rely on goods that do not pollute, such as cars that use solar batteries. Technological and economic barriers to their use, he insisted, would come tumbling down if the federal government funded more research for them.

Further Reading

Kriebel, David, ed. *Barry Commoner's Contribution to the Environmental Movement.* Amityville, N.Y.: Baywood Publishers, 2000.

Coughlin, Charles Edward

(1891–1979) *economic reformer*

A Catholic priest and radio commentator, Charles Edward Coughlin criticized Franklin Roosevelt's New Deal and later promoted anti-Semitic ideas.

He was born on October 25, 1891, in Hamilton, Ontario, Canada, to Thomas J. Coughlin, a seaman, and Amelia Mahoney Coughlin, a seamstress.

Charles Coughlin grew up in a strongly Catholic family and attended Saint Michael's High School, followed by Saint Michael's College, both in Toronto. In 1911 he entered the novitiate at Saint Michael's, and in 1916 he was ordained a priest. For the next seven years he taught English, psychology, and logic at Assumption College in Windsor, Ontario.

In 1923 Coughlin was assigned to the diocese in Detroit, Michigan, and with his personable nature and effective oratory gained a considerable following at Saint Leo's Church. Consequently, Bishop Michael Gallagher chose him to found a new parish in the suburb of Royal Oak.

When Coughlin ran into anti-Catholic hostility in the town—including a Ku Klux Klan (KKK) cross set aflame on the parish lawn—and had a difficult time raising money, he turned to a new technology, the radio, to build support for his church. He first began broadcasting in October 1926 on WJR, a Detroit station that could be heard in 20 states.

The "radio priest," as he soon became known, discussed Catholic doctrine, presented sermons for children, and attacked the KKK. His speaking voice fit radio—rich and warm, with an attractive slight Irish brogue, or what the novelist Wallace Stegner called "a voice made for promises."

After the Great Depression struck, Father Coughlin began making his shows more political. In 1930, the same year he first broadcast over the CBS network, he attacked bolshevism and socialism as anti-Christian and spun tales about an international conspiracy that had caused the depression. According to Coughlin, bankers planned the economic collapse as a way to tighten the money supply, dominate it, and extract greater profits from it. Part of the widespread appeal of his story was that it tapped a long-held distrust of bankers and coincided with attacks by several politicians—including Franklin Roosevelt—on "concentrated wealth" as the source of America's economic problems.

Father Coughlin wanted Congress to abolish the Federal Reserve and nationalize the country's banking system. And he advocated increasing the money supply, though he failed to articulate a specific plan for doing so. He refused a request by CBS to tone down his messages, and the network dropped his show. He then organized his own network, however, and could be heard on 26 stations.

In 1932 Coughlin supported Franklin Roosevelt for president, saying FDR would drive the money changers from the temple of government. But after Roosevelt won the White House and ignored Coughlin's entreaties to listen to him, the radio priest turned on him. He told how New Dealers, communists, and capitalists were all intriguing to grab power for the few and enslave the many. His story found an audience with those disgusted, disheartened, and frightened by the depression.

By 1934 Father Coughlin was receiving thousands of letters a day supporting him, many of them with donations enclosed. That year he founded the National Union for Social Justice to protect the common worker and lobby the government for change. The group wielded its most influence when it helped prevent the United States from joining the World Court, which it attacked as a dangerous internationalist body.

In 1936 Coughlin started a weekly newspaper, *Social Justice,* to endorse political candidates and elaborate on his radio sermons. He also founded the Union Party and predicted that its presidential candidate, William Lemke of North Dakota, would win 10 percent of the popular vote, but the actual count tallied fewer than 1 million.

The loss only emboldened Coughlin and deepened his conspiratorial suspicions. In 1938 his sermons turned anti-Semitic. He blamed Jews for nearly every problem in America and even published portions of "The Protocols of the Elders of Zion," a virulent anti-Semitic tract, in *Social Justice.* According to Coughlin, Jews had financed the communist revolution in Russia, and the Nazis were acting justly in stopping the menace.

That same year, Coughlin organized the Christian Front, a group whose members physically attacked Jews. With these activities, and with his radio speeches turning ever more extreme, in 1940 the National Association of Broadcasters forced him off the air.

When the Japanese attacked Pearl Harbor, and Father Coughlin blamed the outbreak of World War II on a conspiracy among the British, Jews, and Roosevelt, the Catholic Church ordered him to end his rhetoric or face defrocking. In 1942 he agreed to quit the public scene and thereafter, until his retirement in 1966, he said little beyond his usually sedate church sermons.

Father Coughlin died on October 27, 1979, in Birmingham, Michigan. For a part of the 1930s he had been one of the most influential men in America. According to historian Michael Kazin, Coughlin "delivered his messages in a lilting voice that both delighted and inflamed. He translated papal encyclicals about labor and poverty into American vernacular. He unraveled the complexities of banking transactions and legislation concerning the economy. He ridiculed pompous men of wealth." Therein was his appeal.

Further Reading

Carpenter, Ronald H. *Father Charles E. Coughlin: Surrogate Spokesman for the Disaffected.* Westport, Conn.: Greenwood Press, 1998.

Kazin, Michael. *The Populist Persuasion: An American History.* New York: Basic Books, 1995.

Marcus, Sheldon. *Father Coughlin: The Tumultuous Life of the Priest of the Little Flower.* Boston: Little, Brown, 1973.

Warren, Donald I. *Radio Priest: Charles Coughlin, the Father of Hate Radio.* New York: Free Press, 1996.

Cox, Harvey Gallagher, Jr.

(1929–   ) *peace activist, religious reformer*

A Baptist theologian and writer, Harvey Gallagher Cox has helped promote an understanding of religion among the general public. He was born on May 19, 1929, near Philadelphia, Pennsylvania, to Harvey Gallagher Cox, Sr., and Dorothea Dunwoody Cox.

Raised as a Baptist, Harvey Cox, Jr., graduated from the University of Pennsylvania in 1951 and received a bachelor of divinity degree from Yale in 1955. He then became director of religious activities at Oberlin College in Ohio and in 1957 married Nancy Nieburger; they had three children.

The following year he joined the American Baptist Home Missionary Society as a program associate while pursuing his doctorate at Harvard Divinity School, which he received in 1963.

Cox worked as a missionary in Germany for one year and then joined Andover Newton Theological Seminary as an assistant professor of theology. He wrote a study guide for use by the National Student Christian Federation that was published for a larger audience as *The Secular City* (1965), making him internationally prominent. (The book has been translated into 11 languages and has sold about 1 million copies.) Cox concluded that traditional religion was losing its following and would soon disappear. But he claimed that God existed in almost everything that was secular, so that the shift from spirituality to secularization actually enhanced spiritual opportunities.

In *Secular City* Cox stated, "When we look at history as a process of secularization, it becomes for us at the same time meaningful *and* open-ended. It suggests that history has a significance for man, but it does not impose a meaning on him. In fact, it topples inherited metaphysical and religious meanings and turns man loose to compose new ones." He added: "Releasing people to maturity is the work of the God of creation, Exodus and Sinai. Calling them to maturity is the task of the community of faith." As reported in the *New York Times,* "In his vision, the secular world was a natural outgrowth of the Christian doctrine of creation, not the result of sin, evil or a curse on mankind." Cox predicted that Christianity, at least as then structured, would soon disappear.

During the 1960s Cox marched against the Vietnam War, and he supported MARTIN LUTHER KING, JR., in the civil rights movement. He participated in a protest that resulted in his arrest in North Carolina in 1963.

With the publication of *Secular City*, Cox joined Harvard Divinity School as a professor. In the 1980s and 1990s he asserted that America was entering a new religious era, one that was supplanting secular domination, and in his book *Religion in the Secular City* (1984) he reversed his earlier prediction of Christianity's impending demise: "Rather than an age of rampant secularism

and religious decline," Professor Cox wrote, "it appears to be more of an era of religious revival."

In 1998 Cox received the Martin E. Marty Award for contributing to the public understanding of religion. A member of the award committee stated, "Harvey can transcend academic jargon and speak to issues in a language people can understand." About the world's religions dying, Cox said that year, "They will never disappear because we are questioning moral beings."

Further Reading

Cox, Harvey Gallagher. *Just As I Am.* Nashville, Tenn.: Abingdon Press, 1983.

Labbe, Theola S. "Harvey Cox." *Publisher Weekly,* 16 November 1998, S28.

Coxey, Jacob Sechler
(1854–1951) *social reformer*

A businessman and monetary reformer, Jacob Coxey was the leader of "Coxey's Army," a protest group of unemployed men. He was born in Selingsgrove, Pennsylvania, on April 16, 1854, to Thomas Coxey, a sawmill engineer, and Mary Sechler Coxey.

In 1881 Jacob Coxey settled in Massillon, Ohio, where he operated a profitable sandstone quarry. In the meantime, he joined the Greenback Party, and for the rest of his life he advocated the issuance of paper money unsupported by specie.

During those years America's shift from an agricultural economy to an industrial one was anything but smooth; severe depressions punctuated the change. The depression that caused Jacob Coxey to take action began in 1893 with the collapse of the country's railroads. By mid-1894 more than 150 railroads had declared bankruptcy, and as they closed, the steel industry closed with them. Unemployment surpassed 3 million by the end of 1893, and the number of homeless in New York City reached 20,000.

Coxey had a solution to the problem: He wanted Congress to pass the Good Roads Bill, which he had proposed, through which the federal government would employ men to build roads. When Congress refused to act and at the same time rejected his call for a larger public works program, Coxey's friend, Carl Browne, suggested a "petition in boots," meaning a march on Washington of the country's unemployed, and Coxey began developing the plans. Late that winter he publicly announced that he would lead a massive army of the unemployed on Washington.

The scrawny, bespectacled, and articulate Coxey predicted that 100,000 men would join his march, but when the protest began in Massillon on March 25, 1894, only 86 showed up. There were 40 reporters present, though, and as the marchers started out on horses, bicycles, and foot, they received extensive coverage in the country's newspapers. By and large, the reports portrayed the protesters as misguided misfits who were potentially dangerous. The *Akron Beacon* described the group as "poorly clad," and said that "those who had no banners to carry marched along, their hands in their pockets, and many were shivering with cold. It would have been difficult to find among the lot one man who under ordinary circumstances would not be classed as a tramp."

As Coxey's army moved east, it picked up recruits, and by the time it reached Pennsylvania it numbered 600. Thousands of people turned out in the towns through which the army passed, cheering the men on. But in Washington tension prevailed, for in addition to Coxey's army, others were forming. In California, Lewis C. Fry headed a group that left Los Angeles bound for the nation's capital, as did Charles T. Kelly, who organized an army in San Francisco. To make the long journey, these westerners commandeered railroads.

Coxey's army reached Washington on May 1, 1894, only to find the city police out in full force, under the orders of President Grover Cleveland. When Coxey led his men toward Capitol Hill, the police directed them to the outskirts of town. Once Coxey and his men realized they were being diverted, they turned around. Mounted on horses, the police quickly caught up with them.

"What do you want to do here?" the police captain asked Coxey.

"I wish to make an address," he replied.

"But you cannot do that," the captain said.

Coxey was arrested for walking on the grass and for illegally carrying a banner—namely, a lapel button. The other protesters were dispersed with billy clubs. The trial judge subsequently sentenced Coxey to 20 days in jail.

Coxey's army, joined by a few hundred men from the other armies, remained in Washington until August, when the movement disintegrated. President Cleveland used court injunctions, marshals, and even federal troops to break up yet other advancing armies of the unemployed.

In the end, Congress refused to pass any public works legislation. Nevertheless Coxey had changed the course of political debate. In an era when the federal government routinely helped big business but did not create social programs, he insisted it had the duty to provide the unemployed with relief. Much later, during the Great Depression of the 1930s, his idea was accepted.

Coxey, who ran for several different political offices under several different party labels, served as the Republican mayor of Massillon from 1931 to 1934. In 1932 he received 7,000 votes for president as the candidate of the Farmer-Labor Party. Coxey returned to the steps of the Capitol on May 1, 1944, and in a ceremony to commemorate his arrest, he delivered the speech he had intended to give 50 years before. He died on May 18, 1951.

Further Reading

Schwantes, Carlos A. *Coxey's Army: An American Odyssey.* Lincoln: University of Nebraska Press, 1985.

Croly, Herbert David
(1869–1930) *Progressive reformer*

Herbert Croly was the most prominent intellectual force of the early 20th-century Progressive movement. He was born on January 23, 1869, in New York City to David Goodman Croly and Jane Cunningham Croly.

Herbert Croly was weaned on reform. His father edited the *New York World* and the *Daily Graphic* and advocated numerous social programs; his mother did likewise as the country's first regularly working newspaperwoman and the first woman to write a syndicated column. Croly attended private and public schools in New York and then entered the College of the City of New York. In 1886 he enrolled at Harvard, but he interrupted his education several times and did not obtain his bachelor's degree until 1910.

In the meantime, he worked for his father, edited a real-state paper, and wrote for the *Architectural Record*, for which he later served as editor. In 1892 he married Louise Emory, a wealthy socialite and the source of his financial support in the years that followed. The next year he suffered a nervous breakdown and traveled to Europe to recover.

Writing in *Rendezvous with Destiny*, Eric Goldman describes Herbert Croly as "pale and fragile, ugly to the point where he was acutely aware of his looks, speaking with an impediment and so quietly that he could hardly be heard." Croly, he says, would have been ill suited to politics, "but a penetrating mind and an all-absorbing concern with public affairs were bred into this waterish little man."

In 1909, one year before Croly received his Harvard degree, he published *The Promise of American Life*. A commercial flop, it nonetheless provided the philosophical foundation and the intellectual fuel for the Progressive reform movement. He further developed his ideas in *Marcus Alonzo Hanna: His Life and Work* (1912) and *Progressive Democracy* (1914).

Croly thought the Constitution inadequate to handle the complexities of modern life and an enemy to democracy; he believed that only through democracy could society be made better. But he realized that there existed little chance a constitutional convention would ever be held. So he advocated changing the existing system by reinterpreting the founding document.

Croly wanted more democratic politics, a system more responsive to public opinion and better able to correct the abuses inflicted on society by the new corporate industrial economy. Since legislatures such as Congress, he believed, worked as an obstructionist minority to frustrate the majority and its desire for change, he wanted the president to exert executive power on a much larger scale than previously to advance the people's desires. For Croly, the president, as the only political leader truly elected nationally, represented the best hope for change.

The president, however, should always adhere to public opinion, speaking for it and advancing its desires. There should be attached to the president talented, educated administrators whose expertise would carry out the public's agenda and would survive the individual presidencies themselves.

As did other Progressives, Croly found it necessary to address the problem of controlling abusive corporations—the large economic unit previously rare in America, now becoming dominant as industry and transportation expanded. He argued that state regulation meant little; since the power of the corporations transcended state lines, effective regulation required a stronger, more vibrant national government, or what he called a "New Nationalism."

To those who warned that power concentrated in the president and the government's administrators could devolve into dictatorship, Croly's only answer was his faith in democracy. He believed that as presidents reached out to the public, people would see themselves as more effective and participate in politics more often. This would make the government more democratic. Critics discounted this idea and warned that if a powerful national government fell into reactionary hands, Progressive reform would be doomed. Still, Croly said, "My object has not been to recommend a particular plan of . . . political organization as the only plan which will meet the needs and requirements of a progressive democracy. What I have tried to do has been to explain the needs and requirements of a genuinely popular system of representative government."

Croly's ideas influenced Progressive politicians such as Theodore Roosevelt and Woodrow Wilson. To promote Progressive-liberal ideas, in 1914 he founded the magazine *New Republic*, largely with money from his wife. Early on, he exerted considerable influence in the Wilson presidency, and through the magazine he supported American entry into World War I. After the war, however, he broke with Wilson (and in so doing lost many readers) when he opposed the Treaty of Versailles, which he thought required revisions. Presently the Senate rejected the treaty and with it American entry into the League of Nations.

Herbert Croly died on May 17, 1930, in a hospital in Santa Barbara, California. In 1998 Sidney A. Pearson, Jr., writing in *Society* magazine, expressed the assessment of many historians: "Croly helped to give the Progressive Movement some of its most articulate expression in the opening decades of the twentieth century—perhaps better than any other single writer."

Further Reading

Dorreboom, Iris. *"The Challenge of Our Time": Woodrow Wilson, Herbert Croly, Randolph Bourne and the Making of Modern America*. Atlanta, Ga.: Rodopi, 1991.

Goldman, Eric. *Rendezvous with Destiny: A History of Modern American Reform*. Rev. ed. New York: Vintage, 1955.

Stettner, Edward A. *Shaping Modern Liberalism: Herbert Croly and Progressive Thought*. Lawrence: University Press of Kansas, 1993.

Darrow, Clarence Seward
(1857–1938) *labor activist*

A lawyer most known for his role in the Loeb-Leopold murder case and the Scopes trial, Clarence Darrow was also a pacifist and a proponent of labor rights. He was born on April 18, 1857, near Kinsman, Ohio, to Amirus Darrow and Emily Eddy Darrow.

Clarence Darrow graduated from public school in Kinsman and attended Allegheny College in Meadville, Pennsylvania, for one year, followed by a year at the University of Michigan law school. He then read law in Ohio and was admitted to the bar in 1878. Darrow practiced law in Kinsman before moving on to two other Ohio towns. During those years he was attracted to reformist ideas through the writings of HENRY GEORGE and Judge John Peter Altgeld.

Darrow moved to Chicago in 1887, became friends with Altgeld, and showed his sympathy for labor when he joined those who wanted to obtain a commutation for the anarchistic defendants sentenced to death in the Haymarket Square case. Governor Richard Oglesby commuted two of the death sentences to life terms, but four of the defendants were executed. Altgeld won election as governor of Illinois in 1892, causing Darrow's political influence to increase; Altgeld subsequently pardoned the remaining three Haymarket defendants.

Darrow began his legal practice in Chicago as a civil lawyer and in that capacity represented railroads. But he shifted to labor law and in 1906 suc-

cessfully defended WILLIAM DUDLEY HAYWOOD, leader of the socialist Industrial Workers of the World, against a charge of conspiring to murder the former governor of Idaho.

Amid charges that he mishandled a labor case involving the *Los Angeles Times* in 1911, Darrow shifted his legal focus yet again to the practice of criminal law. The many trials he was involved in until 1924, including the Loeb-Leopold case, in which he saved from the death penalty two teenage boys convicted of murdering a young boy, reinforced his reputation as a talented lawyer, but more pertinent to his reform activities was his entry into politics.

In the late 1800s and early 1900s Darrow embraced Progressive reform, and when he ran for Congress as a Democrat in 1894 he condemned the concentration of economic power in an industrializing society. He lost that race but won election as state representative in 1902, and in 1905 he helped to elect Judge Edward F. Dunne as mayor of Chicago. Over the years Darrow supported the closed shop as a way to strengthen unions, opposed capital punishment and child labor, and called for liberal reforms of the judicial and prison systems. He considered civil liberties sacred and opposed any government infringement of them. Yet he criticized such reforms as Prohibition and women's rights.

Darrow supported America's entry into World War I, but he was a pacifist at heart and called war "insane." During the postwar Red Scare of 1919–20, when the federal government persecuted communists and radicals, he defended several persons indicted under state laws for sedition, including communists.

In 1925 Darrow defended John Thomas Scopes, who was indicted for violation of Tennessee law for teaching evolution in a Dayton public school. Darrow sincerely believed in evolution and in free speech, and although Scopes was found guilty of having violated the law, Darrow exposed the narrowness of fundamentalist thinking in a case that made front-page news across the country.

To fight corporate power, Darrow at times called for the breakup of larger businesses into small units; at other times he called for socialism to replace capitalism. His ambivalence was reflected in a report he wrote for the federal government in 1934 about monopolies in which, on the one hand, he praised competition, and on the other, he advocated government ownership of industries.

Darrow died on March 13, 1938, in Chicago. He had been married twice, to Jessie Ohl in 1880 (with whom he had one child), and after their divorce in 1897, to Ruby Hammerstein in 1903.

Further Reading

Darrow, Clarence. *The Story of My Life*. New York: Da Capo Press, 1996.

Sayer, James Edward. *Clarence Darrow: Public Advocate.* Dayton, Ohio: Wright State University, 1978.

Tierney, Kevin. *Darrow: A Biography*. New York: Crowell, 1979.

Davis, Angela Yvonne

(1944–) *black power leader, communist*

A 1960s black power activist, communist, and women's rights advocate, Angela Yvonne Davis has taken on many social challenges. She was born on January 26, 1944, in Birmingham, Alabama, to B. Frank Davis and Sallye E. Davis.

Unlike most African Americans in that heavily segregated city, Angela Davis did not live in poverty. Her mother taught elementary school, and her father owned and operated a service station, so although as an infant she lived in the projects, by the time she was four years old her family was able to move into a comfortable house on Center Street.

Despite Davis's middle-class status, racism stung her. As a child she heard a huge explosion when whites blew up a neighbor's house to protest the intrusion of African Americans into previously white areas. In subsequent years she saw similar vicious acts repeated over and over again, and amid the racist atmosphere she developed a deep dislike for segregation and envied the freedom enjoyed by whites.

Racist Birmingham relegated her and the other African Americans in her neighborhood to Carrie A. Tuggle Elementary School, an all-black facility in disrepair. Her contact there with poor children caused her to realize the economic plight that other families faced. The teachers told her and the other students to work hard and get ahead but warned them that advancement would be more difficult for them than for white children. They taught her that the segregationist system would be permanent, and this she was unwilling to accept. In middle school her history books referred to the Civil War as the War for Southern Independence and portrayed blacks as preferring slavery to freedom. Such racist interpretations contributed to her discontent with the prevailing system.

She excelled in her studies, however, and through the American Friends Service Committee enrolled at Elizabeth Irwin High School in New York City. There Davis heard teachers express socialist ideas; she read the *Communist Manifesto*, which enthralled her; and she attended meetings of Advance, a Marxist-Leninist youth group.

In 1961 Davis received a full scholarship and enrolled at Brandeis University in Massachusetts. In her senior year she veered from her concentration on literature and began studying philosophy under the renowned Marxist Herbert Marcuse. She went to Germany in 1965 to pursue graduate studies at Frankfurt. At the same time, her political activism stirred, and she joined picketers outside the U.S. embassy in demonstrating against the Vietnam War.

In 1967 Davis continued her studies under Marcuse, who had relocated to the University of California at San Diego. That same year she joined the Black Panther Party (BPP). With headquarters in Los Angeles, the Panthers operated independently of the Black Panthers in Oakland. She had become a revolutionary and later said, "For me revolution was never a 'thing to do' before settling down; it was no fashionable club . . . made thrilling by risk and confrontation, made glamorous by costume. Revolution is a serious thing, the most serious thing about a revolutionary's life. When one commits oneself to the struggle, it must be for a lifetime."

The BPP merged with the Student Non-Violent Coordinating Committee (SNCC) in 1968 to form LA-SNCC. Davis worked in the black neighborhoods in Los Angeles, trying to build a mass movement, while continuing research for her doctorate in San Diego. By the spring she had formed a youth corps and a Liberation School, which she directed. After the *Los Angeles Times* reported that LA-SNCC included a prominent communist, and the national SNCC purged the local organization's leadership, Davis resigned from SNCC and joined the Communist Party; she said that she was attracted to its "serious revolutionary" position.

Shortly afterward Davis joined the Oakland-based Black Panthers as well, but differences over policy soon caused her to leave that group. She then traveled in 1969 to Cuba, where on a farm she helped hoe the weeds around coffee plants and harvest sugarcane. The Cuban Revolution greatly impressed her and encouraged her radical commitment.

When she returned to San Diego, the University of California hired her to teach philosophy, but after Governor Ronald Reagan and the board of trustees learned she was a member of the Communist Party, they fired her. Months later the courts ruled unconstitutional the California law that barred Communists from teaching in state universities.

By that time another adventure was unfolding. In 1970 Davis organized a campaign to help George Jackson and two other men imprisoned at Soledad. This bleak fortress, bearing the Spanish name for solitude, had recently experienced considerable turmoil when Jackson led his fellow inmates in condemning its racist practices. Their protest led to a riot, the death of a guard, and mur-

der charges against Jackson and his followers. Davis believed Jackson was innocent, the victim of a government effort to punish him for his outspoken stand.

Then in August, Jonathan Jackson, George's brother, led a group in raiding a courthouse. They captured a judge, a district attorney, and several jurors, whom they held as hostages. Jonathan intended to exchange them for George to get his brother out of jail. The plan backfired when police attacked the assailants and a hail of gunfire resulted in several deaths, including Jonathan's and the judge's. Unfortunately for Angela Davis, Jonathan's .380 automatic was registered in her name. The authorities considered her an accomplice and tried to arrest her. Davis went into hiding and eluded them, but later that year the Federal Bureau of Investigation (FBI) found her in New York City.

Her capture, though, strengthened rather than demoralized her. While she sat in a New York City prison, awaiting extradition shortly before Christmas Day 1970, she heard chants outside: "Free our sisters, free ourselves! Free Angela!" They filled her with excitement, with the possibility that the masses had heard her message, that they could be radicalized and tear down the oppressive social and political structure.

Davis was imprisoned for several weeks and then extradited to California, where she stood trial on charges of murder, conspiracy, and kidnapping. Throughout her confinement, she received strong support from African Americans and from white radicals, and even moderate observers considered the charges against her weak and part of a plan to persecute her. In 1972, after a three-month trial, a jury acquitted her.

Davis then toured the Soviet Union, East Germany, Bulgaria, Czechoslovakia, and Cuba, where she received warm receptions. A few weeks later she returned to the United States and formed the National Alliance against Racist and Political Repression, a Communist-affiliated group that, she claimed, had chapters in 21 states and a diverse but small membership of African Americans, Chicanos, Puerto Ricans, Asians, and Indians.

In 1974 Davis wrote her autobiography, and in the 1990s she remained committed to radical social and political change, as evidenced in her writing and many speaking engagements. Outside her duties at the University of California at Santa Cruz, where she was professor of history and consciousness, Davis spent much of her time working for prison reform. She criticized what she called the "prison industrial complex" by which, she said, "almost two million people are locked up," with "more than 70 percent of the imprisoned population . . . people of color." She claimed that "the dividends that accrue from investment in the punishment industry, like those that accrue from investment in weapons production, only amount to social destruction."

Further Reading

Aptheker, Bettina. *The Morning Breaks: The Trial of Angela Davis.* 2nd ed. Ithaca, N.Y.: Cornell University Press, 1999.

Davis, Angela Yvonne. *Angela Davis: An Autobiography.* New York: Random House, 1974.

Day, Dorothy

(1897–1980) *social worker, pacifist*

Dorothy Day was the founder of the Catholic Worker movement. She was born on November 8, 1897, in Brooklyn, New York, to John Day, a sportswriter, and Grace Satterlee Day.

Dorothy Day grew up alienated and rebellious, characteristics that defined her life. From 1914 to 1916 she attended the University of Illinois in Urbana-Champaign and met other disaffected students, who influenced her with their radical views. She had already declared herself an atheist, and at the university she learned about socialism. Bored with college life and discontent with the injustices she saw in society, she quit the university and moved to New York City, where she began working for *The Call,* a socialist newspaper. In 1917 she joined other protesters in picketing the White House for women's suffrage and was arrested and sent to prison.

In New York she lived in Greenwich Village and met Floyd Dell and MAX EASTMAN, who chose her to edit *Masses,* another socialist publication. In need of money and still living a rootless existence,

in 1918 Day found work as a probationary nurse at Kings County Hospital in Brooklyn. The following year she returned to journalism as a writer for the radical *Liberator.*

She then went through two disastrous relationships with men. The first one led to her becoming pregnant and getting an abortion. The second relationship was with Forster Batterham, a writer more given to drink than to work. They began living together in 1925. Two years later Day bore their child, and at the end of 1927 she converted to Catholicism in search of God. A committed atheist, Batterham left Day at the same time that many of her Greenwich Village friends were also deserting her because of her conversion.

While writing articles for Catholic magazines, in 1932 Day met Peter Maurin, a French émigré, a former Christian Brother, and an intellectual schooled in Catholic humanism. Maurin disliked capitalism and modern technology for their role in undermining community; he hoped that one day people would return to a subsistence economy of agriculture and handmade production, and he believed in helping the poor by living among them. In Maurin, Day saw a commitment to serving society and an attachment to individual freedom and responsibility. Consequently, she dedicated herself to proving that Catholicism could serve the poor. Together they founded *Catholic Worker,* a newspaper to communicate their radical outlook.

The *Catholic Worker,* which first appeared in May 1933, soon expanded its circulation to more than 100,000, and it became the voice of the Catholic Worker movement, which was fast becoming the leader in Catholic reform. Following Maurin's plan, Day established hospitality houses where the homeless could receive food, shelter, and guidance and founded communal farms. Day said, "We [Catholic Workers] believe in an economy based on human needs, rather than the profit motive." She was a tireless worker, and at the *Catholic Worker* she allowed little dissent: An uncompromising pacifist, she insisted that the staff accept her antiwar views without question.

Many future Catholic radicals, such as DANIEL BERRIGAN, PHILIP BERRIGAN, and MICHAEL HARRINGTON, said they owed their moral commitment to Day. To those who asked her how she withstood the challenges of helping the poor, she said, "Pray and endure."

In the 1950s Day led a successful drive in New York City to end compulsory air-raid drills, which she said encouraged a war mentality. In the mid-1960s she joined protests against the Vietnam War, and in fall 1965 she attended the Second Vatican Council's meeting on war and peace in Rome and helped convince the Catholic Church to recognize the right of conscientious objection. And in 1973 Day participated in a strike by the United Farm Workers against growers in California.

Dorothy Day died on November 29, 1980, at Maryhouse, a Catholic Worker shelter for the homeless in New York City. By the late 1990s there were more than 125 Catholic Worker houses and farming communes in the United States.

In response to those who once asked her to define her pacifism, Day said, "I can write no other than this: Unless we use the weapons of the spirit, denying ourselves and taking up our cross and following Jesus, dying with Him and rising with Him, men will go on fighting, and often from the highest motives, believing that they are fighting defensive wars for justice and in self-defense against present or future aggression."

Further Reading

Day, Dorothy. *Loaves and Fishes.* Maryknoll, N.Y.: Orbis Books, 1997.

Forest, James H. *Love Is the Measure: A Biography of Dorothy Day.* Rev. ed. Maryknoll, N.Y.: Orbis Books, 1994.

Klejment, Anne, and Nancy L. Roberts, eds. *American Catholic Pacifism: The Influence of Dorothy Day and the Catholic Worker Movement.* Westport, Conn.: Praeger, 1996.

Miller, William D. *Dorothy Day: A Biography.* San Francisco: Harper & Row, 1982.

De Leon, Daniel
(1852–1914) *socialist*

Leader of the Socialist Labor Party (SLP), Daniel De Leon founded the Social Trade and Labor Alliance. The son of Salomon De Leon and Sara Jesurun De Leon, he was born on December 14, 1852, on the island of Curaçao, a Dutch Caribbean colony.

In 1866, at age 14, Daniel De Leon traveled to Europe to continue his education, first in Germany and then in the Netherlands. He immigrated to the United States in 1872, settling in New York City. After earning a law degree from Columbia University in 1878 and working briefly as a lawyer in Texas, he returned to Columbia as a lecturer and taught Latin American diplomacy for six years. The economic depression of the 1880s and the attendant miserable living conditions of many workers in New York City, caused him to seek social reform.

At first he supported HENRY GEORGE's single-tax plan and campaigned for George when he ran for mayor in 1886. Two years later De Leon joined a union, the Knights of Labor. In 1890 he moved further to the left when he joined the Socialist Labor Party, which had derived from the Socialist First International of 1864. He was elected editor of the party's magazine, *The People,* in 1891 and later that year ran unsuccessfully for governor of New York as the SLP candidate. (He would run several more times for the state assembly and for Congress, losing each race.)

Under De Leon the SLP represented one of the many ideologies then being debated among socialists. He advocated a democratic socialism whereby all laborers would be united under one union and through workers' councils would control the country's industries. He opposed any government action to nationalize industries or any attempt by a political party to take them over in the name of the workers. Such measures would only replace capitalist oppression with state oppression.

The SLP, he insisted, should work to gain control of the government, but once it did so, it should abolish itself and let the workers' councils take over, establishing what he called an "industrial form of government." Unlike some anarchists and socialist extremists, he opposed revolutionary violence; the SLP must win at the ballot box, he said, to prevent a reactionary slaughter by the state that violent tactics would incite, and it must win votes to establish credibility and certify its democratic credentials.

In 1895 De Leon formed the Socialist Trade and Labor Alliance, a union that complemented the work of the SLP and the first union in the United States to proclaim as its goal the replacement of capitalism with workers' ownership of industries. An eloquent writer, De Leon stated many of his socialist views in editorials that he wrote for *The People:*

> The exploiting and idle class struggles upon the lines of their class interests. They aim to conserve the power they now enjoy to live in luxury without work, to ride the proletariat, to fleece the workers.
>
> The working class of America has nothing, no economic or social powers, worth conserving. "Conservatism" can never mean the striving to conserve chains.

De Leon criticized the American Federation of Labor (AFL) for its willingness to work with the capitalist system, asserting that when the AFL talks about "'redemption of the workers from the bondage of industrial slavery,' the words are used as so much claptrap."

In 1901 many members resigned from the SLP, accusing De Leon of exerting dictatorial powers and expressing disagreement with his ideas. The departure crippled the SLP, but De Leon continued as its leader. Four years later he helped found the Industrial Workers of the World (IWW), which also advocated the workers' ownership of businesses, and he presented his "Socialist Reconstruction of Society," later published as a pamphlet, to a rally in Minneapolis, Minnesota. He wrote:

> After thirty years of arduous toil, after thirty years, during which the soil of the land was literally drenched with the sweat and blood and marrow of the workingman; after thirty years during which the American working class produced more heiresses to the square inch than the working class of any other country . . . ; at the end of thirty years during which the working class . . . produced a phenomenal amount of wealth—at the end of these thirty years the American working class is just where it was thirty years before, the wretched retainer of only $20 out of every $100 worth of wealth that it produced!

He continued:

> In the framework of the capitalist social system, the working class and the employing or capitalist class have nothing in common. The principle is a beacon on the track of labor's march to emancipation; the contrary principle is a false light that lures labor to social wreck.

For De Leon and the IWW a "new epoch" had begun, a step toward amassing workers in a crusade that would bring capitalism to its knees.

That same year he outlined the possibility of a more radical strategy when he stated, "If the capitalists should be foolish enough in America to defeat, to thwart the will of the workers expressed by the ballot, then there will be a condition of things by which the working class can absolutely cease production, and thereby starve out the capitalist class, render their present economic means and all their preparations for war absolutely useless."

De Leon allied the SLP with the IWW from 1905 to 1908, yet his hopes for a grand march toward socialism faltered again when factional disputes ended the relationship. Over the next six years of his life he continued to promote his brand of socialism, but his industrial format lost favor with all but a small number of radicals. Daniel De Leon died on May 11, 1914, in New York City. He was married twice, in 1882 to Sara Lobo, who died in 1887, and in 1892 to Bertha Canary, who survived him.

Further Reading

Coleman, Stephen. *Daniel De Leon.* New York: St. Martin's Press, 1990.

Seretan, L. Glen. *Daniel De Leon: The Odyssey of an American Marxist.* Cambridge, Mass.: Harvard University Press, 1979.

Debs, Eugene Victor
(1855–1926) *socialist*

Eugene Victor Debs formed the American Railway Union and became America's foremost socialist. He was born on November 5, 1855, in Terre

Haute, Indiana, to Jean Daniel Debs and Marguerite Marie Bettrich Debs.

In Debs's youth his hometown embraced traditional values far removed from the radical cauldron of "isms"—anarchism, communism, and socialism—that were then making their way from Europe to America. Most people in Terre Haute thought Americans were God's chosen people; they supported business; and they believed that through hard work anyone could advance. Debs attended public school until age 15 and learned these values, along with the others that his neighbors held sacred, namely, democracy and the autonomy and effectiveness of the individual.

In 1870 Debs joined the Terre Haute and Indianapolis Railway, working as a locomotive paint scraper and eventually becoming a locomotive fireman. Four years later he lost his job during an economic depression and found work as a clerk in a wholesale grocery. Still wanting to remain attached to the railroad, in 1875 Debs signed up with the Brotherhood of Locomotive Firemen (BLF), and in 1878 he was appointed editor of its *Firemen's Magazine*. In 1880 he was made the BLF's national secretary. He worked long hours, traveling the country to make the BLF an effective union, and gained a strong reputation as a defender of workers' rights.

During these years changes under way outside Terre Haute infringed on the midwestern town. Businesses grew; some became part of larger corporations directed by absentee owners; increasingly, Terre Haute's residents saw the world as divided between capitalists and workers. The comfortable town boundaries shook with the arrival of the machine, and Debs's life corresponded with these changes.

In 1885 Debs married Kate Metzel; that same year he won election to the Indiana House of Representatives as a Democrat. He disliked the office, though, because it involved making too many compromises, so he refused to seek reelection. A few years later he left the BLF, but for a different reason. He believed that rather than being organized into several different unions based on specialized jobs, railroad workers should enhance their unity and power by uniting into one large union.

With anger among workers growing from economic depressions, low wages, the hiring of immigrants, the use of machines to replace skilled labor, and the corporate practice of making decisions in a manner that made the workers feel replaceable, in 1893 Debs formed the American Railway Union (ARU). In short order, 34 locals were established as membership grew rapidly. Economic conditions, the concept of a united labor force, and Debs's effective appeal produced the startling results.

In April 1894 Debs gained wage increases when he led a strike against the Great Northern Railroad, a victory that made the ARU larger than any other railroad union, with 150,000 members. When soon afterward workers at the Pullman factory in Chicago—a company that made sleeping cars for the railroads—went on strike, members of the ARU urged the union to support them. Debs advised against it, saying the ARU was too new for such an undertaking, but after the membership overrode him, he applied his characteristic energy in organizing the protest. The refusal of the ARU to work on trains using Pullman cars shut down many of the country's railroads—including those carrying the U.S mail—and paralyzed Chicago, the hub of the railroad network.

Dominated by the railroad companies, the federal government acted to crush the strike. On July 2, 1894, it obtained an injunction against the ARU and, over the objections of the governor of Illinois, sent troops into Chicago. As violence flared, Debs was arrested for conspiring to obstruct the mails and for violating the injunction, which he had ignored. In February 1895 the trial judge sentenced him and several others to six months in jail. Debs later portrayed his imprisonment as a great revelatory moment that caused him to abandon capitalism:

> I was to be baptized in Socialism in the roar of the conflict . . . in the gleam of every bayonet and the flash of every rifle the class struggle was revealed.

Such had become the reality of industrial America: a class struggle between capitalists and labor. Actually, Debs had yet to adopt socialism fully, but he dedicated himself to fighting for the freedom and dignity of the individual and began calling for a cooperative society. The government intervention defeated the Pullman workers, but on Debs's release from jail in November 1895 a jubilant crowd of about 100,000 greeted the union leader and listened as he criticized corporate America for assaulting individual autonomy. He said, "So long as one man depends upon the will of another or more often the whims and caprice of another for employment, he is a slave."

In 1897 Debs officially became a socialist, stating, "I am for socialism because I am for humanity." He merged the remains of the ARU—decimated by the Pullman strike—with the Social Democratic Party of America. Debs wanted the wage system replaced with a cooperative scheme in which the workers would own the means of production, running factories for the good of society rather than the profits of a select few—a true community held together by a commitment to the public welfare. He took traditional American ideals, born amid farms and forests; mixed them with the reality of industrial society; and emblazoned them on the country's smokestacks and skyscrapers.

An effective speaker, Debs attracted large audiences for his speeches. He would lean his lanky body toward his listeners, extend his right arm, and move his forefinger about. Time and again he stressed that the true worth of a cooperative commonwealth resided in the dignity it would confer on individuals, a dignity intended by America's founding fathers. He called socialism patriotic and expressed his faith in democracy when he said change could be accomplished through the ballot box. With that view, he parted company with those radicals who insisted that entrenched power would always manipulate voting and voters to prevent any real change, and that the only alternative was a violent overthrow of the government.

Debs ran for president in 1900 as the nominee of the Social Democratic Party and the Socialist Labor Party. In 1901 the Social Democratic Party merged with a faction of the Socialist Labor Party to form the Socialist Party of America, with Debs as its leader. He ran again for president in 1904 and 1908, and yet a fourth time in 1912, when he polled nearly 1 million votes, or 6 percent of the national total.

Debs denounced World War I and supported the stand of the Socialist Party, proclaimed in 1917, when it urged its members to oppose the conflict by whatever means they could. To Debs, the war was sacrificing the lives of workers for the financial benefit of the capitalists. The following year, in a speech at Canton, Ohio, Debs condemned President Woodrow Wilson's administration for arresting war resisters. Several days later he himself was indicted by a federal grand jury in Cleveland for violating the Espionage Act, which forbade acts of sedition.

In September 1918 Debs stood trial and was sentenced to 10 years in prison. On appeal to the Supreme Court in March 1919, the verdict was upheld, and he began his prison term in April. While incarcerated, in 1920 he again ran for president and pulled his highest vote total yet. That same year he called the Russian Revolution a positive step forward. In December 1921 he was pardoned by President Harding and released.

Debs returned to a Socialist Party shattered and weakened by factional disputes. Two of the factions wanted to align the party with the communist movement; a more conservative faction wanted to remain independent of the communists. In 1922 Debs announced his support for the conservatives. He then tried to reconcile the opposing groups, but his health, greatly weakened by his time in prison, deteriorated. He died on October 20, 1926, in Elmhurst, Illinois.

Socialism was more than a minor movement; its power worried the governing elite and encouraged Theodore Roosevelt and other political leaders to pursue Progressive reform lest Debs and his followers gather even greater support. The essential contribution of Debs was to awaken Americans to the threat posed by an emerging corporate economy to the independence and dignity of the individual.

Further Reading

Constantine, J. Robert, ed. *Gentle Rebel: Letters of Eugene V. Debs.* Urbana: University of Illinois Press, 1995.

———. *Letters of Eugene V. Debs.* 3 vols. Urbana: University of Illinois Press, 1990.

Salvatore, Nick. *Eugene V. Debs: Citizen and Socialist.* Urbana: University of Illinois Press, 1982.

Dees, Morris Seligman, Jr.

(1936–   ) *civil rights activist*

Morris Dees is a lawyer who founded the Southern Poverty Law Center to protect individual civil rights and fight hate groups. He was born on December 16, 1936, in Shorter, Alabama, to Morris Seligman Dees, Sr., a farmer and cotton gin operator, and Annie Ruth Frazer Dees.

As a youngster Morris Dees always had some business idea churning inside his head. In high school he made money selling the leftovers from his father's cotton gin as mulch. In 1955, the year he graduated, he owned cattle and hogs and was named one of Alabama's outstanding young farmers.

While an undergraduate at the University of Alabama he began a mail-order order business dealing mainly in book sales. He received a bachelor's degree and pursued a long-held desire by entering the University of Alabama law school. He also continued his mail-order business, and by the time he received his law degree in 1960, his sales were reaching into the millions of dollars.

Altruism motivated Dees to pursue law as a career. He grew up surrounded by Jim Crow racial segregation and, unusual for rural southern whites at the time, he determined to advance African-American civil rights. In 1969 he sold his mail-order business to the Times-Mirror Corporation for $6 million. That same year, he took on his first important civil rights case when, on behalf of two black youths, he won a court case forcing the Young Men's Christian Association of Montgomery, Alabama, to desegregate.

In 1971 Dees cofounded the Southern Poverty Law Center (SPLC) to engage in legal cases involving civil rights. In his first prominent trial, in 1974 he defended Joan Little, a black woman serving time in a North Carolina jail. She had been charged with murdering a white guard but claimed that she had only been defending herself against rape. Dees won the case, but Little later accused him of exploiting her.

Putting his mail-order background to work along with his experience in soliciting money for Democratic senator George McGovern's presidential campaign in 1972, Dees raised millions of dollars for the SPLC. The funds enabled him to handle more civil rights cases and in 1981 to establish Klanwatch. Affiliated with the SPLC, Klanwatch gathered and disseminated information on the Ku Klux Klan (KKK) and other hate groups.

That same year Dees sued the Texas KKK for burning the boats of immigrant Vietnamese fishermen in Galveston Bay and using other scare tactics against them. He won a decision that basically shut down the Texas KKK.

In the 1980s Dees developed a strategy of putting hate groups out of business by using civil suits to get the courts to hold them responsible for violating civil rights and to win financial judgments that would ruin them. One such case in 1986 involved the United Klans of America (UKA) in Mobile, Alabama. James "Tiger" Knowles, a Klan member, admitted his participation in the murder of 19-year-old Michael Donald, an African American who had been hanged and his throat slit. Dees proved that the UKA was responsible for Knowles's actions, and he won for the murder victim's mother, Beulah Mae Donald, $7 million in damages against the organization.

In 1990 he initiated a civil suit against white supremacist Tom Metzger and his group the White Aryan Resistance (WAR) after a group of young men affiliated with WAR were found guilty of the murder of an Ethiopian man, Mulugeta Seraw, in Portland, Oregon. Dees won more than $12 million for the Seraw family and forced WAR to shut down its newspaper, cable TV show, and telephone hot lines.

Dees won a $37 million judgment against the KKK in 1998 for its role in burning a black church three years earlier in Bloomville, South Carolina. At the same time, the SPLC and Klanwatch closely monitored the rise of militia groups. The SPLC reported that 224 militias existed in 39 states, 45 of them with ties to neo-Nazi and white supremacist movements. Although the SPLC reported that most militias were not racist, it warned that many were susceptible to white supremacist takeover and that the more extreme among them were stockpiling weapons to prepare for Armageddon. Yet the SPLC opposed those who wanted intrusive antiterrorist legislation to deal with the militias and other groups, and the SPLC instead called for enforcing the paramilitary laws already on the books in the states.

In the year 2000 Dees turned his attention to Idaho, where several white supremacist groups had located their headquarters. Two years earlier, guards at an Aryan Nations compound had assaulted two passing motorists, who they mistakenly thought had fired shots into the compound. Dees won a $6 million judgment for the motorists that forced Aryan Nations into bankruptcy. Dees said, "We intend to take every single asset from the Aryan Nations now and forever." The defiant Aryan Nations leader, Richard Girnt Butler, said, however, "I'm still in business, and I'll remain in business until the day I die."

In the course of leading the SPLC, Dees, who has been married three times and has three children, has experienced numerous threats against him and his family, yet he has persevered. But he has not been without his critics. Some say that his civil lawsuits for damages stifle free speech by holding people with admittedly repugnant ideas responsible for the actions of others. He has also been criticized for exaggerating the number and range of hate groups to stir people into contributing money to the SPLC. Some have charged the SPLC with mishandling funds.

Dees has ranked among the most prominent leaders in showing how the courts can be used to exert financial pressure on hate groups. He has been determined to send a message to such groups through lawsuits that demonstrate that attacks on the civil rights and dignity of other human beings will no longer be tolerated.

Further Reading

Dees, Morris. *Hate on Trial: The Case against America's Most Dangerous Neo-Nazi.* New York: Villard, 1993.

———. *A Season for Justice: The Life and Times of Civil Rights Lawyer Morris Dees.* New York: Scribner's, 1991.

Delany, Martin Robison
(1812–1885) *abolitionist*

An African-American abolitionist, Martin Delany served as president of the National Emigration Convention. He was born on May 6, 1812, in Charles Town, Virginia (today West Virginia), to Samuel Delany, a slave, and Pati Peace Delany, a free black woman.

As a boy Martin Delany obtained books from peddlers, and with the help of his mother he learned to read. For reasons unclear, in 1822 Pati Delany took Martin and his brother to settle in Chambersburg, Pennsylvania. Samuel Delany soon followed, either by buying his freedom or by running away from his master.

Ambitious and proud of his heritage, Martin often bragged about his black appearance and his lack of mulatto features. In 1831 he moved to Pittsburgh so he could advance his education. In a short time he became a leader in the black community, noted for his participation in philanthropic activities and for his abolitionism. He became an officer in the Pittsburgh Anti-Slavery Society while obtaining training from a white doctor that allowed him to work as a leecher and bleeder, administering what in that age were considered two of the most effective cures for disease.

In March 1843 Delany married Kate A. Richards, a daughter of reportedly the wealthiest black family in Pittsburgh. They had 11 children. That same year he began publishing the *Mystery*, a small newspaper that criticized those African Americans who helped whites catch runaway slaves.

In 1847 he helped FREDERICK DOUGLASS found the *North Star*, an abolitionist paper. As he journeyed through the Midwest gathering stories for publication and lecturing against slavery, he encountered mobs and on one occasion was nearly lynched.

Delany entered Harvard in 1849 to continue his medical studies, but white students protested and forced him to leave after one semester. Nevertheless, he began practicing as a doctor. In 1850 he returned to Pittsburgh and rallied blacks against the Fugitive Slave Act passed earlier that year by Congress. At a meeting held in the city's public square Delany said he would kill any slaveholder who "crossed his threshold."

Delany had previously opposed efforts to send blacks to Africa. He criticized the white-led American Colonization Society and its plan to establish African Americans in Liberia. He called the society

To Martin Delany, the Fugitive Slave Law showed the oppression blacks were suffering and the futility they were encountering in their efforts to find liberty in America.   *(Library of Congress)*

"anti-Christian in its character and misanthropic in its pretended sympathies." He labeled its leaders "arrant hypocrites" who were the enemies of African Americans. They only wanted to rid America of blacks, he said, and he called the Liberian government "a poor *miserable mockery.*"

But the Fugitive Slave Law changed his mind—not about Liberia, but about a home for blacks outside the United States. In his book *The Condition, Elevation, Emigration, and Destiny of the Colored People of the United States, Politically Considered* (1852), he reprinted the entire Fugitive Slave Law to show the oppression blacks were suffering and the futility they were encountering in finding liberty in America. "That there have been people in all ages under certain circumstances, that may be benefited by emigration, will be admitted," he wrote. "And that there are circumstances under which emigration is absolutely necessary to their political elevation, cannot be disputed."

In 1854 Delany was elected president of the National Emigration Convention. In the mid-1850s he moved his family to Chatham, Ontario, Canada, and in 1858 he attended a meeting there called by abolitionist JOHN BROWN. The delegates, who included 34 blacks, adopted a provisional constitution for the United States—one they hoped would replace the existing document—that condemned slavery. Nothing further resulted from the effort, though Brown used the meeting as a springboard to his raid the following year at Harper's Ferry. In 1859 Delany sailed to Africa on behalf of the National Emigration Convention to investigate the valley of the Niger.

In July 1860 Delany arrived in London and attended the International Statistical Conference and a few months after that a meeting of the National Association for the Promotion of Social Science in Glasgow. He returned to Chatham in 1860. While he was working in Brooklyn, New York, in 1861, Southern troops attacked Fort Sumter, beginning the Civil War. When Lincoln finally agreed in 1863 to accept blacks in the Union army, Delany began recruiting African Americans and worked as an examining surgeon in Chicago. In 1864 he and his family moved to Wilberforce, Ohio.

Delany was commissioned a major in the army in February 1865 and ordered to Charleston, South Carolina, that April. With the war over, he served until 1868 in the Freedmen's Bureau. As a liaison between the white and black communities during Reconstruction, he prevented the outbreak of racial violence.

In 1872 Delany ran for lieutenant governor of South Carolina, representing a faction among Republicans at odds with their party's leadership. He lost the election, and his role in causing strife within the party generated the enmity of many African Americans who supported the Republicans for being more able to protect their civil rights.

Delany served as a trial judge in South Carolina from 1875 until 1876, after which accusations that he had defrauded a church of money contributed to his dismissal. He then supported a Democrat, Wade Hampton, for governor, and when Hampton won the office in 1876, he restored Delany as a trial judge.

Delany held that post until 1878, when he again began promoting colonization, this time to Liberia. He practiced medicine in South Carolina before returning in 1884 to Wilberforce, where he died on January 24, 1885.

Further Reading

Andrews, William L., ed. *Two Biographies by African-American Women.* New York: Oxford University Press, 1991.

Griffith, Cyril E. *The African Dream: Martin R. Delany and the Emergence of Pan-African Thought.* University Park: Pennsylvania State University Press, 1975.

Sterling, Dorothy. *The Making of an Afro-American: Martin Robison Delany, 1812–1885.* Garden City, N.Y.: Doubleday, 1971.

Ullman, Victor. *Martin R. Delany: The Beginnings of Black Nationalism.* Boston: Beacon Press, 1971.

Dellinger, David

(1915–   ) *antiwar activist*

During the 1960s, David Dellinger was chairman of the National Mobilization Committee to End the War in Vietnam (MOBE) and since then he has continued in his pacifist activities. He was born on August 12, 1915, in Wakefield, Massachusetts, to Raymond Pennington Dellinger, a prominent Republican lawyer, and Marie Fiske Dellinger.

Like his father, David Dellinger attended Yale, and he graduated magna cum laude in 1936. He studied at Oxford the following year, at Yale Divinity School from 1938 to 1939, and at the Union Theological Seminary in New York City from 1939 to 1940. Although an assistant minister when the United States entered World War II, and thus entitled to a deferment, Dellinger adhered to his strong pacifist principles and refused to register for the draft. As a result, he served three years in prison.

Dellinger adopted a communist ideology, a "pure" one founded on true community, rather than the kind practiced by the Soviet Union. In fact, as much as he disliked capitalism he opposed the Soviets, insisting that Russia had "poisoned the left wing movement with dishonesty, opportunism, and violence."

In 1948 Dellinger merged the Committee for Non-Violent Revolution, a leftist pacifist group that he led, with the Peacemakers, an organization dedicated to participatory democracy and civil disobedience to fight injustice. In 1956 he helped found *Liberation,* a journal dedicated to radical leftist ideas. At the same time, he journeyed to the South, where he participated in numerous civil rights protests.

Dellinger opposed the Vietnam War, as he did all wars, and in the mid-1960s he began speaking at teach-ins on college campuses. In 1965 he called for the "immediate unconditional withdrawal" of American troops from Vietnam. The following year he traveled to North Vietnam (his first of several trips there) and once back home cochaired the Spring Mobilization to End the War in Vietnam, which sponsored large demonstrations in 1967. One in New York City attracted 400,000 protesters; another in San Francisco attracted 75,000.

In October 1967, during a march on the Pentagon, Dellinger, by this time a prominent leader within the New Left, discussed with the activist Rennie Davis the possibility of staging a protest the following August in Chicago to coincide with the Democratic National Convention. Dellinger now chaired his own Spring Mobilization, recently renamed the National Mobilization Committee to End the War in Vietnam, or MOBE, and he and Davis, along with TOM HAYDEN, worked through that organization to create a plan for Chicago.

As August approached, Dellinger feared that Davis and Hayden intended violence at the convention, so he persuaded them to pledge their commitment to a peaceful protest. Although militant himself in wanting to disrupt the war machine, Dellinger deplored bloodshed.

Despite these pledges, developments indicated that peace would be impossible to maintain at Chicago. For one, MOBE was a loose confederacy of political and antiwar groups, and some activists associated with these, and some completely outside the MOBE effort, wanted violence. For another, Chicago's mayor, Richard Daley, refused to allow any permits for demonstrations, making it clear he desired confrontation by forcing the protestors to march illegally.

Violence began at the beginning of the Democratic National Convention, on August 23, 1968, and continued throughout the conclave. At one point Dellinger tried to calm a crowd at Grant Park by organizing it to march on the Amphitheater, where the convention delegates were meeting, but bedlam and police opposition made a peaceful demonstration impossible. Dellinger later said, "We thought if we could hold the MOBE together, we could minimize the damage."

A few months after Chicago, the federal government indicted Dellinger and seven others–a group the press called the Chicago Eight–for conspiracy to riot. At his trial in 1969, Dellinger told the judge:

> You wanted us to be like good Germans supporting the evils of our decade and then when we refused to be good Germans and came to Chicago and demonstrated, now you want us to be like good Jews, going quietly and politely to the concentration camps while you and the court suppress freedom and the truth.

In the end, a jury convicted him of rioting, though it rejected the conspiracy charge. Three years later a higher court overturned the conviction. When the 1960s ended, Dellinger continued his commitment to pacifist and leftist campaigns, including when he led demonstrations in the mid-1980s protesting U.S. military intervention in Central America and when he participated in 1992 in a 42-day fast as part of an attempt to secure "justice and peace in the Americas." In 1996 he returned to Chicago to lead one of several protests at the Democratic National Convention; this time the protests were peaceful.

Further Reading

Dellinger, David. *From Yale to Jail: The Life Story of a Moral Protester.* New York: Pantheon, 1993.

Deloria, Vine, Jr.
(1933–) *Indian rights activist*

Vine Deloria, Jr., of the Hunkpapa Lakota Sioux, is an activist for Indian rights. A prolific writer, he was born on March 26, 1933, in Martin, South Dakota, to Vine Deloria, Sr., and Barbara Eastburn Deloria.

Vine Deloria, Jr., is a member of a prominent Indian family; his great grandfather was a medicine man and leader of the White Swan Band of the Yankton Dakota Sioux; his grandfather was a missionary priest with the Episcopal Church; and his father was the first Indian to hold an executive post with the church. Deloria graduated from high school in Faribault, Minnesota, and served in the Marine Corps from 1954 to 1956. He then attended Iowa State University and received a bachelor's degree in 1958.

Deloria wanted to follow his father and grandfather in the Episcopal Church and in 1963 earned a theology degree from Augustana Lutheran Seminary in Rock Island, Illinois. But he lost faith in Christianity, and in 1964 he served as executive director of the National Congress of American Indians in Washington, D.C. He left the group in 1967 after struggling to help it raise funds and to prevent factions from tearing it apart.

That year Deloria enrolled in law school at the University of Colorado. It was an activist era, when the black civil rights movement was intensifying and American Indians were beginning to organize to ensure their rights. Deloria believed that with a law degree he could represent Indian causes and educate Indians in the ways of the courts.

In 1969 Deloria wrote his first book, *Custer Died for Your Sins: An Indian Manifesto,* in which he condemned the U.S. government's treatment of Native Americans. In this work he advocated a policy central to his beliefs when he stated that he wanted self-rule for Indians and that he wanted them to take pride in their own culture and separate themselves from white culture and politics. In *Custer Died for Your Sins* he decried the insistence that "Indians must be redefined in terms that white men will accept, even if that means re-Indianizing them according to a white man's idea of what they were like in the past and should logically become in the future."

From 1970 to 1972 he handled legal matters for the Northwest Coast tribes as they tried to enlarge their fishing rights. At the same time, he taught at Western Washington State College. From 1972 to 1974 he taught at the University of California at los Angeles and served as chairperson of the Institute for the Development of Indian Law, located in Golden, Colorado.

In his second book, *We Talk, You Listen: New Tribes, New Turf,* published in 1970, he detailed how whites had stereotyped Indians in writings and in movies. He also discussed the Euroamerican taking of land from the Indians and the different perspectives of whites and Indians about land. He asserted that Indians revered the land whereas whites exploited it, a practice that in time produced large cities lacking a heart or soul. "Within our lifetime the difference between the Indian use of land and the white use of land will become crystal clear," Deloria stated. "The Indian lived with his land. *The white destroyed his land. He destroyed the planet earth. . . .* Non-Indians have recently come to realize that the natural world supports the artificial world of which they are so fond. Destruction of nature will result in total extinction of the human race." American society can be saved, he insisted, by embracing the Indian attitude toward the land.

In 1974 Deloria wrote *Behind the Trail of Broken Treaties: An Indian Declaration of Independence,* which aligned him with the militant American Indian Movement (AIM). He described in sympathetic terms the events that led to that group's occupation of Wounded Knee, South Dakota.

From 1978 to 1991 he served as professor of American Indian studies, political science, and history of law at the University of Arizona in Tucson. In 1991 he relocated to the University of Colorado in Boulder, teaching at the Center for Studies of Ethnicity and Race in America.

His 1995 book, *Red Earth, White Lies: Native Americans and the Myth of Scientific Fact,* met with a generally hostile reception. One reviewer, John C. Whittaker, who described himself as an admirer of DeLoria's earlier works, called the new book "a wretched piece of Native American creationist claptrap that has all the flaws of the Biblical creationists [Deloria] disdains." Deloria wrote that Indian traditions provide a better way of understanding the world than does science, and then took this view to the extreme by condemning nearly all archaeological findings about Native American cultures and placing his faith in tribal religious stories about how those cultures developed.

Deloria retired from the University of Colorado at the end of the 1990s but continued to write, publishing in 1999 with David E. Wilkins *Tribes, Treaties, and Constitutional Tribulations.* He remained committed to his belief in the importance of Native Americans learning their culture, as evidenced in an interview he gave in the year 2000. "Young suburban Indians often can't distinguish between the Indians of their tribe and all the information put out about Indians in general," he said:

About six years ago, I brought together traditional people of different tribes for several

conferences on Indian knowledge. . . . Few of the Indians in the audience had heard real Indian storytellers tell about their own traditions. A storyteller would get up and speak for forty minutes and the entire audience would be in tears. People would come up to me and say, "I've never experienced anything like this in my life."

Further Reading

Biolsi, Thomas, and Larry J. Zimmerman. *Indians and Anthropologists: Vine Deloria, Jr., and the Critique of Anthropology.* Tucson: University of Arizona Press, 1997.

Deloria, Vine, Jr. *Behind the Trail of Broken Treaties: An Indian Declaration of Independence.* New York: Delacorte Press, 1974.

———. *Custer Died for Your Sins: An Indian Manifesto.* New York: Macmillan, 1969.

———. *We Talk, You Listen: New Tribes, New Turf.* New York: Macmillan, 1970.

DePugh, Robert
(1923–) *militia leader*

Founder of the right-wing Minutemen militia, Robert DePugh has led a controversial life. He was born in 1923 in Independence, Missouri, where his father served as deputy sheriff.

DePugh graduated from high school in 1941 and a year later enlisted in the army, though he opposed the U.S. entry into World War II for abetting communist Russia. DePugh's stint in the military did not last long; in 1944 he was dismissed for chronic nervousness and depression. In 1946 he enrolled at Kansas State University but left after only 18 months. He then held various jobs from 1947 until 1953, the year he founded the Biolab Corporation in Independence, which produced, most prominently, a dog food supplement. The company went out of business just three years later, at which point DePugh enrolled at Washburn University in Topeka, Kansas.

In 1959 DePugh reactivated Biolab in the small town of Norborne, Missouri. The following year, partly because of his disgust with the rise of Fidel Castro to power in Cuba and the lack of an effective American response to the communist leader, and partly because of the influence of literature issued by the right-wing John Birch Society and the House Un-American Activities Committee, he founded the Minutemen. DePugh described the group as a patriotic organization dedicated to stopping the enemies within the United States who sought to advance communism. At the same time, he was a member of the Birch Society.

DePugh considered the Minutemen a diverse group: a guerrilla warfare outfit ready to fight communists, a nationwide spy network reporting on treasonous activity, and a propaganda group distributing literature about the international socialist conspiracy and showing how to make bombs and ammunition. He said that he wanted to provoke the federal government—which he considered dominated by communist sympathizers—into repressive measures that would, in turn, cause the people to rise up against it. He edited the Minutemen newsletter, *Taking Aim,* which in 1964 advised its readers, "If you are ever going to buy a gun, buy it now."

That same year he held a paramilitary training camp in California that attracted 50 Minutemen of a total membership numbering several hundred. While involved in this, he broke with the John Birch Society after its leaders accused him of trying to take it over. In 1966 he founded the Patriotic Party, a political wing of the Minutemen, intended to be a high-profile public organization running candidates for office. By and large, though, the Minutemen operated in great secrecy, decentralized and divided into small groups. Members of the Minutemen stockpiled weapons, including rifles, submachine guns, and mortars.

In his 1966 book *Blueprint for Victory,* DePugh urged the privatization of government activities to reduce the budget deficit, claimed there must be a broad resistance movement to oppose socialists, charged that labor unions had been infiltrated by an internationalist socialist movement, insisted that the federal bureaucracy would soon destroy states' rights, and urged Americans to regain their freedom through a counterrevolution, violent or otherwise. That same year authorities arrested him for violating federal firearms laws. He was convicted in November 1966 and resigned as head of

the Minutemen in 1967 (though he continued as its unofficial leader). In 1968, while he was free on appeal, a grand jury indicted him of conspiring to rob several banks in Washington state. DePugh fled, and Federal Bureau of Investigation (FBI) agents captured him in New Mexico in July 1969. He served nearly four years of an 11-year prison sentence before receiving parole in February 1973.

Without DePugh, the Minutemen faded into obscurity. In the 1980s he reentered the radical picture by adopting Identity Christianity (the belief that Jews and blacks are inferior to whites and that white Gentiles will one day inherit the world) and published a survivalist book with advice on how to handle the catastrophe that would occur after, he predicted, the Federal Reserve recalled all paper money. He had another encounter with the law in 1991 and was arrested and later convicted on a morals and pornography charge involving an underage girl. In 1992 he was convicted on three counts of federal firearms violations.

The Minutemen revived in the 1990s without DePugh's leadership. DePugh has professed disgust with all politics and has retired from the scene, but his legacy remains one of taking up arms to fight what right-wingers call One World socialism and those within the United States active in promoting it.

Further Reading

Jones, J. Harry. *The Minutemen.* Garden City, N.Y.:Doubleday, 1968.

Stern, Kenneth S. *A Force upon the Plain: The American Militia Movement and the Politics of Hate.* New York: Simon & Schuster, 1996.

Dewey, John
(1859–1952) *education reformer*

A philosopher and writer, John Dewey was a leader of the progressive education movement that advocated students' active participation in learning. He was born on October 20, 1859, in Burlington, Vermont, to Archibald Sprague Dewey, a farmer and shopkeeper, and Lucina Airtimes Rich Dewey.

In 1875 John Dewey entered the University of Vermont. An average student in his early classroom work, he nevertheless developed an interest in philosophy during his senior year and was especially influenced by his teacher, H. A. P. Torrey. Dewey graduated in 1879 and accepted a job teaching at Oil City High School in Pennsylvania. There he continued to study philosophy and wrote an essay that was published in the *Journal of Speculative Philosophy.*

He returned to Vermont in 1881 and taught at a small academy in Charlotte so he could be near Torrey and they could explore philosophical questions. Torrey urged him to enter a doctoral program, and in 1882 Dewey enrolled at Johns Hopkins University in Baltimore, where he obtained a Ph.D. in 1884.

For the next 10 years Dewey taught at the University of Michigan (except for one year at the University of Minnesota) and developed the philosophical views that would lead him to advocate progressive education. He adopted the pragmatism of William James, meaning he believed ideas should be evaluated by their consequences—or how well they worked. But going well beyond James, he believed in using philosophy to advance reform—a type of pragmatism that became known as experimentalism or instrumentalism. He said the experimental methods used in the natural sciences should be applied to politics and social change. Dewey's thoughts coincided with the ferment in America called Progressive reform; he was on the cutting edge of a movement that attempted to correct the worst abuses caused by an industrializing society. As did many other intellectuals, he embraced Charles Darwin's theory of evolution with its environmental rather than supernatural explanation for biological change.

In 1886 Dewey married Alice Chipman; they had seven children. In 1894 he left Michigan to teach at the recently founded University of Chicago, where he served as chair of the department of philosophy, psychology, and pedagogy. With his wife, he began the university's laboratory school, a place to apply his educational methods. Dewey opposed teaching students through rote memorization. According to him, rather than being treated as vessels into which facts were poured, students should engage in analyzing and applying knowledge to practical situations; in

other words, they should "learn by doing." In 1899 he published *The School and Society,* in which he presented his educational methods and raised a storm of controversy over their validity.

In *The Story of Philosophy* (1961), Will Durant writes that for Dewey, "in an industrial society the school should be a miniature workshop and miniature community; it should teach through practice, and through trial and error, the arts and discipline necessary for economic and social order." If a student learned how to think rather than what to think, he or she would be better prepared to meet life's challenges and to grow. Indeed, for Dewey, growth was important and stagnation an abomination. "Not perfection as a final goal," Dewey said, "but the ever-enduring process of perfecting, maturing, refining, is the aim in living. . . . The bad man is the man who, no matter how good he had been, is beginning to deteriorate, to grow less good."

While Dewey continued his teaching and writing, he served from 1899 to 1900 as president of the American Psychological Association. He also engaged in several reforms then under way in the city, including JANE ADDAMS's Hull-House, established to help poor immigrants. In 1905 differences with the president at the University of Chicago caused him to accept an appointment in philosophy at Columbia University in New York City and an appointment in education at the school's Teachers College. He stayed at Columbia for the rest of his career.

While he was at Columbia, his writing—more so than his teaching, which many thought dry and uninspiring—made him America's leading philosopher. Among his many books there appeared *Democracy and Education* (1916), in which he advocated using education as a tool for social reform and said that democracy required widespread participation in politics.

An advocate of unions for teachers, in 1915 he help found the American Association of University Professors and through them strongly defended academic freedom. The following year he became a founding member of the Teachers' Union. He also helped organize the American Civil Liberties Union. Dewey supported America's entry into World War I—a stand that caused other reformers to criticize him—and after the war spent several years traveling and teaching overseas. In 1919 he lectured at Imperial University in Tokyo, and from 1920 to 1922 he presented several lectures in China. In 1924 he visited Turkey as a consultant on that country's school system, and in 1926 he lectured at Mexico's national university. Two years later he traveled to the Soviet Union to study Russian schools.

Dewey retired from teaching at Columbia in 1930, but the university made him a professor emeritus of philosophy in residence, with full pay, and he guided doctoral students in their studies.

Alice Chipman Dewey had died in 1927, and Dewey married a childhood friend, Roberta Lowitz Grant, in 1946; they adopted two children. John Dewey died on June 1, 1952, in New York City.

Further Reading

Fott, David. *John Dewey: America's Philosopher of Education.* Lanham, Md.: Rowman & Littlefield, 1998.

Hook, Sidney. *John Dewey: An Intellectual Portrait.* Amherst, N.Y.: Prometheus Books, 1995.

Ryan, Alan. *John Dewey and the High Tide of American Liberalism.* New York: Norton, 1995.

Dix, Dorothea Lynde

(1802–1887) *mental health reformer*

Dorothea Lynde Dix worked to improve conditions for the mentally ill and to organize hospitals for the Union during the Civil War. In her famous *Memorial to the Legislature of Massachusetts,* published in 1843, she tells how insane persons were held in "*cages, closets, cellars, stalls, pens! Chained, naked, beaten with rods,* and *lashed* into obedience!" Dix was born on April 4, 1802, in Hampden, Maine, to Joseph Dix and Mary Biglow Dix.

In 1812 Dorothea's parents moved their family to Barnard, Vermont, where Joseph, a converted Methodist, opened a wholesale and retail business and sold religious tracts. As Joseph's enterprise faltered and eventually collapsed, so too did Dorothea's relationship with her parents, and later that year, at just 10 years of age, she ran away from home. She returned for a brief period before leaving to live with family friends in Worcester, Mas-

sachusetts. Despite her lack of a formal education, at the young age of 14 she opened a school. She ruled her classes with stern determination and with a stiff countenance that reinforced her inflexible personality. Dix's students thought her dedicated but excessively strict. One of them later said, "It was her nature to use the whip, and use it she did."

In 1821 Dix settled in Boston, where she lived for a while with her grandmother. That same year she opened a school for young women and by 1824 had earned a reputation as a leading schoolmistress known for her ability to instill discipline and commitment in her students. At the same time, she taught needlework at the Boston Female Monitorial School, where teachers used innovative devices, including blackboards and maps. In 1824 Dix wrote *Conversations on Common Things,* a book that instructed young people in a variety of topics through a dialogue she contrived between an imaginary mother and her daughter. One reviewer commented, "We know of few publications which are better adapted for the purpose of family instruction, or for enlivening a winter evening's fireside." In the late 1820s she began writing children's stories, and in the early 1830s she opened a second school in her home to replace her first one, which she had closed.

In 1824 Dix began visiting jails and almshouses in Massachusetts and recording the conditions under which the insane lived. The following year she wrote *Memorial to the Legislature of Massachusetts,* which historian Thomas J. Brown has called "one of the most remarkable documents of the era." She began her report with vivid details meant to draw the reader into the ghastly lives led by the insane, such as a woman "in the horrid process of tearing off her skin by inches; her face, neck, and person, were thus disfigured to hideousness." According to Brown, "The memorial continued in a relentless succession of insane men and women paralyzed by cold, wallowing in filth, and confined in plank sheds without light." Although Dix wrote that most wardens and almshouse keepers were ignorant rather than intentionally cruel, she called them "indifferent" to the barbaric conditions over which they presided.

As Dix proclaimed her commitment to helping insane persons, she insisted that despite their loss of rational abilities they should be provided with improved conditions and treated with respect, for they were still capable of emotional responses. Rather than medical cures, she preferred building a stronger link between the afflicted and God as a way to give them peace. Dix pushed to protect the deranged from society by separating them from the sane in almshouses and jails.

State officials reacted to Dix by calling her descriptions fanciful and by defending their methods of treatment. In 1843 the Massachusetts legislature rejected her call to build an asylum for the incurably insane and instead expanded the hospital at an existing asylum in Worcester. Despite this setback, Dix hailed the legislative action as an achievement that resulted from her *Memorial* and the work of others.

Dix next inspected the mental facilities in several states and continued to present memorials to legislatures in which she urged them to build hospitals for the insane, a shift away from her earlier insistence on additional asylums. Her fame and persistence swayed many political leaders, including some who told about meeting her and becoming "spellbound," and she began insisting that therapy could cure most cases of insanity—though she considered religion, rather than medical science, the most effective remedy. In New Jersey her memorials and lobbying caused the legislature to establish a state mental hospital in March 1845, and one month later Pennsylvania followed suit. "If she had never entered the state," said one of Dix's New Jersey supporters, "this institution would not have been established."

Three years later Dorothea Dix took her crusade to Washington, D.C., urging Congress to raise money for mental hospitals by selling 5 million acres of land from the public domain. She insisted that the insane should be housed and treated in such hospitals rather than in jails or poorhouses. Dix claimed that because competition in a free society contributed to mental illness by placing undue pressure on people, America had a special obligation to the insane, whom she called the "wards of the nation." Reflecting her penchant for order, she believed insanity exemplified the turmoil found in society when reason gave way to passion, and she may well have acted as much from a desire

to prevent social chaos as from any altruistic motive to protect the insane. Dix evoked visions of pandemonium in writing about her travel: "I have myself seen *more than nine thousand idiots, epileptics, and insane, in these United States, destitute of appropriate care and protection.*"

Many congressmen opposed Dix's appeal, preferring to allocate parts of the public domain to economic development, including the building of railroads. Others expressed sectional bias and claimed her proposal would mainly benefit the Northeast. Dix finally convinced Congress in 1854 to pass a bill, but President Franklin Pierce said it allocated money for purposes other than those allowed by the Constitution, so he vetoed it.

When the Civil War erupted in 1861, Dorothea Dix threw herself into the Union cause with the same desire to exert self-control over emotions that she had expressed in her earlier crusade.

Dorothea Dix wrote reports with vivid details meant to draw readers into the ghastly lives led by the insane. *(Library of Congress)*

She even associated the conflict with mental illness when she said, "The South is literally insane on the secession question." Secretary of War Simon Cameron accepted her offer to work as a volunteer and gave her the power to assist in organizing military hospitals, especially in obtaining supplies and recruiting nurses.

Dix immediately went to work preparing facilities in and around Washington for wounded soldiers. In June 1861 she was given the official title of superintendent of woman nurses, but her strict rules, including a requirement that all nurses be in their room by nine each night, and her overbearing manner soon earned her a less flattering nickname, "Dragon Dix." She and the Sanitary Commission, formed by President Abraham Lincoln to help in organizing medical efforts, engaged in numerous battles ignited by her attempt to establish hospitals in the West independently. She also fought the military over her authority to staff army hospitals with nurses.

To Dix, as to her contemporary the Englishwoman Florence Nightingale, famous for her work in the Crimean War, nurses were more than medical assistants: They were the people who created an environment crucial to a patient's recovery. Nurses must maintain their composure, Dix said, and must be "enduring, forbearing; firm but kind." She saw nursing as a calling for women, as an extension of the duty of a wife or mother to care for her husband and children at home.

While Dix complained that "this dreadful civil war has as a huge beast consumed my whole life," her ongoing disputes with others caused her public standing to sink, and by 1863 she had squandered nearly all the goodwill she had cultivated during her crusade for the insane. Some observers thought her intentions good but her medical knowledge lacking. Although in the later stages of the war she continued to recruit nurses, she had little say in determining who would serve in the army hospitals.

Yet Dix stayed at her post beyond the South's surrender at Appomattox and personally tended to Secretary of State William Seward when he was stabbed by an assailant involved in the conspiracy to assassinate President Lincoln. Late in 1865 she returned to Boston and resumed her work with the insane. She lobbied state legislatures to build more mental hospitals, but her influence waned, and her efforts more often met with failure than with success.

Once Dix left the world of the schoolmistress for that of the reformer, she challenged society's traditional dominant value that a woman's proper place was in the home, particularly when her lobbying involved her in politics. Yet she never considered herself a trailblazer for women, nor did she embrace feminism. On the contrary, she criticized the Seneca Falls Convention, held in New York in 1848, that demanded rights for women, including suffrage:

> I do not think that women are oppressed in this country, and if they are intelligently educated, they will do themselves and the country, I think, a truer & nobler service by influencing men in right directions than in attending the polls, and attempting to share abroad, in all masculine pursuits.

She believed that if women strove for legal equality, they would lose their moral superiority.

In October 1881, while visiting the New Jersey State Lunatic Asylum, Dix fell ill with a pain in her lung associated with a recurring bout with malaria. The hospital, whose founding she considered one of her first great achievements, became her last home. She died there on July 18, 1887, her legacy that of having asserted "benevolent womanhood," rather than women's rights, to impose order and help the insane by educating society about their plight and by building mental hospitals.

Further Reading

Brown, Thomas J. *Dorothea Dix: New England Reformer.* Cambridge, Mass.: Harvard University Press, 1998.

Gollaher, David. *Voice for the Mad: The Life of Dorothea Dix.* New York: Free Press, 1995.

Lightner, David L., ed. *Asylum, Prison, and Poorhouse: The Writings and Reform Work of Dorothea Dix in Illinois.* Carbondale: Southern Illinois University Press, 1999.

Schlaifer, Charles. *Heart's War: Civil War Heroine and Champion of the Mentally Ill, Dorothea Lynde Dix.* New York: Paragon House, 1991.

Wilson, Dorothy Clarke. *Stranger and Traveler: The Story of Dorothea Dix, American Reformer.* Boston: Little, Brown, 1975.

Donnelly, Ignatius
(1831–1901) *populist activist*

A leader of the Populist movement and a widely read author, Ignatius Donnelly was labeled a visionary by some and the "Prince of Cranks" by others. He was born on November 3, 1831, in Philadelphia, Pennsylvania, to Philip Carroll Donnelly, an Irish physician, and Catharine Frances Gavin Donnelly.

Ignatius Donnelly attended Philadelphia's public schools and studied law under Benjamin Harris Brewster, later the attorney general of the United States, but he soon abandoned his legal pursuit to participate in a land boom out west. In 1856 he and his wife, Katherine McCaffrey, settled in Nininger, Minnesota, where Donnelly hoped to found a cooperative farm. His utopian venture failed during the Panic of 1857, an economic recession), however, and he turned to operating his own farm and entered politics.

Opposed to slavery, Donnelly joined the Republican Party, and when Minnesota became a state in 1859 he was elected lieutenant governor. Donnelly was reelected in 1861 and two years later won election to Congress; he held the seat until 1869. He supported President Abraham Lincoln's war policies and worked to expand railroad lines in Minnesota.

On the heels of a dispute with Republican leaders, Donnelly quit the party and in the 1870s affiliated with the Grangers and later the Greenbackers (who favored the use of paper money). He called for the country to move beyond the old issues stemming from the Civil War and to confront the new problems being caused by industrialization. He criticized the Republicans for deserting their heritage of caring for the common man so they could more selfishly serve the wealthy. He specifically opposed the high tariff that the Republican Party favored and their efforts to reduce the amount of paper money in circulation in favor of gold specie.

A gifted speaker, known for an oratorical power that kept audiences spellbound and assured a full gallery whenever he rose to address the state legislature, he presented his ideas through his lectures and through a newspaper he edited from 1874 to 1879, the *Anti-Monopolist*. During most of those years he served in the state senate, until he ran for Congress in 1878 as a Greenback-Democrat.

After his loss, Donnelly turned to writing books, and in 1882 he published *Atlantis: The Antediluvian World*, in which he tried to prove the existence of ancient Atlantis, which he insisted was located in the Atlantic Ocean. Among many fantastic claims, presented with disregard even for the archaeological knowledge of the time, Donnelly wrote:

> [Atlantis] became, in the course of the ages, a populous and mighty nation, from whose overflowings the shores of the Gulf of Mexico, the Mississippi River, the Amazon, the Pacific coast of South America, the Mediterranean, the west coast of Europe and Africa, the Baltic, the Black Sea, and the Caspian were populated by civilized nations.
>
> The implements of the "Bronze Age" of Europe were derived from Atlantis. The Atlanteans were also the first manufacturers of iron.
>
> The Phoenician alphabet, parent of all European alphabets, was derived from an Atlantis alphabet, which was also conveyed from Atlantis to the Mayas of Central America.

In 1883 Donnelly's second work, *Ragnarok: The Age of Fire and Gravel*, in which he linked the clay, gravel, and silt found on the Earth's surface to a long-ago contact with a comet, appeared. These two books sold widely and made Donnelly wealthy, yet he returned to politics. In 1884 he lost a race for Congress, then in 1887 he won election to the state legislature. The following year he published *The Great Cryptogram*, in which he tried to prove it was Francis Bacon who wrote the works attributed to Shakespeare.

Donnelly published *Caesar's Column: A Story of the Twentieth Century* in 1891, by which time he was heavily involved in the agricultural reform movement to help farmers suffering from economic hardship and was leader of the Farmers' Alliance. Written as a novel, *Caesar's Column* told of a future society dominated by a wealthy few and filled with greed and violence. A dictatorial plutocracy completely exploits the masses, both farmers and industrial workers, and remains in power through the brutal use of military force. In the end, this society collapses through a great rebellion; only a few people escape, and they begin a utopian Christian socialist state.

Caesar's Column expressed the anger in the farmers' reform movement, the belief that society as constituted in the late 19th century with its disparity in wealth and grasping materialism would end as Donnelly described. The historian Richard Hofstadter has said, "It is perhaps a childish book, but . . . it affords a frightening glimpse into the ugly potential of frustrated popular revolt. . . . It came at a moment when the threat of social apocalypse seemed to many people not at all remote."

Donnelly led the Farmers' Alliance into the Populist Party, organized to change the country's economic system by making it more responsive to farmers and workers, particularly by nationalizing the country's railroads and providing a government system of low-cost loans that would compete with existing banks. Donnelly wrote the preamble to the Populist Party platform, which declared in part: "The fruits of toil of millions are boldly stolen to build up colossal fortunes for a few, unprecedented in the history of mankind; and the possessors of these, in turn, despise the Republic and endanger liberty."

Donnelly ran as the Populist candidate for governor of Minnesota in 1892 but lost by a wide margin. He supported the merger of the Populist and Democratic Parties for the 1896 presidential campaign, but with reservations. Later he regretted his stand, saying that the merger robbed the Populists of their separate identity and prevented the enacting of broader reforms. He ran unsuccessfully for vice president under the Populist banner in 1900, and then he once again served in the Minnesota legislature.

After the death of his first wife, Donnelly married a woman many years his junior, Marian Hanson, on February 22, 1898. He died on January 1, 1901. Ignatius Donnelly was known for his advocacy for the disadvantaged and for his rekindling the public's interest in Atlantis with a story as fantastical as the possibility that the Populist Party would ever replace the Republicans or Democrats.

Further Reading
Anderson, David D. *Ignatius Donnelly.* Boston: Twayne Publishers, 1980.
Ridge, Martin. *Ignatius Donnelly: The Portrait of a Politician.* St. Paul: Minnesota Historical Society Press, 1991.

Douglass, Frederick
(ca. 1818–1895) *abolitionist*

Born into slavery, Frederick Douglass escaped from his master and became a leading abolitionist whose articulate and moving description of his life, in speeches and written narratives, gave strength and direction to the antislavery cause. Douglass was born in a log cabin set among the woods of northern Talbot County, Maryland, most likely in 1818. That he was unsure of the date—he claimed February 14 for his birthday—and that he never knew who his father was stood as testimony to his status as a slave.

Douglass was the son of a white father and a slave mother, Harriet Bailey, who was part Indian. His grandmother, Betsy Bailey, raised him until he reached age six, at which time his master took him from her to Wye House, a plantation along the Wye River, a few miles from his place of birth. Such separations occurred frequently among slaves and contributed to the instability suffered by their families.

In 1825 Frederick's master sent him to live with Hugh and Sophia Auld in Baltimore. Douglass later said he was transferred to the Aulds so he could care for the couple's two-year-old son, but his master may also have seen something special in Douglass and wanted him to expand his horizons beyond the plantation. Several years later Douglass portrayed Sophia in his autobiography as affectionate and kind: "I had been treated as a *pig* on the plantation," he said. "In this new house I was treated as a *child.*"

For reasons unclear, Sophia Auld taught Frederick Douglass to read. She may have done so thinking every child should be educated, or she may have wanted to "experiment" with him to see whether an African American was capable of such learning. When Hugh Auld found out about the lessons, he ordered them stopped. "If you learn him how to read," he said, "he'll want to know how to write; and this accomplished, he'll be running away with himself." Hugh Auld realized the importance of keeping slaves ignorant lest they be exposed to antislavery literature.

Indeed, that happened to Douglass; at age 13 he learned what abolition meant, and in newspaper articles he read about antislavery petitions that were being submitted to Congress. Eight years after being sent to the Aulds, Douglass was ordered back to the plantation in 1833 and sent to Edward Covey, a slave breaker. Covey beat Douglass incessantly until he turned on him, an event that Douglass later remembered as having "revived a sense of my own manhood." In April 1836 he and several other slaves plotted to run away, going so far as to gather their meager possessions in knapsacks. But before they could act, their plan was discovered.

Douglass's master then sent him back to the Aulds in Baltimore, and he worked in shipyards as an independent laborer, meaning that although he was still a slave, he worked for wages. While living in the city, he met Anna Murray, a domestic slave, and determined to marry her.

When Hugh Auld demanded that Douglass quit his job, the young slave decided to run away, and with Anna's help he devised a plan whereby he obtained the papers of a free seaman. Finally, in September 1838 he fled, and traveling by train and ferry, he arrived first in Delaware, then in Pennsylvania, and finally in New York City. It was a close escape: At one point a ship's captain he had known in Baltimore looked straight at him, and Douglass trembled as he thought he would be turned in, but the captain ignored him.

Anna soon followed Douglass to New York City, and as planned, they married. The couple then moved to New Bedford, Massachusetts. By that time Douglass had heard the prominent abolitionist WILLIAM LLOYD GARRISON speak and was reading Garrison's antislavery newspaper, *The Liberator*. In 1839 Douglass arose at a church meeting in New Bedford and declared himself opposed to proposals then circulating to free slaves and colonize them in Africa. Slavery should be ended, he said, but those freed should stay in the United States. He told also about his experiences as a slave.

In 1841 Douglass attended a meeting of the Massachusetts Antislavery Society, in which he again recounted his life as a slave, and his words so moved the audience that they elicited handshakes from Garrison and another abolitionist leader, WENDELL PHILLIPS. Douglass felt as if he had been accepted into the abolitionist movement. The antislavery society hired him as a lecturer, and in his speeches he not only criticized slavery in the South but also Jim Crow segregation practices in the North. One observer, previously skeptical about Douglass's abilities, heard the runaway slave speak and called him "chaste in language, brilliant in thought, truly eloquent in delivery."

In November 1842 Douglass joined the protests surrounding George Latimer, an African American who had been arrested and jailed in Boston on order from a judge in Virginia who claimed the black man was a runaway slave. Abolitionists held Latimer rallies throughout Massachusetts, and Douglass spoke tirelessly on Latimer's behalf, claiming the victim had been "hunted down like a wild beast and ferociously dragged through the streets of Boston."

At the urging of Wendell Phillips, in June 1845 Douglass published his *Narrative of the Life of Frederick Douglass*. A short book of 125 pages with a preface by Garrison and an introductory letter by Phillips, it recounts in a simple and direct style Douglass's life in bondage. In his biography of Douglass, the historian Benjamin Quarles says, "It was absorbing in its sensitive descriptions of persons and places—even an unsympathetic reader would be stirred by its vividness if unmoved by its passion." Many readers, in fact, doubted Douglass could have written it—they considered it so erudite that it was beyond the intellectual and educational ability of a slave. But Douglass was the author and had worked without the help of any ghost writers or editors.

Here photographed some 15 years after the Civil War, Frederick Douglass was the most prominent of the African-American abolitionist leaders. *(National Archives and Records Administration)*

The *Narrative* so endangered Douglass, making it more possible he would be arrested as a fugitive slave, that he traveled to England to escape capture, promote his writing, and advocate abolitionism. In December 1846 British friends Ellen and Anna Richardson of Newcastle raised $700 and purchased Douglass's freedom. The action raised controversy in the United States, though, when many abolitionists criticized its tacit recognition of the legality of slavery. Only William Lloyd Garrison among the prominent abolitionists forcefully defended it. The Philadelphia Female Anti-Slavery Society asserted that the payment cost Douglass "one of the strongest claims to the sympathy of the community."

When Douglass returned to the United States in 1847, he founded *North Star,* an antislavery newspaper, in Rochester, New York. He likely named it after the lyrics in a song sung by runaway slaves: "I kept my eye on the bright north star, And thought of liberty." Residents of Rochester greeted the newspaper with mixed feelings. Quite a few of them thought Douglass should be run out of town; many whites, after all, had no sympathy for blacks, and others saw the abolitionists as troublemakers intent on tearing apart the Union. Nevertheless, the newspaper continued to publish under various names until 1863.

In the controversy then sweeping through the abolitionist movement over whether women should defy social restrictions and join men in fighting slavery, Douglass supported the complete sexual integration of reformist organizations. His stand complemented his support for women's suffrage.

Douglass differed with other abolitionists, most notably Garrison, in his belief that slavery could be ended through participation in the political system, and he supported the formation of the antislavery Liberty Party. At the same time, he spoke out against violence and said blacks should resist arming themselves. Yet he also said, "They who would be free, must themselves strike the blow." In 1849 he claimed, "I should welcome the intelligence tomorrow, should it come, that the slaves had risen in the South." And in 1850 he said, "The only way to make the Fugitive Slave Law a dead letter is to make half a dozen or so dead kidnappers."

In 1856 Douglass met the radical abolitionist JOHN BROWN, who visited him in Rochester. The meeting occurred after Brown had shot and hacked to death three proslavery settlers at Pottawatomie, Kansas. Brown told Douglass about his plans for expansion of the Underground Railroad and the formation of a state in the Appalachian mountains where runaway slaves could live in freedom. (The two had met for the first time in 1848 when Brown outlined for Douglass a plan to arm runaways and others so they could raid plantations.) While staying at Douglass's home early in 1858, Brown wrote letters to sympathizers, asking them to finance an unspecified venture against slavery; apparently Brown tried to interest Douglass in a plot that would use violence to free slaves.

Douglass and Brown conferred again at a quarry in Chambersburg, Pennsylvania, in 1859, when Brown told Douglass about a plan he had devised to capture the federal arsenal at Harper's Ferry, Virginia (today, Harpers Ferry West Virginia), and incite a slave revolt. Brown tried to recruit Douglass, saying, "I want you for a special purpose," but Douglass refused and advised Brown that the plan would fail.

After Brown led the raid and was captured, newspapers published a note seized along with the fiery abolitionist. Dated December 7, 1857, and signed by Douglass, it said, "My dear Cpt. Brown, I am very busy at home. Will you Please, come up with my son Fred and take a mouthful with me?" The note revealed nothing about a conspiracy, but excited by the raid at Harper's Ferry, the governor of Virginia suspected that Douglass had been involved in the plot, and he issued an order for the former slave's capture. Douglass subsequently fled to Canada, then to England and Scotland before returning to the United States.

With the outbreak of the Civil War, Douglass worked to convince President Abraham Lincoln to add to his goal of saving the Union that of ending slavery. He said, "To fight against slaveholders, without fighting against slavery, is but a half-hearted business, and paralyzes the hands engaged in it." He objected to Lincoln's policy of returning runaway slaves to their masters, and he criticized the president for rescinding General John C. Fremont's orders to emancipate slaves in Missouri.

Douglass also worked for acceptance of blacks in the Union army, and he traveled through upstate New York persuading them to enlist. He first signed up his youngest son, Charles, and then recruited more than 100 men to serve in the 54th Massachusetts Regiment. (Another son, Lewis, also joined the regiment.) Douglass denounced the Confederates' claim that they would consider captured black soldiers slave insurrectionaries, a status that would result in their being sentenced to death.

In summer 1863 Douglass met with Lincoln for the first time. He told friends he was impressed with the president and believed that Lincoln was maturing in his views and could be trusted to stand firmly behind African Americans.

After the Civil War Douglass continued his activism. In 1866 he helped begin the American Equal Rights Association to work for women's suffrage and to protect black voting rights. He participated extensively in Republican politics and in 1868 supported Ulysses S. Grant for president. In 1870 he and his sons began publishing the *New National Era,* a newspaper in Washington, D.C. In 1877 President Rutherford B. Hayes appointed him U.S. marshal for the District of Columbia. Over the next few years he held other public offices, most notably minister to Haiti. In 1884 his second marriage, to a white woman, Helen Pitts, evoked criticism from those who opposed interracial marriage.

In 1892 Douglass published *Life and Times of Frederick Douglass,* an expanded version of his autobiography. That same year he scathingly criticized the increased lynchings of blacks in the South. At a meeting with African-American students at Atlanta University, he said, "Be not discouraged. There is a future for you and a future for me. . . . The Negro degraded, indolent, lazy, indifferent to progress, is not objectionable to the average public mind. Only as we rise . . . do we encounter opposition."

On February 20, 1895, Douglass spoke in Washington at a meeting of the Women's Council, a group advocating women's rights. Later that evening he collapsed on the floor of his Cedar Hill home and died. African Americans traveled in large numbers to mourn his passing. As one reporter described, "Here and there in the long, persistent stream of humanity, came one bearing a flower, a fern leaf or a bouquet which was silently laid upon the casket."

Further Reading

Bontemps, Arna. *Free at Last: The Life of Fredrick Douglass.* New York: Dodd, Mead, 1971.

Douglass, Frederick. *Narrative of the Life of Frederick Douglass.* New York: Modern Library, 2000.

Foner, Philip S. *Frederick Douglass: A Biography.* New York: Citadel Press, 1964.

McFeely, William S. *Frederick Douglass.* New York: Touchstone Books, 1991.

Quarles, Benjamin. *Frederick Douglass.* Washington, D.C.: Associated Publishers, 1948.

Dow, Neal
(1804–1897) *prohibitionist*

Author of the "Maine Law," which banned the consumption of alcohol, Neal Dow was a leader in the prohibition movement. He was born on March 20, 1804, in Portland, Maine, to devout Quakers, Josiah Dow and Dorcas Allen Dow.

Neal Dow attended public schools in Portland and the Friends' Academy in New Bedford, Massachusetts, and wanted to enroll in college and study law, but his parents insisted that he enter his father's tanning business, so he did. He eventually became a partner in the firm and one of the leading businessmen in Maine.

Dow's Quaker background, combined with the bad effects of alcohol that he witnessed among the men he employed in his tannery, caused him at age 24 to make his first public address against drinking. Near the same time, he joined the temperance activities of the Maine Charitable Mechanics' Association, formed by skilled workers to promote their self-improvement. The intensity of Dow's commitment was evident in an address he made to the association in July 1829:

> Brethren, why does not our blood chill, when we look upon scenes of misery, and suffering, and wretchedness, which exist every where around us, and which intemperate men bring upon themselves. . . . Facts will support us in asserting that the practice of drinking ardent spirits . . . results in greater misery and suffering to more individuals than any other custom. . . . Not so trifling are the consequence of intemperance . . . for it destroys its unhappy victims as effectually as the flames.

In 1830 Dow married Maria Cornelia Durant Maynard; they had nine children, only five of whom lived past infancy. Dow served as a delegate to the Portland Young Men's Temperance Society in 1834 and helped organize the Maine State Temperance Society. In the late 1830s he formed the Maine Temperance Union to pursue a complete ban on alcohol. The work of this group and others led the state legislature in 1846 to pass a prohibition law, but it contained so many loopholes Dow promised to get a tougher bill passed.

Dow won election as mayor of Portland in 1851 and from that position lobbied the legislature. Later that year both houses passed the bill he desired. The "Maine Law," as it was called, earned Dow a reputation around the country and overseas as America's leading temperance advocate. In 1853 he served as president of the World's Temperance Convention in New York City.

Dow again won election as Portland's mayor in 1855, and a riot broke out in the city to protest prohibition. The uprising caused the legislature to rescind the Maine Law, but in 1858 it was again enacted. Evidence indicates that the riot had been plotted by Dow's opponents, who not only disliked his prohibitionist stand but also his role in helping found the state's Republican Party and his support of other reforms, such as abolition.

Dow served in the Union army during the Civil War and was wounded and captured by the Confederates. After the war he traveled widely in his continued campaign against alcohol. In 1880 he ran for president as the candidate of the Prohibition Party and won a little more than 10,000 votes. In 1884 he campaigned for a prohibition amendment to the Maine constitution, and it was passed. Dow died in Portland on October 2, 1897.

Further Reading
Byrne, Frank L. *Prophet of Prohibition: Neal Dow and His Crusade.* Madison: State Historical Society of Wisconsin, 1961.
"Neal Dow." Available online. URL: http://www.prohibitionists.org/History/votes/Neal Dow bio.htm. Downloaded on March 25, 2002.

Du Bois, W. E. B.
(William Edward Burghardt Du Bois)
(1868–1963) *civil rights activist, communist*

An African-American historian, sociologist, civil rights activist, and communist, W. E. B. Du Bois tried to improve the rights of black Americans. He was born on February 23, 1868, in Great Barrington, Massachusetts, to Alfred Du Bois, who was of French and African descent, and Mary Sylvina Burghardt Du Bois, member of a black family long resident in the town.

Shortly after William's birth, Alfred deserted his family, leaving the youngster to be raised by his mother. He was, by his own account, a dutiful New Englander, attending the Congregational church and working hard at school. He displayed his literary talent at age 15 when he became a correspondent for a black newspaper, the *New York Globe.*

In 1885 Du Bois traveled to Nashville, Tennessee, to attend Fisk University, recently founded as a black college. His exposure to African Americans from different backgrounds broadened him intellectually, while his contact with white racism took him aback. He described the South with its color caste system as barbaric. Du Bois compiled an excellent academic record and graduated from Fisk in 1888, whereupon he entered Harvard to take additional undergraduate courses in philosophy. There he was heavily influenced by the ideas of William James: his liberal views and emphasis on environmental influences in shaping human personality. James discovered in Du Bois a talent for history and encouraged him to pursue that discipline.

Du Bois began graduate study in fall 1890 and in 1892 enrolled as a special student at the University of Berlin. In 1894 he returned to the United States and began teaching at Wilberforce University in Ohio while completing his doctoral dissertation. He taught Latin and Greek but disliked the school's shallowness and preoccupation with religion.

In 1895 Du Bois received his doctorate in history from Harvard, and the following year the college published his dissertation as a book, *The Suppression of the African Slave-Trade to the United States.* In it he argued that economic pressures, rather than moral concerns, had ended the Atlantic slave trade.

In 1896 he married Nina Gomer, a Wilberforce student of German and African-American origins. They had two children. Du Bois then resigned from Wilberforce and agreed to undertake a study of blacks in Philadelphia for the University of Pennsylvania. During his one-year assignment, he lived in the black slums and interviewed some 5,000 people. *The Philadelphia Negro,* published in 1899, attributed African-American behavior to en-

vironmental and historical forces—especially slavery and racism—and not, as some whites alleged, to genetics.

At the time Du Bois was engaged in his study, he wrote an article for *Atlantic Monthly* in which he explained the dual identity of African Americans, an identity he called a double consciousness or a "twoness." The black person, he said, was part American, part Negro, with "two souls, two thoughts, two unreconciled strivings."

In 1897 Du Bois accepted a professorship in economics, sociology, and history at Atlanta University in Georgia, and he agreed to head the annual Atlanta University Conference for the Study of Negro Problems. Three years later he attended his first Pan-African Conference in London, in which he observed that race relations would be the leading problem of the 20th century.

Du Bois became increasingly convinced that for blacks in America to advance, they must be led by a Talented Tenth, a highly trained and scientifically minded African-American elite. Writing in 1903, he explained:

> How then shall the leaders of a struggling people be trained and the hands of the risen few strengthened? There can be but one answer: The best and most capable of their youth must be schooled in the colleges and universities of the land. We will not quarrel as to just what the university of the Negro should teach or how it should teach it—I willingly admit that each soul and each race-soul needs its own peculiar curriculum. But this is true: A university is a human invention for the transmission of knowledge and culture from generation to generation, through the training of quick minds and pure hearts, and for this work no other human invention will suffice, not even trade and industrial schools.

His reference to "trade and industrial schools" displayed his disagreement with his fellow African-American leader, BOOKER TALIAFERRO WASHINGTON. Du Bois contended that in advising blacks to pursue industrial education Washington was relegating them to second-class citizenship; that he was saying, in effect, African Americans were incapable of handling intellectual challenges. In *The*

Souls of Black Folk (1903), Du Bois reviewed Washington's autobiography, *Up from Slavery*, and established himself as Washington's rival.

Du Bois also disliked Washington's accommodationist philosophy, that blacks should forgo seeking civil rights so they could receive economic help from whites. Du Bois believed that blacks should be politically and economically equal to whites, and they should not have to wait for constitutional rights that whites already enjoyed. He expressed his views in 1906 at a meeting of the Niagara movement, which he led, at Harper's Ferry, West Virginia, site of JOHN BROWN'S antislavery raid nearly 40 years earlier:

> In detail our demands are clear and unequivocal. First we would vote; with the right to vote goes everything: Freedom, manhood, the honor of your wives, the chastity of your daughters, the right to work, and the chance to rise, and let no man listen to those who deny this. We want full manhood suffrage, and we want it now, henceforth and forever.
>
> Second. We want discrimination in public accommodation to cease.
>
> Third. We claim the right of freemen to walk, talk, and be with them that wish to be with us. . . .
>
> Fourth. We want the laws enforced against rich as well as poor; against Capitalist as well as Laborer; against white as well as black.

In 1909 a group of liberal whites founded the National Association for the Advancement of Colored People (NAACP) to end racial segregation, obtain equal education for white and black children, ensure the right to vote of African Americans, and secure enforcement of the Fourteenth and Fifteenth Amendments. At a meeting in May 1910 the founders chose the organization's officers; only one African American was selected, and that was W. E. B. Du Bois, as director of publicity and research.

In that post he founded, edited, and wrote articles for the NAACP magazine, *The Crisis*. The first edition appeared in November 1910, and within a few years he built it to a monthly circulation exceeding 100,000. Du Bois wrote with a strident voice, in the form of his Niagara Address, at one point linking the black drive for voting rights with that of women. "Every argument for Negro suffrage is an argument for women's suffrage; every argument for women's suffrage is an argument for Negro suffrage," he said. "There should be on the part of Negroes absolutely no hesitation whatever and wherever responsible human beings are without voice in their government."

The NAACP encountered considerable hostility. After *The Crisis* began appearing, Mississippi prohibited the circulation of materials "favoring social equality." Texas began debating a bill to disband the state NAACP. And in 1910 John Shillady, the national organization's white executive secretary, was brutally assaulted during a visit to Austin. "The haters of black folk beat him and scarred him like a dog," wrote Du Bois in *The Crisis*, "because he tried to talk quiet reason to Texas."

In May 1915 *Atlantic Monthly* published Du Bois's essay "African Roots of the War," in which he offered a Marxist critique of World War I and blamed the conflict on colonialism and imperialism. He antagonized many black liberals, however, when he supported the fight against Germany—they questioned dying for freedom in Europe when they had little freedom at home—and said that blacks should for the moment ignore the injustices they were suffering at the hands of whites.

After the war ended, Du Bois attended three Pan-African Congresses in Europe and one in New York. At the 1921 conference he called for complete racial equality for blacks everywhere and the eventual rule of Africa by Africans.

Near the same time, Du Bois engaged in a feud with the black nationalist leader MARCUS GARVEY. He opposed Garvey's separatist program and thought him a faker out to steal money from African Americans through programs such as his all-black steamship line. "From now on in our new awakening, our self-criticism, our impatience and passion," Du Bois said in allusion to Garvey, "we must expect the Demagog among Negroes more and more. He will come to lead, inflame, lie and steal. He will gather large followings and then burst and disappear." Garvey retaliated by calling Du Bois a "lazy dependent mulatto," who was ashamed of his mixed blood.

Du Bois harbored ambivalent attitudes about the Harlem Renaissance that burst forth in the 1920s. At first he embraced it, but then he worried that whites were glorifying it as a way to say, "Look how far blacks have come; now we do not have to help them." And he objected to the message being sent by the artists and writers through their themes—themes depicting loose morals—and through the way they lived. Daniel Levering Lewis writes in his Pulitzer prize–winning book *W. E. B. Du Bois: The Fight for Equality and the American Century, 1919–1963* (2000), "Du Bois continued to be nagged by misgivings. . . . Whirligig cocktail parties downtown and nightclubbing uptown that substituted for the integration of Manhattan restaurants and hotels, motorcades and Hudson River excursions to A'Lelia Walker's Villa Lewaro, sex in three genders, and demeaning voyeurism—it all began to grate on [his] civil rights nerves." It was a curious criticism in some respects, given Du Bois's own extramarital affairs, well known around the offices of *Crisis.*

While he questioned the Harlem Renaissance, Du Bois's political ideology shifted. In the mid-1920s he praised Russia's communist revolution and declared in *The Crisis,* "I am a Bolshevik." A few years later, he asserted in Garvey-like tones that the attempt to bring about racial integration in America had been a failure. "There seems to be no hope that America in our day will yield in its color or race hatred any substantial ground," he said, "and we have no physical nor economic power, nor any alliance with other social or economic classes that will force compliance with decent civilized ideals in Church, State, industry or art."

In 1934 Du Bois returned to Atlanta University, and the following year he published *Black Reconstruction in America,* a reevaluation of the period immediately after the Civil War. Du Bois argued that far from being a bleak period, Reconstruction was a time of great accomplishment because of the contributions made by the former slaves. Problems certainly existed, but the breath of freedom filled the air, and that mattered most. Of course, he observed, whites often saw it differently:

Of all that most Americans wanted, this freeing of slaves was the last. Everything black was

hideous. Everything Negroes did was wrong. If they fought for freedom they were beasts; if they did not fight, they were born slaves. If they cowered on the plantations, they loved slavery; if they ran away, they were lazy loafers. If they sang they were silly; if they scowled, they were impudent.

Most originally, in *Black Reconstruction* Du Bois said that black labor formed the wealth needed for industrialization. And he claimed that beyond the South, black labor created the foundation "of Northern manufacture and commerce, of the English factory system, of European commerce, of buying and selling on a world-wide scale."

In 1944 pressure from conservatives who disliked Du Bois's socialist views forced him to resign

W. E. B. Du Bois, an integrationist in the early 1900s, ultimately advocated black separation from whites and the adoption of Marxism. *(Library of Congress)*

from Atlanta University, and he returned to the NAACP in an honorary role as director of special research. In 1945 he published *Color and Democracy: Colonies and Peace,* in which he attacked capitalism and colonialism, and in 1947 he published *The World and Africa,* in which he surveyed events on that continent since World War II.

The following year Du Bois defied the NAACP and endorsed the Progressive Party candidate, Henry Wallace, rather than Democrat Harry Truman, for president. For this reason, and for broader ideological differences, the NAACP dismissed him. "Upon his departure from the NAACP in September 1948," David Levering Lewis writes, "he stood on a pedestal occupied by no other American Negro, the senior intellectual of his race and its unexcelled propagandist—idolized or reviled, depending on the region of the United States and the complexion and education of his audience."

In his later years Du Bois moved steadily toward fully embracing communism—and lost the support of all but a few African Americans. He became active in international peace and antinuclear movements, and the federal government indicted him in 1951 as a foreign agent. (That same year he married Shirley McCants Graham; his first wife had died in 1950.) He was acquitted, but his passport was revoked until 1958. That year he toured Western Europe and several communist countries and on May Day 1959 received the Lenin Peace Prize in Moscow.

In 1961 Du Bois officially joined the Communist Party and left the United States for good; at the invitation of Kwame Nkrumah, president of Ghana, he settled in that country. Two years later, after visiting Russia and China, he renounced his U.S. citizenship. He died of natural causes in Accra, Ghana, on August 27, 1963. "Here, then, is the dilemma, and it is a puzzling one, I admit," Du Bois once wrote. "No Negro who has given earnest thought to the situation of his people in America has failed, at some time in his life, to find himself at these cross-roads; has failed to ask himself at some time: what, after all, am I? Am I an American or am I a Negro? Can I be both?" The question would remain at the heart of the modern civil rights movement, blossoming in America at the time Du Bois concluded that he could not be both, that he could not be an American.

Further Reading

Du Bois, W. E. B. *The Autobiography of W. E. B. Du Bois: A Soliloquy on Viewing My Life from the Last Decade of Its First Century.* New York: International Publishers, 1968.

Lewis, David Levering. *W. E. B. Du Bois: Biography of a Race, 1868–1919.* New York: Henry Holt, 1993.

———. *W. E. B. Du Bois: The Fight for Equality and the American Century, 1919–1963.* New York: Henry Holt, 2000.

Rudwick, Elliott M. *W. E. B. Du Bois: Propagandist of the Negro Protest.* New York, Atheneum, 1968.

Dubinsky, David
(Dovid Dobnievski)
(1892–1982)   *union leader*

A former exile in Siberia, David Dubinsky was the leader of the International Ladies' Garment Workers' Union (ILGWU). He was born Dovid Dobnievski on February 22, 1892, in Brest-Litovsk, Russia, to Zallel Dobnievski, a baker, and Shaine Wishingrad Dobnievski.

David Dubinsky, who grew up in Lodz, Poland, which was then under Russian control, became a labor activist while still a teenager. At age 13 he began working in his father's bakery, and two years later he was elected secretary of the bakers' union local, an affiliate of the socialistic General Jewish Workers' Union. His leadership of a strike and his role in other labor protests led to his arrest and exile to a Siberian village.

But Dubinsky sneaked his way back to Lodz and resumed his work as a baker until 1911, when an older brother who lived in New York City helped him immigrate to the United States. He then found a job as a cutter in New York's garment industry and joined the ILGWU, Local 10.

Dubinsky advanced through the union ranks and in 1920 became the president of the local; in 1927 he combined the appointment with the office of secretary-treasurer. A socialist who opposed Marxism, in the 1920s he prevented the Communist Party from gaining control of the

ILGWU. Writing in *The Monthly Labor Review*, Gus Tyler states, "It was thus that Local 10 became the weight that tipped the balance against communist influence in the apparel industry during the 1930s." In 1928 Dubinsky quit the Socialist Party, and in 1932 he supported the Democrat Franklin Roosevelt for president.

That same year Dubinsky won election to the ILGWU national presidency (while also serving as secretary-treasurer, as he had for the local), and his effective leadership, combined with Roosevelt's prounion policies, caused the ILGWU membership to expand from 40,000 to 200,000. Dubinsky improved the union's finances and in 1935 also served as vice president of the American Federation of Labor (AFL), with which the ILGWU was affiliated.

Dubinsky helped found the American Labor Party (ALP), which supported Roosevelt for president in 1936 and again in 1940. When communist influence in the ALP increased, Dubinsky left, and in 1944 he formed the Liberal Party. Impressed by the cooperative spirit he found among workers in Europe, Dubinsky wanted the ILGWU to gain benefits for its members and to create camaraderie and solidarity in the labor movement. Under his leadership the ILGWU effectively ended sweatshops, obtained a 35-hour workweek, and won higher wages, along with insurance and retirement benefits. The ILGWU opened health and recreation centers for its members and sponsored cultural programs, including plays.

He also participated in numerous humanitarian projects. For example, through his leadership the union built an orphanage in China and after World War II provided relief funds to Israel and Italy.

David Dubinsky retired as president of the ILGWU in 1966. He died in New York City on September 17, 1982.

Further Reading

Danish, Max D. *The World of David Dubinsky.* Cleveland, Ohio: World Publishing, 1957.

Dubinsky, David. *David Dubinsky: A Life with Labor.* New York: Simon & Schuster, 1977.

Tyler, Gus. "David Dubinsky: A Life with Social Significance." *Monthly Labor Review,* October 1944, 43+.

Duke, David Ernest

(ca. 1950–   ) *white supremacist*

Leader of the Ku Klux Klan and the National Association for the Advancement of White People (NAAWP), David Ernest Duke briefly served as a state legislator in Louisiana. He was born in about 1950 (sources vary) into a middle-class family in Tulsa, Oklahoma.

After the family's relocation to New Orleans, Louisiana, in the 1960s, Duke completed his high school education there. He entered Louisiana State University in Baton Rouge in 1968 and while a student organized the White Youth Alliance (later renamed the National Party). In one incident Duke wore a Nazi-style uniform and marched outside Tulane University with a picket sign that read, "Gas the Chicago Seven," in reference to leftist political radicals then being tried in Chicago for disruption of the Democratic National Convention.

In 1973 Duke served as national information director and Louisiana Grand Dragon for the Knights of the Ku Klux Klan. He graduated from Louisiana State in 1974, and shortly afterward he traveled to Boston, where he incited angry white crowds to protest court-ordered school desegregation.

When the leader of the Knights was murdered in June 1975, Duke took over as the group's imperial wizard. He soon changed his title to national director to make it more palatable to mainstream audiences. To reach out to a broader following, he often held rallies that featured rock and western bands. And unlike more traditional Klan members he welcomed Catholics into the organization and permitted women to hold leadership positions. His wife, Chloe Duke, even served as an officer in the Klan. Duke filled his speeches with invective against blacks, saying, for example, that he sometimes felt like picking up a gun and shooting them. He urged whites to protect their heritage against the onslaught of African Americans.

Duke made his first run for political office in 1975 while operating his own advertising agency and serving in the Klan. He tried to get elected to the state senate but lost, though he polled a surprisingly high 30 percent of the vote.

The following year an encounter with deputies in Metairie, Louisiana, resulted in his arrest, and in

1977 he was attacked by a mob while visiting Klan members on the Marine Corps base at Camp Pendleton, California. Duke ran for the state senate again in 1979 and again lost. As Klan membership dwindled, a dispute in 1980 with a rival Klan leader led to his quitting the group.

In the early 1980s Duke formed the National Association for the Advancement of White People and published a newsletter, *NAAWP News,* that broadcast his racist views. In the late 1980s he attended meetings of the Institute for Historical Review, a group that believed that the Holocaust had never happened.

In 1987 Duke was arrested for disrupting a civil rights march in Forsyth County, Georgia. He then founded the NAAWP Forsyth County Defense Fund, which raised about $20,000 to help him with his legal challenge. He was released after paying a $55 fine; some observers believe that he kept most of the money that had been raised for his personal use.

When the Republican Party employed the race issue to frighten whites in the late 1980s and gain their votes, David Duke dropped his membership in the Democratic Party. In 1989 he ran as a Republican for the Louisiana House and astounded most observers by winning the primary. Many in the party subsequently disowned him, and the national party censored him, but the state party refused to take any action against him.

During the general election campaign reporters raised questions about his white supremacist views. He insisted that the pro-Nazi statements he had made years earlier had amounted to nothing more than "youthful indiscretion," but during the legislative race he was photographed shaking hands with the vice chairman of the American Nazi Party.

Duke won election to the House and told reporters that he would be tolerant toward all religious and racial groups. Yet from his legislative office he sold pamphlets such as *Hitler Was My Friend,* and he appeared at a rally in Chicago for the Populist Party, an anti-Semitic group. The crowd cheered when he told them that his election represented a victory for the "white majority movement."

Duke obtained his greatest support from those in the middle and working classes who felt squeezed from the top by the wealthy and from the bottom by welfare recipients, those who experienced or feared declining incomes and job opportunities, and those who believed blacks fell short of the standard of hard work and individual initiative that had made America great.

Duke's officeholding ended in 1991 when he lost a bid to become governor. He lost subsequent bids for the U.S. Senate and for the Republican presidential nomination, along with a race for the U.S. House in the year 2000.

Writing in the *Weekly Standard* in April 1999, Matt Labash observed: "Get Duke off the stump, where he almost sounds normal, and into private conversation . . . and you'll be treated to [an] exegesis on the Jews' responsibility for everything from the Russian Revolution to the Gulf War to airport metal detectors." To those who criticized David Duke's earlier affiliations with white supremacist groups, Duke said, "At least my past shows that I've always had the courage of my convictions. I'm a man who hasn't been afraid to stand up and say what I believe."

Further Reading

Bridges, Tyler. *The Rise of David Duke.* Jackson: University Press of Mississippi, 1994.

Klein, Joe. "Deconstructing Duke: What His Appeal Tells Us About the National Narcissism of the Past 25 years." *New York,* December 2, 1991, 627+.

Labash, Matt. "David Duke, Louisiana's Long-Playing Nightmare." *The Weekly Standard,* 26 April 1999, 23+.

E

Eastman, Charles
(Hakadah, Ohiyesa)
(1858–1939) *Indian rights activist*

A Native American doctor, writer, and Indian rights activist, Charles Eastman reflected his upbringing as a traditional Dakota Sioux and as a Christian. He was born in 1858 near Redwood Falls in southwestern Minnesota. His parents were Jacob Eastman, or "Many Lightnings," a Wahpeton Dakota Sioux, and Mary Nancy Eastman, a mixed-blood Sioux. Charles Eastman was given the Dakota name Hakadah, meaning "The Pitiful Last One," because his mother died soon after his birth.

At age four Charles was taken by his family to Canada in the wake of the Sioux Uprising of 1862. "In the general turmoil," he recalled,

> we took flight into British Columbia, and the journey is still vividly remembered by all our family. A yoke of oxen and a lumber-wagon were taken from some white farmer and brought home for our conveyance. . . . In our flight, we little folks were strapped in the saddles or held in front of an older person, and in the long night marches to get away from the soldiers, we suffered from loss of sleep and insufficient food.

It was thought that his father had been hanged by the government for his role in the uprising, but the elder Eastman had been confined to federal prison, where he had converted to Christianity. Following his release, in 1870 he and Charles settled near Flandreau, North Dakota. It was then that Charles followed his father in converting to Christianity and receiving a Christian name.

Charles Eastman attended Flandreau Indian School and from there Beloit College, Knox College, and Dartmouth College, from which he received a bachelor's degree in 1887. At Boston University he studied medicine as "the best way to be of service to my race," he recalled, and he graduated with a medical degree in 1890.

Later that year Eastman returned to the Sioux (Dakota, Lakota, Nakota) people, taking with him to Pine Ridge, South Dakota, his traditional customs and modern medical knowledge. There he saw his people suffer from the brutality inflicted by the U.S. Army in 1890 when it massacred the Sioux at Wounded Knee. He later said, "It took all my nerve to keep my composure in the face of this spectacle, and of the excitement and grief of my Indian companions, nearly every one of whom was crying aloud or singing his death song."

He complained about the massacre and about whites' stealing federal funds owed the Indians, and then left his job (some sources say he resigned, others that he was fired). In 1893 he and his wife, Elaine Goodale, a white teacher and poet, settled in Saint Paul, Minnesota, where he intended to practice medicine. The white authorities prevented him from doing so, however, and he turned to organizing programs for the Young Men's Christian Association (YMCA) on reservations. That year he began writing magazine articles, the first step in a career that would see him author many books.

Eastman resumed practicing medicine in 1900 with the Crow Creek Agency in South Dakota but again sided with Indians in complaints about government policies and was forced to leave his job. At that point writer Hamlin Garland used his influence to obtain employment for Eastman with the Bureau of Indian Affairs in a project to provide the Sioux with English names so they could protect their land titles.

During this time Eastman published four books, *Indian Boyhood, Red Hunters and the Animal People, Old Indian Days,* and *Wigwam Evenings.* His *The Soul of the Indian* appeared in 1911, reflecting the Indian folklore he had collected among people living in the Minnesota woods. These and his later works were known for communicating to whites Sioux legends and history; knowledge of them, he thought, would give whites greater understanding of Indians and cause them to treat Indians better.

In 1923 the government employed Eastman as an inspector in the Indian service, and he traveled to reservations trying to resolve problems. He died of a heart attack in Detroit, Michigan, on January 8, 1939.

Further Reading

Wilson, Raymond. *Ohiyesa: Charles Eastman, Santee Sioux.* Urbana: University of Illinois Press, 1983.

Eastman, Crystal
(1881–1928) *women's rights activist, pacifist*

A lawyer, feminist, and socialist, Crystal Eastman worked to prevent war and to ensure women's rights. She was born on June 25, 1881, in Marlborough, Massachusetts, to Samuel Eastman and Annis Ford Eastman.

Crystal Eastman graduated from Vassar College in Poughkeepsie, New York, in 1903, moved to Greenwich Village in New York City, and in 1904 obtained a master's degree in sociology from Columbia University. Three years later she graduated second in her class from New York University Law School.

She then worked for a private foundation engaged in investigating labor conditions in Pittsburgh, Pennsylvania. In 1910 she wrote a report based on her findings, *Work Accidents and the Law,* the basis for the first workers' compensation law, which she drafted while serving from 1909 to 1911 on the Commission on Employers' Liability and Causes of Industrial Accidents for New York state.

In 1910 Eastman married Walter Benedict, a Wisconsin insurance salesman, and moved to Milwaukee, where she led an unsuccessful campaign for legislation to establish state women's suffrage. The following year she returned to New York and cofounded the Congressional Union, which later became the National Woman's Party.

Eastman helped organize the Women's Peace Party in 1915, with JANE ADDAMS as chair, despite tension between the two activists. (Addams had criticized Eastman's bohemian attitudes for being too impulsively radical and too casual about sex.) Also in 1915 Eastman divorced Benedict, and in 1916 she married Walter Fuller, a poet and political activist. They had two children. From 1917 to 1921, with her brother, MAX EASTMAN, Crystal Eastman edited a radical magazine, *The Liberator.* Eastman opposed America's entry into World War I in 1917 and was executive director of the American Union Against Militarism. At the same time she joined ROGER NASH BALDWIN and others in founding the National Civil Liberties Bureau (for which she served as chief counsel)—later renamed the American Civil Liberties Union—to defend conscientious objectors from the draft.

In 1919 Eastman organized the First Feminist Congress and called for women to fight for their freedom. During the Red Scare of 1919 to 1921 (a hunt launched by Attorney General A. Mitchell Palmer for communists and other radicals), the federal government placed Eastman under surveillance for supposedly radical activities that threatened American security.

After women won the right to vote through the Nineteenth Amendment, Eastman and three other feminists drafted an Equal Rights Amendment in 1923. Presently she moved with her husband to London, where she wrote for feminist journals.

With the death of her husband in 1927, Crystal Eastman returned to New York City. She died there on July 8, 1928, of a kidney ailment. "Life is a big battle for the complete feminist," she once wrote in reference to her commitment.

Further Reading

Beard, Rick, and Leslie Cohen Berlowitz, eds. *Greenwich Village*. Newark, N.J.: Rutgers University Press, 1993.

Cook, Blanche Wiesen, ed. *Crystal Eastman on Women and Revolution*. New York: Oxford University Press, 1978.

Eastman, Max
(1883–1969) *editor, journalist, socialist*

Max Eastman was a socialist who became a reactionary. He was born on January 4, 1883, in Canandaigua, New York, to Samuel Eastman and Annis Ford Eastman.

Handsome, articulate, and intelligent, Max Eastman grew up with what he called a "shadow" hanging over his life from the "irrational emotion" that dominated his early years, a result of his father's debilitating ill health, his mother's episodes of depression, and the death of his older brother. Eastman graduated from Williams College in 1905 and entered the doctoral program at Columbia University, but he left it in 1911 without completing his degree.

Eastman lived in New York City's Greenwich Village, where bohemian habits and radical ideas permeated the social haunts, and he became a leading voice among its intellectuals. In 1913 he began editing a moribund leftist magazine, *The Masses*. Devoid of ponderous political prose, expressive of free thought, and desirous of liberating the individual, it presented a smorgasbord of unconventional views. Eastman recalled about *The Masses*, "I doubt if socialism was ever advocated in a more life-affirming spirit. We did shock the American mores with some gloomy-grim and cruel writing, and with saber-toothed cartoons that set a new style in both art and satire. We spoke our minds with unprecedented candor on both sex and religion."

Eastman so strongly criticized America's entry into World War I that the government closed down *The Masses* in 1917. The following year he was twice prosecuted under the Sedition Act for advising that the military draft be defied—and was twice redeemed by hung juries persuaded by his own brilliant testimony.

Later that year he and his sister, CRYSTAL EASTMAN, founded *The Liberator*, in which Max Eastman supported Russia's Bolshevik Revolution, pushed for women's rights, and called for a socialist government. Eastman was so attracted to Lenin's communist regime that in 1922 he traveled to Russia, married the daughter of a revolutionary official, and advised Bolshevik leader Leon Trotsky. But after Lenin died, Eastman grew disenchanted with the power struggle between Trotsky and Joseph Stalin, and he thought Stalin's rise to power spelled nothing less than disaster for communism.

Eastman returned to the United States in 1927 and found himself rejected by moderates and leftists alike. The moderates considered him a communist; the leftists, or at least those who thought communism promising, considered him a traitor for turning on Stalin. They particularly disliked his release of "Lenin's Testament," in which Lenin stated that he did not want Stalin to succeed him in office. Eastman also wrote several books about the Soviet Union's betrayal of communism.

In the 1940s Eastman worked for the conservative magazine *Reader's Digest* as a contributing editor. The assignment signaled his shift to the political Right, and in the 1950s he defended Senator Joseph McCarthy's hunt for communists and subversives, though he refused to implicate any of his former associates on the Left. Max Eastman died on March 25, 1969, in Barbados of a brain hemorrhage.

Further Reading

Garman, Bryan K. "'Heroic Spiritual Grandfather': Whitman, Sexuality, and the American Left, 1890–1940." *American Quarterly* 52 (March 2000): 90+.

O'Neill, William L. *The Last Romantic: A Life of Max Eastman*. New York: Oxford University Press, 1978.

Echohawk, John
(1945–   ) *Indian rights leader*

John Echohawk has been ranked among the most influential 100 lawyers in the United States while serving as executive director of the Native American Rights Fund, which he cofounded. He was born on August 11, 1945, in Albuquerque, New Mexico. His father, Ernest Echohawk, a Pawnee whose grandfather was a scout for the U.S. Cavalry in the 1870s, held a degree from the University of New Mexico, owned a surveying business, and worked in the oil fields. His mother, Jane Conrad Echohawk, was white.

John Echohawk grew up in Farmington, New Mexico, where he played high school football, was elected student body president, and earned an academic scholarship to his father's alma mater. At that time, in the mid-1960s, MARTIN LUTHER KING, JR.'s, civil rights movement caused Echohawk to realize that the possibilities for racial justice in America applied not only to blacks but also to Indians.

While still in college in 1965, Echohawk married Kathryn Martin, and over the years they had two children. Echohawk obtained a bachelor's degree in 1967 and then enrolled in the University of New Mexico School of Law as part of a new program to train Indians in the legal profession. He graduated in 1970 and was admitted to the Colorado bar at a time when there were only 20 Indian lawyers in the United States.

That same year he cofounded the Native American Rights Fund (NARF), located in California until 1971, when he moved it to its current headquarters in Boulder, Colorado. He formed NARF to ensure that Indians received the rights and privileges due them under various treaties with the United States. He considered Indian nations to be sovereign governments but ones to whom Congress owed special assistance because of treaty obligations.

In 1970 Echohawk worked through NARF to help the Menominee regain their tribal status, which had been revoked by the federal government several years before through a program called Termination. Under pressure from Indian groups such as NARF, President Richard Nixon an-nounced termination would be ended, and he convinced Congress to pass a law to that effect. Echohawk later said, "The salvation for the tribes was right there in the law books—in the federal treaties and promises. They were protected by the Constitution of the United States—it was right there. But most tribes had no money to challenge the termination and NARF was able to help."

Echohawk served as deputy director of NARF from 1972 to 1973, as its executive director from 1973 to 1975, as its vice executive director from 1975 to 1977, and then again as executive director, a post he still held in the year 2001. Under his leadership, in 1980 NARF arranged an agreement whereby the state of Maine returned 300,000 acres to the Passamaquody and paid them $27 million. NARF filed numerous lawsuits to protect Indian water rights in the West, and it has won court rulings affirming and protecting the right of Indians to hunt and fish on and off their reservations. In one instance NARF won damages for the Muckleshoot Tribe after dams built along the White River in Washington state during the early 1900s had destroyed salmon habitats.

NARF helped convince Congress in 1990 to pass legislation requiring that Native American religious items and bodily remains removed from Indian burial sites for display in museums be returned to the tribes. Another bill in 1994 protected the right of Indians to use peyote (a hallucinatory drug) in the ceremonies of the Native American Church.

In the mid-1990s Echohawk and his group filed suit on behalf of five Indian leaders to force the U.S. government to account for Indian trust funds held by the Department of the Interior. The accounts dated back to 1877, when the government began dividing tribal lands into individual lots and began collecting and holding moneys owed the Indians for rent, oil and gas royalties, and grazing fees. By the 1990s government auditors were unable to account for more than $450 million in trust funds, along with tribal assets totaling in the billions.

Senator John McCain of Arizona, chairman of the Indian Affairs Committee, said, "It's absolutely outrageous that the BIA [Bureau of Indian Affairs] cannot account for $2.4 billion of the Indian tribes' own money as a result of shoddy record-keeping." Echohawk commented, "We have all grown up with neglect and abuse. . . . We finally figured we shouldn't have to put up with this anymore." In 1999 a district court held the federal government in breach of trust.

In another case pursued by Echohawk and NARF, an appeals court ruled in summer 2000 that the federal government was responsible for the loss of use of nearly 3 million acres of land over a period of 109 years by the Alabama-Coushatta Tribe in Texas. The court ruled that the government had been given the responsibility to protect the land from encroachment by white settlers between 1845 and 1954, and that it must pay monetary damages for its failure to do so.

John Echohawk, who with his brother, Walter Echohawk, received in 1996 the American Bar Association Spirit of Excellence Award for outstanding achievement by minority lawyers, continues to fight for the treaty rights he believes essential to the pride and prosperity of Native Americans. He has stated, "Tribal governments are the oldest sovereign governments on this continent, and though there were lots more when the white man came, that the tribes are still here is a credit to the United States of America. There is an opportunity for the tribes to prosper again, as the federal government honors its treaties."

Further Reading

Nielsen, Nancy J. *American Indian Lives: Reformers and Activists.* New York: Facts On File, 1997.

Trimble, Stephen. *The People: Indians of the American Southwest.* Santa Fe, N.M.: School of American Research, 1993.

Edelman, Marian Wright
(1939–) *children's rights advocate*

An African-American lawyer, Marian Wright Edelman is the founder of the Children's Defense Fund (CDF). She was born Marian Wright on June 6, 1939, in Bennettsville, South Carolina, to Jerome Wright and Leola Bowen Wright.

Marian grew up in a family who emphasized community service. Her father established the Home for the Aged that helped elderly blacks in Bennettsville, a racially segregated town. Marian graduated from the local black schools and attended Spelman College in Atlanta, Georgia; while enrolled there, she studied at the Sorbonne in Paris, the University of Geneva in Switzerland, and the Soviet Union. During her senior year she engaged in a massive civil rights sit-in at Atlanta's city hall, for which she was arrested. Her experience in the protest and the growth of the civil rights movement convinced her to study law.

Consequently, with her course work at Spelman completed in 1960, she entered Yale University Law School. In 1963 she participated in the Mississippi voting rights drive, and later that year she returned to the state, law degree in hand, and became the first black woman to pass the Mississippi bar. As a lawyer for the National Association for the Advancement of Colored People (NAACP), she spent most of her time defending civil rights protesters who had been arrested. From 1964 to 1968 she headed Mississippi's NAACP Legal Defense and Education Fund. She said, "I realize that I am not fighting just for myself and my people in the South, when I fight for freedom and equality. I realize now that I fight for the moral and political health of America."

In 1968 she married Peter Benjamin Edelman, a staff assistant to the Democratic senator Robert F. Kennedy. They had three children. Later that year the couple moved to Washington, D.C., and Marian Edelman founded the Washington Research Project of the Southern Center for Policy Research to lobby for programs that would help poor children. In 1971 the Edelmans moved to Boston, where Peter served as vice president of the University of Massachusetts and Marian directed the Center for Law and Education at Harvard.

Marian Edelman expanded her work for children in 1973, when she began the Children's Defense Fund, based in Washington. Through the CDF she lobbied politicians and built public support for numerous programs, including those aimed at preventing teenagers from dropping out of school and becoming pregnant and those aimed at fighting child and drug abuse. Her work soon earned her the sobriquet "The Children's Crusader."

With Marian Edelman still at the helm, the CDF began its Leave No Child Behind campaign in 1992, the same year Democrat Bill Clinton won election to the presidency. Given her long-standing friendship with the first lady, Hillary Clinton, Edelman exerted considerable influence in the White House.

In the mid-1990s she expressed great concern about figures showing that the percentage of children living in "extreme poverty" had doubled since 1975 and that in 1992 there had been 850,000 cases of child abuse or neglect. Her Leave No Child Behind effort pushed for medical insurance and vaccinations for children, as well as for more money for Head Start educational programs.

In 1996 she sponsored the Stand For Children march in Washington, which attracted 200,000 supporters. She said, "Children are never going to get what they need until there is a fundamental change in the ethos that says it is not acceptable to cut [them from the budget] first." The following year she criticized President Clinton's welfare reform program, which she said left millions of children behind in poverty.

Edelman insisted in 1998, "The administration and others simply say the reforms are working. It's true that people are leaving the [welfare] rolls, but we don't know where they are going. We don't know whether they have jobs. We do know that a lot of them don't have adequate child care." And she complained, "We are an underdeveloped nation. All the European countries, including the Scandinavian countries—as well as Canada and Japan—do much better. These societies have committed themselves to focusing on children."

On August 9, 2000, President Clinton awarded Marian Edelman the Presidential Medal of Freedom. "I've always been for family first," she once said. "We have never taken a dime of government money at the Children's Defense Fund. We don't believe in government control. We call for families to take charge of their responsibilities, but then we try to help them assume those responsibilities."

Further Reading

Edelman, Marian Wright. *Families in Peril: An Agenda for Social Change.* Cambridge, Mass.: Harvard University Press, 1987.

———. *Guide My Feet: Meditations and Prayers on Loving and Working for Children.* Boston: Beacon Press, 1995.

———. *The Measure of Our Success: A Letter to My Children and Yours.* Boston: Beacon Press, 1992.

———. *Portrait of Inequality: Black and White Children in America.* Washington, D.C.: Children's Defense Fund, 1980.

Eliot, Charles William
(1834–1926) *education reformer*

Elected president of Harvard by a closely divided vote, Charles William Eliot was the initiator of the college's far-reaching reforms. He was born on March 20, 1834, in Boston, Massachusetts, to Samuel Atkins Eliot and Mary Lyman Eliot.

Charles Eliot's family was a distinguished one. His father was treasurer and historian of Harvard, mayor of Boston, a member of the state legislature, and, beginning in 1850, a congressman. His mother descended from one of Boston's leading merchants.

Encouraged in intellectual activities at an early age, Charles Eliot followed his father's example, and after graduating from Boston Latin School in 1849, he entered Harvard. Eliot later described himself at that age as "reserved, industrious, independent, and ambitious." He studied English, mathematics, and science, and he received a degree in 1853. He was appointed a tutor at Harvard in 1854 and an assistant professor of mathematics and chemistry in 1858. That year he married Ellen Derby Peabody.

But Eliot failed to win promotion at Harvard in 1863, so he spent two years in Europe before he was appointed professor of chemistry at the Massachusetts Institute of Technology in 1865. While overseas he had investigated European educational practices, and in 1869 he wrote an article for the *Atlantic Monthly* that advocated reform in America's schools.

Impressed by the article, Harvard's Board of Overseers turned to Eliot that year to fill the college presidency—but only after first rejecting him for the position and then reversing that decision and voting to approve him by a narrow margin.

Eliot assumed the presidency in October 1869 amid pressure from many faculty members to make changes. He firmly believed that Harvard needed to hire talented teachers with diverse backgrounds, and he began recruiting from other colleges in the United States and abroad. He encouraged research by establishing sabbaticals and by beginning the French and German Exchange Professorships. At Harvard's law school he began the practice of teaching by using actual court cases rather than abstract principles; at the medical school he introduced laboratory work and written exams.

In 1872 Harvard began to grant doctoral degrees, and in 1890 Eliot organized the Graduate School of Arts and Sciences. But he achieved his most far-reaching reform when he expanded the elective system. It had begun in a modest and halting way many years before his presidency. Eliot, though, wanted to give students much greater leeway in choosing their course of study, and he wanted modern subjects, such as English, history, and economics, to be placed on an equal footing with the more traditional Latin, Greek, and mathematics. Expansion of the variety of courses worked hand in hand with his desire to attract a diverse faculty, because Harvard would require more teachers from different disciplines.

Over the years Eliot's work extended beyond Harvard and reflected his desire to influence secondary education. In 1892 he served as chairman of the National Education Association's Committee on Secondary School Studies, more commonly called the "Committee of Ten." A report issued by the committee, and largely written by Eliot, recommended topics to be covered in Latin, mathematics, and history courses, and it asserted that secondary schools should prepare all of their students for college, even though a minority of them would continue their education.

The report influenced curriculums across the country and led to the 1906 founding of the College Entrance Examination Board, which established the format and grading system for written examinations required for college admissions. Eliot had advocated such examinations since the 1870s as a means of determining the qualifications of students entering college and pressuring secondary schools into improving their courses.

In 1910 Eliot edited The Harvard Classics, a series of books meant to provide a liberal education for those unable to attend college. He retired from the presidency in 1909 but continued to write and make speeches. He died on August 22, 1926, in Maine. He had married Grace Mellen Hopkinson in 1877, after the death of his first wife in 1869, and was survived by one of his two sons.

Further Reading

Honan, William H. "Looking Back at Forward Thinkers: Thirteen Innovators Who Changed Education." *New York Times*, November 2, 1997, sec. 4a.

James, Henry. *Charles W. Eliot: President of Harvard University, 1869–1909.* 2 vols. Boston: Houghton Mifflin, 1930.

Morison, Samuel Eliot. *The Development of Harvard University Since the Inauguration of President Eliot, 1869–1929.* Cambridge, Mass.: Harvard University Press, 1930.

———. *Three Centuries of Harvard, 1636–1936.* Cambridge, Mass.: Harvard University Press, 1936.

Ely, Richard Theodore

(1854–1943) *Progressive reformer*

An advocate of Progressive economics as a professor, Richard Theodore Ely was known to be temperamental to a fault. He was born on April 13, 1854, in Ripley, New York, to Ezra Sterling Ely, a farmer, and Harriet Gardner Mason Ely.

As a farm boy, Richard Ely carried wood, cleared fields, and milked cows; he also learned to value education from his father, a frustrated academic with a large personal library. Ely graduated from the schools of Fredonia, New York—the town he had relocated to with his family—and enrolled at Dartmouth College in 1872. Dissatisfied with his education, in the following year he transferred to Columbia College in New York City. There he developed an interest in philosophy, obtained a B.A. degree in 1876, and received a scholarship to continue his studies in Germany.

Under the influence of Johannes Conrad, an expert in the German historical school of economics, Ely found his interests shifting away from philosophy. He was attracted to the German theory that economics was not rooted in eternal principles but changed over time in reaction to social developments. Ely earned his doctorate at the University of Heidelberg in 1879 and then returned to the United States. Unable to find a teaching job, he wrote articles for popular magazines and tutored students.

In 1881 Ely obtained a position as instructor of economics at Johns Hopkins University in Baltimore, Maryland. Two years later he married Anna Morris Anderson; the couple had four children. Ely's teaching at Johns Hopkins coincided with the rise of the Progressive reform movement, which stressed that by acting through government, people could change society for the better. The new economics Ely had learned in Germany fit well with this outlook, and he tailored it to the Progressive spirit.

Ely believed that uncontrolled individualism bred greed, selfishness, and a splintering of society; the government, he insisted, should take an active role in regulating the economy. In particular, he said, it should reform factory working conditions and prohibit child labor. Ely supported labor unions, though he favored negotiating with management rather than using strikes as a weapon. At one point he advocated that Americans form a cooperative commonwealth to replace individualistic capitalism, but he later moderated his views to call for nationalization of selected industries, such as utilities, railroads, and mines.

Ely helped found the American Economic Association in 1885 and served as its secretary and later as its president. He was, however, considered by colleagues and students alike to be ill-tempered and prone to equating criticism of his work to a personal attack.

In 1892 Ely left Johns Hopkins to become director of the newly organized School of Economics, Political Science, and History at the University of Wisconsin. Under his guidance the college's economics program earned national acclaim. In 1920 he founded the Institute for Research in Land Economics, but after Progressives attacked him for siding with realtors, he moved the institute to Northwestern University in Evanston, Illinois.

In 1931, at age 77, Ely married 32-year-old Margaret Hahn (his first wife had died in 1923),

and they had two children. In 1933, after a dispute with Northwestern's board of trustees, he moved again, this time taking the institute to New York City, where he established it as an independent organization. Ely died in Old Lyme, Connecticut, on October 4, 1943.

Further Reading

Fink, Leon. "'Intellectual' versus 'Workers': Academic Requirement and the Creation of Labor History." *American Historical Review* 96 (April 1991): 395+.

Rader, Benjamin G. *The Academic Mind and Reform: The Influence of Richard T. Ely in American Life.* Lexington: University of Kentucky Press, 1966.

Evers, Medgar Wiley
(1925–1963) *civil rights leader*

An African-American field worker for the National Association for the Advancement of Colored People (NAACP), Medgar Evers was slain by white supremacist Byron De La Beckwith. Evers was born on July 2, 1925, in Decatur, Mississippi, to James Evers and Jessie Wright Evers.

Medgar Evers grew up in a racially segregated society that consigned African Americans to inferior schools, permanent poverty, and political impotency. Evers, who forever remembered the horror he experienced at age 14 when he witnessed the lynching of one of his father's friends, a black man accused of insulting a white woman, refused to accept this banishment.

He attended a segregated school in Newton, Mississippi; enlisted in the U.S. Army; and fought in World War II. On his return home in 1946, he decided to complete his high school education and toward that end enrolled in special classes at Alcorn Agricultural and Mechanical College in Lorman, Mississippi. His diploma in hand, he continued at the college, majoring in business and playing sports—he excelled as a halfback on the football team—and in 1952 received his bachelor's degree. The previous year he had married Myrlie Beasely (later known as MYRLIE EVERS-WILLIAMS); they had three children.

In July 1952 Evers began working for Theodore Howard as a salesman with Howard's insurance company in Mound Bayou, in the heart of the Mississippi delta. Howard turned out to be a major influence on Evers, convincing him to join the Regional Council of Negro Leadership, a civil rights group. Later that year Evers joined the Mound Bayou branch of the NAACP.

In 1954 Evers was appointed field secretary for the NAACP, a full-time job in which he encouraged blacks in the delta to organize for their civil rights. When during that year the U.S. Supreme Court ordered that public schools be desegregated, Evers demanded that Mississippi enforce the ruling. His high profile caused white supremacists to label him dangerous, and he was subjected to threats, beatings, and arrests.

Trouble began in 1958 when he was thrown into jail for sitting in the white section of a bus in Meridian, Mississippi. Then at a trial for a fellow civil rights protester he applauded the defendant, and the police in the courtroom beat him.

In the early 1960s Evers took his civil rights campaign to Jackson, Mississippi, where he advocated the hiring of black policemen and urged African Americans to exercise their voting rights and engage in economic boycotts. His activism brought yet more threats, to the point that he instructed his wife and children on how to duck should they hear strange sounds. He told Myrlie, "You've got to be strong. I want you to take care of my children. It probably won't be too long." In spring 1963 segregationists firebombed the Evers home; Myrlie, however, was able to put out the fire with a garden hose.

Evers's murder occurred just after midnight on June 12, 1963. He had been out late working for the NAACP when he pulled into the driveway of his home, grabbed some T-shirts emblazoned with the slogan "Jim Crow Must Go" for his children, and stepped from his car. At that point Byron De La Beckwith shot him twice in the back with a rifle. Evers staggered to his front porch and fell face down to the ground; his wife and children came running, the children screaming, "Daddy, get up!" He died later that night.

His death shocked the country and added to the turmoil surrounding the civil rights movement. Just a short time earlier Governor George Wallace of Alabama had vowed he would stand in front of

Civil rights leader Medgar Evers was murdered in 1963 by a white racist in Mississippi. *(Library of Congress)*

the "schoolhouse door" at the University of Alabama to prevent blacks from integrating the college. And just the day before Evers's murder, Wallace had confronted the federal marshals on the Tuscaloosa campus, only to step aside and allow the black students to enter.

The murder caused Congress to quicken its pace on civil rights legislation and caused blacks to intensify their fight in Mississippi for racial equality. Some African Americans began questioning the commitment to nonviolent protest—getting shot at made it hard to turn the other cheek—and the murder contributed to the feeling among whites and blacks alike that American society was hopelessly racist and deeply sick.

The fate of Byron De La Beckwith only reinforced that view. Within hours of the murder, police found the rifle he had used with his fingerprints on it. They arrested him, and he was tried in January 1964, but at a courtroom appearance where Mississippi governor Ross Barnett, an ardent segregationist, patted Beckwith on the back, the jury deadlocked. A second jury deadlocked in April, and Beckwith went free.

Over the years he openly bragged about how he had killed Evers, but it was not until the late 1980s, after the Jackson *Clarion-Ledger* revealed evidence of jury tampering in the second trial, that the case was reopened. A new trial was held early in 1994, and Beckwith was found guilty and sentenced to life in prison. "All I want to do," Myrlie Evers responded, "is say, 'Yeah, Medgar! Yeah Medgar! Yes Yes!'"

Further Reading

Evers, Charles. *Evers.* New York: World Publishing, 1971.

Evers-Williams, Myrlie. *For Us, the Living.* Jackson: University Press of Mississippi, 1996.

Vollers, Maryanne. *Ghosts of Mississippi: The Murder of Medgar Evers, the Trials of Byron De La Beckwith, and the Haunting of the New South.* Boston: Little, Brown, 1995.

Evers-Williams, Myrlie
(Myrlie Beasely Evers)
(1933–) *civil rights leader*

In the decades since a white supremacist murdered her husband, the civil rights activist MEDGAR WILEY EVERS, Myrlie Evers-Williams has compiled a long list of her own accomplishments in her commitment to work for the benefit of African Americans. Born Myrlie Beasely on March 17, 1933, in Vicksburg, Mississippi, to James Van Dyke Beasley, a delivery man, and Mildred Washington Beasely, she grew up in the racially segregated society that characterized the Deep South in her youth.

Because Myrlie's parents separated and her mother left Vicksburg, Myrlie was raised by her grandmother, Annie McCain Beasely, and an aunt, Myrlie Beasely Polk, both of whom were schoolteachers. Myrlie graduated from Magnolia High School in 1950 and enrolled at Alcorn Agricultural and Mechanical College in Lorman, Mis-

sissippi, where she majored in education. There she met Medgar Evers, a fellow student, and they married in December 1951. While Medgar continued his education, Myrlie dropped out. In 1952, Medgar received his degree, and the couple moved to Mound Bayou in the Mississippi Delta.

Two years later Medgar Evers became a field secretary for the National Association for the Advancement of Colored People (NAACP), and Myrlie worked as his assistant. Their jobs engaged them in the fight for black civil rights, including voting rights, equal education, and equal justice.

On numerous occasions white racists physically attacked Medgar and threatened the couple's lives; in spring 1963 their home in Jackson, Mississippi, where they had relocated, was firebombed, and shortly after midnight on June 12, 1963, white supremacist Byron De La Beckwith shot and killed Medgar Evers as the civil rights leader was stepping from his car outside his home.

"The first year after Medgar's death, my fuel for survival was hatred . . .", Myrlie recalled. "Every time I walked out the door, I saw his blood—the place where he had been shot down. I had to move from Mississippi so that my children and I could start anew." They relocated in Claremont, California, where in 1968 she graduated from Pomona College with a degree in sociology.

From 1968 to 1970 Myrlie Evers worked as director of planning at Claremont College, helping high school dropouts obtain diplomas and prepare for college. In 1970 she ran for Congress as a Democrat in the heavily Republican 24th District, but she lost. Shortly afterward she moved to New York City, where she joined the advertising firm of Seligman and Latz as a vice president.

In 1975 she returned to California, settling in Los Angeles as national director for community affairs at the Atlantic Richfield Company (ARCO), an oil and chemical corporation. She supervised outreach programs that were intended to help minorities and women. In 1976 she married Walter Williams, a longshoreman and a civil rights activist. The couple agreed that, in respect for her first husband, she would continue to use Evers as her last name.

Myrlie Evers entered politics again in 1987, when she ran unsuccessfully for the Los Angeles city council. Mayor Tom Bradley then appointed her to a full-time position as a commissioner on the Los Angeles Board of Public Works. She managed a staff of 6,000 that handled problems involving sanitation and air and water quality.

Over the years she worked to reopen her first husband's murder case. Byron De La Beckwith had been tried twice in 1964 for the slaying, and both times all-white juries had deadlocked. With the help of an investigative article in the Jackson [Mississippi] *Clarion-Ledger*, which indicated that the jury in the second trial had been tampered with, the state again prosecuted Beckwith and in 1994 obtained a guilty verdict. He was sentenced to life in prison.

Myrlie Evers remained active in the NAACP, and in 1995, while serving as vice chair of the organization's board, she stepped forward as a candidate to chair the organization. Her entry into the race occurred amid a crisis for the organization: Its former executive director, Benjamin Chavis, had been ousted just months before for sexually harassing employees and mismanaging funds. The NAACP faced a crisis in morale, trouble with its public standing, and $4-million debt.

Part of the reason Evers sought the post was her husband's declining health. When he became ill with cancer in 1993 she began using his last name, along with the last name of her first husband, as a tribute to both; now he urged her to seek the chair of the organization to save the NAACP. But she acted also with the belief that she should continue Medgar Evers's work—"I have been committed to seeing that his legacy and proper place in history are maintained. It's time for me to once again devote my energies to that task," she claimed. She also expressed her strong attach-

ment to the organization: "I am here because I love the NAACP. I believe it must survive. I believe it must thrive." She won by a one-vote margin, 30–29, in February 1995; just days after her victory her husband died.

Myrlie Evers-Williams revived the NAACP; donations increased and confidence among members and the public at large strengthened. At her urging the board hired former congressman KWEISI MFUME as president.

Early in 1998 Evers-Williams announced she would not seek another term as chair. "I believe my mission was to lead [the NAACP] out of the financial, moral and organizational morass in which we found ourselves," she explained. "The NAACP is now solvent, public confidence has been restored and our commitment to equality of opportunity for all Americans is unquestioned."

In 1999 Evers-Williams wrote her autobiography, *Watch Me Fly: What I Learned on the Way to Becoming the Woman I Was Meant to Be*. In the year 2001 she addressed graduates at Simmons College in Massachusetts, telling them about her long struggle to bring Medgar Evers's killer to justice: "All those people said over the years, 'Give up, nothing will happen, you're crazy, here she comes again,'" she said. "But a leader is not always loved or admired. Popularity is not leadership, results are. Leadership is responsibility."

Further Reading

Evers-Williams, Myrlie. *For Us, the Living*. Garden City, N.Y.: Doubleday, 1967.
———. *Watch Me Fly: What I Learned on the Way to Becoming the Woman I Was Meant to Be*. Boston: Little, Brown, 1999.

Farmer, James Leonard, Jr.

(1920–1999) *civil rights leader*

Founder of the Congress of Racial Equality, James Farmer was an organizer of the Freedom Rides that awakened the American conscience about civil rights. He was born on January 12, 1920, in Marshall, Texas, to James Leonard Farmer, Sr., an ordained minister who was the son of a slave, and Pearl Marion Houston Farmer.

James Farmer grew up in an educated family. His father had earned a doctorate at Boston University and his mother a teaching certificate from Bethune-Cookman Institute. Young James possessed his parents' intelligence; he entered the first grade at age four and began attending Wiley College in Texas at age 14. Originally he set his sights on becoming a doctor, but when he discovered that the sight of blood made him queasy, he decided to follow his father into the ministry. So after obtaining a B.A. in chemistry from Wiley in 1938, he studied religion at Howard University in Washington, D.C.

While at Howard, though, Farmer again changed direction. Although he would earn a degree in religion, he thought more about racism and violence in American society and concluded that the church was incapable of doing much about either. "I lost interest in the church very early," Farmer recalled. "Faced with problems on this earth, I looked for answers in the secular world."

He met Howard Thurman, a black professor of theology at the college, and Thurman intro-duced him to the Fellowship of Reconciliation (FOR), a small group led by A. J. MUSTE, that advocated pacifism and racial equality. Farmer became a part-time field organizer for FOR, and through Muste's influence he began learning about the nonviolent direct action practiced by the Indian political protester Mohandas Gandhi.

Farmer then had the idea of applying Gandhi's tactics to fight for black civil rights, and in 1940 Muste authorized the establishment of the Committee of Racial Equality, later renamed the Congress of Racial Equality (CORE). Farmer organized picket lines and sit-ins at segregated businesses, such as a rollerskating rink in Chicago, but for the most part his efforts were ignored. "The technique of nonviolent, direct action received no notoriety," he recalled, "and we were merely considered a few nuts or crackpots sitting in at lunch counters."

Farmer served as national chairman of CORE from 1942 to 1944 and again in 1950, but the organization languished with little money and little staff, and he spent much of his time working for the National Association for the Advancement of Colored People (NAACP). That changed in 1961 when CORE turned to him to take up the cudgel of militant protest. "I left the NAACP to go to CORE as National Director because CORE had been my child and at that point was undergoing reorganization and experiencing some growth," Farmer recalled.

But certainly Farmer realized the atmosphere in the country had changed since the 1940s. For one, the cold war with the Soviet Union had erupted, and in the fight against communism the United States could little afford to have its image sullied by undemocratic practices at home. For another, in 1960 black college students in Greensboro, North Carolina, had generated enormous publicity for the civil rights movement when they staged a sit-in at a Woolworth's lunch counter. Militant tactics were coming to the fore, and Farmer was determined to use them.

In 1961 he proposed staging Freedom Rides to desegregate buses and terminals in the South. Earlier, the Supreme Court had ruled as unconstitutional such racially segregated facilities involved in interstate travel, but southerners had ignored the rulings. Farmer intended to force a change. "We planned the Freedom Ride with the specific intention of creating a crisis," he recalled. "We were counting on the bigots in the South to do our work for us. We figured that the government would have to respond if we created a situation that was headline news all over the world, and affected the nation's image abroad. An international crisis, that was our strategy."

In May 1961 Farmer and 12 other CORE protesters, white and black, boarded two buses and headed into the South. They defied the rules that blacks sit only in the back of the buses, and at the bus depots the black riders used the restrooms and other facilities marked "whites only."

They encountered few problems in the upper South, but when they neared Anniston, Alabama, violence erupted. As one bus pulled into the depot a mob of about 40 whites attacked it with chains, sticks, and iron bars. They broke the windows and slashed its tires. After the bus departed the mob followed it in cars, forced it off the road, and tossed a firebomb into it. While the CORE riders fled the smoke, whites beat them. The second bus encountered similar treatment, and one protester was knocked to the floor and kicked so hard that he suffered permanent brain damage.

Farmer, however, was not present for the violence. He had left the Freedom Ride to care for his dying father. Nevertheless, he was shocked and angered by the news of what had happened at Anniston and additional violence that had occurred in Birmingham.

With the Freedom Riders bloodied, the protest could have ended at that point. But Farmer recruited college students from the Student Non-Violent Coordinating Committee and decided to continue the effort. He later admitted how scared he was to join the new recruits. "I was waving good-bye at the bus, and [the Freedom Riders] looked sort of puzzled," he recalled. "I felt sheepish [about not going with them], so I tried to make excuses. . . . But the real reason was that I was scared shitless. Then a young girl looked out the window and said to me, patronizingly, 'Jim, please.' That's when I got my baggage out of the car and got in."

When the Freedom Riders reached Jackson, Mississippi, they were locked up, but no further violence had occurred, and the protest had attracted widespread coverage in newspapers and on radio and TV. CORE sponsored other Freedom Rides that caused Attorney General Robert Kennedy to pressure the Interstate Commerce Commission into enforcing the court decisions by issuing definite rules banning segregation in interstate bus travel. On a broader level the federal government had now more closely aligned itself with the civil rights movement.

In *Fire in the Streets* (1979), Martin Viorst writes:

> The Freedom Ride accelerated the pace of the civil rights movement. . . . It dramatized, to any who remained doubters, that segregation was a national concern, rather than a series of local problems. It challenged Martin Luther King and other leaders of the movement to find new applications for nonviolence, to push their strategy still closer to its potential as an instrument of social change.

Farmer continued to lead CORE until 1966, when tactical disputes among black activists caused him to resign. He taught at several colleges and in 1968 ran unsuccessfully for Congress from New York's 12th District. In 1969 President Richard Nixon appointed him assistant secretary for administration of the Department of Health, Education and Welfare. He implemented affirmative action programs, but because he was at odds with many of Nixon's policies, he resigned in 1970.

In the 1980s and 1990s Farmer lectured at Mary Washington College in Fredericksburg, Virginia, and wrote books on labor and race relations, along with his autobiography, *Lay Bare the Heart.* In 1998 President Bill Clinton awarded him the Presidential Medal of Freedom. Farmer died on July 9, 1999, in Fredericksburg. About CORE, Farmer had once said, "We dreamed of a mass movement." He certainly had succeeded in igniting one.

Further Reading

Farmer, James. *Lay Bare the Heart: An Autobiography of the Civil Rights Movement.* Fort Worth: Texas Christian University Press, 1998.

Viorst, Milton. *Fire in the Streets: America in the 1960s.* New York: Simon & Schuster, 1979.

Firestone, Shulamith

(1945–   ) *feminist, writer*

Shulamith Firestone is a radical feminist who believes that all forms of social domination, including the oppression of women by men, result from male supremacy. She was born in 1945 in Ottawa, Ontario, Canada.

Before she became involved in the feminist movement, Shulamith Firestone attended Washington University in Saint Louis, Missouri, and transferred to the Art Institute of Chicago, where she received a bachelor of fine arts degree in painting. By that time the 1960s political protests were intensifying, and she became a part of the New Left, which challenged the Vietnam War and believed an evil capitalist system had produced it. Like many other leftists, Firestone at first attributed the oppression of women to capitalism, under which the wealthy exploited everyone else, and concluded that once it was replaced with a socialist system women would be liberated.

But as she experienced male domination and chauvinism within the New Left, she began to change her views. She concluded that radical women should no longer subordinate women's issues to economic ones. So in fall 1967 she and Jo Freeman began the Chicago Westside Group as a feminist organization conforming to her ideas. A few weeks later she left that organization, relocated to New York City, and founded New York Radical Women (NYRW).

In January 1968 she led NYRW in a protest at a gathering of women in Washington, D.C., who were preparing to demonstrate at the Capitol against the Vietnam War. She recalled, "We staged an actual funeral procession with a larger-than-life dummy on a transported bier, complete with a feminine getup. . . . Hanging from the bier were such disposable items as . . . curlers, garters, and hairspray. Streamers floated off it and we also carried large banners, such as 'DON'T CRY: RESIST.'" At the gathering the NYRW distributed a pamphlet that read as follows:

> TRADITIONAL   WOMANHOOD   IS DEAD.
>   TRADITIONAL   WOMEN   WERE BEAUTIFUL . . . BUT   REALLY   POWERLESS.
>   "UPPITY"   WOMEN   WERE   EVEN MORE BEAUTIFUL . . . BUT STILL POWERLESS.
>   SISTERHOOD IS POWERFUL!
>   HUMANHOOD THE ULTIMATE!

The NYRW action was intended to raise women's consciousness and in so doing foreshadowed Firestone's involvement with another protest group, Redstockings.

Speaking to a meeting of radical women's groups at New York's Free University in February 1968, Firestone said:

> In choosing to fight for women's liberation it is not enough . . . to explain it only in general terms of 'the system.' For the system oppresses many groups in many ways. Women must learn that the *specific method* used to keep her oppressed is to convince her that she is at all times secondary to man, and that her life is defined in terms of him. We cannot speak of liberating ourselves until we free ourselves from this myth and accept ourselves as primary.

While with NYRW, Firestone began her career as a writer. In 1968 she edited and contributed articles to *Notes from the First Year: Women's Liberation.*

Two years later she reprised her role in *Notes from the Second Year: Radical Feminism.*

By that time she had left NYRW to found Redstockings, whose name was a takeoff on "bluestocking," a characterization once used to refer to 19th-century feminist intellectuals. Firestone expected Redstockings to be a militant radical feminist group that world advocate the idea that male supremacy rather than class exploitation accounted for women's oppression. This view was reflected in the Redstockings manifesto issued in 1969:

> Women are an oppressed class. Our oppression is total, affecting every facet of our lives. We are exploited as sex objects, breeders, domestic servants, and cheap labor. . . .
> We identify the agents of our oppression as men. . . . All other forms of exploitation and oppression . . . are extensions of male supremacy. . . .
> We call on all of our sisters to unite with us in our struggle.

Redstockings disrupted hearings in the New York legislature on abortion reform, distributed feminist literature, and staged a sit-in at the *Ladies' Home Journal* offices to protest the magazine's sexist content. But Firestone soon thought Redstockings too involved in consciousness raising rather than in pursuing truly radical change. So in 1970 she left the group and with Anne Koedt founded New York Radical Feminists (NYRF). Within months, however, it collapsed from factional fighting.

Firestone's influence remained substantial, however, as reflected by the reaction to her book *Dialectic of Sex,* published in October 1970, in which she argued that women's oppression arose from her biological role as the bearer of children. Ending this oppression required that women control the means of reproduction—and ultimately that they no longer be relied on for reproduction. She advocated using artificial devices such as test-tube conception and gestation in artificial wombs. Sex roles could thus be eliminated, she claimed, and with them the "tyranny of the biological family."

Although since the 1970s Firestone has largely faded from public view, her *Dialectic of Sex* remains in print and is often debated in feminist and academic circles. At one point she said that through her radical actions and those carried out by her supporters, "We . . . confirmed our belief that a real women's movement in this country will come, if only out of the sheer urgent and immediate necessity for one."

Further Reading

Firestone, Shulamith. *The Dialectic of Sex: The Case for Feminist Revolution.* 3rd ed. New York: Morrow, 1993.

Flores Magón, Ricardo
(1874–1942) *anarchist, writer*

A Mexican revolutionary and anarchist, Ricardo Flores Magón fled his home country for the United States. He was born on September 16, 1874, in San Antonio Eloxochitlán in the state of Oaxaca in southern Mexico. His father, Teodoro Flores, was a Zapotec Indian, and his mother, Margarita Magón, was half Spanish and half Indian.

From his father, a liberal and an officer in the Mexican army, Flores Magón learned libertarian ideas as a child, and while a student at the National Preparatory School he participated in protest marches against his country's dictator, Porfirio Díaz. His activism led to his conviction on charges of sedition, and he served five months in jail. On his release in 1893 he entered the National School of Law.

Flores Magón's troubles with Díaz, however, had only begun. While in law school Flores Magón helped publish the newspaper *El Demócrata,* and as police hunted for its staff, he went into hiding for several months. Flores Magón received his law degree in 1895, became an attorney, and in 1900 cofounded the newspaper *La Regeneración.* In several articles he attacked Díaz, and later that year he joined the Liberal Party, further establishing his name in Mexico as a rebel against the government. Díaz had, in fact, formed a cruelly oppressive regime that crushed labor unions and stole communal land from peasants so it could be transferred to wealthy property owners. Under his rule homelessness reached massive proportions while a small elite enjoyed luxury.

Flores Magón wrote about these conditions in *La Regeneración* and in articles for other dissident publications; at the same time he planned labor strikes through the Liberal Party. Hounded by Díaz, his writings officially banned, Flores Magón fled to the United States, settling first in San Antonio, Texas, before moving to Saint Louis, Missouri. In September 1905 Flores Magón and his followers founded the Junta Organizadora del Partido Liberal (PLM), with Flores Magón as president. He continued to publish *La Regeneración*, sending it along with propaganda pamphlets into Mexico. *In Anarchism and the Mexican Revolution: The Political Trials of Ricardo Flores Magón in the United States* (1991), Colin M. MacLachlan states, "Flores Magón hoped that the United States government might tolerate revolutionary activity by Mexican exiles if officials could be convinced that they shared the same democratic principles."

But in advocating the revolutionary overthrow of the Mexican government, Flores Magón sharply criticized the United States for its support of Díaz, and he expressed his commitment to anarchism. When Díaz placed pressure on the United States to silence Flores Magón, the federal authorities arrested him. Out on bail, he hid in Los Angeles and published *Revolución*, another radical newspaper. Arrested again in 1907, he and two other PLM members were convicted of violating neutrality laws and sent to a federal penitentiary in Florence, Arizona.

On his release in 1910, Flores Magón resumed his revolutionary crusade and once again published *La Regeneración*. In November Francisco I. Madero, a member of the Anti-Reelectionist Party, which opposed Díaz, launched a revolution against the dictator. In October 1911 Madero deposed Díaz, but the revolution continued under the PLM and several other groups, including the Zapatistas (rebels led by Emiliano Zapata). One month before Madero's presidency began, in September 1911, Flores Magón and the PLM issued a manifesto that in several passages expressed their commitment to revolutionary change and made it clear they would oppose Madero:

> Capital, Authority, the Church—there you have the somber trinity that makes of this beauteous earth a paradise for those who, by cunning, violence, and crime, have been successful in gathering into their clutches the product of the toiler's sweat, of the blood of the tears and sacrifices of thousands of generations of workers. . . .
>
> Between [the capitalist and working] classes there cannot exist any bond of friendship or fraternity, for the possessing class always seeks to perpetuate the existing economic, political and social system which guarantees it tranquil enjoyment of the fruits of its robberies. . . .
>
> With the disappearance of the last bourgeois and the last agent of authority, and the law which upholds privilege having been shattered, everything having been placed in the hands of the toilers, we shall meet in fraternal embrace and celebrate with cries of joy in inauguration of a system that will guarantee to every human being Bread and Liberty.

In 1912 the U.S. government arrested Flores Magón a second time for violating neutrality laws. As the Mexican Revolution continued and Venustiano Carranza became president, Flores Magón, who had been released from prison in 1914, opposed him, as he had Díaz and Madero. Yet a third arrest followed, and Flores Magón spent 1916–17 in prison.

After the United States entered World War I the government arrested Flores Magón for the fourth and final time in 1918 because he had written an anarchist manifesto (whose ideas, it was feared, would gain a wide appeal) and thus violated an espionage law. He received a 20-year prison term and was sent to Leavenworth in Kansas. He died in his cell on November 22, 1942, under mysterious circumstances, apparently having been beaten to death.

In Mexico City more than 10,000 people turned out in May 1945, when his body was officially interred in the Rotunda of Illustrious Men. While in the United States Flores Magón had written, "It is true that, by birth we are Mexicans, but our minds are not so narrow—our vision not so pitifully small as to regard as aliens or enemies those who have been born under other skies."

Further Reading

Albro, Ward S. *Always a Rebel: Ricardo Flores Magón and the Mexican Revolution*. Fort Worth: Texas Christian University Press, 1992.

Langham, Thomas C. *Border Trials: Ricardo Flores Magón and the Mexican Liberals.* El Paso: Texas Western Press, 1981.

MacLachlan, Colin M. *Anarchism and the Mexican Revolution: The Political Trials of Ricardo Flores Magón in the United States.* Berkeley: University of California Press, 1991.

Flynn, Elizabeth Gurley

(1890–1964) *labor organizer, communist*

A labor organizer for the Industrial Workers of the World (IWW), Elizabeth Gurley Flynn was later a leader of the Communist Party. She was born on August 7, 1890, in Concord, New Hampshire, to Thomas Flynn, a granite worker and civil engineer, and Annie Gurley, a tailor. "My father and mother," she once told an interviewer, "were socialists, were members of the Socialist Party." As a young girl, though, she thought the socialists too stodgy and wanted something bolder. "We felt a desire to have something more militant, more progressive, and more youthful," she said about herself and her friends, "and so we flocked into the . . . IWW."

She joined the IWW after she was expelled from high school in the Bronx in New York City (where her parents had moved in 1900) for blocking traffic while giving a speech on socialism. In 1907 she became a full-time IWW organizer. The IWW had been founded two years earlier by socialists, anarchists, and radical unionists who wanted to unite all of the country's workers into one union and use strikes as a weapon to topple capitalism and put industry into the workers' control. "The IWW believed in the class struggle," she said. "They didn't believe in the brotherhood of capital and labor."

Among the several strikes that Flynn helped organize were those involving textile workers in Lawrence, Massachusetts (1912), and in Paterson (1913) and Passaic (1926), New Jersey. During that time, in 1915, Flynn wrote a pamphlet titled *Sabotage*, in which she advocated "the withdrawal of efficiency" as a weapon in the fight against the capitalists. She stated:

> Sabotage means either to slacken up and interfere with the quantity, or to botch in your skill and interfere with the quality, of capitalist production or to give poor service. Sabotage is not physical violence; sabotage is internal, industrial process. And these three forms of sabotage—to affect the quality, the quantity, and the service, are aimed at affecting the profit of the employer.

Flynn took the lead in fighting for free speech rights at a time when many local laws prohibited IWW members from holding public meetings. She also rallied support and collected money to defend IWW members arrested and held on dubious grounds, among them WILLIAM DUDLEY HAYWOOD and JOE HILL. "I became more and more specialized in what is called labor defense work," she said.

Flynn took an interest in organizing women and children, and she criticized the secondary status assigned to women by some of the men in the IWW. Yet her main concern was not with feminist issues; regarding suffrage, for example, she believed that women should have the right to vote, but she thought the suffrage movement took focus and energy away from the marrow of oppression, namely, the control of the masses by an elite rooted in class differences.

With American entry into World War I in 1917, she defended those arrested for opposing the war, including conscientious objectors, socialists, and IWW members, who were prosecuted under the Sedition Act. That same year she helped found the National Civil Liberties Bureau, which later became the American Civil Liberties Union (ACLU).

When the war ended Flynn led a movement for the release of those imprisoned under the Sedition Act, and in 1924 President Calvin Coolidge granted them amnesty. Suffering from poor health, Flynn largely retired from activism in 1926, but 10 years later she joined the Communist Party and dedicated herself to furthering its program. The ACLU reacted to her communist allegiance in 1940 by removing her from its executive board, a retaliation all the more controversial given the group's commitment to free speech.

Flynn supported the American fight against fascism in World War II, urging people to buy savings bonds and advocating that women be drafted into the military. But after the war federal authorities arrested her for violating the Smith Act (1940), which made it illegal to advocate the forcible overthrow of the U.S. government or to be a member of any group advocating such an action. She was tried and convicted in 1952, and after appealing the verdict she served her prison term from January 1955 to May 1957 at the women's federal penitentiary in Alderson, West Virginia. During her confinement she helped racially integrate facilities at the prison.

On her release Flynn resumed her work with the Communist Party, and in 1961 she became its national chair. Elizabeth Gurley Flynn died on September 5, 1964, during a trip to the Soviet Union and was given a state funeral in Moscow's Red Square. In 1978 the ACLU posthumously rescinded its previous expulsion of her.

Further Reading

Baxandall, Rosalyn Fradd. *Words on Fire: The Life and Writing of Elizabeth Gurley Flynn.* New Brunswick, N.J.: Rutgers University Press, 1987.

Walker, Samuel. *In Defense of Civil Liberties: A History of the ACLU.* 2nd ed. Carbondale: Southern Illinois University Press, 1999.

Foster, William Zebulon

(1881–1961) *labor organizer, communist*

William Zebulon Foster was a leader of the communist movement in the United States as well as a labor organizer. He was born on February 25, 1881, in Taunton, Massachusetts, to James Foster, a carriage washer and livery stableman, and Elizabeth McLaughlin Foster.

Because of his family's poverty, William Foster was forced to leave school at age 10 and work as a sculptor's assistant. That childhood experience stayed with him for the rest of his life: He identified with the hardships suffered by many in the working class and felt inferior to those who were more educated.

For many years Foster worked at jobs that paid little and offered no hope of advancement: He mined ore, loaded merchant ships, and harvested crops. As he did so, he became more political; to him, neither the Republican nor the Democratic

Party truly represented the country's workers, and in 1901 he joined the Socialist Party. He would, over time, change allegiances, but he forever remained committed to radicalism.

In 1909 Foster quit the Socialist Party and joined the Industrial Workers of the World (IWW), which offered the prospect of tearing down capitalism through union activism. The following year he traveled to Europe, and his contacts with labor radicals there, especially in France, led him to embrace their much-used tactic of "boring from within." Using this approach, radicals joined conservative labor unions and worked from inside them to further their agenda. For Foster this meant that IWW members should dismantle their union and infiltrate the more conservative American Federation of Labor (AFL), an association of craft unions, so they could radicalize it.

When Foster returned to the United States in 1911 he pushed his program within the IWW. "I am satisfied from my observation," he said,

> that the only way for the IWW to have workers adopt and practice the principles of revolutionary unionism . . . is to give up its attempt to create a new labor movement, turn itself into a propaganda league, get into the organized labor movement, and by building up better fighting machines within the old unions than those possessed by our reactionary enemies, revolutionize these unions even as our French Syndicalist fellow workers have so successfully done with theirs.

Foster traveled to IWW locals throughout the United States to push his strategy; he rode bitterly cold freight cars in the winter and wore out his body from fatigue. When the IWW rejected his tactic, he resigned from the union in 1912 and formed the Syndicalist League of North America, with him as national secretary, to direct radicals into the AFL craft unions. Yet the league remained small, and in 1914 it disbanded.

The next year Foster, who was working in Chicago's railroad car shops, won election as the business agent for the Chicago District Council of the Railway Carmen. In that union job he learned how to organize and widened his contacts with his fellow workers. In 1917 he unionized the packinghouse workers, and they won an eight-hour workday.

He followed this with an ambitious campaign in the steel industry that by spring 1919 had recruited nearly 100,000 steelworkers under the direction of the National Committee for Organizing Iron and Steel Workers. That year's steel strike, however, damaged Foster, partly because it failed and partly because with the Red Scare (a campaign led by Attorney General A. Mitchell Palmer to jail and deport communists and other radicals) then under way, many Americans believed that the strike was intended to undermine the country.

In 1920 Foster formed the Trade Union Industrial League in another attempt to apply "boring from within" to the AFL. The following year he joined the American Communist Party, but in the 1920s he lost to Earl Browder in a struggle to lead the organization and in 1929 was forced to abandon his boring-from-within tactic and accept the party's decision to organize independent, revolutionary trade unions.

Yet Foster was the party's best-known figure, and he ran for the White House three times as its standard bearer, in 1924, 1928, and 1932, when he won more than 100,000 votes. That same year his overexertion led to a heart attack, and for the next several years he was reduced to writing articles for the party's magazine, *The Communist*.

In 1945, however, the Communist Party repudiated Browder, who had advocated peaceful coexistence with capitalism, and Foster became the organization's leader. The party, whose membership never numbered more than a few thousand, suffered from another Red Scare, this one after World War II, when federal authorities prosecuted its leaders for violating the Smith Act by advocating the forcible overthrow of the government. They were found guilty, further discrediting a party that most considered to be un-American. Foster escaped prosecution only because of his heart condition.

In 1956 the communists blamed their party's decline on Foster, and early in 1957 they ousted him as chairman. In his last years Foster engaged in a long legal battle with the federal government to allow him to go to Moscow and receive medical treatment. On September 1, 1961, he died in Russia and was honored by a state funeral in Red Square.

Foster remained faithful to communism to his very end and in December 1960, while still living in New York City, wrote to his lawyer:

> I am accused of the nonsensical and hypocritical charge of advocating the overthrow of the government by force and violence. This is a flagrant lie . . . the Communist Party of the United States has long distinguished itself in advocating the peaceful road to Socialism. The government has not hesitated to make use of the worst stool pigeons and perjured testimony to convict the political enemies of monopoly capitalism.

Further Reading

Johanningsmeier, Edward P. *Forging American Communism: The Life of William Z. Foster.* Princeton, N.J.: Princeton University Press, 1994.

———. "William Z. Foster and the Syndicalist League of North America." *Labor History* 30 (Summer 1989): 329+.

Fox, Matthew
(Timothy Fox)
(1940–) *religion reformer*

Matthew Fox is a Catholic mystic who was booted from the Dominican priesthood for his beliefs. He was born Timothy Fox on December 21, 1940, in Madison, Wisconsin, to George Fox, an assistant football coach at the University of Wisconsin, and Beatrice Still Fox.

Timothy Fox grew up in a devout Catholic family ruled by his father, a strict disciplinarian. At age 12 Fox contracted polio and was hospitalized for a year. During that time a Catholic brother from the Dominican order visited him and so impressed him that at age 19 Fox joined the order.

Following the Dominican custom of assigning members of the order new first names, Timothy Fox adopted the name Matthew. After a year at the Dominican novitiate in Winona, Minnesota, he entered Aquinas Institute in River Forest, Illinois, where he excelled and earned a master's degree in 1967. He earned a doctorate from the Institut Catholique de Paris in 1970 and then taught theology at several different colleges, including Barat College in Lake Forest, Illinois.

Influenced by creation-oriented theology, in 1976 he founded the Institute in Culture and Creation Spirituality (ICCS) at Mundelein College in Chicago. He taught that before acknowledging original sin, original blessing should be celebrated and people should embrace the sacred quality of nature and experience liberation through a mystical connection with God's creative energy.

In 1983 Fox relocated ICCS to Holy Names College in Oakland, California. His faculty and the teachings they offered became more eclectic and included classes in feminism, Native American rituals, and shamanism. When he hired a witch named Starhawk to join the faculty, the Vatican's Sacred Congregation for the Doctrine of the Faith demanded he be investigated by the Dominicans. A committee review cleared Fox of any wrongdoing or heresy, but Cardinal Joseph Ratzinger rejected the findings and ordered that Fox be temporarily removed as director of ICCS and maintain a year of silence during which he was forbidden to teach, lecture, or publish.

Fox agreed and began his penance in 1988, though shortly before that he published an essay in which he called the Catholic Church "fascist." In 1989 Fox resumed teaching his form of Christian mysticism with its doctrine of creativity over original sin. As a result he was forced to leave the Dominican order in 1993.

Fox was ordained an Episcopal priest in 1994 and set his sights on changing the way that Christians worshiped. He began "rave masses," in which participants danced, played music, and joined in group hugs. Fox continued to insist that doctrinal concerns should be placed second to a deep involvement in environmental and social problems. "Denominations are not that important," he said, "in light of the real issues." In 1996 he founded the University of Creation Spirituality in Oakland, which attracted more than 100 students. He has written extensively and in 1999 published *Sins of the Spirit, Blessings of the Flesh: Lessons for Transforming Evil in Soul and Society.*

Further Reading

Fox, Matthew. *The Coming of the Cosmic Christ.* New York: Harper & Row, 1988.

———. *Sins of the Spirit, Blessings of the Flesh: Lessons for Transforming Evil in Soul and Society.* New York: Harmony Books, 1999.

———. *A Spirituality Named Compassion and the Healing of the Global Village, Humpty Dumpty and Us.* Minneapolis, Minn.: Winston Press, 1979.

———. *Whee! We, Wee All the Way Home: A Guide to the New Sensual Spirituality.* Wilmington, N.C.: Consortium, 1976.

Friedan, Betty
(Bettye Naomi Goldstein)
(1921–) *women's liberationist, writer*

A women's rights activist and author of *The Feminine Mystique*, Betty Friedan is a founding member of the National Organization for Women (NOW). She was born Bettye Naomi Goldstein on February 4, 1921, in Peoria, Illinois, to Harry Goldstein and Miriam Horowitz Goldstein. Her father, a Jewish immigrant, owned a jewelry store, and the family lived in economic comfort.

In her childhood two experiences especially affected Friedan and shaped her consciousness, making her uneasy with some of her middle-class values: the anti-Semitism she experienced in Peoria and her mother's disappointment with having given up her work as a journalist when she married.

Friedan excelled academically in high school, founded a student literary magazine, and after graduation entered Smith College in Massachusetts. There she edited the college newspaper and majored in psychology. She received a B.A. degree in 1942 and accepted a research fellowship to the University of California at Berkeley. One year later she moved to New York City, where she worked as a journalist and met Carl Friedan, a theater producer. They married in 1947, and in 1949 she took maternity leave from her job for the birth of her first child.

According to Friedan (others dispute the account), a personal experience in 1954 stirred her dissatisfaction with society's treatment of women: When she requested a second maternity leave, she was fired from her job. Rather than protest, though, she retreated to her family's home along the Hudson River and tried to follow the role that 1950s society expected of women: a happy, suburban homemaker. At the same time, she wrote articles as a free-lancer in which she portrayed women as satisfied and fulfilled in their duties as homemakers. But Friedan realized this theme conflicted with her own experience, and she wondered whether other suburban women were as unhappy as she. In 1957 Friedan decided to find out by interviewing and surveying her former Smith College classmates.

She published her findings in her 1963 book, *The Feminine Mystique.* This work immediately earned a wide readership because its theme, namely, that many women felt frustrated with their lives, resonated with a large audience and because it coincided with the growth of social and political activism.

Friedan's phrase "feminine mystique" referred to the idealization of the traditional female role of wife and mother. The role in the home that society expected women to fulfill, she claimed, both frustrated and oppressed many women and represented a male conspiracy to limit competition from them.

Friedan used another phrase, "the problem that has no name," to indicate the feeling of emptiness gnawing at women. She said that "as the typical housewife made the beds, shopped for groceries, matched slipcover material, ate peanut butter sandwiches with her children, chauffeured Cub Scouts and Brownies, lay beside her husband at night, she was afraid to ask even of herself the silent question: 'Is this all?'" Friedan continued: "Gradually I came to realize that the problem that has no name was shared by countless women in America. The women who suffer this problem have a hunger that food cannot fill." She insisted:

> If I am right, the problem that has no name stirring in the minds of so many American women today is not a matter of loss of femininity or too much education, or the demands of domesticity. It is far more important than anyone recognizes. . . . It may well be the key to our future as a nation and a culture. We

can no longer ignore that voice within women that says: "I want something more than my husband and my children and my home."

Many women and men applauded Friedan's conclusions, but some reacted negatively to the book and strongly opposed her for undermining traditional middle-class values. Amid the debate that surrounded her work, she toured the nation, making speeches and appearing on television.

Friedan decided that advancing women's liberation required political action. So in 1966 she founded the National Organization for Women, a group devoted to obtaining equal rights for women. This goal, she believed, could be accomplished by enforcing existing legislation, such as the 1964 Civil Rights Act, which made sexual

Betty Friedan founded the National Organization for Women, a moderate group in the fight for women's rights. *(New York World-Telegram and the Sun Newspaper Photograph Collection, Library of Congress)*

discrimination in employment illegal, and by amending the Constitution.

Divisions within NOW hampered Friedan's efforts, however, for as the 1960s political and social protests expanded, younger, more radical women joined the organization and fought with her over issues. Whereas Friedan sought to form alliances with men who supported the cause, these radicals considered men their enemies and opposed cooperating with them. And they also raised sexual issues that Friedan thought alienated many women, such as rights for lesbians and the complete rejection of the family unit as dysfunctional and oppressive. In addition, many radicals outside NOW, such as those affiliated with the group Redstockings, claimed that Friedan was selling out to the male "bourgeois world."

The fighting within NOW grew so intense that in 1970 Friedan retired as the organization's president. She continued her activism, however, and organized a rally later that year, the Women's Strike for Equality, in which the protesters demanded rights equal to men's. The turnout in Washington, D.C., and in other cities made it the largest women's rights rally in many decades. "That was the high point of my political career," she recalled 30 years later. "The strike for equality showed us the great strength, depth, and breadth of the [women's] movement at that time. Political groups that I had started, like the National Organization for Women, numbered under a thousand members. But, as we suspected, this [protest] proved that we spoke for the millions."

In the 1970s Friedan worked through an organization she had founded in the late 1960s, the National Abortion Rights Action League, to lead the fight for safe and legal abortions. In 1971 she joined the feminists GLORIA STEINEM, Bella Abzug, and Congresswoman Shirley Chisholm to found the National Women's Political Caucus, which encouraged women to seek public office.

When many of the 1960s protests lost their momentum in the early 1970s, Friedan helped keep the women's liberation movement alive at the local level by organizing and directing the First Women's Bank and Trust Company in New York City. At the same time, she tried unsuccessfully to begin a new group that could counteract the radi-

calism in NOW. When the requisite number of states failed to ratify the Equal Rights Amendment, she criticized NOW, which she said had caused the defeat by alienating mainstream society.

In the 1980s and 1990s Friedan continued to lecture, and she wrote two books, *The Second Stage* and *The Fountain of Age*. In *The Second Stage* she called for the feminist movement to consider the needs of families; in *The Fountain of Age* she discussed the rights of the elderly and aging. In the year 2000 she published *Life So Far: A Memoir*, in which she discussed the problems in her marriage to Carl Friedan—they had divorced in 1969—including his beating her when he became jealous of her popularity that accompanied the publication of *The Feminine Mystique.*

Betty Friedan remains best remembered for the revolution she stirred in the 1960s that changed women's place in society and ignited a continuing debate over how men and women should relate to each other. "It is twenty years now since *The Feminine Mystique* was published," Betty Friedan observed in 1983. "I am still awed by the revolution that book helped spark."

Further Reading

Friedan, Betty. *Life So Far.* New York: Simon & Schuster, 2000.

Hennessee, Judith Adler. *Betty Friedan: Her Life.* New York: Random House, 1999.

Horowitz, Daniel. *Betty Friedan and the Making of The Feminine Mystique: The American Left, the Cold War, and Modern Feminism.* Amherst: University of Massachusetts Press, 1998.

Fuller, Kathryn Scott
(1946–) *environmentalist*

An attorney with an intense love of the environment, Kathryn Scott Fuller is president and chief executive officer of the World Wildlife Fund (WWF). She was born on July 8, 1946, in New York City to Delbert O. Fuller, a marketing executive, and Carol Fuller.

Although Kathryn Fuller grew up in heavily populated Westchester County, near New York City, she enjoyed outdoor activities from an early age and lost herself in books about naturalists and explorers. In an interview with *Current Biography* in 1994, she said that as a child she was intrigued by the knowledge of strange lands existing in the world.

Kathryn Fuller attended Brown University in Providence, Rhode Island, worked as a model, and thought for a time she would follow her father into a career as an advertising executive. But in 1968 she graduated with a B.A. degree in English and American literature and decided against entering business.

Over the next several years she held a variety of jobs, mainly as a research assistant and as a library assistant at Harvard University's Museum of Comparative Zoology. In 1972 she accompanied two ecologists to Africa for eight weeks to study wildebeests.

The following year Fuller decided to pursue a legal career and entered law school at the University of Texas at Austin. She graduated with honors in 1976 and then served as a law clerk. From 1977 until 1982 she held various positions in the U.S. Department of Justice in Washington, D.C. She helped establish the Wildlife and Marine Resources Section and worked in other posts, before being appointed to the Land and Natural Resources Division, in which she handled cases involving illegal trade in wildlife products. To broaden her scientific knowledge, in 1980 Fuller took graduate courses in marine, estuarine, and environmental studies at the University of Maryland in College Park. In 1981 she conducted research on coral reef crustaceans in the U.S. Virgin Islands.

She then briefly returned to the Justice Department but quit in 1982 so she could have more time to take care of her family. (She had three children, two of them with Stephen P. Boyle, whom she had married in 1977 after a divorce from her first husband. In both instances she kept the name Fuller.) She worked at home as a private consultant, and in that capacity she first had contact with the World Wildlife Federation. The WWF has as its goal to preserve "the diversity and abundance of life" and to protect ecological systems.

Fuller was hired by the WWF in 1982 and was named executive vice president in 1987. She oversaw the organization's many conservation programs and was instrumental in developing the WWF's "debt for nature" program, through which they arranged to have a portion of a developing country's debt forgiven in exchange for its setting aside funds for conservation projects.

In 1989 the WWF board elected Fuller president and chief executive officer, making her the first woman to lead a major international environmental organization. Under her guidance the WWF's membership expanded rapidly and grew from 600,000 in the late 1980s to 1.2 million a decade later. Fuller later said, "We can do great work on the ground—save tigers, getting parks established, and so on—but unless we can also influence opinion leaders, decision makers, those gains aren't consolidated for the long term. That means we need political clout, and 1.2 million members here in the United States gives us a fair amount of voice."

Fuller expanded the WWF's programs, too, so that they included protection of the larger environment. She came to realize that simply to set aside areas to guard wildlife left open the possibility that nearby economic development could still pose a hazard. Consequently, the WWF began advising countries on how to build ecologically friendly businesses that would create jobs while minimizing damage to the environment.

In the mid-1990s Fuller and the WWF helped obtain a ban on the international trade in ivory and convinced Congress to ratify the Convention on Biological Diversity, aimed at slowing the extinction of plant and animal species worldwide. In the late 1990s she insisted that the WWF and other environmental groups must find ways to unite. "The dilemma is that we all need to be distinctive in the public mind because we're all raising money," she said. "At the same time, we need to get beyond individual interests to work collectively."

Further Reading

Staroba, Kristin. "Driving the Mission Home." *Association Management,* 49, no. 4 (April 1997) 48.

Fuller, Richard Buckminster, Jr.

(1895–1983) *technological and social reformer*

An inventor, engineer, and philosopher, Richard Buckminster Fuller, Jr., is best known for his design of the geodesic dome. He was born in Milton, Massachusetts, on July 12, 1895, to Richard Buckminster Fuller, Sr., a wealthy Boston tea and leather merchant, and Caroline Wolcott Andrews Fuller.

Richard, Jr., compiled an outstanding record in science and math at Milton Academy and was expected by his father to follow the family's practice of attending Harvard University. He did—to a point. He enrolled at Harvard in 1913 but was expelled a few weeks later for breaking disciplinary rules. He was then readmitted but kicked out a second time in 1915 for poor attendance and violation of rules. He served in the navy during World War I, and in 1917 he married Anne Hewlett; they had two daughters.

In 1922 Fuller and several investors founded the Stockade Building System in Chicago to produce fibrous building blocks, which he had invented. In 1927, however, the stockholders blamed him for poor profits and fired him. Despondent over his dismissal and over the death of his first daughter, he considered committing suicide but instead decided he would use his architectural talent to find efficient ways to advance society.

In 1927 and 1928 he invented a mass-produced, lightweight apartment house and a single-residence house, both shaped as hexagons, and in 1932 he founded the Dymaxion Corporation to produce these inventions. From 1936 to 1938 he worked as a research and design assistant for the Phelps Dodge Corporation, and from 1938 to 1940 he was a technical consultant for *Fortune* magazine.

In 1947 Fuller developed his most prominent invention: the geodesic dome. This half-sphere had an internal network of interconnected four-sided pyramids that formed a grid with a high strength-to-weight ratio, making it an economical structure. A plastic or fiberglass skin covered the grid.

Most notably, Fuller designed a dome for the American pavilion at the 1967 World's Fair in Montreal, Canada. The military and many industries also used his dome, and the structures appeared in numerous hippie communes in the 1960s.

Over the years Fuller, who held a chair as research professor at Southern Illinois University in Carbondale, wrote more than 25 books. His *Nine Chains to the Moon* was published in 1938 and reis-

sued in 1963, and *Operating Manual for Spaceship Earth* was published in 1969. With its warning about the planet's dwindling resources, this book influenced the environmental movement. In the 1960s countercultural youths who distrusted technology saw in Fuller an alternative to mainstream society's wasteful practices. *The Whole Earth Catalog,* the Bible of the hippie back-to-the-land movement, said, "Fuller's lectures have a raga quality of rich nonlinear endless improvisation full of convergent surprises."

Fuller received 39 honorary doctorates and in 1983 was awarded the Presidential Medal of Freedom. He died that year on July 1 in Los Angeles of a heart attack.

Further Reading

Kenner, Hugh. *Bucky: A Guided Tour of Buckminster Fuller.* New York: Morrow, 1973.

Pawley, Martin. *Buckminster Fuller.* London: Trefoil Publications, 1990.

Zung, T. K., ed. *Buckminster Fuller: Anthology for the New Millennium.* New York: St. Martin's Press, 2001.

Fuller, Sarah Margaret

(1810–1850) *transcendentalist, women's rights activist*

An intellectual who adopted transcendentalist ideas and challenged the social constraints on women through her writing, her teaching, and the sheer dynamics of her personality, Sarah Margaret Fuller could, said one observer, "by the conversation of an hour or two . . . make an epoch in one's life." She was born on May 23, 1810, in Cambridgeport, Massachusetts, near Boston, to Timothy Fuller, a lawyer, and Margaret Crane Fuller.

Timothy Fuller was prominent in Massachusetts politics; he served in the state Senate and as a representative in the U.S. Congress and was determined that Margaret (who went by her middle name) would achieve prominence herself by developing her intellect. Because of his direction—some say his fervent pushing—she learned Latin at age six and at age eight was reading Ovid. By the time she reached her teens she had read Shakespeare, Cervantes, and Molière. She spent two unhappy years at boarding school, and she later blamed her father for forcing her to read too much too early rather than experience a more rounded childhood. The demands placed on her, she said, caused her frequent illnesses.

But as much as Fuller complained, she enjoyed reading, liked intellectual pursuits, and devoured books and ideas; she was a ravenous hunter for knowledge. One observer called her ambitious—"determined on distinction"—and as she moved quickly through European novels and philosophical treatises, she learned Greek, French, Italian, and German so she could read the originals rather than rely on translated works.

She was no wallflower, either, at least not in her midteens. She joined the Boston social scene, and many found her attractive. Fuller's gift for conversation filled with insight made her popular and well liked. She avoided the frivolous and developed friendships with Boston's leading intellectuals, including James Freeman Clarke and William Henry Channing.

Yet Fuller left her teens without any good prospects of finding a husband, and as her friends married, she withdrew from the social swirl. She devoted herself to learning; in her 20s she began writing and had her first works published, mainly book reviews.

Increasingly, she disliked the constraints placed on her as a woman. With all of her learning and intellect, she wondered what she could ever hope to accomplish in a world that expected women to stay at home and leave learning, politics, and social leadership to men. She wanted to be more than a mere object, more than an ornament on society's shelf.

In 1835 her father died, and with her family in financial straits, Fuller found a teaching job at an experimental school in Boston run by transcendentalist AMOS BRONSON ALCOTT. The school closed its doors, however, and she transferred to a girls' school in Providence, Rhode Island. There she developed her confident voice and commanded the classroom.

But Fuller disliked the intellectual barrenness of Providence, and in 1838 she returned to Boston. To earn money she decided to hold what she called "conversations" with the city's educated women. These were weekly colloquiums filled with the transcendentalist ideas she had studied and embraced. Unlike some feminists, such as AN-GELINA GRIMKÉ and SARAH MOORE GRIMKÉ, Fuller never intended or sought to address audiences that included men, an act that would have constituted improper behavior in Boston society.

At first about 25 women attended Fuller's conversations, but that number soon exceeded 100. Fuller wanted to draw women together in an intellectual community, and an open one at that, for although she guided the sessions, she strove to make them truly conversational. Transcendentalists believed in rising above whatever limitations society might impose, and Fuller infused her audience with this belief and urged women to engage in self-discovery. She wanted them to break the bonds of domesticity, meaning that any decision about what they wanted to do with their lives—whether in homemaking or through another type of fulfillment—should be based on their internal desires rather than society's dictates.

Often despondent and unhappy herself, Fuller found great satisfaction in her conversations. "My class is singularly prosperous, I think," she told a friend. "I was so fortunate as to rouse at once the tone of simple earnestness which can scarcely, when once awakened, cease to vibrate. . . . All seem in a glow and quite receptive as I wish."

In 1844 Fuller ended her conversations, wrote *Summer on the Lakes*, and began editing the *Dial*, a transcendentalist magazine. She wrote most of the articles, and Horace Greeley, the editor of the *New York Tribune*, was so impressed with her work that he asked her to join his newspaper.

Fuller agreed, and from 1844 to 1846 she lived in New York City writing articles and reviews. During this time she published *Woman in the Nineteenth Century* in 1845. Largely ignored because of its philosophical content, the book expressed much of what she had taught and learned through her conversations in Boston, revealing the concerns of many women and expressing her belief that women should be liberated. "Ye cannot believe it, men," she wrote, "but the only reason why women ever assume what is more appropriate to you, is because you prevent them from finding out what is fit for themselves."

Through several statements in the book she asserted her belief that women should be allowed to pursue whatever might fulfill them:

> If you ask me what offices they may fill, I reply—any. I do not care what case you put; let them be sea-captains, if you will. I do not doubt there are women well fitted for such an office, and, if so, I should be as glad to see them in it, as to welcome the maid of Saragossa, or the maid of Missolonghi.
>
> In families that I know, some little girls like to saw wood, others to use carpenters' tools. Where these tastes are indulged, cheerfulness and good-humor are promoted. Where they are forbidden, because "such things are not proper for girls," they grow sullen and mischievous.
>
> I think women need, especially at this juncture, a much greater range of occupation than they have, to rouse their latent powers. A party of travelers lately visited a lonely hut on a mountain. There they found an old woman, who told them she and her husband had lived there forty years. "Why," they said, "did you choose so barren a spot?" She "did not know; it was the man's notion."

Women, she wrote, should be true to themselves—much as transcendentalists thought that all people should be true to themselves—and if this meant domesticity, fine. "I have no doubt . . . ," Fuller stated, "that a large proportion of women would give themselves to the same employments as now. . . . Mothers will delight to make the nest soft and warm. Nature would take care of that; no need to clip the wings of any bird that wants to soar and sing, or finds in itself the strength of pinion for a migratory flight unusual to its kind." But the difference in a liberated environment, she wrote, "would be that all need not be constrained to employments for which some are unfit."

In true transcendentalist fashion, she stated that she wanted women to follow "self-reliance" and "self-impulse." She wrote: "By being more a soul, she will not be less a Woman, for nature is perfected through spirit." She had no quarrels with marriage in and of itself but rather with the way society and most couples regarded it. The fault of marriage, she claimed, was "that the woman does belong to the man, instead of forming a whole with him."

In summer 1846 Fuller traveled to Europe. She had long wanted to make the trip in order to meet the intellectual leaders she admired. Among others, she visited Thomas Carlyle, William Wordsworth, George Sand, and Harriet Martineau.

In October 1847 she began an eventful trip to Rome. There she met Angelo Ossoli, a poor Italian who held a title of nobility from his family's more prosperous days. They married, and in September 1848 Margaret Fuller gave birth to a child. She and Ossoli were friends of the Italian nationalist Giuseppe Mazzini and supported his republican revolution. Ossoli even fought in Mazzini's army; in 1849, when the French defeated the Italians, Margaret and her husband fled to Florence. There she began writing a history of the Mazzini revolution.

In May 1850 she and her family left Florence for America to find a publisher for her book. As the ship they were sailing on approached New York harbor, a tremendous storm overtook them. The wind and waves sank the ship off Fire Island on July 19, 1850, killing Margaret, her husband, and her two-year-old child. It was a tragic end to Margaret Fuller's life, but her demise was equal to the mythic status many intellectuals assigned her. "How can you describe a force?" remembered one observer. "How can you write the life of Margaret [Fuller]?"

Further Reading

Capper, Charles. *Margaret Fuller: An American Romantic Life*. New York: Oxford University Press, 1992.

Stern, Madeleine B. *The Life of Margaret Fuller*. 2nd ed. New York: Greenwood Press, 1991.

Von Mehren, Joan. *Minerva and the Muse: A Life of Margaret Fuller*. Amherst: University of Massachusetts Press, 1994.

Galarza, Ernesto, Jr.

(1905–1984) *farm labor organizer, Mexican rights activist*

Ernesto Galarza, Jr., overcame enormous obstacles of immigration and poverty to become a scholar, writer, farm labor organizer, and Mexican rights activist. He was born on August 15, 1905, in Jalcocotán, Mexico, to Ernesto Galarza, Sr., and Henriqueta Galarza.

As the violence of revolution swept across Mexico in 1911, young Ernesto's mother and his two uncles fled from Jalcocotán with the boy, eventually crossing the northern border into Arizona and settling in Sacramento, California. Ernesto learned English quickly and adjusted to the American school system. "I was one of these volunteers," he recalled, "the ones who knew enough English to interpret in court, on a visit to the doctor, a call to the country hospital, and who could make out a money order."

When Galarza was 12, his mother and an uncle died of flu. Despite having to support his surviving uncle and himself by working odd jobs, including laboring in the agricultural fields that surrounded Sacramento, Galarza graduated from Sacramento High School and attended Occidental College on a scholarship. He earned his bachelor's degree in 1927 and completed a master's degree in history and political science at Stanford University in 1929. Shortly thereafter he married Mae Taylor; they had two children.

In 1932 Galarza moved to New York City, where he and his wife directed the Gardiner School, a progressive elementary school in the borough of Queens. Beginning in 1936 he worked as a research assistant with the Pan American Union in Washington, D.C., an organization created to promote international cooperation in the Western Hemisphere and to address economic and social problems in the region. He was soon promoted to director of the union's Division of Labor and Social Information. In that capacity he traveled extensively throughout Latin America, learning much about the problems confronting labor.

Galarza finished his dissertation in economics at Columbia University and received his Ph.D. in 1947, thus culminating his long climb from an impoverished elementary school in Sacramento to a degree from one of America's leading colleges.

At that point he joined the Southern Tenant Farmers Union, later called the National Farm Labor Union (NFLU), as a field organizer. He wanted to help the migrant agricultural workers in California, many of whom had entered the United States under the bracero program, begun by the federal government during World War II. The program allowed growers to import thousands of Mexicans as temporary laborers to work in the fields for little pay. Galarza considered the program exploitive and set out to unionize the migrants.

"I don't know how many opportunities I have had to make money," he wrote to his half-sister as he became more involved in the labor movement:

Each time such a chance had come, my problem was whether I should take it so that I might be able to do something for those I love—sending you to college, for instance. But I have always resolved the conflict against the advantages to my family and always because I could not see myself cutting off from the world that really bore me—my mother's world and that of her people.

Galarza led more than 20 strikes, but in the end they all failed. He was unable to win substantial concessions or build a strong union, largely because the growers had a ready supply of cheap labor and because a congressional committee led by Republican Richard Nixon of California discredited the NFLU, portraying it as engaged in illegal practices.

In 1956 Galarza wrote *Strangers in Our Fields,* the first of his several books that exposed the harsh conditions faced by migrant workers and that attacked the Anglo stereotyping of impoverished Mexicans. Four years later the NFLU disbanded, but Galarza's efforts influenced the later unionizing activities of the Chicano leader CESAR CHAVEZ.

Galarza next worked for Hispanic civil rights. He served as a consultant to the U.S. Commission on Civil Rights, and in 1963 and 1964 he was an adviser to the House Committee on Education and Labor. As the Chicano movement emerged and grew militant, Galarza supported it, helping to form La Raza Unida and the Mexican-American Youth Organization. Through La Raza Unida he guided Chicano communities in developing locally based self-help programs.

In 1971 Galarza published his autobiography, *Barrio Boy,* and during the rest of the decade he taught labor issues at Notre Dame, Harvard, and San Jose State University. He developed bilingual children's books for Hispanics, stemming from his belief that youngsters should retain their ethnic culture while learning to function in Anglo society.

Galarza died on June 22, 1984, in San Jose, California. According to Rose Del Castillo Guilbault, writing in the *San Francisco Chronicle,* he was best remembered "as an organizer and scholar who laid the foundation for the Chicano movement long before the civil rights efforts of the 1960s and 1970s."

Further Reading

Galarza, Ernesto. *Barrio Boy.* South Bend, Ind.: University of Notre Dame Press, 1971.

Saldivar, Ramón. *Chicano Narrative: The Dialectics of Difference.* Madison: University of Wisconsin Press, 1990.

Gale, William Potter
(1917–1988) *right-wing militia leader*

William Potter Gale exerted a considerable influence on America's far Right as one of the promoters of the racist and anti-Semitic Christian Identity movement and founders of the Posse Comitatus. He was born in 1917, but his origins and early life are obscure.

Gale served during World War II on the staff of General Douglas MacArthur and directed guerrilla operations in the Philippine Islands against the Japanese. Soon after the war he retired from the military and began selling securities in California. In 1956 he started his own brokerage business. At the same time he emerged as an outspoken critic of President Dwight D. Eisenhower and the Supreme Court justices, claiming they should be impeached for the decisions that called for the desegregation of public schools. In 1958 he ran for governor of California as the candidate of the Constitution Party, but he received only a small vote.

Two years later Gale founded the California Rangers, a paramilitary group linked to the Christian Identity Church begun by Wesley Swift. To Identity Christians, Jews were the children of Satan and nonwhites were inferior "mud people." Taking the Identity ideology to the extreme, Gale warned that if Jews ever attacked him or his supporters, "every rabbi in Los Angeles will be dead within 24 hours." The Rangers lasted only a short while; the group disbanded several months later, after the state attorney general exposed and condemned them.

Gale, however, continued his extremist activities. With Henry Ward Beach, he founded the Posse Comitatus, an organization that considered the county sheriff to be the highest level of governmental authority. Many in Posse Comitatus adhered to Identity Christianity. In 1982 Gale conducted paramilitary training exercises in Kansas, and in 1984 he founded the Committee of the States, an organization that protested the federal income tax as unconstitutional.

In 1987 a federal grand jury convicted Gale of obstructing the Internal Revenue Service (IRS) and threatening the lives of IRS agents and a Nevada state judge. He was tried in Las Vegas, along with five other defendants, and was sentenced in January 1988 to a one-year prison term. He died, however, a few weeks later, on April 28. As reported in the *New York Times*, Betsy Rosenthal, the western states civil rights director of the Anti-Defamation League of B'nai B'rith, hailed the guilty verdict as a "warning to extremists that the American people will not tolerate the threats of physical harm to our officials and government institutions."

Further Reading

Hamilton, Neil A. *Militias in America: A Reference Handbook*. Santa Barbara, Calif.: ABC-CLIO, 1996.

Garnet, Henry Highland
(1815–1882) *abolitionist*

An African-American abolitionist, Henry Highland Garnet advocated a violent revolution against slavery and the colonizing of American blacks in Africa. He was born on December 23, 1815, near New Market, Maryland, to George Garnet and Henrietta Garnet, who were both slaves on a plantation.

In 1824 the Garnets ran away from their master and settled in New York City. Two years later Henry Garnet enrolled in the African Free School on Mott Street. The horrors of slavery returned to frighten him in 1828 when slave catchers nearly found his family. Garnet thereafter carried a knife for protection and also a deep scar on his soul that would make him a radical abolitionist.

In the mid-1830s Garnet joined the Sunday school of the First Colored Presbyterian Church, and then he met Reverend Theodore Sedgewick Wright, a prominent abolitionist, who encouraged him to join the ministry. Garnet continued his education in 1836, when he enrolled at Oneida Insti-

tute in Whitesboro, New York. In 1840, the same year that he graduated, he attended a meeting of the American Anti-Slavery Society and gave an impassioned abolitionist speech. Later that year, though, he split with his fellow abolitionist WILLIAM LLOYD GARRISON; Garrison called for the antislavery movement to turn its back on politics as hopelessly corrupt, whereas Garnet and others like him engaged in politics to change the system. In the early 1840s Garnet joined the abolitionist Liberty Party.

In 1841 Garnet married Julia Ward Williams; they had three children. Two years later he was ordained a Presbyterian minister and was appointed the first pastor of the Liberty Street Presbyterian Church in Troy, New York. At the same time, he helped edit *The National Watchman*, an abolitionist newspaper, and joined the temperance movement. A formidable speaker, he was a pioneer in advocating that blacks own and operate their own businesses and schools and rely less on whites and more on themselves in determining their future.

In August 1843 Garnet served as a delegate to the National Negro Convention in Albany, New York, and more alienated than before, he presented a stunning speech addressed to "the Slaves of the United States of America." He implored:

> Fellowmen! Patient sufferers! Behold your dearest rights crushed to the earth! See your sons murdered and your wives, mothers, and sisters doomed to prostitution. In the name of the merciful God . . . let it no longer be a debatable question, whether it is better to choose *liberty or death!*
>
> Brethren, arise, arise! Strike for your lives and liberties. Now is the day and the hour. . . . You cannot be more oppressed than you have been—you cannot suffer greater cruelties than you have already. *Rather die freemen than live to be slaves.*

Many in the audience applauded Garnet's call to rebellion, but others criticized its extremism: Black abolitionist FREDERICK DOUGLASS spoke against it; Garrisonians said it violated their principle of opposition to violence; and the convention failed to approve it as an official statement, though only by a single vote.

Shortly afterward Garnet began calling for blacks to be colonized in Africa on a voluntary basis. He said that he wanted black to take Christianity with them to Africa, for it would save the continent. In 1859 he founded the African Civilization Society with the goal of African redemption to be developed by "enterprising colored people."

When the Civil War began, Garnet urged President Abraham Lincoln to enlist African Americans in the army; after Lincoln agreed to do so in 1863, Garnet helped recruit black troops. Having served as pastor of the Shiloh Presbyterian Church in New York City, in 1864 he relocated to Washington to become pastor of the Fifteenth Street Presbyterian Church and engaged in many charitable efforts to help those hurt by the war.

In 1865 Garnet became the first African American to deliver a sermon in the House of Representatives. When the war ended he toured the South, and in 1868 he accepted the presidency of Avery College in Pittsburgh, Pennsylvania. Two years later, though, he returned to Shiloh Church in New York as pastor.

Garnet was appointed minister to the African country of Liberia in 1881 and arrived there in late December. He died shortly thereafter, on February 13, 1882.

Further Reading

Ofari, Earl. *"Let Your Motto Be Resistance": The Life and Thought of Henry Highland Garnet.* Boston: Beacon Press, 1972.

Pasternak, Martin B. *Rise Now and Fly to Arms: The Life of Henry Highland Garnet.* New York: Garland Publishing, 1995.

Garrison, William Lloyd
(1805–1879) *abolitionist*

William Lloyd Garrison embraced several reform movements, but he earned his greatest reputation as an abolitionist who called for the immediate end to slavery and for "no union with slaveholders." Born on December 12, 1805, in Newburyport, Massachusetts, to Abijah Garrison and Frances Maria Lloyd Garrison, William Lloyd Garrison grew up in poverty. When he was only five years

old, his father deserted the family and was never heard from again. Shortly afterward his mother turned him over to relatives while she went to Lynn, Massachusetts, to find work. In his early teens Garrison left school and reunited with his mother while laboring as a shoemaker in Lynn. In 1815 his mother took him to Baltimore, but he grew homesick and returned to Newburyport the following year; there he again lived with relatives and reentered school.

A variety of other jobs followed until he left school in 1818 to work as a printer's devil (an apprentice) for the *Newburyport Herald.* Four years later the paper published one of his essays, and stirred by this journalistic experience, in 1826 he bought the *Essex Courant* from a friend and renamed it the *Free Press.* He gave it up, however, when his political statements put him at odds with his financial backer. Nevertheless, his reputation was already established: Kind and sympathetic on a personal level, he was fiery and combative in public and often picked fights over issues.

By that time Boston's religious and intellectual ferment had worked its influence on him. He listened to Lyman Beecher's calls for morality based on the Scriptures to be employed in government, and he listened to the lectures by William Ellery Channing, a Unitarian who in transcendentalist fashion stressed individual self-reliance. Beecher's sermons in particular, and his family background of alcoholism—his father and a brother both had taken to the bottle—led him into the temperance movement, a path well trod by other future abolitionists who envisioned reforming society in its totality and saw excessive drinking as weakening the country's moral fiber.

At the same time Garrison yearned for greatness, and in 1827 he acquired the *National Philanthropist,* a temperance paper founded by Reverend William Collier, a Baptist preacher. Garrison stated he would "raise the moral tone of the country," with him at the helm of the crusade. In 1828 he met BENJAMIN LUNDY, a Quaker who published a newspaper that called for the abolition of slavery and based his antislavery principles on the Bible and the Declaration of Independence. Lundy's beliefs convinced Garrison to join the crusade, and his reading of *The Book and Slavery Irreconcilable,* written in

1816 by Reverend George Bourne, converted him to immediatism, meaning he advocated ending slavery without delay. Garrison said that if slaves could be held in bondage for even just one more hour, then logic would hold they could be held in bondage forever; he found that unacceptable.

According to Garrison biographer Henry Mayer, writing in *All On Fire* (1998) "Garrison's embrace of immediatism completed his equivalent of a religious conversion. He felt purged of sin, ready to testify about his convictions, and eager to exhort others to repentance."

In fall 1829 Garrison began editing Lundy's newspaper, *Genius of Universal Emancipation*, in Baltimore, but he criticized his friend's belief in colonization. To force blacks to leave the United States, he said, would violate their rights, and, in any event, even voluntary migration would be impractical.

Garrison unloosed his pen in searing attacks on those merchants who engaged in the slave trade. His criticism of Francis Todd, a Newburyport merchant, caused a Baltimore grand jury to indict Garrison for libel. Found guilty, he entered jail in April 1830. He responded, "The court may shackle the body, but it cannot pinion the mind." Garrison was freed 49 days later, after ARTHUR TAPPAN, a New York merchant and reformer, paid his fine.

Unbowed, William Lloyd Garrison returned to Boston in 1830 and lectured against slavery, which he said must be ended through the power of the Gospel. Many fellow abolitionists, meanwhile, urged him to give up his immediatism and support gradual emancipation and colonization. Instead, he found another outlet for his views on January 1, 1831, when he issued the first edition of his newspaper, *The Liberator*. In it he extolled the principles of the Declaration of Independence; said he would recruit persons of all religions to his cause; and called gradualism timid, unjust, and absurd. Public discourse resounded with his firm pronouncement: "I am in earnest—I will not equivocate—I will not excuse—I will not retreat a single inch.—AND I WILL BE HEARD."

Part of what he wanted heard was that the North should leave the Union. He believed such a move would weaken slavery by depriving it of the economic sustenance it received from Northerners and the military protection it received from the federal government. He considered it imperative that Northerners purge their souls of sin by completely dissociating themselves from human bondage.

In addition to advocating abolition, *The Liberator* promoted civil rights for African Americans. In what today would be considered a condescending tone, Garrison called for whites to "respect [blacks] as members of one great family, who may be made useful in society, and honorable in reputation."

Although the circulation of *The Liberator* never topped much more than 3,000, and Garrison had to work at odd jobs to support the publication, it appeared as a weekly for 35 years, ending only with the ratification of the 13th Amendment (which ended slavery) in December 1865. The newspaper raised southern anger; after one issue carried rumors of a slave uprising in the Carolinas, a grand jury in Raleigh, North Carolina, indicted Garrison for "distributing incendiary matter." A vigilance committee in Columbia, South Carolina, offered a $1,500 reward for the apprehension and conviction of any white person found circulating *The Liberator*, and the Georgia legislature offered $5,000 to anyone who took Garrison to the state to be tried for seditious libel.

In 1832 Garrison formed the New England Anti-Slavery Society, the first organization dedicated to immediatism. Its members included Ellis Gay Loring, David Lee Child, and Samuel Sewall from Boston's elite, as well as several persons from the city's black community. That spring Garrison published his *Thoughts on African Colonization*, in which he condemned sending blacks overseas and defended racial equality.

In 1833 Garrison journeyed to England, where he was treated as a leader of the American abolitionist movement. He formed alliances with his British counterparts and gathered information about their tactics. Later that year he founded the American Anti-Slavery Society and wrote its declaration: "We plant ourselves upon the truths of Divine Revelation and the Declaration of Independence as upon the EVERLASTING ROCK." As with his work on *The Liberator*, Garrison's new group elicited a vehement response from the

William Lloyd Garrison condemned the Constitution as a pact with the devil in its recognition of the right of slavery to exist. *(National Archives and Records Administration)*

South. At one point a mob in Charleston, South Carolina, seized mailbags containing pamphlets published by the organization.

Formation of the society represented another step forward for the moralists in the abolitionist movement, those who viewed politics as corrupt. Garrison insisted that political parties took an interest in moral issues only to gain power; he sought purity of thought and deed. He never rejected all political action, but he feared that if antislavery groups began running candidates for office they would degenerate into mere parties and compromise all of their principles. Other abolitionists, however, disagreed, and they formed the Liberty Party to promote a political solution to slavery.

When the American Anti-Slavery Society faltered financially in 1840, Garrison stepped in to

gain control of it. In 1841 he attended the World Anti-Slavery Convention in London—the first meeting of its kind—but refused to participate when the delegates voted to exclude women from the proceedings.

Back in the United States, Garrison pursued the principle on *The Liberator's* masthead: "No Union with Slaveholders." Calling the Constitution an agreement with the devil for its proslavery content, he burned a copy of it at a Fourth of July celebration.

The Compromise of 1850, which allowed California into the Union as a free state but permitted slavery in New Mexico and amended and strengthened the Fugitive Slave Act of 1793, convinced many abolitionists that Garrison was correct about the futility of political action. In short, the compromise strengthened the moralists.

Yet Garrison antagonized many abolitionists with his crusade for other reforms, particularly his advocacy of women's rights, along with his campaigns against the use of tobacco, capital punishment, and imprisonment for debt. Some abolitionists opposed one or more of Garrison's stands on principle; many others feared that engaging in so many different reforms would antagonize mainstream Americans, who should be recruited for the fight against slavery, and would divert attention from abolitionism. Garrison acted during an era of reform, when dissident Americans were engaging in widespread activities ranging from fighting alcoholism to founding communes.

When the radical abolitionist JOHN BROWN raided the federal arsenal at Harper's Ferry, Virginia, in 1859 in an attempt to ignite a slave rebellion, Garrison rushed to his defense. Garrison preferred nonviolence, but he portrayed Brown's fanatical act as an extension of the American Revolution's fight for liberty.

When the Lower South seceded late in 1860, Garrison, despite his earlier advocacy of Northern secession, condemned its refusal to abide by the principles expressed in the Declaration of Independence. He repeatedly turned to this revolutionary document, rather than the more conservative Constitution, to support his argument that slavery violated liberty.

Similarly to other abolitionists, Garrison at first criticized Abraham Lincoln, calling him an ineffective, compromising politician. But with the president's issuance of the Emancipation Proclamation in 1863 Garrison changed his mind. He wished the proclamation had been expressed in moral terms, but he nevertheless accepted it, and in 1864 he supported Lincoln for reelection.

As the war neared its end in 1865, Garrison proposed to dissolve the American Anti-Slavery Society, saying its work had been completed. But his fellow abolitionist WENDELL PHILLIPS disagreed: Phillips insisted the society should fight for black rights as an extension of abolitionism; his view prevailed, and he led the society into the period of postwar Reconstruction.

In the late 1860s Garrison toured Europe, where he recounted his work as an abolitionist. In 1868 he began writing articles for the *New York Herald*. He died on May 24, 1879, in New York City.

An indefatigable leader in the abolitionist movement, he had been willing to attack fellow abolitionists and slaveholders alike. Speaking out of frustration, the antislavery leader Elizur Wright once said of him, "His guns are all turned inward." For Garrison there could be no compromise, nor could there be tolerance of anyone who supported compromise, whatever his or her ideological persuasion. He burned with commitment: "I have need to be all on fire," he said, "for I have mountains of ice about me to melt."

Further Reading

Kraditor, Aileen S. *Means and Ends in American Abolitionism: Garrison and His Critics on Strategy and Tactics, 1834–1850.* New York: Pantheon Books, 1967.

Mayer, Henry. *All on Fire: William Lloyd Garrison and the Abolition of Slavery.* New York: St. Martin's Press, 1998.

Thomas, John L. *The Liberator: William Lloyd Garrison.* Boston: Little, Brown, 1963.

Garvey, Marcus
(1887–1940) *black nationalist*

A black nationalist, Marcus Garvey was the founder of the Universal Negro Improvement Association. He was born on August 17, 1887, at Saint Ann's Bay, Jamaica, to Marcus Moziah Garvey, a mason, and Sarah Jane Richards Garvey. Both of his parents were descended from Maroons, African slaves in Jamaica who had escaped their masters.

Marcus Garvey attended the local elementary school, but his formal education ended when his family's need for more income caused him at age 14 to begin work as a printer's apprentice. Nevertheless, he read extensively, encouraged to do so by his parents and by the access he had to his father's considerable library. At age 17 Garvey moved to Kingston and helped organize a printers' strike. The collapse of the protest caused him to turn against labor unions.

In 1910 Garvey joined the migrant wave looking for work in Central America, and over the next four years he traveled to South America and England, with each stop broadening his awareness of the plight of black people in a world economically and politically dominated by whites. In London he met Duse Mohammed Ali, a half-black Egyptian; worked for his Pan African paper, *Africa Times*; and shared in his thoughts about the oppression of blacks in England and the decline of black culture in Africa.

While Garvey sailed back to Jamaica in 1914 he read BOOKER TALIAFERRO WASHINGTON's *Up from Slavery*, from which he learned about racial pride and the formidable segregation faced by blacks in the United States. In his *Philosophy and Opinions*, Garvey recalled that he began asking: "Where is the black man's Government? Where is his King and his Kingdom? Where is his President, his country, and his ambassador; his army, his navy, his men of big affairs?" He answered his own questions, asserting, "I could not find them, and then I declared, 'I will help to make them.'"

With that, Garvey founded the Universal Negro Improvement and Conservation Association and African Communities League, usually referred to by the shortened name, the Universal Negro Improvement Association (UNIA). He wrote his goals, or "general objects" as he called them, and in a manifesto stated that he wanted "all people of Negro or African parentage" to join his group's crusade to save the race.

In March 1916 Garvey arrived in New York City to raise money for the UNIA and stayed 11 years. He officially relocated the UNIA headquarters to his new location in 1917. His message that blacks should be proud of their past—for it was one of great accomplishments—and look forward to a great future resonated with African Americans then struggling with white racism and turning toward their own culture for identity and guidance. Garvey arrived as Jim Crow segregation descended on the South and as a black exodus from that region to northern and western cities caused a white backlash in places like New York and Detroit. Shut off from white society, African Americans were turning to jazz and the blues—then emerging from traditional black music—and to their own writers and artists. They turned to the black churches, and Marcus Garvey turned to

Black nationalist Marcus Garvey's dispute with W. E. B. Du Bois turned into ugly name calling. *(Library of Congress)*

them, appealing to their Christianity and to their desire for black pride. "Christ died to make men free," he told African Americans. "I shall die to give courage and inspiration to my race."

Garvey said that God was colorblind, but to free His image from white control, blacks must see Him as black. He said he wanted to build a black republic in Africa stretching from Liberia to Capetown—that it would serve as a source of black pride and as a refuge from white oppression. Writing in *Black Moses* (1955), Garvey biographer E. David Cronon states, "It was never Garvey's intention that all Negroes in the New World would return to Africa. . . . Rather he believed like many Zionists that once a strong African nation was established, Negroes everywhere would automatically gain needed prestige and strength and could look to it for protection if necessary."

Garvey showed an impressive ability to bridge the gap between his West Indian culture and American culture, and the UNIA quickly developed a widespread following. In 1918 he founded the *Negro World* newspaper; by the early 1920s its circulation topped 100,000, and at the same time UNIA branches spread to 38 states.

In 1919 Garvey bought an auditorium on 138th Street in Harlem and renamed it Liberty Hall. There his followers gathered to listen to his speeches. Other Liberty Halls were soon established in Philadelphia, Pittsburgh, Cleveland, Detroit, Cincinnati, Chicago, and Los Angeles.

Garvey advocated economic independence for blacks, a separatism that coincided with his belief that they must look out for themselves first. He founded the Negro Factories Corporation to begin black-owned businesses, and in 1919 he obtained a charter to begin the Black Star Line, which he envisioned as a fleet of ships operated by and staffed only with African Americans. The ships would transport passengers and freight between black countries. To raise capital he issued stock and declared in an advertising circular, "Now is the time for the Negro to invest in the Black Star Line so that in the near future he may exert the same influence upon the world as the white man does today."

In short order, he raised more than $600,000. At $10 a share, the stock was priced so that even poorer African Americans could invest, look forward to making money, and contribute to a black company founded for black people. In November 1919 about 5,000 African Americans gathered at New York's 135th Street pier, and as a UNIA band played, they sent off the *Yarmouth*, the first ship of the Black Star Line. Wherever the *Yarmouth* sailed, blacks turned out in large numbers to cheer its arrival.

By that time Garvey's reputation had become practically global; millions of blacks looked to him for leadership. In 1920 he held a massive international convention at Madison Square Garden. Some 25,000 delegates attended from dozens of countries. At the meeting he demanded that whites be expelled from Africa, and the delegates approved a Declaration of Rights of the Negro Peoples of the World. "Nowhere in the world, with few exceptions, are black men accorded equal treatment with white men," the declaration claimed. There began a long list of demands followed by the statement "Be it known that whereas, all men are created equal and entitled to the rights of life, liberty, and the pursuit of happiness . . . [we] do declare all men, women and children of our blood throughout the world free citizens, and do claim them as free citizens of Africa, the Motherland of all Negroes."

Garvey's crusade generated controversy and produced enemies. Some blacks disliked his insistence on racial purity. He caused an uproar in 1922 when he met with leaders of the Ku Klux Klan and told them he supported their fight against miscegenation. To his critics, Garvey responded: "I regard the Klan . . . as better friends of the race than all other hypocritical whites put together. I like honesty and fair play. . . . Potentially every white man is a Klansman, as far as the Negro competition with whites socially, economically and politically is concerned, and there is no use lying about it."

The integrationist National Association for the Advancement of Colored People (NAACP) attacked Garvey's separatism. W. E. B. DU BOIS, a leader of the NAACP, called Garvey ugly for his blackness and labeled him a "lunatic." Garvey called Du Bois a "lazy dependent mulatto." The federal government spied on the UNIA, and at the

urging of several white and black leaders of the NAACP, the Justice Department had Garvey indicted for fraud involving the Black Star Line. The charges held little merit—the shipping company's profits suffered from mismanagement rather than anything illegal—but a jury found Garvey guilty, and a judge who was a member of the NAACP sentenced him to a maximum of five years in prison.

Garvey partisans have claimed that the embattled black nationalist suffered from the prejudice of the judge, yet Garvey represented himself at the trial and often acted arrogantly and with more emphasis on proving the oppression of blacks than answering the charges against him. Garvey's own newspaper called the judge "fair" in his instructions to the jury.

President Calvin Coolidge responded to a flood of letters and petitions and in 1927 commuted Garvey's sentence—but ordered him deported. Garvey returned to Jamaica, edited two newspapers, and in 1929 held another international convention, which was well attended. Back in the United States the UNIA suffered from a factional split.

To many blacks, when Marcus Garvey died on June 10, 1940, he died a hero. Especially in Jamaica and in Africa, monuments were built to him and buildings were named after him. Historian Cronon observes:

> The Black Star Line . . . the Negro Factories Corporation . . . and the other components of the UNIA itself were all a part of the general plan to weld the Negro people into a racially conscious, united group for effective mass action. . . . The importance of this aspect of the movement in restoring the all but shattered Negro self-confidence should not be overlooked. . . .
>
> Garvey exalted everything black and exhorted Negroes to be proud of their distinctive features and color. Negroid characteristics were not shameful marks of inferiority to be camouflaged and altered; they were rather symbols of beauty and grace.

Pride, independence, and unity—these Garvey attributes appealed to African Americans, or in the words of the UNIA official motto: "One Aim! One God! One Destiny!"

Further Reading

Cronon, E. David. *Black Moses: The Story of Marcus Garvey and the Universal Negro Improvement Association.* Madison: University of Wisconsin Press, 1955.

Garvey, Marcus. *Philosophy and Opinions of Marcus Garvey.* 2 vols. New York: Arno Press, 1968–69.

Hill, Robert A., ed. *The Marcus Garvey and UNIA Papers.* Berkeley: University of California Press, 1983.

———, ed. *Marcus Garvey, Life and Lessons: A Centennial Companion to The Marcus Garvey and Universal Negro Improvement Association Papers.* Berkeley: University of California Press, 1987.

Martin, Tony. *Marcus Garvey Hero: A First Biography.* Dover, Mass.: The Majority Press, 1983.

Youssef, Sitamon Mubaraka, ed. *Marcus Garvey: The F.B.I. Investigation Files.* Trenton, N.J.: Africa World Press, 1998.

George, Henry

(1839–1897) *Progressive reformer*

A Progressive reformer, Henry George devised a single-tax scheme that changed the way many Americans looked at their economy. He was born on September 2, 1839, in Philadelphia, Pennsylvania, to Richard George, a shipmaster, and Mary Reid George.

Henry George obtained only a limited education; he attended a private school until age nine and thereafter two elementary schools, followed by several months in a high school, but he quit at age 14 to work as an errand boy. Nevertheless, he read extensively and improved himself by attending public lectures. Raised in a financially strapped family, but one solidly attached to middle-class values, George thought that hard work would lead to success. Try as he might, though, he only encountered setbacks. In 1855 he took to the sea and eventually landed in India. Two years later he sailed from Philadelphia around South America to Oregon. He then made his way to San Francisco, where he set type for a newspaper and headed for California's gold fields, where he hoped to strike it rich but left empty-handed.

Henry George advocated a "single tax" that he believed would eliminate the need for any other tax. *(National Archives and Records Administration)*

In December 1861 George married Annie Fox, and after several more years of odd jobs, in 1866 he found work with the *San Francisco Times* as a reporter. He was soon promoted to editorial writer and then managing editor. In 1869 he became editor of the *Oakland Transcript,* and in 1871 he wrote *Our Land and Land Policy,* which first presented the ideas he would more thoroughly discuss in his more famous book, *Progress and Poverty.*

About that time, however, the *Oakland Transcript* collapsed, leaving George without an income, and when the depression of the 1870s began, he concluded that opportunity for millions of Americans had been destroyed. He reasoned that the country needed a structural change in its economy. With that, he published *Progress and Poverty,* which appeared in 1879. "The present century has been marked by a prodigious increase in wealth-producing power," he wrote, that was expected to "make real poverty a thing of the past." Instead, the country had reaped disappointment. He continued: "The gulf between the employed and the employer is growing wider; social contrasts are becoming sharper; as liveried carriages appear, so do barefooted children."

George bemoaned the loss of the frontier and the public domain, which in the past had provided cheap land and a chance to live independently. There existed, he wrote, only a finite amount of land, and with the rapid population growth then under way it was becoming more expensive and unavailable to the working people. Landowners, he claimed, were getting more of the country's wealth, while laborers were getting less.

To fight this inequity, George proposed a "single tax," a 100 percent tax on increased values of land, the money collected to be used for the public welfare. With such a levy the country would need no other taxes—hence the name *single tax*—and it would have no need to resort to more extreme measures, such as confiscating property or replacing capitalism with communism.

George believed his tax was fair because land increased in value as a result of the community growing up around it, so the community as a whole should enjoy the profits. His tax, he claimed, would prevent people from speculating in land, and since capital and wages would be untaxed, they would increase and poverty would end.

Within a year *Progress and Poverty* sold millions of copies, and its readership extended overseas. One union, the Knights of Labor, claimed, "No man has exercised so great an influence upon the labor movement of to-day as Henry George." A historian has since said that "Henry George's stance was decidedly radical" because it challenged traditional economic theory and embraced the "strongly held beliefs of working people."

Americans formed single-tax clubs, and in 1886 George ran for mayor of New York City; he lost by a narrow margin. He never envisioned forming a single-tax colony, but his followers founded a prominent one in 1894, when they settled the town of Fairhope along Mobile Bay in Alabama.

George died on October 29, 1897, in New York City while again campaigning for mayor, this time as an independent Democrat. By then the popularity of his single-tax idea was waning, and it was soon largely forgotten. The single tax was, after all, a curious attempt to solve urban problems by emphasizing a commodity tied to the rural past, namely, land. Obviously, land remained important in America's development, but the industrial economy focused less on its availability than on that of jobs, along with working conditions and the regulation of capital itself.

Further Reading

Cord, Steven B. *Henry George: Dreamer or Realist?* Philadelphia: University of Pennsylvania Press, 1965.

Rose, Edward J. *Henry George.* New York: Twayne Publishers, 1968.

Wenzer, Kenneth C., ed. *An Anthology of Henry George's Thought.* Rochester, N.Y. University of Rochester Press, 1997.

Gilman, Charlotte Perkins
(Charlotte Perkins Stetson)
(1860–1935) *feminist, writer*

A writer and socialist, Charlotte Perkins Gilman was an advocate of women's economic independence. She was born on July 3, 1860, in Hartford, Connecticut, to Frederick Beecher Perkins and Mary Westcott Perkins.

Because Frederick Perkins deserted his family, Charlotte grew up in poverty and received only a limited education. Yet she read extensively and made money by teaching art. In 1884 she married a fellow artist, Charles Walter Stetson, and they had one child, Katherine Beecher, born the following year. But the unhappiness that dominated Charlotte's childhood continued; she and Charles fought often and in 1894 they divorced.

Influenced by EDWARD BELLAMY's book *Looking Backward,* in the early 1890s Charlotte Perkins joined the Nationalist movement, which sought to apply socialist principles and move society toward the utopian state presented by Bellamy. At the same time, she published a highly acclaimed short story, "The Yellow Wall-Paper," that dealt with insanity and reflected her own episodes of severe depression. She also wrote a volume of poems, *In This Our World.* In the late 1890s she traveled extensively, speaking on women's issues, and in 1898 she published her best-known work, *Women and Economics,* so widely circulated that it eventually was translated into six languages.

In the book Perkins argued that women's oppression stemmed from economics and that to improve their lot women must become independent. "We are the only ... animal species," she wrote, "in which the sex-relation is also an economic relation. With us an entire sex lives in a relation of economic dependence upon the other sex, and the economic relation is combined with the sex-relation." She continued:

Charlotte Perkins Gilman argued that women's oppression stemmed from economic dependency and that to improve their lot women must become independent of men. *(Library of Congress)*

The working power of the mother has always been a prominent factor in human life. She is the worker *par excellence,* but her work is not such as to affect her economic status. Her living, all that she gets—food, clothing, ornaments, amusements, luxuries—these bear no relation to her power to produce wealth, to her services in the house, or to her motherhood. These things bear relation only to the man she marries, the man she depends on.

According to Perkins, the system of the man's being the provider and the ruler had had only ill effects:

The lust for power and conquest, natural to the male of any species, has been fostered in him to an enormous degree by this cheap and easy lordship.... When man's place was maintained by brute force, it made him more brutal; when his place was maintained by purchase, by the power of economic necessity, then he grew into the merciless use of such power as distinguishes him to-day.... Another giant evil engendered by this relation is what we call selfishness.... To have a whole human creature consecrated to his direct personal service, to pleasing and satisfying him in every way possible—this has kept man selfish beyond the degree incidental to our stage of social growth.

In 1900 Charlotte Perkins married her cousin, Houghton Gilman, a lawyer, with the stipulation that she would continue her work. She wrote *The Man-Made World* in 1911, and from 1909 to 1916 she wrote, edited, and published the monthly magazine *Forerunner,* which included in its contents short stories, essays, poems, and book reviews.

Gilman wrote *His Religion and Hers* in 1923 and a few years later completed her autobiography (published after her death). In the early 1930s Charlotte Perkins Gilman contracted cancer, and rather than endure the pain, on August 17, 1935, she committed suicide at her home in Pasadena, California.

In a poem that accompanied *Women and Economics* Gilman wrote that men should not fear the independent woman—trust her to grow, she said, and she will love even more:

Love thee? She will love thee as only freedom knoweth!

Love thee? She will love thee while Love itself doth live!

Fear not the heart of woman! No bitterness
it showeth!

The ages of her sorrow have but taught her
to forgive!

Further Reading

Gilman, Charlotte Perkins. *The Living of Charlotte Perkins Gilman: An Autobiography.* Madison: University of Wisconsin Press, 1991.

Golden, Catherine J., and Joanna Schneider Zangrando, eds. *The Mixed Legacy of Charlotte Perkins Gilman.* Cranbury, N.J.: Associated University Presses, 2000.

Hill, Mary Armfield. *Charlotte Perkins Gilman: The Making of a Radical Feminist.* Philadelphia, Pa.: Temple University Press, 1980.

———, ed. *A Journey from Within: The Love Letters of Charlotte Perkins Gilman, 1897–1900.* Lewisburg, Pa.: Bucknell University Press, 1995.

Goldman, Emma

(1869–1940) *anarchist, women's rights activist*

An anarchist and atheist, Emma Goldman tested the boundaries of society. She was born on June 27, 1869, in Kovno, Lithuania, the daughter of Jewish parents, Abraham Goldman and Taube Goldman.

Emma Goldman's childhood was filled with the violence meted out by her father. He hated having a daughter, rather than a son, (the sons came later, giving Goldman two younger brothers) and when she showed even the slightest inclination to socialize with boys, he beat her. At an early age, then, in an intimate way, she felt the brutality of authority.

She received a limited education and in 1882 moved with her family to Saint Petersburg, Russia, where her father opened a grocery store. At that time Russia was going through tremendous upheaval: The czar had just been assassinated and

revolutionaries were fomenting rebellion. Too young to understand the political tracts then being circulated, Emma nonetheless felt the pace of dissent and liked it. She also was shocked at the retribution against Jews as the Russian government launched anti-Semitic attacks while cracking down on revolutionary activity.

"In this decade of disenchantment and pessimism . . . ," writes the Goldman biographer Alice Wexler in *Emma Goldman in America* (1984), "Emma felt stifled and discontented." So in 1885 she joined her half-sister in immigrating to the United States.

Emma Goldman settled in Rochester, New York, and began attending meetings of a German socialist group while working in a clothing factory. In 1887 she married a fellow worker, Jacob Kershner, but they soon divorced.

Goldman identified strongly with the anarchists accused of exploding a bomb during a labor protest at Chicago's Haymarket Square. Their trial and execution angered her and encouraged her to join the anarchist cause. She began attending their meetings and adopted a modified version of the ideas promoted by the Russian anarchist Peter Kropotkin. Like Kropotkin, Goldman foresaw a utopia in which government would be replaced by voluntary associations and people would be compensated for their work on the basis of their needs. But unlike Kropotkin, Goldman concerned herself less with the shape of a future society than with the destruction of the existing one. In short, she was an antagonist rather than a philosopher.

In 1889 Goldman moved to New York City, where she began collaborating with ALEXANDER BERKMAN, a young Russian anarchist. They fell in love and would remain lovers for many years. But she had at least one other lover in the anarchist movement and believed in free love for some of the same reasons she believed in anarchy: the liberation of the individual. To Goldman anarchy removed government constraints that stunted individual growth. Free love did likewise. She condemned marriage (although she married twice) for its attachment to the state and church and for the pressure it placed on two people to stay together even after they were no longer compatible.

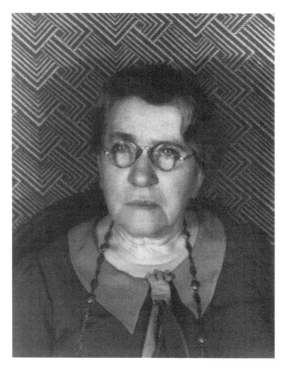

Emma Goldman's anarchist activities caused her to be deported by the federal government shortly after World War I. *(Library of Congress)*

In 1892 Berkman attempted to assassinate Henry Clay Frick, manager of Andrew Carnegie's steel plant in Homestead, Pennsylvania. The deed botched, he was arrested and spent the next 14 years in prison. Many years later, in her autobiography, Goldman claimed she had helped with the plot in support of Berkman's belief that the killing of a tyrant was not murder. "To remove a tyrant," Berkman had said, "is an act of liberation, the giving of life and opportunity to an oppressed people."

The police arrested Goldman in 1893 after she told a mass meeting of unemployed workers in New York City: "Ask for work. If they do not give you work, ask for bread. If they do not give you work or bread, then take bread." Charged with inciting a riot—though there had been no riot—she spent a year in Blackwell's Island prison.

While there she took up nursing, and after her release in August 1894 she traveled to Europe and studied medicine in Vienna. On her return to the United States in 1896 she worked as a nurse and midwife among the immigrant poor in New York City's Lower East Side.

Goldman traveled to Europe a second time in 1899 and met several anarchist leaders, including Peter Kropotkin. Two years later she managed Kropotkin's speaking tour of the United States. After an anarchist assassinated President William McKinley in 1901, she came under intense government scrutiny and so went into seclusion. She had no direct involvement with the killing, but the assassin, Leon Czolgosz, claimed he had been motivated to act after hearing Goldman speak.

By 1906 Emma Goldman had ended her seclusion; she was again lecturing and was editing an anarchist monthly, *Mother Earth,* with the help of Berkman, who had been released from prison.

Added to her anarchistic pronouncements, she spoke out against religion. She thought Christianity especially suited to mind control, producing obedient slaves. Goldman believed religion unnecessary—and even counterproductive—to living as a human being, which required, she said, treating people with respect.

She spoke also about the need for women to be psychologically liberated, meaning they must free themselves from the iron hand of public opinion. She distanced herself from the suffragists, for she thought them too middle class, and in any event, she never had any faith in voting. Yet in her later years she considered herself to be a feminist.

In her public speaking, it was necessary for Goldman to be wary of government interference. Local authorities frequently sent in the police to disrupt her—even when she avoided anarchy as a topic and spoke about theater rather than politics.

In 1910 Goldman wrote *Anarchism and Other Essays.* That year she also advocated birth control and served a 15-day jail sentence in New York City for speaking on the subject. The law at that time prohibited the dissemination of any birth control information or devices.

With the entry of the United States into World War I, Goldman and Berkman advised young men to resist the draft. As a result, they were arrested in June 1917 on charges of conspiracy. At her trial Goldman said to the jury:

Remember that those who fought and bled for your liberties were in their time considered as being against the law, as dangerous disturbers and trouble-makers. They not only preached violence, but they carried out their ideas by throwing tea into the Boston Harbor. They said that "Resistance to tyranny is obedience to God." They were the anarchists of their time.

I for one cannot believe that love of one's country must . . . consist in blindness to its social faults. I know many people—I am one of them—who were not born here, and who yet love America with deeper passion and greater intensity than many natives. Our patriotism is of the man who loves a woman with open eyes. He is enchanted by her beauty, yet sees her faults.

Goldman and Berkman were convicted on July 9 and fined and sentenced to two years in prison. Shortly after Goldman's release from the Missouri state penitentiary in Jefferson City, Attorney General A. Mitchell Palmer began arresting radicals and deported 39 in what became known as the "Red Scare."

The next month the government deported 249 aliens to Russia, and among them were Alexander Berkman and Emma Goldman. J. Edgar Hoover, head of the General Intelligence Division of the Department of Justice (later the Federal Bureau of Investigation [FBI]), had been eager to rid the country of her, and the government formally charged her under a law passed by Congress in 1918 that authorized deportation of any noncitizen immigrant who belonged to an organization that advocated revolution. In early December a federal court had ruled that Goldman did not have the U.S. citizenship she claimed to have acquired through marriage and could be deported to Russia. On December 21 she was placed aboard the transport *Buford*, nicknamed the "Soviet Ark," along with Berkman and the other aliens.

Hoover and several congressman whom he had invited to a bon voyage celebration watched and reveled in their victory. The *New York Times* said good riddance as well, hailing "the sweet sorrow of parting at last with two of the most pernicious anarchists, Emma Goldman and Alexander Berkman, for a generation among the most viru-

lent and dangerous preachers and practicers of the doctrines of destruction."

Goldman had earlier praised the Russian Revolution, but on her arrival in the Soviet Union she began criticizing the government for its oppression. She left the country in 1921 and over the next few years lived in Latvia, Estonia, Sweden, Germany, England, and Canada. While in England she obtained citizenship by marrying James Colton, a Welsh miner. In 1923 she published *My Disillusionment in Russia*.

Goldman briefly visited the United States in 1934 on a temporary visa. When the Spanish Civil War erupted, she sided with the republican forces fighting the fascist Francisco Franco and traveled frequently to England and Canada to raise money for them. In 1940 she suffered a stroke while in Toronto and died there on May 14. Her legacy, says Alice Wexler, was one "of a life dedicated to free speech, free labor, free thought, free love; a life lived in the grip of a powerful libertarian passion. . . . It is the legacy, moreover, of an immigrant who became an American without losing any of her radical commitment."

In her autobiography, Goldman wrote:

> Anarchism alone stresses the importance of the individual, his possibilities and needs in a free society. Instead of telling him that he must fall down and worship before institutions, live and die for abstractions, break his heart and stunt his life for taboos, anarchism insists that the center of gravity in society is the individual—that he must think for himself, act freely, and live fully.

Further Reading

Chalberg, John. *Emma Goldman: American Individualist.* New York: Harper Collins, 1991.

Drinnon, Richard. *Rebel in Paradise: A Biography of Emma Goldman.* Chicago: University of Chicago Press, 1982.

Falk, Candace. *Love, Anarchy, and Emma Goldman.* Rev. ed. New Brunswick, N.J.: Rutgers University Press, 1990.

Glassgold, Peter, ed. *Anarchy! An Anthology of Emma Goldman's Mother Earth.* Washington, D.C.: Counterpoint, 2001.

Haaland, Bonnie. *Emma Goldman: Sexuality and the Impurity of the State.* New York: Black Rose Books, 1993.

Wexler, Alice. *Emma Goldman: An Intimate Life.* New York: Pantheon Books, 1984.

———. *Emma Goldman in Exile: From the Russian Revolution to the Spanish Civil War.* Boston: Beacon Press, 1989.

Gompers, Samuel
(1850–1924) *union organizer*

Samuel Gompers was the founder and first president of the American Federation of Labor. He was born on January 27, 1850, in London to Solomon Gompers, a cigar maker, and Sarah Rood Gompers.

Samuel Gompers attended a Jewish free school until he reached age 10, at which time his family's poverty forced him to work as an apprentice shoemaker. A few years later his father arranged for him to apprentice as a cigar maker. In 1863 Solomon Gompers decided to move his family to New York City, and soon after they arrived Samuel found employment as a journeyman cigar maker. In 1864 he joined the Cigarmakers' Union.

America's economy changed tremendously in the 1860s and 1870s. Industrialization that had begun before the Civil War now accelerated; machines replaced many skilled workers, and the rapid shift away from a farm economy—along with urbanization and the influx of immigrants such as the Gompers family—often meant for laborers low wages and long working hours in the factories and confinement to urban slums.

As labor struggled to come to grips with the economic problems that confronted it, activists promoted several alternatives. The Knights of Labor, which was organized in the 1860s and became the country's largest union, envisioned bringing all workers together in one organization and building a shared commonwealth where wages would be unnecessary. Socialists wanted workers to capture control of the government through a labor party and from there establish the workers' control of industries. Like the socialists, Marxists wanted to see workers run the government, but they thought labor too weak to form a party and instead sought to bolster labor solidarity and class consciousness by helping trade unions fight for improved working conditions through strikes.

The heart of the debate among labor activists was whether to advance workers' rights through political parties or through trade unions. From there the argument centered on whether to seek revolutionary change or the more limited goal of better pay, a shorter workweek, and more benefits.

In the cigar making shop Samuel Gompers became friendly with Ferdinand Laurell, a Marxist from Sweden. Laurell taught Gompers about Marxism and advised him to attend meetings where he could acquaint himself with socialist ideas. At those meetings Gompers met other workers, who later joined him in promoting unionism. But Laurell advised Gompers against becoming a socialist or embracing any utopian plans. Instead he said that Gompers should engage in activities that would result in a stronger union and reject pie-in-the-sky political schemes.

Gompers agreed and chose to build a trade union rather than a political party. He believed that "every political movement must be subordinated to the first great social end, [namely] the economic emancipation of the working classes." He asserted that it was most important to unionize all working people, reduce the length of the workday, and improve wages. Regarding the Marxist insistence that labor should be freed from capitalist "wage slavery," he said that workers must first be freed from poverty and industrial exploitation; he had no interest in overthrowing political systems. (On several occasions, however, he did direct unions to support political candidates who had endorsed labor's views.)

As to the dominant Knights of Labor, Bernard Mandel writes in *Samuel Gompers: A Biography* (1963) that Gompers

> was militant and aggressive where they were conservative and overcautious. He was practical and businesslike, while they were visionary and utopian. He was the worker, and they were middle-class reformers. Gompers could not go along with them in their concern with monetary panaceas, land reforms, and co-operatives, or with their political adventures and their reliance on the state to emancipate the working class.

After the Cigarmakers' Union in New York City staged several disastrous strikes in the 1870s, Gompers and Adolph Strasser, head of the German-speaking branch of the union, took the lead in rebuilding the organization. They established an international union to which local cigar makers' unions would be responsible; they increased dues to form a strike fund; and they set their sights on obtaining sickness, accident, and unemployment benefits. These actions established a model that other trade unions followed.

In 1881 Gompers and Strasser helped form the Federation of Organized Trades and Labor Unions, with Gompers chairman of the committee that wrote the group's constitution. This federation was reorganized in 1886 as the American Federation of Labor (AFL). The AFL consisted of autonomous trade, or craft, unions; only one union was allowed for each craft, such as cigar making, carpentry, and shoemaking. Unskilled workers were excluded.

Gompers believed that the AFL should fight for better working and living conditions through collective action. He supported strikes as an economic weapon, but only as a last resort.

He was elected president of the AFL and worked in that role until his death (except in 1895, when the socialists gained temporary control of the union). As the AFL expanded, Gompers became a political power, much disliked by many businessmen, but recognized as talented, intelligent, and less extreme than the labor radicals.

Unlike most of the socialists, Gompers supported the U.S. entry into World War I, organized a War Committee on Labor that comprised union representatives and employers, and forged a cordial relationship with President Woodrow Wilson. He condemned pacifism and labor groups that embraced it on principle. At the Paris Peace Conference he served on the Commission on International Labor Legislation.

Samuel Gompers had married Sophia Julian in 1867, and they had six children who survived infancy. In 1921, one year after Sophia's death, he married Grace Gleaves Neuscheler. Gompers died on December 13, 1924, in San Antonio, Texas, after a trip to Mexico where he met with that country's political and labor leaders.

Founder and first president of the American Federation of Labor, Samuel Gompers sought to work with emerging corporations rather than attempt to overturn them. *(National Archives and Records Administration)*

His two-volume *Seventy Years of Life and Labor,* one of six books that he wrote, was published posthumously in 1925. He once said, "At no time in my life have I worked out a definitely articulated economic theory." He preferred, instead, to act and to apply trade unionist principles as effectively as he could.

Further Reading

Livesay, Harold C. *Samuel Gompers and Organized Labor in America.* Boston: Little, Brown, 1978.

McKillen, Elizabeth. *Chicago Labor and the Quest for a Democratic Diplomacy, 1914–1924.* Ithaca, N.Y.: Cornell University Press, 1995.

Mandel, Bernard. *Samuel Gompers: A Biography.* Yellow Springs, Ohio: Antioch Press, 1963.

Gonzales, Rodolfo
(Corky Gonzales)
(1928–   ) *Chicano rights leader*

Rodolfo "Corky" Gonzales radicalized the Chicano rights movement with his militant call for separatism. He was born in Denver, Colorado, on June 18, 1928, to parents who worked in the beet fields north of the city.

As a youngster Gonzales attended four different grade schools, three different middle schools, and two different high schools because his family's life as migrant workers required frequent moves from town to town. According to Gonzales, his teachers taught him "how to forget Spanish, to forget my heritage, to forget who I was." He excelled as a boxer, typically reading poetry before a fight to steel his resolve, and at age 19 in 1947 he won the National Athletic Union bantam weight title, an achievement that later earned him induction into the Colorado Sports Hall of Fame. He went on to fight professionally, boxing 125 times in eight years and recording 112 wins against only 12 losses and a draw.

In the 1950s, while owning a bar and a bail bond company, Gonzales entered mainstream politics when he ran as a Democrat for the state legislature. Although he lost, his strong showing resulted in his appointment in 1957 as the first Chicano Democratic district captain. An effective community organizer, in 1960 he was made Colorado coordinator of the "Viva Kennedy!" campaign, the effort by presidential candidate John F. Kennedy to rally Hispanic voters in the state to his bid for the White House.

In 1963 Gonzales founded Los Voluntarios, a group that sought more political representation of Mexican Americans in Denver and protested police brutality in the barrio. The following year he directed the Denver Neighborhood Youth Corps, and in 1965 he headed the city's War on Poverty program. He showed every indication of working within the party system as a liberal and was even criticized by some Chicanos as a puppet of the Anglo establishment.

But in 1966 Gonzales broke with the Democrats in a dispute with Denver's mayor over how the youth corps should be run, and at a rally held by Los Voluntarios he declared, "We are on a crusade for justice." He later said, "We wanted to create a civil rights organization, a human rights organization." Consequently, Gonzales formed a new group, Crusade for Justice, after the main phrase in his declaration.

As American politics radicalized in the 1960s, and as Denver's Hispanic population topped 43,000, Gonzales advocated bilingual education, independent Chicano schools, and economic and political separation from Anglo society. In November 1967 he called for a Chicano nationalistic and ethnic movement and urged Mexican Americans to drop out of politics and teach each other pride in their heritage and culture.

His subsequent protests, carried out through the Crusade for Justice, included a march against the police, who had shot an unarmed 15-year-old Mexican-American youth; a "splash-in" at a white public swimming pool to expose the shoddy facilities in Chicano neighborhoods; and the 1970 founding of Escuela Tlatelolco, a free school dedicated to teaching Chicano children the basics through bilingual classes and promoting social activism and cultural pride. The school, which continues to operate in the year 2002, enrolls students in the first through 12th grades under the auspices of an eastern institution, Goddard College in Vermont.

Gonzales admitted his indebtedness to African-American radicals when he said in 1969: "For the Black brothers, they are practicing the same thing [nationalism] now. And we understand and respect it." He described Chicano separatism, or nationalism, as Mexican Americans' running their own communities and preventing whites from exploiting them economically. He reflected the 1960s antiestablishment spirit when he called the Republicans and Democrats "an animal with two heads eating out of the same trough, that sits on the same boards of directors of the banks and corporations, that shares the same industries that make dollars and profits off wars."

In 1970 Gonzales helped found an independent Mexican American political party, the Colorado State La Raza Unida, and was elected its state chairman. A riot between Chicanos and Denver police in August 1971, which erupted when the police overreacted to a fight, led Gonzales to declare: "We don't want cops in our community anymore. We're going to try and meet with them, but that won't change anything. . . . We're going to create our own community patrols."

But the Crusade for Justice lost much of its support after another confrontation with Denver police in March 1973 resulted in gunfire and an explosion that devastated a building owned by the Chicano organization. Support further weakened in 1975 when the police arrested two crusade activists for plotting to blow up a police substation.

Critics, among them many Mexican Americans, condemned Gonzales for antagonizing Anglos and misguiding his followers with his appeal to separatism. Yet he was popular among Chicano youths, activated them politically, and opened the doors to public office for more Mexican Americans.

Gonzales was severely injured in an auto accident in October 1987 and suffered memory loss. The crusade, though, continued to operate as a nonprofit corporation. Writing in 1999, Ernesto B. Vigil well remembered Gonzales and his Crusade for Justice as "the most powerful and effective organization to fight for the rights of people of Mexican descent in the state of Colorado in this century."

Further Reading

Marin, Christine. *A Spokesman for the Mexican American Movement: Rodolfo "Corky" Gonzales and the Fight for Chicano Liberation, 1966–1972.* San Francisco: R & E Research Associates, 1977.

Vigil, Ernesto B. *The Crusade of Justice: Chicano Militancy and the Government's War on Dissent.* Madison: University of Wisconsin Press, 1999.

Goodman, Paul
(1911–1972) *anarchist, writer*

An anarchist and a lay psychotherapist, Paul Goodman was a prolific writer. He was born in New York's Greenwich Village on September 9, 1911, to Barnett Goodman and Augusta Goodman. Paul Goodman's father deserted the family when the youngster was still an infant, leaving him to be raised by his mother.

Goodman graduated from Townsend Harris High School in 1927 and from the City College of New York in 1931. Later in the decade he entered graduate school at the University of Chicago, but in 1940 financial problems forced him to drop out. He eventually returned to his studies and received his doctorate in 1954.

Influenced by the writing of Peter Kropotkin, Goodman argued for a communitarian anarchism. A pacifist, he avoided military service during World War II. Although he wrote extensively in the 1940s, because of his radical views he was largely ignored. He did, however, team with Frederick Perls and Ralph Hefferline to publish in 1951 a textbook, *Gestalt Therapy*, based on his practice of lay therapy. Goodman believed that mental and emotional health arose from physical contentment.

Openly bisexual, Goodman was socially ostracized for his pronouncements supporting homosexuality and was fired from two teaching positions. Yet he was twice involved in common-law marriages. The first was to Virginia Miller, with whom he had one daughter; it lasted from 1938 to their separation in 1943. The second was to Sally Duchsten, with whom he had another daughter and a son; it lasted from 1945 to his death.

Goodman seemed headed for obscurity despite his attempts to be well published and to find a forum for his ideas. That changed, however, in 1960, when his commentary *Growing Up Absurd* appeared after its rejection by many publishers. The book's content coincided with the maturation of the 1960s baby boomers, and as that decade's counterculture with its New Left politics gained momentum, *Growing Up Absurd* fit the outlook of a restless, rebellious generation.

In the book Goodman argued that America's young people felt alienated because they had been separated from nature and honest work, and he proposed establishing camps where they would be able to experience the natural world and perform jobs that would benefit society. To the counterculture, though, his book was most appealing for its portrayal of modern society as conformist and commercialized to the point of stifling and oppressing individualism. In several subsequent essays, he returned to this theme:

Every element of [President Lyndon Johnson's] . . . Great Society, including its war on poverty and its conservation, is contaminated by, compromised by, and finally determined by lust, greed, and fear of change. . . .

The drive to schooling . . . is not to liberate the children and to insure that we will have independent and intelligent citizens (this was the educational aim of Jefferson); it is apprentice-training of the middle class for the corporations and military, a desperate attempt to make slum children employable and ruly.

The Great Society is to aggrandize the Establishment, the education barons, the broadcasting barons, the automobile barons, the shopping center barons.

Counterculture youths, especially those within the New Left who considered liberalism a sellout to the corporate military state, agreed with Goodman, and he became a sought-after lecturer and consultant. Over the years he taught at the University of Chicago, the University of Wisconsin, Sarah Lawrence College, San Francisco State College, and the University of Hawaii.

In 1964 Goodman wrote *Compulsory Mis-Education*, in which he attacked progressive educators for weakening standards. At the same time, he participated in several antiwar demonstrations against the American presence in Vietnam. Yet Goodman often disagreed with the counterculture, for he believed it was contributing to a decline in education with its destructive antiintellectualism, a view he expressed in his 1970 work, *New Reformation: Notes of a Neolithic Conservative.*

Paul Goodman, who lived on New York City's Lower West Side, died at his summer farm in North Stratford, New Hampshire, on August 2, 1972. He had written more than 40 books, plays, and short stories, along with essays and poems. In addition to those noted, they included *Communitas* (1947), a nonfiction work about urban planning, cowritten with his brother Percival Goodman; *The Structure of Literature* (1954); and *The Empire City* (1959).

Further Reading

Fried, Lewis. *Makers of the City.* Amherst: University of Massachusetts Press, 1990.

Stoehr, Taylor, ed. *Decentralizing Power: Paul Goodman's Social Criticism.* Montreal: Black Rose Books, 1994.

Widmer, Kingsley. *Paul Goodman.* Boston: Twayne Publishers, 1980.

Graham, Sylvester
(1794–1851) *health reformer*

Sylvester Graham was a health reformer who is most famous today for the cracker that was named after him. He was born on July 5, 1794, in West Suffield, Connecticut, to John and Ruth Graham.

John Graham, a clergyman, was 72 years old when Sylvester, the last of his 12 children, was born. When the elder Graham died two years later, he left his wife in poverty, causing her to break up the family and turn Sylvester over to relatives to be raised. Largely ignored by them, Sylvester obtained only a limited schooling, and in his teens and early adulthood he worked at odd jobs. In 1823, however, he entered Amherst Academy in Amherst, Massachusetts, intent on following his father's profession by becoming a minister. The 30-year-old Graham was so derided by his fellow students for his mannerisms that he left Amherst after one term.

He then fell seriously ill and remained debilitated until 1826, when he married one of the women who helped nurse him back to health. Three years later Graham became a Presbyterian minister and a lecturer for the Pennsylvania Society for Discouraging the Use of Ardent Spirits, making him part of the vibrant temperance movement then under way throughout much of the United States.

The 1830s and 1840s were decades of reform, when many reformers tied their doctrines to moral issues in an attempt to rejuvenate a republican society, which they viewed as decadent, and to save individual souls. Graham fit that profile. At first he argued that alcohol destroyed the body and the spirit. Then he expanded his argument to include the excessive use of foods. For him, diet and morality fit together, hand and glove.

Lecturing up and down the East Coast, he advised people to avoid excitement. Graham proscribed spices such as pepper and salt, and he said that Americans should bathe more often, engage in physical exercise, and wear loose-fitting clothing. Stimulation, gluttony, and dirt were evils to be avoided.

Although sizable audiences turned out to hear Graham speak, his appeal remained limited until 1832, when Americans feared that a cholera epidemic would spread from Europe. Graham offered the prescription for health: a proper diet, meaning fruits, vegetables, and coarsely ground whole wheat, along with the avoidance of meat, spices, alcohol, coffee, and tea. Improper diet, Graham claimed, irritated the stomach and allowed cholera to take hold. His *Lecture on Epidemic Disease Generally and Particularly the Spasmodic Cholera*, published in 1833, presented his health proposal.

Graham's followers praised him; his critics questioned his sanity. He generated enormous controversy when he advocated that commercially baked white bread be stricken from diets. He said that it provided only wasted calories and clogged up the digestive system. Graham advised people to eat bread baked at home from "good, unbolted [or unsifted] wheatmeal, coarsely ground" and served "when at least 12 hours old"; he insisted, "There is no article of artificially prepared food known in civic life the use of which more . . . keeps up the regular and healthful functions of the stomach and intestines." From unbolted wheat—or Graham flour, as it was then christened, though it had already existed for many years—appeared the Graham cracker.

His views so angered bakers (and butchers, who disliked his vegetarianism) that when he arrived in Boston to speak, they struck back. They mobbed the hotel where he appeared, only to be turned back by Grahamites who had perched on the roof and dropped lime on their heads.

When Graham discussed the causes of cholera, he added to his list "excessive lewdness." To him, dietary control had to be accompanied by sexual control. His *Chastity*, lectures, published in 1834, condemned masturbation and sexual excess in general, or what he called "venereal indulgence." More than cholera was at issue: Excessive sex caused insanity, debility—even death. In his *Lecture to Young Men* (1834), Graham presented a litany:

Venereal excesses occasion the most loathsome, and horrible, and calamitous diseases that human nature is capable of suffering. . . . By far the worst form of venereal indulgence is self-pollution; or, what is called "Onanism." . . . I am confident that I speak within bounds, when I say, that seven out of every ten boys in this country at the age of twelve, are, at least, acquainted with this debasing practice: and I say, again; the extent to which it prevails in our public schools and colleges, is shocking, beyond measure! I have known boys to leave some of these institutions at the age of twelve and thirteen, almost entirely ruined in health and constitution, by this destructive practice . . . ; many of them went to the still more loathsome and criminal extent of an unnatural commerce with each other!

Graham's popularity led to the opening of Grahamite hotels and restaurants that practiced his dietary regimen. From 1837 to 1839 he edited the *Graham Journal of Health and Longevity*. After 1840 his movement flagged, and although he continued to publish his lectures, he toured less often and his health declined. He died on September 11, 1851. In his waning days the *Northampton Courier* presented a cruel commentary:

The people of Northampton were amused one day last week by seeing this philosopher of sawdust pudding trundled on a wheelbarrow from his house to [another] house, he being infirm and unable to walk the distance. . . . The doctor stands a chance to recover and will be able before long to do without the wheelbarrow . . . his best physician is the keeper of the hotel hard by his dwelling with whom he luxuriates on beef and mutton.

With his advice on health, Sylvester Graham had bridged the religious and secular worlds, making reform less religiously evangelical and more widely accepted; in the process he influenced numerous other reformers, some of whom applied his ideas to their utopian communal experiments, as did AMOS BRONSON ALCOTT in the early 1840s at Fruitlands. In *American Reformers* (1978) Ronald G. Walters concludes that to Graham, "The road to heaven was paved with restraint in food and sex; those who yielded to temptation were doomed."

Further Reading

Gordon, John Steele. "Sawdust Pudding." *American Heritage* 47 (July–August 1996): 16+.

Nissenbaum, Stephen. *Sex, Diet, and Debility in Jacksonian America: Sylvester Graham.* Westport, Conn.: Greenwood Press, 1980.

Sokolow, Jayme A. *Eros and Modernization: Sylvester Graham, Health Reform, and the Origins of Victorian Sexuality in America.* Rutherford, N.J.: Fairleigh Dickinson University Press, 1983.

Walters, Ronald G. *American Reformers, 1815–1860.* New York: Hill and Wang, 1978.

Green, William

(1873–1952) *union leader*

President of the American Federation of Labor for more than 20 years, William Green was a strong voice in the labor movement. He was born on March 3, 1872, in Coshocton, Ohio, to Hugh and Jane Green.

William Green grew up in a poor, working-class family. His father labored in the mines in England, and after he immigrated to the United States, he lived in Coshocton, a bleak town coated more with coal dust than with dreams. For a short while William Green had hoped to leave Coshocton by becoming a minister, but his family's financial straits required that he, like his father, obtain a limited education and then work in the mines.

Yet Green found he could advance within the labor movement. He joined the United Mine Workers of America (UMW), a union affiliated with the American Federation of Labor (AFL), and in 1906 went from president of his subdistrict to president of the entire Ohio district union. In 1913 he won election as UMW secretary-treasurer. At about the same time he served two terms in the Ohio Senate, in which he supported Progressive reforms and sponsored the Workmen's Compensation Act.

After serving as a UMW vice president, Green succeeded SAMUEL GOMPERS in 1924 as president of the AFL. He presided over an organization burdened with declining membership and rent by factional fights. Unable to control the internal conflicts, Green allowed the craft unionists, or skilled workers, to force the industrial unionists, including the UMW, to leave the AFL, whereupon they founded the Congress of Industrial Organizations (CIO). The AFL and CIO would engage in nearly continuous battles until their merger in 1955.

Most analysts classify Green as conservative in his leadership. Some say that he enjoyed the benefits of his union presidency so much that he "sold out" to the corporate managers by agreeing to compliant policies. Yet Green advocated universal health insurance, old-age pensions, and other social and economic programs bold for their time.

Green lived in Washington, D.C., during his presidency, but when his health failed he returned to his hometown of Coshocton. He died there on November 21, 1952, of a heart attack.

Further Reading

Phelan, Craig. *William Green: Biography of a Labor Leader.* Albany: State University of New York Press, 1989.

Grimké, Angelina (1805–1879) and Sarah Moore Grimké (1792–1873)

abolitionists, women's rights activists

Sarah Moore Grimké and Angelina Grimké were sisters who grew up in Charleston, South Carolina, and shocked Southerners by joining the abolitionist fight against slavery during a time of increasing defensiveness in their region over the institution. At the same time, they stirred more controversy when they advocated women's rights. Sarah was born on November 26, 1792, and Angelina on February 20, 1805.

The daughters of Mary Smith Grimké and John Grimké, Sarah and Angelina were raised in material comfort. Their father, who fought against the British in the American Revolution, was a planter and lawyer prominent in South Carolina politics. A member of the elite, over the years he expanded his cotton lands and owned many slaves.

According to historian Gerder Lerner in *The Grimké Sisters* (1967), Sarah expressed discontent with the male-dominated society's oppression of women before she expressed her opposition to slavery. Yet at an early age she questioned why slaves were prohibited from reading and in so doing demonstrated a dissatisfaction with the system. On Angelina's birth she was named the baby's godmother and became closely attached to her sister.

Sarah was also close to her older brother, Thomas, a critic of slavery. Thomas saw the institution as evil, but he believed that blacks were inferior to whites and thought the slaves should be colonized in foreign countries.

Overcome by extreme feelings of loneliness and helplessness, and feeling alienated from a southern society she thought unjust, in 1820 Sarah began reading about the Quaker faith. She exchanged letters with Quaker leader Israel Morris and began attending their meetings in Charleston. Mystical experiences in which she heard inner voices telling her to join the group followed. In 1821 she made a momentous decision: She would leave Charleston to live in Philadelphia, where she could immerse herself in the Quaker community and cleanse herself of all attachment to slavery. In 1823, two years after settling in her new home, she was accepted as a member of the Society of Friends.

Meanwhile, Angelina had her own unsettling experiences with slavery. As a child she once fainted at school after seeing a little slave boy, who had been called in to open the classroom windows, walk awkwardly because his legs had been crippled by lashes from a whip. And she witnessed the cruelties in the workhouses, places where masters sent their slaves for punishment. She saw whippings, and she saw the treadmill, a rapidly turning drum with steps attached to it on which slaves—their hands tied to a railing above them—were forced to stand and keep pace with the movement. Usually, the slaves faltered, and the slamming of the drum against their legs crippled them for days afterward. Repulsed by what she saw at the workhouse, Angelina criticized slavery whenever she could, even making remarks to guests at her mother's house.

In 1829 Angelina followed Sarah in moving to Philadelphia, and two years later she joined the Quakers. But Angelina soon grew discontented with them. She had considered their attachment to social justice a sign of hope in her developing hatred of slavery, but whenever she mentioned the issue at a meeting, the other Quakers silenced her by telling her the matter should be handled by a committee.

In 1834 Angelina began reading two abolitionist newspapers, *The Emancipator* and *The Liberator*. According to Sarah, Angelina "found to her surprise that their principles were her principles, and that they were men and women with whom she could work." Angelina, however, likely was drawn to the abolitionists for more than their antislavery advocacy, for they considered themselves to be engaged in a broader fight to control passions that led to vice. According to Ronald Walters in *The Antislavery Appeal* (1978), the abolitionists "sought to liberate slaves and, at the same time, to control all human beings, to make them moral, to direct their most fearful energies toward their salvation." At the same time, the abolitionist movement was steeped in religion, with frequent references to the Bible, to God, and to the moral imperative stemming from both. Angelina's own piety and religiosity attracted her to this larger abolitionist mesh.

To an extent, abolitionism extolled the traditional belief that women were society's moral guardians and morally superior to men because of their intense emotions and spirituality. *The Emancipator* proclaimed: "The influence of women, under God, is omnipotent." Yet such claims served to encourage some women to believe they should break through society's strictures about women's proper sphere and should actually take the lead, or at least assume a role equal to that of men, in fighting slavery. Many abolitionists, the Grimkés included, classified men by their nature as sexually predatory and oppressive of women. "[T]he very being of a women, like that of a slave," said Sarah, "is absorbed in her master." Angelina approvingly observed that with abolitionism and other reform movements "*woman* [was] rising to that influence and elevation in the world for which she was destined under the Gospel Dispensation."

In short, abolitionists challenged the stereotype of the obedient woman—but within limits, for many abolitionists concluded that although women should speak out, they should maintain proper deference to men and should campaign only among those of their own gender. Consequently, activist women caused the abolitionist movement to split between those who embraced and those who distanced themselves from female involvement. In time, the Grimkés, more than any other women, contributed to the division by challenging the expected deference.

In the mid-1830s Angelina Grimké began making speeches for the American Anti-Slavery Society. Founded in Philadelphia in 1833, the society advocated immediate emancipation along with the education of slaves and the ending of racial prejudice. An interracial organization, it believed blacks should have equal standing with whites in the abolitionist movement.

In 1836 Angelina wrote *An Appeal to the Christian Women of the South,* in which she assured her audience that the antislavery movement was neither fanatical nor delusional, but reasonable. She said, "There is nothing to fear from immediate Emancipation, but *every* thing from the continuance of slavery." She recognized that women did not make law, but she insisted they could still work to end slavery by reading, praying, speaking, and acting; in that way women would exercise the moral qualities attributed to them by society (and given by God) and challenge the social strictures against entering the political arena. She said, "Try to persuade your husband, father, brothers, and sons that slavery is a crime *against God and man."* She insisted:

> The *women of the South can overthrow* this horrible system of oppression and cruelty, licentiousness and wrong. Such appeals to your legislatures would be irresistible, for there is something in the heart of man which *will bend under moral suasion.*

That same year Sarah published *An Epistle to the Clergy of the Southern States,* in which she urged churches to oppose slavery. "What an appalling spectacle do we now present!" she stated. "With one hand we clasp the cross of Christ, and with the other grasp the neck of the down-trodden slave!" She painted a picture of the cruel destruction of slave families:

> We make widows by tearing from the victims of a cruel bondage, the husbands of their bosoms, and then devour the widow herself by robbing her of her freedom, and reducing her to the level of a brute. I solemnly appeal to your consciences.

In 1836 and again in 1837 the sisters toured New England and other northern states and advocated the end to slavery and more: They wanted an end to the oppression of women. Angelina spoke most forcefully against slavery, Sarah most forcefully for women's rights. Nevertheless, Angelina recognized the broader impact of abolitionism when she said: "The discussion of the rights of the slave had opened the way for the discussion of other rights." She forecast "an emancipation more glorious than any the world has ever yet seen."

Many women disagreed with the Grimkés, both about slavery and about women's activism. CATHARINE BEECHER, the eldest daughter of Reverend Lyman Beecher, supported the goal of ending slavery but insisted blacks must be colonized overseas to prevent racial warfare, and in a direct criticism of Angelina Grimké she stated that women should forgo petitioning Congress—that activity, she claimed, was properly the role of men.

Discontented with Quaker moderation and angered by the reprimand they received for sitting on the "colored bench" at a Quaker meeting, the Grimkés left the Society of Friends in 1837. That same year they attended the Anti-Slavery Convention of Women in New York City and offered the controversial view that race prejudice must be fought in the North as much as in the South. To those who said that women should keep quiet on social and political issues, Angelina wrote her *Appeal to the Women of the Nominally Free States,* published by the convention. In it she said, "The denial of our duty to act in this case is a denial of our right to act; and if we have no right to act, then may *we* well be termed 'the white slaves of the North,' for like our brethren in bonds, we must seal our lips in silence and despair."

The following year Sarah wrote *Letters on the Equality of the Sexes*, an appeal for women's rights in which she asserted that God had created women as men's equal. "I ask no favor for my sex . . . ," she said. "All I ask our brethren is that they will take their feet from our necks, and permit us to stand upright on that ground which God designed us to occupy." To the public the Grimké sisters had become the leading proponents of abolitionism and women's rights as a linked movement.

On May 14, 1838, Angelina Grimké married one of America's leading abolitionists, THEODORE DWIGHT WELD. The couple had three children. Both Angelina and Sarah assisted Weld in his work. When poor health and his own dissatisfaction with his activities caused him to retire from the abolitionist crusade in 1843, they carried on the cause, and Sarah helped Weld run an interracial school in New Jersey.

As pacifists, Angelina and Sarah only reluctantly endorsed the Civil War, and they pushed for an immediate declaration of emancipation for all slaves. During the conflict Angelina wrote *A Declaration of War on Slavery*, reputedly a powerful manuscript that has not survived. When the war ended the Grimkés collected money and clothing for the freed persons.

Often given to spiritualism and dream interpretation, Sarah Grimké lived her last days with her sister and Theodore Weld, caring for the Weld children at their home near Boston. She died at the age of 81 on December 23, 1873. Angelina Grimké suffered paralysis from several strokes and died on October 26, 1879.

At Angelina's funeral, abolitionist WENDELL PHILLIPS stated, "No man who remembers 1837 and its lowering clouds will deny that there was hardly any contribution to the anti-slavery movement greater or more impressive than the crusade of the Grimké sisters through the New England States." Add their contribution to the women's rights movement and the tribute stands complete.

Further Reading

Barnes, Gilbert H., and Dwight L. Dumond, eds. *The Letters of Theodore Weld, Angelina Grimké and Sarah Grimké*. 2 vols. New York: D. Appleton-Century, 1934.

Browne, Stephen H. *Angelina Grimké: Rhetoric, Identity, and the Radical Imagination*. East Lansing: Michigan State University Press, 1999.

Ceplair, Larry, ed. *The Public Years of Sarah and Angelina Grimké: Selected Writings, 1835–1839*. New York: Columbia University Press, 1989.

Lerner, Gerder, ed. *The Feminist Thought of Sarah Grimké*. New York: Columbia University Press, 1998.

———. *The Grimké Sisters from South Carolina: Rebels against Slavery*. Boston: Houghton Mifflin, 1967.

Walters, Ronald. *The Antislavery Appeal: American Abolitionism after 1830*. Baltimore: Johns Hopkins University Press, 1976.

Grimké, Charlotte Forten (1837–1914) and Francis James Grimké (1850–1937)
civil rights leaders

Married in 1878, Francis James Grimké and Charlotte Forten Grimké were both instrumental in working for black civil rights—he as a former slave who became a Presbyterian minister and she as an educator and writer.

Francis Grimké was born on November 4, 1852, on a plantation near Charleston, South Carolina, to Henry Grimké, a lawyer and Francis's master, and Nancy Weston, a slave. He had two brothers, John and Archibald Henry, who also became leaders in the fight for black civil rights. After Henry Grimké died Francis lived with his mother in Charleston. In 1860, however, the Grimké family forced him to return to their plantation as a house servant. Two years later Francis ran away but was captured, imprisoned, and then sold to a Confederate officer. When the Civil War ended he returned to Charleston.

With the help of a white abolitionist, Sarah Pillsbury, Francis Grimké attended a secondary school in Charleston and then entered Lincoln University in Pennsylvania. His white aunts, the suffragists and abolitionists SARAH MOORE GRIMKÉ and ANGELINA GRIMKÉ, then stepped in and financed his education. Francis Grimké obtained a bachelor's degree in 1870 and received a master's degree in 1872. He studied law for a year at Howard University in Washington, D.C., but then decided to study for the ministry. He entered Princeton Theological Seminary in 1875, graduated in 1878, and became pastor of the Fifteenth Street Presbyterian Church in Washington, a post he held for the rest of his life, except for a brief tenure as pastor of a church in Jacksonville, Florida, in the 1880s.

Also in 1878, Francis Grimké married Charlotte Forten, an African American descended from a family of abolitionists. In 1893 Francis founded the Afro-Presbyterian Council to represent blacks within the Presbyterian Church. He lectured frequently at all-black Howard University and served as a trustee. In the controversy between BOOKER TALIAFERRO WASHINGTON and W. E. B. DU BOIS over the form of relationship that should exist between African Americans and whites, Grimké sided with Du Bois and the more militant view that blacks should strive for their civil rights immediately, in contrast to Washington's insistence that they defer their crusade as a means to receive economic help from white society. In his book *God and the Race Problem* (1903), Grimké criticized racial discrimination.

Charlotte Forten was born on August 17, 1837, in Philadelphia, Pennsylvania, to Robert Bridges Forten and Mary Virginia Woods Forten. She was tutored at home before being sent to Salem, Massachusetts, to attend Higginson Grammar School and live in the home of Charles L. Redmond, a black antislavery leader. She graduated from Higginson in 1855, completed a one-year course at the State Normal School, and became a teacher—the first black teacher of white students in Salem.

In 1862, at the suggestion of the poet John Greenleaf Whittier, Charlotte Forten traveled to Saint Helena Island, one of South Carolina's Sea Islands, as part of a federally funded project to teach freed slaves. The account she wrote of her mission, published in the *Atlantic Monthly*, revealed her hopeful spirit. "The long, dark night of the Past," she said, "with all its sorrows and its fears, was forgotten; and for the Future—the eyes of these freed children see no clouds in it. It is full of sunlight, they think, and they trust in it, perfectly." She continued:

I shall dwell again among "mine own people." I shall gather my scholars about me, and see smiles of greeting break over their dusky faces. My heart sings a song of thanksgiving, at the thought that even I am permitted to do something for a long-abused race, and aid in promoting a higher, holier, and happier life on the Sea Islands.

Yet Charlotte encountered numerous problems among the freed slaves. She found that many of them spoke in a Gullah dialect, and as a result she had trouble understanding them. She also found that her highly educated background made it difficult for her to relate to either the children or the adults. Exhausted from her efforts and weakened by disease, she left the Sea Islands in 1864.

Her work on Saint Helena and the work of other women like her among the former slaves generated differing assessments. Some southern historians, writing shortly after the Civil War, criticized such "do-gooders" for antagonizing whites who opposed educating blacks. Other historians have seen the missionary crusade as providing much-needed help to the freed persons.

Charlotte Forten settled in Boston, where until 1871 she worked as secretary of the Teacher Committee of the New England branch of the Freedmen's Union Commission, serving as a liaison between teachers in the North and those in the South. She then moved to Washington, D.C., and taught at a black preparatory school. In 1872 she was hired as a clerk in the Treasury Department. It was in Washington that she joined the Fifteenth Street Presbyterian Church and met Francis Grimké. After they married (the couple had one child, who died in infancy), she continued to teach and write, but she spent her later years as an invalid.

Charlotte Grimké died in Washington, D.C. on July 23, 1914. Francis Grimké died in the same city on October 11, 1937.

Further Reading

Barker-Benfield, G. J., and Catherine Clinton, eds. *Portraits of American Women: From Settlement to the Present*. New York: St. Martin's Press, 1991.

Longsworth, Polly. *I, Charlotte Forten, Black and Free*. New York: Crowell, 1970.

Stevenson, Brenda, ed. *The Journals of Charlotte Forten Grimké.* New York: Oxford University Press, 1988.

Trimiew, Darryl M. *Voices of the Silenced: The Responsible Self in a Marginalized Community.* Cleveland, Ohio: Pilgrim Press, 1993.

Gutiérrez, José Angel
(1944–) *Chicano activist*

Founder of the militant Chicano party La Raza Unida, José Angel Gutiérrez has worked to improve conditions for Mexican Americans. He was born on October 25, 1944, in Crystal City, Texas, to Angel Gutiérrez and Concepción Fuentes Gutiérrez.

José Gutiérrez lived in material comfort until age 12, when his father died, leaving the Gutiérrez family financially strapped. Gutiérrez then worked at odd jobs to bring in money, including toiling in the spinach fields that dominated the terrain around Crystal City. "It was a very rude awakening to go from middle class to poverty," he recalled many years later. "We had to take the route all Mexicans took. We became migrant workers." Despite the hard work, Gutiérrez excelled in school and in 1962 entered Uvalde College in Uvalde, Texas. From there he transferred to Texas Arts and Industries University in Kingsville and graduated in 1966 with a bachelor's degree in political science.

Gutiérrez earned a master's degree in the same field from St. Mary's University in San Antonio. In 1976 he earned a doctorate from the University of Texas in Austin.

While at St. Mary's University, Gutiérrez founded the Mexican American Youth Organization (MAYO) in 1967 and served as its president. His activism continued in 1969 when he organized a boycott and walkout by high school students in Crystal City over Anglo discrimination in choosing cheerleaders and the homecoming queen. Like many towns in south Texas, Crystal City was overwhelmingly Chicano (the term then in widespread use to refer to an American of Mexican descent), but the 20 percent Anglo population controlled the economy, the schools, and the political system, keeping the Chicanos in a state of peonage. Gutiérrez determined to change that.

Building on the high school protest, Gutiérrez organized La Raza Unida Party (LRUP). He wanted, he said, to form a political party that, unlike the Democrats or Republicans, would truly represent Mexican Americans. But he intended LRUP to do more than vie for votes: He wanted it to stage marches and economic boycotts so that everything from schools, to city hall, to the local markets would reflect the reality that Chicanos made up 80 percent of the population.

Toward that end he won election as president of the Crystal City school board and engineered the election of two other Chicanos to the board and two to the city council. At a speech in San Antonio in May 1970, Gutiérrez said he had founded LRUP to bring justice to Chicanos. That included better schools, better housing, and better jobs. He stated.

> For a long time we have not been satisfied with the type of leadership that has been picked for us. And this is what a political party does, particularly the ones we have here. I shouldn't use the plural because we only have one, and that's the gringo party. It doesn't matter what name it goes by. It can be Kelloggs, All-Bran, or Shredded Wheat, but its still the same. . . .
>
> So you see that what's happening is not any big miracle. It's just common sense. The trouble is that everybody was always bothered and said, "We can't get out of the Democratic Party. Why bite the hand that feeds you?" Well, you bite it because it feeds you slop. Others say, "Well, why don't you switch over and join the Republican Party?" Well, let's not even touch on that one. . . .
>
> Why can't you begin to think very selfishly as a Chicano? I still haven't found a good argument from anyone as to why we should not have a Chicano party. Particularly when you are the majority. . . .
>
> But there is another, more important reason, and that is that mexicanos need to be in control of their destiny. . . . We have been complacent for too long.

In his speech Gutiérrez denied that by supporting LRUP Chicanos would be segregating themselves or be practicing reverse racism. A united Mexican-

American community, he insisted, could win many political offices. He closed by declaring, "To the gringos in the audience, I have one final message to convey: Up yours, baby. You've had it, from now on."

While serving on the Crystal City school board, Gutiérrez and the other Chicano members began bilingual and bicultural programs for the students. They achieved these and other goals despite immense resistance from Anglos who retaliated against LRUP by firing its members from their jobs.

Yet LRUP fell prey to internal bickering, especially a fight for control between Gutiérrez and RODOLFO GONZALES of Colorado. Gutiérrez prevailed, but the weakened party failed to achieve the degree of electoral success its founder had envisioned.

Nevertheless, in 1974 Gutiérrez won election to a judgeship in Zavala County. An ongoing spirited dispute with Anglo judges and a trip to Cuba to meet with Fidel Castro made Gutiérrez the target of criticism within and outside the Chicano community. He quit the judgeship in 1981 and taught at two colleges in Oregon before returning in 1986 to Texas, where he served as director of the Greater Dallas Legal and Community Development Foundation. He received a law degree from the University of Houston in 1988 and became an administrative law judge in Dallas.

Gutiérrez ran for the U.S. Senate in 1993 as a Democrat but failed to win the primary election. He then founded and served as director of the Center for Mexican American Studies at the University of Texas at Arlington. In 1996 the university president, Robert Witt, removed Gutiérrez from that position, claiming the professor had mismanaged funds. When the center's advisory committee defended Gutiérrez, Witt dismissed all of them. This led to protests by Mexican Americans and to Gutiérrez's filing suit against Witt, accusing him of discriminatory actions. As part of an out-of-court settlement, Gutiérrez received back pay and a job as special adviser for Mexican-American library and research materials; he also continued teaching as a professor of political science.

In the year 2000 Gutiérrez conceded that there was no room in the United States for a third political party and that the Chicano movement "as a social protest movement" had ended, though "as an idea, as a process, as an ideology, as a generation, it continues." Unrepentant, he insisted: "The Anglos have never been counted on to do the right thing. They keep segregating. They keep discriminating. They keep putting us at the end of the line."

Further Reading

Gutiérrez, José Angel. *The Making of a Chicano Militant: Lessons from Cristal.* Madison: University of Wisconsin Press, 1998.

Munoz, Carlos, Jr. *Youth, Identity, Power: The Chicano Movement.* New York: Verso, 1990.

Guttmacher, Alan Frank
(1898–1974) *birth control advocate*

An obstetrician, Alan Frank Guttmacher is remembered for his work as a family planning advocate. He was born on May 18, 1898, in Baltimore, Maryland, one of identical twins, to Adolf Guttmacher, a Reform rabbi, and Laura Oppenheimer Guttmacher, a social worker.

Alan Guttmacher attended the Park School in Baltimore and then entered Johns Hopkins University. He at first intended to major in history but changed his program to premedicine. In 1919 he obtained a bachelor's degree and entered the university's medical school (as did his brother, Manfred). He earned his medical degree in 1923, and while Manfred specialized in psychiatry, Alan Guttmacher taught anatomy at Johns Hopkins, followed by the University of Rochester. In 1925 he married Leonore Gidding; they had three daughters.

Later that year he returned to Baltimore to practice obstetrics and teach at Johns Hopkins. Desiring to popularize the latest findings in reproductive science, in 1933 he wrote his first of several books, *Life in the Making.*

Guttmacher left Johns Hopkins in 1952 to become director of obstetrics and gynecology at New York City's Mount Sinai Hospital. He taught also at the College of Physicians and Surgeons at Columbia University and later at Albert Einstein

Medical School in New York and the School of Public Health at Harvard University in Cambridge, Massachusetts.

Over the years Guttmacher had been greatly concerned with family planning, and in 1962 he became president of the Planned Parenthood Federation of America (PPFA). In that capacity he defended the birth control pill as medically safe, and he and the PPFA convinced Congress to appropriate funds for family planning. He wanted everyone, whether rich or poor, to have access to information about contraception, pregnancy, delivery, and the care of infants. By 1965 the PPFA had centers in 275 locations, and its related organization, the International Planned Parenthood Federation, operated in 28 countries.

Guttmacher also worked to liberalize abortion laws. He recoiled at the old regulations that greatly restricted women's access to abortion, which he maintained hurt poor women by forcing them to see untrained practitioners whose procedures injured or even killed them, whereas wealthy women could travel overseas or find another way to end a pregnancy safely.

In 1969 he began advocating "abortion on demand"; consequently, in 1973 he applauded the Supreme Court's *Roe v. Wade* decision. Guttmacher died on March 18, 1974, in New York City of leukemia. Although he had advocated family planning primarily to help couples and to allow women to have freedom of choice, he warned also about the dangers of overpopulation and believed family planning could alleviate the threat to the Earth's resources.

Further Reading

Grant, George. *Immaculate Deception: The Shifting Agenda of Planned Parenthood.* Chicago: Northfield Publishing, 1996.

Wattleton, Faye. *Life on the Line.* New York: Ballantine, 1996.

H

Hall, Gus
(Gus Halberg)
(1910–2000) *communist activist*

Leader of the American Communist Party, Gus Hall was an unwavering Stalinist. He was born Gus Halberg on October 8, 1910, in Iron, Minnesota, to Matt Halberg and Susannah Halberg. Over the years he used several different aliases before settling on Gus Hall and making it his legal name in the late 1930s.

Gus Hall was introduced to the Communist Party by his father, an impoverished miner who joined the radical labor union Industrial Workers of the World and in 1919 the American Communist Party. In 1927 Gus Hall became a member of the party and attended the Lenin Institute in Moscow, where he learned sabotage techniques. He returned to the United States in 1933, in the heart of the Great Depression, when it appeared capitalism would soon collapse.

Hall gained a reputation among radicals for bravery when he served two jail terms, one of them for inciting a riot in Minneapolis, Minnesota, and the other for plotting to dynamite a company. After his release in 1934 he married Elizabeth Turner; they had two children. As Communist Party leader in Youngstown, Ohio, Hall ran for the city council in 1935 but lost, as he did when he ran for governor a short time later.

During World War II Hall served in the navy; afterward he was elected general secretary of the Ohio Communist Party. In the intensifying cold war atmosphere, however, the federal government arrested him and 11 other Communist Party leaders for violating the Smith Act by conspiring to teach and advocate the overthrow of the U.S. government. A 10-day trial in 1949 resulted in a guilty verdict, and after Hall lost his appeal in 1951 he jumped bail and fled to Mexico. Three months later the Mexican police arrested him, and he served five and a half years in the federal penitentiary at Leavenworth, Kansas.

Hall won election in 1959 to the American Communist Party's highest office, general secretary. By then the party's membership—never more than about 66,000 at its peak in the 1930s—had fallen to 3,000. With political protest increasing in the 1960s, Hall tried to build the Communist Party by aligning it with New Left activists, civil rights crusaders, and disaffected youths. Although he occasionally drew large audiences for rallies, his efforts failed mainly because the 1960s political radicals disliked his uncompromising attachment to the Soviet Union and the legacy of Joseph Stalin.

Hall distanced himself from Soviet president Mikhail Gorbachev in the late 1980s, denouncing the reforms Gorbachev had enacted to save that country's Communist system, claiming they had "literally destroyed the basis for socialism." When reactionary Communists tried to overthrow Gorbachev in 1991, Hall sided with them.

He maintained his fondness for the Soviet Union even after it collapsed later that year. In 1996 he expressed his steadfast attachment to

Marxist dogma—and his stubborn refusal to believe that society would evolve in any other way than as he saw it—when he stated, "The struggle between those who own the wealth is one flaw in capitalism that will lead to socialism."

Gus Hall died on October 13, 2000, in New York City of complications related to diabetes. In evaluating Hall's career, historian Maurice Isserman said that the American Communist had kept his party

> a bastion of Stalinist orthodoxy for four decades, while most of the rest of the international Communist movement was in a state of nearly continuous internally-generated crisis and upheaval. That . . . helps account for the total irrelevance of Communism in American society and politics, save, occasionally, as a bogeyman for conservatives, during the years of Hall's ascendancy.

Further Reading

Isserman, Maurice. *Which Side Were You On? The American Communist Party during the Second World War.* Middletown, Conn. Wesleyan University Press, 1982.

Johnpoll, Bernard K., ed. *A Documentary History of the Communist Party of the United States.* Westport, Conn.: Greenwood Press, 1994.

Ottanelli, Fraser M. *The Communist Party of the United States: From the Depression to World War II.* New Brunswick, N.J.: Rutgers University Press, 1991.

Hamer, Fannie Lou
(Fannie Lou Townsend)
(1917–1977) *civil rights leader*

A civil rights activist who was shot at and beaten by whites, Fannie Lou Hamer joined the movement because she was "tired of being sick and tired." She was born Fannie Lou Townsend on October 6, 1917, in Montgomery County, Mississippi, one of 20 children, to Jim Townsend and Lou Ella Townsend.

Fannie Lou Townsend's hardship began at birth—a hardship imposed by a segregated society with its exploitive sharecropping system. In the eyes of whites most blacks in Mississippi amounted to nothing more than menial laborers, expected to toil in the hot cotton fields for a couple of dollars a day, completely subject to the power of their white overlords, who prevented them from voting and physically abused them.

Fannie Lou Townsend's father worked as a sharecropper, and she herself dropped out of school at an early age to pick cotton. In 1944 she married Perry "Pap" Hamer, a tractor driver; they adopted two children.

Fannie Lou Hamer seemed destined to live her life a sharecropper, but in 1962 she attended a meeting in the small town of Ruleville at which she met civil rights activists from the Southern Christian Leadership Conference and the Student Non-Violent Coordinating Committee. As a result she decided to join a group of black farm workers who intended to register to vote at the courthouse in Indianaola.

On August 31, 1962, she tried to register but was turned away by the white registrar. For her boldness the plantation owner on whose land she sharecropped evicted her, and later that night 16 shots were fired into the house where she was staying.

In June 1963 Hamer attended a voter registration workshop in Charleston, South Carolina. While she was on her way home the police in Winona, Mississippi, arrested her for entering a whites-only restaurant to eat. Once the police threw her into the Montgomery County jail, they forced two black inmates to beat her, leaving her with a blood clot in one eye, a damaged kidney, and a permanently injured leg.

Yet Hamer persevered and attracted national attention in 1964 when she cofounded the Mississippi Freedom Democratic Party and spoke at the Democratic National Convention in Atlantic City, New Jersey. There she told the delegates how she had been beaten and how whites had brutalized the state's African Americans.

That fall she ran for Congress on a Freedom Ballot (one that was separate from the all-white Democratic ticket), and in 1965 she and two other black women appeared on the floor of the House of Representatives to protest the seating of the Mississippi delegation because it had been elected through segregated voting. That same year she helped organize a strike among black cotton pickers, and in 1968 she served as a delegate to the Democratic National Convention in Chicago and as a member of the Democratic National Committee.

By that time she was involved in protesting the Vietnam War, drawing a link between it and racism. "We are sick and tired of our people having to go to Vietnam and other places to fight for something we don't have here," she said. "We want to end the wrongs such as fighting a war in Vietnam and pouring billions over there, while people in . . . Mississippi and Harlem and Detroit are starving to death."

Yet she objected to much of President Lyndon Johnson's War on Poverty, intended to help African Americans and other poor people, claiming that it encouraged black dependence rather than independence. In 1969 she founded the Freedom Farm Cooperative in Sunflower County, Mississippi; shortly afterward she raised funds to build low-income housing in Ruleville and started a daycare center.

While advancing the cause of civil rights, Hamer also advanced the status of black women. In a widely quoted statement, she said they should "work together with the black man, then we will have a better chance to just act as human beings, and to be treated as human beings in our sick society."

Fannie Lou Hamer died on March 15, 1977, in Ruleville. Her biographer, Kay Mills, said about her: "Within the movement, Fannie is not neglected. She ranks up there with Dr. [MARTIN LUTHER] KING."

Further Reading

Mills, Kay. *This Little Light of Mine: The Life of Fannie Lou Hamer.* New York: Dutton, 1993.

Hamilton, Alice

(1869–1970) *health reformer*

A physician, Alice Hamilton was committed to fighting industrial poisoning. She was born on February 27, 1869, in New York City to Mont-

gomery Hamilton, a wholesale grocer, and Gertrude Pond Hamilton.

Raised by her grandmother in Fort Wayne, Indiana, Alice Hamilton lived in material comfort and in 1886 entered a private school in Farmington, Connecticut. She then took science courses at the Fort Wayne College of Medicine and in 1892 entered the University of Michigan. Hamilton received her medical degree in 1893 and interned at hospitals in Minneapolis and Boston. Further training in Europe and at the Johns Hopkins Medical School led to her accepting a teaching position in 1897 at the Woman's Medical School at Northwestern University, near Chicago.

Hamilton began her work in social reform when she decided to live at Chicago's Hull-House, a settlement house begun by JANE ADDAMS to help immigrants. During a typhoid epidemic in 1902 in the Hull-House district, she concluded that the disease was being spread by flies. Later, other researchers disproved her theory, but her findings had alerted Chicagoans to the poor housing in immigrant neighborhoods.

She soon turned her attention to industrial poisoning—the use of chemicals damaging to workers' health. To begin her research she obtained material from European countries that were far ahead of the United States in regulating the problem. In 1909 Governor Charles S. Deneen appointed her to the Illinois Commission on Occupational Diseases. She served on the commission for two years before resigning to become medical investigator for its Survey of Occupational Disease, a job that required her to visit mines, mills, and smelters. She showed that workers suffered from high disease and mortality rates related to lead; in particular, she focused on the making of white lead used in matches, and her investigation of 25 factories revealed 358 cases of lead poisoning, 16 of them fatal, from 1910 to 1911.

Hamilton later found that dyes, acid, arsenic, and carbon monoxide also damaged workers. In a report she noted an obstacle to her research: Unlike England and Germany, Illinois kept few records on workers' illnesses, meaning that "one must simply grope again, and one must carefully check up and control every bit of information one gets." Hamilton had also to contend with plant managers who tried to hide evidence of industrial poisoning; one scraped red lead from a factory ceiling before she inspected the facility.

A pacifist, Hamilton opposed American entry into World War I and revealed the life-threatening conditions in weapons plants. "England and France," she wrote after the war, "facing an emergency infinitely greater than ours, took thought to protect their munitions workers, but we did not."

In 1919 Hamilton participated in the Quaker famine relief effort in war-ravaged Germany. Later that year she joined Harvard Medical School as a part-time assistant professor specializing in industrial medicine, and she criticized the discrimination she faced on campus as the college's first female teacher. She wrote two leading textbooks, *Industrial Poisons in the United States* (1925) and *Industrial Toxicology* (1934), and from 1924 to 1930 she served on the Health Committee of the League of Nations.

Hamilton retired from Harvard in 1935, but she continued her efforts to apply medicine to social reform. She worked as a consultant to the Division of Labor Standards in the federal government's Department of Labor, and from 1944 to 1949 she served as president of the National Consumers' League. In the 1950s she supported an equal rights amendment to the Constitution, and in 1963 she demanded that the United States end its military involvement in Vietnam. Alice Hamilton died on September 22, 1970, in Hadlyme, Connecticut.

Further Reading

Haslett, Diane C. "Hull House and the Birth Control Movement: An Untold Story." *Affilia Journal of Women and Social Work* 12 (Fall 1997): 261+.

Sicherman, Barbara. *Alice Hamilton: A Life in Letters.* Cambridge, Mass.: Harvard University Press, 1984.

Harper, Ida Husted

(1851–1931) *women's suffragist*

A journalist and suffragist, Ida Husted Harper is often remembered as the curator of SUSAN BROWNELL ANTHONY's image. She was born on February 18, 1851, in Fairfield, Indiana, to John Arthur Husted and Cassandra Stoddard Husted.

Ida Husted graduated from high school in Muncie, Indiana—the town to which she had moved with her parents around 1860—and entered Indiana University. She stayed there only a year, however, before leaving in 1869 to become, at age 18, the principal of a high school in Peru, Indiana. Two years later she married Thomas W. Harper, a lawyer, and settled in Terre Haute. They had one daughter and divorced after 19 years of marriage.

In Terre Haute, Ida Harper began contributing articles to newspapers. Her column "A Woman's Opinion" appeared in the *Saturday Evening Mail* for 12 years, and she wrote political articles for the *Indianapolis News*. She wrote also for a union publication, the *Fireman's Magazine* (later called the *Locomotive Fireman's Magazine*), edited by EUGENE VICTOR DEBS.

Ida Harper advocated women's suffrage and in the 1880s became friends with Susan B. Anthony after hearing Anthony speak in Terre Haute. In 1887 Harper was named secretary of the Indiana chapter of the National Woman Suffrage Association (NWSA). She moved to California in 1896 to be near her daughter, who was attending Stanford University, and at Anthony's request led an unsuccessful campaign to attach a woman's suffrage amendment to the state constitution.

Harper moved to Rochester, New York, in 1897 so she could live in Anthony's home and write a book about her friend's life. When it appeared in 1898, the two-volume work (and a later third volume) placed Anthony on a pedestal. According to historian Sara Hunter Graham, in her essay "The Suffrage Renaissance," which appears in Marjorie Spruill Wheeler's *One Woman, One Vote* (1998), Harper wrote a hagiography that converted Anthony into a "suffrage saint."

In a 1902 article for the *North American Review*, Harper discussed the progress made by women in recent years, especially in education; she pointed out that more girls than boys were enrolled in high schools, normal schools, and manual-training schools, and a third of all college students were women. Her intent was to show that such progress should be accompanied by extending voting rights to women.

Harper continued to extol the merits of Susan B. Anthony in several articles, most notably her

"Miss Anthony at Home," which appeared in *Pearson's Magazine* in 1903. The article made Anthony palatable to a middle class concerned that in some way suffragists would undermine household duties and feminine skills. Miss Anthony, or "Aunt Susan," Harper wrote, "has never suggested ways for repairing the damages of society with one-half the skill she employed in teaching her nieces her wonderful method of darning rents in garments and household linens."

Yet in a column Harper wrote near that time for the *New York Sun*, she deplored society's classifying certain traits as "female" qualities and expecting women to sacrifice themselves for men. "The belief has by no means died out," she said, "that it is a woman's sacred duty to marry a dissolute man in order to reform him." Many "feminine virtues," Harper argued, were actually also common in men.

Beginning in 1916 Harper acted as a publicist for the women's suffrage campaign, then nearing its final push in Congress for a constitutional amendment. She opposed those who wanted the National American Woman Suffrage Association (NAWSA, the successor to the NWSA) to admit black members, saying such a move would antagonize southern congressmen whose votes were needed to get the amendment passed. "Many of the Southern members are now willing to surrender their beloved doctrine of State's rights," she wrote to the president of the NAWSA, "and their only obstacle is fear of 'the colored woman's vote' in the State where it is likely to equal or exceed the white woman's vote."

Harper helped Anthony edit *History of Woman Suffrage*, published in 1902, while making speeches for women's suffrage, both alone and with Anthony. After Anthony's death, and after Congress had passed and the states had ratified a constitutional amendment extending the right to vote to women, Harper edited the final two volumes of *History of Woman Suffrage*.

Ida Harper died on March 14, 1931, in Washington, D.C. Her writings had shaped both the substance of the women's suffrage movement and the image that those women who fought for suffrage wanted most remembered.

Further Reading

Wheeler, Marjorie Spruill. *One Woman, One Vote: Rediscovering the Woman Suffrage Movement.* Troutdale, Ore.: NewSage Press, 1998.

Harrington, Michael
(1928–1989) *socialist, antipoverty reformer*

A socialist, Michael Harrington was the author of *The Other America*, a book that changed the way Americans viewed wealth and poverty in their country. He was born on February 24, 1928, in Saint Louis, Missouri, to Edward Michael Harrington, a patent lawyer, and Catherine Fitzgibbon Harrington, a schoolteacher.

Michael Harrington received a bachelor's degree from Holy Cross College in 1947 and a master's degree in English from the University of Chicago in 1949. He became a conscientious objector during the Korean War and from 1951 to 1952 worked as associate editor of DOROTHY DAY's leftist *Catholic Worker*. After leaving both the *Catholic Worker* and the Catholic Church, he became a socialist.

Harrington joined the Workers Defense League, a civil liberties group connected to the trade union movement, and served as its secretary. He also joined the Young Socialist League, where he met Max Shachtman, a Marxist. Harrington embraced Marxist ideology, but he agreed with Shachtman that Stalinism amounted to bureaucratic totalitarianism. An open society required democracy, Harrington claimed, and democracy could only fully exist in a socialist setting.

In the late 1950s Harrington became chairman of the Young People's Socialist League, the student branch of the Socialist Party. In 1964 he was chosen chairman of the League for Industrial Democracy, an affiliate of the party, and served on the editorial board of a socialist magazine, *Dissent*. During the 1950s and 1960s Harrington wrote articles for the *Nation, New Republic, Dissent, Commonweal, Commentary*, and other journals, and he appeared at many peace rallies and civil rights marches.

In 1960 he was elected to a seat on the executive committee of the Socialist Party, and in 1961 and 1962 he served as editor of *New America*, the party's official journal. In May 1963 he married Stephanie Gervis, a writer for the *Village Voice*; they had two sons.

One year prior to Harrington's marriage, his book *The Other America* appeared and exposed how the nation's affluent society had bypassed farm laborers, unskilled urban workers, the elderly, and most blacks. The book ran counter to the conformist atmosphere of the 1950s and early 1960s, and it stunned the middle class, which had been complacent about the substantial poverty that existed. Harrington wrote about an invisible America, the oppressed in society cloaked by television shows that depicted life in the comfortable suburbs; by supermarkets loaded with bounty; and by suburbs that bespoke prosperity. "The new poverty," Harrington said, "is constructed so as to destroy aspiration; it is a system designed to be impervious to hope."

The Other America eventually helped stimulate the War on Poverty, a program of reforms proposed by President Lyndon Johnson. But it did more: It opened the eyes of college students to society's shortcomings and the need to change them through political action and militant protest. In so doing it fueled the rise of many reform movements and the New Left in the 1960s.

In 1973 Harrington and other socialists opposed to the Vietnam War formed the Democratic Socialist Organizing Committee (DSOC), which comprised progressive groups representing labor, minorities, environmentalists, feminists, and peace activists. DSOC merged with the New American movement in 1982 to form the Democratic Socialists of America, with Harrington as cochair.

Michael Harrington taught political science at Queens College, City University of New York, from 1972 until his death on July 31, 1989, in Larchmont, New York.

Further Reading

Gorman, Robert A. *Michael Harrington—Speaking American.* New York: Routledge, 1995.

Harrington, Michael. *The Long-Distance Runner: An Autobiography.* New York: Holt, 1988.

Isserman, Maurice. *The Other American: The Life of Michael Harrington.* New York: Public Affairs, 2000.

Harris, LaDonna

(1931–) *Indian rights leader*

A fighter for Indian and women's rights, LaDonna Harris once said about Native Americans: "We are not just another minority. We are political governmental entities and nobody—not the state, not the general public—knows how all these odd little Indians fit in. But the Supreme Court continues to uphold the fact that we are sovereign governments and that we have to be dealt with." She was born on February 15, 1931, in Temple, Oklahoma.

Of mixed blood, LaDonna grew up on the Kiowa-Comanche-Apache Reservation in southwestern Oklahoma. Her mother, Lily Tabbyite, was a Comanche, and her father, Don Crawford, was an Irishman. Crawford deserted the family soon after LaDonna's birth, and Lily Tabbyite's parents stepped in to raise the youngster on a small farm outside Walters, Oklahoma. LaDonna's grandparents influenced her greatly with their traditional customs. A medicine man, her grandfather wore his hair in braids, held tightly to tribal legends, and spoke only Comanche.

While LaDonna was in her teens she boarded with a family in Walters so she could attend the local high school. She graduated in 1949 and married Fred Harris, the 19-year-old son of a sharecropper, whom she had been dating for two years. They moved to Norman, Oklahoma, where he could attend college, and over the years the couple raised two daughters and a son.

Fred Harris graduated from law school in 1954, and they moved to Lawton, Oklahoma, where he established a legal firm and entered politics. With LaDonna Harris's help, in 1956 he won election to the state senate as a Democrat. At the same time, she worked to expand educational and economic opportunities for Native Americans and civil rights both for them and for African Americans. She began to organize groups that met weekly to talk about racism and develop plans to end segregation. Fred Harris later recalled that "LaDonna took part in the civil rights efforts in a personal way." At one point she and her group stood with protest signs outside a segregated swimming pool and several restaurants, demanding that the facilities be integrated. In 1963 she was appointed to the board of the Southwest Center for Human Relations Studies at the University of Oklahoma, where she oversaw programs in career counseling and leadership training for Indian students.

The following year LaDonna Harris organized a meeting for representatives from 68 Oklahoma Indian tribes who gathered to discuss problems common to them. LaDonna Harris remembered, "We didn't know what to expect. We didn't know if anyone would come. . . . It was the first time in the twentieth century that eastern and western Oklahoma tribes had ever met together." From this meeting emerged Oklahomans for Indian Opportunity, a group that sought to create jobs for Native Americans. She served as its first president. When Fred Harris won election to the U.S. Senate that fall, she followed her husband to Washington.

Through LaDonna Harris's efforts, in the mid-1960s the Peace Corps established the Peace Pipe Project, a program whereby Indians in North America worked with those in Latin America. In 1968 President Lyndon Johnson appointed Harris to his newly established National Council for Indian Opportunity (NCIO). Two years later she lobbied for a bill to transfer Blue Lake near Taos, New Mexico, from Carson National Forest back to the Taos Indians, who had once controlled it and considered it a sacred place. Congress passed this legislation in December 1970, ending a 75-year struggle by the Indians of Taos for their land.

In 1970 Harris convinced President Richard Nixon and Congress to end a termination policy by which Indian tribes had lost their tribal status. At the same time, as Native American activism intensified, she criticized the Bureau of Indian Affairs, calling the agency slow and paternalistic.

Also in 1970 Harris founded Americans for Indian Opportunity and through it promoted programs to protect tribal lands, establish health care systems, and encourage Indian children to take pride in their culture. She looked at the tribes as sovereign and wanted them to be strong and self-sufficient. With that in mind, she sympathized with the American Indian Movement, which through the work of DENNIS JAMES BANKS and RUSSELL MEANS was taking militant action to protect Indian civil rights and was siding with tradi-

tionalists in a violent conflict involving federal agents on South Dakota's Pine Ridge Reservation.

Harris joined the board of the National Organization for Women and participated in a feminist demonstration against the Vietnam War. In 1971 she helped found the National Women's Political Caucus. Five years later she supported her husband in his unsuccessful campaign for the Democratic presidential nomination. In 1979 the magazine *Ladies' Home Journal* recognized Harris's many achievements when it named her "Woman of the Year and of the Decade."

Then in 1980 LaDonna Harris launched her own bid for office when she ran for the vice presidency on the Citizen's Party ticket headed by the environmentalist BARRY COMMONER. She did so, she said, because the party offered a progressive alternative to the conservatism of the Democrats and the Republicans and because she felt frustrated by the lack of choice between the two major parties. She recalled: "When the presidential campaign started and I was watching it on television, I became very angry. I was literally screaming at the television, feeling frustrated and helpless."

During the campaign she said, "We are not running to be elected. We are running to establish a party and to focus attention on the issue we consider imperative, economic justice." She expressed also a commitment to environmental reform: "As an Indian I grew up with the sense that all living things are interdependent, that everything, including rock and stone, should be protected, and that if you break that cycle you will cause the downfall of your society—or your world."

In the 1980s Harris fought the many budget cuts that hurt federal programs intended for Indians, and she organized meetings on reservations that called together federal, state, and tribal officials to discuss Native American issues. She and Fred Harris divorced in the mid-1980s.

Over the years LaDonna Harris served on the Commission on Mental Health and in the United Nations Education, Science, and Culture Organization (UNESCO). In 1994 she moved the headquarters of Americans for Indian Opportunity to Bernalillo, New Mexico, on the Santa Ana Pueblo Reservation. Soon afterward she began INDIANnet, a computer network formed to provide Internet access to Native Americans. Indian tribes, she said, must progress in the 21st century by embracing new technology while holding on to their values and offering them as an alternative way of life to the world at large.

Further Reading

Gordon-McCutchan, R. C. *The Taos Indians and the Battle for Blue Lake.* Santa Fe, N.M.: Red Crane Books, 1991.

Harris, LaDonna. *LaDonna Harris: A Comanche Life.* Lincoln: University of Nebraska Press, 2000.

Hayden, Tom
(Thomas Hayden)
(1940–) *antiwar activist*

Thomas Hayden—known as Tom—emerged as one of the most prominent New Left leaders during the great countercultural upheaval of the 1960s. He helped organize Students for a Democratic Society; wrote the group's initial Port Huron Statement; worked in northern ghettos; made highly publicized trips to Communist Cuba and North Vietnam; and endured arrest for his part in a massive antiwar protest in Chicago. He was born on December 12, 1940, in Royal Oak, Michigan, to Jack Hayden, an accountant, and Genevieve Garity Hayden.

At Royal Oak High School in Michigan, Tom Hayden's interest turned to journalism, and he gained a reputation for a feisty, rebellious attitude. As a senior he wrote an editorial criticizing overcrowding in the school and positioned the first letters of the first words in the subheadings to spell "GO TO HELL." Hayden entered the University of Michigan in 1957, expecting to earn a degree in journalism and become a foreign correspondent. The rebelliousness he displayed in high school carried over to college as he opposed the authoritarian policies of the administration that, typical for those days, set strict rules for students and allowed them little say in campus governance.

The larger scene in America influenced Hayden as well. He disliked the materialistic conformity that characterized the 1950s and started reading Jack Kerouac, whose novel *On the Road* fed his rebelliousness. In June 1960 Hayden hitch-hiked to California, thinking he might live the type of dropout existence portrayed by Kerouac.

But he was much too political for that. His journey was prompted in part by a protest that had occurred a month earlier in San Francisco, where college students from Berkeley demonstrated against hearings held by the House Un-American Activities Committee. The police had reacted by hosing down the demonstrators and forcing them from the stairways in city hall while the committee called the students communists. To Hayden the episode displayed the country's oppression and its callous disregard for the ideas young people could offer society.

Hayden's politics grew more radical during his California trip. He stayed with friends who took him into the countryside to see the poverty suffered by farm workers—a contrast to the pleasant images of suburbia prevalent on television and the environment in which he had been raised—and taught him about nuclear research under way at Livermore, a nearby laboratory.

Then in August 1960 he covered the Democratic National Convention in Los Angeles for the *Michigan Daily,* the student newspaper, and experienced the civil rights movement for the first time when he met protesters outside the meeting. In the stories he sent back to Michigan, Hayden called for student activism, a message university officials disliked.

In his senior year Hayden served as editor of the *Michigan Daily.* His activism intensified when Al Haber, a founder of Students for a Democratic Society (SDS), convinced him to help the Student Non-Violent Coordinating Committee (SNCC) in its fight for civil rights. Hayden graduated in 1961 and worked as a field worker for SDS and as a volunteer for SNCC in Georgia and Mississippi. As a result he saw racism firsthand and grew angry when President John Kennedy dragged his feet in pushing for civil rights legislation.

Through SDS Hayden had found an outlet for his protest and his desire to change American society. In 1962 he drafted the Port Huron Statement, a manifesto expressing the criticisms, ideals, and principles of SDS. The statement attacked both liberalism and right-wing anticommunism. Hayden asserted that liberalism had sold out to a big military state, and right wingers had promoted extremism to the point of stifling dissent. He called for a new, participatory democracy, a system in which domination by the elite would be replaced by widespread participation, open expression, and greater power for the oppressed.

From 1962 to 1963 Hayden served as president of SDS while completing his master's degree in sociology at the University of Michigan. The following year he helped begin the Economic Research and Action Project (ERAP), an SDS program to help the poor people in America's cities. Hayden opened an ERAP office in the all-black Central Ward of Newark, New Jersey, and as did other ERAP volunteers, lived in the decrepit housing that characterized the ghettos. He and some 30 coworkers organized rent strikes and pressured the local government to repair neighborhood streets. He recalled, "We believed that people can solve problems by themselves." Yet he found it difficult to organize the residents, many of whom considered him a white interloper.

Near the same time Hayden participated in protests against the Vietnam War. At the invitation of STAUGHTON LYND, a left-wing historian, in 1965 Hayden made his first of several trips to North Vietnam. He did so with some second thoughts, worrying that he was a traitor, but finally concluding that the best way to support American soldiers would be by ending the war.

Hayden praised the stamina of the Vietnamese people and the integrity of their revolutionary fight. Back in the United States in 1966 and 1967 he spoke at campus teach-ins organized to protest the war. Later in 1967 he traveled to Cuba and praised Fidel Castro.

Hayden left Newark in 1967, after the ghetto had exploded into riots, and dedicated himself full-time to the antiwar movement. He had earlier participated in an SDS-sponsored protest march in Washington, D.C., and now began planning a large-scale demonstration for the 1968 Democratic National Convention in Chicago. At the same time, during a student strike in spring 1968 at Columbia University, he helped resolve conflicts within one of the protest groups, a move that earned praise from some leftists, whereas others accused him of grandstanding. One protester com-

mented, "Like the Lone Ranger, he didn't even wave goodbye, but quietly slipped away, taking his silver protest button to another beleaguered campus."

Still planning for Chicago, Hayden worked with representatives from other radical groups that had organized the National Mobilization Committee to End the War in Vietnam (MOBE). Hayden and MOBE (which included the activists Rennie Davis and DAVID DELLINGER) organized the protest despite warnings that fringe groups committed to violence would likely show up, and that the Chicago police would crush any demonstrations, peaceful or otherwise. Hayden later stated that the assassination of Senator Robert Kennedy that year had affected him deeply, reinforcing his belief that a violent society understood only force.

Yet Hayden took an ambivalent position toward the Chicago protests—stating he had no wish for violence but expressing a desire to shut down the Democratic Convention and "confront" the oppressors. Shortly before the protest began, he said the national government must be destroyed and claimed, "The government of the United States is an outlaw institution under the control of war criminals."

When the Chicago protest deteriorated into rock and bottle throwing by the demonstrators and unrestrained tear gassing and beating by the police, Hayden declared: "The city and the military machinery it has aimed at us won't permit us to protest in an organized fashion. Therefore . . . we must turn this over-heated military machine against itself. Let us make sure if blood flows, it flows all over the city." Evidence uncovered later found that the federal government had infiltrated the protest groups and that secret agents likely provoked at least some of the violence.

Shortly after the Democratic Convention, the government arrested Hayden and seven other radicals for planning and inciting a riot; newspapers called them the Chicago Eight (on trial as the Chicago Seven after one defendant was granted a separate hearing). In February 1970 Hayden was found guilty, but two years later the Seventh Circuit Court of Appeals overturned his conviction on the grounds that the presiding judge had been biased against the defense. Looking back on his involvement, Hayden said, "Chicago was part of a decisive upsurge which, we thought, faster than any of us could predict, was going to bring down the American government."

In the early 1970s Hayden and his second wife, Jane Fonda (whom he had married in 1973 after divorcing Sandra Carson; he and Fonda would also later divorce), led several efforts to end America's continuing military presence in Vietnam. Hayden wrote articles for the magazines *Ramparts* and *Rolling Stone,* as well as a book recounting his Chicago experience. In 1976 he ran for the U.S. Senate from California but lost in the Democratic primary. In the 1980s and 1990s he served in the California legislature and in 1997 was defeated in his bid to become mayor of Los Angeles. His service in the legislature ended in the year 2001 because of a term-limit law.

During the 1960s Hayden had worked tirelessly to promote change. When a friend once asked him where he got his energy, he replied, "I have an ideology." The antiwar movement, he still insisted years later, had been right.

Further Reading

Bunzel, John H. *New Force on the Left: Tom Hayden and the Campaign against Corporate America.* Stanford, Calif.: Hoover Institution Press, 1983.

Hayden, Tom. *Reunion: A Memoir.* New York: Random House, 1988.

Rodriguez, Emelyn. "Packing It up and Heading Home." *California Journal* 32 (January 2001): 30+.

Haywood, William Dudley
(Big Bill Haywood)
(1869–1928) *labor organizer*

A miner and labor leader, William Dudley Haywood, often called "Big Bill" Haywood, was at various times a socialist, syndicalist, and revolutionary agitator. He was born on February 4, 1869, in Salt Lake City, Utah. His father was a miner who was also named William Dudley Haywood, and his mother was a Scotch-Irish woman named Elizabeth, whose maiden name is unknown.

Haywood faced several childhood challenges. When he was three, his father died; at age 9 he lost his right eye when a knife he was using to carve wood lodged in it; and at age 15 he was forced to leave school and work full time in the mines, where except for a brief fling as a cowboy and homesteader, he would remain for the next 16 years.

In 1889 Haywood married Jane Minor (known as "Nevada Jane") in Pocatello, Idaho; they had three children, one of whom died at birth. Haywood, though, was never emotionally close to his wife; away from home for long periods, he preferred to socialize with miners and prostitutes.

Influenced by the Haymarket Trial of 1886, in which eight anarchists were arrested for exploding a bomb during a labor protest in Chicago, and four were hanged for the crime on the basis of flimsy evidence, Haywood developed a radical outlook. From his standpoint what had happened to the Haymarket anarchists exemplified government and business combining to oppress the masses.

Yet his entry into labor activism awaited his recuperation from a work-related injury, during which he gave more thought to the oppression endured by him and other miners. In 1896, after hearing Ed Boyce, president of the Western Federation of Miners (WFM), urge the mine workers to join the union as the only way to end their exploitation, Haywood became a charter member of Local 66 in Silver City, Idaho. Two years later he was elected a delegate to the WFM national convention, and in 1899 he was made a member of the national executive board. The following year he was elected secretary treasurer and worked at the union headquarters in Denver, Colorado.

In addition, Haywood edited the WFM's *Miners' Magazine* and wrote several articles for it. They reveal his commitment not only to the WFM but also to socialism; over time his articles became more strident, more radical.

With Boyce as WFM president and Haywood as secretary treasurer, the union grew rapidly in membership and income, but in 1902 Haywood miscalculated its strength. That year the WFM began organizing smelter and mill workers in Colorado City. When J. D. Hawkins, superintendent of the Standard Mill, fired workers who joined the WFM, Haywood went to see him. "Whether you like it or not," Haywood told him, "these mills are going to be organized." "Well it is up to you," Hawkins replied. "Go ahead."

Go ahead he did. When the Standard Mill continued to fire WFM members, Haywood rallied the miners in Cripple Creek, Colorado, to stop providing ore to the company. Standard Mill, though, struck back; allied with other mining companies and the state government, it acted to crush the union. The governor mobilized the militia, whose expenses were paid for in part by the mining companies, and by 1904 the WFM was humbled, its membership reduced, and its funds depleted.

Haywood lost the strike, but he emerged from it a dedicated revolutionary. Several years later he recalled: "It was during the period of those strikes that the Western Federation of Miners realized the necessity of labor getting together in one big union. . . . There seemed to be no hope for such a thing as that [solidarity] among any of the existing labor organizations."

Soon after the strike Haywood presided over a convention that met in Chicago in 1905 to found the Industrial Workers of the World (IWW). He said in his opening speech, "This organization will be formed, based, and founded on the class struggle, having in view no compromise and no surrender, and but one object and one purpose and that is to bring the workers of the country into the possession of the full value of the product of their toil." Because the IWW sought to encompass all workers, the WFM became a part of it.

A few months later sensational charges embroiled Haywood in a criminal case when an IWW member, Harry Orchard, was arrested for assassinating Frank E. Steunenberg, the former governor of Idaho. Orchard claimed that Haywood and two other men had told him to commit the murder. The police then arrested Haywood.

Thousands of workers rose to Haywood's defense, staging rallies and raising money for him. In November 1906 the Colorado Socialist Party ran Haywood for governor, and he polled some 16,000 votes. Since Haywood was defended by the famed attorney CLARENCE SEWARD DARROW, his trial in Boise received national coverage. "I sometimes wonder whether here in Idaho or anywhere else in the country, broad and free," Darrow said in his closing statement, "a man can be placed on trial and lawyers seriously ask to take away the life of a human being upon the testimony of Harry Orchard. Lawyers come here and ask you, upon the word of that sort of man, to send this man to the gallows, to make his wife a widow and his children orphans." In July 1907 Haywood was acquitted. Haywood's biographer Melvyn Dubofsky writes, "The Steunenberg trial had made William D. Haywood for the first time in his life a national and even international personality."

Despite the socialist support for Haywood and his membership in the party's national executive committee, he soon broke with them as his views grew more radical, and he adopted a "syndicalist" stand, meaning that rather than acting through political parties he favored furthering the workers' cause by uniting them behind militant protest. Speaking at Cooper Union in New York City on December 21, 1911, Haywood dismissed the socialists for their "parliamentary politics." "I believe in direct action . . . ," he said, his voice booming from his 200-pound-plus frame. "Do you blame me when I say I despise the law? I am not a law-abiding citizen. Those of us who are in jail—those of us who have been in jail—all of us who are willing to go to jail—care not what you say or do! We despise your hypocrisy. . . . We are the Revolution! It is our purpose to overthrow the capitalist system by forcible means if necessary."

In February 1912 the Socialist Party booted Haywood from its national executive committee, saying it was getting rid of a "turbulent element." Haywood strengthened his position in the IWW, though, and despite an occasional verbal retreat from his Cooper Union statement, he continued to embrace militant tactics. He advocated that workers "engage in passive resistance and sabotage, use the ordinary strike, the intermittent strike, the silent strike, and finally labor's ultimate weapon, the general strike." But, he insisted, "I, for one, have turned my back on violence. It wins nothing. When we strike now, we strike with our hands in our pockets. We have a new kind of violence—the havoc we raise with money by laying down our tools."

That same year Haywood and the IWW scored a tremendous victory when they led textile mill workers in a strike at Lawrenceville, Massachusetts, and obtained a settlement that raised wages and paid for overtime. Haywood, who liked to socialize with the anarchists EMMA GOLDMAN and ALEXANDER BERKMAN, continued to travel and organize and to be harassed by the police, who often threw him in to jail.

When in 1913 strikes in Paterson, New Jersey, Akron, Ohio, and Detroit, Michigan, ended in defeats for the IWW and cost the union many members, questions about Haywood's tactics were raised. Yet in 1914 the membership elected him to the union's highest post as general secretary, and two years later his control over the IWW deepened when he gained more authority over its affiliated industrial unions.

Haywood talked more about obtaining higher wages and shorter hours for the workers than about dismantling capitalism. He did not abandon his belief in revolutionary change, but it ran head-on into the practical need to do something immediate for the workers.

When the United States entered World War I in April 1917 Haywood took a moderate stand toward the entanglement. At heart opposed to the war as a conflict intended to benefit the capitalist class, he nonetheless turned back those within the IWW who wanted the union to defy the draft and instead insisted that the IWW stay its course in organizing workers and, where necessary, staging strikes.

The federal government, though, had other ideas; after IWW strikes erupted in several localities, it moved to crush the union. One congressman reflected widespread public opinion when he linked the IWW to the German kaiser, calling it "Imperial Wilhelm's Warriors."

Charging the IWW with conspiracy to destroy war production, the Justice Department sent its agents into IWW offices across the country, and, using search warrants unprecedented in their broad scope, they seized nearly everything. In September 1917 grand juries indicted Haywood and 165 other IWW members on charges of criminal conspiracy and conspiracy to defy the conscription act.

Convicted and sentenced to a 20-year term in Leavenworth prison, his health failing, Haywood doubted he would live to see freedom again. His spirits revived, though, when JOHN SILAS REED, a Marxist journalist, sent him a copy of his book *Ten Days That Shook the World*, which presented Russia's Bolshevik Revolution in a glorious light. Haywood longed for the day he would be able to meet the revolution's leader, Vladimir Lenin.

Then in 1919 the government granted him his petition for a new trial, and he left Leavenworth under an appeal bond. Once released, Haywood found his every move watched by federal agents, and after Attorney General A. Mitchell Palmer attempted to arrest him in January 1920, in the period of the Red Scare (when Palmer was hunting down communists and other radicals), he turned himself in to face the newly filed charge of criminal syndicalism. Out on bail, he learned that his appeal for his original arrest had been denied by a U.S. circuit court.

For Haywood the future looked bleak. So in late March 1921 he donned a disguise and boarded a ship for Russia. There he received a hero's welcome from Lenin. Haywood joined an attempt to develop an industrial colony near the Ural Mountains, but his failing health hampered him; he found the frigid weather and poor housing intolerable and the cultural differences between him and the Russians insurmountable. In late 1926 Haywood married a 37-year-old Russian woman (his first wife had died), but he remained largely isolated from the surrounding society and psychologically depressed.

Big Bill Haywood died on March 16, 1928, in Moscow after suffering a stroke. His years in Russia produced a torment that made his ending tragic. To a newspaper reporter he defended his life in exile, saying, "I am an open country man, I couldn't live . . . cooped up in a prison." Yet ELIZABETH GURLEY FLYNN, an American Communist, captured his essence after his death:

> He longed for the land of baseball and burlesque, big steaks and cigars, cowboys and rodeos, strikes and picket lines, to see the Mississippi and the Rocky Mountains. He was flesh and blood of America, he belonged here in its militant struggles against Capitalism.

Further Reading

Carlson, Peter. *Roughneck: The Life and Times of Big Bill Haywood.* New York: Norton, 1983.

Conlin, Joseph Robert. *Big Bill Haywood and the Radical Union Movement.* Syracuse, N.Y.: Syracuse University Press, 1969.

Dubofsky, Melvyn. *"Big Bill" Haywood.* New York: St. Martin's Press, 1987.

Renshaw, Patrick. *The Wobblies: The Story of the IWW and Syndicalism in the United States.* Chicago: Ivan R. Dee, 1999.

Hernandez, Aileen Clarke

(1926–) *civil rights leader, women's rights leader*

A civil rights activist, Aileen Clarke Hernandez served for a time as president of the National Organization for Women. She was born on May 23, 1926, in Brooklyn, New York, to Charles Henry Clarke and Ethel Louise Hall Clarke, both of whom were immigrants from Jamaica.

Charles and Ethel Clarke struggled to raise Aileen and her two brothers during the Great Depression. He worked as a brush maker, and she as a seamstress; their work ethic instilled in Aileen a similar commitment, and she excelled in school, graduating in 1943 as class salutatorian from Bay Ridge High School. During her undergraduate studies at Howard University in Washington, D.C., she joined the campus branch of the National Association for the Advancement of Colored People (NAACP) and protested racial segregation by taking part in picketing the National Theater and a restaurant chain.

Clarke obtained her bachelor's degree from Howard in 1947 and entered graduate school at California State University in Los Angeles, where she interned with the International Ladies Garment Workers Union (ILGWU). In 1951 she accepted a job with the union's West Coast division first as an organizer and assistant education director and later as its education and public relations director. She married Alfonso Hernandez, a garment cutter, in the 1950s, but they divorced in 1961.

That same year Aileen Clarke Hernandez left the ILGWU to work in Democrat Alan Cranston's campaign for state comptroller, and after he won, Governor Edmund Brown, a fellow Democrat, appointed her assistant chief of the California Division of Fair Employment practices, charged with enforcing the state antidiscrimination law. Under her leadership employers ended the use of racially biased tests for hiring workers.

In 1965 President Lyndon Johnson selected Hernandez as the first woman to serve on the U.S. Equal Employment Opportunities Commission, which enforced laws that prohibited employers from discriminating in their hiring on the basis of race, color, religion, national origin, or sex.

Her work convinced her that women needed an organization to protect their rights, so in 1966 she quit her government job and in 1967 joined the recently formed National Organization for Women (NOW) as its western regional vice president, making her the first black woman to hold an appointive position within the organization. At the same time she began her own consulting firm, Aileen C. Hernandez and Associates, in San Francisco. It specialized in advising employers on how to abide by antidiscrimination laws.

In 1970 Hernandez succeeded BETTY FRIEDAN, NOW's founder, as the group's president. Her appointment was controversial in the black community; many African Americans saw NOW as largely a white middle-class organization competing with the civil rights movement and, by and large, irrelevant to the special problems faced by African-American women.

In 1971 Hernandez helped found the National Women's Political Caucus to encourage women to seek public office. She left the NOW presidency in September of that year and in 1972 conducted a study of NOW that showed it had attracted few minority women.

Discontented with NOW's racial tokenism, in 1979 Hernandez left the organization and joined the Women's Caucus of the Black American Political Association of California. Into the 1980s and early 1990s she continued to expand her consulting firm, employing as many as 30 people.

Mayor Willie Brown of San Francisco appointed Hernandez to a three-person panel in 1999 to find ways to improve the city's Human Rights Commission, which had as its duties selecting minority groups for its affirmative action contracts. Brown acted after Hernandez complained about possible illegal practices and as the federal government began investigating alleged wrongdoing by the commission. The following year the panel recommended that the Human Rights Commission no longer handle affirmative action contracts.

Further Reading
Smith, Jessie Carney, ed. *Notable Black American Women.* 2 vols. Detroit: Gale Research, 1992–96.

Higginson, Thomas Wentworth
(1823–1911) *abolitionist, women's rights leader*

An eclectic reformer, Thomas Wentworth Higginson advocated abolitionism, women's rights, and physical exercise. He was born on December 22, 1823, in Cambridge, Massachusetts, to Stephen Higginson, a wealthy Boston merchant, and Louisa Storrow Higginson.

Thomas Wentworth Higginson was more inclined to slaying social demons than pursuing a run-of-the-mill career. A voracious reader with a steel-trap mind, he enrolled at Harvard in 1841, at the age of 13. While excelling at his studies, he liked the outdoors and participated avidly in swimming, skating, and other sports. He graduated from Harvard and taught school for two years but disliked teaching. Rudderless, he returned to Harvard in 1843 and for three years indulged his fondness for reading while enrolled as a graduate student. Looking at an empty future, he finally decided to pursue courses in Harvard's divinity school, though without enthusiasm.

Higginson graduated in 1847 and became minister at the Unitarian First Religious Society in Newburyport, Massachusetts. But his greatest attachment was to social reform, in particular abolition and women's rights. On the slavery issue he took a radical stand: Much as WILLIAM LLOYD GARRISON did, he favored dissolving the Union rather than the North's continuing to coexist with the slaveholding South.

His zeal for reform even included diet and exercise. He advocated the "vigorous life" for health and was so emphatic that his championing of ice skating led to wags' calling the activity "Higginson's Revival."

In 1850 Higginson ran for Congress as a candidate of the Free-Soil Party, the political party that opposed extending slavery into the western territories. He lost that race and then lost his ministry when his controversial political views resulted in his being forced to leave Newburyport Church.

But he found a new religious home in 1852, when he became pastor of the nonsectarian Free Church in Worcester, Massachusetts. He had earlier joined a Boston vigilance committee to prevent slave catchers from retrieving runaways. In 1854 his name circulated in newspapers across New England for his part in the daring rescue of a fugitive slave, Anthony Burns. To free Burns, Higginson and several colleagues battered down a courthouse door and fought with the police—a battle that left him with a deep gash on his chin.

In the later 1850s Higginson traveled to Kansas, where he aided free soil settlers and developed a friendship with the radical abolitionist JOHN BROWN. At the same time he took up writing, and over the years he published many magazine articles and numerous books. His "Ought Women to Learn the Alphabet?" which appeared in the *Atlantic Monthly* in 1859, expressed his support for women's rights. "What rational woman can be really convinced by the nonsense which is talked in ordinary society around her," he asked, "as that it is right to admit girls to common schools, and equally right to exclude them from colleges; that it is proper for a woman to sing in public, but indelicate for her to speak in public; that a post-office box is an unexceptionable place to drop a bit of paper into, but a ballot-box terribly dangerous?" He added:

> As matters now stand among us, there is no aristocracy but of sex: all men are born patrician, all women are legally plebeian; all men are equal in having political power, and all women in having none. This is a paradox so evident, and such an anomaly in human progress, that it cannot last forever.

In the Civil War Higginson served in the Union army as colonel of the First South Carolina

Volunteers, which was the first African-American regiment. Complications from a wound forced him to leave the regiment in May 1864.

With slavery ended, Higginson focused on women's rights. He joined several suffrage groups and from 1870 to 1884 edited *Woman's Journal*, published by the Massachusetts Suffrage Association. He served in the state legislature from 1880 to 1881 and on the floor called for women to have the right to vote.

Higginson died on May 9, 1911. He had married twice—Mary Channing, who died in 1877, and Marry Potter Thatcher in 1879—and had several children. Not without good reason, Ronald G. Walters opens his book *American Reformers, 1815–1860* (1978) by noting Higginson's reference to a phrase that prevailed in the antebellum period namely, "'the Sisterhood of Reforms.'" It meant, Higginson stated, "a variety of social and physiological theories of which one was expected to accept all, if any." Of these it can be said that Higginson accepted many, with purpose and commitment.

Further Reading

Higginson, Thomas Wentworth. *Army Life in a Black Regiment, and Other Writings*. New York: Penguin Books, 1997.

Meyer, Howard N. *Colonel of the Black Regiment: The Life of Thomas Wentworth Higginson*. New York: Norton, 1967.

Wells, Anna Mary. *Dear Preceptor: The Life and Times of Thomas Wentworth Higginson*. Boston: Houghton Mifflin, 1963.

Hill, Joe
(Joel Haggland, Joseph Hillstrom)
(1879–1915) *union organizer*

An organizer and a songwriter for the Industrial Workers of the World (IWW), Joe Hill was executed for murder. He was born Joel Haggland in Gavle, Sweden, on October, 7, 1879, to Olof Haggland, a railroad worker, and Margareta Haggland.

Joe Hill's past is shrouded in so much myth and legend that the details surrounding his life are a mystery. It is known that he grew up in poverty; that at some time around 1900 his father died; and that in 1902 his mother died. These tragic events caused him and his brother to immigrate to the United States in 1902. He spent some time in New York City and then went out West, working at itinerant jobs—a longshoreman, miner, logger, fruit picker. Between 1906 and 1910 he changed his name to Joseph Hillstrom, for reasons in dispute. Some historians say he was trying to change his identity because he had engaged in petty crime; others say it was because he was being persecuted by company bosses who disliked his labor activism.

Hillstrom joined the San Pedro, California, local of the Industrial Workers of the World in 1910. The following year he joined his fellow Wobblies (the nickname for IWW members) in plotting in Tijuana, Mexico, to overthrow the Mexican government. Back in the United States, his labor protests resulted in several skirmishes with the police, and he later admitted that he had spent 30 days in the San Pedro, California, jail for vagrancy.

By that time he was using Hill as his last name and writing songs intended to rally Wobblies as they organized and engaged in strikes. Usually he wrote lyrics that he set to popular tunes of the day. His songs began appearing in the *Little Red Song Book*, an annual published by the IWW, which sold for 10 cents. Bearing the slogan "To Fan the Flames of Discontent," the *Little Red Song Book* urged the workers to rise up against the company bosses. Some in the IWW criticized the resort to music as frivolous, but Hill said, "If a person can put a few cold, common sense facts into a song and dress them . . . up in a cloak of humor to take the dryness out of them, he will succeed in reaching a great number of workers who are too unintelligent or too indifferent to read a pamphlet or an editorial on economic science."

Hill's songs certainly succeeded. His "Casey Jones—the Union Scab," a parody set to another song about Jones, was widely popular with Wobblies and other workers, as was his "The Preacher and the Slave." By 1913 he had become the most frequent contributor to the *Little Red Song Book*.

That year he went to Utah, where he may have worked briefly in the silver mines at Park City. On the wintry night of January 10, 1914, at about 10 o'clock, two men wearing dark hats and coats, and with handkerchiefs pulled up to cover their faces, entered a Salt Lake City grocery store owned by John G. Morrison. When Arling Morrison, John's son, pulled out a revolver and shot at them, they fired back, killing both John and Arling. As 13-year-old Merlin Morrison rushed from a backroom to see what was going on, the two men fled. Merlin later gave only vague descriptions of the intruders.

Later that night Joe Hill appeared at a doctor's house, bleeding from a gunshot wound. He always insisted the wound was inflicted during an argument he had with a woman. On hearing the police request for help in the killings, the doctor turned in Hill, and he was arrested.

Only circumstantial evidence had been collected to convict Hill. Merlin Morrison offered nothing positive; another witness who saw one of the gunmen fleeing the store said he saw a scar on the intruder's face that resembled the one on Joe Hill's face. Inexplicably, Hill refused to testify and identify the woman who he claimed had shot him. The jury deliberated four hours before finding him guilty. Hill had his choice of execution—a hanging or a firing squad. "I'll take the shooting," he told the judge. "I've been shot a couple times before, and I think I can take it."

Had Joe Hill been framed by enemies who wanted to eliminate a labor agitator? If he had been engaged previously in petty crime, he may have resorted to robbery. And evidence indicates that at the time of his arrest, the police had no idea he was a Wobbly and so had no political motive for jailing him. Yet other facts nag at the jury's verdict. For one, John Morrison was an ex-policeman who admitted that in his years on the local force he had angered many criminals, some of whom threatened to get him. For another, the grocery store gunmen took no money, either because they panicked and forgot it or because they intended to kill Morrison rather than rob him. Finally, added to the circumstantial evidence was the feeling of the community against unions and its disdain for the IWW's sponsoring of strikes in 1912 and 1913 at three mines. Writing in May 1914, Hill's lawyers said, "The main thing the state has against Hill is that he is an IWW and *therefore* sure to be guilty."

As Hill's trial approached, the IWW claimed he had been victimized, and it called for workers to rally behind him. The guilty verdict resulted in letters pouring into the office of the Utah governor, William Spry, from around the country and around the world, pleading that he grant Hill clemency. The Swedish ambassador to the United States protested, as did President Woodrow Wilson, who asked that Hill's case be "reconsidered." Spry responded by asking Hill whether he had anything to say in his defense; the convicted man refused to speak. On November 19, 1915, at 7:44 A.M., at the Utah State Penitentiary in Salt Lake City, a firing squad executed Joe Hill.

In Chicago 30,000 people turned out for a funeral procession to honor Hill. One reporter wrote, "What kind of man is this whose death is celebrated with songs of revolt and who has at his bier more mourners than any prince or potentate?" For many workers Joe Hill became a martyr, and his image would be resurrected numerous times during labor, antiwar, and other protests.

Shortly before Joe Hill was executed, he wrote to a fellow Wobbly, Bill Haywood, these words: "Goodbye Bill. I die like a true rebel. Don't waste time mourning—organize!"

Further Reading

Foner, Philip Sheldon. *The Case of Joe Hill.* New York: International Publishers, 1965.

Smith, Gibbs M. *Joe Hill.* Salt Lake City: University of Utah Press, 1969.

Hempill, Thomas. "To Be Found Dead in Utah." *Journal of the West* 39 (Fall 2000): 72+.

Hillman, Sidney
(1887–1946) *union leader*

A labor pragmatist, Sidney Hillman was president of the Amalgamated Clothing Workers of America (ACWA) and a founder of the Congress of Industrial Organizations (CIO). He was born on March 23, 1887, in Zagare, Lithuania, to Samuel Hillman and Judith Paiken Hillman.

Since Sidney Hillman hailed from a family whose sons traditionally studied to become rabbis, in 1901 he entered the Hebrew seminary at

Kovno. But a year later he left, attracted to the political upheaval then gripping Russian-controlled Lithuania. Hillman began organizing typesetters for the illegal Jewish trade union movement, and after serving time in prison for his labor activities, he joined the 1905 revolution. When the Russian government crushed the revolutionaries, Hillman fled to England, and in 1907 he immigrated to the United States.

In Chicago his labor activism flared anew. Working as an apprentice cutter at Hart, Shaffner, and Marx, a men's clothing factory, he took over a strike that had begun spontaneously and gave it direction. His advice that the strikers arbitrate with management caused the workers to support him and the company to respect him.

Hillman moved to New York City in 1914 to serve as chief clerk in the International Ladies Garment Workers Union. Late that year several locals founded a new union, the Amalgamated Clothing Workers of America. They asked Hillman to become its president, and he agreed.

This renegade organization, operating outside the American Federation of Labor (AFL), needed firm, shrewd, and practical leadership, and Hillman provided it. He led strikes in several cities while also inveighing against revolutionary demands. To Hillman the union should win better pay, shorter hours, and more benefits. Unlike some radical labor leaders who embraced pacifism and opposed World War I, Hillman supported America's entry into the conflict and cooperated with the federal government to establish standards for army clothing.

By 1920 Hillman had boosted membership in the ACWA to 177,000; fully 85 percent of the industry was under an ACWA contract, and he had won the 44-hour workweek. In 1916 Hillman married Bessie Abramowitz, a labor leader with Local 152; they had two daughters.

In the 1920s Hillman developed several innovative programs for the ACWA, including low-cost housing and the union's own bank. Ever the pragmatist, he claimed he had no desire to build a socialist society or lead a revolution; he was willing to cooperate with big business rather than to overthrow it and to obtain for the workers a bigger slice of the economic pie.

Although the Great Depression caused the ACWA to lose some members in the 1930s, Hillman embraced President Franklin Roosevelt's New Deal legislation that helped labor and encouraged unionization. He led the ACWA into the AFL in 1933, but he took the stand that labor leaders should diversify beyond the skilled trades and unionize workers in the mass assembly industries. Toward that end he cooperated with JOHN LLEWELLYN LEWIS in founding the Committee for Industrial Organization in 1935, which became the Congress of Industrial Organizations after it split with the AFL. Beginning in 1937 Hillman directed a new campaign to organize the textile industry.

Hillman rallied union members behind Franklin Roosevelt, forming the Non-Partisan League to recruit the more radical workers to the Democratic Party. His enthusiastic effort for Roosevelt made him the president's leading labor adviser. In 1943 Hillman became chairman and director of the CIO's Political Action Committee, formed to raise money for Democratic candidates and recruit volunteers to work for them.

Sidney Hillman suffered a heart attack in 1942 and died of a second heart attack on July 10, 1946, at Point Lookout, Long Island, New York.

Further Reading

Fraser, Steve. *Labor Will Rule: Sidney Hillman and the Rise of American Labor.* New York: Free Press, 1993.

Hine, Lewis Wickes
(1874–1940) *child labor reformer*

Lewis Wickes Hine was a photographer whose stark portrayal of working conditions contributed to the child labor reform movement. He was born on September 26, 1874, in Oshkosh, Wisconsin, the son of Douglas Hill Hine, a sign painter, and Sarah Hayes Hine.

Lewis Hine quit school at age 15 and held a variety of odd jobs until Frank A. Manny, the head of the psychology and education department at the state normal school in Oshkosh, encouraged him to take up teaching as a career. Hine then studied at the University of Chicago from 1900 until 1901, when Manny, who had been hired as the principal of the Ethical Culture School in New York City, re-cruited Hine to join his staff. At the same time Hine continued his studies at Columbia University and at New York University, and in 1904 he married Sara Ann Rich; they had one child.

At Manny's suggestion Lewis Hine began taking photographs of the immigrants as they arrived at Ellis Island. At that time photography was still in its infant stage: Matthew Brady had gained national attention 40 years earlier with his Civil War photographs, and JACOB RIIS was applying photography to social reform, but the act of taking pictures was still a difficult one, requiring the hauling around of heavy cameras mounted on tripods and attached to cumbersome flash pans that, when ignited, exploded into a choking haze of black smoke.

Hine soon took his camera beyond Ellis Island and began photographing the new arrivals in the tenements where they lived and the sweatshops where they worked. Then in 1908 the National Child Labor Committee (NCLC) hired him as an investigator and photographer. For the next several years he took photos of children laboring in factories, selling newspapers on street corners, and picking fruits and vegetables as hired hands on large farms. Usually, the managers and foremen banned Hine from the premises, and he had to pose as a fire inspector or a salesman to gain entry. In one 12-month period he traveled 12,000 miles taking pictures.

Hine told an audience: "Perhaps you are weary of child labor pictures. Well, so are the rest of us, but we propose to make you and the whole country so sick and tired of the whole business that when the time for action comes, child labor pictures will be records of the past." He accompanied his published photos with captions that he wrote, often containing direct quotations from the children. The combination of pictures and words stirred emotions:

Fuhrman Owens, 12 years old. Can't read. Doesn't know his A, B, C's. Said, "Yes I want to learn but can't when I work all the time." Been in the mills 4 years, 3 years in the Olympia Mill. Columbia, S.C.

One of the spinners in the Whitnel Cotton Mill. She was 51 inches high. Has been in the mill one year. Sometimes works at night.

Runs 4 sides—48 cents a day. When asked how old she was, she hesitated, then said, "I don't remember," then added confidentially, "I'm not old enough to work, but I do just the same."

Cutting fish in a sardine cannery. Large sharp knives are used with a cutting and sometimes chopping motion. The slippery floors and benches and careless bumping into each other increase the liability of accidents. "The salt water gets into the cuts and they ache," said one boy.

Hine's photos enhanced support for the movement for child labor reform, and in 1916 Congress passed the Keating-Owen Act, which restricted the employment of children below age 14 in factories and shops by prohibiting interstate shipment of goods that had been produced by child labor. (Two years later the Supreme Court overturned the act.) Owen Lovejoy, chairman of the NCLC, claimed, "The work Hine did for this reform was more responsible than all other efforts in bringing the need to public attention."

After World War I Hine accepted an assignment from the Red Cross to photograph conditions in war-devastated Europe. In the United States in the 1920s and 1930s he took pictures of working people; in one dramatic series taken in 1931 he recorded the construction of the Empire State Building. These photographs extolled the bravery and dedication of the workers; they also unintentionally revealed Hine's bravery, for he had to drag his bulky camera along steel girders, many stories above the street. For his final shot, a photo of the last rivet being driven into the metal, he dangled midair from a crane.

A number of Hine's photos appeared in *Men at Work,* published in 1932, and he compiled a photo essay for the magazine *Fortune* in 1939. But Lewis Hine found it difficult to make a living as a photographer, and he died on November 3, 1940, while living in dire poverty.

Further Reading

Curtis, Verna Posever, and Stanley Mallach. *Photography and Reform: Lewis Hine and the National Child Labor Committee.* Milwaukee, Wis.: Milwaukee Art Museum, 1984.

Gutman, Judith Mara. *Lewis W. Hine and the American Social Conscience.* New York: Walker, 1967.

Hine, Lewis Wickes. *The Empire State Building.* Munich: Prestel, 1998.

Kaplan, Daile, ed. *Photo Story: Selected Letters and Photographs of Lewis W. Hine.* Washington, D.C.: Smithsonian Institution Press, 1992.

Hoffa, Jimmy
(James Riddle Hoffa)
(1913–ca. 1975) *union leader*

A leader of the Teamsters Union, who was convicted of several crimes, James "Jimmy" Riddle Hoffa was likely killed by mobsters in 1975. He was born on February 14, 1913, in Brazil, Indiana, to John Cleveland Hoffa, a miner, and Viola Riddle Hoffa.

Raised in a poor family, Jimmy Hoffa was forced to drop out of school in the ninth grade—eight years after his father had died of lung disease—so he could earn enough money to support his mother and siblings. Living in Detroit at that time, he worked first as a stock boy and then obtained a job on a warehouse loading dock at the Kroger Grocery and Baking Company. Hoffa helped form a union local connected to the International Brotherhood of Teamsters, and in 1932 he became a full-time organizer.

Hoffa attached himself to the union with an avidity that later underscored his comment that the Teamsters "was all I've got." The union was his way to move beyond the loading docks and out of poverty. He organized truckers by walking up to their cabs and presenting a union spiel dosed with his friendly personality. His success in recruiting members was no small feat since his potential recruits were known for their fierce independence. But Hoffa was determined to give order to a largely chaotic industry by building a strong, centralized union.

Hoffa organized during the Great Depression by turning to gangsters for help in quashing factional fights and maintaining discipline during strikes. Bloody noses and broken arms were administered by his henchmen on numerous occasions, and Hoffa himself received his share of injuries in beatings by police and labor opponents.

In *Out of the Jungle: Jimmy Hoffa and the Remaking of the American Working Class* (2001), Thaddeus Russell describes Teamsters tactics: "Rather than devoting their time to signing up workers and petitioning for representation elections . . . the local's business agents first approached the owner of a firm and told him that if he did not enroll his employees with the union, his trucks would be bombed. Next, if the employer refused to capitulate, they bombed his trucks."

Hoffa married Josephine Poszywak in 1936; they had two children. In 1937 he landed in jail for the first time when he was convicted of assault and battery; another conviction occurred in 1940 for conspiracy. But Teamsters president Daniel J. Tobin liked Hoffa and used him to cleanse a union local in Minneapolis, Minnesota, of its left-wing members. Job accomplished, Tobin made Hoffa vice president of the Teamsters' Central State Drivers Council. In that post Hoffa worked as chief negotiator for interstate truck drivers in the Midwest. His ability to win higher wages and better benefits led to a strong following among union members, and in 1952 they elected him vice president and placed him on the executive board.

In his new post Hoffa helped negotiate a labor contract in 1955 that created a central states Teamster pension fund. He soon gained control over the board of trustees who administered the fund and used the money to make loans to gangsters—in return for their support in the union—and to invest in Las Vegas casinos and various real estate deals.

As reports spread about corruption in the handling of pension fund moneys, the U.S. Senate's Select Committee on Improper Activities in the Labor or Management Field, led by Democratic senator John L. McClellan, investigated Hoffa, and during televised hearings Senator John F. Kennedy and the committee's chief counsel, Robert F. Kennedy, grilled the beleaguered union leader. The investigation resulted in Teamsters president Dave Beck's being charged with and convicted of grand larceny and Hoffa's being charged with, but found innocent of, attempting to bribe a member of the McClellan committee. Hoffa never forgave the Kennedys for the treatment he received—over the years he maintained a deep hatred of them.

With Beck in prison, in 1957 Hoffa won election as Teamsters president, but the federal government stepped in and nullified the vote after finding it had been rigged. Court action, though, restored Hoffa to office, and he was reelected in 1961. The AFL-CIO, however, expelled the Teamsters, claiming the union had failed to dissociate itself from criminals.

Hoffa's popularity among the Teamsters only grew as he won yet more concessions from trucking companies. At the same time, from the late 1950s to 1971, he tightened his control over the union, centralizing power in the presidency. Hoffa organized nearly 90 percent of long-haul truckers and effectively combined strikes with negotiations to gain ever more favorable contracts, yet he maintained a good working relationship with the trucking companies. He wanted eventually to combine the many different contracts negotiated by the union into one all-encompassing contract; he never achieved that goal, but he did reduce their number.

Legal troubles again burdened Hoffa in 1962 when the Justice Department, led by Attorney General Robert F. Kennedy, investigated the Teamsters, and Hoffa was tried on charges he had received illegal payments from a trucking company. A jury acquitted him, but a federal grand jury indicted him on tampering with the trial jury, and he was convicted on that charge in March 1964. Later that year he was also convicted on charges of conspiracy and mail fraud.

Hoffa tried to get these convictions overturned on the basis that the federal government had used illegal wiretaps against him, but he failed. As he headed to prison in March 1967, he told reporters: "This is a very unhappy day in my life . . . the Government has wire-tapped, room-bugged, surveilled and done everything unconstitutional it could do. . . . They have temporarily been able to do so. . . . I hope to be back."

With Hoffa in jail, his friend Frank Fitzsimmons headed the Teamsters. At first compliant and largely taking orders from Hoffa, Fitzsimmons soon displayed increasing independence. Hoffa, meanwhile, pressed for an early release from prison—he had been sentenced to 13 years—and in December 1971 President Richard Nixon commuted his sentence to time served, provided that he refrain from engaging in any union activity until 1980, the year he would have been released from prison under the original judgment. Hoffa agreed, though he disliked the conditional release and unsuccessfully fought it in court.

Despite the restriction on his union activities, Hoffa tried to regain control of the Teamsters with a plan to unseat Fitzsimmons and install someone loyal in his place. Then on July 30, 1975, he drove to the Machus Red Fox restaurant near Detroit to meet "somebody," as he had told a friend, and disappeared, never to be seen or heard from again. Shortly before his disappearance his wife received a phone call from him in which he said, "Where the hell is Tony Giacalone? I'm being stood up."

The mysterious disappearance of Jimmy Hoffa (left) remains unsolved as speculation continues that he was killed as part of an underworld plot to eliminate him. Here he is shown with his son, James P. Hoffa, at a testimonial dinner in 1965. (*New York World-Telegram and the Sun Newspaper Collection, Library of Congress*)

The Federal Bureau of Investigation (FBI) investigated Hoffa's disappearance but came up empty-handed. Although lacking sufficient evidence to indict anyone, FBI agents involved in the case think they know what happened. They believe that a reputed New Jersey mobster, Tony Provenzano, and his gang killed Hoffa and then disposed of his body by placing it in a 55-gallon drum and burying it in a landfill. Provenzano did this, they think, largely because he thought Hoffa would get in the way of the mob's access to the Teamsters pension fund.

Hoffa's unsolved disappearance was like his middle name, a riddle. Yet what cannot be doubted is that through all his legal battles he remained enormously popular with Teamster members. While he was in jail their trucks displayed bumper stickers saying, "Bring Back Jimmy Hoffa," and in one random poll, 83 percent of the truck drivers said they would vote for Hoffa as the next Teamsters president.

Further Reading

Russell, Thaddeus. *Out of the Jungle: Jimmy Hoffa and the Remaking of the American Working Class.* New York: Knopf, 2001.

Sheridan, Walter. *The Fall and Rise of Jimmy Hoffa.* New York: Saturday Review Books, 1972.

Sloane, Arthur A. *Hoffa.* Cambridge, Mass.: MIT Press, 1991.

Hoffman, Abbie
(Abbott Hoffman)

(1936–1989) *antiwar leader, counterculture leader*

An antiwar protester and founder of the Yippies, Abbie Hoffman was an artist at using the absurd in protest. He was born Abbott Hoffman on November 30, 1936, in Worcester, Massachusetts, to John Hoffman, a pharmacist who provided his family with middle-class comfort, and Florence Schanberg Hoffman.

As a high school student, Abbie Hoffman once got into trouble for striking a teacher, but he did well enough in his studies to enroll at Brandeis University in Waltham, Massachusetts, where he received a bachelor's degree in 1959. Hoffman continued his education at the University of California at Berkeley, and the following year obtained a master's degree in psychology. He then began working as a psychologist at the Massachusetts State Hospital.

By that time Hoffman had adopted radical political views, which he later attributed to social injustice, to his Jewish heritage, and to the lesson he learned from the failure of Jews in 1930s Germany to stand up to their Nazi oppressors forcefully. He said: "Six million dead and except for the Warsaw ghetto hardly a bullet fired in resistance." Rejecting what he saw as his ancestors' passivity, he intended to fight oppression in America and end the insanity of war.

Hoffman claimed his real birth occurred in May 1960, when two "generation-shaking" events "molded my consciousness forever." The first was a protest he joined in California against the death penalty. The second happened a few days later when he demonstrated in San Francisco at hearings held by the House Un-American Activities Committee and police attacked him and other protesters with clubs and water hoses.

Back in Massachusetts, Hoffman worked for the civil rights movement in Worcester as an activist with the National Association for the Advancement of Colored People. In summers 1964 and 1965 he traveled to Mississippi, where he helped the Student Non-Violent Coordinating Committee (SNCC) register black voters. The following year he moved to New York City and operated Liberty House, an SNCC store that sold goods handmade by African Americans who lived in a cooperative in the South. In 1966 his six-year marriage to Sheila Karklin, with whom he had two children, ended in divorce.

When SNCC decided in 1967 to expel its white workers, Hoffman plunged into street theater, an artistic endeavor first developed by a San Francisco hippie group, the Diggers. Street theater involved staging outrageous acts to attract media attention and expose straight society's absurdities. Although it had a political goal, namely, revolutionizing people, it emphasized cultural activities, so it rejected picketing and sit-ins. Hoffman saw street theater as a creative way to make statements against oppression without relying on wordiness and a way to draw the hippies, who disdained political activity as useless, into a greater crusade to change America. In effect, he wanted to build a bridge between the political and cultural radicals. "I always held my flower in a clenched fist," he said. "A semi–structure freak among the love children, I was determined to bring the hippie movement into a broader protest."

With regard to media appeal, Hoffman stated, "I trained for the one-liner, the retort jab, or sudden knockout put-ons." He exploited those television interview shows intent on ridiculing him, and he turned the tables on others through stunts, as when, during David Susskind's program, he let loose a duck wearing a sign reading, "I AM A HIPPIE." "The goal of this nameless art form—part vaudeville, part insurrection, part communal recreation—was to shatter the pretense of objectivity," he later said. "We learned to sneak onto the airwaves with Conceptual Art pieces that roused viewers from their video stupor."

Hoffman staged his first widely reported put-on early in 1967 when he threw dollar bills from the balcony of the New York Stock Exchange to the floor below, causing stockbrokers to scramble after the money in a chaotic frenzy that paralyzed trading for several minutes. He claimed that this act said "more than thousands of anti-capitalist tracts and essays." That spring Hoffman married Anita Kushner; they had one son and were divorced in 1980.

In October 1967 Abbie Hoffman and JERRY RUBIN worked together to enliven the antiwar march on the Pentagon. They led a band of self-proclaimed witches, wore outlandish outfits, and declared their intention to levitate the Pentagon and purge its evil spirits. Needless to say, the press widely publicized the antics.

The following month Hoffman organized a War Is Over demonstration at Washington Square in New York City. About 3,000 young people gathered and on cue ran down the streets from Grand Central Station to Times Square and back, shouting "The war is over!" Hoffman wanted straight society to think about Vietnam and how liberating ending the bloodshed would be.

In December 1967, on New Year's Eve, Hoffman, Rubin, and several others decided to plan a street theater action to be held at the Democratic National Convention scheduled for August in Chicago. They called it the Festival of Life, to contrast with their name for the Democratic Party's meeting, the Convention of Death, and they formed an organization to promote their concept, the Yippies. Hoffman later called the Yippies a myth devised to manipulate the media. "How do you do this starting from scratch, with no organization, no money, nothing?" he said. "Well, the answer is that you create a myth. Something that people can play a role in and relate to."

In the spring and summer Hoffman publicized the Yippies by distributing buttons bearing the word *Yippie!* in pink psychedelic letters set on a purple background and by staging several events to excite people and get them and the media involved. For example, the Yippies held a Yip-in at Grand Central Station, a largely unorganized party that attracted several thousand youths.

At Chicago, however, Hoffman and the Yippies failed to pull off their Festival of Life. Instead, the entire scene decayed into violence as a result of several factors, including tension between Hoffman and Rubin over tactics; differences between the Yippies and other protesters, most notably the National Mobilization Committee to End the War in Vietnam, which wanted a more serious political demonstration; and the decision by the Chicago police to use force. Shortly after the protest Hoffman made another controversial move when in response to a subpoena from the House Un-American Activities Committee he showed up at their hearing wearing boots, buckskin pants, and an American flag shirt.

Within weeks after Chicago the federal government arrested Hoffman and seven other prominent protesters for conspiracy to riot during the Democratic National Convention. The press called this group the Chicago Eight. (It soon became the Chicago Seven when one of the defendants was tried separately.) At their trial in 1969, known for its counterculture celebrity witnesses, uproarious actions by the defendants, and intolerant decisions by the judge, Abbie Hoffman professed his innocence. Although a jury acquitted him of conspiracy, it convicted him of rioting. Three years later, however, a higher court overturned the conviction, citing several errors of law committed by the trial judge.

In 1973 undercover police in New York City arrested Hoffman for selling cocaine. Rather than face the charges, he disappeared from view. Living in upstate New York under the alias Barry Freed, he wrote articles and worked as an environmentalist. In typical Hoffman outrageousness, he disguised himself and pulled off an appearance before a U.S. Senate subcommittee as Freed.

Through the 1980s he never deserted his earlier social commitment; always the activist, he said: "Democracy is not something you believe in or a place you hang your hat . . . it's something you do. You participate. If you stop doing it, democracy crumbles."

On April 12, 1989, Hoffman was found dead in his motel room in New Hope, Pennsylvania, a victim of an overdose of phenobarbital. Hoffman had, for some time, suffered from manic depression, and the authorities ruled his death a suicide.

Abbie Hoffman's outlook appeared in its usual satirical garb during testimony he offered at his 1969 trial:

> Attorney Weinglass: Would you state your name?
>
> Witness: My name is Abbie. I'm an orphan of America.
>
> Attorney: Where do you reside?
>
> Witness: Woodstock nation.
>
> Judge: What state is that in?
>
> Witness: The state of mind. It's a nation of alienated young people, which we carry in our minds, just as the Sioux Indians carried around the Sioux nation in their minds.

Further Reading

Hoffman, Abbie. *Soon to Be a Major Motion Picture: The Autobiography of Abbie Hoffman.* New York: Four Walls Eight Windows, 2000.

Jezer, Marty. *Abbie Hoffman: American Rebel.* New Brunswick, N.J.: Rutgers University Press, 1992.

Raskin, Jonah. *For the Hell of It: The Life and Times of Abbie Hoffman.* Berkeley: University of California Press, 1996.

Sloman, Larry. *Steal This Dream: Abbie Hoffman and the Countercultural Revolution in America.* New York: Doubleday, 1998.

Hooks, Benjamin Lawson
(1925–) *civil rights leader*

An African-American lawyer and preacher, Benjamin Lawson Hooks served as executive director of the National Association for the Advancement of Colored People (NAACP). He was born on January 31, 1925, in Memphis, Tennessee, to Robert Hooks, a photographer, and Bessie White Hooks.

Benjamin Hooks graduated from all-black Booker T. Washington High School in 1941 and then attended LeMoyne College in Memphis, but his higher education was interrupted when he was drafted into the U.S. Army during World War II and sent to Italy to fight. On his return he enrolled at Howard University in Washington, D.C.; after his graduation he received a law degree in 1948 from DePaul University in Chicago.

Hooks then returned home to Memphis and practiced law in the racially segregated court system. In 1951 he married Frances Dancy, and three years later he was ordained as a Baptist minister. In 1956 he was chosen pastor of the Middle Baptist Church in Memphis, a post he would hold until 1972, while continuing his legal career and working in the civil rights movement.

In 1961 Hooks won appointment as the assistant public defender for Shelby County, Tennessee. His job, his involvement in lunch counter sit-ins, and his service on the board of MARTIN LUTHER KING, JR.'s, Southern Christian Leadership Conference antagonized whites and generated numerous threats to his safety.

The governor of Tennessee appointed Hooks in 1965 to a vacancy on the county criminal court, to which he was elected the following year. He was the first black criminal court judge in the South since Reconstruction. He resigned, however, in 1968 to go into business as the president of the Mahalia Jackson Fried Chicken franchises. Unfortunately for Hooks, and for Mahalia Jackson, the company quickly folded.

In 1972 President Richard Nixon acted to fulfill a campaign promise by appointing an African American to the Federal Communications Commission (FCC), and for this job he chose Hooks. While on the commission Hooks criticized the stereotyping of blacks on television and favored granting more TV and radio broadcasting licenses to African Americans to introduce more of the black perspective to the industry.

When ROY WILKINS retired as executive director of the NAACP in 1976, the organization turned to Benjamin Hooks as his replacement, whereupon he quit the FCC and accepted the job with enthusiasm. "I didn't think twice before agreeing," Hooks recalled. "I wanted to play a continuing role in the evolution of freeing blacks from the sting of racial prejudice and discrimination."

To boost membership, Hooks increased the number of NAACP youth, college, and prison chapters, and he expanded Project Rebound, which helped parolees readjust to society. He also worked to improve the NAACP's finances. When he took over the organization, its debt exceeded $1 million; by the end of 1978 that had been cut in half.

Under his leadership the NAACP lobbied Congress to pass the Martin Luther King federal holiday bill, an extension of the 1965 Voting Rights Act, sanctions against segregationist South Africa, and the 1991 Civil Rights Act. The last measure he thought to be a great accomplishment in an era of conservatism that he viewed as damaging to African Americans. "I'm glad we had the 1991 Civil Rights Bill passed and signed," he recalled a year later, "but I can't help wondering if we would not have needed it but for the backward movement of the Supreme Court. If the court had not absolutely moved [that way], we would not have had to restore the status quo. That's disturbing."

Hooks retired from the NAACP executive directorship in 1992, though he announced he would continue to support the organization. He left a solid record of accomplishment, one that contrasted markedly with the several years of economic hardship and scandal that nearly destroyed the NAACP in the late 1990s.

Yet for all of his accomplishments, many African Americans thought it time for a change, for fresh and vigorous leadership. A nationwide poll conducted in 1992 by the *Detroit News*/Gannett News Service found that most of the blacks questioned thought the NAACP needed to address more pressing problems involving jobs, crime, and education. Writing in the *Cleveland Plain Dealer* in 1993, one observer asked, "Can the NAACP regain any of its former influence? It can if it confronts reality. The old civil rights agenda—securing new laws to combat racism—is inadequate. The NAACP must find the candor and the courage to campaign boldly against self-destructive behavior in blacks just as it fights racism in whites."

Hooks next accepted a teaching position at Fisk University in Nashville, Tennessee, as distinguished professor of the Benjamin L. Hooks Chair for Social Justice. In 1994 he scaled back his activities after suffering a severe heart attack and undergoing quadruple bypass surgery.

Further Readings

Bradley, David, and Shelby Fisher, eds. *Encyclopedia of Civil Rights in America.* New York: Sharpe Reference, 1998.

Hostos, Eugenio María de
(1839–1903) *Puerto Rican nationalist*

Eugenio María de Hostos was an educator, writer, and Puerto Rican nationalist. He was born on January 11, 1839, in Rio Canas, Puerto Rico, to Eugenio María de Hostos y Rodrigo de Velasco, a Spanish lawyer and planter, and Hilaria de Bonilla y Cintrón.

Eugenio María de Hostos received an elementary education in San Juan, Puerto Rico, and attended high school in Bilbao, Spain. From there he entered the University of Madrid Law School and in 1860 obtained a law degree. During those years he wrote several articles advocating independence for Spain's colonies in Latin America. He hoped that his home island of Puerto Rico could be united with Cuba and Santo Domingo into a confederation, and for the rest of his life he worked to fulfill that plan.

While in Spain Hostos campaigned for a change from a primarily monarchical government to a republican one, believing that once the republicans took power they would grant the Spanish West Indies their independence. In 1863 he wrote *La Peregrinación de Bayoan,* a novel that historians believe had an enormous impact on the cause of Cuban independence. As it turned out, a republican government did rise to power in Spain, but it refused to relinquish the colonies, and in 1869 it expelled Hostos from the country for his views.

Hostos then immigrated to the United States and joined the Cuban Revolutionary Junta, operated by Cuban exiles in New York City who were seeking independence for their island. He edited the junta's newspaper, *La Revolución,* before leaving in 1870 for South America. In the early 1870s he taught at the University of Santiago in Chile and wrote many articles that gained him a wide following in Latin America.

Hostos returned to New York City in 1874 and joined a revolutionary expedition to Cuba, but the group was shipwrecked before it could leave Long Island Sound. In 1875 he moved to the Dominican Republic and published a magazine. The following year he taught in Venezuela, and in 1877 he married Belinda Otilia de Ayala, the daughter of a Cuban émigré doctor. They had six children.

When the Cuban revolt ended in 1878 without gaining independence, Hostos began teaching at the National University in the Dominican Republic. In 1887 he published *Lecciones de Derecho Constitucional* (constitutional law), followed the next year by his *Moral Social,* a book of essays dealing with ethics.

Expelled from Santo Domingo in 1888 by the dictator Ulises Heureaux, Hostos returned to Chile and from 1890 to 1898 taught international law at the University of Chile in Santiago. When Cuba finally won its independence from Spain in 1898 as a result of the Spanish-American War, Hostos traveled to Washington, D.C., to convince the United States to grant Puerto Rico independence.

In a January 17, 1899, interview in the San Juan newspaper, *El País,* Hostos said: "Puerto Rico is now in a position to become a territory of the American Union. It cannot go back to being a colony without the benefits of an ample autonomy. We want to be brothers of the Americans, not servants. We have the right to be first-class Americans, with all the prerogatives of a free country. So, let's hope for a civil government." Instead, President William McKinley decided that the island should become an American possession and that status was arranged through the treaty that ended the war.

Shattered by this turn of events, Hostos organized the short-lived Puerto Rican Patriots to resist American control, and he again traveled to Washington in 1899 to ask McKinley to reconsider, giving him a book that he had written that presented his argument, *The Case of Puerto Rico.* Hostos wanted the Americans to hold a plebiscite on the island. He said, "We will accept annexation if it is the will of the Puerto Ricans. If not, we will give the Federation of the North the best tribute any nation could receive by asking for a temporary 20-year protectorate. It will not be a protectorate of force and power but one of guidance to liberty and progress."

Rejected a second time, Hostos refused to live under American rule; he left Puerto Rico and moved back to the Dominican Republic. Hostos worked as inspector general of that country's schools until his death in Santo Domingo on August 11, 1903. Hailed for his writing and for his contributions to education, Hostos nevertheless died disappointed that he had been unable to gain Puerto Rican independence and establish the confederation he so deeply wanted. He thought himself a failure, though history has judged him a success in his endeavors.

Further Reading

Balseire, Jose Agustin. *Eugenio Maria de Hostos, Hispanic America's Public Servant.* Coral Gables, Fla.: University of Miami Press, 1949.

Hostos, Eugenio Carlos de, ed. *Eugenio María de Hostos, Promoter of Pan Americanism: A Collection of Writings and a Bibliography.* Madrid: Litografía y Encuadernación, 1954.

Howe, Julia Ward
(1819–1910) *women's suffragist, peace activist*

Julia Ward was a writer, women's suffragist, and peace activist. She was born on May 27, 1819, in

New York City to Samuel Ward, a banker, and Julia Rush Cutler Ward.

Raised in a wealthy family, Julia Ward was educated in a private school and by tutors. As a child she showed a talent for writing poems that she would continue to develop as an adult. In 1843 she married Samuel Gridley Howe, a Boston reformer some 20 years her senior; they had five children. Through him her intellectual contacts expanded, and she became well known among the city's philosophers and writers. Samuel Gridley Howe's prominent role in the abolitionist movement stirred her own dislike for slavery, but although she helped him edit *The Commonwealth,* an antislavery newspaper, for the most part she remained in the movement's background.

In 1854 Julia Ward Howe published her first volume of poems, *Passion Flowers,* followed three years later by *Words for the Hour.* During the Civil War she accompanied her husband on a trip to Washington, D.C., where they studied the sanitary conditions among the Union troops. At one camp the sight of the soldiers and the burning watch fires so infused her with patriotic feelings that she sat down in her dark tent at night and wrote a poem, "The Battle Hymn of the Republic," subsequently set to the music of "John Brown's Body" and made into a stirring song filled with Christian imagery and expressing the righteousness of the Northern cause.

In the 1870s, as Howe's children reached adulthood and began leaving home, she moved out of her husband's reformist shadow and took the lead in the women's suffrage and peace movements. In 1868, the year that the New England Woman's Club made her its vice president (she would later hold office as president nearly continuously from 1871 to 1910), she joined the newly formed New England Woman Suffrage Association and began serving the first of two terms as its president.

The following year she helped found the American Woman Suffrage Association (AWSA). More moderate than its rival group, the National American Woman Suffrage Association (NAWSA), the AWSA emphasized working at the state level to secure women's right to vote and shied away from the numerous feminist reforms advocated by the NAWSA, along with its penchant for direct action. From 1870 to 1878, and again from 1891 to 1893, Howe also served as president of the Massachusetts Woman Suffrage Association.

Like many other suffragists, Howe entered the peace movement, and in 1870 she issued her "Appeal to Womanhood throughout the World." The idea for the essay, she said, arose from her visit to France that year and her disgust with the Franco-Prussian War. "While the war was still in progress," she recalled,

> I was visited by a sudden feeling of the cruel and unnecessary character of the contest. It seemed to me a return to barbarism, the issue having been one which might easily have been settled without bloodshed. The question forced itself upon me, "Why do not the mothers of mankind interfere in these matters, to

Like many other women's suffrage activists, Julia Ward Howe, here pictured in her old age, entered the peace movement. *(Library of Congress)*

prevent the waste of that human life of which they alone bear and know the cost."

The appeal drew heavily on women's attachment to motherhood and called for a worldwide meeting:

> Arise . . . Christian women of this day! Arise, all women who have hearts, whether your baptism be that of water or of tears! Say firmly: "We will not have great questions decided by irrelevant agencies. Our husbands shall not come to us, reeking with carnage, for caresses and applause. Our sons shall not be taken from us to unlearn all that we have been able to teach them of charity, mercy, and patience . . . ."
>
> In the name of womanhood and humanity, I earnestly ask that a general congress of women, without limit of nationality, may be appointed and held at some place deemed most convenient . . . to promote . . . the great and general interests of peace.

There followed in December 1870 the commencement of the World's Congress of Women in New York City, at which Howe made the opening address. "So I repeat my call and cry to women," she said. "Let it pierce through dirt and rags, let it pierce through velvet and cashmere. It is the call of humanity. It says: 'Help others, and you help yourselves.'" The following year at a meeting in Boston held at the New England Woman's Club, Howe and her fellow peace advocates founded the American Branch of the International Peace Association, and she was chosen president.

In 1873 Howe joined in founding the Association for the Advancement of Women (AAW), which brought together female scientists, educators, lawyers, reformers, and others to discuss their works and seek ways to solve problems faced by women in pursuing their endeavors. She served as president of the organization in 1881 and of the General Federation of Women's Clubs in the 1890s, after it had replaced the AAW.

Amid her reform work, Howe continued writing poems, essays, and fiction. These included *Memoir of Dr. Samuel Gridley Howe* (1876), *Modern Society* (1881), *Margaret Fuller* (1883), *From Sunset Ridge: Poems Old and New* (1898), and *Reminis-*

cences (1899). In 1908 she became the first woman elected to the American Academy of Arts and Letters.

Still, her greatest impact, beyond the "Battle Hymn of the Republic," resulted from her reform activities. In these she sought to exert the force of women and of womanhood and reduce the power of men. "The present style of woman has been fashioned by man," she wrote as both an observation and complaint, "and is only *quasi* feminine."

Further Reading

Clifford, Deborah Pickman. *Mine Eyes Have Seen the Glory: A Biography of Julia Ward Howe*. Boston: Little, Brown, 1979.

Grant, Mary Hetherington. *Private Woman, Public Person: An Account of the Life of Julia Ward Howe from 1819–1868*. Brooklyn, N.Y.: Carlson, 1994.

Huerta, Dolores Fernandez
(1930–) *labor organizer*

Cofounder of the United Farm Workers (UFW), Dolores Fernandez Huerta was called by her admirers "Madonna of the Fields." She was born Dolores Fernandez on April 10, 1930, in Dawson, a small mining town in northern New Mexico, to Juan Fernandez and Alicia Chavez Fernandez.

Because Dolores Fernandez's parents divorced while she was still an infant, Dolores was raised primarily by her mother. At first the family struggled financially, but during World War II Dolores's mother remarried, and with her new husband she ran a modest hotel in Stockton, California. Dolores graduated from Stockton High School and received an associate of arts degree from Stockton College. During those years she held a variety of odd jobs, and after receiving her A.A. degree she briefly taught school.

Dolores began her reform activities in the mid-1950s, when she joined the Community Service Organization (CSO), a self-help group founded by Fred Ross, a liberal activist. She helped register voters, form citizenship classes, and lobby local governments. Impressed with her results, the CSO hired her to lobby at the state capital in Sacramento. At that time Dolores married her second husband (a brief first marriage had ended in divorce), Ventura Huerta. Pressure on the marriage exerted by her activist commitments eventually caused them to divorce.

Around 1960 Dolores Huerta joined the Agricultural Workers Association to help Mexican-American farm workers. After it merged with the Agricultural Workers Organizing Committee, she served as the group's secretary-treasurer.

In that capacity Huerta met CESAR CHAVEZ, and they collaborated in trying to persuade the CSO to add rural issues to its largely urban agenda; they especially wanted it to organize farm workers. When it refused, they founded the National Farm Workers Association, which later became the United Farm Workers, in 1962.

Huerta was instrumental in organizing the UFW, developing strategy, and planning strikes. From the union's home base in Delano, California, she scoured the pool halls and the front steps of workers' shacks, recruiting members. When the UFW began a table-grape strike in 1965, she joined the picket lines and rallied the workers in the fields. And when the growers formed an alliance with the Teamsters Union against the strike, she sat down outside the apartment of the Teamster leader JIMMY HOFFA in Miami Beach, demanding that he change the union's policy—to no avail, as it turned out, but a move that gave the UFW considerable exposure.

During the strike Huerta coordinated the table-grape boycott. When the first grape grower finally agreed to recognize the UFW in 1966, she was the one who negotiated the contract. As the boycott continued in the late 1960s, she mobilized other unions, political activists, student groups, and many others to support it. Finally, in 1970 the growers in Delano agreed to sign contracts with the UFW. One UFW leader recalled: "She went about this stuff with an amazing confidence. She went face to face with these lawyers or professional management people and she was just very impressive. She more than held her own." Chavez once described her as "totally fearless, both mentally and physically."

In the early 1970s Huerta directed a boycott against lettuce growers and against the Gallo wine company. The UFW achieved a victory in 1975 when the California legislature passed the Agricultural Labor Relations Act, which recognized the collective bargaining rights of the state's farm workers.

Huerta directed the UFW's Citizenship Participation Day Department, the political arm of the union that lobbied the California state legislature, in the late 1970s. In 1988 she suffered a severe injury when, during a protest in San Francisco against President George Bush, the police clubbed her and ruptured her spleen. She subsequently settled a suit out of court, winning $825,000 in damages, and the San Francisco police reformed their policies on crowd control.

In the late 1990s the UFW struggled to maintain its membership against conservative politicians and intransigent growers, and despite the union's gains an estimated 75 percent of all field workers earned less than the minimum wage and fewer than 33 percent received health insurance. To address that abuse, Huerta and the UFW began a drive to unionize strawberry field workers in California's Ventura County. "It's a disgrace that here we are going into the 21st century and farm workers can't get decent sanitary conditions," Huerta said. "There's no clean toilets, toilet paper, soap or paper towels. They don't have clean water to drink or wash their hands." At that time in her 70s, Huerta still traveled from coast to coast, attended rallies and marches, and met with politicians.

In the *Los Angeles Times* in 1999, reporter James Rainey wrote, "Today, the Left heralds Huerta as a hero. Mexican Americans consider her a seminal figure in the Chicano power movement." One of Huerta's colleagues has added: "Dolores . . . has an ability to inspire you and urge you to do things you could not think were possible. She is one of those life-changers."

Further Reading

De Ruiz, Dana Catharine. *La Causa: The Migrant Farmworkers' Story*. Austin: Raintree Steck-Vaughn, 1993.

Perez, Frank. *Dolores Huerta*. Austin: Raintree Steck-Vaughn; 1996.

I

Ingersoll, Robert Green
(1833–1899) *free thought reformer*

A lawyer and lecturer, Robert Green Ingersoll was called "the Great Agnostic" by his contemporaries. He was born on August 11, 1833, in Dresden, New York, to John Ingersoll and Mary Livingston Ingersoll.

Robert Ingersoll never knew his mother, for she died while he was still an infant. And since his father was a preacher who served in many different churches, Robert moved frequently, settling in Ohio, Wisconsin, and then Illinois. At Shawneetown, Illinois, in 1854 he entered the bar. Three years later he moved to Peoria and gained widespread notice for his commanding presence in the courtroom.

Originally a Democrat in politics, Robert Ingersoll switched to the Republicans when his opposition to slavery corresponded with their views. In 1861 Ingersoll joined the Union army, serving in the 11th Illinois Volunteer Cavalry Regiment. He saw duty at Shiloh and Corinth in Tennessee. He and several hundred fellow soldiers were captured in December 1862 by Confederate general Nathan Bedford Forrest. He was paroled a few weeks later and received a discharge from the army in June 1863.

During his military service he had married Eva Amelia Parker; the couple had two children. In 1867 he was appointed attorney general of Illinois, and he held the office for two years. In the atmosphere that surrounded publication of Charles Darwin's *Origin of Species*, which put in question traditional religious belief and encouraged rational thought over acceptance of the supernatural, Ingersoll embraced agnosticism, forcefully and proudly using the word *agnostic* to describe himself. He said that his belief had liberated him. "When I became convinced that . . . all the ghosts and gods are myths, there entered into my brain, into my soul, into every drop of my blood, the sense, the feeling, the joy of freedom." Whereas Ingersoll admitted that God might exist, and that there might be life after death for human beings, he denied all divine intervention in earthly affairs and the existence of a supernatural entity who listened to prayers.

Ingersoll lectured widely, and his controversial views, coupled with his commanding ability as a speaker, meant that he drew large audiences. A delegate to the Republican National Convention in 1876, he gave the nominating speech for presidential candidate James G. Blaine. Blaine lost to Rutherford B. Hayes, but Ingersoll had presented the most memorable of all the convention speeches, affirming his status as a leading orator. That fall he campaigned extensively for Hayes, who won the presidency. In 1879 Ingersoll moved to Washington, D.C., where his law practice became even more lucrative.

Most observers believe that Ingersoll could have won public office in his own right but that his pronounced agnosticism prevented him from doing so. In response to the claims by Christians that in human history infidels had accomplished little, Ingersoll offered his mixture of intelligence and wit:

To answer the interrogatory often flung at us from the pulpit, What institutions have infidels built? In the first place, there have not been many infidels for many years and, as a rule, a known Infidel cannot get very rich, for the reason that Christians are so forgiving and loving they boycott him. . . . But as a matter of fact, there have been some Infidels who have done some good, even from a Christian standpoint. . . .

Most of the colleges in this country have, I admit, been founded by Christians, and the money for their support has been donated by Christians, but most of the colleges . . . have simply classified ignorance, and I think the United States would be more learned than it is to-day if there never had been a Christian college in it. . . . The best college in this country . . . was the institution founded by Ezra Cornell. That is a school where people try to teach what they know instead of what they guess. Yet Cornell University was attacked by every orthodox college in the United States at the time it was founded, because they said it was without religion.

In answer to the question "What would you substitute for the Bible as a moral guide?" Ingersoll said, "There are many good precepts, many wise sayings and many good regulations and laws in the Bible, and these are mingled with bad precepts, with foolish sayings, with absurd rules and cruel laws." His indictment included the following:

Pentateuch upholds nearly all crimes, and to call it a moral guide is as absurd as to say that it is merciful or true.

In first and second Samuel there is not one word calculated to develop the brain or conscience.

Jehovah murdered seventy thousand Jews because David took a census of the people. David, according to the account, was the guilty one, but only the innocent were killed.

His ultimate answer to the question was "Intelligence is the only moral guide."

Ingersoll also supported women's suffrage and said that women should be paid the same wages as men for the same jobs performed. He died at Dobbs Ferry, New York, on July 21, 1899.

Further Reading

Cramer, C. H. *Royal Bob: The Life of Robert G. Ingersoll.* Indianapolis, Ind.: Bobbs-Merrill, 1952.

Larson, Orvin Prentiss. *American Infidel: Robert G. Ingersoll, a Biography.* New York: Citadel Press, 1962.

Smith, Frank. *Robert G. Ingersoll: A Life.* Buffalo, N.Y.: Prometheus Books, 1990.

Innis, Roy
(1934–) *black nationalist*

A controversial black nationalist and later a conservative, Roy Innis is a leader of the Congress of Racial Equality (CORE). He was born on June 6, 1934, in Saint Croix, United States Virgin Islands, to Alexander Innis and Georgiana Thomas Innis.

In 1947 Roy Innis relocated to New York City to join his mother, who had moved there after the death of his father. He attended Stuyvesant High School but dropped out at age 16 to join the army. Innis served in Korea, resumed his education, received his high school diploma, and then majored in chemistry at the City College of New York. He graduated in 1956 and shortly afterward worked as a researcher at the Vicks Chemical Company.

Innis's first marriage ended in divorce, and he subsequently married civil rights activist Doris Funnye. Through her he became acquainted with the Congress of Racial Equality and joined the group's Harlem chapter. CORE had been founded in the early 1940s as a biracial organization intended to advance black civil rights through direct action, such as sit-ins at segregated lunch counters and the famous Freedom Rides of the early 1960s, when white and black bus riders challenged segregated bus terminals in southern cities.

Differing with CORE's leaders, Innis criticized the integrationist civil rights movement. Instead, he advocated black nationalism with African Americans operating their own businesses, taking pride in black culture, and attending all-black schools. In 1965 he won election as chairman of CORE's Harlem chapter, and in 1966 he helped elect Floyd McKissick as national chair. A fiery black nationalist, McKissick struck the word *multiracial* from the CORE constitution. One year later he appointed Innis as associate national director, thus extending the black nationalist hold on the group.

Innis took McKissick's place in 1969, a move that split CORE and caused those who favored integration over nationalism to leave the organization. As a result of the turmoil, CORE lost many members, yet Innis forged ahead with programs to create black-owned businesses in Harlem. In 1968 he told *U.S. News & World Report* that African Americans should have their own schools, completely equal in quality to white schools.

Adding to his controversial reputation, in 1973 Innis toured Uganda; met with its dictator, Idi Amin, a leader widely reviled for his human rights abuses; and presented Amin with life membership in CORE. In 1978 the state of New York charged Innis with having misused CORE funds, and three years later he agreed to an out-of-court settlement that required him to contribute $35,000 to CORE.

Near that time Innis was changing and adopting a right-wing ideology, and in 1984 he urged African Americans to vote for the conservative Republican presidential candidate, Ronald Reagan, rather than the liberal Democrat, Walter Mondale.

Innis ran for Congress in 1985 but lost, in part because one month before the election the Internal Revenue Service fined him for failure to report more than $100,000 in income he had received from CORE. Three years later Innis generated national headlines when he appeared on the *Geraldo Rivera Show,* a television program, and engaged in a melee with white supremacist Tom Metzger. Members of the audience joined in the fight, sending punches and chairs flying everywhere.

In 1991 Innis told the *Wall Street Journal* that he opposed gun control. He stated that blacks needed handguns to protect themselves in the typically high-crime districts where they lived. He ran unsuccessfully for mayor of New York City in 1993, while telling the *National Review* that the problems of the black community rested in "a racial solidarity that apologizes for crimes and black failure." And he complained that "many black children are taught to be black before they're taught to be American, or even before they're taught to be human."

Roy Innis and his son Niger Innis supported fellow African American Alan Keyes, a conservative, for the 2000 Republican presidential nomination. Keyes, however, came nowhere close to winning. In a speech the following year Innis complained that blacks had rejected the Republican Party and remained solidly Democratic: "Blacks were the only group to vote so strongly to one side," he said. About affirmative action, he added, "I hope it goes away."

Further Reading

"Civil Rights Leader Roy Innis for Governor of New York." *Jet,* March 14, 1994, 8.

Meier, August, and Elliott Rudwick. *CORE: A Study in the Civil Rights Movement, 1942–1968.* Urbana: University of Illinois Press, 1975.

Ireland, Patricia
(1945–) *women's rights leader*

Patricia Ireland is a lawyer and former president of the National Organization for Women (NOW). She was born on October 19, 1945, in Oak Park, Illinois, to James Ireland and Joan Filipek Ireland.

Raised in a middle-class family, Patricia Ireland in her early years showed nothing of the feminist consciousness she later adopted. On the contrary, she questioned little as a child and in high school won a beauty contest. She entered DePauw University at age 16 but left when she became pregnant. She then had an abortion and ended her brief marriage before enrolling at the University of Tennessee at Knoxville, where in 1966 she earned a bachelor's degree in German. Over the following two years she took graduate courses at the university and married James Humble, an artist.

In 1968 Ireland and her husband moved to Miami, Florida; she became a stewardess (as flight attendants were called at the time) at Pan American Airlines. Soon an event awakened her to the discrimination faced by women: When her husband needed dental care, she realized that employee health insurance polices at Pan Am covered the wives of men who worked for the airline but not the husbands of women who worked for it. She informed members of the Dade County chapter of the National Organization for Women of the practice, and they convinced Pan Am in 1969 to change its health insurance. Ireland then joined NOW's feminist campaign.

Because the episode made her see the power that could be wielded by lawyers, she entered law school at Florida State University in Tallahassee while keeping her job as a stewardess. She then transferred to the University of Miami in Coral Gables and in 1975 received her law degree.

Ireland worked for the Miami law firm of Arky, Freed, Stearns, Watson & Greer while engaged in volunteer work for NOW. In 1983 she was elected to chair NOW's lesbian rights task force in Florida. To fight the right-to-life movement she organized NOW's Stand Up for Women committee on abortion rights, and in 1987 she won election as NOW's vice president. Ireland won reelection in 1989 and in May 1991 was named acting president after the sitting president suffered a stroke. By that time Ireland had left the Miami law firm to work full time for NOW. In December she won election to the NOW presidency, and five months later she offered a stunning revelation to the magazine *Advocate*: Even though she was married to Humble, she had engaged in a long-term relationship with a woman in Washington, D.C.

Ireland later admitted she had worried that by revealing her lesbianism she would provide ammunition to conservative critics of NOW who liked to condemn the organization as far outside the American mainstream. But she felt that she could no longer be active in the women's movement and argue that women should not be labeled because of their sexuality while at the same time hiding her own affair.

As NOW president Ireland pursued what she called an "inside-outside strategy." This meant fighting sexual discrimination two ways: At times NOW used external pressure through high-profile media stands, such as opposing the Supreme Court nominee Clarence Thomas by criticizing him on TV and, in another protest, by picketing Mitsubishi car dealerships over sexual harassment. At other times NOW worked quietly behind the scenes, as when it resolved sexual harassment complaints with the Ford Motor Company by meeting with its chief executive officer.

In 1992 Ireland organized the Global Feminist Conference, and later that year she backed a massive prochoice demonstration in Washington attended by nearly 1 million protesters. She and NOW were criticized in the mid-1990s by some activists who called the group's close relationship with President Bill Clinton a sellout to the establishment.

The criticism increased after NOW appeared to defend Clinton in a scandal involving White House intern Monica Lewinsky that abounded in sexual exploitation, if not outright sexual harassment. In a 1999 interview with *The Progressive* magazine, however, Ireland insisted, "I have called [Clinton] everything on television. I have said that we weren't defending him, that his actions were indefensible. You know, I've been very hard-edged about what he's done. . . . Clinton is beyond what even the worst of the culture of men usually behave like."

In the year 2000 Ireland led a NOW attack on sexist stereotypes on network TV. Although some shows presented "multidimensional female characters," most failed to do so, and Ireland said that if programming did not change, NOW might have to boycott advertisers.

In August 2001 Ireland retired from the NOW presidency. She said that in the campaign for women's rights "we have a long way to go." She added: "When I was a young feminist, I felt angry all the time. But I found an outlet for that. If you're always angry, you feel helpless and hopeless. We've done too much to feel helpless and hopeless."

Further Reading
Ireland, Patricia. *What Women Want.* New York: Dutton, 1996.

Irons, Martin
(1827–1900) *labor organizer*

Martin Irons was a leader of the Great Southwestern Strike sponsored by the Knights of Labor. He was born in Dundee, Scotland, in 1827 and immigrated to the United States in 1841.

Irons served as an apprentice in New York City before becoming a machinist and moving from town to town in Texas and elsewhere in the Southwest. In the early 1880s he found work in the railroad shops at Sedalia, Missouri. In an article that he wrote for *Lippincott's Magazine* in 1886, Irons recalled how in his wanderings he had come across the slogan of the Knights of Labor, "An injury to one is the concern of all," and how it motivated him to join the union:

> When that beautiful watchword . . . resounded through my life, when I learned that the Knighthood embraced every grade of honest toil in its height and depths—when I learned that it meant broad and comprehensive union for labor on a basis that would counter-balance the power of aggregated and incorporated wealth and give to the creator of wealth the wealth he creates—then I felt that I had reached a field in which I was ready to spend the remaining energies of my life.

Irons joined the Knights in 1884, but unlike the union's leader, TERENCE VINCENT POWDERLY, he embraced a radical ideology, namely, socialism, and a belief in militant tactics. Within the Knights Irons organized District Assembly 101, composed of workers from the southwestern railroads owned by the financier Jay Gould. The assembly called for Gould's railroads to recognize the Knights as the workers' bargaining organization and to establish a minimum wage of $1.50 a day for unskilled labor. When Gould rejected the demands, and when the Texas and Pacific line arbitrarily fired a master workman in February 1886, the assembly called a strike and made Irons the leader of the walkout.

In Saint Louis, Kansas City, and other southwestern cities, the railroads came to a standstill. Powderly, however, believed strikes were more damaging than beneficial, and without first conferring with Irons he announced an agreement whereby Gould would submit the dispute to mediation. When Gould insisted he had made no such promise, the strikers rallied around Irons and continued their protest.

Two developments, though, worked against them. For one, Gould caused a split among the la-

borers when he gave the skilled workers higher wages than the unskilled. For another, he unleashed the newspapers and police against the strikers. Grabbing onto Irons's socialist background, the papers called the strikers un-American; the police, meanwhile, arrested them on minor charges and often beat the men senseless.

On May 4, 1886, the strike ended with the workers in full retreat. Powderly said, "The strike in the Southwest will be over this evening and I am glad of it." But the workers received nothing for their sacrifice, and without protection many, among them Irons, were blacklisted and denied employment on all railroads.

Once again he moved about, finally settling in Fort Worth, Texas, where he lectured for the state's Social Democratic Party. Martin Irons died in 1900 and was buried in Bruceville.

Further Reading

Allen, Ruth A. *The Great Southwest Strike.* Austin: University of Texas Press, 1942.

Allen, Ruth A. "Martin Irons." Available online. URL: http://www.tsha.utexas.edu/handbook/online/articles/view/II/fir7.htm/. Downloaded on March 25, 2002.

Itliong, Larry Dulay
(1913–1977) *labor leader*

Larry Dulay Itliong was the founder of the Filipino Farm Labor Union. He was born on October 25, 1913, in San Nicolas, Pangasinan, Philippines, and after completing the sixth grade immigrated to the United States.

On arriving in Seattle, Washington, Itliong worked on the nearby farms as a child laborer and later in the Alaskan salmon canneries. He moved to California in the late 1930s and joined the ranks of Filipinos working in the huge agricultural fields in the central part of the state. Growers had recruited thousands of Chinese, Japanese, Mexican, and Filipino workers as a cheap, migratory labor supply. The California Filipino population, which numbered only 5 in 1900, reached 30,000 in 1930, with nearly all of the increase from the importation of farm laborers. By that year Filipinos made up almost 15 percent of the state's agricultural workers.

They labored long hours in the fields, stooped over in the hot sun, picking celery, lettuce, asparagus, and grapes. The growers paid them about $1 an hour with few, if any, benefits but little feared that the workers might organize because they thought the Filipinos lacked initiative. Had the growers looked across the Pacific, however, they would have discovered that in 1919 Japanese and Filipino farm workers in Hawaii had gone on strike and won higher wages. In the 1930s they began organizing in California, founding the Filipino Labor Union in 1933 and staging a massive lettuce strike. Three years later the Filipino Agricultural Laborers Association staged a successful strike against the asparagus growers.

Itliong built on that heritage. In 1956 he founded the Filipino Farm Labor Union, and in 1959 he served as organizer for the American Federation of Labor-Congress of Industrial Organizations (AFL-CIO)–affiliated Agricultural Workers Organizing Committee (AWOC). In the early 1960s Itliong united Filipino vegetable and grape workers into a cohesive group and established a union headquarters in Delano, California.

Under Itliong's leadership, in summer 1965 Filipino farm workers began demanding an increase in pay from $1.20 an hour and 15 cents a box to $1.40 an hour and 25 cents a box. When the growers resisted, Itliong led a sit-down strike in the fields. Within a few days the larger National Farm Workers Association (NFWA), led by CESAR CHAVEZ and representing Mexican laborers, joined the strike. About two years later the AWOC merged with the NFWA, forming the United Farm Workers Union (UFW), with Chavez as national director and Itliong as his assistant.

To bolster the union and rally support for the ongoing strike, Itliong recruited members, met with political leaders, and spoke to community organizations. Working with Chavez, he convinced consumers in many parts of the country to boycott California table grapes. The UFW finally won a contract with the Delano growers in 1970, though the strike continued elsewhere. The workers obtained $1.80 an hour, plus 20 cents a box and contributions to the union's health and welfare fund.

Itliong quit the UFW in 1971, complaining that it had become too bureaucratic and too far removed from the workers. He continued to live in Delano and worked with the Filipino Service Center to help retired Filipino farm workers. Itliong also served as president of the Filipino American Political Association and in 1972 attended the Democratic National Convention as a delegate.

Larry Itliong died in Delano on February 8, 1977, of Lou Gehrig's disease.

Further Reading

Griswold del Castillo, Richard, and Richard A. Garcia. *Cesar Chavez: A Triumph of Spirit.* Norman: University of Oklahoma Press, 1995.

Rodriguez, Consuelo. *Cesar Chavez.* New York: Chelsea House, 1991.

J

Jackson, Helen Hunt
(Helen Maria Fiske)
(1830–1885) *Indian rights advocate*

Helen Hunt Jackson was a writer and advocate for Indian rights. She was born Helen Maria Fiske on October 15, 1830, in Amherst, Massachusetts, to Nathan Welby Fiske and Deborah Vinal Fiske.

Helen received a limited education at Ipswich Academy in Massachusetts and at a school in New York City before marrying in 1852 Edward Bissell Hunt, a soldier who eventually became a major in the army corps of engineers. Tragedy led her to writing. In 1863 her husband died in an accident while testing a submarine; two years later her young son, Warren, known as "Rennie," died. (Another son had died in 1854 at age 11 months.) In grief, Helen moved in 1866 to Newport, Rhode Island, where she wrote a poem that appeared in *The Nation*.

She followed that with other poems and with romance stories. Her *Verses* was published in 1870. Three years later, while living in Colorado Springs, Colorado, she met William Sharpless Jackson, a banker, financier, and railroad executive. They married in October 1875.

In 1879 Helen Hunt Jackson attended a lecture given in Boston by Chief Standing Bear. She listened to him tell the story of how the Ponca had been forcibly moved from Nebraska to the Indian Territory (today Oklahoma), and how they had suffered from disease, starvation, and sorrow. Motivated by his story, she researched extensively at the Astor Library in New York City and then published *A Century of Dishonor* (1881). She wanted it to influence public opinion and cause Congress to change its policies toward Indians.

The book was published at a time when the wars against Native Americans were coming to a close. (The last battle, actually a massacre, of Lakota Sioux Indians by the U.S. Army would occur at Wounded Knee, South Dakota, in 1890.) With the deepening destitution of the surviving Indians, liberals were trying to stir the American conscience. *The Nation* had lamented in 1876 the horrid conditions facing Indians in the taking of their lands by whites, calling the development "shocking . . . [with] nothing in our religion, or manners, or laws, or tradition, or policy, to give it any countenance or support."

Jackson fully intended to stir that conscience further; her book detailed the treatment of seven Indian tribes: the Cheyenne, Cherokee, Delaware (Lenni Lenape), Nez Perce, Ponca, Sioux (Dakota, Lakota, Nakota), and Winnebago (Ho-Chunn). In some passages she unleashed a straightforward barrage, searing in tone:

> It makes little difference . . . where one opens the record of the history of the Indians; every page and every year has its dark stain. . . .
>
> The history of the Government connections with the Indians is a shameful record of broken treaties and unfulfilled promises. The history of the border white man's connection with the Indians is a sickening record of murder, outrage, robbery, and wrongs.

In other passages she presented a poignant account, as in her summation of testimony provided by a Cheyenne to a government committee:

> When asked by Senator Jon T. Morgan, "Did you ever really suffer from hunger?" one of the chiefs replied, "We were always hungry; we never had enough. When they that were sick once in a while felt as though they could eat something, we had nothing to give them."
>
> "Did you not go out on the plains sometimes and hunt buffalo without the consent of the agent?"
>
> "We went out on a buffalo-hunt, and nearly starved while out; we could not find any buffalo hardly . . . we had to kill a good many of our ponies to eat, to save ourselves from starving."
>
> "How many children got sick and died?"
>
> "Between the fall of 1877 and 1878 we lost fifty children. A great many of our finest young men died, as well as many women."

Jackson's prescription to help the Indians relied in part on ending "cheating, robbing, and breaking promises," and it relied also on the assimilation of Indians into white culture. To a great extent, she wanted to eliminate through peaceful measures the way of life others were eliminating through warfare.

Her book sold so widely that the government made her a special commissioner to investigate conditions among the Mission Indians of California. But her 56-page report was ignored by the secretary of the interior, so she decided to write a novel that would stir Americans to understand the plight of the Indians and help them: She intended *Ramona* (1884) to do for them what *Uncle Tom's Cabin* had done for black slaves, but although it sold well, most readers related to its romantic content rather than its social criticism.

Helen Hunt Jackson died on August 12, 1885, just two years before Congress passed the Dawes Act. The legislation represented the assimilationist view that Jackson had championed; it ended the policy of defining Indian tribes as legal entities and divided land among individual Indians to make them property owners as whites were. The Dawes Act, which was rescinded in 1934, greatly damaged Indian culture and caused many Native

Helen Hunt Jackson described the horrid conditions facing Indians in her book *A Century of Dishonor.* *(Library of Congress)*

Americans to lose their land through fraudulent actions by whites.

Further Reading

Banning, Evelyn I. *Helen Hunt Jackson.* New York: Vanguard Press, 1973.

Senier, Siobhan. *Voices of American Indian Assimilation and Resistance: Helen Hunt Jackson, Sarah Winnemucca, and Victoria Howard.* Norman: University of Oklahoma Press, 2001.

Jackson, Jesse Louis
(1941–) *civil rights leader*

An African-American Baptist minister, civil rights leader, and presidential candidate, Jesse Louis Jackson has been called innovative and bold by his supporters and brash and opportunistic by his critics. He was born out of wedlock on October 8, 1941, in Greenville, South Carolina, to Helen Burns and Noah Robinson. Burns was 16 years old at the time; Robinson was married and lived next door to her. Shortly before Jesse's third birthday, Helen Burns married Charles Jackson, a shoe shine attendant. Jesse considered Charles Jackson, who adopted him when he was in his teens, to be his father.

In his childhood Jesse was energetic, ambitious, and eager to help others. He delivered stove wood, caddied at a nearby country club, waited on tables, and read newspapers to adults unable to read. At Sterling High School Jackson excelled academically and athletically. Elected to the honor society, he graduated 10th in his class, and he played football, baseball, and basketball. Jackson later said about his high school years, "I never lacked for anything, I was the star quarterback and made the honor roll as a student. I could get about any girl I liked. I was a leader."

In 1959 the Chicago White Sox offered him a contract to play professional baseball, but he decided instead to attend the University of Illinois on a football scholarship. One year later, though, disheartened by the way white students were treating him, he transferred to all-black North Carolina Agricultural and Technical State University in Greensboro, North Carolina.

He arrived at North Carolina A&T in fall 1960 at a momentous time: The previous winter students at the college had begun a sit-in at the local Woolworth's store to protest its refusal to serve blacks at the lunch counter. The protest ignited a stage of the civil rights movement in which young people no longer settled for following their elders; rather, they took the lead themselves in fighting racial injustice.

Under parental pressure to stay out of trouble, Jackson at first kept away from the upheaval. But in 1963 he joined the Congress of Racial Equality (CORE) and led a 10-month-long protest that involved marches, sit-ins, and boycotts of businesses that practiced racial segregation. The following year Jackson married Jacqueline Livinia Brown, graduated with a bachelor's degree in sociology, and was named field representative for CORE's southeast region.

In 1965 Jackson left the South to study under a Rockefeller grant at the University of Chicago's theological seminary. "I decided to go . . . ," Jackson recalled, "to learn how to do without the law to change society, change it in deeper ways." While at the seminary he worked as a volunteer for the Coordinating Committee of Community Organizations, which joined civic with civil rights groups.

That same year Jackson joined the voting rights protest in Selma, Alabama, then being led by MARTIN LUTHER KING, JR., and his Southern Christian Leadership Conference (SCLC). Shortly after Jackson met King, he joined the SCLC. When King decided to take his civil rights crusade into Chicago, Jackson provided him with contacts in the black community and organized local ministers to support King's effort to end racial segregation in the city's housing.

Jackson soon quit the seminary, and beginning in 1966 he coordinated the SCLC's Operation Breadbasket, a program founded to unite African Americans in placing pressure on manufacturers and retailers to hire more black workers. One of Jackson's colleagues recalled about him: "We were working with a very open and, in worldly ways, unsophisticated person. But he had a power that could only be classified as supernatural."

Jackson persuaded the High-Low grocery chain to hire 183 blacks; Jewel Tea, to hire 662; and A&P, to hire 970. Saying, "We have a monopoly on rats in the ghetto, and we're gonna have a monopoly on killing 'em," he obtained contracts at white businesses for black-owned exterminating companies. In less than two years Operation Breadbasket had produced about 3,000 jobs for African Americans. With these accomplishments the SCLC named Jackson national director of the program.

When in 1968 striking African-American sanitation workers in Memphis, Tennessee, called for the SCLC to help them, King responded and traveled to the city. He had at that time an ambivalent relationship with Jackson: He liked his talent, energy, and commitment, but he disliked his ambition and his tendency to grandstand. One of King's aides later said, "Jesse could never pass a reflective surface without pausing—whether it was a store window or just a shiny car, he'd have to stop a second and check himself out again."

At the Lorraine Hotel on April 4, 1968, a gunman assassinated King while the civil rights leader stood on a balcony. Jackson later said that he held King in his arms and heard his last words as the fallen man's blood stained his shirt. Others disputed the account and said Jackson exaggerated the story to make it appear that the SCLC leadership should be handed to him.

Although RALPH DAVID ABERNATHY became the new leader, Jackson, who was ordained a Baptist minister in 1968, continued to work for the SCLC. At the same time, in 1969 and 1970 he led marches on the Illinois state capitol at Springfield to demand programs to help fight hunger. The legislature subsequently agreed to fund school lunch programs. When Chicago mayor Richard Daley resisted Jackson's reform efforts, Jackson decided to unseat him, and in 1971 he ran for mayor. He lost, but he may have paved the way for the city to elect its first black mayor in 1983, when Harold Washington won the office.

With tension mounting in the SCLC between Jackson and Abernathy and some SCLC staffers criticizing Jackson as overly aggressive and antagonistic, he quit the organization in 1971 and founded People United to Save Humanity (PUSH). Jackson was proud of his heritage, which was one of black blood mixed with Cherokee and Irish, and he intended PUSH to help people of many different colors and nationalities, though it focused on African Americans. In the early 1970s he obtained agreements with Burger King and Kentucky Fried Chicken to employ more blacks. Soon other companies signed similar agreements, and PUSH chapters appeared in several cities.

In the mid-1970s Jackson established PUSH EXCEL to encourage minority students to stay in school. He said in 1976, "Black Americans must begin to accept a larger share of responsibility for their lives. . . . We black Americans can rebuild our communities with moral authority. . . . Parents, teachers, superintendents, school boards have all failed to impose discipline."

In early 1984 Jesse Jackson earned national acclaim for intervening with the Syrian government and securing the release of a black navy pilot, captured when his plane was shot down over eastern Lebanon. Later that year Jackson launched a massive black voter registration drive and made his first run for the presidency by entering the Democratic primary. Despite controversy about Jackson's closeness to Louis Farrakhan, the Black Muslim leader known for his anti-Semitism, Jackson won a surprising 21 percent of the popular and caucus votes and 80 percent of the African-American vote. In 1986 he organized the National Rainbow Coalition to secure social justice, jobs, and education for minorities by electing to office politicians who supported such goals. A campaign led by the coalition registered 2 million voters.

Jackson ran a second time for president in 1988, saying he would work for expanded health care, better housing, and more jobs. Once again he surprised the pundits in the Democratic primary when he won in Michigan and the victory briefly made him the front runner for the nomination. According to Jackson's biographer Marshall Frady in *Jesse* (1996), "These campaigns amounted to the first genuinely serious presidential runs by a black candidate ever."

After Jackson failed to win the Democratic nomination, he moved his home from Chicago to Washington, D.C. There he led a movement to help the homeless, and in 1990 he won election as "statehood senator," a position created by the district to lobby Congress for statehood. He also intervened overseas to secure the release of Americans being held hostage by Iraq after that country invaded Kuwait.

Jackson traveled through 27 states in 1992 urging people to register to vote while also condemning the violence in American cities and urging the presidential candidates to commit themselves to solving the problem. In 1997 Jackson began the Wall Street Project, whereby he encouraged blacks to buy stocks and use their status as shareholders to pressure corporations to provide more jobs and other opportunities for African Americans.

Two years later Jackson led an interfaith delegation to Yugoslavia to obtain the release of three American soldiers being held captive by that country's army. He met with Yugoslav president Slobodan Milosovic and secured their release. In May 1999 he traveled to Sierra Leone, where he negotiated a cease-fire between rebel and government forces and arranged the release of 2,000 prisoners of war.

In the year 2001 Jackson, working as president of the Rainbow/PUSH Coalition, which he had organized in 1996 to merge the PUSH and Rainbow programs, convinced Toyota Motor Sales to suspend an ad campaign that many blacks had found racist. But that year proved challenging in other ways: The *National Enquirer* revealed in a story that Jackson had fathered a child out of wedlock, and he was forced to admit the affair. Other critics attacked him for lavish living and questioned whether he was draining funds from his organizations to his own bank account. Jackson denied the charges. As for all the criticism, he said: "I can take the hits because God has blessed me."

Despite his accomplishments, to many Jackson remains a puzzle. How much has he been motivated by selflessness, how much by self-aggrandizement? His biographer Frady states:

> In attempting to transfer the [civil rights] movement's moral gospel into an actual presidential competition, he had become a much larger . . . enigma. That may have accounted, in part, for much of the disquiet about him: no one was certain exactly who he was. He had [obtained an] increasing conspicuousness in our national experience since the early seventies, to the point where polls indicated he had become one of the most recognizable public figures in the land, but a kind of familiar stranger whose exact nature remained unclear.

Further Reading

Colton, Elizabeth O. *The Jackson Phenomenon: The Man, the Power, the Message.* New York: Doubleday, 1989.

Frady, Marshall. *Jesse: The Life and Pilgrimage of Jesse Jackson.* New York: Random House, 1996.

Jones, Mary Harris
(Mother Jones)
(1830–1930) *labor activist*

Mary Harris Jones was a labor activist known as "Mother Jones." She was born Mary Harris on May 1, 1830, in Cork, Ireland, to Richard Harris and Mary Harris. She later said, "I was born in revolution," because as a young girl she had witnessed clashes between British soldiers and Irish farmers. She immigrated to the United States in the mid-1830s after her father had immigrated to America and found employment on the railroad. Shortly thereafter she relocated with her family to Toronto, Canada, where she attended high school and a normal (teacher training) school.

Mary's teaching career took her to Memphis, Tennessee, in 1860. There she met and married Robert Jones, an iron worker and union member. Then tragedy struck, not once, but twice. First, a yellow fever epidemic in 1867 killed her husband and all of her children. "One by one, my four little children sickened and died," she wrote in her autobiography. "I washed their little bodies and got them ready for burial. My husband caught the fever and died. I sat alone through nights of grief." Distraught, she moved to Chicago and opened a dressmaking shop, only to be hit by the second tragedy: In 1871 a citywide fire destroyed her business.

Her life took a different direction when she was helped by her husband's friends and through them became an organizer for the Knights of Labor, the largest union in the country to that time. An effective speaker—despite her high-pitched voice—she went from one meeting hall to another, calling for worker solidarity.

As the fissure between industrial workers and capitalists darkened and deepened and led to a strike in December 1874 among the miners in western Pennsylvania's anthracite coal fields, the Knights sent Mary Jones into the battle to rally the workers. They lived under the rubble heap of an unstable economy in which capitalists exploited a cheap source of labor, largely immigrant and uneducated. An economic depression that had begun a year earlier caused wages and jobs to be cut. Any miner who joined a union could easily be fired—there were many more workers willing to fill the places of those departed.

Five years earlier the miners had succeeded in convincing the mine operators to sign a contract with their union, the Workingmen's Benevolent Association. But taking advantage of the economic downturn, Franklin B. Gowen, leader of the mine operators, determined to crush the union. He blamed its activities on foreign agitators, whom he called "emissaries of the [socialist] International."

It was during the anthracite coal strike of 1874–75 that Mary Harris got her name "Mother Jones" for combining her stamina with a maternal concern for the workers. One labor radical later said of her work:

> She might have been any coal miner's wife ablaze with righteous fury when her brood was in danger. Her voice shrilled as she shook her fist at the coal operators, the mine guards, the union officials, and all others responsible for the situation. She prayed and cursed and pleaded, raising her clenched and trembling hands, asking heaven to bear witness. . . . The miners loved it and laughed, cheered, hooted, and even cried as she spoke to them.

Despite Mother Jones's exhortations, in 1875 the strike failed; the union was broken and wages were cut 20 percent.

In 1877 Mother Jones participated in a railroad strike in Pittsburgh, and in the 1880s she pushed for the eight-hour workday. Some other radicals criticized her; Marxists, for one, thought her appeals about hours and wages too limited; the workers, they insisted, must overthrow the capitalist system to gain true liberation. Jones eventually supported the Socialist Party, but she was not an ideologue, and she rejected doctrinal disputes. To her the important strategy was to organize and agitate.

In 1891 Mother Jones became an organizer for the United Mine Workers (UMW) under its president, John Mitchell. Once again she went into Pennsylvania's anthracite coal fields, where no union had existed since the failed strike more than a decade earlier, and she rallied the workers. To elude the Coal and Iron Police, assembled by the mine operators to crush all union activity, she traveled in disguise.

During a strike of miners in Arnot, Pennsylvania, in 1899–1900, she recruited the miners' wives to protest, knowing the owners would be less likely to use physical violence against them than against the men. Mother Jones described the scene in her autobiography: "The women kept continual watch of the mines to see that the company did not bring in scabs. Every day women with brooms and mops in one hand and babies in the other arm wrapped in little blankets, went to the mines and watched that no one went in. And all night long they kept watch. They were heroic women."

The mine operators soon convinced the farmers nearby to withhold food from the miners, causing Jones to travel the countryside in a buggy, persuading the farmers to change their minds. "Sometimes it was twelve or one o'clock in the morning when I would get home . . . ," she said. "Sometimes it was several degrees below zero. . . . The wind whistled down the mountains and drove the snow and sleet. . . . My hands and feet were often numb."

This time the strike ended successfully for the workers when they received a wage increase. Jones broke with Mitchell, though, over a strike among Colorado miners in 1903. The miners were demanding the eight-hour day and payment for their labor in cash rather than company scrip. When the mine operators agreed to terms for some of the miners but not for others, Mitchell accepted the offer, calling it the best that could be arranged. Mother Jones, however, called it a sellout and accused him of ingratiating himself with the rich and powerful; she said that he lived in splendor while the miners were living in tents and getting 63 cents a week.

Mother Jones next organized a spectacular children's march in spring 1903, during a strike by 75,000 textile workers in Kensington, Pennsylvania. "Every day little children came into Union Headquarters," she recalled, "some with their hands off, some with thumbs missing, some with their fingers off at the knuckle." She decided, with the help of the mothers, to lead the children on a march from Philadelphia to New York City to demand more effective child labor laws. Thus, at age 73 she showed her genius in appealing to the public's heart. "A great crowd gathered in . . . front of the city hall," she wrote in her autobiography. "I put the little boys with their finger off and hands crushed and maimed on a platform. I held up their mutilated hands and showed them to the crowd, and made the statement that

Philadelphia's mansions were built on the broken bones, the quivering hearts and drooping heads of these children."

As the procession continued north, crowds turned out to see the marchers and hear Mother Jones. "I called on the mayor of Princeton [New Jersey]," she wrote, "and asked for permission to speak opposite the campus of the University. . . . The mayor gave me permission. A great crowd gathered, professors and students and the people; and I told them that the rich robbed these little children of any education . . . that they might send their sons and daughters to places of higher education." She continued:

"Here's a textbook on economics," I said pointing to a little chap . . . who was ten years old and was stooped over like an old man from carrying bundles of yarn that weighed seventy-five pounds. "He gets three dollars a week and his sister who is fourteen gets six dollars. They work in a carpet factory ten hours a day while the children of the rich get their higher education."

Although Mother Jones failed to achieve her goal of obtaining an audience with President Theodore Roosevelt, the state of Pennsylvania passed a law in 1904 that prohibited employers from hiring children under age 14.

Popularly known as "Mother Jones," Mary Jones endured several arrests as a labor organizer and remained active until just days before her death at age 100. Here she is speaking to President Calvin Coolidge in 1924. *(Library of Congress)*

Mother Jones rejoined the UMW as an organizer in 1912—at age 82—and was arrested in a district where martial law had been declared. Consequently, she was tried before a military court and sentenced to 20 years in prison. A massive public outcry over this act, however, caused the governor to pardon her in March 1913. On her release she joined miners striking in Colorado and was again arrested. When women in the town of Trinidad marched in the streets to protest her confinement, the militia ran them down with horses. Nevertheless, the protests continued, and under public pressure the government released Jones.

The following year she announced her opposition to women's suffrage, asserting that protest was more important than voting: "The plutocrats have organized their women," she said. "They keep them busy with suffrage and prohibition and charity. I don't belong to the women's club. I belong to the fighting army of the working class." (Curiously, for all of her union activity, she maintained the view that a woman's proper place was in the home.)

In 1915 she spoke at rallies for striking New York City transit workers and did the same for steel workers in 1919. In 1930, at age 100, she made a radio address in which she urged labor to organize and build a more humane society. Later that year, on November 30, she died.

Further Reading

Fetherling, Dale. *Mother Jones: The Miners' Angel.* Carbondale: Southern Illinois University Press, 1974.

Foner, Philip, ed. *Mother Jones Speaks.* New York: Monad Press, 1983.

Josephson, Judith P. *Mother Jones: Fierce Fighter for Workers' Rights.* Minneapolis: Lerner Publications, 1997.

Kameny, Franklin
(1925–) *gay rights activist*

An astronomer, Franklin Kameny has made important contributions to gay rights. The son of an electrical engineer, he was born on May 21, 1925, in Queens, New York.

Kameny developed an interest in astronomy while still a child, and his precocity allowed him to enter Queens College at age 16. He later said that he knew as a teen that he was gay but that he dutifully followed society's conformist rules in high school and college by dating women.

In 1943 World War II interrupted his college education, and he enlisted in the Army Special Training Program and served in Germany as part of an armored infantry battalion. After the war he returned to Queens College and graduated in 1948 with a bachelor's degree in physics and a specialization in optics.

He then entered Harvard graduate school, and in 1953 and 1954 he worked in astronomical research at the University of Arizona in Tucson. There he engaged in his first homosexual relationships. Kameny next worked at an observatory in Armagh, Northern Ireland, and then completed his doctorate at Harvard in 1956.

He served briefly on the faculty at Georgetown University before joining the U.S. Army Map Service in 1957 as a civil service employee. He received outstanding job evaluations, and his future in the government looked promising, but in 1958 an investigator for the Civil Service Commission called him in and told him that his homosexuality had been discovered and because of it he was being fired from his job and prohibited from holding any other job with the federal government.

The shock of the dismissal made Kameny a gay rights activist. He contested his firing in the federal courts, and when his lawyer quit the case, Kameny personally took his appeal to the Supreme Court. In 1961, however, the court refused to hear his petition, whereupon he founded a Washington chapter of the Mattachine Society (a national organization founded 10 years earlier in Los Angeles) committed to obtaining for homosexuals the "basic rights and liberties guaranteed to all Americans." Under Kameny the society pursued a high-profile strategy and lobbied Congress. In 1963 Kameny helped establish a regional federation, the East Coast Homophile Organizations, and he appeared before a subcommittee of the U.S. Civil Rights Commission to condemn job discrimination against homosexuals.

In 1965 the Mattachine Society began picketing the White House, the Pentagon, the State Department, and the Civil Service Commission. Influenced by the phrase "Black Is Beautiful," coined by African Americans" in the black power movement, Kameny coined "Gay Is Good" for the homosexual rights movement. His campaign corresponded with increasing militancy among gays, evident in the 1969 Stonewall Uprising in Greenwich Village when they rebelled against police harassment at nightclubs.

After Congress allowed the District of Columbia to elect a nonvoting delegate to the House of Representatives, Kameny ran for the office in 1971. He lost, but his campaign educated the public about homosexual rights and involved gays in the political system.

Kameny won an important victory in 1973 when the American Psychiatric Association removed homosexuality from its list of mental disorders. "This represents the culmination of a decade-long battle," Kameny said. Later that year he succeeded in persuading the District of Columbia to repeal its sodomy law. When the Mattachine Society dissolved, Kameny served on the board of directors of the National Gay Task Force. In 1975 the Civil Service Commission ended its ban on gays' holding federal jobs, and Kameny focused on convincing the military to openly accept gay recruits. That battle continued to be waged in the year 2002.

Further Reading

Katz, Jonathan Ned. *Gay American History: Lesbians and Gay Men in the U.S.A.* New York: Penguin Books, 1992.

Marcus, Eric. *Making History: The Struggle for Gay and Lesbian Equal Rights: An Oral History.* New York: HarperCollins, 1992.

Keller, Helen

(1880–1968) *author, lecturer, socialist*

Famous for overcoming her handicap as a blind and deaf person, Helen Keller embraced socialism and promoted a radical labor union, the Industrial Workers of the World (IWW). Born on June 27, 1880, in Tuscumbia, Alabama, to Arthur Keller and Kate Adams Keller, Helen Keller lost her sight and hearing when she was 19 months old as a result of a disease, possibly scarlet fever.

When Helen was six her parents took her to Baltimore, Maryland, to see an eye specialist. He could do nothing about her blindness, but he recommended that she see Dr. Alexander Graham Bell, who was known for his work with the deaf. Keller and Bell immediately liked each other, and Bell suggested to her parents that they contact the Perkins Institution for the Blind to arrange a tutor for Helen.

This led to a long relationship between Helen Keller and Anne Sullivan. In March 1887 Sullivan arrived at the Keller home in Alabama and began teaching Helen the manual alphabet, whereby messages were conveyed by moving the fingers to spell words in Helen's hand. Helen learned the alphabet within six months and was soon reading Braille and raised type, as well as writing letters with a specially made typewriter. Anne Sullivan's work with Keller earned the tutor the nickname "the Miracle Worker."

When Bell and Michael Anagnos, the director of the Perkins Institution, brought Keller to public notice, she became at age 10 a national figure and in 1888 met President Grover Cleveland, jurist Oliver Wendell Holmes, and poet John Greenleaf Whittier.

From 1894 to 1895 Keller attended the Wright-Humason School in New York City, where she improved her lip reading (accomplished by hand) and worked on the rudimentary speaking ability she had earlier developed. Keller attended a preparatory school and in 1900 enrolled at Radcliffe College. Once again Sullivan proved essential to Helen's development, accompanying her to classes and acting as an interpreter. Keller, though, had to take all exams on her own.

Helen Keller wanted to become a writer, and in 1903, with the help of John Macy, a Harvard professor who had married Sullivan, she published *The Story of My Life.* She would eventually write 14 books and numerous magazine articles.

Her writing, and almost everything else she did, soon became embroiled in the controversy surrounding her political ideology. In 1909 she joined the Socialist Party and wrote articles that promoted its platform. Her motivation for becoming a socialist has long been debated. Many historians believe that Macy and Sullivan indoctrinated her. Conservatives at the time severely criticized her, and whereas they had once praised her as an example of what hard work could accomplish in overcoming great odds, they now implied that her handicap had impaired her thinking.

Writing in the leftist magazine *Call* in 1912, Keller said she became a socialist through her reading. "The first book I read was [H. G.] Well's *New World for Old*," she recounted. "I read it on Mrs. Macy's [Anne Sullivan's] recommendation. She was attracted by its imaginative quality, and hoped that its electric style might stimulate and interest me. When she gave me the book, she was not a Socialist and she is not a Socialist now." Keller said about Sullivan: "The periodical which I have most often requested her lively fingers communicate to my eager one is the *National Socialist*. She gives the titles of the articles and I tell her when to read on and when to omit." Responding to the attack of a conservative newspaper, Keller wrote:

> *The Brooklyn Eagle* says, apropos of me, and socialism, that Helen Keller's "mistakes spring out of the manifest limitations of her development." Some years ago I met a gentleman who was introduced to me as Mr. McKelway, editor of the *Brooklyn Eagle*. . . . At that time the compliments he paid me were so generous that I blush to remember them. But now that I have come out for socialism he reminds me and the public that I am blind and deaf and especially liable to error. I must have shrunk in intelligence during the years since I met him.

Shortly before World War I Keller declared the socialists too moderate and deserted them for a radical revolutionary labor union, the Industrial Workers of the World. During the winter of 1913–14, when unemployment climbed in many cities, the IWW organized protest marches, and in March 1914 IWW members joined an "army" of unemployed who organized in Sacramento, California, to head east and protest in Washington, D.C. When the marchers gathered, the Sacramento police bludgeoned them.

Keller, who was scheduled to speak in Sacramento as part of a lecture tour, heard about the brutality and announced that she would speak on behalf of the IWW. When the police threatened to arrest her, she stood her ground. She told reporters, "I think their treatment was outrageous. It is not a crime to protest for your fellows. It is not a crime to be without bread. . . . I honor these men for their protest, and I am going to say that in Sacramento tonight." She did, and the authorities left her alone.

Keller supported the women's suffrage movement too. When that goal was achieved through a constitutional amendment, she gradually quieted her political comments. In 1924 the American Foundation for the Blind asked her to help in raising money, and for the next three years she lectured for them.

Keller wrote *Midstream: My Later Life* in 1929 and then returned to the lecture circuit to help the foundation. On Anne Sullivan's death in 1936, the foundation established a trust to support Keller.

Helen Keller was awarded the Medal of Freedom by President Lyndon Johnson in 1964. She died on June 1, 1968, at her home in Westport, Connecticut. She once said: "If I ever contribute to the Socialist movement the book that I sometimes dream of, I know what I shall name it: Industrial Blindness and Social Deafness."

Further Reading

Einhorn, Lois J. *Helen Keller, Public Speaker: Sightless but Seen, Deaf but Heard.* Westport, Conn.: Greenwood Press, 1998.

Herrmann, Dorothy. *Helen Keller: A Life.* New York: Knopf, 1998.

Lash, Joseph P. *Helen and Teacher: The Story of Helen Keller and Anne Sullivan Macy.* New York: Delta, 1981.

Kelley, Florence
(1859–1932) *labor reformer*

Florence Kelley was a crusader for child labor laws and improved working conditions for women. She was born on September 12, 1859, in Philadelphia, Pennsylvania, to William Darrah Kelley, a Republican congressman, and Caroline Bartram Bonsall Kelley.

Growing up in a privileged family with ties to mainstream politics, it may be surprising to find that Florence Kelley adopted not only reformist views but also socialist ones. Intelligent and given to extensive reading, she entered Cornell University in 1876, at a time when women were just beginning to study at American colleges in small numbers. Poor health hampered her educational progress, but she graduated with a bachelor's degree in 1882. At that point she wanted to enter graduate school but found the doors locked to women.

So she went overseas and studied at the University of Zurich. There she socialized with Marxists, and in 1884 she married one of them, Lazare Wischnewetzky, a Jewish doctor. While raising three children, Kelley began translating Friedrich Engels's *The Condition of the Working-Class in England in 1844* into English; it was published in 1887.

One year before her book was released, she and her husband moved to New York City, where she sought to become active in the Socialist Party, only to be disappointed by the group's ongoing factional fights. Consequently, she taught economics at a settlement house (established to help immigrants) and wrote letters to newspapers urging child labor reform.

While she was so involved, her marriage deteriorated as she suffered numerous beatings from her husband. In 1891 she took her children and fled to Chicago. There she began working at Hull-House, the settlement house founded by JANE ADDAMS. She observed sweatshops and in 1892 led a campaign against them. A report she wrote for the Bureau of Labor Statistics of Illinois resulted in the state legislature passing a bill that established the eight-hour workday for women and banned tenement labor and employment of children less than 14 years old.

Kelley's work caused Governor John Peter Altgeld, a reformer, to appoint her as the state's first factory inspector. She held that post from 1893 to 1897; she left it after conservatives regained power in the state government and limited her efforts. During her work as factory inspector, she earned a law degree from Northwestern University; she believed that her degree would enable her to deal more effectively with government attorneys.

In 1899 Kelley was named general secretary of the National Consumers' League, which sought to rally consumers to place pressure on manufacturers so they would improve factory working conditions. She then moved back to New York City and joined the Henry Street Settlement House. At the same time she lectured widely and encouraged local consumer leagues to lobby their legislatures, an effort that led to nine states' passing laws establishing minimum wages for women and protection for child laborers.

Kelley advocated women's suffrage and with LILLIAN WALD convinced the federal government to found the United States Children's Bureau. She supported the Keating-Owen Child Labor Act passed by Congress in 1916 and the Sheppard-Towner Maternity and Infancy Protection Act passed in 1921.

Historians debate whether Kelley and other reformers were motivated to act so they could help working women or whether they were seeking to advance their own political power. Most likely, they wanted both, but Kelley's efforts had the condescending tinge of a wealthy white woman trying to tell poorer women how to run their lives. Interestingly, while she worked to assist working women, her efforts benefited working men, for as legislators established minimum wages for women, they thought the same should be done for men.

Florence Kelley died on February 17, 1932, at her summer home in Maine after a long illness. Her biographer Kathryn Kish Sklar states that Kelley and her friends were "a voice that served no master but the public welfare."

Further Reading

Sklar, Kathryn Kish. *Florence Kelley and the Nation's Work: The Rise of Women's Political Culture, 1830–1900*. New Haven, Conn.: Yale University Press, 1995.

Kellogg, John Harvey
(1852–1943) *health reformer*

A surgeon and health reformer, John Harvey Kellogg was an inventor of flaked cereal. He was born on February 26, 1852, in Tyrone, Michigan, to John Preston Kellogg, a Seventh-Day Adventist, and Ann Janette Stanley Kellogg.

John Harvey Kellogg moved with his family to Battle Creek in 1856 and spent his youth receiving a sporadic early education while working first in his father's broom factory and then, beginning at age 12, in the Adventist publishing business, where he started as a printer's devil, or assistant, and advanced to editorial assistant. Articles he published that were written by Ellen G. White, the leader of the church, dealt with health topics, and Kellogg began adopting some of her practices, most notably vegetarianism. This influence stayed with him, greatly affecting his later life.

Kellogg graduated from high school in 1872 and enrolled at Michigan State Normal College in Ypsilanti. He intended to become a teacher, but by this time Ellen White had opened the Western Health Reform Institute in Battle Creek, which combined Adventist theology with health foods and a health regimen, and she paid for him to attend the Hygeio-Therapeutic College in Florence Heights, New Jersey. He stayed at the college only a brief time, however, before opting to study more traditional medicine at the University of Michigan Medical School. He later attended Bellevue Hospital Medical College in New York City, where he received a degree in 1875 with a thesis that claimed disease acted as the body's natural defense mechanism.

In 1876 the Adventist church appointed Kellogg the medical superintendent of the Health Reform Institute. To popularize the institute he changed its name to the Battle Creek Sanitarium and, much to the disdain of many Adventists, pushed religion into the background while applying his health program, called "the Battle Creek Idea." Guests who stayed at the sanitarium were restricted to a diet that eliminated meats and only sparingly used milk, cheese, eggs, and refined sugar. Instead, Kellogg's regimen offered nuts, fruits, vegetables, and whole grains. He advised that these items be consumed in moderation—and slowly and fully chewed before swallowing. He disliked drugs and said that the best medicine was his diet, correct posture, regular exercise and rest, and plenty of fresh air.

Yet he included in his regimen some unusual practices. He subjected his guests to wearing athletic diapers, having multiple daily enemas, and dunking themselves in electrified water pools.

Kellogg wrote many works, and his early sex education manual, *Plain Facts about Sexual Life,*

published in 1877, sold more than 500,000 copies. In one widely quoted passage he warned about masturbation. He said the practice caused "irritation of the spinal cord," along with "numerous pains in the limbs" and "spasmodic twitching of the muscles." He claimed, "Paralysis, partial or complete, of the lower limbs, and even of the whole body, is not a rare occurrence. We have seen a number of cases in which this is well marked. Two of the patients were small boys who began to excite the genital organs at a very early age." One solution: circumcision. "The operation," he said, "should be performed by a surgeon without administering an anaesthetic. . . . The soreness which continues for several weeks interrupts the practice [of masturbation], and if it had not previously become too firmly fixed, it may be forgotten and not resumed."

Kellogg was himself an accomplished surgeon. In the 1890s he performed a record 165 successive abdominal operations without a fatality, and during his career he performed more than 22,000 operations with an outstanding recovery rate.

Also during the 1890s Kellogg and his brother Will inadvertently invented the first flaked cereal. They had been experimenting with boiled wheat, pressing it through rollers to make sheets of food, when they mistakenly left some of it on top of a baking tin overnight. The next morning, when they passed the wheat through the rollers, it crumbled into flakes. Will then applied the new method to corn and rice and began making corn flakes as a packaged breakfast cereal. The brothers fought over policies, however, and after many court battles Will obtained the exclusive right to market his products under the Kellogg name.

With support from the Adventists, in 1895 John Harvey Kellogg founded the American Medical Missionary College in Chicago to train doctors. (It later merged with the University of Illinois Medical School.) About 1900 Kellogg drifted away from Adventist doctrine and caused a rift with the church; as a result in November 1907 he was excommunicated. A long battle then ensued between Kellogg and the Adventists for control of the sanitarium. Kellogg continued to direct it, and for several years it prospered, attracting many prominent guests, including businessmen

J. C. Penney and S. S. Kresge, inventor Thomas Edison, explorer Richard Byrd, and aviator Amelia Earhart. In the late 1920s, however, Kellogg overexpanded the sanitarium, and when the Great Depression began and its patronage dwindled, its glory days ended.

John Harvey Kellogg died on December 14, 1943, in Battle Creek of pneumonia. He had married Ella Ervilla Eaton in 1879, and though they had no children, they raised 42 foster children, some of whom they adopted. "Eat what the monkey eats," Kellogg had advised, "simple food and not too much of it."

Further Reading

Butler, Mary. *The Battle Creek Idea: John Harvey Kellogg and the Battle Creek Sanitarium.* Battle Creek, Mich.: Heritage Publications, 1994.

Kellogg, Paul Underwood

(1879–1958) *social reformer, Progressivist*

Paul Underwood Kellogg was an innovator in sociological research, a proponent of Progressive reform, and the editor of *Survey* magazine. He was born on September 30, 1879, in Kalamazoo, Michigan, to Frank Israel Kellogg and Mary Foster Underwood Kellogg.

Paul Kellogg got his first taste of journalism at Kalamazoo High School, when he and his older brother, Arthur, edited the student newspaper. He graduated in 1897, became a reporter for the *Kalamazoo Daily Telegraph,* and in 1898 was promoted to city editor.

Kellogg left Kalamazoo in 1901 to enroll at Columbia University. While taking courses part time, in 1903 he joined the staff of *Charities* as assistant editor. Published by the New York Charity Organization Society, *Charities* was originally a journal aimed at discussing charitable services. But Kellogg changed it to discuss broader social issues, and in 1905 *Charities* merged with the journal *Commons,* published by the settlement house movement, to become *Charities and the Commons.*

This was a time when the Progressive reform movement was challenging the injustices generated by the country's industrial society, and Kellogg joined the crusade while also influencing its course. In 1907 he took a leave of absence from *Charities and the Commons,* gathered together scholars and community leaders, and over the next several years studied life and labor in Pittsburgh, Pennsylvania. That endeavor produced the "Pittsburgh Survey," published as a series of articles and later, between 1910 and 1914, as six large volumes. Historian Cara Finnegan states that the survey "became the model for a new kind of social research based upon 'modern' methods of information-gathering, investigation, and analysis." The findings encouraged Progressives who wanted to reform housing and factory conditions; they now had the information to back their efforts and a research technique they could apply to other localities.

Kellogg returned to *Charities and the Commons* in 1909, and to reflect the magazine's extended coverage and honor the work done with the Pittsburgh Survey, he changed its name to *The Survey.* The publication appealed mainly to social workers, but its articles went beyond industrial problems to discuss racial discrimination, women's suffrage, and birth control. Kellogg said that *The Survey* was intended to investigate and interpret "the objective conditions of life and labor" and chronicle the "undertakings to improve them."

To reach a wider audience, in 1921 Kellogg founded *Survey Graphic.* In combining narratives with graphics, especially photographs, it built on the Progressive tradition started by JACOB RIIS and LEWIS WICKES HINE (who contributed to the magazine); making topics more immediate and more memorable by showing life through the camera lens. Historian Kay Davis has observed, "Writers gave common men names and personalities. Photographers gave them faces."

The photographs showed factory workers, child laborers, immigrants, but also in the 1930s, the theater and paintings produced by artists in the New Deal programs. "We present the heart of experience," Kellogg said, while effusively comparing the magazine to a "voyage of discovery" founded on the belief "that the destiny of a million new citizens, the struggle for public health, the aspirations of workaday men and women are as colorful as a trip to the Fortunate Isles."

Survey and *Survey Graphic* foundered, however, after their business manager, Arthur Kellogg, died in 1934. Paul Kellogg lacked the financial acumen of his brother and was unable to find a suitable replacement. In the late 1940s *Survey Graphic* merged with *Survey*, but the publication folded in 1952.

Paul Kellogg was also active in the American Civil Liberties Union, on whose board he served for many years. He died in New York City on November 1, 1958. He had been married twice, in 1909 to Marion Pearce Sherwood, with whom he had two children, and in 1935, one year after a divorce, to Helen Hall.

Further Reading

Chambers, Clarke A. *Paul U. Kellogg and the Survey: Voices for Social Welfare and Social Justice.* Minneapolis: University of Minnesota Press, 1971.

Guimond, James. *American Photography and the American Dream.* Chapel Hill: University of North Carolina Press, 1991.

Kellor, Frances

(1873–1952) *Progressive reformer*

A Progressive reformer, Frances Kellor advocated an activist government that could address social problems. She was born on October 20, 1873, in Columbus, Ohio, to Daniel Kellor and Mary Sprau Kellor.

After Daniel Kellor abandoned his family, Frances Kellor and her mother moved to Coldwater, Michigan. Their economic straits prevented Frances from finishing high school, but she eventually attended adult education classes and entered Cornell University in Ithaca, New York.

Kellor graduated in 1897 and moved to Chicago, where she lived at Hull-House, the settlement house founded by JANE ADDAMS to help immigrants. In 1900 she traveled to the South and investigated living and working conditions among African Americans. Articles that she based on her findings recommended improving schools, establishing vocational training institutes, and setting up employment bureaus. In her book *Out of Work: A Study of Employment Agencies* (1904), she advo-

cated that the federal government intervene to tackle the economic problems that led to unemployment. Her stand signaled her commitment to a vibrant government that would advance social reform while accepting the general outline of the capitalist economy, a position many Progressives embraced, but one that radicals who believed capitalism must be completely torn down and replaced with a socialist system rejected.

In 1906, one year after Kellor moved to New York City to live with fellow reformer Mary Dreier, she organized the National League for the Protection of Colored Women. The league helped black women who had recently moved to New York from the South to find housing and jobs. Appointed to the New York State Immigration Commission in 1908, Kellor investigated immigrant housing and employment. She called for a state bureau to address the many problems she had uncovered and was appointed in 1910 to direct the newly created New York State Bureau of Industries and Immigration.

The bureau advised immigrants on how to adjust to the American environment and avoid unscrupulous landlords and employment agents. It also promoted laws, passed by the state legislature, to regulate immigrant banks and steamship companies that often exploited the newcomers.

An assimilationist, Kellor believed that immigrants should be merged quickly into American society and abandon their foreign cultures. She created the North American Civic League for Immigrants and through it held English classes for adults. "The English language is a highway of loyalty," she said. "It is the open door to opportunity."

An enthusiastic supporter of the Progressive Party, Kellor headed its administrative board, the National Service Committee, and handled much of the party's publicity in 1912 when its candidate, Theodore Roosevelt, sought the presidency. She did much to make Roosevelt aware of the plight facing urban immigrants.

When World War I began, Kellor supported American preparedness and thought it even more important to assimilate immigrants to foster national unity. In 1915 she promoted National Americanization Day, held on July 4; in Pittsburgh

10,000 immigrants gathered to hear children sing patriotic songs and form a giant American flag.

In the mid-1920s Kellor helped found the American Arbitration Association, dedicated to avoiding war by seeking international arbitration of disputes among countries. Keller was the author of several books; her later volumes established her reputation as an expert in arbitration. She died in New York City on January 4, 1952.

Further Reading
Fitzpatrick, Ellen. *Endless Crusade: Women Social Scientists and Progressive Reform.* New York: Oxford University Press, 1990.

King, Coretta Scott
(1927–) *civil rights leader*

The wife of the slain civil rights leader MARTIN LUTHER KING, JR., Coretta Scott King is a civil rights leader in her own right. She was born on April 27, 1927, in Heiberger, Alabama, near the Mississippi border, to Obidiah Scott and Bernice McMurray Scott.

Coretta Scott was raised on a farm and at an early age harvested vegetables and picked cotton. As a child she experienced the sting of racism when she was required to walk to a one-room schoolhouse several miles from her home while the white children rode buses to classes in a modern building. In her teens she attended Lincoln High School, a private all-black school in nearby Marion that charged a modest tuition. Already musically gifted, she played the piano and sang in the school chorus.

Scott graduated in 1945 as class valedictorian and then enrolled at Antioch College in Yellow Springs, Ohio. There she pursued a degree in education and music and lived for the first time in a white community. The white students accepted her, but racism again hurt her when the local school board refused to allow her into its classrooms so she could complete her student teaching. Although the Yellow Springs schools had admitted black students, they had yet to desegregate the faculty. Such discrimination encouraged her to join the campus chapter of the National Association for the Advancement of Colored People, along with committees on race relations and civil liberties.

Despite her conflict with the Yellow Springs schools, in 1951 Scott graduated and received a fellowship to study at the New England Conservatory of Music. While living with a white family on Boston's elite Beacon Hill, she held odd jobs, including working as a file clerk in a mail-order business.

In February 1952 a friend arranged for Scott to meet a young Baptist preacher, MARTIN LUTHER KING, JR. Stephen B. Oates recounts in *Let the Trumpet Sound* (1982) that at first she thought him unimpressive, but as he talked she found him to be sincere, eloquent, confident, and smart. According to Oates, when they returned to the conservatory from their first date, he said to her:

> "You have everything I have ever wanted in a wife. There are only four things, and you have them all."
>
> "I don't see how you can say that," she responded. "You don't even know me."
>
> "Yes, I can tell. The four things that I look for in a wife are character, intelligence, personality, and beauty. And you have them all."

They married on June 18, 1953, at Coretta Scott's family home in Alabama. Then they returned to Boston so Martin could finish his doctoral degree at Boston University and Coretta could finish her bachelor's degree at the conservatory. She graduated in June 1954, whereupon Martin agreed to preach at Dexter Avenue Baptist Church in Montgomery, Alabama (while completing his dissertation).

One year after the couple arrived, Martin Luther King, Jr., became leader of the bus boycott touched off when ROSA PARKS refused to give up her seat on a city bus and move to the black section. Coretta participated extensively in the boycott, handling mail and other administrative work and holding Freedom Concerts at which she sang to raise money for the Southern Christian Leadership Conference (SCLC), which had been established by Martin Luther King, Jr.

She experienced enormous pressure and frayed nerves from the many threatening phone calls and anonymous letters that she received. These warned the Kings to quit their protests or face death. Then in a frightening attack their home was bombed in 1956 while she was in it caring for the couple's first child, Yolanda, then a baby. No one was hurt, but the threats would continue.

When an assassin shot and killed Martin Luther King, Jr., in Memphis, Tennessee, on April 4, 1968, Coretta King vowed to continue his crusade. Four days later she led a march in Memphis that Martin had planned. In June she spoke at the Poor People's Campaign in Washington, D.C., another protest that the slain leader had been organizing, and in May 1969 she led a demonstration of striking hospital workers in Charleston, South Carolina.

Before her husband's death Coretta King had been active in the Women's International League for Peace and Freedom; had attended a disarmament conference in Geneva, Switzerland; and had addressed an antiwar rally in California; now she intensified her criticism of the Vietnam War.

She served on the SCLC board of directors, and in January 1969 she announced that she would establish the Martin Luther King, Jr., Center for Nonviolent Social Change in Atlanta, Georgia. The center, originally housed in the basement of her home, became in 1981 a large complex, complete with a library, museum, and auditorium, near Martin Luther King, Jr.'s, birthplace, which had been designated a National Historic Site.

Coretta King led the campaign to have her husband's birthday declared a national holiday. Congress passed a bill to that effect in 1983, and she served as chair of the Martin Luther King, Jr., Federal Holiday Commission, which coordinated observances to honor her late husband.

Coretta King and her four children became embroiled in a controversy in the late 1990s when critics charged them with exerting control over Martin Luther King, Jr.,'s image and works to make money. In the year 2000 Coretta King spoke at a civil rights march on Washington, held to replicate the one at which Martin Luther King, Jr., had spoken in 1963. "Today, we have a new generation coming forward," she said. "I am just as happy as I can be to see these younger men and women taking the torch and running with it."

Further Reading

King, Coretta Scott. *My Life with Martin Luther King, Jr.* New York: Avon Books, 1970.

Press, Petra. *Coretta Scott King: An Unauthorized Biography.* Des Plaines, Ill.: Heinemann Library, 1999.

King, Martin Luther, Jr.
(1929–1968) *civil rights leader*

America's preeminent civil rights leader, Martin Luther King, Jr., was the founder of the Southern Christian Leadership Conference. He was born on January 15, 1929, in Atlanta, Georgia, the son of the Reverend Martin Luther King, Sr., and Alberta Williams King.

Religion was an integral part of Martin Luther King, Jr.'s, lineage. His maternal grandfather, Adam Daniel Williams, had served as the pastor of Ebenezer Baptist Church in Atlanta for more than 30 years, until his death in 1931; his father was assistant pastor of the church at the time of young Martin's birth and became pastor on the death of Reverend Williams; and his older sister, Christine, and his younger brother, Alfred Daniel, both became ministers.

Intelligent and precocious, King entered Morehouse College, an all-black school, as part of a program that accepted bright high school students for early admission. So at age 15 he was studying for a bachelor's degree and reading Henry David Thoreau's essay *Civil Disobedience* (1849), which he later said "left a deep impression on me." In those years immediately after World War II, with the modern civil rights movement beginning to stir, Thoreau showed King how to defy authority peacefully for the sake of liberty.

In 1947, one year before King graduated, he was ordained a Baptist minister and served as assistant pastor to his father. With his bachelor's degree in sociology in hand the following year, King enrolled at Crozer Theological Seminary in Chester, Pennsylvania, a predominantly white school. Here the philosophical basis of his later crusade for civil rights fell into place. King read the writings of Walter Rauschenbusch, a proponent of the social gospel, who assailed capitalism for encouraging selfishness and an imbalance of wealth that left many people impoverished; he called on Christians to replace capitalist competitiveness with a new morality dedicated to harmony and community.

King studied Karl Marx and accepted the philosopher's critique of capitalism—a decision that later contributed to his enemies labeling him a communist. But King was no communist. He saw in Marx what he had seen in Rauschenbusch, namely, that capitalism encouraged selfishness, that it lacked a moral center. He disliked, however, communism's atheism and its authoritarianism—both inimical to the fulfillment of human potential—and the ruthless tactics used by the Soviet Union's leaders.

But until King attended a lecture devoted to the ideas of the Indian leader Mohandas Gandhi, he doubted that Christian love could be used to reform the world. Excited by what he heard, King delved into books about Gandhi and into Gandhi's autobiography, and he discovered *Satyagraha,* a Sanskrit word for "persistent truth"—which Gandhi applied to his tactic of nonviolent protest—along with *agape,* or the love for fellow human beings. To King, that love could be found in Christ's teachings as an antidote to the selfishness bred by capitalism and the hatred generated by racism.

King studied Gandhi's use of nonviolent protest against British oppression in India, and he concluded it could be used by blacks against racist oppression in America. He liked the tactic because it rejected violence as a weapon by emulating the "turn the other cheek" precept of Christianity and because it called attention to injustice in a dramatic way and purged both the oppressor and the oppressed of hatred. Yet for King nonviolent protest rooted in Christian love was always more than a tactic—it was a way of life, the way that he tried to live, and the way he hoped others would live to expand social justice.

Martin Luther King, Jr., graduated from Crozer at the top of his class in 1951 with a divinity degree, and with a fellowship from the seminary he entered Boston University as a graduate student in the philosophy department. Two years later he married Coretta Scott, a voice student at the New England Conservatory. The couple had four children. CORETTA SCOTT KING later joined her husband in his civil rights campaign, providing him with crucial support and advice.

King wrote his doctoral dissertation on the concept of God as presented by Paul Tillich and H. N. Wieman, while taking additional philosophy courses at Harvard and preaching in Boston churches. In 1954, one year before King completed his Ph.D., the Dexter Avenue Baptist Church in Montgomery, Alabama, recruited him to serve as their preacher, so he returned to the Deep South and its fiercely segregated society.

He was at Dexter little more than a year when on December 1, 1955, ROSA PARKS, an African-American seamstress, was arrested when she refused to abide by a bus driver's order to give up her seat to a white passenger. Blacks in Montgomery, led by E. D. Nixon, had for some time been looking for a case that would allow them to protest the city's bus segregation. Now they had it, and with the newcomer King as eager as they were to press for reform, the city's black ministers gathered at the Dexter Avenue Church and decided to begin a boycott on December 5. Later that day they organized the Montgomery Improvement Association (MIA) to run the boycott and chose King as its president.

With the bus boycott King applied his nonviolent protest; he urged blacks who were harassed by whites and detained by the police to react with peace rather than violence. He always thought that violence promoted hate, and hate more violence, and he told a rally:

> Love your enemies, bless them that curse you, and pray for them that despitefully use you. If we fail to do this our protest will end up as a meaningless drama on the stage of history, and its memory will be shrouded with the ugly garments of shame. In spite of the mistreatment that we have confronted we must not become bitter, and end up by hating our white brothers. As BOOKER T[ALIAFERRO] WASHINGTON said, "Let no man pull you so low as to make you hate him."

Using his rich voice and the cadence of the Baptist preacher—qualities that over the years would mesmerize many audiences—King continued:

If we protest courageously, and yet with dignity and Christian love, when the history books are written in the future, somebody will have to say, "There live a race of people, of black people, of people who had the moral courage to stand up for their rights. And thereby they injected a new meaning into the veins of history and civilization."

King's philosophy was sorely tried when whites bombed his house, but he held to a steady course. The bus boycott drew national attention to the city's segregation, and the national spotlight illuminated King as the charismatic young leader of the civil rights movement. When in November 1956 the U.S. Supreme Court declared Montgomery's segregationist bus laws unconstitutional, blacks and white liberals hailed King and his nonviolent strategy. That December King and several MIA colleagues rode Montgomery's first desegregated bus.

Pictured here during the 1963 civil rights march on Washington, Martin Luther King, Jr., promoted nonviolent resistance. *(National Archives and Records Administration)*

In January 1957 King and some 60 black leaders met at the Ebenezer Baptist Church and founded the Southern Christian Leadership Conference (SCLC). As its name indicated, the SCLC applied to the civil rights movement Christian values and King's nonviolent philosophy, both as a strategy and as a vision for a more humane society. In May he led a prayer pilgrimage of 25,000 people in Washington, D.C., demanding that Congress pass a civil rights bill.

In January 1958 King's book *Stride toward Freedom* appeared. In it he told about the Montgomery bus boycott, and the following month the SCLC launched the Crusade for Citizenship with the goal of enrolling 3 million black southerners as voters over two years. King said, "History has demonstrated that inadequate legislation supported by mass action can accomplish more than adequate legislation which remains unenforced for lack of a determined mass movement." The SCLC held workshops, clinics, and rallies throughout the South, but strong white resistance to the crusade caused it to fall far short of its goals—only 160,000 blacks registered to vote.

King resigned as pastor of the Dexter Avenue Church in January 1960 so he could devote himself full-time to the SCLC. That October black college students in Atlanta began a series of sit-ins to tear down the city's racial segregation—the "Second Battle of Atlanta," they called it—and they asked King, as the most prominent civil rights leader, to join them. He did so and was arrested. He had been jailed before, but this time he was sentenced to four months hard labor and thrown into Reidsville Penitentiary for violation of a one-year probation given him several months earlier for a minor traffic incident. The stunningly harsh sentence was reversed, and King was released only after Democratic senator John Kennedy of Massachusetts intervened on his behalf.

That action led King and many other African Americans to support Kennedy for president in 1960. With Kennedy victorious, King expected the new president to act quickly on civil rights. But Kennedy, worried about antagonizing southern congressmen, dragged his feet—a move that greatly disappointed many black leaders.

In spring 1963 King launched a campaign to desegregate Birmingham, Alabama. Under Sheriff Eugene "Bull" Connor, the police retaliated against the protesters who were attempting to march peacefully by unleashing on them dogs, cattle prods, and fire hoses. Pictures of the brutal assault appeared on national TV—and on televisions and in newspapers around the world—greatly damaging America's standing in its cold war with Russia.

King was arrested and thrown into a solitary cell, during which he wrote, on April 16, 1963, his "Letter from a Birmingham Jail," since considered to be among the most important protest documents in American history. King wrote the letter in response to criticism from eight white Christian and Jewish clergymen who thought nonviolent street protests too extreme. To those who said he was wrong to be breaking the law, he explained when it was proper to do so:

> Since we so diligently urge people to obey the Supreme Court's decision of 1954 outlawing segregation in the public schools, at first glance it may seem rather paradoxical for us consciously to break laws. One may well ask: "How can you advocate breaking some laws and obeying others?" The answer lies in the fact that there are two types of laws: just and unjust. I would be the first to advocate obeying just laws. One has not only a legal but a moral responsibility to obey just laws. Conversely, one has a moral responsibility to disobey unjust laws. I would agree with St. Agustine that "an unjust law is no law at all."
>
> Now, what is the difference between the two? How does one determine whether a law is just or unjust? A just law is a man-made code that squares with the moral law or the law of God. An unjust law is a code that is out of harmony with the moral law. . . . Any law that uplifts human personality is just. Any law that degrades human personality is unjust. All segregation statutes are unjust because segregation distorts the soul and damages the personality. It gives the segregator a false sense of superiority and the segregated a false sense of inferiority.

His statement reflected his belief that segregation damaged blacks *and* whites by degrading the personalities of *both*. Segregation damaged whites by calling forth the worst within them, by calling forth hate.

In early May Birmingham officials met most of the demands made by King and the SCLC and desegregated the city's public facilities. A few weeks later, on August 28, 1963, King participated in the March on Washington for civil rights, organized by ASA PHILIP RANDOLPH, and addressed 200,000 people with his "I Have a Dream" speech:

> I say to you today, my friends, that in spite of the difficulties and frustrations of the moment I still have a dream. It is a dream deeply rooted in the American dream. I have a dream that one day this nation will rise up and live out the true meaning of its creed: "We hold these truths to be self-evident—that all men are created equal. . . . "
>
> Let freedom ring from every hill and mole hill of Mississippi. From every mountaintop, let freedom ring. When we let freedom ring, when we let it ring from every village and every hamlet, from every state and every city, we will be able to speed up that day when all of God's children, black men and white men, Jews and Gentiles, Protestants and Catholics, will be able to join hands and sing in the words of the old Negro spiritual, "Free at last! Free at last! Thank God almighty, we are free at last!"

In 1964 King received the Nobel Peace Prize and said that the award added credence to nonviolent protest. His efforts contributed substantially to Congress's passage of the Civil Rights Act of 1964 and the Voting Rights Act of 1965. Over the next several months he continued to press his fight for expanded voting rights and a complete end to segregation.

But additional controversy arose from two different quarters. For one, many young blacks thought his civil rights gains inadequate. This was especially true of blacks living in northern and western urban ghettos. The SCLC was largely southern in focus, and ghetto blacks argued that King had done nothing to bring about economic gains for them. In effect, they were saying it meant little to use the same water fountain as a white person when white economic domination meant few jobs in the ghettos.

Many young African Americans embraced the militant Black Power movement, which stressed black self-determination, black culture, and black strength separate from the white community. This was exactly opposite to King's integrationist approach, and the dislike for nonviolence as a way of life that ran through Black Power only added to the challenge posed to King's leadership.

King did take his civil rights campaign into the North. Most notably, early in 1966 he entered Chicago and vowed to force an end to policies that perpetuated the slums. "We're going to organize to make Chicago a model city," he told his supporters. "Remember, living in a slum is robbery. It's a robbery of dignity, and the right to participate creatively in the political process. It's wrong to live with rats."

The other controversy arose from his remarks about the Vietnam War. He condemned the war as racist and so earned the enmity of President Lyndon Johnson, who thought King should have shown more gratitude for all the White House had done to advance civil rights.

As during the Montgomery bus boycott, King had received many death threats over the years, and the possibility of assassination stalked him. In spring 1968 he traveled to Memphis, Tennessee, to support striking sanitation workers. On April 4 he was standing on a balcony at the Lorraine Motel when a gunman shot and killed him. James Earl Ray was later arrested and confessed to the crime. In the late 1970s evidence compiled by the Select Committee on Assassinations of the U.S. House of Representatives portrayed Ray as King's lone assassin. But while in jail Ray recanted his story, and the King family and others have long thought him innocent—or part of a much larger conspiracy.

Some skeptics have even questioned the role of the federal government in the killing, suggesting its complicity given the animosity shown by the Federal Bureau of Investigation (FBI) toward King and its extensive surveillance of him. Ever since King had gained prominence, FBI director J. Edgar Hoover had ordered that information be gathered about him and used to discredit him. Hoover dis-

liked blacks in general, considered the civil rights movement a threat to order, and thought King a closet communist.

With the approval of Attorney General Robert Kennedy, agents tapped King's home telephone and those located at the SCLC offices. They even planted unauthorized and illegal microphones in his hotel rooms and then gave journalists and political and religious leaders a report that accused him of sexual and financial misconduct. They sent King an audio-tape of his sexual indiscretions, with a note hinting that he should kill himself. Such secret and sordid activity by the federal government was not uncommon—political dissidents were typically surveilled and harassed to restrict their liberties and destroy their influence.

In *Let the Trumpet Sound: The Life of Martin Luther King, Jr.* (1982), Stephen Oates writes about a black janitor in Montgomery who at the time of the bus boycott said about King's effort and the Supreme Court decision ending bus segregation: "We got our heads up now, and we won't ever bow down again—no, sir—except before God!"

Further Reading

Carson, Clayborne, ed. *The Autobiography of Martin Luther King, Jr.* New York: Warner Books, 1998.

Friedly, Michael. *Martin Luther King, Jr.: The FBI File.* New York: Carroll & Graf, 1993.

Lewis, David L. *King: A Biography.* 2nd ed. Urbana: University of Illinois Press, 1978.

Millner, Sandra. *The Dream Lives On: Martin Luther King, Jr.* New York: Metro Books, 1999.

Oates, Stephen B. *Let the Trumpet Sound: The Life of Martin Luther King, Jr.* New York: Harper & Row, 1982.

Kramer, Larry

(1935–) *AIDS activist*

The playwright Larry Kramer is the founder of the Gay Men's Health Crisis (GMHC) and the militant group ACT UP. He was born in 1935 in Bridgeport, Connecticut, to George L. Kramer, an attorney, and Rea Wishengrad Kramer.

Larry Kramer graduated from Yale University in 1957 with a bachelor of arts degree and first received national attention in 1970, when his adaptation to screen of D. H. Lawrence's *Women in Love* earned four Oscar nominations. His novel *Faggots*, published in 1978, satirized gay men involved in dangerous sexual practices.

Kramer's activism began in 1981 when at a meeting in his Manhattan apartment he founded Gay Men's Health Crisis to help homosexuals deal with the deadly disease called acquired immunodeficiency syndrome (AIDS). Since that time GMHC has been the largest nonprofit group to serve those suffering from AIDS, assisting 11,000 people in the year 2000 alone.

With the formation of GMHC, Kramer began a strident, vociferous campaign to awaken the public to the threat posed by AIDS. He found many gays ignorant on the subject and many heterosexuals dismissing it as something peculiar to gays, with extreme conservatives even labeling it just retribution for a sinful way of life. Kramer advised gays to practice safe sex and warned about the devastating effects of AIDS as a sexually transmitted disease.

In 1985 Kramer wrote *The Normal Heart*, a play that became an international hit. The drama depicted an abrasive gay activist waging war against the apathy and political maneuvers hindering efforts to fight an unnamed plague.

Many labeled Kramer abrasive. One fellow activist called him "disruptive and accusatory and unforgiving, even egotistical." Kramer, though, believed the AIDS crisis required loudness. He once declared, "We must do nothing less now than remake the soul of our time."

As more AIDS patients died, Kramer demanded that political leaders pressure the medical community into finding a treatment for the disease. In 1987 a speech that he gave caused about 350 people to gather at a town meeting, and from that Kramer founded ACT UP (AIDS Coalition to Unleash Power). He intended ACT UP to engage in civil disobedience—to sponsor picketing, marches, and sit-down demonstrations to force research on AIDS and make drugs more readily available. In *Newsweek* David France wrote about ACT UP:

Its members shut down Wall Street to protest drug costs; they pulled a huge condom over [Senator] Jesse Helms's home in North Carolina to demand prevention funds; they staged die-ins and political funerals, carrying the bodies of their dead comrades to the gates of the White House in wide-open coffins, shocking the government to action.

In 1996 Kramer offered to donate $250,000 to Yale to begin a gay studies program. When Yale rejected the gift, calling the money insufficient and stating that gay studies lacked credibility, Kramer accused the school of being "homophobic." But in spring 2001 he and Yale finally reached an agreement whereby his family would donate $1 million to the university, along with Kramer's manuscripts, in return for which Yale would establish the Larry Kramer Initiative for Lesbian and Gay Studies. Diagnosed as human immunodeficiency virus (HIV)–positive, Kramer was, by that time, suffering from end-stage liver disease. Doctors predicted he had about 18 more months to live.

Critics of Kramer's strident activism said that he was diverting attention from other diseases just as serious as AIDS that also needed money for research. They cautioned that the "notion of exceptionalism" was causing a backlash against the AIDS activists. But Roger McFarlane, Kramer's former lover, said of him, "This is a rich and very successful man who could have had a different career. . . . He devoted his life to fighting for people, and in fighting for AIDS he won a battle for all sick people. Medicine will never be the same. Now the medical consumer doesn't just accept what the doctor says. He reads and challenges everything. Larry gave birth to consumer activism in medicine."

Further Reading

Kramer, Larry. *Reports from the Holocaust: The Story of an AIDS Activist*. London: Cassell, 1995.

Mass, Lawrence, ed. *We Must Love One Another or Die: The Life and Legacies of Larry Kramer*. New York: St. Martin's Press, 1997.

L

Ladd, William
(1778–1841) *pacifist*

William Ladd earned a reputation as the "apostle of peace" for his untiring effort to spread pacifist ideas and establish a body of nations that would work to lessen their stores of armaments and encourage international arbitration. He was born on May 10, 1778, in Exeter, New Hampshire, to Eliphalet Ladd and Abigail Hill.

The son of a wealthy sea captain, Ladd as a young man followed his father's profession and after graduating from Harvard in 1798 commanded a brig based in Portsmouth, New Hampshire. In 1813 Ladd and his wife, Sophia Ann Augusta Stidolph, settled in Minot, Maine, where he owned and operated a farm of several hundred acres dedicated to scientific agriculture.

Six years later Ladd happened on the peace movement through the influence of Jesse Appleton, the president of Bowdoin College. Appleton had dedicated himself to peace and told Ladd about several societies then forming that were dedicated to the cause. According to Ladd, "This was almost the first time I ever heard of them. The idea then passed over my mind as the day-dream of benevolence." He stated that his reading on the subject further stimulated his interest, riveting his attention "in such a manner as to make it the principal object of my life to promote the cause of Peace on earth and good-will to man."

Ladd contributed to the reading material related to those ideas when he wrote the series "Essays on Peace and War," which began appearing in the *Christian Mirror* of Portland, Maine, in 1823. The 32 essays were published as a book in 1825.

Ladd originated the idea for a national peace society, and in 1827 he convinced the societies of Maine, Massachusetts, and New Hampshire to pass resolutions supporting his effort. Finally, on May 8, 1828, the American Peace Society was organized, and Ladd agreed to serve as chairman of its board of directors. The group had as its goal educating the public to the "evils of war" and showing how best to abolish such conflicts. Most of the local peace societies were subsequently absorbed by the national group.

Although the American Peace Society never numbered more than a few hundred members, it printed and distributed numerous tracts. Ladd traveled widely, promoting the society, presenting lectures, and raising money. He wrote articles for newspapers and magazines, and he edited the society's periodical, *Harbinger of Peace*, later renamed *Calumet*.

Ladd promoted the idea for a Congress of Nations, an international deliberative body, and in 1832 published a pamphlet on the subject. In 1840 he wrote an essay in which he broke new ground by advocating that the proposed Congress of Nations be split into two parts: a Congress of Ambassadors that would devise plans for preserving peace and a Court of Nations that would arbitrate disputes between countries. He was responding to critics who said that diplomats would take control of any international court and work for their self-interest rather than for justice. In words that reflected the separation of powers in the American political system, Ladd said his plan would divide "the diplomatic from the judicial functions." He stated, "I consider the Congress as the legislature, and the Court as the judiciary, in the government of nations." The U.S. Senate refused to adopt Ladd's plan, but his ideas served as an outline for the later World Court, League of Nations, and United Nations.

When Ladd formed the American Peace Society he avoided the controversial issue of whether pacifists should condemn defensive wars. If anything, he at first supported the fighting of such wars. But he changed his mind when he realized that some of the world's greatest aggressors had portrayed their combat as defensive. To Ladd all wars were immoral and to accept one would mean accepting them all.

Ladd won only a few converts to his cause in an era when the idea of manifest destiny prevailed and Americans were eager to take up arms to expand their territory. Yet he continued his campaign for peace right up to his death. On April 8, 1841, he spoke to a group in Boston; the following day he died, partly as a result of exhaustion that had worsened his declining health.

Further Reading

Curti, Merle Eugene. *The American Peace Crusade, 1815–1860*. New York: Octagon Books, 1965.

Hemmenway, John. *The Apostle of Peace: Memoir of Wm. Ladd*. Boston: American Peace Society, 1872.

Lathrop, Julia Clifford
(1858–1932) *child welfare reformer*

Julia Clifford Lathrop was a reformer who helped establish America's first juvenile court. She was born on June 29, 1858, in Rockford, Illinois, to William Lathrop and Adeline Potter Lathrop.

Julia Lathrop grew up in a reformist family; her father fought against slavery, and her mother advocated women's suffrage. Lathrop studied briefly at Rockford Seminary and then entered Vassar College, where she graduated in 1880.

She worked in her father's law office and in 1890 moved to Chicago to live at Hull-House, the settlement house founded by JANE ADDAMS to help immigrants. In 1893, as a terrible depression gripped Chicago and the country, Lathrop studied relief work in Cook County and wrote a report that appeared in *Hull-House Maps and Papers* (1895).

Also in 1895 she began serving on the Illinois Board of Public Charities. She visited almshouses and other facilities to ascertain the best means to care for the blind, the deaf, prisoners, juvenile delinquents, and the mentally ill. In articles and speeches she criticized the assigning of the sick and mentally ill to the same institutions; mental illness, she insisted, should be treated in specialized hospitals.

Lathrop joined Jane Addams in pushing Illinois to enact a juvenile court act. Before it took effect in 1899, the same courts handled offenses committed by adults and children. In Chicago children who were unable to provide bail were placed in cells at police stations with adults, and if convicted they were sent to Bridewell, the city prison. Lathrop recalled, "Not only in Cook County but throughout the state of Illinois . . . boys were kept in 'lockups' and jail in the company of adult prisoners, under circumstances which were a guarantee of ruined character."

The 1899 act established the first juvenile court in the United States. Lathrop later wrote, "The combination of a separate court, a separate detention for children, the abolition of fines, and the system of returning the child to his home and providing probation officers to help him there, was probably new, and was certainly unprecedented in a city as large as Chicago." That development reflected, Lathrop said, the "popular conviction that the growing child must not be treated by those rigid rules of criminal procedure which confessedly fail to prevent offenses on the part of adults or cure adult offenders." She added, "The great primary service of the court is that it lifts up the truth and compels us to see the wastage of human life whose sign is the child in court."

Lathrop resigned from the Board of Public Charities in 1901 to protest the use of state charitable institutions as dumping grounds for political appointees. She returned to the board, though, in 1905 and served until 1909, when the board was replaced by a restructured administrative board proposed by her.

Meanwhile, Lathrop took part in beginning a series of courses to help social workers, which became known as the Chicago School of Civics and Philanthropy. In 1912 President William Howard Taft appointed her head of the newly created Children's Bureau of the Department of Labor. In that post she investigated infant mortality, child labor, mothers' pensions, juvenile crime, and other problems related to children. Her work led to Congress passing the Sheppard-Towner Act shortly after she had resigned from the Children's Bureau in 1921 because of poor health. The act authorized appropriations of $1 million to the states to promote the health of expectant mothers and of infants.

Lathrop also campaigned for women's suffrage and in 1922 became president of the Illinois chapter of the League of Women Voters. In the 1920s she fought in vain for a constitutional amendment that would prevent child labor. Julia Lathrop died on April 15, 1932.

Further Reading

Abel, Emily K. "Correspondence Between Julia C. Lathrop, Chief of the Children's Bureau, and a Working-Class Woman, 1914–1915." *Journal of Women's History* 5 (Spring 1993): 10+.

Addams, Jane. *My Friend, Julia Lathrop.* New York: Macmillan, 1935.

Chambers, Clarke A. *Seedtime of Reform: American Social Service and Social Action.* Minneapolis: University of Minnesota Press, 1963.

Lease, Mary Elizabeth Clyens

(1853–1933) *Populist reformer*

Mary Elizabeth Lease—famous for the thundering statement she once made to farmers, "Raise less corn and more hell!"—has been called the most effective of the Populist orators. Born Mary Elizabeth Clyens on September 11, 1853, in Ridgway, Pennsylvania, to Joseph P. Clyens and Mary Elizabeth Murray Clyens, Irish immigrants, she grew up on the family farm and taught school for two years before moving to Kansas, where she resumed her teaching and married Charles L. Lease. They bought and worked a farm but lost it, causing her to turn to studying law; in 1889 she was admitted to the Wichita bar.

The previous year Lease had joined the Union Labor Party, a forerunner to the People's (Populist) Party, and even though women were ineligible to vote, she ran for a county office. She later edited the party's publication, the *Union Labor Press.* In 1892 she helped found the national People's Party when delegates from various state farm and people's parties, including the one in Kansas, met in Saint Louis, Missouri.

A typical Lease speech was filled with fire in assaulting eastern money men and depicting the suffering experienced by farmers and city workers alike. She claimed:

> Wall Street owns the country. It is no longer a government of the people, by the people, and for the people, but a government of Wall Street, by Wall Street, and for Wall Street. . . .
>
> The [political] parties lie to us and the political speakers mislead us. . . . The politicians said we suffered from overproduction. Overproduction, when 10,000 little children . . . starve to death every year in the United States, and over 100,000 shop girls in New York are forced to sell their virtue for the bread their niggardly wages deny them. . . .
>
> We will stand by our homes and stay by our firesides by force if necessary. . . . The people are at bay; let the bloodhounds of money who dogged us thus far beware.

Lease left the People's Party in 1896 because it supported the Democratic candidate, William Jennings Bryan, for president. She moved to New York City, joined the *New York World* as a political reporter, and lectured frequently, advocating women's suffrage, prohibition, and birth control.

Mary Elizabeth Lease died on October 29, 1933.

Further Reading

"Mary Lease." Available online. URL: http://beria.vassar.edu/1896/lease.html. Downloaded on March 25, 2002.

Stiller, Richard. *The Queen of the Populists: The Story of Mary Elizabeth Lease.* New York: Crowell, 1970.

Lens, Sidney
(Sidney Okun)
(1912–1986) *labor organizer, peace activist*

Sidney Lens was a writer, labor organizer, peace activist, and senior editor of *Progressive* magazine. He was born Sidney Okun on January 28, 1912, in Newark, New Jersey. His father, a pharmacist, died when Sidney was only three years old, and his mother supported the family by working as a seamstress in New York City.

Lens obtained his high school diploma before working in 1930 at Hecht Brothers, a New York department store, where he wrote advertising copy. With the Great Depression then under way, he launched his first foray into activism when he formed a union for the store's workers. Over the following two decades he organized sit-ins and strikes in Detroit, Washington, and New York City. In 1946 he married Shirley Ruben.

In the early 1950s Lens began writing for the *Progressive.* In 1962 he ran for president of the United States as a peace candidate, and in the late 1960s he became a contributing editor at the *Progressive.*

At that time Lens was a leader in protests against the Vietnam War. He spoke to students on college campuses and helped organize the Mobilization to End the War in Vietnam, which he cochaired. In 1976 he joined other antiwar activists in founding Mobilization for Survival, a national peace organization. Two years later the *Progressive* named him its senior editor.

A prolific author, Lens wrote more than 20 books and numerous articles. In several of them he condemned the cold war buildup of nuclear weapons. Writing in the *Progressive* in 1976, he stated: "The decision makers understand how frightful a nuclear war would be—they understand it much better than the rest of us do. But they are motivated by considerations that are never openly expressed, and that are therefore difficult for the average citizen to divine."

He lamented that Americans had accepted the nuclear crisis as habit. "Because of its catastrophic scope," he wrote, "the nuclear menace is neither believable nor believed by the general public. It has been absorbed, grain by grain, over a period of thirty years, so that its impact has been lost. Americans have become immunized to the permanent emergency, the permanent war economy, the permanent national security state." He concluded:

> We are confronted by a lunatic process, in which every participant is sane but all collectively are trapped in psychosis. The process propels itself, like a machine gone mad.

Lens died of cancer on June 18, 1986, in Chicago. The city's mayor, Harold Washington, called him a "warrior for justice. . . . He has . . . fought the tireless fight and been an inspiration to us all."

Further Reading

Lens, Sidney. *Unrepentant Radical: An American Activist's Account of His Five Turbulent Decades.* Boston: Beacon Press, 1980.

Lewis, John Llewellyn
(1880–1969) *union leader*

A supporter of Republican presidents and of Democrat Franklin D. Roosevelt, John Llewellyn Lewis is revered as a founder of the Congress of Industrial Organizations. He was born on February 12, 1880, in Cleveland, Iowa, to Welsh immigrants Thomas H. Lewis and Ann Louis Watkins Lewis.

Cleveland was a small coal-mining town, and the Lewis family moved several times during John's childhood as Thomas sought to find work in the mines after having been placed on a blacklist by the companies for his role in a strike. Then in 1897 they returned to Cleveland and rented a farm just outside town. John Lewis, who left high school in his junior year, worked in the Cleveland coal mines and by 1901 had become secretary of the United Mine Workers (UMW) local. Shortly afterward he traveled out West, holding various

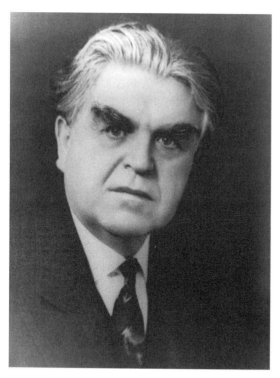

Important in building the United Mine Workers into a large union, John Llewellyn Lewis later collaborated with big business. *(National Archives and Records Administration)*

jobs, until like his father before him he returned to Cleveland. Lewis tried to escape his blue-collar status by opening a feed and grain business, but in 1907—the year he married Myrta Edit Bell, with whom he would have three children—his business failed.

The following year Lewis moved again, settling in Panama, Illinois, another coal-mining town. There he set his sights on a career in trade unionism, and after being chosen president of the UMW Panama local, he became a lobbyist for the union in the state legislature.

In 1911 SAMUEL GOMPERS, the head of the American Federation of Labor (AFL), which encompassed the UMW, made Lewis a union organizer. His success caused the AFL in 1916 to appoint him to a committee and assign him to blunting a drive by the socialists to take over the union. His ruthless tactics in fulfilling his assignment earned him the sobriquet "Ironjaw."

The following year the union officials appointed him UMW statistician and editor of the union journal. In 1918 the executive board made him vice president, an appointment tantamount to making him president, since the sitting chief executive was largely ignoring his duties. Just one year later Lewis became acting president, capping his rapid rise to the union's highest post. He immediately led a national coal strike that ended in a compromise agreement, and in 1920 the rank and file elected him president.

The decade of the 20s, however, turned out to be devastating to Lewis and the UMW. While many Americans enjoyed the country's economic boom, mining companies produced too much coal, causing prices to drop and miners to lose their jobs. As a result UMW membership declined. In 1922 Lewis led the largest coal strike in America's history, but the effort collapsed. Two years later he negotiated a no-strike contract that won few benefits for the workers.

Yet Lewis tightened his grip on the union, assumed dictatorial power, and in 1928 endorsed Republican candidate Herbert Hoover for president. Lewis said about him, "Labor and industry require his services and genius for constructive industrial statesmanship, so that the unprecedented industrial and business prosperity which he inaugurated [as secretary of commerce] may be properly developed and stabilized." He endorsed Hoover again in 1932 as the Great Depression worsened the living conditions of miners.

But Franklin Roosevelt won the presidency that year, and once in the White House, FDR provided a big boost to unions by convincing Congress to pass a law recognizing the right of workers to bargain collectively. Lewis wasted no time in shifting his support to Roosevelt and moving to organize not only miners but steel workers and other laborers. He quickly boosted UMW membership from 100,000—to which it had declined in the 1920s—to 300,000, and as vice president of the AFL from 1935, he stated:

We [miners] are anxious to have collective bargaining established in the steel industry, and our interest in that is, to a degree, selfish because our people know that, if the workers were organized . . . it would remove the incentives of the great captains of the steel industry to destroy and punish our people who work in the captive coal mines throughout the country, owned by the steel industry.

At the AFL national convention in 1935 Lewis tried to convince the delegates to organize millions of blue-collar workers who did not fit into the AFL's existing craft union structure. His demand produced an acrimonious battle that at one point caused him to shout angrily at an opponent on the convention floor and hit him in the mouth.

Lewis had already thought about bolting the AFL, and when the convention rejected his demand he organized the Committee for Industrial Organizations in November 1935, which became the Congress of Industrial Organizations (CIO) and included the UMW as one of its member unions. Over the next two years Lewis sought to organize two of the world's biggest corporations, General Motors (GM) and United States Steel. A massive sit-down strike at Flint, Michigan, caused GM to agree to a collective bargaining contract; U.S. Steel witnessed the CIO's power and decided to reach an agreement before a strike could be called.

In 1936 Lewis directed the UMW to support Roosevelt in his reelection bid, and by the following year Roosevelt's victory and a boost in CIO membership made Lewis a powerful leader. But in 1937 he sponsored an unsuccessful steel strike that cost the CIO dearly in prestige and members. Then as war approached in Europe he took an isolationist stand at odds with Roosevelt and lost much of his influence in the White House. In 1940 he broke with Roosevelt completely when he supported Republican Wendell Willkie for president. Lewis said that if Willkie lost, he would quit the CIO presidency; Willkie lost, and Lewis quit.

In 1942 Lewis pulled the UMW out of the CIO, and during World War II he led the miners' union in several strikes that produced economic gains for the workers but antagonized many Americans by making the union appear to be unpatriotic and selfish when sacrifices were needed to fight the war. Lewis restored the UMW to the AFL in

1946, but he pulled it out a second time the following year, when the AFL refused to join him in defying the antiunion Taft Hartley Act. Through the 1950s Lewis obtained collective bargaining contracts for the UMW that boosted wages and benefits for miners, but he did so by becoming a collaborator with big business and at one point even loaned funds from the UMW bank to coal companies that used the money to replace miners with machinery.

In fact, mechanized mining produced more coal than the country could use and caused the UMW again to lose members. By the time Lewis retired from the UMW presidency in 1960, it was a union clearly in decline despite its financial stability. John L. Lewis died on June 11, 1969, having led the UMW to great prominence and a bleak future.

Further Reading

Dubofsky, Melvyn, and Warren Van Tine. *John L. Lewis: A Biography.* Urbana: University of Illinois Press, 1986.

McFarland, Charles K. *Roosevelt, Lewis, and the New Deal, 1933–1940.* Fort Worth: Texas Christian University Press, 1970.

Roberts, Ron E. "The Rook of Labor's Demiurge: Iowa's John L. Lewis." *Journal of the West* 35 (April 1996): 10+.

Waschler, James A. *Labor Baron: A Portrait of John L. Lewis.* New York: Morrow, 1944.

Lewis, John Robert
(1940–) *civil rights leader, congressman*

An African-American civil rights leader who was bloodied by police and white mobs during protests in the 1960s, John Robert Lewis later served as a congressman known for his unflagging support of racial integration. He was born on February 21, 1940, in Troy, Alabama, to Eddie Lewis and Willie Mae Lewis.

Raised in a sharecropping family amid dusty cottonfields near Troy, John Lewis showed at an early age a desire to become a preacher; at seven years old he would stand in front of the chickens on his farm and preach to them (and become upset whenever one of them was taken away to be slaughtered). Throughout his childhood Lewis attended racially segregated schools. He recalled:

> When I was fourteen years old, the Supreme Court issued its decision on school desegregation [in *Brown v. Board of Education*]. I remember it very well. I thought that the next year I would go to a real high school, and not the kind of training school that blacks were sent to. I thought I wouldn't have to be bused forty miles each day, past white schools, to maintain a system of segregation. I thought we would have new buses.
>   But integration didn't happen . . . I went all the way through high school and graduated in 1957, without attending a single desegregated school.

Pursuing his desire to preach, Lewis briefly attended the American Baptist Theological Seminary in Nashville, Tennessee, but then decided he wanted to break the color barrier back home at Troy State College. Since Lewis had avidly followed the Montgomery bus boycott and admired MARTIN LUTHER KING, JR., he asked King to support his intended attempt to enter Troy State. Lewis's plans collapsed, however, when his parents objected to his doing anything that might cause trouble. So he instead enrolled at all-black Fisk University in Nashville.

Ironically, at Fisk he had intimate contact with the "trouble" his parents had wanted him to avoid. He learned about theories of nonviolent protest, especially after he began attending student workshops run by James Lawson, a black pacifist theologian. Then in February 1960, stirred by the sit-ins staged by African-American college students at a segregated Woolworth's lunch counter in Greensboro, North Carolina, he joined other protesters at sit-ins in Nashville. Over a span of six weeks he was arrested four times but held steadfast to his goal of destroying segregation.

In April 1960 Lewis attended the founding meeting of the Student Nonviolent Coordinating Committee (SNCC) in Raleigh, North Carolina. The following year he volunteered to participate in the Freedom Rides campaign, whereby white and black civil rights workers aimed to challenge the segregated bus terminals common in the South by defying the laws that required the races to use separate restrooms, restaurants, and waiting areas. Lewis may well have been thinking back to his childhood when he peered into the clean washroom reserved for whites at the Troy bus station and then had to use the dirty washroom set aside for blacks.

The Freedom Riders knew that once the buses they were on reached the Deep South, their lives would be in danger. And they were right; at Rock Hill, South Carolina, a white mob bloodied Lewis and several other Freedom Riders. More violence followed at Anniston, Alabama, and then again at Montgomery, where club-wielding thugs smashed Lewis over the head. But he stayed with the Freedom Ride to its final stop, in Jackson, Mississippi, where the police threw him into jail, and he spent 30 days at the Parchment Prison Farm.

Soon after Lewis obtained his release, the Interstate Commerce Commission ordered the South to desegregate its bus lines. Back in Nashville, Lewis continued to demonstrate, and the city's segregation laws came tumbling down. Impressed by his accomplishments and bravery, in 1963 fellow SNCC members elected him chairman.

In 1964 Lewis went to Mississippi to take part in Freedom Summer, the drive to register black voters in that state, and in 1965, acting independently of SNCC, he joined King's voting rights march from Selma, Alabama, to Montgomery. As the marchers left Selma and approached the Edmund Pettus Bridge, about 200 state troopers, sheriff's deputies, and posse members assaulted them with tear gas, fire hoses, and clubs wrapped in barbed wire. Lewis was knocked to the ground, and his skull fractured. He still bears a scar from the attack.

The Selma slaughter caused Congress to pass the Voting Rights Act later that year and made Lewis a hero among civil rights workers. Yet his goal of integrating U.S. society was criticized by blacks within SNCC who demanded black power. Lewis agreed with them that African Americans should run the civil rights campaign and whites should be kicked out of SNCC, but he adhered to his desire to integrate society at large and to his nonviolent beliefs. As a result in 1966 black-power advocate STOKELY CARMICHAEL wrested the SNCC chairmanship away from Lewis, and, shortly thereafter, Lewis quit the group.

Lewis then worked for the Voter Education Project (VEP) sponsored by a private foundation in Atlanta, Georgia. While still engaged in that effort, in 1968 he joined Robert F. Kennedy's presidential campaign. From 1970 to 1977 Lewis served as director of VEP and then was appointed by President Jimmy Carter to head a federal agency, Action, which supervised community-based economic recovery programs.

Lewis lost a race for Georgia's Fifth Congressional District and then ran for the Atlanta City Council, wining a seat in 1982 by promising to help the poor and elderly. He ran again for Congress in 1986, this time going up against a fellow black civil rights worker, JULIAN BOND, in the Democratic primary. Most observers expected Bond to win, but Lewis waged a strong, even vicious, campaign, in which he accused Bond of using drugs. After winning the primary, Lewis easily won the general election.

As a congressman Lewis continued to pursue his civil rights agenda, tied to his belief in a racially integrated society. He stuck to his program even after blacks who had lost faith in integration and wanted to maintain distinctive black institutions accused him of being a dinosaur.

In the mid-1990s Lewis vigorously attacked Republican conservatives intent on dismantling civil rights and welfare legislation. About them, in 1995 he warned, "They're coming for the children. They're coming for the poor. They're coming for the sick, the elderly, and the disabled." In 1998 Lewis published his book *Walking with the Wind: A Memoir of the Movement,* and in 2001 he and Republican congressman J. C. Watts of Oklahoma convinced Congress to pass legislation honoring the slaves who had helped build the Capitol.

Despite Lewis's record in Congress, he will likely be most remembered for his fortitude in the 1960s civil rights struggle, much as historian Sean Wilentz described him in a 1996 article for *The New Republic* as "a valiant, bloodied hero of the nation's greatest domestic struggle" in the 20th century.

Further Reading
Lewis, John. *Walking with the Wind: A Memoir of the Movement.* New York: Simon & Schuster, 1998.

Limbaugh, Rush Hudson
(1951–) *conservative reformer*

A radio talk show host and commentator from the late 1980s into the year 2002, Rush Hudson Limbaugh has stimulated a conservative reaction against liberal policies. He was born in Cape Girardeau, Missouri, in 1951 to Rush Hudson Limbaugh II and Millie Limbaugh.

Rush Limbaugh knew as a teenager that he wanted to be on the radio. He was a member of a wealthy Republican family, and his father, an attorney, expected that Rush would one day earn a college degree and go to law school. But in 1967, at age 16, Rush broadcast for the first time on station KGMO in Cape Girardeau, and he immediately wanted more. About shows that he tuned in to, Limbaugh recalled: "I'd be sitting at the breakfast table, dreading school and meanwhile listening to some guy on the radio who sounded like he was having a great time." Limbaugh attended Southeast Missouri State University but quit after one year and moved from place to place holding various radio jobs as a disc jockey (DJ), newsreader, and commentator.

With a medical deferment in hand, he managed to avoid the Vietnam War draft, and in 1971 he landed a broadcasting job at KQV in Pittsburgh, Pennsylvania. Shortly thereafter the manager told him he lacked talent and should get a job in sales. He soon did and went to work as a marketing executive for the Kansas City Royals baseball team, a position he held until 1983. "That was not a high point in my life," he recalled. "I was going nowhere. . . . I was not cut out for corporate conformity." So he returned to radio at station KMBZ in Chicago but was fired for being too controversial.

Limbaugh's big break occurred in 1984, when station KFBK in Sacramento, California, hired him to take the place of talk show host Morton Downey, Jr., who had accepted another job. Sacramento listeners liked Limbaugh's conservative attack on liberals and his wit, and his became the most listened to show in the city.

In 1988 producer Ed McLaughlin convinced Limbaugh to syndicate his broadcast across the country. McLaughlin brought him to New York City, and before long Limbaugh's show was being heard on hundreds of radio stations. His high ratings coincided with the country's conservative mood—the popularity of President Ronald Reagan, the discontentment with big government, even the sharp reactionary turn toward the militia movement in the early to mid-1990s.

Yet as much as the times made Limbaugh, he has made his own success. His humor and his talent for pithy but barbed comments have won over millions of fans. At various moments he has said:

> Feminism was established so that unattractive women could have access to the mainstream of society.
>
> I like the women's movement—from behind.
>
> If [pacifists] want to protest something, let them protest the wheel. It kills more people each year than nuclear bombs do.

Limbaugh once remarked that he considered himself more an entertainer than anything else, but clearly he has aimed his commentary at changing America, at steering it on a more conservative course. "I don't use this program for activism," Limbaugh said, "but if people act on what I say, then that's the icing on the cake." *U.S. News and World Report* stated in 1993, "However he is defined, Limbaugh is a growing force in American politics. When congressmen go home to their districts, Democrats and Republicans alike find themselves berated by constituents spouting Limbaughisms."

Yet Limbaugh has polarized society: One survey has found that whereas 33 percent of Americans like him, 30 percent dislike him. And his acerbic assaults that have favored Republicans over Democrats have contributed to intolerance in political debate (though by most accounts Limbaugh himself has been tolerant of opposing views).

In the late 1990s critics attacked Limbaugh for his many factual inaccuracies, and the waning conservative fervor weakened his ratings. But in 2002 Limbaugh was still attracting a large audi-

ence, and in July 2001 he signed a contract with Clear Channel radio for a salary of $250 million over eight years, making him, in the words of one analyst, "the highest paid voice in the history of radio." In January 2002 Limbaugh announced that an implant in his left ear had cured him of near total deafness, which had overtaken him a few months earlier.

Further Reading

Colford, Paul D. *The Rush Limbaugh Story: Talent on Loan from God: An Unauthorized Biography.* New York: St. Martin's Press, 1993.

Limbaugh, Rush H. *See, I Told You So.* New York: Pocket Books, 1993.

———. *The Way Things Ought to Be.* New York: Pocket Books, 1992.

Perkins, Ray, Jr. *Logic and Mr. Limbaugh: A Dittohead's Guide to Fallacious Reasoning.* Chicago: Open Court, 1995.

Seib, Philip. *Rush Hour: Talk Radio, Politics, and the Rise of Rush Limbaugh.* Fort Worth, Tex.: Summit Group, 1993.

Livermore, Mary Ashton Rice

(1820–1905) *women's suffragist, temperance crusader*

Mary Ashton Rice Livermore was a writer, temperance crusader, and leader in the fight for women's suffrage. She was born Mary Ashton Rice on December 19, 1820, in Boston, Massachusetts, to Timothy Rice and Zebiah Vose Glover Ashton Rice.

Mary Rice graduated from the Hancock Grammar School in 1834 and entered the Female Seminary of Charlestown, near Boston. She completed her coursework there and continued at the school as a teacher. In 1845 she married Daniel Parker Livermore, a minister in the Universalist Church; they had two children. Eventually, Daniel Livermore's advocacy of temperance caused trouble with his congregation, who disagreed with him, and in 1857 the Livermores moved to Chicago.

When Daniel became editor of the *New Covenant,* a Universalist publication, Mary assisted him as associate editor. Abolitionist in outlook, the

This photo shows woman's suffragist Mary Ashton Rice Livermore around the year 1901. *(Library of Congress)*

Livermores sided with the Union in the Civil War, and during the conflict Mary volunteered to work for the Chicago (later Northwestern) Sanitary Commission, which had been formed to help the army acquire medical supplies for battlefield hospitals. She toured the North raising money for the commission and in that endeavor gained valuable experience as a public speaker.

Livermore's work in the Civil War convinced her that to be truly influential women must have the right to vote. So in 1868 she helped found the Illinois Woman Suffrage Association and became its first president. A year later she began a suffrage newspaper, *The Agitator*, which soon merged with *Woman's Journal*. She served as the new publication's editor and helped organize the American Woman Suffrage Association.

Mary Livermore and her family soon returned to Boston, settling in nearby Melrose, and she took part in 1870 in starting the Massachusetts Woman Suffrage Association. That year, working under the management of James Redpath, a promoter, she began touring the country as a speaker. In 1872 she gave up her editorship of the *Woman's Journal* to concentrate full time on her public speaking. In her most famous lecture, "What Shall We Do with Our Daughters?" she advocated that women receive higher education and professional training.

Livermore continued lecturing until 1895. She also served for 10 years as president of the Massachusetts Women's Christian Temperance Union. Mary Livermore died on May 23, 1905.

Further Reading

Livermore, Mary Ashton Rice. *The Story of My Life: Or, the Sunshine and Shadow of Seventy Years.* New York: Arno Press, 1974.

———. *My Story of the War: The Civil War Memories of the Famous Nurse, Relief Organizer, and Suffragette.* New York: De Capo Press, 1995.

Lovejoy, Elijah Parish
(1802–1837) *abolitionist*

Influenced by the Presbyterian faith, Elijah Parish Lovejoy became an abolitionist and died defending his views. He was born on November 9, 1802, in Albion, Maine, to Reverend Daniel Lovejoy and Elizabeth Pattee Lovejoy.

Lovejoy graduated from Waterville (today Colby) College in 1826. The following year he moved to Saint Louis, Missouri, where he taught school and edited a newspaper. In 1832 he decided to follow his father into the ministry and entered the seminary at Princeton in New Jersey. He received his license to preach in April 1833 and returned to Saint Louis, where he edited a Presbyterian weekly, the *St. Louis Observer*. In 1835 he married Celia Ann French.

That same year several residents met with him and demanded that he end his editorial comments in the *Observer* that called for the abolition of slavery. Although at that time Lovejoy advocated only a gradual end to slavery, in Saint Louis even such a limited proposal met with strong resistance.

Lovejoy refused to accede to the demands, however, and in 1836 published a story about the lynching of a free African American in the city. When he was then threatened with physical attack, he moved in 1837 to Alton, Illinois, about 25 miles up the Mississippi River. A town settled in part by New Englanders, Alton contained a greater number of people sympathetic to his views.

Yet many still opposed him. During his move he left his printing press unguarded on the Alton wharf, and his enemies dumped it into the river. Several citizens of Alton subsequently raised money for a new press, and Lovejoy began publishing and editing the *Alton Observer*.

His views grew more radical, however, and elicited yet more protests when he called for the immediate end to slavery. (In a convoluted argument he had for years linked the evils of human bondage to the pope and condemned the Catholic Church.) On July 4, 1837, he printed a call for a meeting in Alton to form a state chapter of the American Anti-Slavery Society. Mobs then attacked Lovejoy's printing press and destroyed it, whereupon the Ohio Anti-Slavery Society sent him a new one, only to have it destroyed by another mob. To demands that he leave Alton, Lovejoy said, "Should I attempt it, I should feel that the angel of the Lord, with his flaming sword, was pursuing me wherever I went. It is because I fear God that I am not afraid of all who oppose me in this city."

Yet another press was sent to Lovejoy, and this time 60 abolitionists guarded it as it sat in a warehouse. On the night of November 7 an armed mob assaulted the building. When they started to set fire to it, Lovejoy rushed outside, and as he tried to prevent the torching, he was shot and killed.

Lovejoy's death shocked northerners and caused a wave of indignation in the region. Some who later joined the abolitionist movement recalled this event as the one that awakened them to the evil of slavery, an institution that slaveholders would protect to the point of using violence to destroy freedom of speech and of the press.

Further Reading

Merton L. Dillon. *Elijah P. Lovejoy: Abolitionist Editor.* Urbana: University of Illinois Press, 1961.

Gill, John. *Tide without Turning: Elijah P. Lovejoy and Freedom of the Press.* Boston: Starr King Press, 1958.

Simon, Paul. *Freedom's Champion: Elijah Lovejoy.* Carbondale: Southern Illinois University Press, 1994.

Lundy, Benjamin
(1789–1839) *abolitionist*

Through his newspaper publishing and pamphlet writing, Benjamin Lundy became what one historian has called the "greatest of pioneer abolitionists." He was born on January 7, 1789, to Quaker parents Joseph Lundy and Eliza Shotwell Lundy.

Benjamin Lundy received only an elementary education before leaving his hometown of Philadelphia in 1808 and settling in Wheeling, Virginia. There he learned the saddler's trade and for the first time saw slaves chained together as they passed through town on their way to be sold at markets. He moved to Saint Clairsville, Ohio, married Esther Lewis, and founded the Union Humane Society, an early organization dedicated to rallying political support for ending slavery, in 1815. He was among the first social activists to call for the formation of antislavery societies throughout the country.

Lundy contributed abolitionist articles to *The Philanthropist*, a newspaper published at Mount Pleasant, Ohio, by Charles Osborn, and traveled to Missouri in 1819; there he campaigned against that territory's entering the Union as a slave state, a battle that he lost. In January 1821 he returned to Mount Pleasant and began publishing *The Genius of Universal Emancipation*. Shortly thereafter he relocated to Greeneville, Tennessee, and in 1824 to Baltimore, Maryland. Lundy advocated the gradual emancipation of blacks and believed they should be resettled in colonies outside the United States. He subsequently visited Haiti, Canada, and Texas in search of suitable locations for colonization.

In 1828 Lundy lectured in several northern states and met the young abolitionist WILLIAM LLOYD GARRISON. Lundy invited Garrison to join him in publishing *The Genius*, and in 1829 the young man became the newspaper's associate editor. Differences soon separated them, however, as Garrison called for an immediate end to slavery— a more radical stand than the one held by Lundy—and through his uncompromising pen involved Lundy in lawsuits filed by slaveowners.

Lundy continued to publish *The Genius* until 1835. The following year he moved to Philadelphia and began *The National Enquirer and Constitutional Advocate of Universal Liberty*, in whose pages he exposed what he called a plot by slaveowners to take Texas from Mexico and add it to the United States as a slave state.

At the same time he published his influential pamphlet *The War in Texas* (1836), which began with the words "PEOPLE OF AMERICA!—Again I entreat you. . . . Let your voice be heard, immediately, in the strongest language of reprobation, and denunciation of the UNHALLOWED SCHEME." In describing the war for independence then being fought by Anglos in Texas against Mexican rule, Lundy stated:

> The prime cause, and the real objects of this war, are not distinctly understood by a large portion of . . . the well-meaning citizens of the United States. . . . They have been induced to believe that the inhabitants of Texas were engaged in a legitimate contest for the maintenance of the sacred principles of Liberty, and the natural, inalienable Rights of Man. . . . [But] the immediate cause and the leading object of this contest originated in a settled design, among the slaveholders of this country . . . to wrest the large and valuable territory of Texas from the Mexican Republic, in order to re-establish the SYSTEM OF SLAVERY: to open a vast and profitable SLAVE MARKET therein; and, ultimately, to annex it to the United States.

Among those influenced by the pamphlet was Congressman John Quincy Adams of Massachusetts, who on the floor of the House of Representatives echoed Lundy's opposition to annexation. Lundy published *The Enquirer* until 1838; later that year an antiabolitionist mob besieged him, and in 1839 he moved to Lowell, Illi-

nois. There he resumed publishing *The Genius*. After a brief illness he died on August 22, 1839.

Further Reading

Dillon, Merton L. *Benjamin Lundy and the Struggle for Negro Freedom*. Urbana: University of Illinois Press, 1966.

Lynd, Staughton
(1929–) *peace activist, antiwar activist*

A historian and peace and antiwar activist, Staughton Lynd condemned American fighting in Vietnam. He was born on November 22, 1929, in Philadelphia, Pennsylvania, to Robert S. Lynd and Helen Merrell Lynd, sociologists famous for their book *Middletown* (1929).

A bright child, Staughton Lynd benefited from his parents' emphasis on intellectual development and from their Quaker heritage. His father was a professor of sociology at Columbia University in New York City, and his mother held the rank of professor at Sarah Lawrence College in Bronxville, New York. Young Staughton received his education at the Ethical Culture School in Manhattan and Fieldston School, a private institution in the Bronx, New York. In the late 1940s he attended Harvard University on an academic scholarship; there he joined left-wing political groups and at one point affiliated with a communist organization.

Lynd obtained a B.A. degree from Harvard in 1951 with a major in history and entered graduate school at the University of Chicago. Two years later, however, the army drafted him. This caused a predicament: On the one hand, his devout Quaker beliefs made him a pacifist; on the other, he was reluctant to avoid all military service while men his age were fighting in Korea. So he accepted induction but took a noncombatant assignment. But one year later he received a dishonorable discharge because of his previous communist affiliation.

Lynd and his wife, Alice Niles, then moved to a Quaker commune in Georgia. In 1958 they relocated to New York City, where Lynd engaged in community work on the Lower East Side. The following year, after a Supreme Court ruling overturned his dishonorable discharge, changing it to an honorable one and making him eligible for government issue (GI) benefits, he entered graduate school at Columbia University.

In 1962 Lynd received a doctorate in American history and began teaching at a black school, Spelman College, in Atlanta, Georgia. At the same time he engaged in the civil rights demonstrations then spreading across the South. Among his activities, he headed the Freedom Schools project in Mississippi, where he taught African Americans about their constitutional rights, including their voting rights.

Lynd remained dedicated to his scholarly work and produced several impressive articles and books for academic publishers and a wider audience. His *Anti-Federalism in Dutchess County, New York: A Study of Democracy and Class Conflict in the Revolutionary Era* (1962) earned favorable reviews, and articles he wrote appeared in *Commentary, The Nation,* and *New Republic.*

In 1964 Yale University hired Lynd to teach American history, and he moved to Connecticut; there he joined the antiwar movement to protest America's involvement in Vietnam. In April 1965 he and several other demonstrators were arrested in Washington, D.C., when they tried to barge onto the floor of the House of Representatives.

Later that year Lynd took a trip to North Vietnam that raised a storm of controversy. He traveled there with TOM HAYDEN, a left-wing activist prominent with Students for a Democratic Society, and Herbert Aptheker, a pronounced communist. Lynd worried about traveling to North Vietnam with Aptheker, fearing that their association would appear to be an endorsement of communism, but the North Vietnamese had issued the invitation and set the rules: A communist must accompany him.

Lynd believed his journey could lead to successful negotiations between the United States and North Vietnam to end the war. Instead, the trip changed his career. While in North Vietnam Lynd, although wary of Vietnamese deceit in the war, compared the revolution there to democracy in the United States. In *The Other Side* (1967), a book he wrote with Hayden, he stated: "We suspect the colonial American town meetings and current village meetings . . . have much in common, especially the concept of 'grass-roots' or 'rice-roots' democracy."

On an even more controversial note, while in North Vietnam he pronounced the American military presence immoral and antidemocratic. This assessment received widespread press coverage in the United States and angered conservatives, especially wealthy alumni at Yale. When Lynd returned home, he found his job in jeopardy. Officially, he took an extended leave of absence (without pay); unofficially, Yale's administration had let it be known he should find a job elsewhere.

Rejected by Yale and widely criticized by others, Lynd was a hero and a leading figure in the developing New Left political movement. Searching for a place in academia, he applied while on his leave for teaching positions at other colleges, at first to no avail. Finally, in 1967 Chicago State University agreed to hire him for one year.

Lynd moved to Illinois, only to have the Board of Governors of State Colleges and Universities refuse to grant him a contract, basing its decision on his antiwar activity in North Vietnam. He then sued the board, a move that caused it to relent and allowed him to be hired.

In 1968 Lynd's contract at Chicago State expired, and as expected Yale, the college from which he was still on leave, refused to grant him tenure despite his scholarly achievements. He then formally resigned and concentrated on his antiwar activities. That same year he published two historical works praised by historians, *Class Conflict, Slavery, and the United States Constitution* and *Intellectual Origins of American Radicalism.* Written from a New Left viewpoint, these established Lynd's credentials as a radical historian.

Lynd participated in antiwar demonstrations held at the 1968 Democratic National Convention in Chicago and was arrested. Several months later he testified on behalf of the Chicago Seven—Hayden and six other radicals who were on trial for conspiring to incite a riot outside the convention—and favorably compared the radicals' actions to the activities of the resistance to Britain during the American Revolution. Nevertheless, Lynd had serious misgivings about the New Left: Ever since 1966 he had been disenchanted with its internal divisions and its penchant for repeating communist dogma and resorting to violence.

Since Lynd had no hope of ever being hired by a college, he decided to change professions and in 1973 enrolled in law school at the University of Chicago. Three years later he graduated and began representing workers as a labor lawyer.

In the 1980s Lynd continued his law career and wrote a book about the steel industry and labor's place in it. He also joined steelworkers in Youngstown, Ohio, in fighting the closing of the plants where they worked. Into the 1990s he wrote books aimed at motivating workers to stand up for their rights. He broke with many liberals when he urged leftists to oppose President Bill Clinton as a sellout and a hypocrite, someone who talked about compassion but did little to correct economic injustice. Clearly, Lynd was holding on to the principles and humanitarianism he had embraced as a young man.

Further Reading

Lynd, Staughton. *Solidarity Unionism: Rebuilding the Labor Movement from Below.* Chicago: Charles H. Kerr, 1992.

———. *"We Are All Leaders": The Alternative Unionism of the Early 1930s.* Urbana: University of Illinois Press, 1996.

Lynd, Staughton, and Alice Lynd, eds. *The New Rank and File.* Ithaca, N.Y.: ILR Press, 2000.

M

Magón, Ricardo Flores   See FLORES MAGÓN, RICARDO.

Malcolm X
(Malcolm Little, "Detroit Red," El-Hajj Malik El-Shabazz)
(1925–1965) *black nationalist*

A dynamic organizer for the Nation of Islam, Malcolm X had a short but controversial life. He was born Malcolm Little on May 19, 1925, in Omaha, Nebraska, to Earl Little and Louise Norton Little.

In 1965 Malcolm X began his autobiography (as told to Alex Haley) with the following words:

> When my mother was pregnant with me, she told me later, a party of hooded Ku Klux Klan riders galloped up to our home in Omaha, Nebraska, one night. Surrounding the house, brandishing their shotguns and rifles, they shouted for my father to come out. My mother went to the front door and opened it. Standing where they could see her pregnant condition, she told them that she was alone with her three small children, and that my father was away, preaching, in Milwaukee. The Klansmen shouted threats and warnings at her that we had better get out of town because "the good Christian white people" were not going to stand for my father's "spreading trouble" among the "good" Negroes of Omaha with the "back to Africa" preachings of MARCUS GARVEY.

In that paragraph Malcolm X revealed the racism, and his consciousness of it, that defined his life. His father was a Baptist minister and organizer for Marcus Garvey's Universal Negro Improvement Association, which extolled black pride. For reasons unclear, Earl Little moved his family to Lansing, Michigan, and shortly afterward the white racists appeared again, this time as the Black Legionnaires, who set fire to the family's home. "I remember," Malcolm X recalled, "we were outside in the night in our underwear, crying and yelling our heads off. The white police and firemen came and stood around watching as the house burned down to the ground."

Earl Little frequently beat his wife and children, except his son Malcolm. As the youngster remembered it, that may have been because he was the lightest of the children, and because blacks were "brainwashed" by white society to think of white as better, they treated their lighter-skinned children leniently. In 1931 Reverend Little was found dead near a streetcar line; the police called it a suicide, but many others, Malcolm included, believed he had been murdered.

Devastated by her husband's death, Louise Little was evaluated by state officials as psychologically unstable, and Malcolm and his siblings were placed in foster homes. Despite that disruption, he excelled at school and began to think about becoming a lawyer. When he revealed his aspiration to his white junior high school teacher, he was told that his goal was unsuitable "for a nigger" and was advised to think about becoming a carpenter.

Again racism had shattered Malcolm Little's life, and when he finished the eighth grade he dropped out of school. At age 17 he went to Boston to live with his half-sister. To make money he worked on a railroad that ran to New York City, and he spent more and more time in Harlem. He began to engage in a variety of activities, some legal and some illegal. He waited on tables, shined shoes, gambled, sold bootleg liquor, dealt drugs, and pimped. He swore, he drank, and he tried to look more white by dying and straightening his hair. Malcolm recalled: "The mirror reflected [my friend] Shorty behind me. We both were grinning. . . . And on top of my head was this thick, smooth sheen of shining red hair—real red—as straight as any white man's." On the streets he was called "Detroit Red."

In 1946 Malcolm Little was arrested in Boston for burglary and sentenced to 10 years in prison. He later said that when he began his sentence he was an atheist and uncouth, with a vocabulary of no more than 200 words. All of that changed. In 1948 he received two letters. One, from his brother Philbert, told about how he had discovered a new religion, the Nation of Islam. It was, Philbert Little said, the only real religion for a black person. Another letter, from his brother Reginald Little, advised him to quit smoking cigarettes and refrain from eating pork. Malcolm did not understand why Reginald had emphasized those points, nor did he see a connection between the two letters.

But then Reginald visited him and told him that members of the Nation of Islam stayed away from cigarettes, pork, and drugs, and anything else harmful to the body; moreover, they did not drink alcohol and refrained from sex outside marriage. Malcolm finally put Philbert's letter together with Reginald's and realized how they had both been talking about the same religion and had both converted to it.

Reginald told Malcolm that the Nation of Islam, through its spiritual leader, Elijah Muhammad, believed that God, or Allah, had created blacks as the first race, and in ancient times Yacub, a black scientist, had rebelled against Allah by creating a devilish people with bleached skin—the white race. Whites had ruled the Earth for 6,000 years, but their time was nearing an end; the original black race would soon give birth to a leader instilled with wisdom and unlimited power.

These ideas from the Nation of Islam made it clear to Malcolm why he had been treated so brutally by whites and why blacks had suffered at the hands of white people. Whites were created to be that way; it was innate to them; they could be no different. "The white people I had known marched before my mind's eye . . . ," Malcolm recalled:

> The white people who kept calling my mother "crazy" to her face and before me and my brothers and sisters, until she was finally taken off by white people to the Kalamazoo asylum . . . the white judge and others who had split up the children . . . white youngsters I was in school . . . with, and the teachers—the one who told me in the eighth grade to "be a carpenter" because thinking of being a lawyer was foolish for a Negro.

Reginald told Malcolm that whites had robbed blacks of their names and their identities and had erased from their memories nearly all knowledge of their African homeland. Other relatives who wrote to Malcolm revealed that they, too, had converted to the Nation of Islam; that they had become Black Muslims. They urged him to "accept the teachings of The Honorable Elijah Muhammad."

Through literature that they sent him, Malcolm learned about the great civilizations once built by blacks in Africa. He learned that whites had perpetrated the greatest crime in history by enslaving blacks and forcibly taking them to the Americas. He learned that whites had raped black women and had diluted the black race by creating mulattoes. And he learned that Christianity equated black with evil and white with good, causing black people to be reviled. Furthermore, Christianity taught blacks to be servile to whites—to sing and pray and do whatever white people wanted.

Malcolm read more than Black Muslim literature. He read classic and modern intellectual works—philosophies, histories, political treatises. He read so much and in such poor light in prison that his eyesight deteriorated. But he kept on reading, a veritable library, and kept on learning:

Herodotus, Harriet Beecher Stowe, Mohandas Gandhi, Will Durant, Schopenhauer.

Malcolm wrote:

> I preferred reading in the total isolation of my own room.
>
> Ten guards and the warden couldn't have torn me out of those books.
>
> I never will forget how shocked I was when I began reading about slavery's total horror.

Malcolm concluded: "History has been so 'whitened' by the white man that even the black professors have known little more than the most ignorant black man about the talents and rich civilizations and cultures of the black man of millenniums ago." He would leave prison a Black Muslim in outlook, as well as educated, articulate, and freed of the profanity and crime that had been his previous life.

Within weeks after his parole in 1952, Malcolm Little met Elijah Muhammad at the headquarters of the Nation of Islam in Chicago. Shortly after that meeting he converted and replaced his last name Little, the one given his family by whites, with X, representing the African name he never would be able to know. The following summer Malcolm X was made assistant minister of Detroit's Temple Number One.

Malcolm X organized temples in Boston and Philadelphia, and he showed his considerable skill as a public speaker, whereupon in 1954 Elijah Muhammad appointed him minister of Harlem's Temple Number Seven, one of the most important temples within the Nation of Islam.

Although the growth of the Black Muslims in the 1950s resulted in great measure from the work and influence of Malcolm X, other factors contributed to the change: the general belief among blacks that they should no longer accept a second-class citizenship, the population surge among young African Americans, and the very nature of Black Muslim beliefs and activities, which offered a source of pride. The Nation of Islam was, after all, more than a religion: It operated black-owned farms, bakeries, supermarkets, and restaurants.

Malcolm wrote a widely read column for the *Amsterdam News* and later the *Los Angeles Herald Dispatch,* both prominent black newspapers. In 1961 he founded *Muhammad Speaks,* the official organ of the Nation of Islam. Meanwhile, in 1958 he married Betty Shabazz (born Betty Dean Sanders). They had their first child in 1959 and would have five more.

Malcolm X and the Black Muslims disagreed with the civil rights movement as led by MARTIN LUTHER KING, JR., and his Southern Christian Leadership Conference. Whereas King wanted integration with whites, the Black Muslims wanted separation from them. They were black nationalists who believed that the devil—white people—could never be reformed and that blacks should stay away from such evil.

Malcolm X's rising star in the Nation of Islam came tumbling down in 1963. At a rally on De-

After a dispute with the leader of the Nation of Islam, Malcolm X was slain while attempting to speak to his followers in Harlem. *(New York World-Telegram and the Sun Newspaper Photograph Collection, Library of Congress)*

cember 1 he referred to President John F. Kennedy's assassination as a case of "the chickens coming home to roost," meaning that the same hatred that whites had directed at blacks had felled the president. Whites and blacks labeled the remark insensitive, and Elijah Muhammad ordered that Black Muslims disown the statement and that Malcolm X be prohibited from speaking publicly for 90 days. Muhammad's anger, however, was a response to more than that statement: He feared that his protégé was becoming too popular and too powerful and so must be contained.

For his part, Malcolm X had heard rumors about Muhammad's jealousy and had also heard that Muhammad had engaged in extramarital affairs, a practice that to Malcolm X made Muhammad a hypocrite. Malcolm X was also discontented with the separationist stand of the Black Muslims, which he felt did nothing to alleviate the racial discrimination blacks suffered and put the Black Muslims in agreement with the Ku Klux Klan (KKK) and other white supremacists who said blacks and whites should live segregated from each other. Indeed, back in 1961 Muhammad had sent him to meet with leaders of the KKK to win white supremacist support for a separate black state.

So in 1964 Malcolm X quit the Black Muslims and formed his own group, Muslim Mosque, Inc. That April he took a trip that proved to be another turning point in his life: a pilgrimage to Mecca, the holy city of Islam.

The pilgrimage, and his journeys elsewhere in the Middle East and in Africa, revealed to him how wrong he and the Black Muslims had been about the issue of race. Malcolm X still believed that whites were oppressive and that blacks must fight for their rights. But everywhere he went among Muslims he found no discrimination based on race and certainly no belief that whites were the devil. Islam, he concluded, had been corrupted in America by the Nation of Islam. Whites, he now said, did evil things, but rather than the result of innate characteristics, their evil was the result of racial prejudice rampant in Western culture. As a result, whites could change.

In June 1964 Malcolm X formed the Organization of Afro-American Unity to draw together blacks of different faiths and ideologies. He called for blacks to control their economies, and he stated that in both developing nations and America capitalistic exploitation and racist oppression relied on each other.

Malcolm X changed his name to El-Hajj Malik El-Shabazz and met with prominent black leaders, including Martin Luther King, Jr.; JOHN ROBERT LEWIS; FANNIE LOU HAMER; and ROSA PARKS, to build relations with them. But in so doing he antagonized the Black Muslims. At the same time the Federal Bureau of Investigation (FBI) worried that he might prove to be a dynamic black leader who would lead African Americans to rebel against the government.

While the FBI watched him, the Black Muslims attacked him. At Elijah Muhammad's behest Louis X, later known as Louis Farrakhan, wrote in *Muhammad Speaks* that Malcolm had accepted nonbelievers as his friends and that "no Muslim is a Muslim who accepts such people as his brothers." He warned: "Such a man as Malcolm is worthy of death."

Malcolm had long predicted that he would die violently. That prophecy was reinforced on February 14, 1965, when his home was firebombed. He believed that the Nation of Islam and the federal government wanted him killed. The next Sunday, on February 21, 1965, he was scheduled to address his followers gathered at the Audubon Ballroom in New York City. As he rose to speak three men stood up and fired 16 shots at him. He died 90 minutes later. Two of the three assassins were Black Muslims, but at the trial where they were sentenced to life terms it was not proven that they had been ordered by the Nation of Islam to kill Malcolm.

In the year 2000 Louis Farrakhan, by then head of the Black Muslims, admitted to television correspondent Mike Wallace, "I may have been complicit in words that I spoke leading up to February 21. I acknowledge that and regret that any word that I have said caused the loss of life of a human being."

About his trip to Mecca, Malcolm X had said it was "the first time I had ever stood before the Creator of All and felt like a complete human being." He added "I'm a human being first and foremost, and as such I'm for whoever and whatever benefits humanity as a whole."

Further Reading

Evanzz, Karl. *The Judas Factor: The Plot to Kill Malcolm X.* New York: Thunder's Mouth Press, 1992.

Friedly, MIchael. *Malcolm X: The Assassination.* New York: Carroll & Graf, 1992.

Goldman, Peter Louis. *The Death and Life of Malcolm X.* 2nd ed. Urbana: University of Illinois Press, 1979.

Karim, Benjamin. *Remembering Malcolm.* New York: Carroll & Graf, 1992.

Malcolm X. *The Autobiography of Malcolm X, with the Assistance of Alex Haley.* New York, Grove Press, 1965.

Wood, Joe, ed. *Malcolm X: In Our Own Image.* New York: St. Martin's Press, 1992.

Mann, Horace
(1796–1859) *education reformer*

A politician and educator, Horace Mann led reforms that revolutionized schooling in Massachusetts and in other states. He was born on May 4, 1796, in Franklin, Massachusetts, to Thomas Mann and Rebecca Stanley Mann.

Horace Mann grew up in great poverty on his father's farm amid a stern Puritanism that made him, as a child, fear God and, as an adult, accept the need for moral guidance in society. He received little formal education, but in 1816, over a span of a few months, he studied so assiduously under a tutor that he gained acceptance to Brown University in Providence, Rhode Island. He graduated from there in 1819 with high honors, entered the Litchfield Law School in Connecticut in 1821, and was admitted to the bar in Massachusetts in 1823.

Mann began his law practice in Dedham before moving several years later to Boston. At the same time he entered politics, winning election in 1827 to the state House of Representatives, where he held office for six years. While serving in the legislature, he married Charlotte Messer, the daughter of Asa Messer, president of Brown University, in 1830. Her death in August 1832 shattered Mann and left him scrambling to find meaning and direction in his life.

The following year he won election to the state Senate, but he remained dissatisfied with his political and law career. Still suffering the emptiness that followed his wife's death and raised to believe that people should, at some point in their lives, serve humanity, in 1837 he left the Senate to accept appointment as secretary, or director, of the recently created state board of education.

Mann wanted to improve an educational system long neglected and in poor shape. In Massachusetts—as indeed in many states—schools were open only a few weeks each year, teachers were unqualified, and school houses were so dilapidated that Mann once said "astronomy . . . could be studied in them to advantage, for through the rents in the roof the stars might all be seen as they came to zenith."

To interest the public in educational problems, he organized annual conventions in every county, at which clergymen, lawyers, and college professors addressed audiences consisting of teachers, school officials, and the general public. About teacher training Mann said, "Every teacher ought to know vastly more than he is required to teach, so they may be furnished, on every subject, with copious illustration and instructive anecdote; and so that the pupils may be disabused of the notion that they are apt to acquire, that they carry all knowledge in their satchels. . . . Every teacher should be possessed of a facility at explanation." Toward that end he worked with the legislature to fund normal schools where teachers could be trained. As a result Massachusetts established the first state-run normal schools in the country, beginning with one at Lexington.

In 1838 Mann founded the *Common School Journal*, dedicated to discussing school problems, and was its editor for 10 years. More important were his 12 annual reports, from 1837 to 1848, that thoroughly and clearly discussed school problems and possible solutions to them. Taken together, these reports provided the state with a coherent reform program.

Beginning in 1839 Massachusetts required that the school year last at least six months, and the legislature doubled appropriations for public school systems while increasing the pay for teachers. Although the state had passed a law in 1827 to establish high schools, it had been largely ignored; now under Mann's guidance 50 high schools were opened.

On the topic of religion, Mann stated that Bible instruction should take place at home; the Bible, he said, could be read in the public schools, but no lessons in it should be given. His stand raised the wrath of ministers, but he stood his ground in insisting that his policy be followed.

In 1843 Mann married Mary Tyler Peabody and traveled to Europe, where he studied the schools in several countries. He returned praising the German method for training teachers and instructing students.

Mann viewed public education as essential to democracy. He said that society would suffer if voters were ignorant. To him, education made the person. "As an apple is not in any proper sense an apple until it is ripe," he said, "so a human being is not in any proper sense a human being until he is educated." He also saw the schools as playing a crucial role in preventing economic exploitation:

> Universal education can counterwork [the] tendency to the domination of capital and the servility of labor. If one class possesses all the wealth and the education, while the residue of society is ignorant and poor, it matters not by what name the relation between them may be called: the latter, in fact and in truth, will be the servile dependents and subjects of the former. But if education can be equally diffused, it will draw property after it by the strongest of attractions; for such a thing never did happen, and never can happen, as that an intelligent and practical body of men should be permanently poor. . . .
> Education, then, beyond all other devices of human origin, is a great equalizer of the conditions of men—the balance wheel of the social machinery.

And despite his aversion to biblical lessons, Mann believed the schools should teach moral values. According to historian Louis Filler, the educational leader "believed that people had souls, and that these souls could be perverted to produce devils." Mann thought that education without moral values created only a monster, more dangerous than an illiterate devil.

Horace Mann returned to politics in 1848, winning election to the U.S. House of Representatives. He resigned as secretary of the state board of education and while in Congress spoke out against slavery. In 1852 he lost his bid to become governor of Massachusetts as the Free Soil candidate.

He then accepted the presidency of Antioch College in Yellow Springs, Ohio—a school known for its openness to all students regardless of race, sex, or religion—but his tenure turned out to be disappointing. During Mann's presidency the college suffered from mismanagement and poor finances, and in 1859 he returned to Massachusetts.

Exhausted from his experience at Antioch and from his many years of working for educational reform, Mann suffered declining health. He died on August 2, 1859, survived by his wife and three sons. "Even on the atheistic hypothesis of no God," Horace Mann once wrote, "it could be shown that Duty is expedient; but on the theistic hypothesis of a God, it can be demonstrated that the knowledge and performance of Duty are the highest moral necessities for every human being."

Further Reading

Eakin, Sybil. "Giants of American Education: Horace Mann." *Technos: Quarterly for Education and Technology* 9 (Summer 2000): 4+.

Filler, Louis, ed. *Horace Mann on the Crisis in Education.* Boston: University Press of America, 1965.

Messerli, Jonathan. *Horace Mann: A Biography.* New York: Knopf, 1972.

Williams, Edward Irwin Franklin. *Horace Mann, Educational Statesman.* New York: Macmillan, 1937.

McDowell, Mary Eliza

(1854–1936) *immigrant advocate, health reformer*

Mary Eliza McDowell was the director of a Chicago settlement house and crusader for public health reform in that city's Packingtown district. She was born on November 30, 1854, in Cincinnati, Ohio, to Malcolm McDowell and Jane Welch Gordon McDowell.

In the mid-1860s Mary McDowell moved to Chicago when her father established a steel mill

As a Progressive, Mary McDowell helped to improve Chicago's polluted Packingtown district. *(Library of Congress)*

there. Her involvement in social causes began in 1871, when she helped provide relief for those displaced by the great Chicago fire. After her family moved to Evanston, she met temperance leader FRANCES ELIZABETH CAROLINE WILLARD during a gathering in that town and joined the Woman's Christian Temperance Union.

In 1890 McDowell moved to Hull-House, a settlement house founded in Chicago by JANE ADDAMS to assist immigrants. With that action McDowell joined the Progressive reform movement then gaining momentum in America's cities and aimed at correcting numerous abuses arising from industrial and urban growth. Four years later faculty at the University of Chicago asked her to head

a new settlement house to be located behind the Union Stockyards, and she agreed.

"Packingtown," as the district was called, encompassed one square mile and on three sides was bordered by industrial debris: stockyards and slaughterhouses on the east, a garbage dump on the west, and Bubbly Creek, a polluted arm of the Chicago River, on the north. At the settlement house McDowell provided classes in arts and crafts, sewing, and cooking, and she established a library and formed various clubs and groups to help immigrants adjust to American society. Outside the settlement house she launched a campaign to improve Packingtown. Having visited Europe in 1911 and investigated garbage disposal there, she convinced Chicago's leaders to build incinerators and persuaded the city and the meat packers to finance a sewer that would alleviate the flow of refuse from the stockyards into Bubbly Creek.

Meanwhile, McDowell encouraged workers to join labor unions, and she founded the Illinois Women's Trade Union League in 1903, the same year she helped organize the National Women's Trade Union League. She served as president of the Illinois group from 1904 to 1907. McDowell played an important role in persuading President Theodore Roosevelt to start a government investigation of women and child labor in industry.

The Chicago race riots of 1919 caused her to found the Interracial Cooperative Committee to promote greater civic contact between whites and blacks. She was also active in the National Association for the Advancement of Colored People, the Urban League of Chicago, and the Immigrant's Protection League. In 1923 Mayor William E. Dever appointed her commissioner of public welfare; four years later a conservative mayor removed her from office.

Mary McDowell continued as director of the University of Chicago Settlement House until her retirement in 1929. She died on October 14, 1936, from a paralytic stroke.

Further Reading

Davis, Allen Freeman. *Spearheads for Reform: The Social Settlements and the Progressive Movement, 1890–1914.* New Brunswick, N.J.: Rutgers University Press, 1984.

Spain, Daphne. *How Women Saved the City.* Minneapolis: University of Minnesota Press, 2001.

Wilson, Howard Eugene. *Mary McDowell, Neighbor.* Chicago: University of Chicago Press, 1928.

McNickle, William D'Arcy

(1904–1977) *Indian rights advocate*

William D'Arcy McNickle was a writer and Indian rights activist. He was born on January 18, 1904, at Saint Ignatius on the Flathead Indian reservation in northwestern Montana and went by the name D'Arcy. His father was William McNickle, an Irish rancher, and his mother was Philomene Parenteau, a mixed blood Canadian woman of Cree descent who had been adopted into the Flathead tribe.

William D'Arcy McNickle felt drawn to his Indian heritage, and the conflict between that heritage and white values shaped his life and his writing. As a boy McNickle was sent for three years to the Chemawa Indian School, run by the Bureau of Indian Affairs (BIA) in Salem, Oregon. At that time the U.S. government used the schools to eradicate Indian culture from Native American children, and the students suffered beatings whenever they followed Indian practices.

In 1921 McNickle entered the University of Montana, where he began to write poetry and short stories, and as a senior he won a statewide poetry contest. Bachelor's degree in hand, he studied at Oxford University in England, but he left there when his finances ran low. He briefly resided in Paris before settling in New York City, where from 1928 to 1934 he worked as an editor for the *Encyclopaedia Britannica* and the *National Cyclopedia of American Biography.* At the same time he took courses at Columbia University and the New School for Social Research.

McNickle moved to Washington, D.C., in 1935 to work for the Federal Writers Project, a New Deal program. The following year his first novel, *The Surrounded*, was published to critical acclaim. The story tells of a young man, half Indian and half Spanish, torn by his conflicting attachment to both cultures.

Also in 1936 John Collier, commissioner of the BIA, appointed McNickle to his staff. In 18 years with the agency, McNickle worked as Collier's personal assistant, as a field representative, and as director of tribal relations. He helped protect Indian water rights and organize tribal councils and courts. And he served in 1940 as a representative to the first Pan-American Conference on Indian Life at Patzcuaro, Mexico. Four years later McNickle cofounded the National Congress of American Indians, intended to unite tribes into a politically influential group.

In 1949 McNickle published his book *They Came Here First: The Epic of the American Indian,* which used anthropological evidence to detail Native American history, including early contacts between Indians and whites. Dissatisfied with the BIA's increasing conservatism, he quit the agency in 1954, the same year his *Runner in the Sun: A Story of Indian Maize* was published.

McNickle moved to Boulder, Colorado, and founded the American Indian Development Corporation (AID) to raise private funds for health and education projects. While directing AID he wrote *Two Ways of Life Meet* (1959), with Harold Fey, and *Indian Tribes of North America* (1962).

In 1966 the University of Saskatchewan in Regina, Canada, appointed him professor of anthropology and chairman of the department. In 1971 he wrote *Indian Man: A Life of Oliver La Farge* and retired from the university to reside in Albuquerque, New Mexico, and concentrate on writing. He served also as founding director of the Center for the History of the American Indian at the Newberry Library in Chicago, to which he commuted.

William D'Arcy McNickle died of a heart attack on October 15, 1977. He was survived by two daughters from two marriages.

Further Reading

Parker, Dorothy. *Singing an Indian Song: A Biography of D'Arcy McNickle.* Lincoln: University of Nebraska Press, 1992.

Purdy, John Lloyd. *WordWays: The Novels of D'Arcy McNickle.* Tucson: University of Arizona Press, 1990.

Ruppert, James. *D'Arcy McNickle.* Boise, Idaho: Boise State University Press, 1988.

Means, Russell
(1939–) *Indian rights leader*

Russell Means emerged as a leader in the American Indian Movement (AIM) during the 1970s and continued over the next two decades to protest the white oppression of Native Americans. He was born near Greenwood, South Dakota, on the Pine Ridge Reservation on November 10, 1939. His father, Harold Means, was a mixed-blood Oglala Lakota Sioux, and his mother, Theodora Means, was a full-blooded Yankton Sioux.

According to Russell Means, his father endured an insufferable life as a youngster in Indian boarding schools. "They beat him with rubber hoses for speaking his language," Means recalled. "He was ashamed of being an Indian—of being himself." That experience left a deep impression on Means, as did the influence of his maternal grandfather, John Feather, who taught him to be proud of his Indian heritage.

At age three Russell Means moved with his family to Oakland, California, where his father worked in the shipyards as a welder and battled a continuing problem with alcoholism. At first Russell excelled in school, but then his family relocated to San Leandro, and he began skipping class, stealing, and drinking. His parents then sent him to the Winnebago Reservation in Nebraska, hoping that sending him there would improve his behavior, but when he returned to California he again fell into trouble and in 1958 barely graduated from San Leandro High School. Means later recalled that while he was growing up white kids would watch TV westerns in which Indians were portrayed as barbaric, and then they would taunt and fight him. "Every time some wise guy would mouth off," he said, "I'd figure I had to defend myself for bein' Indian."

Means moved to Los Angeles, kicked a drug habit, but then followed his father's path into alcoholism. He jumped from job to job and at one point worked as a dance instructor in San Francisco. He married and returned to the Pine Ridge Reservation when he found employment as a construction worker. In 1965 he attended Iowa Technical College in Ottumwa and in 1966 Arizona State University in Tempe; he never graduated.

Soon thereafter Means moved to Cleveland, Ohio, where he directed the government-funded American Indian Center and met Clyde Bellecourt and DENNIS JAMES BANKS, founders of the recently formed American Indian Movement. He embraced their militancy, later saying that he joined AIM because he had been frustrated by the loss of Indian culture. Begun in Minneapolis, Minnesota, AIM modeled itself after the California-based Black Panthers, patrolling the city's Indian ghetto to monitor police actions and prevent false arrests, harassment, and brutality—much as the Panthers had in African-American neighborhoods.

Means organized the Cleveland chapter of AIM, and on Thanksgiving Day 1970 he and several followers seized control of the ship *Mayflower II* in Plymouth, Massachusetts. As they protested the honoring of early America's Pilgrims, who had stolen Indian land, the national media covered the event, and the publicity propelled Means into the forefront of the radical Indian movement.

Over the next few months Means led a prayer vigil atop Mount Rushmore to protest the taking of land in South Dakota's Black Hills in the late 1800s (land considered sacred), and he filed a damage suit against the Cleveland Indians baseball club for its use of a mascot, Chief Wahoo, whose caricature Means claimed demeaned Native Americans.

Then in February 1972 Means led about 1,000 Indians into Gordon, Nebraska, where they protested the refusal of the town's authorities to file charges against two white men implicated in the murder of an Oglala Lakota. As was typical in other states, white persons who committed crimes against Indians seldom faced prosecution. The protest resulted in the two men's being tried, found guilty, and sentenced to prison; in the eyes of many Indians AIM's prestige, and that of Russell Means, rose to new heights. AIM, however, drew the attention of the federal government, and within a short time the Federal Bureau of Investigation (FBI) secretly infiltrated the group; as it did with other protest organizations in the 1960s and 1970s, it began illegal activities to destroy it. This action was consistent with long-standing federal policy to humble and discipline noncompliant Indians.

In 1972 Means resigned from his job at the American Indian Center and returned to the Pine Ridge Reservation. That summer he helped organize a caravan of about 2,000 Indians from more than 100 reservations who arrived in Washington, D.C., to stage a protest, the Trail of Broken Treaties. They wanted to expose the federal government's failure over the years to abide by its promises and treaty obligations.

Officials refused to meet with the protesters, however, leading about 400 of them to occupy the building that housed the Bureau of Indian Affairs. In the event that the government rejected AIM's demands, Means supported burning the building. But as it turned out President Richard Nixon agreed to consider the group's Twenty Points, which included a call for new treaties, changes in the law to protect existing treaty rights, and land reform. When the Indians evacuated the building they took with them government documents that showed that the BIA had violated Indian land and mineral rights on several reservations. Nixon subsequently ignored the Twenty Points.

A more violent confrontation erupted in 1973 at Wounded Knee on the Pine Ridge Reservation. For the Indians, Wounded Knee held special meaning: It was there in 1890 that the U.S. Army massacred more than 200 Lakota Sioux—largely elderly men, women, and children. Now in February 1973 Means and other members of AIM rallied at Wounded Knee to protest an alliance between the tribal president, Richard "Dickie" Wilson, and the federal government that threatened to result in white ranchers' gaining more rights to reservation lands and the government's acquiring access to rich uranium deposits.

Wilson's police force reacted to the protesters by surrounding them, and Means and some 200 Indians confiscated weapons from a trading post and erected barricades, thus creating a standoff. The federal government reacted by deploying marshals and enormous firepower, including armored personnel carriers, helicopters, and grenade launchers. When shots rang out—no one knows who fired first—the government forces assaulted AIM, and over the next few weeks sporadic fighting left two Indians dead in the AIM compound. As the government entered into talks with AIM, Means emerged as a negotiator, and in meetings with the press he strongly denounced federal actions. He joined six other AIM protesters in signing an agreement with federal officials, sealed with a traditional peace pipe ceremony, that called for a government investigation into the reservation leadership but provided no amnesty for the insurgents. He surrendered to U.S. marshals after the signing ceremony and was arraigned and then released on bond so he could attend meetings with the Nixon administration in Washington.

Although Means described the agreement as "a small victory, a preliminary victory, in our war with the U.S. over treaty rights," nothing resulted from an AIM demand that the government recognize the Fort Laramie Treaty signed in 1868. Yet Means claimed that the Wounded Knee occupation, which had lasted from February 28 to May 7, 1973, taught Indian youths to take pride in their heritage. Several years later he said, "Wounded Knee woke up America. We're still here, and we're resisting. John Wayne did not kill us all."

Means was arrested in late August 1973 in Winner, South Dakota, on charges of assault, conspiracy to commit arson, and participation in a riot stemming from his role in a protest earlier that year in the town of Custer. He eventually was convicted and served 43 days in jail.

In October 1973 Means stood trial in Saint Paul, Minnesota, for his role at Wounded Knee. At the same time he ran against Dickie Wilson for the Pine Ridge tribal presidency. Means lost in an election widely viewed as tainted by Wilson's corrupt tactics, but he won his case at Saint Paul when the judge threw out the charges against him and Dennis Banks on the grounds that the FBI had violated the wiretap law and that the federal government had engaged in numerous illegal activities.

Means returned to the Pine Ridge Reservation despite threats to his life by Wilson's supporters. In conflicts with tribal police he was shot in the back and in the chest, and his eye was gouged by a rifle. From 1978 to 1979 he served time in the South Dakota State Penitentiary for an altercation he engaged in with the police outside the Minnehaha County Courthouse in Sioux Falls.

In 1981 Means led another protest seeking the return of the Black Hills to the Sioux, during which he and several of his supporters occupied Yellow Thunder Camp. Two years later Means tried again to run for tribal president at Pine Ridge, but opponents blocked him, citing his prison record.

Over the years Means engaged in numerous disputes with AIM leaders, and as the group split into factions, he resigned, rejoined, and resigned from it on several occasions. In the mid-1980s he worsened the rift within AIM when he decided to support the Miskito Indians in Nicaragua in their fight against the leftist Sandinista government. Many AIM members backed the Sandinistas and criticized Means for taking a stand that supported the foreign policy of a conservative American president, Ronald Reagan. In November 1985 Means declared, "I do not support the racist policies of the United States of America, the same as I do not support the racist policies of Nicaragua."

In 1986 Means sought but failed to win the presidential nomination of the Libertarian Party. Five years later he again stirred controversy among his fellow Indians when he appeared in the movie *The Last of the Mohicans* as Chingachgook. Many Native Americans considered James Fenimore Cooper's novel, on which the movie was based, to be racist, and they claimed that Means had sold out to make big money in Hollywood. Means insisted that by making the movie he was actually fighting racism, but he admitted his fondness for his new career. "During *Mohicans,* I fell in love with acting," he said. "I hadn't realized I was an artist until I became an actor."

Yet Means returned to protesting in 1992 when he organized demonstrations against the Columbus Day parade in Denver, Colorado. According to Means, Columbus had begun the tactics of "relocation and extermination—the policy toward the Indians since 1492." As a result of the Means-led effort, Denver ended the annual parade.

In 1993 Means intensified the factional dispute within AIM when he organized the International Confederation of Autonomous Chapters of the American Indian Movement and in the Edge-

wood Declaration labeled the AIM Grand Governing Council in Minneapolis a "fringe element." Two years later he drew more criticism when he provided the voice for the character Chief Powhatan in the Disney cartoon movie *Pocahontas.* Fellow Native Americans compared his part to his *Last of the Mohicans* role and called the production a distortion and an insult to their culture. Means said he took the job to connect children to the world of Indians.

In an interview in May 1997, Means said, "Since 40 percent of America's mineral reserves are under Indian lands, white society and the government are still trying to eradicate my people with genocidal policies." He claimed, "I remain the most hated man in my home state of South Dakota, and wherever white men oppress Indians."

While the AIM Grand Governing Council attacked Means's "clownish antics," in 1999 he led a protest in Whiteclay, Nebraska, near the Pine Ridge Reservation, to demand that the police investigate the unsolved killings of several Indians. He also advocated restrictions on the sale of alcohol and recognition of the claim that, under the Fort Laramie Treaty, Whiteclay rightfully belonged to the Sioux. Some 250 marchers took part in the protest, in which Means declared: "We're here to tell all Nebraska—from the governor on down and especially the commissioners of Sheridan County—that we're going back to our agreement. We're going to force the government to give back our land." He was joined by two of his opponents from AIM, Dennis Banks and Clyde Bellecourt.

Russell Means spoke to the national convention of the Libertarian Party in summer 2000, and that fall he again led a protest against the Denver Columbus Day parade after Italian groups decided to revive the event. In 2002 he announced his candidacy for governor of New Mexico as an independent. Still the activist, Means insisted in his autobiography, "I am not a leader. I *am* an Oglala Lakota patriot. That is all I want and all I need to be."

Further Reading

Matthiessen, Peter. *In the Spirit of Crazy Horse.* New York: Viking Press, 1983.

Means, Russell. *Where White Men Fear to Tread: The Autobiography of Russell Means.* New York: St. Martin's Press, 1995.

Meany, George
(1894–1980) *union leader*

George Meany was a leader of the American Federation of Labor (AFL), an architect of its merger with the Congress of Industrial Organizations (CIO), and the destroyer of the new union's vitality. He was born on August 16, 1894, in New York City to Michael Joseph Meany, a plumber, and Anne Cullen Meany.

At age 16 George Meany quit school to enter his father's profession of plumber. After passing his journeyman's examination he emulated him in joining the Plumbers International Union (PIU), in which the elder Meany served as president of the Bronx chapter. In 1919 George Meany married Eugenia McMahon, a member of the International Ladies Garment Workers Union.

Meany won election in 1922 as business agent for the PIU Bronx chapter, which was affiliated with the American Federation of Labor, and he then spent the rest of his career as a full-time union official. In 1923 he added to his duties that of secretary of the New York City Building Trades Council, a position that gave him contact with local, state, and national labor leaders and politicians. From that base in 1934 he became president of the New York State Federation of Labor and lobbied the legislature for prounion bills.

A staunch Democrat, Meany supported Franklin D. Roosevelt and his New Deal program to fight the Great Depression. In 1940 he was elected secretary treasurer of the AFL, and the following year Roosevelt appointed him to serve on the National Defense Mediation Board, established to resolve differences between workers and management and to avert strikes as Americans prepared themselves for World War II.

Strongly anticommunist in the cold war, Meany nevertheless opposed the reactionary tactics of Senator Joseph McCarthy during the Red Scare of the early 1950s in which the federal government and state governments hunted down

George Meany was the architect of the merger between the American Federation of Labor and the Congress of Industrial Organizations. *(American Federation of Labor-Congress of Industrial Organizations, National Archives and Records Administration)*

communists and other radicals. In 1952 Meany was elected to succeed WILLIAM GREEN as president of the AFL. For his top goal he wanted to unite the AFL with the rival Congress of Industrial Organizations, and in 1955 the two unions completed their merger, thus forming the AFL-CIO. He worked hard to rid the union of corruption, a move that in 1957 resulted in the AFL-CIO's expelling from its ranks the International Brotherhood of Teamsters, then being led by JIMMY HOFFA.

For Meany the union mattered more than almost anything else; he had little concern or compassion beyond its confines. About nonunion workers he once said, "They could drop dead."

Meany supported the Vietnam War. Although he eventually cooled to it when he learned about the killing of civilians by American forces, according to historian Paul Buhle he called New York Democrats who opposed the war a "dirty-mouth group of kooks." Meany largely ignored the civil rights movement, and in the late 1960s he criticized radical protesters within it.

Overall, Meany embraced conservative social views and presided over a centralization of the AFL-CIO that decreased the power of the rank and file, making the union inflexible and unable to respond adequately to the changing labor market. As a result by the time he resigned the presidency in 1979, the AFL-CIO was in serious decline. Meany died on January 10, 1980.

Further Reading

Buhle, Paul. *Taking Care of Business: Samuel Gompers, George Meany, Lane Kirkland, and the Tragedy of American Labor.* New York: Monthly Review Press, 1999.

Goulden, Joseph C. *Meany.* New York: Atheneum, 1972.

Robinson, Archie. *George Meany and His Times.* New York: Simon & Schuster, 1981.

Meredith, James Howard

(1933–) *civil rights activist*

The African American James Meredith integrated the University of Mississippi in 1963, but he endorsed a white racist for political office in the 1990s. His was a strange odyssey marked by outrageous behavior and instability. Meredith was born on June 25, 1933, in Kosciusko, Mississippi, to Moses "Cap" Meredith, a farmer, and Roxie Smith Meredith.

As required of blacks in Mississippi at the time, James Meredith attended a racially segregated school in Kosciusko far inferior in quality to the white school. In 1950 his parents sent him to Saint Petersburg, Florida, to complete his last two years of secondary education at Gibbs High School. He graduated in 1951, joined the U.S. Air Force, and for the next nine years worked in the service as a clerk-typist while taking some college courses. In 1956 he married Mary June Wiggins; they had three children.

Meredith left the Air Force and completed his college courses at Jackson State, an all-black school in Jackson, Mississippi. But he wanted to break the color barrier at the University of Mississippi in Oxford, and with that in mind he refused to graduate from Jackson State so he could instead transfer. Meredith recalled, "The Negro in Mississippi was dead because he could not live. I was fighting to live." He conferred with MEDGAR WILEY EVERS, field secretary for the Mississippi branch of the National Association for the Advancement of Colored People (NAACP), and Thurgood Marshall of the Legal Defense and Educational Fund and filed his application to enter Ole Miss on January 31, 1961.

By that time the civil rights movement had entered a new phase. In February 1960 several black college students in Greensboro, North Carolina, had staged a sit-in at a segregated lunch counter in the local Woolworth's store. There followed similar sit-ins in cities across the South, as young people took the lead in the fight for civil rights. And in March 1961 black students from Tougaloo College demonstrated against the segregated Jackson Public Library. Although older than those students—he was 29 when he entered Ole Miss—Meredith was young enough and conscientious enough to be influenced by them.

On September 13 Supreme Court justice Hugo Black issued an injunction ordering university officials to admit Meredith and prohibiting them from engaging in racial discrimination against him. In response, Mississippi governor, Ross Barnett, insisted, "There is no case in history where the Caucasian race has survived total integration. We must either submit to the awful dictate of the federal government or stand up like men and tell them, 'Never.'"

On September 20 Barnett denied Meredith admission. Six days later Lieutenant Governor Paul Johnson defied Meredith and the federal marshals who accompanied him by turning him away from the university. A federal court then found both Barnett and Johnson guilty of contempt, and when violence erupted on campus, President John Kennedy ordered troops to join the marshals in protecting Meredith. About the harrowing atmosphere, Meredith later said:

> I knew that in a man-to-man encounter there were few men in the world that I could not subdue, both mentally and physically. . . . I had nine years of training in military service, and few men possessed greater potential for doing bodily harm than myself. Why then should I fear any man? My belief in my supernatural or superhuman powers was another important factor. Whether it was true or not, I had always thought that I could stop a mob with the uplift of a hand.

Meredith finally entered Ole Miss on September 30, 1961. The patrol car that was used to transport him to class was none too reassuring: "It was battered and smashed," Meredith recalled; "bullet holes had riddled the sides; the windows were all shot out." White rage had spoken in acts of violence, and that night it spoke again when rioters injured 160 marshals, 28 of them with gunshots, and killed two people, including a newspaper reporter. Army troops went into action, tear gas filled the air, and 200 arrests were made. Federal marshals would remain on campus until August 1963, when Meredith graduated.

Meredith took graduate courses at Ibadan University in Nigeria in 1965, returned to Mississippi, and on June 6, 1966, led the March against Fear to advance black voting rights and show that blacks would not be intimidated. On the second day of the protest along Highway 51, James Aubrey Norvell, a white segregationist, shot Meredith. While Meredith recuperated, MARTIN LUTHER KING, JR., and other civil rights leaders stepped in to continue the march.

Meredith, who had begun studying law at Columbia University in New York City obtained his degree in 1968. While in New York he ran for Congress against black incumbent Adam Clayton Powell, Jr., but lost.

Returning to Mississippi in 1971, Meredith behaved erratically. He dropped law for business and then dropped business for farming. None of his endeavors earned much money, and during the decade he ran for public office five times and lost each time.

Meredith accepted a position in 1984 as visiting professor at the University of Cincinnati in Ohio. But he antagonized nearly everyone by making wild charges about racism at the college and claiming, "God sent me to Cincinnati." The college refused to renew his contract, and he later moved to San Diego, California.

Having recently worked for the Republican Party, Meredith was hired in 1989 by Senator Jesse Helms of North Carolina as a domestic policy adviser. To many it seemed an odd match—Helms had long been an archconservative and an enemy to many federal civil rights programs. Ralph Neas, head of the Leadership Conference on Civil Rights, reacted: "Without question, Senator Helms has one of the worst civil rights records in the Congress. For years he has led the right-wing opposition to effective civil rights laws and remedies."

But Meredith's views coincided with those held by Helms. "It is the specific intent of the liberal elite to establish on a permanent basis a dual citizenship in the United States," Meredith said. "They need to keep blacks in a non-full-citizenship status." And he told a reporter for the *Washington Post*, "Integration is the biggest con job ever pulled on any group of people. . . . It was a plot by white liberals to gain political power for themselves." In 1990 he outraged many African Americans when he accused a majority of delegates to the NAACP national convention of being drug users or engaging in immoral acts.

Helms defended Meredith, but by the next year he was gone from the senator's staff and back in San Diego running for president. Meredith vowed to win the Republican nomination, or at least influence party policy, by appealing to "born-again Christians" who were "appalled" by big government intrusions into family life, but few voters took notice.

In 1991, the year Meredith married Judy Alsobrooks (his first wife had died in 1989, and with Alsobrooks he would have two children), he offered to team with the white racist DAVID ERNEST DUKE as Duke's vice-presidential running mate should Duke seek the presidency. "His positions are my positions," Meredith said. Nothing came of the offer because Duke decided against seeking the White House. In 1997 Meredith founded the Meredith Institute at Ole Miss, which offered a weekend class to blacks so they could learn standard English and eradicate what he called unacceptable black English.

Soon after the University of Mississippi integrated, Meredith said, "I had the feeling that my personal battle was over." But his battle actually continued in his struggle to find an ideological home.

Further Reading

Bradley, John. "The Man Who Would Be King." *Esquire,* December 1992, 101+.

Branch, Taylor. *Parting the Waters.* New York: Simon & Schuster, 1988.

Meredith, James. *Three Years in Mississippi.* Bloomington: Indiana University Press, 1966.

Merton, Thomas
(1915–1968) *peace activist*

A Trappist monk and writer, Thomas Merton was known for his opposition to the nuclear arms race and the Vietnam War. He was born on January 31, 1915, in Prades, France, to Owen Merton, a New Zealand–born painter, and Ruth Jenkins Merton, an American.

After Ruth Merton's death in 1921, Owen Merton took his son to Bermuda, then to New York City, and finally back to France, where in 1925 the youngster enrolled at the Lycée Ingres at Montauban. When Owen moved to England, Thomas transferred to London's Oakham School, and in 1933 he entered Cambridge. There he stayed until 1934, when, for reasons unclear, his guardian at the time—his father had died—removed him from the college and in 1935 took him to the United States. In New York Merton studied at Columbia University and received a B.A. in 1938 and an M.A. 1939.

Merton then began work on a doctorate but converted to Catholicism and in 1941 entered a Trappist monastery near Bardstown, Kentucky. In 1944 he published his first of many works, *Thirty Poems*. The story of his conversion, *The Seven Storey Mountain*, appeared in 1948 and became a best-seller. The following year he was ordained in the priesthood.

It was in *The Seven Storey Mountain* that Merton extolled the contemplative life that over the years others would admire and seek to learn more about. Merton wrote: "Whether you teach or live in the cloister or nurse the sick, whether you are in religion or out of it, married or single . . . you are called to the summit of perfection: you are called to a deep interior life, perhaps even to a mystical prayer, and to pass the fruits of your contemplation on to others. And if you cannot do so by works, then by example."

In the 1960s Merton lived as a hermit in a small cottage on the grounds of the Abbey of Gethsemani. Yet he received many visitors, especially social activists, among them his fellow priest DANIEL BERRIGAN and the folk singer JOAN BAEZ. His writings in the 1960s increasingly linked religion with politics, an emphasis that angered church authorities.

Merton read RACHEL LOUISE CARSON's *Silent Spring* (1962) and embraced the environmental movement. In his journal he wrote:

> I have been shocked at a notice of a new book by Rachel Carson, on what is happening to birds as a result of indiscriminate use of poisons. . . . Someone will say: you worry about birds: why not worry about people. I worry about *both* birds and people. We are in the world and part of it and are destroying everything because we are destroying ourselves, spiritually, morally, and in every way. It is all part of the same sickness, and it all hangs together.

He criticized racism and wrote against the Vietnam War in a critique linked to his opposition to the arms race and the dangerous influence of the military-industrial complex. In the essay "Christian Action in World Crisis," he stated:

> Christians have got to speak by their actions. Their political action must not be confined to the privacy of the polling booth. . . . It is crucially important for Christians today to adopt a clear position and to be prepared to defend that truth with sacrifice, accepting . . . even imprisonment and death.

In 1968 Merton traveled to Thailand to meet with contemplative monks. On December 10, near Bangkok, he accidentally electrocuted himself and died.

Further Reading

Furlong, Monica. *Merton: A Biography*. San Francisco: Harper & Row, 1980.

Higgins, Michael W. *Heretic Blood: The Spiritual Geography of Thomas Merton*. Toronto: Stoddart, 1998.

Inchausti, Robert. *Thomas Merton's American Prophecy*. Albany: State University of New York Press, 1998.

Shannon, William Henry. *"Something of a Rebel": Thomas Merton, His Life and Works: An Introduction*. Cincinnati: St. Anthony Messenger Press, 1997.

———. *Thomas Merton's Paradise Journey: Writings on Contemplation*. Cincinnati: St. Anthony Messenger Press, 2000.

Mfume, Kweisi
(Frizzell Gray)
(1948–) *civil rights leader*

A former member of a street gang, the African American Kweisi Mfume changed his life when he decided to complete school and, as he put it, make something of himself. He then became a radio announcer, city councilman, congressman, and president of the National Association for the Advancement of Colored People (NAACP). Mfume was born Frizzell Gray on October 24, 1948, in Turners Station, Maryland, near Baltimore, to Mary Elizabeth Willis Gray and Rufus Tate. He was given the last name Gray, however, because he was raised by his stepfather, Clifton Gray.

Frizzell Gray experienced a difficult childhood filled with poverty. His mother worked at odd jobs, and his stepfather worked as a truck driver. But when Frizzell was 11 his stepfather deserted the family, and the following year his mother moved with him and his siblings to Baltimore.

Frizzell idolized his mother, who worked long hours; in 1964 she died of cancer. That blow forced him to leave school and find work. He toiled in a bread factory and in a grocery, but angry with his circumstances, he began running with a street gang. He had five children by various women, none of whom he married.

Then in the late 1960s he changed his life. According to him, he saw a vision of his mother, and he interpreted it as God's indicating that he should reform himself. He left the gang, left the streets, earned a general equivalency diploma (GED), and enrolled at the Community College of Baltimore. At the same time he worked as a disc jockey for WEBB, a black radio station owned by singer James Brown, and won a wide following for his unconventional habit of playing social protest songs by Gil Scott-Heron, reading poems, and discussing politics.

In the early 1970s, at the suggestion of a relative, he changed his name to Kweisi Mfume, an African Ibo phrase that means "conquering son of kings." For him it signified his awareness of African culture and his developing social consciousness.

Mfume earned a bachelor's degree from Morgan State University in 1976 and was hired as pro-gram director for the college's noncommercial radio station. At the same time he hosted a political talk show and attacked the Baltimore mayor, William Donald Schaefer, for ignoring poor neighborhoods.

Mfume's popularity grew, and in 1978 he won a seat on the city council. He quickly developed a reputation for confronting Schaefer, and both men became so angry at times that they nearly engaged in fistfights Presently, Mfume moderated his tactics, learning, he later said, that more could be accomplished through cooperation.

In 1984 Mfume obtained a master's degree from Johns Hopkins University, and two years later he won election to the U.S. House of Representatives as a Democrat from Maryland's Seventh Congressional District. He quickly earned a reputation as a fast study and specialized in problems facing inner cities. Mfume served on three committees: Banking, Finance, and Urban Affairs; Small Business; and the Select Committee on Hunger. He also served as treasurer of the Congressional Black Caucus (CBC). In 1993 he became the CBC chairman, and he directed it to emphasize economic issues, especially tax breaks for the working poor.

In February 1996 Mfume surprised political observers by resigning from Congress to become president of the NAACP. "I'm a true believer," he said, and pointed out that his mother had taught him, "What you do between [your] birth date and [your] death date should have substance and worth."

The NAACP desperately needed his leadership. It was suffering from declining membership and internal bickering, along with a controversy over misused funds and a $4.5-million debt. Mfume said, "There is much work to be done and the time for such work is now. I am convinced . . . that I can best effect social, economic, and political change in the broader capacity that the NAACP represents."

Within one year he eliminated the debt, stirred the group out of its dormancy, and restored confidence in it. In April 2000 he led the NAACP in reaching an agreement with the NBC, ABC, CBS, and Fox television networks whereby they promised to make their programs more accurately reflect the country's racial diversity. The civil rights group had complained that of 26 new shows in 1999, none was geared toward African Americans or featured a minority lead character. Mfume said, "The NAACP has worked extremely hard with our coalition partners over the last several months to create opportunities for qualified men and women of color."

Further Reading

Mfume, Kweisi, and Ron Stodghill II. *No Free Ride: From the Mean Streets to the Mainstream.* New York: Ballantine, 1996.

Swan, Carl M. *Black Faces, Black Interests: The Representation of African Americans in Congress.* Cambridge, Mass.: Harvard University Press, 1995.

Milk, Harvey
(1930–1978) *gay rights activist*

A financier, Harvey Milk was quite possibly the country's first openly homosexual elected official. He was born on May 22, 1930, in Woodmere on the south shore of Long Island, near New York City, to William Milk and Minerva Karns Milk.

At high school in Bay Shore, Harvey Milk compiled a solid academic record and played basketball and football. In 1951 he graduated from New York State Teachers College in Albany and enlisted in the U.S. Navy. He attended the Officers Candidate School in Newport, Rhode Island, and by 1953 had been promoted to lieutenant junior grade on an aircraft carrier. But he was dishonorably discharged in 1955 after the navy discovered that he was gay.

Milk taught at Woodmere High School before finding work as a statistician for an insurance company. In 1963 he became a researcher for Bache & Company, a Wall Street investment firm. His talent for making profitable investments made him a wealthy man, and he began financing Broadway shows.

In 1969 Milk moved to San Francisco, where he worked as a financial analyst. He had been conservative in his political views but was now becoming more liberal and lost his job in 1970 after he participated in a protest against the Vietnam War.

Two years later his life changed when he opened a camera shop on San Francisco's Castro Street, in the heart of a gay community. His popularity encouraged him in 1973 to run for the city's board of supervisors. At the beginning of the campaign he publicly admitted his homosexuality. Milk believed that as long as gays kept their sexual orientation secret, they would be unable to do anything about protecting their rights.

Milk lost the 1973 race, ran again in 1975 and lost a second time, and in 1976 ran for the state assembly and lost that race, too. But in 1977 he created a solid coalition of liberals and gays and finally won election to the board of supervisors. A Democrat, he promised to work for improved child care programs, subsidized housing, and an effective civilian police review board. At his swearing-in ceremony he defied conventional political wisdom by introducing Jack Lira as his lover and partner.

Milk achieved his most notable success on the board when he sponsored a citywide gay-rights ordinance to forbid discrimination against gays in jobs, housing, or public accommodations. The board passed the ordinance with only one dissenting vote, that of conservative Dan White.

On November 27, 1978, a disgruntled White walked into city hall and shot and killed Mayor George Moscone and Harvey Milk. At White's trial his lawyers presented the "Twinkie defense," arguing that White's depressive state had been worsened by his eating of junk food.

A jury found White guilty of a lesser charge of manslaughter, rather than murder, and the trial judge sentenced him to seven years in prison. The verdict caused riots in San Francisco as enraged gays assailed what they called White's lenient treatment. White served his time in prison, and one year after his release in 1984 he killed himself.

Shortly before Harvey Milk died he recorded his will on three tapes. On one of them he said, "If a bullet should enter my brain, let that bullet destroy every closet door."

Further Reading

Cloud, John. "The Pioneer: Harvey Milk." *Time,* June 14, 1999, 183+.

Shilts, Randy. *Mayor of Castro Street: The Life and Times of Harvey Milk.* New York: St. Martin's Press, 1982.

Weiss, Mike. *Double Play: The San Francisco City Hall Killings.* Reading, Mass.: Addison-Wesley, 1984.

Millett, Kate
(1934–) *feminist, writer*

A sculptor and writer, Kate Millett wrote *Sexual Politics*, a work known as "the feminist manifesto." She was born on September 14, 1934, in Saint Paul, Minnesota, to James Albert Millett, an engineer, and Helen Feely Millett.

By Kate Millett's own account, she had an unhappy childhood characterized by little money and by beatings administered by her father, a man she described as "mind-blowing frightening." She attended parochial elementary and high schools— part of her strict Catholic upbringing—and in 1956 obtained a B.A. degree with honors from the University of Minnesota. She then entered Saint Hilda's College at the University of Oxford and in 1958 earned first class honors in English literature. She then returned to the United States and settled in New York City, where she supported herself by teaching kindergarten while taking up painting and sculpting.

In 1961 she traveled to Japan to sculpt and exhibit her artwork. There she met another sculptor, Fumio Yoshimura, and in 1965 they married. Returning again to New York in 1967, she exhibited her work and taught English at Barnard College. In 1968 she entered the graduate school at Columbia University and in 1970 obtained her doctorate in comparative literature.

By that time she had become involved in the civil rights movement, participating in protests sponsored by the Congress of Racial Equality, and had joined the women's rights movement, serving as chair of the education committee of the National Organization for Women (NOW). She never expected that her doctoral dissertation would make her a feminist icon, but it did; published in August 1970 as *Sexual Politics*, it became a best-seller.

Writing at a time when women were only 7 percent of all doctors, 3 percent of all lawyers, and 1 percent of all engineers, and when they held only 300 of nearly 9,000 federal judgeships, Millett offered a radical feminist theory, namely, that Western civilizations were patriarchies driven by an ideology of male supremacy. That ideology, she wrote, permeated every institution and social practice. She called romantic love "a means of emotional manipulation which the male is free to exploit" and monogamous marriage and the family "patriarchy's chief institution."

Time magazine called *Sexual Politics* "a remarkable book" for providing the feminist movement with a coherent theory. In a 1970 article *Time* quoted George Stade, assistant professor of English at Columbia and one of Millett's doctoral advisers, as stating, "Reading the book is like sitting with your testicles in a nutcracker."

Millett followed *Sexual Politics* with several other books, among them *Flying*, in which she told about the effect fame had had on her and revealed her lesbianism, a confession that several leaders of the feminist movement said diminished her influence by revealing deviancy, and *Going to Iran* (1981), in which she wrote about her trip in 1979 to address that country's feminists.

Kate Millett and Yoshimura divorced in 1985. She continued to write articles and books and in 1990 published the *Looney Bin Trip*, an autobiographical account of her manic-depression and submission to electroshock treatments. In 1994 she published her most noted work since *Sexual Politics*, *The Politics of Cruelty*, in which she exposed the use of state-sanctioned torture in several countries. Her *Mother Millett*, published in the year 2001, discussed the challenges she faced in caring for her dying mother.

In 1970 Millett had said, "Women's liberation is my life." But by 2001 she had been bypassed as a feminist figure, less remembered than BETTY FRIEDAN or GLORIA STEINEM. Her admonition from *Sexual Politics* echoed in obscurity: that unless women and men destroy the patriarchal system, they will "remain imprisoned in the vast gray stockades of sexual reaction. There is no way out but to rebel and be broken, stigmatized, and cured."

Further Reading

Millett, Kate. *A.D.: A Memoir.* New York: Norton, 1995.
———. *The Loony-Bin Trip.* New York: Simon & Schuster, 1990.
———. *Mother Millett.* New York: Verso, 2001.
———. *Sexual Politics.* Garden City, N.Y.: Doubleday, 1970.

Montezuma, Carlos
(Wassaja)
(ca. 1865–1923) *Indian rights activist*

A physician and Indian rights activist, Carlos Montezuma favored assimilation of Native Americans into white society. He was born with the name Wassaja around the year 1865 near Mesa, Arizona. He was the son of Cocuyevah, a Yavapai man, and a mother who was likely also a Yavapai but whose name is unknown.

When Wassaja was only three years old, he was captured by Pima Indians and sold for $30 to Carlos Gentile, a traveling photographer. According to some stories Wassaja's mother was killed while trying to rescue her son.

Wassaja traveled east with Gentile, and during that time, perhaps after the two had settled in Chicago, he took a new name: Carlos, after his guardian, and Montezuma after the ancient ruins found in Arizona. Gentile, though, committed suicide after suffering some business losses, and Montezuma soon lived with W. H. Steadman, a Baptist minister in Urbana, Illinois, who converted him to the faith.

Montezuma had been enrolled in several different schools, and with Steadman's guidance he entered the University of Illinois, where in 1884 he earned a B.S. His work for a druggist caused Montezuma to decide to study medicine, so he enrolled in the Chicago Medical College of Northwestern University and in 1889 received an M.D. degree.

He then headed out West, working for the federal government's Indian Service on reservations in North Dakota, Nevada, and Washington. The poverty and isolation he witnessed appalled him, and he concluded that the reservations entrapped Indians and guaranteed that they would live short lives filled with unemployment, disease, and despair. So he began advocating an end to the reservations system and to the Bureau of Indian Affairs (BIA) that oversaw the reservations and that, through its white paternalism, kept the Indians in a servile state.

In 1896 Montezuma moved to Chicago and established his own medical practice in gastroenterology (dealing with stomach disorders) while teaching at the College of Physicians and Surgeons. When President Theodore Roosevelt asked him in 1906 to head the BIA, he refused, citing his opposition to it and the reservation system. That same year he published *Indians of Today and Tomorrow*, in which he advocated moving Indians away from the reservations and from tribal culture.

When several Indian leaders formed the Society of American Indians in 1911, he refused to join, saying that it supported the BIA and the status quo. In 1913 he changed his mind and served on the society's executive committee. Montezuma intended to use his presence within the group to change it. He spoke often and forcefully against the reservations, and in one speech, delivered in September 1915 to a meeting in Lawrence, Kansas, he said:

> American Indians are not free. We are not free! We are hoodwinked, duped more and more each year; we are made to feel that we are free when we are not. We are chained hand and foot. . . .
>
> Better, far better for the Indians had there never been a [BIA]. Then self-preservation would have led the individual Indian to find his true place and his real emancipation would have been speedily consummated. . . .
>
> The Reservation is a sludgepond . . . a demoralizing prison of idleness, beggary, gambling, pauperism, and ruin, where the Indians remain as Indians, a barrier against enlightenment and knowledge. There is not one redeeming feature on the Indian reservations for the Indians.

In 1916 Montezuma began publishing a magazine called *Wassaja*, bearing the motto "Let My People Go." He wrote articles for it in which he criticized the Society of American Indians and repeated his anti-BIA, antireservation theme. When in 1918 the society finally called for dismantling the BIA, Montezuma praised its new direction.

During World War I he was imprisoned for criticizing the government's decision to draft Native Americans into the military. President Woodrow Wilson, however, arranged his release. Shortly afterward Montezuma contracted tuberculosis, and the man who had been so far removed from his people returned to Arizona in 1922 with his wife, Marie Keller (a Romanian, whom he had married in 1913). There he lived at Fort McDowell among the Yavapai in a brush shelter. He died on January 31, 1923.

Further Reading

Iverson, Peter. *Carlos Montezuma and the Changing World of American Indians.* Albuquerque: University of New Mexico Press, 1982.

Spack, Ruth. "Disengagement: Zitkala-Sa's Letters to Carlos Montezuma, 1901–1902." *MELUS* 26 (Spring 2001): 173.

Morgan, Robin

(1941–) *feminist, writer*

A writer and feminist, Robin Morgan described herself in the late 1970s as "one of the women who helped start this wave of feminism back in the Pleistocene Age of the middle and late 1960s." She was born on January 29, 1941, in Lake Worth, Florida, and grew up in a one-parent family headed by her mother, Faith Berkely Morgan.

Robin Morgan graduated from Columbia University in the early 1960s; married a poet, Kenneth Pitchford; and worked as a lexicographer for a book publisher while doing free-lance editing. She participated in civil rights and antiwar demonstrations and in the mid-1960s adopted a socialist ideology and wrote articles for New Left publications, among them *Liberation, Win, Rat,* and *The Guardian.* Yet she found the New Left discriminatory and oppressive because, much as mainstream society did, it relegated women to a secondary status.

As her feminist consciousness developed, Morgan helped organize New York Radical Women, a group that protested the 1968 Miss America Pageant in Atlantic City, New Jersey. According to Morgan, "Each work meeting with the organizers of the protesters was an excitement fix: whether we were lettering posters or writing leaflets or deciding who would deal with which reporter requesting an interview, we were affirming our mutual feelings of outrage, hope, and readiness to conquer the world." Solidarity and feminism abounded among the demonstrators as they called

national attention to the commercial and sexual oppression of women. "It announced our existence to the world," Morgan said, "and is often taken as the date of birth of this feminist wave."

Morgan claimed she never deserted the New Left but wanted to take it further and confront sexism. She did so pointedly in late 1969 when she announced she would cease writing for the leftist publication *Rat* because she could no longer tolerate its sexist hierarchy. Shortly afterward, in January 1970, Morgan supported feminists who forcibly took over the paper, and she wrote an article for the conquered *Rat,* a subsequently widely quoted tract in the women's movement, "Goodbye to All That." In it she stated:

> White males are most responsible for the destruction of human life and environment on the planet today. Yet who is controlling the supposed revolution to change all that? White males. . . . It just could make one a bit uneasy. It seems obvious that a legitimate revolution must be led by, made by those who have been most oppressed: black, brown, and white women—with men relating to that the best they can. . . .
>
> Goodbye, Goodbye. The hell with the simplistic notion that automatic freedom for women—or nonwhite peoples—will come about ZAP! with the advent of a socialist revolution. . . . Two evils predate capitalism and have been clearly able to survive and postdate socialism: sexism and racism. . . .
>
> We are rising with a fury older and potentially greater than any force in history, and this time we will be free or no one will survive. *Power to all the people or to none.* All the way down, this time.

In 1970 Morgan edited *Sisterhood Is Powerful: An Anthology of Writings from the Women's Liberation Movement,* which included historic documents related to feminist activism and articles pertaining to sexism. Her book influenced many women both within and outside the movement, opening their eyes to oppression.

Morgan, in fact, claimed *Sisterhood Is Powerful* deeply affected her, for as she toured the nation to speak with women about the book, she discovered their widespread work on issues such as child care and abortion. "I felt as if I had discovered a whole new continent," she said, "the authentic Women's Movement."

At the same time she encountered another influence: *The Dialectic of Sex* written by SHULAMITH FIRESTONE, which criticized the National Organization for Women (NOW), a moderate women's rights group. Consequently, Morgan considered NOW's approach deficient because it sought only limited reforms in women's second-class citizenship. She defined her radical feminism as a drive to uproot oppression and prevent it from continuing to "put forth the branches of racism, class hatred, ageism, competition, ecological disaster, and economic exploitation."

Morgan was hired in 1990 as editor of the feminist magazine *Ms.* but resigned a few years later. During the 1990s she continued to write, including poetry and *The Anatomy of Freedom,* an exploration of feminist consciousness. Through her writing she remains committed to the radical feminism born in the "Pleistocene Age" of the 1960s protests.

Further Reading

Morgan, Robin. *The Anatomy of Freedom: Feminism in Four Dimensions.* 2nd ed. New York: Norton, 1994.

———. *Going Too Far: The Personal Chronicle of a Feminist.* New York: Random House, 1977.

———. *Saturday's Child: A Memoir.* New York: Norton, 2001.

———, ed. *Sisterhood Is Powerful: An Anthology of Writings from the Women's Liberation Movement.* New York: Random House, 1970.

Moses, Robert

(1935–) *civil rights leader*

A teacher and leader in the Student Non-Violent Coordinating Committee (SNCC), Robert Moses is best known for his civil rights work during the 1960s. He was born on January 23, 1935, in New York City's Harlem district to Gregory Moses and Louise Parris Moses.

Although the elder Moses worked as a janitor, he pushed his sons to obtain a higher education, and Robert Moses responded by showing a remarkable intellect. He performed so well on an entry exam that he was able to enroll at Stuyvesant High School for gifted children. He graduated in 1952 and received a scholarship to attend Hamilton College in Clinton, New York. There he majored in philosophy and adopted Albert Camus's existentialist belief that only the individual can distinguish good from evil and that the individual defines himself or herself through actions. In his junior year he attended a Quaker workshop in France and absorbed its pacifist ideology.

Moses graduated from Hamilton College in 1956 and enrolled in the doctoral program at Harvard, but he had to leave the following year after his mother died and his father became ill. To help pay for his father's medical care, he obtained a job as a math teacher at Horace Mann High School in New York City.

In 1960 Moses closely followed the sit-ins being staged by black college students in Greensboro, North Carolina, against a Woolworth's store and its segregated lunch counter. As the protests spread beyond Greensboro, Moses marveled at the energy and commitment of the young people involved and wanted to become a part of it.

That summer he joined SNCC as a field representative after ELLA JOSEPHINE BAKER recruited him. In Cleveland, Mississippi, Moses met Amzie Moore, who headed the local chapter of the National Association for the Advancement of Colored People (NAACP). Moore convinced Moses that for blacks in the state to gain their freedom and improve their economic standing they must be registered to vote, and Moses must lead them in the effort.

Both men knew full well the obstacles they faced. Whites in Mississippi had used intimidation and violence to prevent blacks from voting; they would use both weapons against anyone who tried to change the system. But Moses exuded charisma; a reluctant leader susceptible to the mental stress that resulted from commanding others, he was described by a fellow SNCC member as a person "you could sit down and talk with. After talking to him, you would really understand. . . . He also had this thing about him, like if it was Bob who said it, you knew it had to be done. I think a lot of other people felt the same way about him. He was just one of those persons."

In August 1961 Moses began an SNCC voter registration drive in McComb, Mississippi. He opened a citizenship school to teach blacks the state's byzantine registration system and boost their morale. But as he took them to the courthouse to register, and as other blacks staged rallies, harassment and violence shadowed him: A highway patrolman followed him in his car and arrested him for obstructing justice; after another arrest a judge sentenced him to six months in jail for contributing to the delinquency of a minor; in February 1963 whites fired 14 bullets into a car in which he was riding.

With the voter registration drive failing, Moses contrived the Freedom Vote—a mock election in which black candidates would "run" for state office. He wanted to show that if given the chance blacks would vote; as it turned out, more than 80,000 cast ballots—an impressive performance, but one that in the short run put no African Americans in public office.

In 1964 SNCC launched Freedom Summer, a renewed effort to register black voters. When the group fell to bickering over whether to allow white college students to join the crusade, Moses rejected those who argued that whites should be banned because they tended to take control and knew little about black culture, and he supported those who wanted a racially integrated strategy.

That same year Bob Moses and James Forman created the Mississippi Freedom Democratic Party (MFDP) as a parallel organization that would operate within the Democratic Party. It eventually sent black delegates to the Democratic National Convention to challenge the all-white delegation chosen through segregated voting.

As white and black students put Freedom Summer into action, violence recurred; this time white segregationists, working with the police in the town of Philadelphia, Mississippi, murdered three of the civil rights workers. Freedom Summer continued, but voter registration lagged, and then in August President Lyndon Johnson refused to let the MFDP delegation be seated at the Democratic convention. Instead he offered a compromise that would recognize two MFDP delegates and would ban racially segregated delegations in the future. The MFDP rejected the offer, leaving the group without represen-

tation. On network television Moses explained why he had opposed the compromise: "We are here for the people . . . and they don't want symbolic votes. They want to vote for themselves."

The defeat was too much for him. He quit SNCC; divorced his wife, Dona Richards; and to avoid the military draft and fighting in Vietnam, fled to Canada. In 1968 he married Janet Jemott, and they soon moved to Tanzania, where Moses taught school in a village.

Moses returned to the Unites States in 1976, and in 1982 the MacArthur Foundation awarded him a grant to launch his Algebra Project, a program to enable inner-city and minority children to learn college-level math. He began the Algebra Project in Mississippi, traversing the same towns where two decades earlier he had been physically beaten. Moses said, "Economic access and full citizenship depend on math and science literacy." And he saw his project as a way to draw entire communities together, enabling them to be effective beyond the schoolroom walls. In the late 1980s the Algebra Project spread to Boston and Atlanta.

In the year 2001 Moses and Charles E. Cobb, Jr., detailed the founding of the project and outlined its hopes in *Radical Equations: Math, Literacy, and Civil Rights*. While teaching at a middle school in Jackson, Mississippi, Moses stated, "Taking responsibility for your own life, your own learning, can change a person."

Further Reading

Moses, Bob, and Charles E. Cobb, Jr. *Radical Equations: Math, Literacy, and Civil Rights*. Boston: Beacon Press, 2001.

Viorst, Milton. *Fire in the Streets: America in the 1960s*. New York: Simon & Schuster, 1979.

Walter, Mildred Pitts. *Mississippi Challenge*. New York: Aladdin, 1992.

Mott, Lucretia Coffin
(1793–1880) *abolitionist, women's rights advocate*

A Quaker minister, Lucretia Coffin Mott supported abolitionism and women's rights, radical ideas for her time. She was born on January 3, 1793, on the island of Nantucket, Massachusetts, to Quaker parents Thomas Coffin, a businessman, and Anna Folger Coffin.

When Lucretia was 11 her father moved the family to Boston, where she attended public school before enrolling, at age 13, in the Friends' boarding school at Nine Partners, near Poughkeepsie, New York. She spent two years at the school as a student and an additional two years there as a teacher, and then she moved with her family to Philadelphia, Pennsylvania. In 1811 she married James Mott, her father's business partner; the couple had six children.

In April 1817 their baby, Tommy, contracted a fever and died. The loss so shattered Lucretia that she experienced a spiritual rebirth in a way that Quakers called "an appearance in the ministry," so in 1821 they formally recognized her as a minister. At about the same time, she took a trip to Virginia, where she witnessed plantation slavery on a large scale. The sight sickened her, and with what she had also seen in Philadelphia, namely planters hunting down their runaway slaves, she vowed to oppose slavery. A Quaker minister, Elias Hicks, also influenced her as he inveighed against those Friends who had become too satisfied with material comfort and had lost their moral commitment to ending human bondage. In the mid-1820s Mott decided she would no longer consume any items derived from slave labor, including cotton, molasses, and sugar.

In 1827 her friendship with Hicks embroiled her in a religious controversy when Philadelphia's Quaker elders sought to prevent him from preaching because of his criticism that too many Friends had lost the inner light, a light that must, more than any written matter, guide people in their lives. In the dispute Lucretia and her husband sided with Hicks; her decision and her influence in the church made a schism inevitable. According to historian Margaret Hope Beacon, in her later years Lucretia recalled how difficult it had been for her "to find that she must part with old friends for the truth, and to have meeting houses closed to her in which she loved to meet them."

Mott was chosen clerk of the Philadelphia Women's Yearly Meeting in 1830 and stunned fellow Quakers by denouncing a recent resolution by male Quakers that repudiated Hicks and his followers. Typically, women went along with what men decided, making her statement all the more controversial.

A meeting with the abolitionist WILLIAM LLOYD GARRISON encouraged Mott's own abolitionism, and in 1833 she attended the founding convention of the American Anti-Slavery Society in Philadelphia. In keeping with the prevailing view that on political issues men and women should never mix, the group forbade women to become members, whereupon Mott helped form a women's auxiliary, the Philadelphia Female Anti-Slavery Society. In 1837 Mott attended the First Anti-Slavery Convention of American Women, held in New York City.

The following year she witnessed directly the fury generated by abolitionism. When the Second Anti-Slavery Convention of Women, a meeting she had helped organize, convened at Philadelphia Hall, those who opposed abolitionism and thought that abolitionists wanted racial amalgamation demanded that black women be barred from attending the convention. Mott answered them by arranging for the white and black women to march together, arm in arm.

Later that night a mob nearly 20,000 strong ransacked Philadelphia Hall and burned it to the ground. The Mott home was saved from destruction only because a friend of the abolitionists—shouting "On to the Motts!"—tricked the mob by pointing it in the wrong direction.

Many women who joined the abolitionist movement also advocated women's rights, and some of them insisted that women working within their own antislavery organizations, apart from men, only encouraged separation and a secondary status based on sex. Mott supported women's rights, but she disagreed with this view, thinking it would disrupt the fight against slavery.

In 1840 Mott attended the World Anti-Slavery Convention in London, but she was prohibited from taking part as a voting member because of her sex, and at that point she and ELIZABETH CADY STANTON decided to organize a women's rights convention. From that resolve came the famous 1848 convention at Seneca Falls, New York, where men and women delegates approved a Declaration of Sentiments that claimed equal rights for women, including the right to vote. Mott once recalled of the earlier Philadelphia Female Anti-Slavery Society, "At that time I had no idea of the meaning of preambles and resolutions and voting. Women had never been in assemblies of the kind." The Seneca Falls Convention showed how far she and other women had progressed in organizational ability.

Mott regularly attended the succeeding women's rights conventions and in 1852 was elected president of the convention at Syracuse, New York. In 1861 she appeared before the New York state legislature, and insisting that marriage was a sacred union over which the state had no authority, she called for an end to all laws governing marriage and divorce.

With the outbreak of the Civil War and with the ratification of the Thirteenth Amendment ending slavery, Mott worked for the civil rights of blacks and served in the Friends Association of Philadelphia for the Aid and Elevation of the Freedmen. In addition she raised money for Swarthmore College, which opened in 1864, and was elected vice president of the Pennsylvania Peace Society. She remained active in the women's rights movement, even defending extremists such as VICTORIA WOODHULL.

Although Mott remained a Quaker, in the 1870s she joined the Free Religious Association, a nonsectarian radical group through which she insisted that the internal light knew no one religion. There existed, she said, a higher power: "Let it be called the Great Spirit of the Indian, the Quaker's 'Inward Light' of George Fox, the 'Blessed Mary, Mother of Jesus' of the Catholics, or Brahma, the Hindoo's [sic] God—they will all be one, and there will come to be such faith and such liberty as shall redeem the world."

Lucretia Mott died on November 11, 1880, at her home, "Roadside," near Philadelphia. A friend wrote about her: "She was more closely connected with Deity than anyone I ever met. Now there is the higher work she always craved. She used to say she never wanted to be so at rest that she would have nothing to do."

Further Reading

Beacon, Margaret Hope. *Valiant Friend: The Life of Lucretia Mott.* New York: Walker, 1980.

Graham, Maureen. *Women of Power and Presence: The Spiritual Formation of Four Quaker Women Ministers.* Wallingford, Pa.: Pendle Hill Publications, 1990.

Venet, Wendy Hamand. *Neither Ballots nor Bullets: Women Abolitionists and the Civil War.* Charlottesville: University Press of Virginia, 1991.

Muir, John
(1838–1914) *environmentalist*

An explorer and writer, John Muir was a preservationist within the environmental movement. He was born on April 21, 1838, in Dunbar, Scotland, to Daniel Muir and Ann Gilrye Muir.

John Muir received his earliest education in the Scottish Highlands; in 1849 he immigrated with his family to America, where his father took up farming near Portage, Wisconsin. A stern Presbyterian, the elder Muir worked his children hard and expected their complete obedience. Between doing chores John Muir found time to wander among the Great Lakes and to read books; he loved them, and they and nature became his talismans and served as an escape from his father's sternness.

In 1860 he left the farm and entered the University of Wisconsin. But when in 1863 the Civil War threatened to violate his pacifism by causing him to be drafted into the military, he fled to Canada and began hiking through the wilderness, enthralled with nature's beauty and its filling of the senses with a mystical, religiouslike wonder.

In 1867, while working at a wagon factory in Indianapolis, Indiana, Muir experienced a frightening event: He was accidentally stabbed in the eye with a metal file and for several months suffered near-total blindness. He feared that he would never again be able to see nature, and he vowed that he would have nothing more to do with mechanical inventions.

Later that year he entered what he called the "University of the Wilderness" and hiked from Indiana through Kentucky, Tennessee, Georgia, and Florida—1,000 miles in all. Then he continued his

Pictured here around 1902 in the natural setting he so strongly loved and defended, John Muir founded the modern conservation movement. *(Library of Congress)*

journey, catching a boat to Cuba, through the Isthmus of Panama, and up the Pacific Coast to San Francisco. He arrived there in 1868, and seeing the summits of the Sierra Nevada, he believed he had found a home in God's country.

As he hiked through the mountains he encountered the splendor of the Yosemite Valley. Muir bathed in the aesthetics of the wilderness, yet he surveyed the environment with a scientific eye—he had studied botany and geology—and in 1871 theorized that Yosemite Valley had been created by glaciers that had sculpted the rock. Most professional geologists rejected his idea; they claimed the valley had resulted from a cataclysmic event. In time, evidence supported Muir's analysis, and the story of the valley's origin was changed.

In *The Quiet Crisis and the Next Generation* (1988), Stewart Udall states that Muir compared wilderness freedom to political freedom in that it, too, required eternal vigilance or it would be stolen from the people. Muir advocated preserving large tracts of land for public ownership, tracts where nearly all development would be forbidden. He thought it impossible to compromise natural beauty: to even partially develop an area would ruin it completely; it would be as ridiculous as placing a billboard on a wall of the Sistine Chapel and asserting that the ceiling could still be enjoyed. Muir accepted some development in pristine areas, mainly farming, but according to Udall, he "gave first priority to preserving the finest landscapes of the public domain as temples unspoiled and intact."

In 1879 Muir explored Alaska and discovered Glacier Bay, where a glacier was named for him. A prolific writer, he wove nature's grandeur and enchantment into his narratives. About Alaska, he wrote:

> To the lover of wildness Alaska offers a glorious field for either work or rest: landscape beauty in a thousand forms, things great and small, novel and familiar, as wild and pure as paradise. Wander where you may, wildness ever fresh and ever beautiful meets you in endless variety: ice-laden mountains, hundreds of miles of them peaked and pinnacled and crowded together like trees in groves, and so high and so divinely clad in clouds and air that they seem to belong more to heaven than to earth; inland plains grassy and flowery, dotted with groves and extending like seas all around to the rim of the sky; lakes and streams shining and singing, outspread in sheets of mazy embroidery in untraceable, measureless abundance, brightening every landscape, and keeping the ground fresh and fruitful forever; forests of evergreens growing close together like leaves of grass, girdling a thousand islands and mountains in glorious array; mountains that are monuments of the work of ice, mountains monuments of volcanic fires; gardens filled with the fairest flowers, giving their fragrance to every wandering wind; and far to the north thousands of miles of ocean ice, now wrapped in fog, now glowing in sunshine through nightless days, and again shining in wintry splendor beneath the beams of the aurora.

In 1880 Muir married Louie Wanda Strentzel and moved to Alhambra, California, where the couple raised two daughters and he tended his orchard. Muir continued to write, though less often. Yet as he hiked the snow-covered mountains and lush meadows surrounding Yosemite Valley, he found, from year to year, a marked decline in the land. Sheepherding (at which Muir had once worked part-time) had turned the ground into barren rock. He later wrote, "Nine-tenths of the whole surface of the Sierra has been swept by the scourge." Adding to the assault, lumber companies were cutting down sequoia trees hundreds of years old and blasting the felled trunks with gunpowder to make them smaller and more manageable.

Muir took Robert Underwood Johnson, the editor of *Century* magazine, to Yosemite in 1889, and Johnson agreed that something had to be done to halt the decline. Others before Muir had been impressed with Yosemite, and in 1864 Congress had passed an act declaring it a scenic reserve to be administered by the state of California. But in a series of articles published in *Century*, Muir advocated setting aside and protecting the entire Yosemite region.

President Benjamin Harrison and his secretary of the interior agreed, and in 1890 Congress passed a bill that reserved more than a million acres, placing them under federal control, while leaving other land under California's jurisdiction. Muir then proposed additional protection for stands of sequoia trees, and Congress created two more reserves. He had proved to be an indefatigable fighter for the wilderness, though also intransigent, or what critics called hard-headed, a trait that he had inherited from his father.

With these victories in hand, in 1892 Muir helped establish the Sierra Club to protect wilderness freedom. That same year he became involved in a huge battle in the nations's capital as the House of Representatives passed a bill to reduce the size of the Yosemite reserve by more than half. With Muir leading the way, the Sierra Club lobbied the Senate and defeated the bill.

With the help of a friend, William E. Colby, Muir built the Sierra Club into a formidable organization. In 1894 he published his first book, *The Mountains of California*, which presented his aesthetic outlook. One reviewer said to him, "I have never read descriptions of trees that so picture them to the mind as yours do."

Muir's fight to protect Yosemite took another turn in the late 1890s. By then that part of the valley administered by the state of California had come under assault by developers. While the state stood by, land was plowed by farmers, trees were chopped down by lumber companies, and a lake was dammed for irrigation. Muir wanted the federal government to step in, and in 1903 he and President Theodore Roosevelt, an avid outdoorsman, camped beneath the stars at Yosemite. Muir told the president about the destruction and the need to protect Yosemite's beauty, and Roosevelt returned to the White House a believer. In 1905, the same year that Louie Muir died, John Muir, Theodore Roosevelt, and railroad president Edward H. Harriman convinced Congress to go beyond reserving land at Yosemite and create Yosemite National Park.

That action, however, failed to quiet the demands that Yosemite be exploited. Political and business leaders in San Francisco looked at it as a water source and asked Congress for permission to dam the Tuolumne River, which ran through a valley called Hetch Hetchy. Muir had called the Hetch Hetchy a land of "sublime rocks and waterfalls" studded with "gardens, groves, and meadows." The proponents of the dam, however, called it "mosquito-ridden."

The battle over Hetch Hetchy revealed a split within the environmental movement. On one side stood the federal government's chief forester, Gifford Pinchot, who in setting aside national forests (as opposed to national parks) had placed controlled scientific use above the protection of natural beauty. Pinchot wanted forestlands and other natural resources used scientifically to protect them from damaging effects and wasteful use, but nevertheless he wanted them exploited. He applied this view to Hetch Hetchy, and as a powerful influence on presidents in the early 1900s, he tried to persuade them to accept his position.

On the other side, Muir and his supporters in the environmental movement, sometimes called preservationists, thought Hetch Hetchy and other locations that qualified as natural wonders should be preserved inviolate. Muir said, "Everybody needs beauty as well as bread, places to play in and pray in where nature may heal and cheer and give strength to body and soul alike." Pinchot responded that the valley's scenic beauty was "altogether unimportant compared with the benefits to be derived from its use as a reservoir."

Throughout the battle Muir suspected that the politicians and financiers promoting San Francisco's plan had more in mind than a reservoir; they wanted to make money by generating electricity. The dam's supporters, however, kept the hydroelectric issue in the background. Muir called his opponents "temple destroyers" and said that "instead of lifting their eyes to the God of the Mountains, [they] lift them to the Almighty Dollar." He also claimed that if Yosemite could be so assaulted, then no national park would be safe.

In 1913 the House of Representatives passed a bill to build a dam in Hetch Hetchy. Muir summoned his strength to do battle in the Senate in what had become a national issue. On December 6, 1913, the Senate voted 43–25 to pass the House bill. Hetch Hetchy was flooded, and the loss devastated Muir.

As it turned out, the bill, called the Raker Act, granted San Francisco both water and power rights in Hetch Hetchy. In his biography of Muir, Thurman Wilkins states:

> It would take eighteen years for Tuolumne River water to reach the city. The reservoir itself would never become, as the dam defenders had promised, "a beautiful mountain lake, blue, deep, and clear, in which fishes swim and on the surface of which rowboats and sailboats glide." Rather it would become a perpetual eyesore, a synonym for error along the lines of Muir's prediction of how "it would be gradually drained [in summer], exposing the slimy sides of the basin and the shallower parts of the bottom with the gathered drift of waste, death and decay."

On December 24, 1914, just one year after the Raker Act passed Congress, John Muir died of pneumonia. He was hailed as the leader of the preservation movement. Fifty years later *Time* magazine called him "the real father of conservation." Muir had once written about climbing a 100-foot Douglas fir to its upper branches during a gale:

> Never before did I enjoy so noble an exhilaration of motion. . . . My eye roved over the piny hills and dales as over fields of waving grain, and felt the light running in ripples and broad swelling undulations across the valley from ridge to ridge, as the shining foliage was stirred by corresponding waves of air.

Further Reading

Ehrlich, Gretel. *John Muir: Nature's Visionary.* Washington, D.C.: National Geographic Society, 2000.

Gifford, Terry, ed. *John Muir: His Life and Letters and Other Writings.* London: Baton Wicks, 1996.

Miller, Sally M., ed. *John Muir in Historical Perspective.* New York: Peter Lang, 1999.

Wilkins, Thurman. *John Muir: Apostle of Nature.* Norman: University of Oklahoma Press, 1995.

Muñoz Rivera, Luis

(1859–1916) *Puerto Rican political activist*

Luis Muñoz Rivera was an advocate of autonomy for his homeland of Puerto Rico. He was born on July 17, 1859, in Barranquitas to Luis Ramon Muñoz-Barrios and Monserrate Rivera-Vasquez.

Luis Muñoz Rivera attended elementary school and then educated himself and began writing poetry that expressed the patriotism he felt and wanted others to feel for Puerto Rico. In 1887 he served as a representative in an assembly that demanded autonomy for Puerto Rico from Spain. Three years later he began publishing *La Democracia* to express his views.

Muñoz soon headed the Autonomist Party, and in 1896 he reached an agreement with the Liberal Party in Spain stipulating that when the liberals regained power they would grant autonomy, though not independence, to Puerto Rico. Muñoz and others who supported the agreement organized the Insular Liberal Party, and he began publishing *El Liberal* in San Juan as the group's newspaper.

Soon the liberals regained power in Spain, and in November 1897 they granted autonomy to Puerto Rico. In an Autonomist cabinet, appointed in February 1898, Muñoz served as secretary of grace, justice, and government. But war erupted between Spain and the United States, and in July American troops invaded the island and placed it under military rule.

In October 1898 Spain transferred sovereignty over Puerto Rico to the United States. Muñoz and the rest of the cabinet remained until 1899, serving under the military governor. In 1900 he organized the Federal Party and founded a new paper, *El Diario da Puerto Rico,* both of which opposed the

Foraker Act, which had replaced the military government with a civilian one. Muñoz believed the act had failed to grant enough power to Puerto Ricans. In 1901 he founded in New York City the English-language *Puerto Rico Herald* to reach a wider audience in the United States and report on problems facing his island homeland.

The following year the Federal Party merged with dissidents from the Republican Party and formed the Unionist Party. In 1906 he campaigned for a seat in the House of Delegates under that party's banner and won. He left that post in 1910, when the Unionists elected him resident commissioner for Puerto Rico in the United States, and he relocated to Washington, D.C. His new position allowed him to make speeches in Congress and vote in committees.

He supported the Jones-Shafroth Act, which granted U.S. citizenship to Puerto Ricans, allowed the Puerto Rican government to establish its own suffrage laws, and provided for a bill of rights similar to that in the U.S. Constitution. In addition, it maintained U.S. control over Puerto Rico's fiscal policies and the island's defense, and it allowed Congress to overrule the Puerto Rican legislature. Muñoz died at Santurce, near San Juan, on November 15, 1916. He was survived by Amalia Marín, whom he had married in 1893.

Further Reading

Norris, Marianna. *Father and Son for Freedom.* New York: Dodd, Mead, 1968.

Tuck, Jay Nelson, and Norma Coolen Vergara. *Heroes of Puerto Rico.* New York: Fleet Press, 1970.

Murray, Philip

(1886–1952) *union leader*

Philip Murray served for more than 20 years as the vice president of the United Mine Workers (UMW) and later president of the Congress of Industrial Organizations (CIO) and the United Steel Workers of America. He was born on May 25, 1886, in New Glasgow, Scotland, to William Murray and Rose Ann Layden Murray.

At age 16 Philip Murray immigrated to the United States with his father (his mother had died several years earlier, and his stepmother and the rest of the family immigrated to the United States later), and they settled near Pittsburgh, Pennsylvania, where they went to work in the coal mines. A dispute with one of his bosses caused Murray to be fired from the job and convinced him to join the UMW; at age 18 he was elected president of the local. Because Murray had quit school when he was 10, he took correspondence courses. In 1910 he married Elizabeth Lavery, and in 1911 he was naturalized a U.S. citizen.

The following year Murray was elected to the UMW's international executive board and in 1916 became president of District 5. JOHN LLEWELLYN LEWIS assumed the UMW presidency in 1920; Murray became vice president and for more than 20 years worked closely with Lewis.

Murray proved himself to be a talented negotiator and an effective spokesman for the UMW before congressional committees. Whereas Lewis was known for his gruffness and his desire to amass power for the sake of gratifying his ego, Murray was congenial and disdained power grabbing. During World War I President Woodrow Wilson appointed Murray to the War Labor Board. In the 1920s, at the request of President Warren G. Harding, he stepped in and resolved a violent coal strike in West Virginia.

In 1935 Murray joined Lewis in arguing before the American Federation of Labor (AFL), of which the UMW was a part, that workers in the mass production industries should be allowed to form their own industrial unions rather than be forced to join the existing craft unions. When the AFL decided against them, Lewis withdrew the UMW from the organization and formed the CIO, with himself as president.

The CIO then tapped Lewis to chair the Steel Workers' Organizing Committee (SWOC), created to unionize United States Steel and other steel companies. In 1937 SWOC obtained a contract with the steel giant, but other smaller companies, known as Little Steel, refused to sign.

At that point Philip Murray called for a strike, and on the afternoon of May 30—Memorial Day—about 1,200 workers and some 200 women and children rallied to hear SWOC leaders urge them to support the right to organize. Republic

Steel's use of the Chicago police as a strike-breaking force, one leader said, had violated the Wagner Act, which prohibited businesses from engaging in unfair labor practices.

The crowd then approved resolutions protesting recent police conduct, whereupon someone moved that they march to Republic's gate. The others agreed, and they began marching behind two American flags. They trekked along a dirt road and headed across the open prairie under a hot sun while chanting "CIO, CIO!"

Labor sympathizer Howard Fast describes the scene:

> About two hundred and fifty yards from the plant, the police closed in on the strikers. Billies and clubs were out already, prodding, striking, nightsticks edging into women's breasts and groins. But the cops were also somewhat afraid and they began to jerk guns out of holsters.
>
> "Stand fast! Stand fast!" the line leaders cried. "We got our rights! We got our legal rights to picket!"
>
> The cops said, "You got no rights. You red bastards, you got no rights. . . . "
>
> Grenades began to sail now; tear gas settled like an ugly cloud. Children suddenly cried with panic, and the whole picket line gave back, men stumbling, cursing, gasping for breath. Here and there a cop tore out his pistol and began to fire; it was pop, pop, pop at first, like toy favors at some horrible party, and then as the strikers broke under the gunfire and began to run, the contagion of killing ran like fire through the police.
>
> They began to shoot in volleys at these unarmed men and women and children who could not strike back or fight back. The cops squealed with excitement. They ran after fleeing pickets, pressed revolvers to their backs, shot them down, and then continued to shoot as the victims lay on their faces, retching blood.

The police shot and killed 10 strikers, and they wounded another 30, including three children. Another 28 were hospitalized with injuries delivered by police wielding billy clubs and axe handles.

Murray and the SWOC reeled from the violence, and for the moment they failed to induce Little Steel to recognize the union. Adding to their woes, a resurgent depression put jobs at a premium and made strikes less attractive than job security. By the end of 1937 Murray felt chastened and was ready to try a different approach. In the 1940s he would rely less on militant action and more on government regulatory bodies, mainly the National Labor Relations Board (NLRB), to which the SWOC appealed for favorable rulings. In 1941 Republic and the other Little Steel companies agreed to end what the NLRB said were unfair labor practices, and in 1942 they signed contracts with the SWOC, which by then had been reorganized as the United Steelworkers of America.

Meanwhile, in the 1940 presidential election John L. Lewis opposed Franklin D. Roosevelt's reelection and vowed that if the Republican candidate, Wendell Willkie, lost, he would quit as CIO president. Willkie lost, and Lewis kept his promise. As a result Murray was elected to the CIO presidency.

In short order Lewis, who was still president of the UMW, and Murray, who was still the union's vice president, clashed, and in 1942, after Lewis forced Murray from the vice presidency and withdrew the UMW from the CIO, the two men ended their friendship.

But Murray continued as president of the CIO, and when the SWOC became the United Steel Workers of America he was made its president as well. Murray supported President Roosevelt during World War II and served on the National Defense Mediation Board.

Long opposed to racism, Murray was a member of the National Association for the Advancement of Colored People, and he directed the CIO to establish the Committee to Abolish Racial Discrimination to fight racism within the organization's member unions. In 1943 he founded the CIO's Political Action Committee (PAC) to register union members as voters and provide endorsements and volunteers for political candidates endorsed by the CIO. Through PAC he lobbied for guaranteed annual wages. During the cold war he adamantly opposed communism and expelled several communist-led unions from the CIO.

In 1952 Murray endorsed the Democrat Adlai Stevenson for the White House, only to see the Republican Dwight Eisenhower win. Just a few days after the election, on November 9, 1952, Murray died of a heart attack.

Further Reading

Clark, Paul F., Peter Gottlieb, and Donald Kennedy, eds. *Forging a Union of Steel: Philip Murray, SWOC, and the United Steelworkers* Ithaca, N.Y.: ILR Press, 1987.

Muste, A. J.
(Abraham Johannes Muste)
(1885–1967) *pacifist*

A pacifist, A. J. Muste embraced revolutionary Marxism. Abraham Johannes Muste was born in Zierikzee, the Netherlands, on January 8, 1885, to Martin Muste, a coachman, and Adriana Jonker Muste.

In 1891 A. J. Muste immigrated with his family to Grand Rapids, Michigan. He obtained a bachelor's degree from Hope College in Holland, Michigan, in 1905. Four years later he graduated from New Brunswick (New Jersey) Theological Seminary, which was affiliated with the Dutch Reformed Church; married Anna Huizenga; was ordained; and became minister of the Fort Washington Collegiate Church in New York City.

Muste received a bachelor of divinity degree from Union Theological Seminary in 1913, and in 1915 he broke with the Dutch Reformed Church and became minister of the Central Congregational Church in Newtonville, Massachusetts. When the United States entered World War I, he was influenced by Christian mystics and Quaker writers and took a pacifist stand.

In the 1920s Muste directed Brookwood Labor College in Katonah, New York, an alternative school founded by radicals. He disliked traditional universities for their reliance on corporate funds, their preparation of students to serve the corporate economy unquestioningly, and their "bourgeois mentality." One of the teachers, Helen G. Norton, recalled, "The labor college curriculum prepared students to serve the labor movement as active organizers and leaders instead of as union bureaucrats."

Housed in a large white-pillared building, Brookwood offered a two-year course in history, English, sociology, economics, and speech, along with labor tactics and a study of the working class. The students wrote and performed their own labor plays—*Starvation Army, Mill Shadows,* and *Sit-Down*—sang labor songs, and celebrated Karl Marx.

The college closed in 1937 for several reasons: The American Federation of Labor withdrew its funding; ideological factions had erupted within the college; and big business and conservatives condemned the school as un-American.

In the 1950s Muste chaired the Committee for Nonviolent Action and opposed nuclear arms testing. When college students began protesting the Vietnam War in the 1960s, he supported them and wholeheartedly endorsed the most prominent New Left organization, Students for a Democratic Society. At one point he traveled to Hanoi with two other clergymen to meet with North Vietnam's leaders and discuss the possibility of ending the war. A few weeks later, on February 11, 1967, Muste died.

Further Reading

Cochran, David. "An Underground Tradition." *The Progressive,* April 1995, 37.

Robinson, Jo Ann Ooiman. *Abraham Went Out: A Biography of A. J. Muste.* Philadelphia, Pa: Temple University Press, 1981.

N

Nader, Ralph

(1934–   ) *consumer activist, environmental activist*

Ralph Nader is a crusader for consumer protection and environmental regulation. He was born on February 27, 1934, in Winsted, Connecticut, the son of Lebanese immigrants Nadra Nader, a restaurant owner, and Rose Bouzine Nader. His father, strong-willed and self-righteous, instilled in him a commitment to social justice.

Ralph Nader graduated in 1951 from Winsted's Gilbert School and then enrolled in the Woodrow Wilson School of Public and International Affairs at Princeton University. There he displayed his trademark behavior: battling the authorities, in this instance fighting the school administration over the spraying of campus trees with dichloro-diphenyl-trichloroethane (DDT). He tried, but failed, to persuade the university to stop using the chemical.

Nader graduated magna cum laude from Princeton in 1955 and entered Harvard Law School, where he was appointed editor of the law review and used the publication as a forum for social issues. He received a law degree in 1958 and served briefly in the army before starting a small private practice in Hartford, Connecticut. At the same time, he traveled as a freelance writer to the Soviet Union, Africa, and South America, trips that exposed him to the great disparity in wealth between haves and have-nots and convinced him

that American corporations, wielding enormous power overseas, acted oppressively.

In 1964 Nader moved to Washington, D.C., where he worked as a staff consultant on highway safety to Daniel Patrick Moynihan, an assistant secretary of labor. He studied automobile manufacturers and discovered that for the sake of speed, appearance, and profits they made unsafe cars. His book *Unsafe at Any Speed,* published in 1965, recounted his findings and reached the best-seller list.

General Motors, whom Nader criticized for making the dangerous Chevrolet Corvair, reacted by hiring detectives to secretly investigate and harass him. They compiled a dossier about his personal life but found nothing scandalous. When uncovered, the corporation's actions caused a storm of controversy and assured passage of the Traffic and Motor Vehicle Safety Act of 1966, which set safety standards for new cars. At the same time, sales of the Corvair plunged 93 percent, and the company was forced to end its production of the maligned car.

To many Americans Nader's showdown with General Motors made him a hero; young people who were already discontented with an impersonal and exploitive society were especially drawn to him. His unorthodox way of living also made him attractive to many youths: He resided in an efficiency apartment (made all the more possible by his remaining single), owned no car, and used only $5,000 annually to meet his personal expenses.

In the late 1960s Nader toured the nation speaking about consumer rights, recruiting ordinary citizens to fight abuses committed by government and big business, and motivating many law students to think about social issues rather than corporate jobs. He urged workers to become "whistle-blowers" and expose immoral or illegal acts by corporations. His statement "There is a revolt against aristocratic uses of technology and a demand for democratic uses" corresponded with the distaste within the 1960s counterculture for a technocratic society in which experts had great authority and the average citizen had little.

Reacting to Nader's efforts, Congress passed legislation establishing meat inspection and setting safety standards for natural gas pipelines. In 1969 Nader helped found the Center for the Study of Responsive Law in Washington, D.C., which investigated the influence wielded by corporations over federal regulatory agencies intended to protect the public.

In 1970 he began the Public Interest Research Group to work for consumer reform, and the following year Public Citizen, a consumer lobbying organization intended to counteract corporate lobbies. He and his associates, dubbed "Nader's Raiders," exposed many harmful business practices and numerous government failings. The raiders helped create several regulatory agencies, such as the Occupational Safety and Health Administration, the Environmental Protection Agency, and the Consumer Product Safety Commission.

Although Nader's popularity and influence waned in the late 1970s, the reformer continued to fight for consumer rights over the next two decades, and in 1996 he ran unsuccessfully for president on the Green Party ticket. He ran again in the year 2000, challenging the Democratic nominee, Al Gore, and the conservative Republican nominee, George W. Bush, with a platform that called for stricter environmental regulation, protection of women's right to abortion, and a more equitable adjustment to America's high concentration of wealth. Nader criticized his two opponents for offering no real choice, and he urged voters, "Don't go for the lesser of two evils, because at the end of the day you wind up with evil."

When the election ended with Bush's winning by a margin of a few hundred votes in Florida and as a result capturing the White House, critics claimed that Nader had assured the Republicans' victory by draining votes away from Gore. "This changes his legacy as a person," said Deborah Callahan, president of the League of Conservation Voters. And Kate Michleman, president of the National Abortion and Reproductive Rights Action League, declared, "Ralph Nader is no friend of American women." Nader responded by saying, "I'm sorry that Bush and Gore took the election from us."

Nader had hoped to win 5 percent of the popular vote so the Green Party could qualify for federal campaign financing in the 2004 presidential election, but he fell short. He blamed that result in part on the failure of the media to cover his presidential campaign. "That's corporate power at work," he said. "They didn't like it that I included a relentless daily critique of the mass media on the campaign trail. Maybe they take that personally."

In August 2001 Nader founded a new group, Democracy Rising, intended to heal the rift among liberals stemming from his run for president and rally those seeking widespread reform. ""We have to replenish the well," Nader said, "find the young generation of leaders and galvanize existing citizen groups."

Further Reading

Gorey, Hays. *Nader and the Power of Everyman.* New York: Grosset & Dunlap, 1975.

Griffin, Kelley. *Ralph Nader Presents More Action for a Change.* New York: Dembner Books, 1987.

Nader, Ralph. *Cutting Corporate Welfare.* New York: Seven Stories Press, 2000.

———. *Unsafe at Any Speed: The Designed-in Dangers of the American Automobile.* New York: Grossman, 1965.

Nation, Carry
(Carry Amelia Moore, Carry Gloyed)
(1846–1911) *temperance leader*

Carry Nation (in some sources spelled Carrie) is remembered for being a fiery temperance leader. She was born Carry Amelia Moore in Garrard County, Kentucky, on November 25, 1846, to George Moore and Mary Campbell Moore. She grew up in an unusual household; among other oddities, her mother suffered from delusions that made her think she was Queen Victoria. At age 10 Carry experienced a religious conversion, and in subsequent years she claimed to have had visions.

In 1867 she married Charles Gloyed, a physician who preferred alcohol to doctoring. At their wedding—a most miserable event as she later called it—he was drunk before the ceremony even began. They spent several trying months together before Carry abandoned him. In another bad choice of a mate, she married David Nation, a lawyer and minister nearly 20 years her senior, in 1877. The couple had little in common and fought frequently.

Settling in Medicine Lodge, Kansas, in the 1890s with her husband, Carry Nation founded a sewing circle to make clothes for the poor, and she provided meals for them at Thanksgiving and Christmas. Kansas was a dry state, and after the Supreme Court ruled in 1890 that no state could prohibit the sale of alcohol that was in its original packaging (for to do so would place an unconstitutional restriction on interstate commerce), she formed a branch of the Woman's Christian Temperance Union. Carry planned to make sure the state stayed legally dry, and she wanted to make it completely dry in practice by forcing illegal saloons to close.

At first she relied on peaceful protest, but little came of it. Then in 1899 she experienced visions in which, she claimed, God told her to go to Kiowa, Kansas, and smash its saloon to pieces. "I'll stand by you," God said. On June 7, 1899, Carry entered the saloon, presented a brief lecture on the evils of drink, and then threw rocks at the mirrors, glasses, and bottles.

In spring 1900 she attacked the saloon in Wichita's Hotel Carey, this time with a hatchet that she applied to the windows, furniture, pornographic paintings, and liquor bottles. Newspapers covered her crusade extensively, and she became the most talked-about woman in the country.

Onward she marched into other towns in Kansas and on to New York, Washington, Pitts-

Axe-wielding prohibitionist Carry Nation, here photographed in 1904, died after a severe beating by a female saloon owner in Montana. *(Library of Congress)*

burgh, San Francisco, and elsewhere. Arrested numerous times, she continued her violent attacks, often striking fear in saloonkeepers as her sharp tongue and even sharper axe combined with her large-armed, six-foot-tall body to devastate the barrooms.

As she gained more publicity she earned some money by lecturing and selling souvenir hatchets. She operated several short-lived publications to spread her message, including *The Smasher's Mail* and *The Hatchet*.

Carry Nation died on June 9, 1911, as a result of a severe beating by a female saloon owner in Montana. Her death occurred before national prohibition took effect in 1920, but through her sensational tactics she had kept the issue burning in the public's mind.

Further Reading

Grace, Fran. *Carry A. Nation: Retelling the Life.* Bloomington: Indiana University Press, 2001.

Taylor, Robert Lewis. *Vessel of Wrath: The Life and Times of Carry Nation.* New York: New American Library, 1966.

Nearing, Scott

(1883–1983) *social activist*

In a life that lasted 100 years and that witnessed two world wars, wars in Korea and Vietnam, and technological change from the automobile to astronauts in space, Scott Nearing taught and lived a radical gospel that at various times included socialism, Marxism, pacifism, and back-to-the-land simplicity. Born on August 6, 1883, in Morris Run, Pennsylvania, to Louis Nearing, a businessman and stockbroker, and Minnie Zabriskie Nearing, he grew up in wealth.

Scott Nearing received a doctorate from the Wharton School of Finance and Economy at the University of Pennsylvania in 1906, and he stayed on at the college as an instructor. He once wrote that as a teacher, "I felt I had a mission to carry out, to teach the truth as it was, or at least as I saw it."

Such principles, mixed with his stubborn personality, caused him trouble. As the Progressive movement gained prominence and reformers exposed exploitation within the industrial economy, Nearing wrote *Solution of the Child Labor Problem* (1911) and spoke out against the abuse of child labor by local businesses. Wharton's administrators told him to quiet his criticism and conform to the corporate mentality, but Nearing refused to be silenced. Consequently, in 1915 the college declined to renew his contract.

There followed a frustrating search for a teaching position at another college before Nearing accepted appointment as professor of social science at the University of Toledo. He moved to Ohio with his wife Nellie Marguerite Seeds, a feminist and pacifist whom he had married in 1908. When the United States entered World War I in April 1917, Nearing expressed his own pacifist principles and condemned the involvement. The college's board of trustees reacted by firing him, and while he was away from home that summer teaching at the Chautauqua Summer School in New York, federal authorities raided his house and confiscated all of his papers. He later wrote: "Since that day I have not kept files of personal records or letters. Living as an unwilling citizen in a warfare state, I feel that the fewer records one has, the better."

As Americans lost their lives in the war, Nearing chaired the People's Council of America for Democracy and Peace. In 1918 he ran for Congress from New York's 14th District as a socialist. Shortly before the election a federal grand jury indicted him for violating the Espionage Act because he had criticized of the government's role in the war. Partly for that reason, Nearing lost the election to Fiorello La Guardia and then faced his trial—not with fear, but with an expectation that he could use it as a platform from which to express his views. The trial began on February 6, 1919, and at its end on February 19 Nearing addressed the jury:

> I do not care for the prosperity of this country if we are going to have gag laws. I care not for the wealth of this country if we are going to be forbidden to have free speech. . . . In America we want liberty. And I believe that as an American citizen, that is the dearest possession for which I can contend. That is my right constitutionally and legally. But if there were no constitution and no law, it would be my right as a member of a democratic society.

Persuaded by his argument, the jurors acquitted him.

Sympathetic to the Bolshevik Revolution in Russia, Nearing left the Socialist Party in 1922 after it denounced the Communists. In 1927 he joined the Communist Party but quit it three years later because it allowed no room for individual liberty.

In 1932 Nearing walked out on his wife, Nellie, to live with Helen Knothe on a 65-acre farm in

Vermont. The move occurred as book publishers and magazine editors were rejecting his writing—a rejection that he explained as the result of big business wanting to censor any news that disagreed with what he called "the business-politicos-military-public relations oligarchy"—and as his finances were dwindling. "If one is to be poor," he said, "it is better to be poor in the country than in the city because one can at least grow . . . food instead of having to buy it from barrows or pick it out of garbage cans on city streets."

Nearing resided on the Vermont homestead without electricity or telephone. He wanted to accomplish more than to live frugally: He wanted to prove that he could live with minimal reliance on modern technology and modern markets. In 1950 he and his wife Helen wrote *The Maple Sugar Book*, whose title belied its full content; it was as much a book about living a basic life as it was about maple sugaring.

When land developers appeared on Nearing's horizon in 1952, he and Helen moved to a farm in Harborside, Maine. By then in his late 60s, he continued to chop wood, raise vegetables, and write books and articles.

In 1954 Nearing wrote *Living the Good Life,* and after the countercultural back-to-the-land movement emerged in the late 1960s, his publisher reissued the book in 1970, and it became a bible for alternative living. His autobiographical *Making of a Radical* (1972) influenced political activists.

Nearing kept tilling his land, built a stone farmhouse, and erected a stone wall that enclosed an organic garden. As his 100th birthday approached, he told his wife that he was ready to die, and after his birthday passed, he simply went to his bed and gave up. He died on August 24, 1983.

Further Reading

Nearing, Helen. *Loving and Leaving the Good Life.* Post Mills, Vt.: Chelsea Green, 1992.

Saltmarsh, John A. *Scott Nearing: An Intellectual Biography.* Philadelphia: Temple University Press, 1991.

Sherman, Steve, ed. *A Scott Nearing Reader: The Good Life in Bad Times.* Metuchen, N.J.: Scarecrow Press, 1989.

Newton, Huey Percy
(1942–1989) *black power activist, writer*

Huey Percy Newton was a founder of the militant Black Panthers during the 1960s counterculture. He was born on February 17, 1942, in New Orleans, Louisiana, to Walter Newton and Armelia Johnson Newton.

Huey Newton grew up in Oakland, California, where his father worked as a laborer for the city. He barely graduated from high school but decided to overcome his poor academic record, and to accomplish this he enrolled at Merritt College, a two-year school. His friend BOBBY SEALE introduced him to *The Wretched of the Earth*, a book by the black psychologist Frantz Fanon, and Newton endorsed Fanon's idea that violence could educate oppressed people and develop leadership. Raised in the ghetto, Newton was already well acquainted with violence, and while at Merritt he formed a gang and served six months in jail for felonious assault with a knife.

Also while at Merritt, he organized the Soul Students' Advisory Council, through which he advocated that oppressed blacks defend themselves with guns and develop a revolutionary program to tear down capitalism and establish socialism. Most of the group's members rejected his call to arms, and although some of them advocated cultural nationalism—the idea that whites should be condemned for being white—Newton insisted that alliances should be forged with radical whites who wanted to advance leftist revolution.

In October 1966 Newton and Seale wrote a 10-point program that included demands for freedom, black self-determination, and the end of police brutality. Specifically, they stated:

1. We want freedom. We want power to determine the destiny of our black community.
2. We want full employment for our people.
3. We want an end to the robbery by the white man of our black community.
4. We want decent housing fit for shelter of human beings.
5. We want education for our people that exposes the true nature of this decadent

American society. We want education that teaches us our true history and our role in the present day society.

6. We want all black men to be exempt from military service.

7. We want an immediate end to *police brutality* and *murder* of black people.

8. We want freedom for all black men and women held in federal, state, county, and city prisons and jails.

9. We want all black people, when brought to trial, to be tried in court, by a jury of their peer group or people from their black communities, as defined by the Constitution of the United States.

10. We want land, bread, housing, education, clothing, justice, and peace.

They went on to state, "We believe that the federal government is responsible and obligated to give every man employment or a guaranteed income." And they said:

We believe that this racist government has robbed us, and now we are demanding the overdue debt of forty acres and two mules. Forty acres and two mules was promised 100 years ago as retribution for slave labor and mass murder of black people.... The Germans murdered 6 million Jews. The American racist has taken part in the slaughter of over 50 million black people; therefore, we feel that this is a modest demand that we make.

Newton and Seal adopted the name Black Panther Party and opened an office in Oakland on January 1, 1967, with Seale as chairman of the party and Newton as minister of defense. Newton soon declared that to be a "revolutionary nationalist" a person would "have to be a socialist."

Newton began armed patrols in Oakland to monitor the arrests of blacks. The police hated the tactic, but Newton understood his rights (critics said he flaunted them), for California law allowed the carrying of loaded guns, and he was determined to use the patrols to reduce police brutality. The Panthers wore combat jackets, raised clenched fists, and shouted, "Black Power!" and "Power to the People!" Newton talked about "rev-

olutionary suicide," meaning that the revolutionary must act against reactionaries even at the risk of death. Then in October 1967, shortly after the Panthers had staged a sensational demonstration in the state legislature, two policemen, one known for his poor relations with ghetto residents, stopped Newton and a friend. A struggle ensued between one of the police and Newton, and the policeman's gun went off, killing him and wounding Newton.

Newton's arrest generated widespread protests from radicals and even moderates who considered him a political prisoner. Nevertheless, he was tried for murder and found guilty of manslaughter.

In May 1970 a higher California court set aside Newton's conviction and released him. By that time the Federal Bureau of Investigation (FBI) and police had weakened the Panthers through harassment and raids so intense that one of Newton's close friends later claimed the attacks changed the Panther leader's personality, making him forever paranoid. Whatever the case, the Panthers suffered from their members' dealing drugs and committing petty crimes.

In 1971 Newton announced that the Panthers would forgo guns and revolution in favor of education, community programs, and nonviolent protests. That same year he visited Communist China, and in 1972 and 1973 he published two books of essays, *To Die for the People* and *Revolutionary Suicide*. Newton received a B.A. degree from the University of California at Santa Cruz in 1974.

By that year Newton had become addicted to cocaine, and he was arrested on charges of murdering a prostitute, gun whipping a tailor, and illegally possessing weapons. Rather than face trial he fled the country. He returned, however, in July 1977, and his trial for murder resulted in a hung jury. That same year he married Gwen Fontaine.

Although Newton suffered from drug and alcohol abuse, he still managed in 1980 to earn a doctorate in social philosophy at the University of California at Santa Cruz. Having divorced his first wife, he married Fredericka Slaughter in 1984.

Newton's legal problems flared anew when he was arrested in 1985 for embezzlement of funds from a nutritional program. His conviction in 1988 for violation of parole resulted in his serving time at San Quentin prison. In 1989 he pleaded no contest to the embezzlement charges; then on August 22 a street gang member killed him on a ghetto street in Oakland.

Huey Newton well recognized the risk of being a radical in America. "The first lesson a revolutionary must learn," he said in 1973, "is that he is a doomed man. Unless he understands this, he does not grasp the essential meaning of his life."

Further Reading

Newton, Huey P. *Revolutionary Suicide.* New York: Writers and Readers Publishing, 1995.

———. *War against the Panthers: A Study of Repression in America.* New York: Writers and Readers Publishing, 1996.

Pearson, Hugh. *The Shadow of the Panther: Huey Newton and the Price of Black Power in America.* Reading, Mass.: Addison-Wesley, 1994.

Noyes, John Humphrey

(1811–1866) *utopian reformer*

A religious utopian, John Humphrey Noyes advocated perfect holiness and founded communes at Putney, Vermont, and Oneida, New York. He was born on September 3, 1811, in Brattleboro, Vermont, to John and Polly Noyes. "Why should it be an incredible thing that God should raise the dead?" Noyes would ask in 1847. "Pride, envy, anger, sensuality, &c., are but limbs of the tree of sin, the stock of which is that *unbelief which rejects the righteousness of God.*"

Noyes's father moved frequently and held many different jobs over the years—teacher, tutor, minister, and businessman—and in 1815 was elected by Vermonters to one term in the U.S. House of Representatives. Young John was closer to his mother, a deeply pious woman who taught him to fear the Lord.

Sensitive to criticism, preoccupied with his speech and appearance, shy yet yearning to be assertive, John Humphrey Noyes entered Dartmouth College in the late 1820s. He graduated in 1830, studied and practiced law in New Hampshire, and

in 1831 prepared to join his uncle's law firm in Brattleboro.

But then the unexpected happened. As industrialization took hold in the Northeast and republican politics gave way to an opportunistic democratic system, disorder threatened to undermine society, and critics assailed the United States for failure to measure up to its ideals and for sinfulness in allowing slavery to continue. In that atmosphere, a religious revival, the Second Great Awakening, swept New England, and it attracted Noyes. As a result, rather than practice law he experienced a conversion and entered Andover Theological Seminary in Massachusetts.

One year after beginning his studies at Andover, Noyes transferred to Yale. He received his license to preach in 1833 and joined a small Congregational church in New Salem, New York, as its pastor. Noyes believed that even a person who had lived a wicked and sinful life could start anew, provided he or she surrender completely to God. Beginning in 1834 he sank into despair over his own weaknesses, and in an unshaven and bedraggled state he wandered among drunks and prostitutes in New York City, talking to them about salvation. To one of them he gave a Bible, to another some money, and to all he offered compassion.

Noyes experienced a vision, of which he said, "On my bed [one] night, I received the baptism which I desired and expected. Three times in quick succession a stream of eternal love gushed through my heart and rolled back again to its source." There followed such a complete breakdown that his relatives thought him deranged. In 1835 one said about him: "He would not reason at all, but denounced everything and everybody. He looked haggard and care-worn." Noyes denied he was mad and insisted that spiritual growth required suffering.

Amid society's problems, some Americans embraced perfectionism, a belief that moral or spiritual perfection could be achieved by individuals or groups. Perfectionism took different forms, such as WILLIAM LLOYD GARRISON's striving for an immediate end to slavery. For Noyes it meant proclaiming that he had reached a state without sin and that others could do the same. He said that "men were either totally pure and perfect of

Christ or they were sinners," and he placed himself among the pure. With that the Congregational church expelled him.

Noyes began proclaiming that the millennium had occurred in A.D. 70, so no one had any need to fear sin. "The kingdom of Heaven," he declared, "could be realized on earth." In 1837 he wrote his Battleaxe Letter, in which he outlined his views about sex and marriage. He stated that a higher morality would develop once sex was "elevated to spirituality." Noyes refrained from advocating uncontrolled sexual pleasure and in that way distanced himself from the free love movement. But he said that in a godly community sexual intercourse should be no more restrained by law than "eating and drinking should be—and there is as little occasion for shame in the one case as in the other."

In 1838 Noyes married Harriet A. Holton, who had contributed money to his newspaper, *Witness,* and he founded a perfectionist community in Putney, Vermont, where some 30 followers operated two farms and a store. He instructed his adherents to study the Bible three times a day, and said to one, "I would much rather that our land should run to waste than that you should fail of a spiritual harvest."

As a result of the stillbirth of all but one of his five children, he developed his concept of male continence. Although he said, "To be ashamed of the sexual organs is to be ashamed of God's workmanship . . . of the most perfect instruments of love and unity," he insisted that the human sex drive be controlled to prevent moral collapse and painful childbirth for women. Since men were morally superior to women, he said, they must take the lead in exerting sexual self-control and therefore must during intercourse avoid ejaculation while maintaining an erection. To those who called the practice impossible, he proclaimed he had accomplished it through willpower granted to him by God.

Noyes formulated what he called his concept of "complex marriage" in 1846, after he and his wife had engaged in sexual relations with another couple. Noyes had concluded that monogamous marriages produced jealousy and selfishness, and he saw his idea as a compromise between tradi-

tional marriage and free love. He said, "The human heart is capable of loving more than one at the same time." Under his plan all men and women in the commune were married to each other. He linked complex marriage to ascending and descending fellowship, in which spiritually advanced members were paired with those less advanced.

In complex marriage, children belonged to the entire community, and procreation, done by community decision, had as its goal the siring of stronger offspring. "We believe the time will come when involuntary and random propagation will cease," Noyes said, "and when scientific combination will be applied to human generation as freely and successfully as it is to that of other animals."

The authorities, however, disagreed with Noyes and indicted him for adultery. He and his group then fled Putney and in 1848 founded the Oneida Perfectionists in Oneida, New York. They built a Bible communist economic system in which no one person owned property, and they engaged in farming, sawmilling, blacksmithing, and silk production. Most of their money, though, was generated by making steel traps used by hunters in the beaver trade. When that trade declined, they turned to making silverware.

Despite initial prosperity, dissension gradually overtook the group, and in 1879 its members abandoned their system of complex marriage. Shortly afterward Noyes immigrated to Canada to escape legal action, and the Oneida Perfectionists disbanded in 1881 and formed the Oneida Community, a joint stock company that thrived in continuing to make silverware.

John Humphrey Noyes died in Niagara Falls, Ontario, Canada, on April 13, 1886. According to historian Robert David Thomas, the visionary "had tried to deal with the disruptive circumstances of a rapidly changing society through . . . a community based on devotion, sentiment, obedience, and hierarchy."

Further Reading

DeMaria, Richard. *Communal Love at Oneida: A Perfectionist Vision of Authority, Property, and Sexual Order.* New York: E. Mellen Press, 1978.

Jacoby, John E. *Two Mystic Communities in America.* Westport, Conn.: Hyperion Press, 1975.

Klaw, Spencer. *Without Sin: The Life and Death of the Oneida Community.* New York: Allen Lane, 1993.

Thomas, Robert David. *The Man Who Would Be Perfect: John Humphrey Noyes and the Utopian Impulse.* Philadelphia: University of Pennsylvania Press, 1977.

O'Leary, Jean
(1948–) *gay rights activist*

A nun who left her convent because of her lesbianism, Jean O'Leary then became a leader in the gay rights movement. She was born on March 3, 1948, in Cleveland, Ohio, to Jim O'Leary, an advertising sales manager, and Betty Higgins O'Leary.

Jean O'Leary surprised all of her friends when she announced at her graduation from Magnificat High School in 1966 that she would be joining a convent, for they knew her as an outgoing member of rock'n'roll bands. But later that year she became a novice in the convent of the Sisters of the Holy Humility of Mary, in Youngstown, a teaching and nursing order. She wanted, she said, to make a difference in the world.

O'Leary took her temporary vows, studied psychology at Youngstown University, transferred to the Lourdes Convent in Cleveland, and graduated in 1971 from Cleveland State University with a B.A. She left the order, however, later that year after having become involved in sexual relationships with several women.

She then moved to Greenwich Village in New York City, which she knew to be a haven for gays. She enrolled in the doctoral program at Yeshiva University and began attending meetings of the Gay Activists Alliance (GAA). Discontented with men's domination of the GAA, she helped form the Lesbian Liberation Committee (LLC) within the GAA and served as its chairwoman. In that capacity she lobbied state legislators in Albany for laws that would protect gays from discrimination. In 1973 O'Leary withdrew the LLC from the GAA and established the Lesbian Feminists Liberation. Three years later she and Bruce Voeller were made co–executive directors of the National Gay Task Force.

In 1977 O'Leary organized meetings of leaders of gay groups with government officials, including those in the Department of State and the Department of Justice, and with Margaret Costanza, an aide to President Jimmy Carter, to discuss gay issues and work at ending discrimination against gays in federal agencies. O'Leary complained about policies that barred homosexuals from serving in the military, and she demanded more money for gay social and research programs and an end to the ban on granting U.S. citizenship to gay immigrants.

O'Leary also tried to build a bridge between the National Gay Task Force and groups involved in the civil rights and women's rights movements. At a meeting in Washington, D.C., she and Voeller met with the leaders of the American Civil Liberties Union, the League of Women Voters, the National Organization for Women, the National Women's Political Caucus, and the Women's Action League. "We are all facing common enemies," O'Leary said. She warned, "A new [conservative] right is forming opposed to an equal rights amendment, abortion, and gay rights." And she said, "As a minority group we have a lot in common with women and blacks but there are differences, so our remedies have to be different." Also in 1977 President Jimmy Carter appointed her to the National Commission on the Observance of International

Woman's Year, and she helped arrange the National Women's Conference, held in Houston, Texas.

O'Leary moved to Los Angeles in 1979 to serve on the board of directors of National Gay Rights Advocates (NGRA); a nonprofit law firm dedicated to protecting gay rights, it was also the country's largest organization working for gay rights in general. Two years later she became the group's executive director. Under her leadership the NGRA won a lawsuit against several federal agencies, including the Food and Drug Administration, that compelled the government to quicken its evaluation of drugs used to treat acquired immunodeficiency syndrome (AIDS). In the 1990s O'Leary headed a computer supply firm and continued to work for gay rights. In the year 2000 she chaired the Democratic National Committee's Gay and Lesbian Caucus.

Further Reading

Marcus, Eric. *Making History: The Struggle for Gay and Lesbian Equal Rights.* New York: HarperCollins, 1992.

Oppenheimer, Julius Robert
(1904–1967) *antinuclear activist, scientist*

A physicist best known as the inventor of the atomic bomb, Julius Robert Oppenheimer also warned against an arms race with the Soviet Union and the development in America of a garrison state. He was born on April 22, 1904, in New York City to Julius Oppenheimer, a textile importer, and Ella Freidman Oppenheimer.

Robert Oppenheimer grew up in wealth, being chauffeured to a private school every day. In 1922, after a bout with dysentery, he entered Harvard. His voracious intellect showed in his pattern of taking four or five courses each semester for credit and another two or three for the purpose of expanding his mind culturally. He spent many hours in the library reading an eclectic assortment of books.

Oppenheimer graduated with a B.A. summa cum laude in 1925, with his main interest in physics (though he majored in chemistry). In 1927 he received a Ph.D. from the University of Göttingen in Germany, where with his major professor, Max Born, he wrote a thesis that advanced a quantum theory of molecules, called the Born-Oppenheimer approximation.

Having completed postdoctoral work, Oppenheimer accepted a joint appointment in 1929 as assistant professor at the University of California and the California Institute of Technology. He developed into an engaging teacher, a wiry man adeptly handling both a cigarette and chalk while lecturing and known for communicating enthusiasm for his subject. During the 1930s his prodigious research resulted in numerous papers on quantum mechanics, nuclear physics, and cosmic rays.

At the same time, the Great Depression caused him to investigate alternatives to capitalism. He associated with left-wingers and communists and later admitted that he had belonged to "just about every Communist front organization on the West Coast." He concluded that a cooperative society would work much better than a competitive one. On November 1, 1940, he married Katherine Puening Harrison; they had two children.

Oppenheimer's involvement with the atomic bomb began in October 1941 when fellow physicist Ernest O. Lawrence advised the federal government that it consult Oppenheimer about fast-neutron reactions. In May 1942 the government put him in charge of fast-neutron research, and later that year General Leslie R. Groves, head of the Manhattan Project, a secret program to develop an atomic bomb, appointed him director of the central laboratory for bomb design to be established at Los Alamos, New Mexico. Writing in *The Wilson Quarterly* (August 1994), Robert Erwin states that Oppenheimer's "reputation for bridging theoretical and experimental physics appealed to the can-do spirit of the armed forces."

Oppenheimer recruited the nation's leading physicists, or what Groves called "the greatest collection of eggheads ever." In taking charge at Los Alamos, Oppenheimer effectively balanced the secrecy required by the program with the scientific need for open investigation, and he established an atmosphere that encouraged the scientists to put aside their clashing personalities and work cooperatively.

At 5:30 A.M. on July 16, 1945, at the Alamogordo Bombing Range in New Mexico, the scientists detonated a nuclear explosion, unleashing a fireball and a mushroom cloud 40,000 feet high. Oppenheimer watched with mixed emotions, convinced an A-bomb must be built before Hitler completed one but distraught over the potential for massive destruction.

As it turned out, Germany surrendered and withdrew from World War II before the A-bomb could be completed. By the time it was ready for use, Japan had become the target. When some scientists at Los Alamos suggested that lives be spared by demonstrating a test explosion to the Japanese rather than bombing one of their cities, Oppenheimer opposed the idea as impractical.

Robert Oppenheimer helped develop the atomic bomb and then opposed the nuclear arms race with the Soviet Union. *(Library of Congress)*

In 1947 Oppenheimer became director of the Institute for Advanced Study in Princeton, New Jersey. Under his leadership the institute emerged as the world center for theoretical physics; at the same time he developed its solid reputation for liberal studies. Oppenheimer began writing articles for the lay public, exploring the link between science and society, and as a member of the General Advisory Committee established by the Atomic Energy Commission (AEC) in 1949 he recommended to President Harry Truman that he forgo a rapid program to develop a hydrogen bomb. Truman, however, ignored his advice.

Oppenheimer opposed the arms race that developed with the Soviet Union. He said that he "must tell" about it but complained that he could not reveal government secrets. Robert Erwin writes, "His position hindered his ability to talk openly about using an arms race as an excuse for imposing a garrison state in peacetime, replete with loyalty oaths, spy networks, and the large standing army that Americans had traditionally rejected." He believed that countries involved in the arms race were acquiring many more weapons than defenses required.

In June 1954 the AEC revoked Oppenheimer's security clearance with the explanation that his leftist associations prior to World War II made him a security risk. It was a conclusion reached without sound evidence to support it, and many scientists and laypersons protested. The government, however, was more interested in eliminating from its inner circles individuals opposed to its arms policy.

Nevertheless, Oppenheimer continued to direct the Institute for Advanced Study and lectured frequently both within the United States and overseas. In 1963 he received the AEC's Enrico Fermi Award for outstanding contributions to atomic energy.

Oppenheimer died on February 18, 1967, in Princeton, New Jersey. He had never wavered from his belief in military preparedness, but as Lewis states, he had advised: "Don't waste resources competing in corners of the world where the United States has no vital interest. Don't imagine you are hurting your enemies by making schoolteachers sign loyalty oaths."

Further Reading

Kunetka, James W. *Oppenheimer: The Years of Risk*. Englewood Cliffs, N.J.: Prentice-Hall, 1982.

Schweber, S. S. *In the Shadow of the Bomb: Bethe, Oppenheimer, and the Moral Responsibility of the Scientist*. Princeton, N.J.: Princeton University Press, 2000.

Smith, Alice Kimball, and Charles Weiner, eds. *Robert Oppenheimer, Letters and Recollections*. Stanford, Calif.: Stanford University Press, 1995.

Ortiz, Alfonso Alex

(1939–1997) *Indian rights activist*

Alfonso Alex Ortiz was an anthropologist, folklorist, and activist. He was born on April 30, 1939, at San Juan Pueblo north of Santa Fe, New Mexico, to Sam Ortiz, a Tewa Indian, and Lupe Naranjo Ortiz, a Spanish American.

Alfonso Ortiz was raised by his Tewa grandparents and graduated from Espanola High School with a National Merit Scholarship that allowed him to attend the University of New Mexico in Albuquerque. In 1961, the same year he obtained a B.A. in sociology, he married Margaret Davisson; they had three children.

The following year Ortiz received a fellowship and enrolled at the University of Chicago to study anthropology. When one of the college's professors, Fred Eggan, the leading authority on the Pueblo Indians, suggested to Ortiz that he study his own people, Ortiz agreed. Over the next five years he did fieldwork in New Mexico and in 1967 earned his doctorate. He modified his dissertation and in 1969 published it as his first book, *Tewa World: Space, Time, Being and Becoming in a Pueblo Society*.

Meanwhile, he had begun teaching at Princeton University in New Jersey as an assistant professor of anthropology, and in 1971 he was elected vice president of the Association on American Indian Affairs (AAIA). Two years later he became its president, a post he held until 1988. Under him the AAIA succeeded in its effort to have the sacred Blue Lake returned to the Taos Pueblo people and convinced Congress to pass the Indian Child Welfare Act.

Ortiz left Princeton in 1974 to teach at his alma mater, the University of New Mexico. He edited two volumes of the *Handbook of North American Indians*, published by the Smithsonian Institution, and in 1984 joined Richard Erdoes to write *American Indian Myths and Legends*, which has since become a classic work in contemporary anthropology. He served also on the advisory board of the Native American Rights Fund, which provided legal help to Indian communities. Alfonso Ortiz died of heart failure on January 27, 1997, in Santa Fe, New Mexico.

Further Reading

Erdoes, Richard, and Alfonso Ortiz, eds. *American Indian Myths and Legends*. New York: Pantheon Books, 1984.

Jojola, Ted. "A Tribute to Alfonso Ortiz, 1939–1997." *Wicazo Sa Review* 12 (Fall 1997) 9+.

Owen, Robert

(1771–1858) *communal reformer*

Robert Owen took the money that he amassed from his management of a textile mill and applied it to a communal experiment in Indiana noted for its secular arrangement and its rapid collapse. He was born on May 14, 1771, in Newton, Wales.

Owen was the son of a shopkeeper, and though he left school at age nine, he excelled at business. By age 18 he had risen from working as a clerk to managing one of the largest textile mills in Manchester, England. In 1799 he and several partners purchased the mills at New Lanark, Scotland. Disturbed by the working conditions he found there and by those conditions that had developed in Britain's industrializing economy as a whole, he determined to make changes. For the 2,000 workers at the mills he renovated the housing, established safety procedures, provided insurance plans through payroll deductions, and founded schools.

But Owen was in a quandary. He had made tremendous money in industry, yet he disliked the degrading conditions the industrial economy had produced and thought that the factory system was brutal and competitive. To a certain extent, he looked backward to an idealized preindustrial past when people lived in small towns and coexisted in harmony.

Primarily, though, he was a rationalist; whereas other reformers turned to religion for guidance, Owen relied on the mind. True to the words that appeared on the masthead of a newspaper he published, "The character of a man is formed for him, not by him," Owen embraced a philosophy that said the environment exerted the most influence in shaping people's actions, and in *A New View of Society* (1813) he advocated government programs to help those living in poverty.

Parliament, however, rejected his proposals for unemployment and poor relief, causing him to doubt that government could ever enact substantial reform. As a result he advocated the founding of villages where workers would live in comfortable housing, with good schools and a cooperative environment. His proposals profoundly affected American reformers, particularly in causing them to see the value of his environmental argument and the limitations to their own belief in individualism.

In 1824 the Harmony Society, operating the Harmony commune in southern Indiana, contacted Owen about selling their property to him. He bought the nearly 20,000 acres and 200 buildings and called it New Harmony. Owen arrived in the United States in November 1824 with grand plans to apply his ideas to the settlement. His program excited reformers and mainstream Americans alike; he even addressed Congress twice and met with President James Monroe and President-elect John Quincy Adams. Here, after all, was a man with an alternative to the industrial blight that had overcome England and that threatened to appear in America as its agricultural economy encountered the intrusion of factories.

Years later, Owen's son, Robert Dale Owen, described the terrain at New Harmony as his father began his social experiment:

> The land around the village, of which three thousand acres were under cultivation, was of the richest quality of alluvial soil, level but above the highest water mark, and in good farming order. This valley-land was surrounded by a semicircular range of undulating hills, rising sixty or seventy feet above the plain below, and sweeping round about half a mile from the village on its southern side.

As verdant as the land may have been, Owen's plans grew only brambles. At first New Harmony seemed destined for greatness. About 800 settlers arrived in 1825, more than the buildings could house. These included renowned intellectuals and activists. Robert Dale Owen remembered them as "Thomas Say, who six years before had accompanied Major Long on his expedition to the Rocky Mountains as its naturalist; Charles Lesueur, a French naturalist and designer . . . Gerard Troost, a native of Holland and a distinguished chemist and geologist," and William Maclure, president of the Philadelphia Academy of Sciences.

But most of the settlers had little commitment to Owen's ideas; many were even wastrels. Writing in New Harmony's newspaper, the *Gazette*, Robert Dale Owen recalled: "Our opinion is that Robert Owen ascribed too little influence to the early anti-social circumstances that had surrounded many of the quickly collected inhabitants of New Harmony before their arrival there." In short, Owen had failed to screen his initiates.

Other problems bedeviled the settlement. Most important, Owen believed that families and private property ownership were barriers to community, but he never completely decided how they should be handled and was often blocked in making changes. Owen owned New Harmony outright, and when several settlers pressured him to turn it into a true commune in which the property would be held by the "true believers," others imposed their own views. Speaking in 1827, Owen recounted that "it was proposed, that a community of common property and equality should be formed from among the members of the preliminary society" most fully committed to his ideas. But, he said, "this intention was frustrated by a motion . . . that *all* the members of the preliminary society should be admitted members of the community."

Owen contributed to New Harmony's problems by failing to provide effective leadership. He spent little time at the settlement, relying too much on his son, Robert Dale Owen, to communicate his directives through the *Gazette*.

Owen's experiment encouraged the formation of 16 Owenite communities in the United States between 1825 and 1829. None lasted more than a short time, and New Harmony itself failed in 1828. Back in England by that year, less $200,000 he had lost in the collapse of New Harmony, Owen continued to pursue reforms that would help the working class. He died in Newtown on November 17, 1858.

Despite New Harmony's brief existence, Owen had challenged the industrial capitalist ethic with ideas that stressed community over selfishness and encouraged society to recognize the environmental influences at work in shaping human beings. Other reformers had previously attempted utopian communities in America, but they usually had done so by relying on religion; Owen, however, used reason as the building block for a community that would serve as a beacon for the rest of the world.

Further Reading

Barker, Paul. "In New Lanark Robert Owen Tried to Forge a New Society." *New Statesman,* August 7, 1998, 54.

Harrison, John Fletcher Clews. *Quest for the New Moral World: Robert Owen and the Owenites in Britain and America.* New York: Scribner, 1969.

Harvey, Rowland Hill. *Robert Owen, Social Idealist.* Berkeley: University of California Press, 1949.

Johnson, Oakley C. *Robert Owen in the United States.* New York: Humanities Press, 1970.

Owen, Robert. *The Life of Robert Owen: Written by Himself with Selections from His Writings and Correspondence.* Fairfield, N.J.: A. M. Kelly, 1977.

Paine, Thomas
(1737–1809) *political philosopher, revolutionary, writer*

An international revolutionary, Thomas Paine wrote *Common Sense* and *The Age of Reason.* He was born on January 29, 1737, in Thetford, England, to Joseph Paine, a stay maker (a person who fashioned whalebone used in corsets), and Frances Cocke Paine.

Thomas Paine's family was a poor one, so although he was enrolled in 1743 at the Thetford Grammar School, his education ended seven years later when economic hardship forced him to work as an apprentice in his father's trade. Paine then labored for 12 years, interrupted only by a brief stint in 1757 as a privateer. He opened his own stay-making shop, and in 1759 he married Mary Lambert, but one year later she and their child died during childbirth. In 1762 he became an excise tax officer and collected taxes, but he was soon dismissed after an accusation that he had filed an improper report.

From 1766 to 1768 Paine taught school in London and then obtained reappointment as an excise tax officer. He again ran into trouble, though, when he organized his fellow workers to demand higher wages. During this dispute he wrote his first pamphlet, *The Case of the Officers of Excise,* in which he expressed ideas he would discuss in later writings, especially his discontent with the poverty in England and dislike for the wealthy. In 1771 Paine married Elizabeth Ollive and ran a tobacconist shop that had been owned by his re-cently deceased father-in-law. He had little interest in business, however, and spent considerable time reading and attending lectures. He liked to meet with the White Hart Evening Club to debate political issues and was, in fact, considered to be the best debater in the group.

In 1774 Paine suffered another reversal when his tobacconist shop folded, he and his wife separated, and he lost yet another job with the excise service. As the times tried his soul, he decided to sail for America. In London he had met Benjamin Franklin, then an agent for several of the British North American colonies, and the Pennsylvanian provided him with letters of introduction to prominent colonists.

Paine arrived in Philadelphia on November 30, 1774, and soon afterward began writing for the *Pennsylvania Magazine,* which he eventually edited. By this time differences between the colonies and Britain had reached a critical point. The colonists were rejecting Parliament's attempts to tax them, and the Boston Tea Party, led by the radical Samuel Adams, had pushed events closer to revolution. Then, after the first shots rang out in 1775 at Lexington and Concord, Paine issued a work that removed the last restraints on the colonists, namely, his pamphlet *Common Sense;* it changed the political debate and went through 25 editions within one year, reaching a circulation of 500,000.

In *Common Sense* Paine argued that the colonies should be independent and that a republican government was superior to a monarchy. He insisted that power should reside largely in the people, and with that view he took the most radical position among America's founders. In promoting independence, his words rang clear as a liberty bell, rallying common people and elite leaders alike:

> There is something absurd in supposing a continent to be perpetually governed by an island.
>
> France and Spain never were, nor perhaps ever will be, our enemies as *Americans,* but as our being the subjects of Great Britain.
>
> I challenge the warmest advocate for conciliation to show a single advantage that this continent can reap being connected with Great Britain.

The stir caused by his pamphlet impressed George Washington, Thomas Jefferson, James Madison, and Alexander Hamilton, even though to varying degrees they worried that he had gone too far in advocating popular power. John Adams, the Massachusetts patriot, disliked Paine's excesses but said of him: "Without the pen of Paine the sword of Washington would have been wielded in vain."

Paine's pamphlet helped weaken fears that the colonists would stand no chance of winning a war against Britain, and, more important, it helped the colonists see themselves as Americans rather than Britons. In *Tom Paine and Revolutionary America* (1976), Eric Foner claims that *Common Sense* did something else: that in extolling a republican government, "Paine literally transformed the political language. 'Republic' had previously been used as a term of abuse in political writing; Paine made it a living political issue and a utopian ideal."

Tom Paine provided crucial leadership in guiding Pennsylvania to support independence and adopt the most democratic constitution of all the states. Indeed, he desired more than separation from Britain: He wanted radical political change, and that occurred when the Pennsylvania convention adopted a state constitution that largely followed the ideas he had outlined in *Common Sense.* The document provided for a one-house legislature with no executive branch, annual elections, no property qualifications for holding office, and nearly universal male suffrage. Although conservatives dismantled the constitution in 1787 (enact-

Thomas Paine died a forgotten and disliked man in the country he helped to create, the United States. *(Library of Congress)*

ing changes even Paine considered necessary), the document nevertheless signified the radical stream of the Revolution, one that distrusted the elite and challenged the traditional power structure by advancing popular power.

In 1776, while the Pennsylvania convention met, Paine enlisted in the army, and as aide-de-camp to General Nathanael Greene he retreated with the Continental troops when the British advanced across New Jersey. In that inglorious time, he wrote *The American Crisis,* with its famous lines about summer soldiers and sunshine patriots. Before crossing the Delaware River at Christmas in 1776 to attack Hessian soldiers, General Washington ordered that the pamphlet be read to his troops. The work's stirring sentiments lifted their spirits, as it did those of other revolutionaries.

"These are the times that try men's souls," Paine wrote. "The summer soldier and the sunshine patriot will, in this crisis, shrink from the service of their country; but he that stand it *now,* deserves the love and thanks of man and woman."

With the recommendation of Massachusetts leader John Adams, in 1777 Congress appointed Paine secretary to its foreign affairs committee. He resigned, however, in 1779 after a messy controversy in which he had publicly revealed that the French had sent supplies to the United States at a time when France and Britain were at peace—a transaction the French government wanted hidden from the British.

That November the Pennsylvania Assembly made Paine its clerk, and he continued to write his *Crisis* pamphlets while diverting part of his salary to support the Revolution. With the British surrender in 1783, Paine bought a small farm in New York, where he lived until 1787. He largely avoided politics, but he did speak out in 1785 to voice his support for the Bank of North America, the first "national" bank, which he considered important to stabilize America's currency and provide capital for economic expansion.

Paine sailed for England in 1787 seeking to win acceptance for his innovative plan for an iron bridge. Financiers eventually built the bridge, but by then the French Revolution had erupted. Convinced that his help was needed to spread revolutionary ideals, in 1789 he journeyed to Paris. Two years later Paine wrote *The Rights of Man,* a reply to *Reflections on the Revolution in France,* written by the English conservative Edmund Burke, who had attacked the overthrow of the French monarchy as destroying traditional wisdom and promoting riotous disorder. Paine supported the radical break with tradition, insisting that each generation must reinvent institutions or be tyrannized by the past.

In 1792 Paine issued *The Rights of Man, Part Second,* in which he condemned monarchy and promoted the concept of democracy, at that time labeled a dangerous ideology. He also insisted that each individual possessed natural rights and that a bill of rights should exist to protect them. He hoped that his works would lead to the end of the monarchy in England, but the British government

censored him and in 1792 convicted him in absentia of treason.

Paine was by then in Paris, and in September he won election to the French Assembly. After the moderate group, or Girondins, with which he associated fell from power in June 1793, he no longer attended the assembly. In December radical revolutionaries arrested him, and he was imprisoned in Luxembourg. During his confinement Paine completed *The Age of Reason,* in which he presented his deism, or belief in an impersonal God, and pilloried churches and the Bible as representing or promoting superstition. Paine believed that a rational, reasoned world would best promote human welfare, and he presented Christianity and deism as incompatible. The clergy in Europe and America widely attacked him.

In July 1795 Paine returned to his seat in the French Assembly. The following year he wrote *Agrarian Justice,* in which he said that economic activities should be regulated for society's welfare and stressed the urgency of alleviating the worsening poverty in Europe. Nevertheless, Paine stopped short of calling for the end to private property.

At the invitation of President Thomas Jefferson, Paine returned to America in 1802 and settled on his farm in New Rochelle, New York. He had little money, and most of his revolutionary colleagues ignored him, saying he was too radical, particularly since stories circulated—incorrect ones, as it turned out—that he was an atheist. In 1808 he moved to Greenwich Village. He died there on June 8, 1809, largely forgotten, his funeral attended by only six mourners. A final indignity occurred in 1819 when William Cobbett, a British journalist who hoped to build a memorial to honor the revolutionary, removed Paine's remains from their burial spot and took them to England; he then died before the project could be completed, and Paine's bones were lost.

The historian Eric Foner has written about Paine: "More than any other individual, [he] set an example of the radical cast of mind [with] his . . . revolutionary internationalism and defiance of existing institutions, his rationalism and faith in human nature, and his belief in casting off the burden of the past and remaking institutions."

Paine said in *The Rights of Man:* "From what we now see, nothing of reform in the political world ought to be held improbable. It is an age of revolutions, in which everything may be looked for."

Further Reading

Ayer, A. J. *Thomas Paine.* London: Secker & Warburg, 1988.

Foner, Eric, ed. *Thomas Paine, Collected Writings.* New York: Library of America, 1995.

———. *Tom Paine and Revolutionary America.* New York: Oxford University Press, 1976.

Keane, John. *Tom Paine: A Political Life.* Boston: Little, Brown, 1995.

Parks, Rosa
(Rosa Louise McCauley)
(1913–   ) *civil rights activist*

An activist for the National Association for the Advancement of Colored People (NAACP), Rosa Parks has been most remembered for her refusal to obey a segregationist law governing buses. She was born Rosa Louise McCauley on February 4, 1913, in Tuskegee, Alabama, to James McCauley, an African American with Indian blood who was a skilled carpenter and stonemason, and Leona Edwards McCauley, a mulatto.

In *Rosa Parks* (2000) historian Douglas Brinkley writes, "To understand the African-American condition when Rosa McCauley was born, it is illuminating to read the February 1913 edition of the NAACP's monthly journal, *The Crisis.* . . . [It] published a harrowing tally of the names and hometowns of blacks lynched or burned for supposed crimes—sixty-three documented cases in 1912 alone."

Rosa McCauley had lived in Tuskegee for only two years when her father briefly moved her and the rest of the family to Abbeville to live with his extended family; then he deserted them, and her mother took her to Pine Level.

As a teenager Rosa attended the high school affiliated with Alabama State Teachers College in Montgomery, the state capital, and in 1932 she married Raymond Parks, a barber. He was a member of the NAACP, and although he quit the group over a dispute, she, too, joined the civil rights organization.

With the American entry into World War II, Rosa Parks fumed over the hypocrisy evident in fighting against racism in Europe while enforcing it in the South, and she concluded that black voting was essential to tearing down segregation. "From the start the NAACP, to me at least, was about empowerment through the ballot box," she recalled. "With the vote would come economic improvements. We would have a voice."

As secretary of the Montgomery NAACP, she helped begin a voter registration drive and tried several times herself to register. Each time the registrars told her she had failed the literacy test; the rejection only strengthened her resolve to vote and to advance black rights, and in 1945 the authorities relented and granted her a voting certificate. While battling for suffrage, in 1943 Parks encountered a bigoted bus driver, James Blake. When she boarded Blake's bus through the front door, he demanded that she reenter through the back, the customary entry point for African Americans. Known for his viciousness toward blacks, Blake flew into a rage during the incident, and though Parks gave in to his demand, she vowed never again to ride a bus driven by him.

In 1947 the normally quiet Parks impressed her colleagues in the NAACP with an impassioned speech at the state convention in Mobile. She criticized those African Americans who promoted the South: "No one should feel proud of a place," she said, "as long as Negroes are intimidated."

Parks continued to work for the Montgomery NAACP while employed as a seamstress. During that time the organization decided to challenge the city's most offensive from of discrimination: the segregated public buses. The indignity that African Americans suffered by being forced to give up their seats to white riders when the whites-only section of a bus overflowed hurt all the more with the realization that blacks made up 70 percent of the riders and were thus the economic lifeblood of the bus system.

When in March 1955 a black female riding home from high school was arrested for violating the segregation law, it looked as if the NAACP had the case it could use to challenge the law in court. But the group's leaders refused to pursue it—the young woman, it turned out, was short-tempered and pregnant, and an unwed pregnant woman's trial would damage the NAACP in its attempt to influence public opinion. "They'd call her a bad girl," Parks recalled, "and her case wouldn't have a chance."

In summer 1955 Parks attended the Highlander Folk School near Chattanooga, Tennessee. Founded to protest social injustice, the school taught Gandhian nonviolent resistance and encouraged blacks and whites to use it in the fight for civil rights. Douglas Brinkley writes, "Parks left Tennessee feeling empowered to be one of many African Americans who would no longer tolerate racist bullying and who would use the federal courts to dismantle American apartheid."

On the evening of December 1, 1955, Rosa Parks, tired after a long day at work, boarded a Montgomery bus. As the front of the bus filled with whites, the driver turned around and ordered blacks sitting behind them to move to the back. Only then did Parks realize that she had boarded a bus she had vowed never to board again—one driven by James Blake.

Several blacks obeyed Blake. Parks, however, refused to budge. Blake demanded again; Parks refused again. He then called the police, and they removed her from the bus and arrested her. "Why do you all push us around?" Parks asked one of the policemen. "I don't know," he answered, "but the law is the law, and you're under arrest."

Parks had intended that day to ride home in peace; she never intended to become the NAACP "test case" in challenging the segregationist law. But she neither wanted to give in to Blake, whom she detested, nor compromise her principles. She later explained:

> These other persons had got on the bus after I did. It meant that I didn't have a right to do anything but get on the bus, give them my fare, and then be pushed wherever they wanted me. . . . There had to be a stopping place, and this seemed to have been the place for me to stop being pushed around and to find out what human rights I had, if any.

With the case headed to court, an even more significant development occurred: The Montgomery NAACP under the guidance of E. D. Nixon decided to boycott the city's buses.

Nixon and the other protesters recruited a young Baptist preacher, MARTIN LUTHER KING, JR., to lead the boycott and formed an organization to coordinate it, the Montgomery Improvement Association (MIA). The protesters made modest demands, stopping short of calling for complete desegregation of the buses. But the city refused, and on February 1, 1956, the MIA said it wanted the buses integrated.

The bus boycott was perilous. Those who joined it—and nearly all African Americans did—risked losing their jobs, being harassed by the police, and being physically attacked. Rosa Parks was fired from her job, yet she persevered and helped coordinate the boycott.

On November 13, 1956, the U.S. Supreme Court declared bus segregation unconstitutional, and on December 21 the city of Montgomery complied with the ruling. The boycott established a milestone victory in the fight for black civil rights.

In 1957 Rosa Parks moved with her husband to Detroit, Michigan. Once again working as a seamstress, she also helped raise money for the NAACP. In 1965 John Conyers, Jr., a black congressman from Michigan, hired her as his office manager.

In 1987, at age 74, she founded the Rosa and Raymond Parks Institute for Self-Development, which had as its goal helping black youths. In 1994 she entered the national headlines again, this time when a young black man brutally beat her and stole her money. Americans of all races expressed outrage over an incident that so vividly bespoke the horrors of urban crime.

In 1999 a seriously ill Parks, confined to a wheelchair, received a congressional medal for lifetime achievement; in 2000 the Rosa Parks Museum and Library opened in Montgomery.

Martin Luther King, Jr., once wrote about Parks and her refusal in 1955 to vacate her seat on the Montgomery bus:

> It was an individual expression of a timeless longing for human dignity and freedom. She

wasn't "planted" there by the NAACP . . . she was planted there by her personal sense of dignity and self-respect. She was anchored to that seat by the accumulated indignities of days gone and the boundless aspirations of generations yet unborn. She was a victim of both the forces of history and the forces of destiny. She had been tracked down by . . . the spirit of the time.

Further Reading

Brinkley, Douglas. *Rosa Parks*. New York: Penguin Books, 2000.

Parks, Rosa, with Jim Haskins. *Rosa Parks: My Story*. New York: Dial Books, 1992.

Paul, Alice

(1885–1977) *women's rights activist, suffragist*

An advocate of women's suffrage, Alice Paul was an author of the equal rights amendment. She was born on January 11, 1885, in Moorestown, New Jersey, to Quaker parents William Mickle Paul and Tacie Parry Paul.

Alice Paul attended private schools before entering Swarthmore College in Pennsylvania. She graduated from there in 1905 and for the next year took graduate courses at the New York School of Social Work while living at a settlement house, which had been founded to help the immigrant poor. In 1906 she went to England to continue her education; there her roots in Quakerism and Progressive reform blended with the local suffrage movement and caused her to join her host country's militant wing in the fight for women's voting rights.

With her studies completed in England, Paul received a master's degree in absentia from the University of Pennsylvania. On her return home she resumed her course work and in 1912 earned a doctorate, also from the University of Pennsylvania.

Paul transferred her suffrage activism to the United States and in 1912 led the congressional committee of the National American Woman Suffrage Association (NAWSA). But she favored more militant tactics than those practiced by

NAWSA and preferred to work at the national level rather than on a state-by-state basis for voting rights, so in 1913 she formed and chaired the Congressional Union for Woman Suffrage.

Pledging to work against Democratic congressional candidates who failed to support women's right to vote, Paul placed intense pressure on Congress, and in 1914 the House of Representatives passed a women's suffrage bill. The Senate, however, defeated it by one vote.

Even though the federal government demanded an end to political dissent during World War I, Paul and the Congressional Union decided to picket the White House for suffrage. They denounced the hypocrisy behind statements made by President Woodrow Wilson such as "We shall fight for the things which we have always held nearest our hearts—for democracy, for the right of those who submit to authority to have a voice in their own government." They called him "dictatorial and oppressive" toward women and chided him as "Kaiser Wilson."

In June 1917 the government began arresting the suffragists on charges of obstructing traffic. At first they received only minor sentences, but after they kept picketing—even withstanding an assault by a mob in July—Alice Paul was arrested and sentenced to seven months at the Occoquan Workhouse in Virginia.

The government ignored her request and those of other arrested picketers to be recognized as "political prisoners," and she and her colleagues began a hunger strike. "From the moment we undertook the hunger strike," she recalled, "a policy of unremitting intimidation began. One authority after another, high and low, in and out of prison, came to attempt to force me to break [it]."

Paul was placed in a psychopathic ward, and when she still refused to eat, she was force fed. For Paul and the other hunger strikers that tactic involved more than, as the government said, an attempt to "save them"; it was painful punishment as tubes were jammed down their nostrils and throats.

On November 14 the police arrested 33 more picketers, and in what has been called a "night of terror," the women were clubbed, handcuffed to iron bars, and denied access to toilets. Later that

As a suffragist, Alice Paul raised the ire of President Woodrow Wilson by campaigning for women's voting rights during World War I. *(Library of Congress)*

month a judge released Paul and the other protesters.

The government persecution, though, failed to intimidate or dissuade them. Instead, they reacted with anger and commitment. Texas suffragist Lucille Shields commented: "In jail . . . you realize more keenly the years that women have struggled to be free and the tasks that they have been forced to leave undone for lack of power to do them." They resumed picketing the White House and displayed signs stating, "President Wilson is deceiving the world when he appears as the prophet of democracy."

In 1917 the Congressional Union joined the Woman's Party to form the National Woman's Party, with Paul as head of its national executive committee. President Wilson finally announced his support for women's suffrage on January 9, 1918, and the next day the House of Representatives passed a constitutional amendment giving women the right to vote. The Senate did likewise in June 1919, and in August 1920, Tennessee became the 36th state to ratify the change, putting it into effect as the Nineteenth Amendment.

With that accomplishment in hand, Alice Paul earned a law degree from the Washington College of Law in 1922, and she drafted an Equal Rights Amendment (ERA) that was introduced into Congress in 1923. The amendment read: "Men and women shall have equal rights throughout the United States and every place subject to its jurisdiction. Congress shall have the power to enforce this article by appropriate legislation."

Paul earned another master's degree and another doctorate, both from American University, in 1927 and 1928, and from 1930 to 1933 she served as head of the nationality committee of the Inter-American Commission of Women, an organization formed to gain equal rights for women in Latin America. She also served on the Women's Consultative Committee on Nationality of the League of Nations, as well as on the executive committee of the World's Women Party.

Paul continued her fight for the ERA, and in 1944 both the Democratic and Republican Parties included support for the amendment in their platforms. But in 1946 the Senate failed to pass it. The issue then remained largely dormant until the women's liberation movement picked it up in the 1960s, whereupon Paul, though in her 80s, once again worked to get it passed. Congress finally approved an ERA amendment in 1970, but it failed to win ratification by the states.

Beginning in 1972 Paul's failing health limited her political activity. She died on July 10, 1977, in Moorestown.

Further Reading

Barker-Benfield, G. J., and Catherine Clinton, eds. *Portraits of American Women: From Settlement to the Present.* New York: St. Martin's Press, 1991.

Lunardini, Christine A. *From Equal Suffrage to Equal Rights: Alice Paul and the National Woman's Party,*

1910–1928. New York: New York University Press, 1986.

Pauling, Linus Carl
(1901–1994) *peace activist*

Ranked among the leading American scientists of the 20th century, Linus Carl Pauling was a prominent critic of nuclear proliferation and the Vietnam War. He was born on February 28, 1901, in Portland, Oregon, to Herman Henry William Pauling and Lucy Isabelle Darling Pauling.

Struggling to make a living as a druggist, the elder Pauling moved his family several times, first to Oswego, seven miles south of Portland, in 1903; then to Salem in 1904; to Condon, in northern Oregon in 1905; and finally back to Portland in 1909. One year later Linus Pauling's father died of a perforated ulcer, leaving Lucy Pauling to care for Linus and his two siblings.

A voracious reader as a child, Pauling also had a small chemistry laboratory in his bedroom. Even though a dispute over course credits prevented him from receiving a high school diploma, in 1917 he entered Oregon State Agricultural College (today Oregon State University) and five years later obtained a bachelor's degree in chemistry and physics. In 1925 he received a doctorate in chemistry from the California Institute of Technology (Cal Tech). With a Guggenheim fellowship in hand, he spent a year in the cities of Munich, Zurich, and Copenhagen, and there, under Europe's leading physicists, he studied quantum mechanics, a new discipline that sought to describe the nature of matter.

Pauling returned to Cal Tech as an assistant professor in 1927, and he studied the joining of atoms into molecules. He developed a theory of resonance in bonding that he presented in his book *The Nature of the Chemical Bond and the Structure of Molecules and Crystals* (1939). When applied, his theory led to the development of new drugs, plastics, and synthetic fibers. His book became a standard chemistry text for several decades.

Pauling also worked in molecular biology and biochemistry, expanding knowledge about the structure of protein molecules and showing connections between molecular irregularities and hereditary diseases. As he concentrated on complex chemical elements, in 1951 he discovered the alpha helix structure of several protein molecules. That, in turn, led to advances in disease control. In 1954 he won the Nobel Prize in chemistry for his work on chemical bonds and molecular structure.

With the outbreak of the cold war and the nuclear arms race between the United States and the Soviet Union, Pauling became an outspoken proponent of disarmament. His scientific work had made him aware of the dangers of excessive radiation and the destruction that nuclear weapons could inflict. Along with his wife, Ava Helen Miller, he joined the international peace movement and was attacked during the Red Scare (the government hunt for Communists and other radicals) by Senator Joseph R. McCarthy, who accused him of being a communist. Despite that attempt at intimidation, in 1958 Pauling wrote *No More War!* This book added warnings about the spread of biological and chemical weapons to concerns about nuclear weapons. That same year he presented a petition to the United Nations signed by more than 11,000 scientists calling for an end to nuclear testing. Because of his efforts he was awarded the 1962 Nobel Peace Prize.

In 1963 Pauling left Cal Tech to join the Center for the Study of Democratic Institutions in Santa Barbara, California. In 1965 he released a letter signed by eight other Nobel Prize winners demanding that the United States withdraw its troops from Vietnam. Shortly afterward he denounced the Vietnam War as unconstitutional and urged young men to resist the draft.

In 1967 Pauling left Santa Barbara for San Diego, where he became research professor of chemistry at the University of California; two years later he became professor of chemistry at Stanford University. His work with vitamin C caused a stir in 1970 when he claimed that large doses of it could help the human body's immune system and protect people from numerous infectious diseases.

The following year the government revealed that its army chief of intelligence had kept a file on Pauling, along with 125,000 other Americans, as alleged subversives. Pauling retired from teaching in 1973 and founded the Linus Pauling Institute of Science and Medicine in Palo Alto, California.

In the 1980s Linus Pauling lectured frequently on social issues. He died on August 19, 1994, at Palo Alto of prostate cancer.

Further Reading

Goertzel, Ted George. *Linus Pauling: A Life in Science and Politics.* New York: Basic Books, 1995.

Hager, Thomas. *Force of Nature: The Life of Linus Pauling.* New York: Simon & Schuster, 1995.

Marinacci, Barbara, and Ramesh Krishnamurthy, eds. *Linus Pauling on Peace: A Scientist Speaks Out on Humanism and World Survival: Writings and Talks by Linus Pauling.* Los Altos, Calif.: Rising Star Press, 1998.

Serafini, Anthony. *Linus Pauling: A Man and His Science.* New York: Paragon House, 1989.

Payne, Roger Searle

(1935–) *conservationist*

A biologist and conservationist, Roger Searle Payne is known for his recording of the songs of humpback whales. He was born on January 29, 1935, in New York City to Edward Payne, an electrical engineer, and Elizabeth Payne, a violinist.

Despite Roger Payne's urban upbringing, the youngster developed an interest in nature, which grew stronger after his parents moved the family to a less densely populated location in New Jersey. Payne majored in biology at Harvard University and earned a bachelor's degree in 1957. He then entered Cornell University in Ithaca, New York, where he studied animal behavior and wrote his doctoral dissertation on owls' use of sound to locate their prey in the dark. While at Cornell, Payne married Katy Boynton in 1960, and they would, over the years, collaborate in the study of whales.

Roger Payne first became interested in sealife in the mid-1960s. While teaching at Tufts University in Medford, Massachusetts, he heard about a dead porpoise that had become beached. When he went to see the porpoise, he discovered that human beings had desecrated its body. That convinced him to study and protect the creatures and their cousins, the whales.

In 1967 Payne met Frank Watlington, an engineer with the Lamont Geophysical Field Station in Bermuda. Watlington asked Payne to listen to some recordings he had made of humpback whales. Payne was astonished to hear the sounds, and after he analyzed them more closely concluded they were songs. Made mostly, if not exclusively, by the males, these songs changed over time and contained tonal variations generally associated with human music. The whale songs, Payne said, "were divided into repeating phrases called themes" with up to nine themes in a song. He theorized that the songs were likely used by males to attract females during courtship.

Payne soon began making his own tapes of the humpbacks. "The first time I ever recorded the songs . . . was off Bermuda," he recalled.

It was also the first time I heard the abyss. Normally, you don't hear the size of the ocean when you are listening, but I heard it that night. It was a bit like walking into a dark cave, dropping your flashlight and hearing wave after wave of echoes cascading from the darkness beyond, realizing for the first time that you are standing at the entrance to an enormous room. The cave has spoken to you. That's what whales do; they give the ocean its voice, and the voice they give it is ethereal and unearthly.

He stated:

When you swim up next to a singing whale through the blue water, the song is so loud, so thundering in your chest and head, you feel as if someone is pressing you to a wall with their open palms, shaking you until your teeth rattle. When you swim close enough to touch the singer, you doubt whether you will be able to stand the intensity of the sound. But you can.

In 1968 Payne joined the New York Zoological Society's Institute for Research in Animal Behavior and taught as an assistant professor of biology at Rockefeller University in New York City. In 1971 he founded the Whale Conservation

Institute, dedicated to protecting whales through education and research.

Payne began studying a population of right whales that wintered off the coast of Argentina at Peninsula Valdes, noted for its two nearly land-locked bays. Most scientists believed it would be impossible to study such a population intensively because whales spend most of their time beneath the water surface and they migrate. But Payne found a method to pinpoint and follow individual whales. He explained: "We have learned to identify individuals by callosities—patches of thickened skin distributed on the top, front, and sides of a whale's head—which make a whale recognizable from all directions except from below."

In the late 1960s Payne released recordings of the humpback songs to the public so they could share in the beauty of the music and be drawn into the complexity of the whales' lives. He hoped that would make people receptive to saving the whales from hunters and from the chemical pollution that was injuring their oceanic habitats. Payne has since worked with composers to integrate the songs of the humpback whales into music, such as the orchestral piece *And God Created Great Whales* by Alan Hovhaness,, presented by the New York Philharmonic in 1970.

In a 1994 interview Payne said, "Whales make us feel small, and I think that's an important experience for humans to have at the hands of nature. We need to recognize that we are not the stars of the show. We're just another pretty face, just one species among millions more. The star of the show is nature." In the year 2002 he continued his studies. He once said, "Much of my life has been spent among whales. Above all, I have tried to understand the messages that their songs and calls contain."

Further Reading

Payne, Roger. *Among Whales*. New York: Scribners, 1995.

Peltier, Leonard
(1944–   ) *Indian rights activist*

A charismatic leader in the American Indian Movement (AIM), Leonard Peltier fought for Indian treaty and civil rights until his arrest and conviction for killing two Federal Bureau of Investigation (FBI) agents. Peltier was born on September 12, 1944, to Leo and Alvina Peltier in Grand Forks, North Dakota. His father was an Ojibway and his mother was Lakota Sioux. After his parents separated when he was four years old, he was raised by his paternal grandparents, Alex and Mary Peltier.

Leonard Peltier grew up in poverty, moving with his family from one mining and logging camp to another. At age nine he attended the government-run Wahpeton Indian School in North Dakota, which taught the students that Native American culture was inferior to white culture. At age 14 he quit school (he would later earn a general equivalency diploma) and worked at odd jobs until the mid-1960s, when he owned an auto body shop in Seattle, Washington.

In 1972 Peltier joined AIM, a new organization formed to protect Indian rights through a militant strategy modeled on that of the Black Panthers. Peltier became friends with DENNIS JAMES BANKS, an AIM founder, and helped raise money for the group. He took part in several AIM protests, among them the Trail of Broken Treaties caravan in 1972 that journeyed to Washington, D.C. Peltier was among the 400 protesters who occupied the Bureau of Indian Affairs (BIA) building after officials reneged on a promise to meet with them.

By that time the FBI had started an extensive program to infiltrate, harass, and destroy AIM, and tension mounted on the Pine Ridge Reservation in South Dakota, where federal officials in the BIA allied with a Sioux faction under Dickie Wilson. The officials intended to cooperate with white interests to obtain reservation land and to obtain concessions that would allow the national government to mine for uranium.

This crisis led to violent confrontations between AIM and the government-Wilson alliance. On June 26, 1975, federal agents intruded on an AIM encampment near the reservation village of Oglala in pursuit of Jimmy Eagle, an Indian who, it was alleged, had stolen a pair of cowboy boots. The firefight that ensued—no one knows who shot first—resulted in the deaths of one AIM member and two FBI agents. In November 1975 the government indicted Peltier, along with Bob Robideau, Darrelle Butler, and Jimmy Eagle, for the killing of the agents. Fearing he would not get a fair trial, Peltier fled, at first hiding with friends at Pine Ridge and then slipping into Canada. He was captured early the following year, however, in Alberta and extradited to the United States.

The federal government dropped its charges against Eagle and decided to try Peltier separately from Robideau and Butler. His trial began on March 4, 1977, in Fargo, North Dakota, and was presided over by Judge Paul Benson, known for holding biased views toward Indians.

Most observers believe that the prosecutors and judge validated Peltier's fears about his trial. Highly dubious judicial rulings prevented Peltier from using a self-defense strategy—one that had led to the acquittal of Robideau and Butler. Judge Benson forbade Peltier to present evidence that the FBI had waged war against AIM and had tampered with evidence relating to the case. Further, he permitted the prosecution to submit an affidavit from a witness, Myrtle Poor Bear, despite her inconsistent testimony. (She has since claimed that the FBI coerced her into making statements detrimental to Peltier.)

The all-white jury found Peltier guilty of murder, and he received two consecutive life terms. On appeal, a court upheld the conviction, although the government officials have since admitted that they have no idea who killed the agents. He was sentenced to the federal penitentiary at Marion, Illinois.

In 1994 about 3,000 people participated in a 3,800-mile-long walk for justice to protest Peltier's continued imprisonment. In 1999 Peltier wrote *My Life Is My Sun Dance*, in which he discussed the importance to him of his Indian heritage. That same year the European Parliament asked President Bill Clinton to grant clemency to Peltier.

Many observers thought Clinton would agree to such an act, for by the time he was preparing to leave office in January 2001, Peltier had suffered a stroke. But Clinton refused to grant clemency. A disappointed Peltier then wrote the following to his supporters through the Leonard Peltier Defense Committee (LPDC):

> January 20, 2001, was a sad day for all of us. I know that this denial of clemency has affected many of you as much as it has affected both my family and myself. It is a terrible feeling and disappointment knowing that this nightmare has not ended and will continue for many months to come.
>
> When I received the news, I felt my stomach curl and a feeling of nausea rolled over me. It took a while for me to refocus. For some reason I had thought I might be having dinner with my family that night. It was an especially disappointing day for all of us.
>
> The White House gave my attorneys indications that there was a good chance for my clemency to be granted. I had to prepare myself for being released because there was no sign that my petition would be denied.
>
> The LPDC bought me clothes, my grandson prepared his bedroom for me to sleep in and other preparations were made for my homecoming . . .
>
> January 19, came and still, they kept us in nervous anticipation saying the more difficult clemencies are still being worked on and would be announced the next morning. Then January 20 came and went! The White House never even told us what the decision was. We had to find out through the press that my name was not on the list of clemencies. To leave a person's life and so many peoples' hopes hanging in the balance like that is truly hardhearted.

Thus Peltier still languishes in prison. Many activists, including the group Amnesty International, consider him to be a political prisoner, a talented leader persecuted because he challenged the compliant Indian model federal officials mandated on the reservations.

Further Reading

Matthiessen, Peter. *In the Spirit of Crazy Horse*. New York: Viking, 1991.

Peltier, Leonard. *Prison Writings: My Life Is My Sun Dance*. New York: St. Martin's Press, 1999.

Penn, William
(1644–1718) *civil liberties activist*

Through his influence on the settlers of New Jersey and his founding of Pennsylvania, William Penn stands out as the great promoter of civil liberties in colonial America. He was born on October 14, 1644, in London to Sir William Penn, an admiral who had extensive landholdings, and Margaret Jasper Penn.

From his time as a college student, William Penn was in trouble with the English authorities because of his religious beliefs. In 1660 he entered Christ Church College, Oxford, where he was influenced by Puritan ideas, but he was expelled in 1662 for criticizing the rituals of the official state church, the Church of England. Penn's father sent the young man to the European continent, hoping he would see the light and abide by the teachings of the Church of England, but Penn remained recalcitrant. He returned home and studied law for a year at Lincoln's Inn; then in 1667 he heard Thomas Loe preach in Cork, Ireland, and converted to the Quaker faith.

The Quakers, or Society of Friends, believe that every person has the potential for salvation, that all authority arises from the soul rather than the church, and that every person should be directed by an inner light. These claims greatly threatened the English monarchy, which exerted its authority through the Anglican Church. Added to the list of heresies, the Friends embraced political equality and pacifism, and they refused to swear oaths.

Penn wrote several religious tracts, and his *No Cross, No Crown* (1669), in which he stated that all religion emanated from the soul, landed him in the Tower of London. He was arrested in 1670 for public preaching and was placed on trial for inciting an unlawful assembly. He handled his own defense so effectively that the jury acquitted him. Then the judge ordered the jurors to change their verdict, and when they refused, he fined them. Later a chief justice upheld the jury's original decision, taking a stand for the freedom of English juries.

In April 1672 Penn married Gulielma Maria Springett, with whom he had four children. Between 1675 and 1680 he made a pilgrimage to the European continent to learn more about the Quaker faith and to spread the word, and he wrote political pamphlets that advocated toleration for religious dissenters, frequent elections, and Parliament's freedom from royal control.

When in 1677 a group of Friends obtained a grant to settle West Jersey in America, they carried with them the Concessions and Agreements, a charter largely written by Penn. The charter both affirmed English liberties and extended them. It guaranteed religious freedom (such toleration was not only unknown in England but limited in the North American colonies, as evidenced by the persecution of dissenters by Puritans in Massachusetts Bay), the right to trial by jury, and the right to petition. It included an innovative requirement that in jury trials in which Indians were involved the jury must be composed of six whites and six Indians.

William Penn petitioned King Charles II for a land grant north of Maryland to compensate for a debt owed his late father by the Crown and received a large tract, which was named Pennsylvania. He was required to pay the king two beaver

William Penn was the great promoter of civil liberties in colonial America. *(Library of Congress)*

pelts annually and one-fifth of any gold or silver that might be discovered in the new land. As with West Jersey, the charter, issued in March 1681, contained liberal principles that guaranteed religious freedom, established an elective assembly and an appointive council, and expressed Penn's opposition to dictatorial rule: "Any Government is free to the People under it . . . where the Laws rule, and the People are a Party to those Laws." Penn called Pennsylvania a "Holy Experiment":

> For my Country, I eyed the Lord in the obtaining of it . . . and desire to keep it; that I may not be unworthy of His love; but . . . serve His Truth and people; that an example may be set up to the nations; there may be room there, though not here, for such an holy experiment.

Although Penn wanted Quakers to settle his new colony, he recruited a diverse group that included Dutch, German, and Welsh colonists, some of them Quakers and some of other faiths. Growth was rapid, and by 1684 Philadelphia comprised 150 houses. The original charter was revised several times, and in 1701 the Charter of Privileges took legislative power away from the council and vested it in a one-house assembly, thus expanding the people's influence.

Penn established a humanitarian policy toward the Indians. He told them that he had "great Love and Regard towards you," and though they could not understand the English concept of land ownership, in negotiations for their lands he tried to treat them fairly and keep his promises. He opposed slavery, though he owned slaves himself, whom he freed on his death, and he advised against slave labor in Pennsylvania.

Because Penn had to defend the Pennsylvania charter in England from the Crown (from 1692 to 1694 the king controlled it as a royal colony), he spent little time in the settlement. Nevertheless, while in Philadelphia he supervised the laying out of the town and preached at Quaker meetings.

Penn suffered an apoplectic attack in 1712 that left him so mentally impaired that his wife had to take over his affairs. He died in London on July 30, 1718. A statement he once made while imprisoned in the Tower of London expressed his commitment to principles and independence: "My prison shall be my grave before I will budge a jot, for I owe my conscience to no mortal man."

Further Reading

Bronner, Edwin B. *William Penn's Holy Experiment: The Founding of Pennsylvania, 1681–1701.* New York: Columbia University Press, 1962.

Fantel, Hans. *William Penn: Apostle of Dissent.* New York: Morrow, 1974.

Peare, Catherine Owens. *William Penn: A Biography.* Ann Arbor: University of Michigan Press, 1956.

Soderlund, Jean R., et al., eds. *William Penn and the Founding of Pennsylvania, 1680–1684: A Documentary History.* Philadelphia: University of Pennsylvania Press, 1983.

Wood, Richard R. *William Penn: A Twentieth-Century Perspective.* Philadelphia: Philadelphia Yearly Meeting, Publications Committee, 1994.

Phillips, Wendell
(1811–1884) *abolitionist*

Athletic, handsome, and a stunning orator, Wendell Phillips ranked among America's leading abolitionists. He was born on November 9, 1811, in Boston, Massachusetts, to John Phillips, a wealthy lawyer and political figure who served as mayor of that city in the early 1820s, and Sarah Walley Phillips.

With his pedigree, Phillips attended the finest schools. He graduated from Boston Latin School and entered Harvard, where he obtained a bachelor's degree in 1831 and a law degree in 1833. He then opened a legal practice in Boston, but after finding his work confining and wanting to make a greater contribution to society, he searched for another way in which he could fulfill his father's admonition to provide leadership.

At first Phillips paid little attention to the antislavery movement. He later said: "I did not understand the country in which I lived. My eyes were sealed, so that, although I knew the Adamses and Otises of 1776, and the Mary Dyers and Ann Hutchinsons of older times, I could not recognize the Adamses and Otises, the Dyers and Hutchinsons, whom I met in the street of [1835]."

That changed in 1836 when he began court-ing Ann Terry Greene, a member of one of Boston's wealthiest families. Frail and sickly, Ann belonged to the Boston Female Anti-Slavery Society. A few months later the couple married, and long after that Phillips recollected: "My wife made me an out and out abolitionist, and she always preceded me in the adoption of the various causes I have advocated."

Yet for all the guidance Ann provided, other influences affected Phillips. For one, the controversy over slavery was reaching a feverish pitch with the expansion of settlers into the West, and the rebellion by Americans in Texas against Mexican rule was raising the prospect that the United States one day would annex that slave territory. For another, New England transcendentalists such as Ralph Waldo Emerson and Henry David Thoreau were advising people to pursue individual conscience, irrespective of society's restraints. Finally, Jacksonian democracy was gaining momentum; in an era when leaders emphasized the importance of the voice of the people, Phillips determined to shape that voice.

Phillips at first said little publicly about slavery, but then a dramatic development in 1837 caused him to speak out. In November ELIJAH PARISH LOVEJOY, the publisher of an abolitionist newspaper in Illinois, was attacked and killed by a mob. Lovejoy's death stirred the country, and Bostonians met at Faneuil Hall to debate the tragedy. James T. Austin, the state attorney general, defended the killing of Lovejoy by likening the mob to the colonists who had stood up to British tyranny in 1776, causing Phillips to respond with such succinct oratory that he destroyed Austin's argument. "To draw the conduct of our ancestors into a precedent for mobs . . . is an insult to their memory," he said. Referring to Austin, he added: "For the sentiments he has uttered, on soil consecrated by the prayers of Puritans and the blood of patriots, the earth should have yawned and swallowed him up."

Phillips then took to the lecture circuit, speaking on a variety of subjects, for which he received fees, and on abolitionism, for which he received no money. (Over the years, Phillips and his wife gave away nearly all of their considerable

Wendell Phillips applied his talent as "one of the first orators of the century" to the abolitionist movement. *(Library of Congress)*

wealth to charities.) According to observers, he typically began his speeches in a low voice before reaching a conversational level. He rejected formal lectern speeches and instead used a casual and friendly style. Yet he was foremost a powerful speaker, and his contemporary, the writer James Bryce, said he was "one of the first orators of the century, and not more remarkable for the finish than for the transparent simplicity of the style, which attained its highest effects by the most direct and natural methods."

So fervently did Phillips pursue his abolitionist ideas that for a time his family feared he was insane. He was an agitator and prided himself on being one. In fact, he wanted to be remembered as the greatest agitator of his time. In that vein, he cared little for politics or compromise; he wanted to shape public opinion through unadulterated moral principles.

Phillips developed a friendship and philosophical affinity with his fellow abolitionist WILLIAM LLOYD GARRISON. Like Garrison, Phillips insisted there existed a higher law than the Constitution, a moral law that judged slavery as evil. Thus he considered the Constitution nothing less than a pact with the devil for countenancing slavery. An immediatist who insisted there could be no accommodation with sin, he wanted slavery ended right away. "Immoral laws are doubtless void, and should not be obeyed," he said.

Whereas other abolitionists pursued a political strategy in the fight to end slavery by forming the Liberty Party and later the Free Soil Party, Phillips took the Garrisonian view that to participate in elections was to dance with the devil. Again in agreement with Garrison, he argued that the North should secede from the Union. Phillips was unclear as to how this would help the slaves (presumably slavery would vanish once denied northern military protection and economic ties), but he thought it would remove the North from any complicity with human bondage since existing federal law required northerners to return runaway slaves to their masters.

To an extent Phillips differed with Garrison on the issue of violence. Unlike his colleague, he stated that rebellion was a right sanctified by the Declaration of Independence, and so slaves could revolt, much as America's revolutionary leaders had risen up against England. (Never mind his earlier criticism of mob action—here liberty was the issue.) On one occasion he said, "I do not believe that . . . we shall see the total abolition of slavery, unless it comes on some critical conjunction of national affairs, when the slave, taking advantage of a crisis in the fate of his masters, shall dictate his own terms." But in agreement with Garrison's desire for nonviolence, he preferred peaceful change.

In 1840 the Phillipses attended the World Anti-Slavery Conference in London. Pursuing his belief that by advancing women's rights he would also be advancing abolition—because, he assumed, most women disliked slavery—he pushed for women to be admitted to the conference as voting delegates but failed in his effort. In 1845 Phillips closed his law office rather than take an oath to the Constitution. That same year he published a pamphlet for the American Anti-Slavery Society, *Can Abolitionists Vote or Take Office under the United States Constitution?*

When the Southern states seceded from the Union in 1860 and 1861, Phillips at first said they should be allowed to leave peacefully. But after Southern troops fired on Fort Sumter, he said the North must fight, both to defend itself and to end slavery. At first he criticized President Abraham Lincoln for limiting the ensuing war to one of preserving the Union. But after Lincoln issued the Emancipation Proclamation, Phillips supported the president, saying that although Lincoln had moved slowly, at least he had moved.

Phillips broke with Garrison in 1865 when Garrison sought to disband the Anti-Slavery Society on the ground that its work had been completed. Phillips argued that the organization must be kept alive to help the freedmen win land and the ballot. The society then continued to operate with Phillips as its president.

When the Civil War ended Wendell Phillips added to his moral crusades a fight for the rights of labor. He criticized big money and big businesses for controlling legislatures, with the result, he said, that voting meant nothing. He campaigned for the eight-hour workday and called for workers to own railroads, mills, and other means of production. He urged them to form their own political party, and in 1871 he ran unsuccessfully for governor of Massachusetts as the candidate of the Labor-Reform Party. He proclaimed that his party "declare[d] war with the wages system . . . war with the present system of finance, which robs labor and gorges capital, makes the rich richer and the poor poorer, and turns a republic into an aristocracy of capital." He praised the growth of the communist movement in France and advocated socialism.

When Wendell Phillips died on February 3, 1884, northern newspapers printed numerous eulogies. In one salute the Massachusetts legislature called him a man "full of the generous spirit of self-sacrifice . . . standing firm against any and every injustice like the hills of his native State."

Further Reading

Bartlett, Irving H. *Wendell and Ann Phillips: The Community of Reform, 1840–1880.* New York: Norton, 1979.

———. *Wendell Phillips: Brahmin Radical.* Boston: Beacon Press, 1961.

Stewart, James Brewer. *Wendell Phillips: Liberty's Hero.* Reprint. Baton Rouge: Louisiana State University Press, 1998.

Pierce, William Luther
(1933–) *white supremacist*

William Luther Pierce is the author of the racist and anti-Semitic *The Turner Diaries* and is a promoter of right-wing militia activity. He was born on September 11, 1933, in Atlanta, Georgia, to William Luther Pierce, an insurance agent, and Marguerite Ferrell Pierce.

Young Pierce grew up in Atlanta, Georgia, and in 1955 earned a bachelor's degree from Rice University in Houston, Texas. In 1962 he obtained a doctorate in physics from the University of Colorado at Boulder and then worked as a science laboratory researcher. Later that year he became an assistant physics professor at Oregon State University; in 1965 he moved to Connecticut, where he worked in a science lab at Pratt and Whitney. Pierce quit the company in 1966 to devote his energies to the American Nazi Party.

By the following year he had become one of the main leaders in the Nazi organization, renamed the National Socialist White People's Party. In 1970 he began the National Alliance, which appealed to young people to protect the white race against Jews and what he called other "undesirables."

In 1978 Pierce published *The Turner Diaries* (under the pen name Andrew Macdonald), a novel derived from a series he had written in a tabloid. Steeped in anti-Semitism and racism, the book tells of a world ruined by a Jewish conspiracy, then saved by a fearless fighter who leads "the Organization," dedicated to killing Jews and non-whites. On "Day of the Rope," the Organization hangs tens of thousands of white traitors who had associated with the members of other races. In the end a New Era emerges in which society is redeemed by white supremacy.

The Turner Diaries gained a wide audience within the far Right, selling more than 200,000 copies, and exerted considerable influence among militia leaders in the 1980s and 1990s. Timothy McVeigh, who bombed the Murrah Federal Building in Oklahoma City in 1995, treated the book as his Bible. Most Americans had never heard of *The Turner Diaries* until after the bombing, when observers pointed out the similarity between the explosion that leveled the office building and a tactic used by the main character in the book.

In 2002 Pierce continued to promote his extremist literature on a 400-acre farm near Hillsboro, West Virginia, and provided what he called a training ground for his followers to prepare for the great fight to save white civilization. "My purpose from the beginning has been the dissemination of ideas," Pierce told *Contemporary Authors,* "ideas about right and wrong behavior, about individual responsibility, about identity, about purpose, and about the significance of our lives in a cosmic context."

Further Reading

Blythe, Will. "The Guru of White Hate." *Rolling Stone,* June 8, 2000, 98+.

Mollins, Carl. "At Home with a Racist Guru: William Pierce Anticipated the Oklahoma Bomb." *Maclean's,* May 8, 1995, 42+.

Pierce, William. *The Turner Diaries.* Hillsboro, W. Va.: Barricade Books, 1978.

Powderly, Terence Vincent
(1849–1924) *union leader*

Terence Vincent Powderly was a leader of the Knights of Labor, America's largest union in the 19th century. He was born on January 22, 1849, in Carbondale, Pennsylvania, to Terence Powderly and Margery Walsh Powderly.

Terence Powderly attended school until age 13, when he began working on the railroad. At age

17 he became a machinist, and in 1871 he joined the Machinists' and Blacksmiths' Union, in which he took an active role. In 1872 he married Hannah Dever.

Just two years before Powderly joined the union, URIAH SMITH STEPHENS had founded the Knights of Labor as a grand secret organization to join all workers, skilled and unskilled, white and black, male and female, to build a cooperative society in which the wage system would disappear. Powderly joined the Knights in 1874 and advanced quickly in its ranks; by 1877 he was corresponding secretary for the district assembly in the region that included Oil City, Pennsylvania. The following year he helped draft a constitution for the Knights, which was adopted by the group's general assembly.

In 1879 Stephens retired as leader of the Knights, and Powderly replaced him, with the official title Grand Master Workman. The 1870s had been a time of numerous strikes called by workers as the economy adjusted to the rapid growth of industrial production with harsh results, including exploitive factory working conditions and severe depressions. The general failure of the strikes reinforced Powderly's views that workers should use them only as a last resort. Powderly insisted in 1882 that strikes could never solve labor's problems, because "strikes cannot change the apprentice system, a strike cannot remove the unjust technicalities in the administration of justice, a strike cannot regulate the laws of supply and demand, for if it cuts off the supply it also cuts off the demand by throwing consumers out of work, thereby curtailing their purchasing power."

To Powderly the Knights would work best as an educational group, teaching workers the necessity for solidarity and developing a cooperative society, and he insisted that the Knights should arrange contracts with industries through conciliation rather than confrontation. According to Philip S. Foner in *History of the Labor Movement in the United States* (1947), unlike more radical labor unions, the Knights proclaimed "the identity of interest between labor and capital."

In 1881 the Knights no longer operated as a secret organization, and as a result membership grew from fewer than 10,000 in 1878 to several hundred thousand by 1885. At the same time the Knights were faced with competition from the recently created Federation of Organized Trades and Labor Unions, which later became the American Federation of Labor (AFL), and had to confront the problem of whether to encourage the formation of trade unions and allow them to join the Knights.

Powderly believed that trade unions made the development of a cooperative society more difficult by separating workers into groups on the basis of their skills. In 1880 he wrote, "All men who labor have been brought by the hard times to one level and should have the good sense to remain on that level." The Knights, however, vacillated on the issue and then declared in 1882 that they would accept trade locals.

Throughout the 1880s Powderly pursued his policy of handling labor disputes without resorting to strikes. In several instances, however, the rank and file defied him and struck anyway. They often showed more interest than Powderly in immediate issues such as wages and hours; for Powderly these paled in significance in relation to the goal of building a cooperative society.

In the early 1890s the Knights declined rapidly, hurt by their failure to gain concessions from several industries, by the desire of some workers to pursue more militant tactics, by competition from the AFL, and by Powderly's own increasing remoteness from the membership. They rebelled against him and in 1893 forced him to vacate his leadership position.

The following year he began practicing law in Pennsylvania, and in 1896 he campaigned for the Republican presidential candidate, William McKinley. Once in the White House, McKinley appointed Powderly the United States commissioner-general of immigration, a post he held until 1902.

In 1907 President Theodore Roosevelt named Powderly chief of the Division of Information of the Bureau of Immigration. He resigned in 1921 to serve as commissioner of conciliation in the Labor Department, a post he held until 1924, when he resigned because of poor health.

Terence Powderly died on January 10, 1928, in Washington, D.C. He was survived by his second wife, Emma Fickenscher, whom he had married in 1919, after the death of Hannah Dever.

Further Reading

Phelan, Craig. *Grand Master Workman: Terence Powderly and the Knights of Labor.* Westport, Conn.: Greenwood Press, 2000.

Weir, Robert. "Powderly and the Home Club: The Knights of Labor Joust Among Themselves." *Labor History* 34 (Winter 1993): 84+.

Randolph, Asa Philip (A. Philip Randolph)
(1889–1979) *labor and civil rights leader*

Asa Philip Randolph was an organizer of the Brotherhood of Sleeping Car Porters and a civil rights activist. He was born on April 15, 1889, in Crescent City, Florida, to James William Randolph, a minister in the African Methodist Episcopal Church, and Elizabeth Robinson Randolph.

Raised in Jacksonville, Florida, Asa Philip Randolph left there in 1911 to find work in New York City as an actor. He failed to land any major stage roles, but while living in Harlem he attended classes at City College and at the Rand School of Social Science, where he learned about socialism and Marxism.

Randolph's move to the North occurred at a time of great demographic and economic change: In the early 1900s tens of thousands of blacks were leaving the South, making Harlem a largely African-American community; once in their new home they obtained jobs in industry.

During those years Randolph earned a following among blacks for his strident denunciation of racial segregation. In 1914 he became friends with Chandler Owen, a writer, and met Lucille Green, a widow. Later that year he married Green, and in 1917 he and Owen founded the *Messenger,* which they called "the only radical Negro magazine in America." And radical it was, espousing socialism, praising the Bolshevik Revolution in Russia, condemning the lynchings of blacks in the South, criticizing U.S. entry into World War I, and urging African Americans to resist service in the military until they had rights equal to those of whites.

Oddly, given his later labor leadership, Randolph at first thought unions incapable of helping black Americans. But in 1925 a group of porters (workers on the trains who handled baggage, shined shoes, and cleaned cars) asked him to organize them, and he grew to believe that union membership could advance blacks economically and secure their civil rights.

So in 1925 Randolph founded the Brotherhood of Sleeping Car Porters (BSCP). At first he made little progress; the Pullman Car Company, which employed many porters, ignored him, as did the white-dominated American Federation of Labor (AFL). But in 1926 and 1929 Randolph bargained for wage agreements with the company, and in the 1930s New Deal legislation made it easier to unionize. Finally, in 1935 the AFL granted a charter to the BSCP.

Although Randolph embraced socialism, he disagreed with the argument that the oppression suffered by blacks could be solved through economic measures alone; racism, he said, defied a pure economic argument. And by the 1930s he opposed communism, saying the Bolsheviks had taken the wrong path by turning to dictatorship, and he warned that communist influence in the BSCP would open it to charges of un-Americanism and destroy it.

Randolph supported the entry of the United States into World War II, but he threatened to hold a huge protest march in Washington, D.C., organized by the BSCP against racial discrimination unless President Franklin Roosevelt ended segregation in employment and in the military. He envisioned it as an all-black protest. "We shall not call upon our white friends to march with us," he said. "There are some things Negroes must do alone." Roosevelt prevented the march by agreeing to a limited response: He signed an executive order prohibiting the federal government from entering into contracts with businesses or unions that practiced racial discrimination. Many blacks thought that when Randolph accepted Roosevelt's compromise the labor leader gave up too much; Randolph, though, considered it a great step forward.

Randolph finally organized a massive march on Washington for civil rights—this one in 1963,

A. Philip Randolph, a pioneering labor leader among African Americans, organized the 1963 civil rights march on Washington, D.C. *(National Archives and Records Administration)*

when 200,000 protesters gathered and heard MARTIN LUTHER KING, JR.'s "I Have a Dream" speech. The march contributed to Congress's passing the Civil Rights Act of 1964 and the Voting Rights Act of 1965.

Randolph continued as president of the BSCP until he retired in 1968. As the civil rights movement grew more heated, he sensed that it would lead to radical upheaval. He said, "The Negro's protest today is but the first rumbling of the 'under-class.' As the Negro has taken to the streets, so will the unemployed of all races take to the streets." Yet, integrationist in outlook, he criticized black power leaders for their separatism. Randolph died in New York City on May 16, 1979.

Further Reading

Davis, Daniel S. Mr. *Black Labor: The Story of A. Philip Randolph, Father of the Civil Rights Movement.* New York: E.P. Dutton, 1972.

Patterson, Lillie. *A. Philip Randolph: Messenger for the Masses.* New York: Facts On File, 1996.

Pfeffer, Paula F. *A. Philip Randolph: Pioneer of the Civil Rights Movement.* Baton Rouge: Louisiana State University Press, 1990.

Reed, John Silas

(1887–1920) *communist, journalist*

A journalist and communist, John Silas Reed wrote a book about the Russian Revolution, *Ten Days That Shook the World,* that galvanized left-wing activists in the United States. He was born in Portland, Oregon, on October 20, 1887, to Charles Jerome Reed, a wealthy businessman, and Margaret Green Reed.

John Reed attended Harvard University, where he wrote plays and was named the college orator and poet. He graduated in 1910, whereupon the Progressive reformer Lincoln Steffens helped him get a job on the staff of *American Magazine.* The young journalist, influenced by the Progressives but traveling well to their Left, began writing in 1913 for *The Masses,* a socialist publication.

Later that year *Metropolitan* magazine sent him to Mexico to report on Pancho Villa's peasant uprising against the dictator Victoriano Huerta.

Casting all objectivity aside, he joined the fight to topple Huerta and reported events in writing that exploded across the page:

> The sharpshooter running in front stopped suddenly, swaying, as if he had run against a solid wall. . . . He shook his head impatiently, like a dog with a hurt ear. Blood drops flew from it. Bellowing with rage, he shot the rest of his clip, and then slumped to the ground and thrashed to and fro for a minute. . . . Now the trench was boiling with men scrambling to their feet, like worms when you turn over a log.

His attachment to the downtrodden affirmed, in 1914 Reed traveled to Russia, where his socialist views antagonized the czarist regime. He returned there in 1917, arriving in the capital of Saint Petersburg to witness the October Revolution that overthrew Czar Nicholas. He attended the rally at the Great Hall of the Smolny Institute, where Vladimir Lenin proclaimed the founding of the Workers and Peasants Government.

When Reed sought to return to the United States in 1918, the federal authorities, then involved in crushing domestic dissent to maintain unity during World War I, prevented his reentry. Reed stayed in Norway, where he wrote *Ten Days That Shook the World*, in which he described Lenin rallying the workers and peasants to the Bolshevik cause and how the Red mob stormed the Winter Palace. Reed's fervor for the revolution saturated his book as strongly as had his fervor for Villa, placing the reader on the scene:

> Besides the organized and peaceful demonstrations there were many of a different kind—tumultuous, ardent, violent, anarchical, drawing in hundreds of thousands, even millions of participants—the succession of these demonstrations marking the advance of the revolution.
>
> Every street corner was a public tribune. In railway trains, street cars, always the spurting up of impromptu debate, everywhere.
>
> It was just 8:40 when a thundering wave of cheers announced the entrance of the presidium, with Lenin—great Lenin—among them. A short, stocky figure, with a big head

set down in his shoulders, bald and bulging. Little eyes, a snubbish nose, wide, generous mouth, and heavy chin; clean-shaven now, but already beginning to bristle with the well-known beard of his past and future. . . . Unimpressive, to be the idol of a mob, loved and revered as perhaps few leaders in history have been.

Friendly with Lenin, Reed obtained inside information about political leaders and their plans and even wrote propaganda for the Bolsheviks. He finally reentered the United States in 1919, when he appeared before a Senate committee investigating sedition. His radicalism caused him to be expelled from the Socialist Party, and he became an organizer for the Communist Labor Party (CLP), writing its manifesto and editing its paper, the *Voice of Labor*. The CLP, however, was at odds with other leftists, who formed the Communist Party.

Reed was indicted for sedition, but he returned again to Russia and made numerous speeches in Moscow. In 1920 he contracted typhus, and on October 27 he died. He was buried near Red Square; in the 1960s the Soviet government removed his remains to a privileged spot within the Kremlin walls.

Back in the United States, *Ten Days That Shook the World* gave rise to John Reed Clubs, founded in 1929 by the Communist Party to promote its ideology through art and literature "of a proletarian character" and, as the party stated, through "agitational and propagandistic writing, art, and activities." The clubs proclaimed, "Art Is Propaganda" and "Art Is a Class Weapon."

John Reed died despondent that the workers in America would ever rise up against their capitalist exploiters, yet he was hopeful they would somehow change the system. He said, "I cannot give up the idea that out of democracy will be born the new world—richer, braver, freer, more beautiful." Even for the many radicals who rejected communism, Reed's spirit of challenging the system served as a beacon.

Further Reading

Homberger, Eric. *John Reed.* New York: St. Martin's Press, 1990.

Newsinger, John, ed. *Shaking the World: John Reed's Revolutionary Journalism*. Chicago: Bookmarks, 1998.

Rosenstone, Robert A. *Romantic Revolutionary: A Biography of John Reed*. New York: Knopf, 1975.

Reich, Wilhelm
(1897–1957) *health reformer*

A psychoanalyst, Wilhelm Reich promoted the idea that an invisible energy force, called orgone, permeated the universe. He was born on March 24, 1897, in Dobrzcynica, Galicia, to a farming family.

According to Reich's autobiography, his childhood was characterized by beatings by his father and by a massive preoccupation with sex. Reich claims that he spied on his mother's affair with his tutor and that at age 11 he had daily sexual intercourse with a servant cook. He claimed to have frequented brothels at age 14 and that his experience sent him in search of the perfect woman, one who would live with him as "both mother and whore."

Reich served in World War I and obtained an M.D. degree in 1922 from the University of Vienna. He completed additional courses in neurology and psychiatry and became the first clinical assistant at Sigmund Freud's Psychoanalytic Polyclinic. Reich joined the Austrian Socialist Party in 1924 and in his research concluded that neurosis generally was caused by poverty. In 1928 he was named vice president of the polyclinic, and he joined the Communist Party; shortly afterward he became disillusioned with the party and in 1933 was expelled from it.

In 1939 Reich fled Hitler's Nazi regime and immigrated to the United States, eventually settling at Oregon, Maine, where he founded the Orgone Institute Laboratories. Reich claimed that he had discovered an energy force that differentiated living from nonliving matter; he called it orgone and said it exists in all living things and throughout the universe.

To trap the energy he built an "orgone accumulator," a large box made of alternating layers of an organic material, usually plywood, and a metallic layer of steel wool, in which a person could sit to benefit from orgone's therapeutic qualities. He thought it would especially help cancer sufferers. Reich restricted use of the orgone accumulator to those who recognized it as no more than an experimental instrument.

Reich also believed that human beings must release the orgone within them through sexual activity and that to do otherwise would result in neuroses. Professional psychologists ridiculed Reich and refused to consider his research valid.

Along with the orgone accumulator, Reich developed the Cloudbuster to produce rain. In 1953 a blueberry farmer in Maine claimed that Reich's machine had saved his crop from a drought.

But Reich's orgone accumulator led the Food and Drug Administration (FDA) to prosecute him for fraud. Reich called the action a "smear" and said that answering the government's complaint "would, in my mind, imply admission of the authority of this special branch of the government to pass judgment on primordial, pre-atomic cosmic orgone energy."

Reich insisted, "Inquiry in this realm of Basic Natural Law is outside the judicial domain of this or ANY OTHER KIND OF SOCIAL ADMINISTRATION ANYWHERE ON THIS GLOBE, IN ANY LAND, NATION, OR REGION." And he stated, "My discovery of the Life Energy is today widely known all over the globe in hundreds of institutions, whether acclaimed or accursed. It can no longer be stopped by anyone, no matter what happens to me."

The Justice Department ordered Reich's orgone accumulator destroyed, and on at least two occasions the authorities burned the books he had written. When one of Reich's associates shipped an orgone accumulator across state lines, Reich was tried for contempt of a 1955 court injunction that prohibited him from engaging in such activities, and he was sentenced to two years in jail. Reich—who had married Lore Kahn and, after divorcing her, Annie Pink, with whom he had two children—was incarcerated at the federal penitentiary in Lewisburg, Pennsylvania, where he died on November 3, 1957. While in custody he expressed regret: "I have 'done wrong' to have disclosed to mankind the cosmic primordial mass-free energy which fills the universe."

Further Reading

Higgins, Mary Boyd, ed. *American Odyssey: Letters and Journals, 1940–1947.* New York: Farrar, Straus & Giroux, 1999.

———. *Beyond Psychology: Letters and Journals, 1934–1939.* New York: Farrar, Straus & Giroux, 1994.

———. *Passion of Youth: An Autobiography, 1897–1922.* New York: Farrar, Straus & Giroux, 1988.

Reich, Wilhelm. *The Discovery of the Orgone: The Function of the Orgasm.* New York: Orgone Institute Press, 1942.

———. *The Discovery of Orgone: The Cancer Biopathy.* New York: Orgone Institute Press, 1948.

Sharaf, Myron. *Fury on Earth: A Biography of Wilhelm Reich.* New York: St. Martin's Press, 1983.

Reuther, Walter Philip

(1907–1970) *union leader*

Leader of the United Automobile Workers of America (UAW), Walter Philip Reuther worked to improve conditions for union members. He was born on September 1, 1907, in Wheeling, West Virginia, to Valentine Reuther, a brewery worker, and Anna Stocker Reuther.

From his parents Walter Reuther imbibed a socialist outlook and a trade union mentality. He learned tool and die making, quit high school at age 16, and found work at the Wheeling Steel Company as an apprentice. But when he led a protest against working conditions in 1926 the company fired him. Reuther then moved to Detroit, Michigan, and worked for the Ford Motor Company. He was soon promoted to a supervisor die maker. At the same time he completed his high school education and in 1930 entered Detroit City College.

In 1932 he supported NORMAN MATTOON THOMAS, the socialist candidate for president, and engaged in union activity that caused Ford to fire him. Reuther and his brother Victor then traveled to Europe and the Soviet Union. At Gorki, in Russia, he taught workers to use equipment that had been purchased from Ford. Reuther was attracted to Soviet-style economic planning, but he disliked the absolutist government.

Walter Reuther (left) opposed the attempt by communists to take over the United Auto Workers. *(American Federation of Labor-Congress of Industrial Organizations, National Archives and Records Administration)*

Walter Reuther returned to the United States in 1935 and found work at General Motors (GM). Once again the union beckoned to him, and he helped organize the UAW. In 1936 he married May Wolf.

Later that year Reuther, president of UAW Local 174 in Detroit, helped lead one of the greatest and most successful strikes in American history, the sit-down at GM in Flint, Michigan. The militant tactic, in which workers took over three factories, suspended production, and refused to leave, caused GM, the largest corporation in the country, to recognize the UAW as the workers' union. Subsequently, UAW membership reached 400,000.

In May 1936 Reuther and the UAW undertook the daunting task of organizing the workers at Ford's River Rouge plant in Detroit. The company hated unions and fired anyone who participated in them. It also used a private police force to intimidate workers. While standing outside the River Rouge plant with other union leaders, waiting to get his picture taken by a photographer for *Time* magazine, Reuther was brutally beaten by Ford's police. His bloodied portrait appeared around the country, making him a national figure.

In 1939 Reuther was named director of the UAW's General Motors department. As noncommunists battled within the union with communists, Reuther opposed the Reds. In 1942 he became vice president of the UAW, which by then had joined the Congress of Industrial Organizations (CIO). During World War II Reuther served on several government boards and earned renown for his plan to convert plants from making autos to making aircraft. He made sure that union members honored their no-strike pledge to prevent economic disruption.

Once the war ended, though, Reuther led the UAW in a strike that in 1946 won them a substantial pay raise. A liberal in politics, he organized Americans for Democratic Action in 1947 and in 1948 supported Democrat Harry S. Truman's candidacy for president. That year he barely escaped death when an assassin shot him, leaving his right arm crippled.

After the CIO leader PHILIP MURRAY died in 1952, Reuther was elected president of the organization. Three years later he helped merge the CIO with the American Federation of Labor (AFL), creating the AFL-CIO. He served as its vice president and director of its industrial union department.

Powerful within the Democratic Party, Reuther backed John F. Kennedy for the 1960 presidential nomination, and after Kennedy's assassination he strongly supported President Lyndon Johnson's Great Society program. Opposed to racism, he participated in civil rights demonstrations.

Reuther withdrew the UAW from the AFL-CIO in 1968 and allied with the Teamsters Union to form the Alliance for Labor Action. On May 9, 1970, Reuther, his wife, and several union officials boarded a chartered plane to inspect a recreational center being built for union members on Black Lake in northern Michigan. The plane crashed, killing everyone aboard.

Walter Reuther had made the UAW a strong and prominent union, winning for its members pay raises, pensions, cost-of-living increases, and profit sharing. His death cost the labor movement one of its greatest leaders.

Further Reading

Barnard, John. *Walter Reuther and the Rise of the Auto Workers*. Boston: Little, Brown, 1983.

Carew, Anthony. *Walter Reuther*. New York: St. Martin's Press, 1993.

Goode, Bill. *Infighting in the UAW: The 1946 Election and the Ascendancy of Walter Reuther*. Westport, Conn.: Greenwood Press, 1994.

Lichtenstein, Nelson. *The Most Dangerous Man in Detroit: Walter Reuther and the Fate of American Labor*. New York: Basic Books, 1995.

Reuther, Victor G. *The Brothers Reuther and the Story of the UAW: A Memoir*. Boston: Houghton Mifflin, 1976.

Rickard, Clinton

(1882–1971) *Indian rights activist*

Clinton Rickard was the founder of the Indian Defense League of America, a group dedicated to protecting border crossing rights and other rights of Native Americans. He was born on May 19, 1882, the third son of George and Lucy Rickard, on the Tuscarora Reservation in upstate New York.

As a child Clinton Rickard experienced the poverty endemic to Indians. When he was four his father joined Buffalo Bill Cody's Wild West Show, leaving Lucy Rickard in dire straits as she struggled to feed her children. When the elder Rickard returned to his family two years later, conditions remained bad. Clinton recalled: "I remember many times in my childhood, even when my father was home, that food was scarce. Often we lived only on Indian corn bread with no meat to eat. My mother would also cook a green which grew wild in the yard and which we called pig weed." George Rickard took to the bottle, and in alcoholic rages he often beat Lucy and abused Clinton and his brothers. The boys ended the drunken behavior when they jumped on him during one of his rampages and pinned him to the floor—a physical declaration that they would no longer tolerate his attacks.

Clinton Rickard tried to join the army when the Spanish-American War began in 1898, but he was only 16 and was rejected for being too young. He finally enlisted three years later to get away from his father, who had taken money from him. Rickard was sent to the Philippines, where he fought against armed rebels who opposed the U.S. takeover of the islands. At one point he saved the life of his captain by blocking the blow of a bolo-wielding enemy.

Rickard returned home in 1904 and later that year married Ivy Onstott. Tragedy struck twice in 1913: first, when his wife died, along with one of their two sons, and second, when a flood destroyed all of his possessions while he was passing through Waverly, Iowa. Rickard married Elizabeth Patterson in 1916, and they had three sons, one of whom died in infancy.

A full-time farmer, Rickard raised milk cows and made maple syrup from his sugar bushes. In the 1920s he became a chief and represented his clan on the Chiefs' Council. A traditionalist, he criticized those who adopted white society's materialistic values, as evidenced in his political battle on the reservation with Chief Grant Mount Pleasant, who had accumulated considerable land and money at the expense of the community's welfare.

Rickard began his fight for Indian rights in 1924, when he opposed the coercive nature of the Citizenship Act that made all Indians U.S. citizens. "This was a violation of our sovereignty," he later explained. "Our citizenship was in our own nations. We had a great attachment to our style of government."

An even larger battle began the next year, a "long struggle," as Rickard called it, "to secure the crossing rights for our Indian people as guaranteed by the old treaties, which were still in existence." He meant the right of Indians, stipulated in Article 3 of Jay's Treaty (1794) and Article 9 of the Treaty of Ghent (1814), to cross the border between the United States and Canada unmolested. Because an immigration act passed by Congress in 1924 stated that "no alien ineligible for citizenship

shall be admitted to the United States" and the Citizenship Act placed American Indians born in Canada in the ineligible category, Canadian Indians found their movement into the United States prohibited. Some who attempted to enter anyway were jailed for months. (Indians had commonly crossed back and forth over the border in that area, which was near Niagara Falls, where many sold crafts to tourists.)

Rickard's protests caused the U.S. Department of Labor to rule in 1925 that American Indians born in Canada could be admitted across the border, provided they were entering the United States temporarily. With that partial victory, in 1926 Rickard organized the Six Nations Defense League, later called the Indian Defense League of America, to advocate full border crossing rights. Finally, in 1928 Congress passed legislation that allowed free passage, and beginning that year Rickard staged an annual Border Crossing Celebration in Niagara Falls (which is still held). He continued the work of the Defense League to fight for other Indian rights.

During the border crossing controversy, some Tuscarora who disliked Canadian Indians entering their reservation opposed Rickard. But he held steadfast to his crusade and later said, "The reason I was so certain of the rightness of my work was because I had always appealed to the Great Spirit to bestow upon me the knowledge and wisdom to defend the rights of my people."

In 1929 Rickard obtained an appropriation from the state of New York for the Cayuga people to compensate them for annuity payments required by a treaty signed in 1795. He became council president in 1930 and obtained increased funding for schools on the Tuscarora Reservation and for Indians who attended high schools elsewhere. In 1931, after the death of Elizabeth Rickard, Rickard married Beulah Mount Pleasant. They had seven children and struggled through the hardship of the Great Depression.

Rickard defended the Tuscarora in March 1957 when the New York State Power Authority (SPA) requested permission to survey reservation land as part of its plan to build a reservoir related to an electric project. The SPA wanted to obtain several hundred acres and flood them, and it offered

$1,100 an acre for the land it wanted. The Tuscarora, however, rejected the money, and Clinton Rickard, joined by his son, William, led a resistance movement. The New York state legislature passed a bill in April 1958 authorizing the taking of 1,383 acres, but the Indians refused to allow SPA workers, backed by state troopers, onto the reservation. The SPA then offered the Tuscarora new roads, a community center, and free electricity; still they rejected any deal.

Rickard and the Tuscarora defeated the SPA in a court case, but on appeal in March 1960 the U.S. Supreme Court voted 4–3 against them. The SPA subsequently redesigned the reservoir to take less land, but it still flooded hundreds of acres. Rickard engaged in a similar fight in the early 1960s when he helped the Seneca resist the building of the Kinzua Dam on their land, but again the authorities obtained the acreage they wanted.

Clinton Rickard died in Buffalo on June 14, 1971, of heart disease. He had written his autobiography in cooperation with Barbara Graymont, a professor at Nyack College in Nyack, New York. Graymont called Rickard "an Indian patriot" and said, "More than that, he was a great humanitarian."

Further Reading

Graymont, Barbara, ed. *Fighting Tuscarora: The Autobiography of Clinton Rickard.* Syracuse, N.Y.: Syracuse University Press, 1973.

"Indian Defense League of America." Available online. URL: http://tuscaroras.com/IDLA/. Downloaded on March 25, 2002.

Riis, Jacob

(1849–1914) *social reformer, journalist, photographer*

A journalist, Jacob Riis exposed the slum conditions among New York City's immigrant poor and his work inspired numerous reforms. He was himself born to foreign parents, Niels Edward Riis and Caroline Lundholm Riis, in Ribe, Denmark, on May 3, 1849.

Jacob Riis was a member of a large family of 14 children and as a boy received only a limited education while training to become a carpenter and helping his father prepare copy for a weekly newspaper. Riis immigrated to New York City in 1870, and like those people he described in his later articles and books, he lived in poverty, even resorting to flophouses for lodging. Optimistic, ambitious, and determined, he eventually used his experience at laying out pages to secure a job at a small newspaper on Long Island. Unfortunately, the paper failed to meet its payroll.

Riis held several other jobs during that period. In 1876 he married Elizabeth Nielsen, with whom he had five children, before finding employment in 1877 at the *New York Tribune* as a police reporter. He quit that job in 1888 to work as a reporter for the *New York Evening Sun,* a position he held until 1899. Riis wrote mainly about crime and slums. He wandered among the poor—their streets, their shelters, their tenements. Particularly concerned with children, he told about how the squalor in which they lived doomed them.

Riis's book *How the Other Half Lives* (1890) established his reputation in the United States and in Europe as a reformer, though he disliked the word *reformer* because, he said, it implied that he wanted to change people, whereas he really wanted to give them a chance. In that work Riis's narrative style breathed compassion and disgust. "In the tenements all the influences make for evil," he wrote,

> because they are . . . the nurseries of pauperism and crime that fill our jails and police courts; that throw off a scum of forty thousand human wrecks to the island asylums and workhouses year by year; . . . that maintain a standing army of ten thousand tramps with all that that implies; because, above all, they touch the family life with deadly moral contagion.

In several passages Riis placed the reader at the scene of slum horrors:

> Be a little careful, please! The hall is dark and you might stumble over the children pitching pennies there. . . . The sinks are in the hallway, that all the tenants may have access—and all be poisoned alike—by their summer stenches. Hear the pump squeak! It is the lullaby of tenement-house babes.

Six cents for his bed, six for his breakfast of bread and coffee, and six for his supper of pork and beans . . . are the rate of the boys' "hotel" for those who bunk together in the great dormitories that sometimes hold more than a hundred berths, two tiers high. . . .

Two [boys] were found making their nest once in the end of a big iron pipe up by the Harlem Bridge, and an old boiler at the East River served as an elegant flat for another couple.

Beyond Riis's words, the effect of *How the Other Half Lives* was due to the photographs used to support his assertions. At that time photography was new, only recently popularized by Mathew Brady and his Civil War pictures, and those who promoted the technology claimed it would reveal the truth: that "pictures never lie." Riis's photographs, then, gave his book more credibility, more power, more influence.

Yet claims of objectivity can be misleading, and so it was for photography. Mathew Brady had rearranged dead bodies on battlefields to add drama to his shots; Jacob Riis asked slum dwellers to pose for some scenes, including poor "Street Arabs," young boys, who reenacted their technique in rolling a drunk.

Riis's writing continued with *Out of Mulberry Street* (1898), *The Battle with the Slum* (1902), and *Children of the Tenement* (1903). His work led to the tearing down of the squalid Mulberry Bend tenement block and the building of a center, named after him, to help the poor. He exposed corruption in the police department and contaminants in the city water supply. Reformers embraced him, and several, particularly Theodore Roosevelt, tried to persuade him to enter politics, but he refused.

Yet Riis's concern for the poor had limits. As a native of northern Europe, he was prejudiced against immigrants from southern and eastern Europe, such as Italians, and stereotyped them in ways that debased them. Further, although he acted from altruism, he acted also from a desire to achieve order by imposing middle-class values on others and eliminating their native cultures.

How the Other Half Lives appealed to a primarily well-to-do audience, and Riis minced no words in instilling in them the fear that without changes, the lower orders would rise up and attack the elite. One passage in the book describes a poor man who is standing on a street corner watching the carriages of the wealthy pass by. The man starts thinking about "little ones crying for bread around the cold and cheerless hearth," and with that he moves through the crowd and slashes "those around him with a knife, blindly seeking to kill, to revenge." Clearly, Riis implies that the mad act of one could become the mad act of many.

Riis lectured extensively, and in his later years his demanding work load worsened a serious heart condition. His wife Elizabeth died in 1905, and he married Mary A. Phillips in 1907. Riis died at his country home in Barre, Massachusetts, on May 26, 1914.

Whatever Riis's motivation, he galvanized Progressive reformers with *How the Other Half Lives*, which was bold in its technique, and with ideas that challenged the conservative view that nothing could or should be done about slums. To ignore the slums, Riis said, would only breed suffering for wealthy and poor alike.

Further Reading

Lane, James B. *Jacob A. Riis and the American City*. Port Washington, N.Y.: Kennikat Press, 1974.

Meyer, Edith Patterson. *"Not Charity, but Justice": The Story of Jacob A. Riis*. New York: Vanguard Press, 1974.

Ryan, Susan M. "Rough Ways and Rough Work: Jacob Riis, Social Reform, and the Rhetoric of Benevolent Violence." *ATQ (The American Transcendental Quarterly)* 11 (September 1997): 191+.

Rivera, Luis Muñoz See MUÑOZ RIVERA, LUIS.

Robeson, Paul Leroy

(1898–1976) *civil rights activist, communist, singer, actor*

A singer and actor, Paul Leroy Robeson was also a left-wing political activist. He was born on April 9, 1898, in Princeton, New Jersey, to William Drew Robeson and Maria Louisa Bustill Robeson. His father was a former slave and college graduate who became an ordained minister; his mother was part black, Indian, and white.

Tragedy struck the Robesons in 1904 when Maria Louisa died in a household fire. The family moved in 1910 to Somerville, where Paul Robeson compiled an excellent high school academic and athletic record. In 1915 he entered Rutgers College and in 1918 was chosen to be on the All-American college football team. He graduated the following year with academic honors.

From Rutgers Robeson moved to New York City and studied law at Columbia University. To help pay for his tuition he coached football at Lincoln University and played on a Harlem basketball team. In 1921 he married Eslanda "Essie" Cardozo Goode; they had one child.

Robeson received his degree in 1923 and worked for a law firm, but he disliked the racism he encountered in dealing with clients. With the support of his wife he decided to pursue an acting career, and later that year he accepted the lead in a new Eugene O'Neill play, *All God's Chillun Got Wings,* a controversial production because of its topic of interracial marriage. Praise for his performance earned him national recognition.

In April 1925 he made his major singing debut in New York, performing black spirituals and folk songs. Again he received acclaim, and he signed a recording contract with the Victor Talking Machine Company. Even greater fame resulted, however, in 1928 when he appeared in the play *Show Boat* in London and sang "Ol' Man River."

The English loved Robeson, and in the 1930s he made several movies for British film companies. In 1934 and again in 1936 he visited the Soviet Union and marveled at the country's lack of racism; he said that in Russia his dignity was restored. While there he studied Marxism and decided to send his son to a Russian school.

Robeson's first significant political foray occurred in 1936 when he declared his support for the Popular Front Republican forces fighting Francisco Franco in the Spanish Civil War. Over the next three years he raised money for the Popular Front, only to see Franco win.

During World War II Robeson sang a stirring song, "Ballad for Americans," on national radio in the United States; it increased his fame and caused

Americans to hail him as a true patriot. Audiences praised his performance as Othello in the Broadway production of Shakespeare's play, and in 1945 the National Association for the Advancement of Colored People (NAACP) awarded him its Spingarn Medal.

In 1946 Robeson visited President Harry Truman and urged him to support a bill that would make the lynching of blacks a federal crime. The meeting with the president, though, went poorly when Robeson criticized American foreign policy and defended the Soviet Union. That October he appeared before the California Legislative Committee on Un-American Activities, and he testified that although he was not a communist, he found much to support in their fight for equality.

The following year Robeson suspended his concert tours to campaign for the Progressive Party presidential candidate, Henry Wallace. In 1948 the singer traveled through Europe and again condemned American foreign policy. The State Department and other government agencies began spying on him, and when he stated in 1949 that African Americans would never support a war by the United States against the Soviet Union, a barrage of criticism descended on him from whites and blacks alike.

Several cities reacted to Robeson's political beliefs and statements by banning his concerts. The bans became more extensive after violence erupted at one of his shows sponsored by left wingers in Peekskill, New York, in August 1949. Many cities feared that if Robeson appeared his supporters and opponents would clash.

In 1950 the State Department revoked Robeson's passport, thus preventing him from traveling overseas. With the Red Scare, whereby the government was hunting down communists and other radicals, few organizations sided with Robeson or wanted to be even remotely affiliated with him; the NAACP, for one, condemned him. His reaction to most criticism was to defend his beliefs more strongly.

Robeson regained his passport in 1958 after the Supreme Court declared such suspensions unconstitutional, and he staged concerts in England and other European countries. Shortly afterward he stayed at an East Berlin sanatorium to receive treatment for physical and emotional problems. He returned to the United States in 1963 only to find that many Americans still shunned him. The civil rights movement, however, rehabilitated his reputation as a fighter for freedom, and in 1965 several black actors and writers held a salute in his honor. In 1973 they were joined by civil rights leaders in staging a birthday celebration for him at Carnegie Hall.

After Essie Robeson died in 1965, Paul Robeson lived in seclusion with his sister in Philadelphia. He died there on January 23, 1976.

Further Reading

Duberman, Martin B. *Paul Robeson.* New York: Knopf, 1989.
Robeson, Paul. *Here I Stand.* Boston: Beacon Press, 1958.
Stewart, Jeffrey C., ed. *Paul Robeson: Artist and Citizen.* New Brunswick, N.J.: Rutgers University Press, 1998.

Rockwell, George Lincoln
(1918–1967) *white supremacist*

A virulent anti-Semite and racist, George Lincoln Rockwell was head of the American Nazi Party. He was born on March 9, 1918, in Bloomington, Illinois, to George Rockwell and Claire Schade Rockwell, vaudeville performers.

George Lincoln Rockwell graduated from Central High School in Providence, Rhode Island, in 1937 and attended Brown University. He left there in 1940 to join the navy as a pilot and served in World War II. In 1943 he married Judith Aultman; they had three children.

After the war Rockwell attended Pratt Institute in New York City and showed talent as an illustrator, but he quit without graduating. He then briefly owned and managed an advertising agency in Portland, Maine, before rejoining the navy and serving in the Korean War with the rank of commander. While stationed in Iceland he met Thora Hallgrimsson, and in October 1953 he divorced Judith and married Thora. They had four children, but in 1959 their marriage also ended in divorce.

While in the navy Rockwell read books written by Gerald L. K. Smith, an anti-Semite. Later

he claimed to have read Hitler's *Mein Kampf* several times. In 1958 he founded the American Nazi Party in Arlington, Virginia.

Rockwell wanted all Jews exterminated and all blacks sent to Africa. His comments reveal the intolerant mentality of the far Right racists:

> When two people prove incompatible in marriage and they can't live together, they separate; and the mass of average niggers simply don't "fit" in modern American society.
>
> Jews want to run the white people just the way they run the niggers. Once they get the white people mixed with the black people, the white people will be just as easy to run as the niggers.
>
> I have an affidavit from a Jewish doctor, a prisoner at Auschwitz, who says there were no gas chambers. . . . I believe the gas chambers in these concentration camps were built after the war—by Jewish Army officers.

Rockwell's American Nazi Party never attracted more than 100 members, yet their appearance in Nazi uniforms with swastika armbands caused a sensation. Rockwell was stoned in 1961 while attempting to picket the pro-Israeli movie *Exodus,* and he was arrested in 1965 in Selma, Alabama, for disturbing the peace at a civil rights meeting.

That same year he ran for governor of Virginia but polled just 5,730 votes of more than 500,000 cast. In 1966 he changed the name of the party to National Socialist White People's Party and tried to build its membership by capitalizing on the backlash against the civil rights movement. Still nearly everyone ignored him.

On August 25, 1967, Rockwell was shot to death by John Patler, a disgruntled former member of the Nazi group. George Lincoln Rockwell's ideology represented the most vicious of America's hatemongers. Writing in *The Historian* (Spring 1995), Frederick J. Simonelli says,

> From its founding to the day of Rockwell's death, the [American Nazi Party] was little more than Rockwell's personal vehicle for the promotion of his ideas. It never evolved into a political movement or political party in any conventional sense. He worked and agitated

and marched until the day he died, but [to use another person's] colorful phrase, "whatever Hitler's ghost promised him never showed up."

Further Reading

Schmaltz, William H. *Hate: George Lincoln Rockwell and the American Nazi Party*. Washington, D.C.: Brassey's, 1999.

Simonelli, Frederick J. *American Fuehrer: George Lincoln Rockwell and the American Nazi Party*. Urbana: University of Illinois Press, 1999.

Roosevelt, Eleanor

(1884–1962) *social reformer*

As first lady, Eleanor Roosevelt became the voice of America's disadvantaged, but her activism continued after she left the White House, most notably in convincing the United Nations to adopt the Universal Declaration of Rights. Eleanor Roosevelt was born in New York City on October 11, 1884, the daughter of Elliot Roosevelt and Anna Ludlow Hall Roosevelt, a descendant of the prominent Livingstone family.

Eleanor Roosevelt's biographer Joseph Lash has stated that Eleanor was born into a ruling class. Although she grew up in wealth and attended the finest schools, her childhood was anything but idyllic. Her father was an alcoholic, and her mother often verbally abused her, calling her ugly. When Eleanor was 8 her father died, and when she was 10 her mother died. Eleanor was raised by her maternal grandmother and at age 15 was sent to Mademoiselle Souvestre's finishing school in South Fields, England. She learned from Souvestre the importance of serving society, and when she returned to New York she preferred charitable work to the debutante scene in which she also took part.

In March 1905 Eleanor Roosevelt married her fifth cousin, Franklin Roosevelt, and between 1906 and 1916 they had six children, one of whom died in infancy. The family lived on the Roosevelt estate at Hyde Park on the Hudson River. Meanwhile, Franklin's political career moved ahead; he won election to the state legislature as a Democrat in 1910 and was appointed secretary of the navy by President Woodrow Wilson in 1913.

Eleanor Roosevelt's relationship with her husband took a dramatic turn in 1918, when in September she discovered that he was having an affair with her friend and personal secretary, Lucy Mercer. Eleanor considered divorce, but she and Franklin decided to maintain their marriage, partly to protect their children and partly to protect Franklin Roosevelt's political career. From that point forward the couple maintained a relationship of convenience rather than love. Eleanor Roosevelt turned for support to her close female friends, many of whom were lesbians. Her biographer Blanche Wiesen Cook believes that Eleanor Roosevelt likely had a lesbian relationship with Lorena Hickcock.

Yet when Franklin Roosevelt contracted polio in 1921, she supported him, encouraged him, and advised him to continue his life in public office. He never regained the use of his legs, but in 1928 he was elected governor of New York, and four years later he won the presidency.

In the White House Eleanor, as first lady, represented groups often neglected in the councils of government: women, factory workers, poor farmers, the unemployed, African Americans. Historians generally credit her with exerting a liberal influence on President Roosevelt, shaping the New Deal along those lines. When, for example, he developed the Works Progress Administration to provide jobs for the unemployed, she made sure that those hired included writers and artists. In 1936 she began a syndicated newspaper column, "My Day," in which she discussed social and political issues.

As Europe armed itself in the late 1930s, Eleanor Roosevelt opposed war—she said, "I have never believed that war settled anything satisfactorily"—but she backed her husband's preparedness policies, and with the outbreak of combat in 1939 she agreed that the United States needed to stand up to Adolf Hitler. To support American troops after the attack at Pearl Harbor, in 1943 she toured battle sites in the Pacific, traveling 23,000 miles.

In the wake of Franklin Roosevelt's death in April 1945, Eleanor Roosevelt remained politically active. Later that year President Harry Truman appointed her a delegate to the newly formed United Nations (UN). She was, in turn, made chair of the UN Human Rights Commission and in that post pushed for member nations to ratify the Universal Declaration of Human Rights. The General Assembly finally approved it in December 1948. She recalled: "We wanted as many nations as possible to accept the fact that men, for one reason or another, were born free and equal . . . that they were endowed with reason and conscience, and should act toward one another in a spirit of brotherhood. The way to do that was to find words that everyone would accept."

The declaration stated in part:

> All human beings are born free and equal in dignity and rights. They are endowed with

reason and conscience and should act towards one another in a spirit of brotherhood. . . .

> Everyone has the right to life, liberty and security of person.

> No one shall be subjected to torture or to cruel, inhuman or degrading treatment or punishment.

> Everyone has the right to freedom of thought, conscience and religion; this right includes freedom to change his religion or belief, and freedom, either alone or in community with others and in public or private, to manifest his religion or belief in teaching, practice, worship and observance.

When the Republican Dwight Eisenhower entered the White House in 1953, he replaced Eleanor Roosevelt in the UN post. Yet she continued to pursue humanitarian issues. She bravely spoke out against Senator Joseph McCarthy during the Red Scare (the nationwide hunt for communists and other radicals) and called for improved relations with the Soviet Union. Her political views caused the Federal Bureau of Investigation (FBI) to investigate and keep a file on her, as it did on thousands of other Americans who supported liberal causes in the 1950s.

In 1960 she supported John F. Kennedy for president, and after the Democrat won he made Roosevelt a delegate to a special session of the United Nations General Assembly and appointed her to lead his Commission on the Status of Women. She also served as adviser to the Peace Corps.

Eleanor Roosevelt died on November 6, 1962, in New York City of a bone marrow disease. She left a legacy of justice rooted in her belief in equal rights and compassion for all. The former Democratic presidential candidate Adlai Stevenson once said of Eleanor Roosevelt, "She would rather light a candle than curse the darkness."

Far from being an obscure first lady, Eleanor Roosevelt worked tirelessly for blacks' and women's rights and for the benefit of the downtrodden in American society. *(Library of Congress)*

Further Reading

Cook, Blanche Wiesen. *Eleanor Roosevelt: Volume One, 1884–1933.* New York: Viking, 1992.

Lash, Joseph P. *Eleanor and Franklin: The Story of Their Relationship, Based on Eleanor Roosevelt's Private Papers.* New York: Norton, 1971.

———. *Eleanor: The Years Alone.* New York: New American Library, 1972.

Rubin, Jerry

(1938–1994) *antiwar activist*

Jerry Rubin was a flamboyant protester for the 1960s counterculture and founder of the Yippies. He grew up in Cincinnati, Ohio, where he was born on July 14, 1938, to Robert Rubin and Ester Katz Rubin.

Rubin's mother was well educated; his father drove a truck and worked as a business agent for the Teamsters Union. They provided their son with a comfortable upbringing and the opportunity for a college education. In the late 1950s Jerry Rubin enrolled at the University of Cincinnati. He graduated in 1961 and worked as a newspaper reporter in his hometown.

Rubin read widely, especially about politics, and developed an interest in socialist ideas. Late in 1961 he traveled to Israel and began graduate studies in Jerusalem. As he surveyed the scene there, he found himself identifying more and more with the Palestinians; at the same time he associated with socialists who deepened his discontent with capitalism.

In 1964 Rubin left Israel for the University of California at Berkeley, where he began studying for a doctorate in sociology. He never completed the course work, but his arrival on campus and his newfound leftist ideology meshed with the free speech movement that was then erupting, and he joined the fight against oppression.

The following year Rubin helped organize Berkeley's first teach-in to protest the Vietnam War. He then founded the Vietnam Day Committee (VDC), which attracted college militants and held several highly publicized confrontations. In one instance VDC members lay across railroad tracks in Oakland, California, in an attempt to stop troop trains carrying soldiers bound for the war.

Rubin typified New Left activists in his belief that Vietnam exposed an oppressive capitalist society that needed revolutionary change. Many New Leftists admired him for his ability to create visual action that communicated their ideas more effectively than did speeches. For example, the VDC protested the manufacture of napalm by painting an old truck dark gray; placing a large bright yellow sign on it that warned "Danger, Napalm Bombs Ahead"; and then using it to follow delivery vehicles.

Rubin increasingly talked about exploiting the popular media to change consciousness, and he began to move toward cultural radicalism and the street theater tactics developed by the anarchistic Diggers in San Francisco's Haight-Ashbury district. These practices involved staging outrageous stunts to draw media attention and show society its absurdities. In 1966 he answered a summons to the House Un-American Activities Committee by appearing in the uniform of an American revolutionary soldier.

The following year Rubin did an about-face and mounted a serious campaign for mayor of Berkeley. Anyone who thought he had entered the mainstream, however, was mistaken. After losing he rejected traditional politics, and when DAVID DELLINGER, chairman of the National Mobilization Committee to End the War in Vietnam (MOBE), asked him to direct an antiwar march in Washington, D.C., he agreed. Rubin joined his friend ABBIE HOFFMAN in injecting street theater into the event. As a result the demonstration included a rock band—the Fugs—and a satirical attempt to levitate the Pentagon and exorcise its evil spirits.

As 1967 ended Rubin joined Hoffman and several others in forming the Yippies. They intended to stage an outrageous protest, the Festival of Life, at the 1968 Democratic National Convention in Chicago, but disagreement surfaced on two fronts. For one, tension existed between Rubin and Hoffman, as Rubin stressed politics, and Hoffman preferred street theater. For another, MOBE feared the presence of the Yippies would detract from a serious antiwar protest.

In any event, violence broke out at the convention in late August, and the Festival of Life never got off the ground. Rubin, however, had managed to make a sensational appearance a few days before the convention when he paraded outside the Chicago Civic Center with "Pigasus," a 200-pound pig that he and the Yippies nominated as their presidential candidate. The event drew enormous media coverage, conforming with what Rubin thought about television and demonstrations in general, as he stated in his book *Do It!*:

Have you ever seen a boring demonstration on TV? Just being on TV makes it exciting. Even picket lines look breathtaking. Television creates myths bigger than reality.

Demonstrations last for hours, and most of that time nothing happens. After the demonstration we rush home for the six o'clock news. The drama review. TV packs all the action into two minutes—a commercial for the revolution.

In the wake of the Chicago protest, the federal government arrested Rubin, Hoffman, and six other prominent protesters on grounds of conspiracy to riot. The media called them the Chicago Eight. (They became the Chicago Seven when one of the defendants was tried separately.) At his trial in 1969 Rubin defended himself. He was found guilty of rioting, though not of conspiracy. Three years later a higher court overturned the verdict.

In the 1970s Rubin plunged into self-help techniques. He tried Esalen, meditation, massage, acupuncture, hypnotism, health foods, and tantric yoga. The following decade he joined Wall Street, citadel of the capitalism he had earlier attacked; worked as a stockbroker with John Muir & Company; and said he had no apologies for making money. He had learned, he claimed, that in order to change the world, he first had to have cash. Secretly, he may still have been committed to his countercultural principles, for he had once stated, "Every guerrilla must know how to use the terrain of the culture that he is trying to destroy."

Rubin told a *National Review* reporter in 1983:

The whole idea of promotion is myth. In the Sixties we created a myth of disruption. There was disruption, but the country was nowhere near as disrupted as people believed it to be. And the myth that I created about myself was not the truth—but I didn't really create it either. The media took it. Today, obviously, although I don't like it, I'm playing the "anti-capitalist goes capitalist" myth. The world's playing on it. They'll play on it forever.

He admitted, though, "People are working out their own problems, and I represent the part of themselves that is no longer radical." Whatever the explanation, many observers believed that in selling stocks, Rubin had simply sold out.

In founding Business Networking Salons, Incorporated, with his wife, Mimi, he hosted weekly parties at New York City's Studio 54 for the business elite. For a slight fee, those who attended could swap business cards, discuss deals, and otherwise rub elbows. In 1991 Rubin moved to Denver, Colorado, and worked as a distributor for Wow!, a nutritional drink company. On November 14, 1994, Rubin was struck by a car while jaywalking in Hollywood. He died on November 28.

Further Reading

Cavallo, Dominick. *A Fiction of the Past: The Sixties in American History.* New York: St. Martin's Press, 1999.

Kessler, Lauren. *After All These Years: Sixties Ideals in a Different World.* New York: Thunder's Mouth Press, 1990.

Kimball, Roger. *The Long March: How the Cultural Revolution of the 1960s Changed America.* San Francisco: Encounter Books, 2000.

Rubin, Jerry. *Do It! Scenarios of the Revolution.* New York: Simon & Schuster, 1970.

———. *Growing Up at Thirty-Seven.* New York: M. Evans, 1976.

Rudd, Mark
(1947–   ) *New Left activist*

Mark Rudd was a New Left activist who once led a spectacular student strike at Columbia University. He was born on June 2, 1947, in Irvington, New Jersey, and grew up in a tree-shaded upper-middle-class neighborhood that bespoke an idyllic future attached to the American dream.

Following a traditional route for success, Rudd enrolled at Columbia University in New York City in 1966. But within two years he became radically politicized and chaired the college chapter of Students for a Democratic Society (SDS), a New Left organization that advocated greater democracy in American society and, at least as espoused by some of its members, a socialist economy. On the surface Columbia appeared to be a benign institution, but students had grown disenchanted with three policies: severe limitations on participation in college governance; ties to war industry, primarily the Institute for Defense; and the administration's decision to build a gym in Harlem without consulting the neighborhood's residents. In addition, many of them had become totally opposed to the war in Vietnam.

In April 1968 Rudd disrupted a university memorial service to MARTIN LUTHER KING, JR., the civil rights leader, who had been slain just days earlier. He seized the pulpit and denounced Columbia as hypocritical for pretending to care about blacks while disrupting Harlem and paying African-American workers practically nothing. He singled out, too, the college's relationship with the Institute for Defense Analysis, a research group funded by the Central Intelligence Agency and engaged in developing weapons used in the Vietnam War. On April 22, 1968, Rudd wrote a letter to Columbia's president, Grayson Kirk, in which he said:

> You want to know what is wrong with this society. . . . We can point to the war in Vietnam as an example of the unimaginable wars of aggression you are prepared to fight to maintain your control over your empire. . . . We can point to your using us as cannon fodder to fight your war. We can point . . . to the ghetto . . . you've helped to create through your racist University expansion policies, through your unfair labor practices, through your city government and your police. We can point to this University, your University which trains us to be lawyers and engineers, and managers for your IBM, your Socony Mobil, your IDA, your Con Edison. . . . We can point, in short, to our own meaningless studies, our identity crises, cogs in your corporate machines as a product of and reaction to a basically sick society.

With Rudd's denunciations, students seized campus buildings and declared a strike. Later that month, over the course of two days, about 1,000 joined the occupation. They demanded numerous changes, and a prolonged and bloody encounter that included massive arrests by the police resulted in some concessions. Soon after the strike Rudd

dropped out of Columbia to work as a full-time political organizer.

In 1969 Rudd allied with Third World Marxists, a faction within SDS that had formed to battle another faction, Progressive Labor (PL), for control of the national organization. That summer he helped lead a successful effort to boot PL from SDS. Third World Marxists, in turn, evolved into Weatherman, dedicated to revolution, and Rudd won election as its national secretary. In October he helped lead the Days of Rage, an assault on police and property in Chicago. During the upheaval the police beat and arrested him.

Along with other radicals, Rudd considered Weatherman a separate entity from SDS and grew disenchanted with SDS's campus chapters. He criticized their constant debates and compromises. "I hate SDS," he proclaimed. "I hate this weird liberal mass of nothingness." He wanted militant action; he wanted violence to tear down the capitalist system. He later recalled, "Our goal was the violent overthrow of the government of the United States." Late in 1969 he declared: "It's a wonderful feeling to hit a pig. It must be a really wonderful feeling to kill a pig or blow up a building."

He soon got his chance. Facing charges from the Days of Rage for conspiring to riot, he and most other Weathermen went underground, and in the early 1970s they bombed government facilities. Rudd surrendered himself to the authorities in 1977, and for his actions in Chicago he was sentenced to two years' probation.

During his underground period Rudd had lived in New Mexico. He later returned there and in 2002 was teaching math at the Albuquerque Technical Vocational Institute. "We were hopeful that it was a revolutionary time," Rudd told a reporter that March. "It was not."

Further Reading

Cavallo, Dominick. *A Fiction of the Past: The Sixties in American History.* New York: St. Martin's Press, 1999.

Kahn, Roger. *The Battle for Morningside Heights: Why Students Rebel.* New York: Morrow, 1970.

Kunen, James S. *The Strawberry Statement: Notes of a College Revolutionary.* New York: Random House, 1969.

Ruffin, Edmund

(1794–1865) *agricultural reformer,*
secessionist

An advocate of changes in the way Southerners
treated agricultural land, Edmund Ruffin was a
staunch supporter of slavery and secession. He was
born on January 5, 1794, in Prince George County,
Virginia, to George Ruffin, a wealthy planter, and
Jane Lucas Ruffin.

Edmund Ruffin quit school at age 16 and
spent a few fruitless months at the College of
William and Mary before marrying Susan Travis in
1813 (they had 11 children) and inheriting his recently deceased father's plantation, called Coggin's
Point. Ruffin immediately encountered a problem
common to many Virginia farms: poor plowing and
planting methods had depleted the soil and damaged the crop yield. To find a solution to the

Edmund Ruffin advocated that southerners reform their
agricultural practices; during the Civil War he
supported the Confederacy. *(National Archives and
Records Administration)*

predicament, he started to experiment. In about
1815 he discovered that marl, a calcium-rich sub-
strate, could benefit the soil. So he began advocating that farmers dig for large amounts of marl;
spread it, along with organic material, across their
fields; and plow it under.

Ruffin presented his findings to the Prince
George Agricultural Society in 1818 and printed
them in 1821 as *American Farmer.* From 1823 to
1826 he served in the Virginia senate, and in 1833
he began the *Farmer's Register,* a publication that
over its 10-year existence printed articles, written
by both him and others, who advocated experimental farming methods.

Ruffin hoped to ignite an agricultural revolution, but most farmers resisted his ideas. Quite
likely slavery contributed to their intransigence:
They either could not get slaves to do the work or
did not want to break the pattern of slave labor.

In 1841 Ruffin was appointed to the newly
founded Virginia State Board of Agriculture and
served as its first corresponding secretary. The following year he became agricultural surveyor for
South Carolina and in 1854 commissioner for the
Virginia State Agricultural Society. In the meantime he had moved to a new house, Marlbourne,
in Hanover County, Virginia, where until his retirement from agricultural reform in 1855 he wrote
numerous works calling for improved farming
methods.

For all his reformist ideas about treating the
soil, Ruffin staunchly defended slavery. He considered neither the treatment of slaves to be inhu-
mane nor the practices inherent in slave labor
inimical to better farming methods. Quite the opposite, Ruffin thought blacks inferior to whites and
use of slaves superior to employment of wage laborers. He held these views even though Virginia
itself was suffering from an excessive number of
slaves and the system had become a burden to
many farmers. To embrace any reform that would
not be based on slavery would challenge white
supremacy, a possibility Ruffin could never support.

Ruffin stood at the forefront of Virginia secession. He wrote many articles and several pamphlets advocating that the South secede from the
Union and arguing that an independent South

would flourish. Toward that end in 1858 he organized the League of United Southerners.

Legend has it that Ruffin fired the first shot on Fort Sumter in the battle that began the Civil War. He served briefly in the Confederate army and spent considerable time defending his lands from enemy attacks. Despondent after the Confederacy fell, he committed suicide on June 18, 1865. Shortly before his death he had written in his diary:

> I here declare my unmitigated hatred to Yankee rule—to all political, social and business connection with the Yankees and the Yankee race. Would that I impress these sentiments, in their full force, on every living Southerner and bequeath them to every one yet to be born! May such sentiments be held universally in the outraged and down-trodden South, though in silence and stillness, until the now far-distant day shall arrive for just retribution for Yankee usurpation, oppression and atrocious outrages, and for deliverance and vengeance from the now ruined, subjugated and enslaved Southern States!

Further Reading

Allmendinger, David F., Jr. *Ruffin: Family and Reform in the Old South.* New York: Oxford University Press, 1990.

Mathew, William M. *Edmund Ruffin and the Crisis of Slavery in the Old South: The Failure of Agricultural Reform.* Athens: University of Georgia Press, 1988.

Rush, Benjamin

(1745–1813) *social reformer*

Benjamin Rush was a physician, revolutionary patriot, and social reformer. He was born in Byberry, Pennsylvania, on December 24, 1745, the son of John Rush, a farmer, and Susanna Hall Harvey Rush. Benjamin Rush grew up in nearby Philadelphia, where his father had moved the family so he could pursue his trade as a gunsmith.

Rush graduated from the College of New Jersey in 1760 and studied medicine, first under Dr. John Redman from 1761 to 1766, and then under

prominent physicians in Edinburgh, Scotland. He obtained his medical degree in 1768, trained for a year at Saint Thomas's Hospital in London, and returned to Philadelphia in 1769. The following year he wrote the first American chemistry text, *A Syllabus of a Course of Lectures on Chemistry.*

As events propelled the colonists toward a revolution with Britain, Rush supported the Patriot side and developed friendships with THOMAS PAINE, John Adams, and Thomas Jefferson. His reformist zeal extended beyond imperial politics when in 1773 he wrote "An Address to the Inhabitants of the British Settlements in America, upon Slave-keeping." Despite his ownership of a slave, Rush said, "Slavery is so foreign to the human mind, that the moral faculties, as well as those of the understanding, are debased and rendered torpid by it."

He insisted that blacks were the intellectual equals to whites and that slavery was holding them back. His solution: End the importation of slaves, teach young blacks to read and write, and provide for their gradual emancipation. In a statement directed at the Pennsylvania legislature, which was then considering a measure that would restrict the importing of slaves into the colony, Rush said, "Remember, the eyes of all Europe are fixed upon you to preserve an asylum for freedom in this country, after the last pillars of it are fallen in every other quarter of the globe." Recognizing his own fault, he agreed to free his slave, and in 1774 he helped organize the Pennsylvania Society for Promoting the Abolition of Slavery.

In 1776, the same year Rush married Julia Stockton (they had 13 children), he was elected to the Continental Congress, in which he signed the Declaration of Independence. He was appointed the surgeon general for the Middle Division of the Continental army in 1777; in that post he became involved in an unnerving dispute. Appalled by medical conditions in the military hospitals, he accused Dr. William Shippen, Jr., of maladministration. Although Congress absolved Shippen of any wrongdoing, Rush continued to press his case with George Washington, asserting in a letter to him that 708 patient deaths had occurred at a time Shippen was claiming there had been only a few.

Benjamin Rush was a Revolutionary patriot who later advocated numerous social reforms, including the end to capital punishment. *(National Archives and Records Administration)*

Washington ignored him, for by that time Rush's dispute with Shippen had become entangled in one with the general when Rush accused Washington of incompetence and urged he be replaced by Horatio Gates or Thomas Conway. In a letter to John Adams, Rush said, "I am daily looking out for some great military character to start up, perhaps from the plow, to save this country." When Washington heard of Rush's remarks, he accused Rush of personal disloyalty. (Rush later expressed regret for his attack and apologized to Washington.)

In 1777 Rush opposed the radical Pennsylvania constitution of the previous year and worked hard to replace it. His complaints, however, stemmed from a desire to protect popular power, not diminish it. He disparaged the lack of checks and balances and claimed that the one-house legislature made it easier for the wealthy to control the government.

Rush resigned from the military in 1778 and resumed his medical practice. In 1783 he joined the staff of the Pennsylvania Hospital in Philadelphia. His observations of the poor, coupled with the postrevolutionary spirit of social change, caused him to engage in more reform. In 1786 he established the first free dispensary to help the poor. The following year he campaigned for adoption of the Constitution and served in the Pennsylvania ratifying convention. When the document went into effect, he said proudly, "I am now a citizen of every state."

Rush condemned capital punishment and worked for prison reform. He so strongly promoted temperance that he became known as the "father of the American temperance movement." His *An Enquiry into the Effects of Spirituous Liquor Upon the Human Body, and Their Influence upon the Happiness of Society* (1785) included a vivid description of a drunk: "He opens his eyes and closes them again—he gapes and stretches his limbs—he then coughs and pukes."

Rush advocated education for girls, establishment of a national university, and changes in pedagogy to teach children science and subjects they could apply to their lives, rather than the classical education then offered. In 1793 he risked his life by staying in Philadelphia to help those afflicted by a yellow fever epidemic while most of the city's doctors fled. In September he wrote to his wife: "I have lived to see the close of another day, more awful than any I have yet seen. Forty persons it is said have been buried this day, and I have visited and prescribed for more than 100 patients."

In 1803 he was elected president of the Pennsylvania Society for Promoting Abolition of Slavery. His work with the insane at the Pennsylvania Hospital displayed a compassion toward their plight that was unusual for the time. He was the first to use a rudimentary form of psychoanalysis.

During these years and later he continued to advance his medical career. In 1787 he helped organize the Philadelphia College of Physicians, and in 1789 he was appointed chair of theory and practice at the University of Pennsylvania. Three years later he was named professor of that college's institutes of medicine and clinical practice. He was by far the most prominent physician of his time, and students flocked to his classes. As a result they increased in size from about 45 annually in 1790 to about 3,000 in 1812.

Benjamin Rush died in Philadelphia on April 19, 1813. Some contemporaries criticized his moral certitude as overbearing; others marveled at the scope of his reform activities. One compared him to a fictional character who "attacks without mercy all the giants, hydras, hobgoblins, etc."

Further Reading

Binger, Carl Alfred Lanning. *Revolutionary Doctor: Benjamin Rush, 1746–1813.* New York: Norton, 1966.

Hawke, David Freeman. *Benjamin Rush: Revolutionary Gadfly.* Indianapolis: Bobbs-Merrill, 1971.

Katcher, Brian S. "Benjamin Rush's Educational Campaign Against Hard Drinking." *The American Journal of Public Health* 83 (February 1993): 273+

Rustin, Bayard

(ca.1910–1987) *civil rights leader, pacifist*

A civil rights leader known for his intellect and eloquence, Bayard Rustin was hailed as a "tactical genius." He was born out of wedlock on March 17,1910 (some sources say 1912), to Archie Hopkins and Florence Rustin in West Chester, Pennsylvania. He was adopted by his maternal grandparents and grew up in their household.

As a child Bayard was deeply influenced by his grandmother's Quaker faith, and he adopted her concern for social justice and her pacifist views. At West Chester High School he excelled academically and athletically. He also exhibited a powerful voice in the glee club as a tenor. He graduated in 1932 and received a music scholarship from Wilberforce University in Ohio, where he matriculated for a few months before transferring to Cheyney State Teachers College in Pennsylvania and then in 1938 to the City College of New York. He never earned a degree, but during his two years at City College he joined the Young Communist League (YCL). Rustin recalled that when the "Scottsboro boys" faced hanging in Alabama, it was the Communists who went to their assistance. "When it came to speaking out against Jim Crow, it was the Communists. Every black who got into

trouble, the Communists made a great deal of fuss about. So I got involved in the Young Communist League."

While at City College Rustin worked as an usher in movie theaters, as a waiter, and as a substitute teacher. He also sang at nightclubs and in plays, and some observers claim he could have become a famous singer had he not decided on a career as a social activist.

In 1941 Rustin quit the YCL. He later explained, "I raised a series of questions with them, to have it revealed to me that at that moment the Communists were interested only in what was good for the Soviet Union. They were not really interested in justice, as I had thought. I therefore resigned."

He applied his reform zeal to a nonviolent antiwar group, the Fellowship of Reconciliation (FOR), and he served as its secretary for race relations. In 1942 he also joined the Congress of Racial Equality (CORE). CORE was a group sponsored by FOR, which sought to advance black civil rights through nonviolent direct action. As early as his teenage years Rustin had protested racial discrimination. In West Chester he had sat in the white section of a movie theater and was arrested when he refused to move. Now he had found an organization that would allow him to pursue civil rights through the Quaker-based nonviolent methods he preferred.

When the United States entered World War II, Rustin declared himself a conscientious objector and refused to serve either in combat or in a civilian work camp as a noncombatant. Consequently, he was imprisoned from 1944 to 1946 at the Ashland Correctional Institute in Kentucky and the Lewisburg Penitentiary in Pennsylvania.

After his prison sentence ended, he chaired the Free India Committee to protest British rule in India, traveled to that country, and studied Mohandas Gandhi's nonviolent protest tactics. In 1947 he participated in the Journey of Reconciliation (JOR), organized by CORE, and joined 15 other protesters, white and black, on buses as they pulled into depots in the South and challenged the segregationist laws that required the two races to use separate bathrooms, restaurants, and waiting rooms. During the trip Rustin was arrested in

Chapel Hill, North Carolina, for violation of the segregationist statutes, and he served 30 days on a chain gang.

In 1953 Rustin quit FOR and became executive director of the War Resisters League, a post he held for 12 years. At the same time he continued his civil rights activities. At the invitation of MARTIN LUTHER KING, JR., he helped organize the bus boycott in Montgomery, Alabama, and from 1955 until 1960, and again shortly thereafter, he served as King's special assistant. In that capacity he helped King and other black ministers form the Southern Christian Leadership Council, one of the country's most influential civil rights groups and a proponent of King's Gandhian nonviolent protest, in 1957.

In 1963 ASA PHILIP RANDOLPH, who had greatly influenced Rustin in his commitment to civil rights, asked him to serve as deputy director of the March on Washington. Rustin agreed and coordinated the event that sent 200,000 demonstrators to the nation's capital.

By the mid-1960s the Vietnam War was placing a great strain on Rustin. He sympathized with the war's critics but strongly supported President Lyndon Johnson for his War on Poverty and the masterful way in which he had convinced Congress to pass the Civil Rights Act of 1964 and the Voting Rights Act of 1965. He wanted, too, to make the Democratic Party a more progressive institution by working within it. Alienating its leaders, he felt, would only make that impossible.

Rustin was also moving away from his pacifist roots and quit the War Resisters League to join the newly founded A. Philip Randolph Institute as its director. Rustin's biographer Daniel Levine says in *Bayard Rustin and the Civil Rights Movement* (2000), "Exactly when he stopped being a pacifist is hard to say, but certainly by 1966 his old pacifist friends realized that they had lost him for their cause."

When King condemned the Vietnam War, Rustin demurred. He often made contradictory statements as he struggled with his conscience. Finally, in 1967 he stated that he could not

> go along with those who favor immediate U.S. withdrawal, or who absolve Hanoi and the Vietcong from all guilt. A military takeover by those forces would impose a totalitarian regime on South Vietnam and there is no doubt in my mind that the regime would wipe out independent democratic elements in the country. Of these there may not be many, but they deserve our support.

And directing his remarks at King, he said, "I would consider the involvement of the civil rights organizations as such in peace activities as unprofitable and perhaps even suicidal."

Rustin opposed black power militants who were calling for African Americans to distance themselves from whites. He agreed with them that blacks must move beyond political issues to achieve economic gains, but he wanted greater alliances with whites. In 1975 he founded the Organization for Black Americans to Support Israel Committee, a group intended to build a bridge between the black and Jewish communities. In so doing, he again antagonized black militants.

While in Israel in 1982, Rustin defended that nation's invasion of Lebanon and condemned the Palestine Liberation Organization. He insisted that for there to be peace, Arabs must accept Israel's existence (though he said the Israeli government must show more willingness to compromise on issues).

A member of the Socialist International, Rustin attended their meetings in the United States and overseas. He chaired the Social Democrats, U.S.A., which was a faction of the Socialist Party. In the 1980s he also spoke publicly about his homosexuality. Rustin's first homosexual experience had occurred when he was 14, but he had kept silent about his sexual preference, though he had been arrested in the 1950s on a public sex charge. Other black leaders had encouraged his silence, for they feared the government would use his homosexuality to smear the entire civil rights movement. Rustin never became prominent in the gay rights movement, but he made a few speeches in the mid-1980s supporting it.

Rustin took up the cause of Haitian refugees and democracy within Haiti and in 1987 traveled there. He returned to the Untied States ill and thinking he had contracted a tropical disease, but his appendix had burst, and on August 24, 1987, he died of cardiac arrest at a hospital in New York City.

As a civil rights leader, Rustin had wanted to take protest beyond the streets to develop it into a force influential with government and businesses. Historian John D'Emilio states, "He wanted the outside to become the inside. He wanted the protesters to become the policy makers, and the visionaries to become the builders of a new world of social and economic justice."

Further Reading

Anderson, Jervis. *Bayard Rustin: Troubles I've Seen: A Biography.* New York: HarperCollins, 1997.

Levine, Daniel. *Bayard Rustin and the Civil Rights Movement.* New Brunswick, N.J.: Rutgers University Press, 2000.

S

Sanger, Margaret Higgins

(1879–1966) *women's rights activist, birth control activist*

Margaret Sanger was an advocate of liberating women through birth control. She was born Margaret Higgins on September 14, 1879, in Corning, New York, to Michael Hennessy Higgins, a stonemason, and Anne Purcell Higgins.

While growing up Margaret Higgins was greatly influenced by her father's fervent attachment to socialism. She even attended a large open field rally that was condemned by the Catholic Church and bred in her a preference for free expression over religious authority. Margaret was also influenced by her mother's declining health, a result of the birth of her 11 children, and though she would eventually have two sons and a daughter of her own, she thought that too many women were bearing too many children.

Margaret attended Claverack College in upstate New York and in 1899 began studying nursing. She quit, however, in 1902 when she married William Sanger, an architect and socialist. Ten years later she moved to New York City, made friends with radical intellectuals, joined the Socialist Party, wrote articles for the socialist magazine *Call*, and marched in the picket lines during strikes declared by the Industrial Workers of the World, a revolutionary socialist union. She also believed that women should be liberated from suppressing their erotic desires, so she enthusiastically promoted free love. One observer reported:

Margaret Sanger was a Madonna type of woman, with soft brown hair parted over a quiet brow, and crystal-clear brown eyes. . . . It was as if she had been more or less arbitrarily chosen by the powers that be to voice a new gospel of not only sex knowledge in regard to contraception, but sex knowledge about copulation and its intrinsic importance. . . . She was the first person I knew who was openly an ardent propagandist for the joys of the flesh.

In 1914 Sanger began publishing *Woman Rebel*, a rabidly anticapitalist magazine that also denounced marriage and defended political assassination. Federal authorities arrested her for violation of antiobscenity laws, and to avoid prosecution she fled to Europe. Sanger had already shown an interest in the issue of birth control, partly because her own health made it risky for her to become pregnant again. Now Havelock Ellis, a British philosopher who became her lover, convinced her to abandon her other issues for that one.

She returned to the United States in 1915, and the charges against her were dropped. But she plunged determinedly into the birth control campaign then under way and confronted a divided movement. Mary Ware Dennett had founded the National Birth Control League, a group that sought congressional repeal of the Comstock Act, which classified birth control literature as obscene and illegal. Unlike Sanger, Dennett opposed direct action in favor of such procedures as petitioning. Sanger disagreed with that approach and disliked anyone's challenging her leadership in the birth control movement. She wanted to dominate the campaign and considered her leadership absolutely essential to its success.

In October 1916 Sanger decided she would engage in a direct-action challenge to the New York state law that made it illegal to distribute birth control devices or information. For Sanger and many other women, those laws represented an attempt by men to dictate when children would be born and how many children a couple would have; devices or information that would allow women to take the initiative in conception would weaken male authority and liberate women sexually and spiritually.

On October 16, 1916, in the Brownsville section of Brooklyn, Sanger, her sister, Ethel Byrne, who was a registered nurse, and Fania Mindell, a Russian woman willing to act as an interpreter with the neighborhood's immigrants, opened the Brownsville Clinic. Any woman could enter the facility and for 10 cents buy a pamphlet written by Sanger—entitled *What Every Girl Should Know*—along with instructions on how to use contraceptives. Handbills that advertised the clinic announced:

> MOTHERS
> Can you afford to have a large family?
> Do you want any more children?
> If not, why do you have them?
> DO NOT KILL. DO NOT TAKE LIFE,
>   BUT PREVENT.

On October 26 an undercover policewoman arrested Sanger, Byrne, and Mindell. Sanger reopened the clinic but was arrested a second time on November 14. She opened the clinic yet again and was arrested on November 16. This time the police forced the landlord to evict her, and the clinic closed for good.

Shortly before Sanger went to trial in January 1917, several prominent women organized the Committee of 100 to help her, Byrne, and Mindell. They raised money for lawyers and rallied public opinion. Byrne was tried, convicted, and sent to prison at Blackwell's Island, but she began a hunger strike, and the Committee of 100 held a protest rally at Carnegie Hall. Sanger appeared before the group and declared: "I come to you

Margaret Sanger advocated free sexual expression for women and founded a birth control clinic in New York City, an act that resulted in her arrest. *(Library of Congress)*

tonight from a vortex of persecution. I come not from the stake of Salem where women were once burned for blasphemy, but from the shadow of Blackwell's Island where women are tortured for so-called obscenity."

Sanger was herself convicted and served a 30-day sentence from February to March 1917. The New York court of appeals upheld her conviction, but it interpreted the law in a way that made it easier for doctors to prescribe contraceptives.

Margaret Sanger continued her birth control campaign but with some changes in outlook. She identified more closely with eugenics, arguing that birth control should be used to prevent the working class from "overbreeding" and to limit the number of "unfit" persons. In an article she wrote in 1919, "Hard Facts," she depicted the difficulties facing poor women burdened by large families:

A woman living in three dark rooms in the lower East Side, makes her living as janitress of the house. She has been married sixteen years and has eight living, and two dead children in that time. The husband is an habitual drunkard and a gambler. The financial status of this family is nil. The oldest child is fifteen and helps support the family, as she earns nine dollars a week. A younger boy of thirteen works after school and earns a little toward the support of the family. The other children are sick and so underfed that they cannot resist stealing food from push carts in the street.

If this woman has another baby she is not physically fit to produce a healthy one. Her children have no chance for an education and can only grow up, if they live, as demoralized, degraded men and women, unworthy citizens and menaces to the community. This mother is nothing but a human breeding machine, an unwilling one at that. . . .

When will our government see the necessity of allowing the practices of Birth Control for such a woman . . . ?

Despite her interest in the poor—often based on a frightening picture that their continual breeding would overwhelm the respectable class—Sanger abandoned her sympathies for leftists. In 1922 she divorced William Sanger and married James Noah Henry Slee, a wealthy oilman, and circulated in high society. His money bankrolled the American Birth Control League that she had founded the previous year.

In 1923 she opened the Clinical Research Bureau in New York, which provided contraceptive devices to women. She remained active in the birth control movement into the 1950s, when she campaigned for federal funding of contraceptive services. Sanger died on September 6, 1966, at her home in Tucson, Arizona.

Margaret Sanger never doubted that birth control would liberate women: "The basic freedom of the world is woman's freedom," she wrote in *Woman and the New Race* (1920). "A free race cannot be born of slave mothers. . . . No woman can call herself free who does not own and control her body."

Further Reading

Chesler, Ellen. *Woman of Valor: Margaret Sanger and the Birth Control Movement in America.* New York: Simon & Schuster, 1992.

Douglas, Emily Taft. *Margaret Sanger: Pioneer of the Future.* New York: Holt, Rinehart & Winston, 1969.

Gray, Madeline. *Margaret Sanger: A Biography of the Champion of Birth Control.* New York: R. Marek, 1979.

Savio, Mario
(1942–1996) *free speech activist*

Mario Savio was an ardent fighter for free speech during the 1960s counterculture. He was born on December 8, 1942, into a Catholic Italian-American working-class family in New York City. He attended Queens College until his junior year, in 1963, when he transferred to Berkeley after his parents moved to California.

As did many political activists in the 1960s counterculture, Savio worked in the civil rights movement. His teaching during the summer of 1964 at a Freedom School for black children in McComb, Mississippi, affected him deeply, making him angry about racism and oppression in a nation that proclaimed itself free.

This anger extended to his experiences at Berkeley. As he continued to study for a degree in philosophy, the impersonal red tape at the university and its restrictions on speech disturbed him; his concern was reinforced and intensified when he read Karl Marx's assertion that alienation emerged in response to bureaucratic institutions. In fall 1964 Savio, who had worked briefly in the Young People's Socialist League, won election as chair of the University Friends of the Student Non-Violent Coordinating Committee, a prominent civil rights organization.

He was in that position when conflict erupted on campus over the administration's refusal to let students use a narrow strip of sidewalk at the university's south entrance as a place where they could recruit volunteers for off-campus social causes, especially civil rights activities. Savio and several student leaders opposed the ban and formed the United Front to set up tables and defy it. The administration reacted on October 1, 1964, by suspending Savio and seven other students.

Later that afternoon police arrested a member of a civil rights group for sitting at a table near the administration building. Students then surrounded a police car that had arrived and prevented it from leaving. Soon the crowd reached several thousand, and Savio climbed atop the car and gave a speech that made him the leader of the protest.

Savio had the ability to combine rational argument with angry epithets. He called the administrators a "bunch of bastards" and said about the police: "They have a job to do! . . . Like [Nazi executioner] Adolph Eichmann. He had a job to do. He fit into the machinery."

During the sit-down Savio played only a minor role in the negotiations to end the crisis. Finally, an agreement reached on October 2 by the students and administration ended the sit-down. Savio then won election to the steering committee of the Free Speech Movement (FSM), formed to protect the right of students to express their ideas and organize as they desired.

In late November the Board of Regents made clear its intention to continue restrictions on student advocacy, and the administration brought charges against Savio for his actions during the sit-down, causing the FSM to call a mass rally. More than 6,000 students turned out on December 2, at which time Savio spoke and encouraged the crowd to occupy the administration building, Sproul Hall. "There is a time," Savio said:

> when the operation of the machine becomes so odious, makes you so sick at heart, that you can't take part; and you've got to put your bodies upon the gears and upon the wheels, upon the levers, upon all the apparatus and you've got to make it stop. And you've got to indicate to the people who run it, to the people who own it, that unless you're free, the machine will be prevented from working at all.

He and about 800 demonstrators stayed the night at Sproul Hall, and the following morning police and state troopers evicted and arrested them.

On December 3 a campus strike began and lasted five days. During it, on December 7, Savio approached a microphone to address a rally of more than 18,000, and campus police grabbed him and forced him from the stage. They relented, however, when the crowd grew angry. Savio and the FSM gained concessions later that month when the board of regents agreed to recognize as primary those First Amendment rights governing speech and assembly.

In June 1965 Savio and 154 other students were convicted on charges relating to their political protests, and he served four months in jail. The university refused to readmit him in November 1966, because as a nonstudent he had violated rules by distributing leaflets on campus. Later that month he participated in a sit-in to protest the administration's refusal to allow nonstudents to set up an antiwar table at the student union. Soon after that he largely withdrew from politics.

In 1984 Savio earned a bachelor's degree from San Francisco State University, followed five years later by a master's degree in physics from the same college. In 1995, while working as a mathematics and critical thinking professor at Sonoma State College in California, Savio organized the Campus Coalition for Human Rights and Justice. The group opposed those seeking to end affirmative-action programs. In November 1996 he organized students at Sonoma State to resist a tuition increase.

At about that time Savio denounced the Rightward turn in American politics. He labeled House Speaker Newt Gingrich and North Carolina senator Jesse Helms "crypto-fascists" and said, "Occasionally something comes down the pike that is just so horrible, that you . . . have to do something."

Savio died on November 6, 1996, of a heart attack caused by moving furniture at his house. He had been married twice. His first marriage, to Suzanne Goldberg, ended in divorce. He was survived by his second wife, Lynne Hollander, and three sons.

At a memorial to Savio one 1960s political activist said, "He was the personification of our passions and commitment to justice."

Further Reading

Rorabaugh, W. J. *Berkeley at War: The 1960s.* New York: Oxford University Press, 1989.

Rosen, Ruth. "A Passion for Justice: A Gentle Warrior's Fight for Free Speech." *Chronicle of Higher Education* 10 January 1997, B7.

Scheffer, Victor Blanchard
(1906–   ) *environmentalist, zoologist, writer*

A zoologist and writer, Victor Blanchard Scheffer is known for his environmentalist work. He was born on November 27, 1906, in Manhattan, Kansas, to Theophilus Scheffer, a biologist, and Celia Blanchard Scheffer, an elementary school teacher.

When Victor Scheffer was eight years old his father began working for the United States Biological Survey, and the Scheffer family moved to Puyallup, Washington. In 1925 Scheffer graduated from Stadium High School in nearby Tacoma and enrolled at the University of Washington in Seattle. There he took a course in entomology taught by Trevor Kincaid. Kincaid greatly influenced Scheffer with his enthusiasm, his love for discovery, and his belief that all living things lived together in a community.

Scheffer graduated with a B.S. in zoology in 1930; he earned a master's degree from the University of Washington in 1932, and a doctorate from the same school in 1935. Later that year he married Mary Elizabeth MacInnes (who died in 1989), and they had three children. With the Great Depression then under way he had difficulty finding a full-time job, but for several years he served as a part-time ranger and naturalist at Mount Rainier National Park in Washington state. Scheffer later credited that job with showing him how to reach beyond his fellow scientists and speak to a general audience. In 1937 he began working full-time with the United States Biological Survey as a junior biologist.

Over the ensuing years Scheffer engaged in many scientific studies of wildlife. In the late 1930s he investigated the state of several endangered species in Washington and Alaska. In 1940 he went to the Pribilof Islands in the Bering Sea and studied northern fur seals. In the late 1940s and early 1950s he studied sea otters, whales, and sharks. In 1964 the United States ratified the international Antarctic Treaty, and Scheffer served on the first team of observers sent to that conti-

nent to enforce the pact's provisions by looking for any signs of violations.

Scheffer's name became known to the general public in 1969 when his book *The Year of the Whale* won praise from reviewers for its poetic writing. The book became a best-seller and was eventually translated into seven languages. It helped awaken people to the lives and plight of whales. *The Year of the Seal* followed in 1970. Scheffer wrote *A Voice for Wildlife* in 1974; in it he surveyed existing wildlife management and called for a greater understanding of animals. Other books followed into the 1990s.

From 1972 to 1973 Scheffer served as consultant to the National Oceanic and Atmospheric Administration, and he became the first chairperson of the Marine Mammal Commission to regulate the killing of ocean mammals. From 1978 to 1983 he served on the board of directors of the Scientists Center for Animal Welfare, a group formed to increase the awareness of scientists and the general public of issues concerning the treatment of animals. Beginning in 1982 he served on the advisory committee of Friends of the Sea Otter.

Scheffer has criticized those who believe wildlife should be managed as a resource for human beings; he has insisted that they instead should be recognized and treated as part of an interdependent ecosystem. In *The Shaping of Environmentalism in America* (1991) he wrote that the goal of the environmental movement is "to strike a balance between idealism and realism, to preserve the diversity and wondrous beauty of our world while recognizing that billions must steadily draw upon its substance for survival."

Further Reading
Scheffer, Victor. *The Year of the Whale.* New York: Scribner's, 1969.
———. *The Year of the Seal.* New York: Scribner's, 1970.
———. *The Shaping of Environmentalism in America.* Seattle: University of Washington Press, 1991.

Schlafly, Phyllis Stewart
(1924–   ) *conservative activist*

An archconservative anticommunist in the 1950s, Phyllis Schlafly was a crusader against the Equal

Rights Amendment and is an advocate of traditional family values. She was born Phyllis Stewart on August 15, 1924, in Saint Louis, Missouri, to John Bruce, an engineer, and Odille Dodge Stewart.

In 1941 Phyllis Stewart graduated from the Academy of the Sacred Heart in Saint Louis and remained in her home city to attend Washington University. She earned a B.A. in 1944 and an M.A. the following year from Radcliffe College.

Schlafly worked for one year at the conservative American Enterprise Association in Washington, D.C., before returning to Saint Louis and employment as a research director for two banks. In 1949 she married Fred Schlafly, a wealthy lawyer and right-winger, and moved to his hometown of Alton, Illinois. With her marriage she quit her job to raise a family. Over the years the couple had six children.

In 1952, however, Phyllis Schlafly ran for Congress as an ultraconservative who opposed big government and warned about the communist menace within America. She lost, but she maintained her prominence within the political Right by traveling the state and making speeches as an officer with the Daughters of the American Revolution. She also conducted research for Joseph McCarthy as the Wisconsin senator hunted for communists in the early 1950s.

Turning her hand to publishing, Schlafly issued two pamphlets, *A Reading List for Americans* (1954) and *Inside the Communist Conspiracy* (1959), both of which guided readers to conservative literature. She served as president of the Illinois Federation of Republican Women from 1956 to 1964 and as a delegate to the Republican National Convention.

It was at the 1964 convention in San Francisco that she supported conservative Arizona senator Barry Goldwater for president. She entered the convention as the author of *A Choice Not an Echo,* which claimed conservatives had been thwarted at previous conventions by an eastern elite that had imposed on the delegates its choice for the presidential candidate. Some observers credited the book with helping Goldwater win the nomination.

Goldwater's landslide loss to President Lyndon Johnson in the general election resulted in

Schlaflys becoming involved in a power struggle between conservatives and moderates within the Republican Party. Consequently, in 1967 she lost her bid to become president of the National Federation of Republican Women. She went on to found the *Phyllis Schlafly Report,* a newsletter that appealed to women on the far Right.

Schlafly ran for Congress again in 1970 on a platform that attacked the welfare system and the turmoil of the 1960s counterculture. Like many in the counterculture, she opposed the Vietnam War, but for a different reason: She thought it a trap set by the communists to tie down America's military and weaken it through attrition.

Between 1964 and 1976 Schlafly joined retired rear admiral Chester Ward to write five books on national defense. They had as their theme that certain leaders in the U.S. government, notably National Security Adviser and Secretary of State Henry Kissinger, had undermined the country's security through a policy of détente, or cooperation, with the Soviet Union and through agreements to limit the spread of nuclear weapons.

But the issue that gained Schlafly the most notice in the 1970s was the Equal Rights Amendment (ERA). The amendment passed Congress in 1972, and Schlafly reacted by forming a Stop ERA organization and taking to the lecture circuit to urge state legislatures to reject the constitutional change. She said it would destroy labor regulations that protected working women, force women into military service, and lead to laws that would make homosexual marriage and abortion legal.

In 1975 she founded Eagle Forum to recruit conservative women to oppose feminist groups. Schlafly praised traditional family values and said women should stay at home and take care of their children—an interesting statement given the many hours she had spent on the road championing conservative causes. (Several years later she was embarrassed when newspapers reported that one of her sons was a homosexual.)

In the mid-1970s Schlafly broadcast her own talk show on the CBS radio network and served as a commentator on the Cable News Network. In 1977 she published *The Positive Woman,* which extolled the traditional wife and homemaker roles and attacked feminist values. The following year she earned a law degree from Washington University. In 1982 her fight against the ERA paid off when the amendment languished as the deadline passed for states to ratify it.

Schlafly continued to lead the Eagle Forum in the 1990s, and she wrote a syndicated newspaper column and broadcast a radio show. In the year 2000 she formed an unusual alliance with the progressive advocate RALPH NADER when they both worked to end the broadcasting of television network Channel One into public school classrooms. The network provided current events and other news features to students, but the shows were accompanied with commercials. Schlafly and Nader opposed the exploitation, though Schlafly did so more for the "immoral" content of the commercials and the shows themselves, which presented such issues as whether drugs should be legalized. Schlafly commented about her alliance with Nader: "We agree that the public schools should not be used for commercial purposes. A captive audience of students should not be sold for profit."

Further Reading

Felsenthal, Carol. *The Sweetheart of the Silent Majority: The Biography of Phyllis Schlafly.* Garden City, N.Y.: Doubleday, 1981.

Marley, David John. "Phyllis Schlafly's Battle Against the ERA and Women in the Military." *Minerva: Quarterly Report on Women and the Military* 18 (Summer 2000): 17.

Schneiderman, Rose

(1882–1972) *union organizer*

Rose Schneiderman is remembered as a union organizer for women. She was born on April 6, 1882, in Saven, Poland, to Samuel Schneiderman and Deborah Rothman Schneiderman.

At age eight Rose Schneiderman immigrated to the United States with her parents, and they settled on New York City's Lower East Side in a neighborhood heavily populated by European Jews. Two years later Rose's father died, and she was forced to leave school and find work to help her family financially. She loved books, however, and continued her education through reading.

Schneiderman worked as an errand girl and as a cashier before landing a job in 1898 as a lining maker in a cap factory. She was paid six dollars a week and had to furnish her own thread and buy her own sewing machine.

In 1903 Schneiderman met Bessie Braut, a fellow worker at the factory who was an anarchist. From Braut Schneiderman learned about unions, and later that year the two formed a women's local of the Jewish Socialist cap makers union. A few months later they joined the local to the previously all-male United Cloth Hat and Cap Makers Union.

By 1904 the local numbered several hundred members, and Schneiderman was chosen to serve on the national union's executive board—the first woman in the United States to hold such a position. In 1905 she joined the New York Women's Trade Union League (WTUL) and organized a cap makers' strike. Devoting herself full-time to labor organizing, in 1909–10 she led a strike of 25,000 shirtwaist makers. In 1913 she directed a general strike while serving as president of the International Ladies Garment Workers Union (ILGWU).

Schneiderman supported women's suffrage, believing that if women could vote they would be able to exert greater political leverage within the unions. But she preferred to focus on organizing women and so never took a prominent role in the movement. In 1915 she became national organizer for the ILGWU.

Beginning in 1918 Schneiderman shifted her strategy away from strikes and emphasized lobbying state legislatures to pass laws setting maximum work hours and minimum wages for women. In the 1920s she opposed the Equal Rights Amendment (ERA) then being promoted by many women's groups. Schneiderman believed that if it were passed working women would lose the protection afforded them by the laws and the opportunity to gain additional protective legislation.

When Democrat Franklin Roosevelt became president in 1933, he appointed Schneiderman to the National Recovery Administration's Labor Advisory Board. She exerted considerable influence on the president as a member of his "brain trust," an informal group of advisers.

In 1937 New York governor Herbert Lehman appointed her secretary of the state's Department of Labor, a post she held until 1944. She remained president of the New York WTUL until 1949 and of the national WTUL until 1950. Rose Schneiderman died on August 11, 1972, at the Jewish Home and Hospital for the Aged in New York City.

Further Reading

Barker-Benfield, G. J., and Catherine Clinton, eds. *Portraits of American Women: From Settlement to the Present.* New York: St. Martin's Press, 1991.

Seale, Bobby
(Robert George Seale)
(1936–) *black power leader*

Robert "Bobby" George Seale was one of the founders of the 1960s radical African-American group the Black Panthers. He was born into a poor family on October 22, 1937, in Dallas, Texas, but grew up in Oakland, California.

Discontented with high school, Bobby Seale dropped out and joined the air force. His stint, however, proved short—after a fight with an officer, he was dishonorably discharged. He then enrolled in night classes, obtained a high school diploma, and in 1965 entered Merritt College, a small two-year school on the edge of the Oakland ghetto where he lived. Seale immersed himself in the writings of left-wing radicals and black nationalists, especially Frantz Fanon and MALCOLM X. While at Merritt he met HUEY PERCY NEWTON, and they exchanged ideas and shared their anger about oppression.

Seale helped Newton organize the Soul Students' Advisory Council and advocated a militant revolutionary agenda that espoused opposition to capitalism and insisted blacks should arm themselves for self-defense. When many in the group opposed that stand, he and Newton wrote a 10-point program, and in October 1966 they founded the Black Panther Party. Seale and Newton demanded freedom for blacks, economic improvements, socialist development, and an end to police brutality. Seale recalled: "We wanted power to determine our own destiny in our own black commu-

nity. And what we had done is, we wanted to write a program that was straightforward to the people."

About Marxism, Seale recalled in a 1996 interview for the Cable News Network that one day he and Newton opened up Chairman Mao Tse-tung's "Little Red Book" (*The Sayings of Mao Tse-tung*) and said to each other,

> Hey, man, this is pretty good stuff. . . . Mao . . . says "You should not steal a needle and piece of thread from the people." I says, "That's something we could teach the party members." Because we were a young organization: We weren't more than about four or five months old. And that's where we began to have what we would call a lot of study in that [Marxist] direction. . . . What I developed best was a concept of community-controlled cooperatives in the black community, which largely I picked up from W. E. B. DU BOIS. So I mean, I sort of got there from W. E. B. Du Bois and a few other reads. But Marxist-Leninism per se was really a later development: not until 1968 that we really considered the Red Book required reading.

Seale served as the group's chairman and Newton as minister of defense. The two men antagonized the police when they organized armed patrols to monitor arrests in the ghettos. Seale and the Panthers gained national attention in May 1967 when they protested a legislative proposal to prohibit the carrying of guns in public; they barged onto the floor of the California Assembly in Sacramento while armed with rifles, shotguns, and pistols. Panther membership subsequently surged, though the authorities arrested Seale for disrupting the legislature, and he served six months in jail. After his release Seale helped forge ties with white radicals and joined them in forming the Peace and Freedom Party, under whose banner Newton ran for president in 1968.

That same year Seale joined a protest outside the Democratic National Convention in Chicago and was arrested for inciting a riot on the basis of an emotional speech he had presented to a crowd in which he condemned oppression. He stood trial with seven other radicals, a group newspapers called the "Chicago Eight." During the proceedings Seale protested so vociferously about rulings that went against him that the judge ordered him gagged and bound to a chair. Seale was later prosecuted separately, changing the Chicago Eight to the Chicago Seven. He was sentenced to four years in jail for 16 counts of contempt of court, but he served only half his term when the government suspended the contempt charges.

With Newton in jail from 1968 to 1970 on charges of manslaughter for killing a police officer (an appeals court later set aside his conviction), Seale assumed greater power in the Panther organization. By that time, though, the Federal Bureau of Investigation (FBI) had infiltrated the group with spies and agent provocateurs, and in cooperation with local police departments it launched violent and illegal attacks on the Panthers. In 1996 Seale told the Cable News Network:

> Why did the FBI [come] down on us? We started working coalitions with other organizations at the beginning of 1968. Those coalitions solidified themselves. We had the Peace and Freedom Party working in coalition with the Black Panther Party; Students for a Democratic Society, all the anti-war movement people; numerous other organizations. In late 1968, we had a working coalition with the Poor People's March through Rev. RALPH [DAVID] ABERNATHY, with SCLC [Southern Christian Leadership Conference]; we had a coalition with the Brown Berets, the Chicano organization, CESAR CHAVEZ and others in the labor [movement]; AIM: American Indian Movement; Young Puerto Rican Brothers, the Young Lords—we coalesced with everybody, you see. Because remember, we were dealing with "all power to all the people," not just black power. . . .
>
> They came down on us because we had a grassroots, real people's revolution, complete with the programs, complete with the unity, complete with the working coalitions, where we crossed racial lines. That synergetic statement of "All power to all the People," "Down with the racist pig power structure."

Seale acted to purge the government spies, but his action contributed to schisms within the group over policies, including how far to pursue the revolutionary socialist program desired by

Seale and Newton, and distrust mounted. In 1971 Seale went on trial, charged with ordering the execution, two years earlier, of a Panther who was actually a government informer. Radicals considered the trial an attempt by the authorities to silence Seale by putting him away in prison. A hung jury resulted, and the charges were dropped.

Back in Oakland, with the Panthers in disarray, Seale and Newton deemphasized militancy and developed neighborhood programs. In 1973 Seale ran for mayor of Oakland, and although he lost, he won many votes in the ghetto. As the Panthers faded in the 1980s, he engaged in social work to help ghetto youths. In 1987 he published a best-selling cookbook, *Barbecue with Bobby,* the proceeds of which he donated to social organizations. In the 1990s Seale (married and the father of one child) worked in Philadelphia, Pennsylvania, as a recruiter for the African-American Studies Program at Temple University. In the year 2002 he had his own web page at which he advocated a future world of "cooperational humanism" and sold videos along with his barbecue books.

Michael Tigar, a radical activist in the 1960s, said about Bobby Seale and the Black Panthers, "The Panthers started with the notion of the gun and the law book together. That's what Bobby and [Huey] Newton were really about. . . . You could organize all you want and be represented in court, but people first had to know you were serious"

Further Reading

Newton, Huey P. *War against the Panthers: A Study of Repression in America.* New York: Writers and Readers Publishing, 1996.

Pearson, Hugh. *The Shadow of the Panther: Huey Newton and the Price of Black Power in America.* Reading, Mass.: Addison-Wesley, 1994.

Seale, Bobby. *A Lonely Rage: The Autobiography of Bobby Seale.* New York: Times Books, 1978.

Sharpton, Al
(Alfred Charles Sharpton)
(1954–) *civil rights leader*

A controversial civil rights leader, Al Sharpton is noted for boldness that often crosses over to opportunism. He was born Alfred Charles Sharpton on October 3, 1954, to Alfred Sharpton, Sr., and Josephine Sharpton in the Brownsville section of Brooklyn, a borough of New York City.

Al Sharpton began appealing to people at an early age. At 10 he began preaching after he was ordained by a Pentecostal minister. That same year his father deserted the family, and he and his mother moved to the Crown Heights section of Brooklyn, where she worked as a cleaning woman and lived on welfare. At about age 14 Sharpton met two individuals who greatly influenced his life: the civil rights leader JESSE JACKSON and the soul singer James Brown. Jackson appointed Sharpton youth director of his newly formed Operation Breadbasket, a program intended to unite African Americans in using boycotts to place pressure on manufacturers and retailers to hire more black workers. Brown hired the already heavy-set Sharpton as one of his bodyguards.

Sharpton graduated from Brooklyn's Tilden High School in 1973 and briefly attended Brooklyn College before dropping out. The following year he met the boxing promoter Don King, and they joined to protest a concert tour by the singer Michael Jackson for hiring too few blacks, a move that won them a contract to promote him.

At about the same time Sharpton founded the National Youth Movement, later renamed the United African Movement, to fight drugs in inner city black neighborhoods. His gift for hyperbole became evident when he claimed that the organization had 30,000 members in 16 cities, whereas it actually was much smaller.

Sharpton first gained widespread attention in New York City in 1974, when he organized a demonstration that protested the shooting death of a 14-year-old African-American youth by police. But for all his activity, Al Sharpton remained a local phenomenon until 1984. That year he demanded that Bernhard Goetz, a white man who had shot four black teenagers on a subway train in what Goetz called self-defense, be indicted for murder. When Goetz was indeed indicted, Sharpton began standing on the courthouse steps daily, calling for him to be found guilty. The jury, however, convicted Goetz only of minor gun possession charges.

In 1985 Sharpton married Kathy Jordan; they had two daughters. The following year he again resorted to street protest in the aftermath of the Howard Beach racial killing, an incident in which bat-wielding white youths in the neighborhood had attacked three black men and killed one of them. Sharpton led the Days of Outrage protest, which blocked the Brooklyn Bridge.

By then the media had found in Sharpton someone who could provide blunt sound bites, often guaranteed to raise controversy. His aggressive and confrontational manner nearly destroyed him in 1987 when he became involved in the Tawana Brawley case. Brawley, a 15-year-old black girl, claimed that she had been raped by five or six white men, one of whom carried a police officer's badge. Sharpton publicly criticized the investigation of the crime and advised Brawley to refrain from cooperating with the police. There followed days of headlines in New York's newspapers, and it finally came out that Brawley had made up the entire story. The *Philadelphia Inquirer* accused Sharpton of unscrupulous behavior in his disregard for the facts. (In 1998 a New York jury found Sharpton liable for defaming one of the prosecutors involved in the Brawley affair.)

Sharpton's reputation suffered another blow when he confirmed in 1988 that he had been an informant for the Federal Bureau of Investigation (FBI), in which capacity he had supplied the agency secret information about Don King and various black leaders. In 1989 the federal government indicated him for income tax evasion, but he was acquitted; in 1990 he was charged with misuse of funds collected for the United African Movement, but he was again acquitted.

He then reaffirmed his commanding position in the black community when he led demonstrators through the Bensonhurst neighborhood to protest the killing of Yusef Hawkins, a 16-year-old black teenager, by a white mob. As two white youths stood trial for the murder, Sharpton made a thinly veiled threat to burn down the city if they were acquitted. As it turned out, one of the defendants was convicted of murder.

While getting ready to lead another protest in January 1991, Sharpton was knifed by a white man and hospitalized with a wound in his chest. That spring he returned to protesting, and in 1992 he entered the Democratic primary for the U.S. Senate. He lost, but he polled a respectable 166,000 votes. He ran again for the Senate in 1994 but was unable to unseat the Democratic incumbent, Daniel Patrick Moynihan.

By the mid-1990s Sharpton had mellowed, perhaps from a desire to reach more voters in his next political campaign: a race in 1997 for mayor of New York City. Sharpton finished behind Ruth Messinger in the Democratic primary.

In 1999 Sharpton led nonviolent protests against the killing of Amadou Diallo, a black immigrant gunned down by the police while standing unarmed in the vestibule of his apartment building. At about the same time he protested the police brutalization of Haitian immigrant Abner Louima, and in March 2002 he denounced a court decision that overturned the conviction of three offices found guilty of participating in the assault.

Meanwhile, Sharpton ran the Madison Avenue Initiative, formed to win contracts for minority-owned businesses, and ignited a dispute with Jesse Jackson when he accused him of siding with Burger King against a black franchisee who had sued the corporation for racial discrimination. Many observers believed that Sharpton was seeking to replace Jackson as the most prominent leader of black America.

In May 2001 Sharpton announced he would seek the Democratic presidential nomination in 2004. That same month he was imprisoned, along with others, for trespassing on naval property in a protest to force the U.S. Navy to end its use of the island of Vieques, Puerto Rico, as a bombing range. In June he began a hunger strike that he resolved to continue until the government changed its policy. Bowing to widespread protests, President George W. Bush announced that the Vieques site would soon be closed.

Sharpton was released in mid-August proclaiming, "We went into jail struggling and we've come out continuing to struggle. They didn't give me nothing but a recharge of my batteries!"

Further Reading

Sharpton, Al. *Go and Tell Pharaoh: The Autobiography of the Reverend Al Sharpton.* New York: Doubleday,1996.

Shays, Daniel

(1747–1825) *American revolutionary, insurgent*

Daniel Shays was a soldier in the American Revolution and an insurgent in the 1780s. He was born in Hopkinton, Massachusetts, in about the year 1747 to Patrick Shays and Margaret Dempsey Shays.

Little is known about Daniel Shays prior to the American Revolution. In 1772 he married Abigail Gilbert, and when the Revolution began he rallied to the Patriot cause, fighting both at Lexington and at Bunker Hill. He saw action at Ticonderoga, Saratoga, and Stony Point, and in January 1777 he was commissioned a captain in the Fifth Massachusetts Regiment. He resigned from the army in 1780 and settled in Pelham, Massachusetts, where he served on the revolutionary Committee of Safety.

In the 1780s Shays's Rebellion began in an atmosphere of widespread economic distress and intense instability. With a postwar depression gripping the country, farmers suffered from falling prices for their foodstuffs. At the same time creditors wanted them to pay their debts in hard currency rather than less valuable paper money. Shays was one of those who lived in debt and struggled economically.

In Massachusetts the legislature increased taxes to eliminate the state's Revolutionary War debt; between 1783 and 1786 taxes on land rose 60 percent. With that, farmers in many parts of the state, but especially in the west, began demanding reduced levies and stay laws that would prevent foreclosures on their property. The lower house responded by passing relief measures, but the upper house, under the influence of eastern creditors, rejected them.

As the economic crisis worsened, the legislature announced in July 1786 that it would adjourn until January 1787. Many farmers felt frustrated and held town conventions at which they wrote down their grievances. But with the legislature refusing to meet, they concluded that the Massachusetts government was as unresponsive in 1786 as had been the British Crown in 1776.

In the east armed mobs formed. One operating in Northampton in August 1786 prevented a court from meeting. In September mobs under the direction of Job Shattuck disrupted court sessions in Concord. In late November, however, government troops arrested Shattuck and quelled the disturbances.

In the west, though, insurrection spread throughout the Berkshires; farmers gathered in armed groups, including some 1,500 who organized under Daniel Shays. They marched on the courts to prevent mortgage foreclosure hearings and broke into jails to release debtors. A contemporary observer outlined the reasons for the protest, referring to "the present expensive mode of collecting debts, which, by reason of the great scarcity of cash, will of necessity fill our gaols with unhappy debtors."

A leader of the Massachusetts elite, Benjamin Lincoln, observed:

> The proportion of debtors runs high in this State. Too many of them are against the government. The men of property . . . are generally abettors of our present constitution, but few of them have been in the field, and it remains quite problematical whether they will in time fully discover their own interests . . . [and] lend for a season out of their property for the security of the remainder.

But they did "lend for a season out of their property" when eastern creditors provided the money for the state to raise an army, with the troops commanded by Lincoln. On January 25, 1787, Shays tried to capture the arsenal at Springfield but was turned back by an artillery barrage, and on February 4 the uprising effectively ended when Lincoln's army defeated Shays's force at Petersham.

At a trial of four of the rebels, Massachusetts chief justice William Cushing said that they had tried "to overturn all government and order" and that they had given in "to the power of the most

restless, malevolent, destructive, tormenting passions." Daniel Shays avoided trial by fleeing to New Hampshire and then Vermont before settling in western New York. The Massachusetts government eventually pardoned him and all of the rebels.

Shays's Rebellion shook the political system. In Massachusetts the voters threw out the conservative leadership in the spring of 1787 and replaced it with one more representative of the farmers. The legislature subsequently passed several reforms, including a law that exempted clothing, household goods, and tools of trade from impoundment for debt.

In the country as a whole, Shays's Rebellion stunned conservatives, who called it an instance of the rabble gaining too much power and threatening anarchy. One member of the elite said: "The natural effects of pure democracy are already produced among us. It is a war against virtue, talents, and property carried on by the dregs and scum of mankind."

These conservatives acted to form a stronger national government that could contain democratic impulses and secure order by righting the economy and, if necessary, using military force. In 1787 they met in Philadelphia, where they dumped the Articles of Confederation and replaced them with the Constitution.

Daniel Shays died in poverty and obscurity at age 78, but his rebellion had raised the banner of liberty against tyranny. Although many Americans, including the Revolutionary leader Sam Adams, thought that Shays had gone too far and had threatened to unleash lawlessness and even class warfare, Shays and his followers saw themselves as acting consistently with the precedent of the American Revolution. Thomas Jefferson said in defense of Shays's Rebellion: "The tree of liberty must be refreshed from time to time with the blood of patriots and tyrants. It is its natural manure." That indeed was the radical alternative Daniel Shays had provided.

Further Reading

Feer, Robert A. *Shays's Rebellion*. New York: Garland, 1988.

Gross, Robert A., ed. *In Debt to Shays: The Bicentennial of an Agrarian Rebellion.* Charlottesville: University Press of Virginia, 1993.

Sinclair, Upton
(1878–1968) *socialist*

Upton Sinclair was a writer and socialist. He was born on September 20, 1878, in Baltimore, Maryland, to Upton Beall Sinclair, a successful wholesale liquor salesman, and Priscilla Augusta Harden Sinclair.

When Upton Sinclair was 10 years old his family moved to New York City, and he attended grammar school there for three years. He entered the College of the City of New York at age 14.

Sinclair began writing for publication while he was still in college, putting pen to paper to earn money for tuition by cranking out stories for pulp magazines. At the same time he read widely and inquired deeply, showing as he did so an idealistic faith in the human ability to improve the world. He graduated from college in 1897 and turned to more serious writing, producing two nondescript novels, one in 1901 and the other in 1903.

By then George D. Herron, a writer and lecturer, had interested Sinclair in the socialist movement. So, too, had Jack London's novel *People of the Abyss*—a story about how the author lived incognito in the East End of London, England, to study poverty. In 1902 Sinclair joined the Socialist Party. One historian has said, "Socialism came to him as more than an intellectual conviction; it came as a magnificent discovery, as a combined religious conversion and revelation, in the light of which he saw clearly the ends for which he might live."

With that background, Sinclair wrote *The Jungle.* The idea was first presented to him by J. A. Wayland, the editor of a Socialist weekly, *Appeal to Reason.* Wayland gave Sinclair a small advance to write about the meatpacking industry, and he spent seven weeks in Chicago researching the topic. Sinclair talked to factory workers and some officials, but never entered a slaughterhouse or meatpacking plant. His work first appeared in *Appeal to Reason* as a serial; then *The Jungle* was pub-lished as a book in February 1906 by Doubleday, Page and Company.

The Jungle caused an immediate sensation, but less for its depiction of exploited workers, such as Jurgis and other Lithuanian immigrants, than for what Sinclair had to say about meatpacking itself—an account that took only about 12 pages of the entire novel but that sent stomachs churning and tempers flaring over the poison being fed consumers in the guise of meat. Even today the vividness of some passages strikes with force:

> As for the . . . men who worked in tank rooms full of steam, and in some of which there were open vats near the level of the floor, their peculiar trouble was that they fell into the vats; and when they were fished out, there was never enough of them left to be worth exhibiting—sometimes they would be overcooked for days, till all but the bones of them had gone out of the world as Durham's Pure Leaf Lard!
>
> There was never the least attention paid to what was cut up for sausage; there would come back from Europe old sausage that had been rejected, and that was mouldy and white—it could be dosed with borax and glycerine, and dumped into the hoppers, and made over for home consumption.
>
> [The] rats were nuisances, and the packers would put poisoned bread out for them; they would die, and the rats, bread and meat would go into the hoppers together. . . .

Critics accused Sinclair of exaggerating conditions, and a report in 1906 by the Department of Agriculture's Bureau of Animal Husbandry concluded he had engaged in "willful and deliberate misrepresentations of fact." But a congressional investigation of the meat packing conditions supported him, and although he had written a novel, he defended his story as factually accurate.

The Jungle created such a public outcry that in 1907 Congress passed the Meat Inspection Act. Sinclair, however, had wanted to expose the oppression suffered by workers under capitalism. A promotion for the work, written by Jack London and approved by Sinclair, stated in part: "Take notice and remember, comrades, this book is straight proletarian. It is written by an intellectual proletarian, for the proletarian. . . . It is to be read by the proletariat. What *Uncle Tom's Cabin* did for the black slaves *The Jungle* has a large chance to do for the white slaves of today."

Disappointed by his failure to ignite a mass movement toward socialism, Sinclair said, "I aimed at the public's heart, and by accident hit it in the stomach." In fact, leaders in the Republican and Democratic Parties concluded that *The Jungle* had the potential to wreck capitalism. That notion, as much as any desire to help society, propelled President Theodore Roosevelt to push for the Meat Inspection Act; he concluded that if capitalism failed to show it could correct its worst abuses, then socialism would take over. The Meat Inspection Act was a small bandage on the wound inflicted by Sinclair on capitalism.

Upton Sinclair went on to write many more novels, along with a series of nonfiction works that showed how capitalism shaped the church, the press, and the schools to serve its ends. But he was an activist beyond the writer's desk. In 1906 he ran for Congress as a socialist from New Jersey. He lost that race, as he did several others when he ran under the Socialist Party banner.

He came closest to winning office during the Great Depression in 1934, when he ran for governor of California as a Democrat. He won the primary under the slogan "End Poverty in California," but he lost the general election to conservative Republican incumbent Frank Merriam after corporate leaders, most prominently Louis Mayer at MGM movie studios, misrepresented his proposals and warned that a Sinclair victory would produce socialism and cause poor people from all over the country to descend on California.

Sinclair died on November 25, 1968, survived by his third wife, Mary Elizabeth Hard Willis. He had married Meta A. Fuller in 1900 and had one child, but they divorced in 1913. He married Mary Craig Kimbrough later that year; she died in 1961. Sinclair's death did not end the popularity of his books; they remained in print, not only in the United States but also in many other countries.

Further Reading

Harris, Leon. *Upton Sinclair: American Rebel.* New York: Crowell, 1975.

Mitchell, Greg. *The Campaign of the Century: Upton Sinclair's Race for Governor of California and the Birth of Media Politics.* New York: Random House, 1992.

Sinclair, Upton. *Autobiography.* New York: Harcourt, Brace & World, 1962.

Spingarn, Joel Elias
(1875–1939) *civil rights activist, writer*

A literary critic, editor and poet, Joel Elias Spingarn served as president of the National Association for the Advancement of Colored People (NAACP). He was born on May 17, 1875, in New York City to Elias Spingarn and Sarah Barnett Spingarn.

Joel Spingarn knew no material want as a child; his father, a wholesale tobacco merchant, provided an affluent upbringing. Spingarn spent a year at the City College of New York and then entered Columbia College, where he received his degree in 1895. Later that year he married Amy Einstein; they had four children.

Spingarn received a Ph.D. from Columbia in 1899, when the college appointed him to teach in the department of comparative literature. In 1910 he became department head, but in 1911 he clashed with Columbia's president, NICHOLAS MURRAY BUTLER, over a plan to merge the department with the English department, a move Spingarn opposed, and Butler fired him.

A Progressive politically and an enthusiastic supporter of Theodore Roosevelt, Spingarn supported the former president's unsuccessful campaign to return to the White House in 1912 and served as a delegate to the Progressive Party's national convention both that year and in 1916. At the same time he wrote books of literary criticism.

When the African-American leader W. E. B. DU BOIS and several whites formed the NAACP in 1909, Spingarn began contributing money to it, and he soon became an activist within the organization. In 1913 he was named chairman of the board and established the Spingarn Medal, awarded each year to the country's most outstanding African American.

Spingarn became treasurer of the NAACP in 1919; he held the post while helping to found the publishing firm of Harcourt, Brace, and Company. In the 1920s he wrote three books of poetry and served as the scholarly editor of the 25-volume European Library. He was president of the NAACP from 1930. Joel Spingarn died on July 26, 1939, in New York City of a cerebral thrombosis.

Further Reading

Ross, Barbara Joyce. *J. E. Spingarn and the Rise of the NAACP, 1911–1939.* New York: Atheneum, 1972.

Spock, Benjamin
(1903–1998) *peace activist, antiwar activist*

Benjamin Spock was a pediatrician, widely read author, and peace activist. He was born on May 2, 1903, in New Haven, Connecticut, silver spoon in mouth, to Benjamin Ives Spock, a corporate lawyer for the New Haven Railroad, and Mildred Louise Stoughton Spock.

Benjamin Spock completed two years of college preparatory work at the exclusive Phillips Academy in Andover, Massachusetts, and then enrolled at Yale University, where he excelled academically and earned recognition as an oarsman on the crew that won a gold medal at the 1924 Olympics in Paris. Spock obtained a B.A. the following year and enrolled at the Yale Medical School and later the Columbia University College of Physicians and Surgeons, where he graduated in 1929 at the head of his class.

He then completed his residencies, trained at the New York Psychoanalytic Institute, and began a private practice in pediatrics. The parents who took their children to his office in New York City praised his ability to set their youngsters at ease.

Spock served in the navy during World War II as a psychiatrist in the medical corps. During that time he began writing his monumental book *Baby and Child Care* (originally titled *Common Sense Book of Baby and Child Care)*. First published in 1946, it instructed mothers to create a warm, intimate atmosphere for their children and advised parents to use reasoned discussion rather than physical punishment to enforce discipline. Critics called Spock's book a primer in permissiveness, and in reaction to them he wrote a revision in

which he insisted that parents deserved respect from their children and that there should be firm parental standards.

Later, those who disagreed with the 1960s counterculture blamed youthful rebelliousness on Spock's influential book (as if the upheaval could be separated from the influences of economic prosperity and social problems). They claimed Spock had created a spoiled, irresponsible generation. Nevertheless, between its first appearance in 1946 and the mid-1960s, *Baby and Child Care* outsold every other book except the Bible.

Spock's moneyed background might suggest that he would be conservative politically. And at first he was; he considered, for example, nuclear arms important in order to contain the Soviet Union. But he changed his views in the early 1960s, when he opposed nuclear testing and nuclear weapons in general as a threat to children. He joined the National Committee for a Sane Nuclear Policy (SANE) in 1962 as a member of its national board. He later said he did so because he "was reluctantly convinced we had to have a test-ban treaty." He added, "Otherwise more and more children would be born with mental and physical defects."

Spock recalled that another turning point in his life occurred after President Lyndon Johnson betrayed him and the nation by sending American troops to fight in Vietnam despite assurances to the contrary. Spock reacted by leading numerous demonstrations against the war.

He grabbed national headlines in late 1967, when the Department of Justice decided to prosecute him and four other prominent activists for encouraging young men to resist the draft and burn their draft cards. The government based its charge on a document Spock had written and signed with the other activists, "Call to Resist Illegitimate Authority." The document said in part:

> We . . . believe that the war is unconstitutional and illegal. Congress has not declared a war as required by the Constitution. Moreover . . . the Charter [of the United Nations] specifically obligates the United States to refrain from force or the threat of force in international relations. It requires member states to

exhaust every peaceful means of settling disputes and to submit disputes which cannot be settled peacefully to the Security Council. The United States has systematically violated all of these Charter provisions for thirteen years. . . .

Moreover . . . the combat role of the United States . . . violates the Geneva Accords of 1954 which our government pledged to support but has since subverted. . . .

Therefore, we believe on all these grounds that every free man has a legal right and a moral duty to exert every effort to end this war, to avoid collusion with it, and to encourage others to do the same.

Thus, in explaining why the draft should be resisted, the statement declared the Vietnam War illegal and immoral.

Formally charged with aiding young men to violate the Selective Service Act, Spock and the other defendants were tried, and in June 1968 they were found guilty. Spock received a two-year prison sentence, but he appealed his case, and a higher court reversed the convictions, claiming the presiding judge had improperly instructed the jury and in so doing had made a fair trial impossible. The case stirred enormous controversy, partly because Spock's views drove a wedge between those who supported and those who opposed the Vietnam War, but also because of the realization that out of the thousands of protesters who could have been put on trial, the government had clearly selected a few high-profile activists to prosecute in an attempt to intimidate others into silence.

Dr. Benjamin Spock died on March 15, 1998, at his home in La Jolla, California. He had been married twice, first in 1927 to Jane Davenport Cheney, with whom he had two sons. They divorced in 1976, and he married the feminist Mary Morgan, about 40 years his junior. In reflecting on his protests against the Vietnam War, Spock said, "What is the use of physicians like myself trying to help parents to bring up children healthy and happy, to have them killed in such numbers for a cause that is ignoble?"

Further Reading

Maier, Thomas. *Dr. Spock: An American Life.* New York: Harcourt Brace, 1998.

Mitford, Jessica. *The Trial of Dr. Spock, the Rev. William Sloane Coffin, Jr., Michael Ferber, Mitchell Goodman, and Marcus Raskin.* New York, Knopf, 1969.

Stanton, Elizabeth Cady
(1815–1902) *women's suffragist*

In many instances abolitionists and women's rights advocates crusaded hand in hand in the mid-1800s, and such was the case for Elizabeth Cady Stanton, who embraced both movements. Born in Johnstown, New York, on November 12, 1815, to Daniel Cady and Margaret Livingston Cady, young Elizabeth became a feminist when her father, who served as a judge, angered her by ruling that women had no legal recourse to enduring mistreatment by their husbands and fathers. At the same time, under the influence of a cousin, she became involved in the antislavery movement.

In 1840 Elizabeth Cady married Henry B. Stanton, a prominent abolitionist. The marriage ceremony omitted the promise to "obey." That same year she and her husband attended the World Antislavery Convention held in London. Outside the subjugation that women suffered, no greater catalyst existed for the rise of the women's rights movement than abolitionism. Through the fight against slavery, women developed a greater sense of their own oppression and mustered the fortitude to do something about it. Abolitionist Abby Kelly said about women and their effort to free the slaves that in "striving to strike his irons off, we found most surely, that we were manacled *ourselves.*"

More pointedly, events at the World Antislavery Convention motivated Elizabeth Cady Stanton and LUCRETIA COFFIN MOTT to organize a meeting at Seneca Falls, New York. Stanton was appalled when she and other women were denied seating as delegates to the convention, and while in London she met and became good friends with Mott, who was also discontented with the discriminatory act. According to Stanton, she and Mott "resolved to hold a convention as soon as we returned home, and form a society to advocate the rights of women."

At that time women suffered second-class status in America's male-dominated society. They

An abolitionist and women's rights advocate, Elizabeth Cady (left) married Henry B. Stanton, a prominent abolitionist, in a ceremony in which they agreed to omit the promise to "obey." She is shown here with Susan B. Anthony. *(Library of Congress)*

were prohibited from voting, had no legal control over their property, could obtain no formal education beyond the elementary level, and, if divorced, had to relinquish custody of their children to their former husbands.

Various events delayed Stanton and Mott in forging ahead with the convention, but in July 1848 they at last assembled more than 200 men and women at Seneca Falls. There the delegates drafted a Declaration of Sentiments, written by Stanton and Mott, that followed the format and spirit of the Declaration of Independence. "We hold these truths to be self-evident," the Seneca document stated, "that all men are created equal; that they are endowed by their Creator with cer-

tain inalienable rights; that among these are life, liberty, and the pursuit of happiness." The document continued: "The history of mankind is a history of repeated injuries and usurpations on the part of man toward woman, having in direct object the establishment of absolute tyranny over her."

The Declaration of Sentiments outlined the oppressive acts suffered by women, including the following:

> He has never permitted her to exercise her inalienable right to the elective franchise.
> He has made her, if married, in the eye of the law civilly dead.
> He has taken from her all right in property, even to the wages she earns.

The document resolved "that woman is man's equal—was intended so by the Creator, and the highest good of the race demands that she should be recognized as such." The reference to equal voting rights raised the most controversy at the convention, but still 100 of the delegates signed the Declaration of Sentiments.

The Seneca Falls convention led to other women's rights meetings in the 1850s, most notably the "first national convention" at Worcester, Massachusetts, in 1850 and the Ohio Women's Rights Convention at Akron in 1851, when the former slave SOJOURNER TRUTH spoke.

That same year Stanton met SUSAN BROWNELL ANTHONY, whom Stanton convinced to enter the fight for women's rights. Thereafter, Stanton and Anthony maintained a close working relationship. They planned campaign programs, organizational projects, and speeches, and they appeared together at public debates and before legislative and congressional committees.

In 1860 Stanton became the first woman to address a joint session of the New York State legislature when she argued on behalf of a married woman's property bill. The legislation passed, and later that year she proposed liberalized divorce laws.

Although Stanton hated war and thus disliked the Civil War, she saw the conflict between the North and South as necessary to abolish slavery. During the fighting she helped to found the

Women's Loyal National League to support the Union effort and secure a constitutional amendment that would end slavery. She also served as the organization's president.

Despite those abolitionist activities, Stanton ultimately opposed the Fourteenth and Fifteenth Amendments because they extended civil rights to African Americans and in the case of the Fifteenth Amendment voting rights to African-American males, while ignoring women's suffrage. In 1868 she and Parker Pillsbury began publishing *Revolution*, a weekly that promoted women's rights. Stanton advocated suffrage, greater employment opportunities, and the right to serve on juries. In May 1869 Stanton and Anthony founded the National Woman Suffrage Association, and Stanton served as its president. Later, when the group merged with another in 1890 to form the National American Woman Suffrage Association, she served as its president.

Meanwhile, Stanton and Anthony campaigned in California in 1871 for women's suffrage, and in the 1880s they joined Matilda Joslyn Gage to write the three-volume *History of Woman Suffrage* (1881–86). In 1895 Stanton raised a storm of controversy when she published *Woman's Bible*, in which she revised the Bible to eliminate passages that she said degraded women.

Stanton devoted her later years to advocating changes in divorce laws. She died in New York City on October 26, 1902. She was survived by six children.

Elizabeth Cady Stanton is best remembered for the Seneca Falls Convention. Although a constitutional amendment to establish and protect women's suffrage would not be enacted until after World War I, Seneca Falls assembled men and women in a quest to reshape American society by ending sexually based oppression. In that way the convention in upstate New York transcended the suffrage issue and laid the groundwork for the modern women's rights movement.

Further Reading

Banner, Lois W. *Elizabeth Cady Stanton: A Radical for Woman's Rights*. Glenview, Ill.: Scott Foresman, 1980.

Griffith, Elisabeth. *In Her Own Right: The Life of Elizabeth Cady Stanton*. New York: Oxford University Press, 1984.

Kern, Kathi. *Stanton's Bible*. Ithaca N.Y.: Cornell University Press, 2001.

Stanton, Elizabeth Cady. *Eighty Years and More: Reminiscences, 1815–1897*. Boston: Northeastern University Press, 1993.

Venet, Wendy Hamand. *Neither Ballots nor Bullets: Women Abolitionists and the Civil War*. Charlottesville: University Press of Virginia, 1991.

Ward, Geoffrey C. *Not for Ourselves Alone: The Story of Elizabeth Cady Stanton and Susan B. Anthony: An Illustrated History*. New York: Knopf, 1999.

Steinem, Gloria
(1934–   ) *feminist*

A leading feminist and journalist, Gloria Steinem was the founding editor of *Ms.* magazine. She was born on March 25, 1934, in Toledo, Ohio, to Leo Steinem, an antiques dealer, operator of a summer resort, and itinerant who traveled in a house trailer with his family, and Ruth Nunevillar Steinem.

Gloria's mother and father divorced in 1946, and she and her mother then lived in a run-down house in East Toledo. For years she took care of her mother, a near-invalid who suffered from anxiety and depression. As a teenager Steinem tap-danced at the neighborhood Elks Club, and she entered and won a local television talent contest, hoping it might provide an escape from her life in Toledo.

The escape occurred in 1952 when she attended Smith College in Massachusetts. She worked hard, won scholarships, and graduated magna cum laude in 1956 with a degree in political science. That summer she traveled to India under a fellowship she had received to study in Delhi and Calcutta. Little did she realize that the trip would change her, helping shape her social outlook. Steinem's biographer, Carolyn G. Heilbrun, states in *The Education of a Woman: A Life of Gloria Steinem* (1995) that Steinem discovered in India "the political focus of her life," namely, "a strong concern for the disadvantaged." Steinem found, too, that as she published free-lance articles in Indian newspapers, she could earn a living through writing and advocacy.

On her return to the United States in 1958, Steinem was unable to find work as a reporter. She eventually was hired as codirector of the Independent Research Service in Cambridge, Massachusetts. This organization operated in conjunction with the National Student Association (NSA), which employed leaders of college student governments. But the NSA was receiving money from the Central Intelligence Agency (CIA), and in the 1960s Steinem's enemies accused her of having been a government spy. This charge, however, amounted to no more than political mudslinging, as Steinem did not know about the CIA connection at that time.

Steinem landed her first job with a magazine in 1960; her first article appeared two years later when *Esquire* carried her story about the sexual revolution. In 1963 she wrote an article published in *Show* based on her work as an undercover Playboy bunny. The article preceded her conversion to feminism by several years, but her future course was revealed by her observations that women were sex objects, worth something to men only as bunnies.

Steinem free-lanced for other magazines—she later said that an editor at *Ladies' Home Journal* called that publication's readers "mental defectives with curlers in their hair"—but her writing gained little recognition until, beginning in 1968, her "City Politic" column appeared in *New York*. According to Heilbrun, with this column Steinem "was on her way to becoming a serious journalist, reporting events affecting women, as well as other dispossessed groups."

The 1960s countercultural protests encouraged Steinem's feminist outlook. This was evident in March 1969, when she attended a meeting on abortion organized by the radical feminist group Redstockings. There she spoke out and confessed that she had once had an abortion, and she objected to women's having to feel criminal about undergoing the procedure.

Steinem next wrote the article "After Black Power, Women's Liberation," in which she took an openly feminist stand. Her writing ability and the knack she had for presenting ideas without being confrontational moved her to the forefront of the emerging women's liberation movement. In 1971 she joined BETTY FRIEDAN, Bella Abzug, and Congresswoman Shirley Chisholm in founding the National Women's Political Caucus (NWPC), which recruited women to run for public office.

At the same time her journalistic career took a new turn when she decided to found a feminist magazine. The idea for the publication arose from a meeting she had with other feminists in 1971 to begin the Women's Action Alliance, an organization dedicated to developing educational programs for women. Several of the participants at the meeting suggested that a national magazine be started.

When Steinem first pursued the idea, she doubted she would find any advertisers, but she contacted women who were editors, journalists, and opinion makers and found them all supportive. The publisher Clay S. Felker then agreed to run a 30-page sample publication, called *Ms.*, as an insert in the December 1971 issue of his magazine, *New York*. The favorable response it received convinced him to finance a full issue of *Ms.*, which appeared in January 1972, with Steinem serving as editor, as she had for the supplement. The first issue, which contained a petition calling for making abortions legal, sold out within eight days.

During the following summer *Ms.* appeared on a regular monthly basis and featured articles such as "Down with Sexist Upbringing" and "Why Women Fear Success." Within a few months the magazine's circulation had reached half a million.

Steinem believed that the oppression of women prevented men from living fuller lives, and she expressed this view in her work at *Ms.* She also believed that men and women should share responsibility for child rearing and household chores.

In 1972 Steinem campaigned to convince the necessary number of states to ratify the Equal Rights Amendment in an effort that eventually failed. At the same time radicals within the women's liberation movement, primarily Redstockings, attacked her and *Ms.* for selling out to male-dominated corporations. While parrying the criticism, she continued to edit the magazine.

In 1975 Steinem attended the International Women's Year Conference in Mexico City as an observer. Two years later she served on President Jimmy Carter's commission to organize an American Conference on Women. In 1980 she received a Woodrow Wilson Fellowship and moved to Washington, D.C., to study the effects of feminism on political theory.

Steinem published her first book, *Outrageous Acts,* in 1983. Her *Revolution from Within: A Book of Self-Esteem* appeared in 1992. She worked also as a contributing editor at Random House publishers. In 1998 Steinem and 14 other women purchased *Ms.,* by then a failing magazine, from MacDonald Communications. They were able to revive it and begin a *Ms.* website.

Later in the decade Steinem was heavily criticized for defending President Bill Clinton on charges he had sexually harassed women. Some said that Steinem, who opposed sexual harassment, was making a special case for Clinton because he had supported women's groups on several issues. She did, however, condemn Clinton's welfare reform program for abandoning poor women and children.

In September 2000 Steinem, who once said, "A woman needs a man like a fish needs a bicycle," married David Bale, a businessman and political activist; on the political front she criticized the Green Party candidate, RALPH NADER, for entering the presidential race. She said that the Democratic candidate, Al Gore, should be elected over the Republican George W. Bush as the true friend of women's rights, and that Nader would only take votes away from Gore and cause Bush to be elected. (Her prediction about the election results turned out to be correct.) "If I were to run for president in the same symbolic way," she said, "I would hope my friends and colleagues would have the sense to vote against me, . . . saving me from waking up to discover that I had helped send Bush to the most powerful position in the world."

Further Reading

Heilbrun, Carolyn G. *The Education of a Woman: A Life of Gloria Steinem.* New York: Dial Press, 1995.

Henry, Sondra, and Emily Taitz. *One Woman's Power: A Biography of Gloria Steinem.* Minneapolis, Minn.: Dillon Press, 1987.

Steinem, Gloria. *Outrageous Acts and Everyday Rebellions.* New York: Holt, Rinehart & Winston, 1983.

———. *Revolution from Within: A Book of Self-Esteem.* Boston: Little, Brown, 1992.

Stephens, Uriah Smith
(1821–1882) *labor organizer*

Uriah Stephens was a utopian visionary who founded the Knights of Labor. He was born on August 3, 1821, in Cape May, New Jersey. He intended to become a Baptist minister, but his training for such a career abruptly ended in 1837 when the nation's economic panic forced him to apprentice as a tailor. A short time later he taught school for a while in New Jersey, and in 1845 he moved to Philadelphia, Pennsylvania, where he returned to tailoring.

Stephens hated slavery, supported the abolitionists, and in the 1850s joined the Republican Party. He backed Abraham Lincoln for president, but when the Civil War broke out he opposed the conflict as injurious to workers.

Stephens began organizing laborers in 1862, when he formed a trade association of garment cutters in Philadelphia. When that group collapsed in 1869 he concluded that for workers to amass power while avoiding harassment from business they must operate in secrecy. On December 9, 1869, he and eight other former members of the garment cutters formed the Knights of Labor. Each took an oath of secrecy and set to work on a clandestine plan to build the union.

The Knights were steeped in secret ritual: an oath, handshakes, and passwords. They communicated through mysterious symbols and messages scrawled in chalk on sidewalks.

Stephens thought it important to build the workers' solidarity. For that reason he disliked trade unions because they were too narrow and too divisive. Although he sought to improve wages, in the long run he aimed to replace capitalism with a cooperative economic system. That, he said, would free the "wealth producers," as he called the workers, from "the thraldom and loss of wage slavery."

He wanted the Knights to educate all of its members to the common goals and interests of the workers, and he wanted the group to encompass all workers regardless of race or sex—a radical concept in an age of widespread discrimination. According to one report, he said, "I don't claim any power of prophecy, but I can see ahead of me an organization that will cover the globe. It will include men and women of every craft, creed, and color; it will cover every race worth saving."

For a while it appeared that Stephens's vision would be realized. The Knights quadrupled in size during the 1870s, and by 1878 it was the largest labor organization in the nation. Yet in time the secrecy of the Knights exposed them to charges of being subversive and forced them to become open (a move Stephens opposed). More important, the aversion of the Knights' leadership to using strikes—Stephens and his successor as head of the Knights, TERENCE VINCENT POWDERLY, opposed them—crippled the group's effectiveness. When the Knights did call several strikes in 1886, they lost out to management, and the defeat cost them dearly in prestige and members.

Stephens, however, had left the Knights before then. An interest in running for political office led him to resign his leadership position as grand master workman in 1878. On February 13, 1882, he died in Philadelphia.

Further Reading

Fink, Leon. *Workingmen's Democracy: The Knights of Labor and American Politics*. Urbana: University of Illinois Press, 1983.

Voss, Kim. *The Making of American Exceptionalism: The Knights of Labor and Class Formation in the Nineteenth Century*. Ithaca, N.Y.: Cornell University Press, 1993.

Weir, Robert E. *Beyond Labor's Veil: The Culture of the Knights of Labor*. University Park: Pennsylvania State University Press, 1996.

Still, William
(William Steel)
(1821–1902) *abolitionist*

William Still was an abolitionist who was instrumental in the running of the Underground Railroad. He was born on October 7, 1821, to runaway slaves Levin Steel and Sidney Steel. To elude slave hunters, the family had changed its name to Still prior to William's birth.

William grew up among the pine forests of Shamong, New Jersey, the town where his parents had fled in escaping their master in Maryland. He received little formal education and in 1844 settled in Philadelphia, Pennsylvania, where he worked as a handyman. Three years later he married Letitia George, and they had four children.

Still obtained a job as clerk in the office of the Pennsylvania Society for the Abolition of Slavery in 1847. In that position he began helping slaves flee the South along the Underground Railroad, a network of safe havens where sympathetic participants provided food, shelter, and other help.

In 1852 Philadelphia abolitionists appointed Still secretary and chairman of the General Vigilance Committee to raise funds for, and in other ways assist, the Underground Railroad. Under his guidance some 500 fugitive slaves were aided in their escape between 1852 and 1857, among them his brother, Peter. Still talked with many of the fugitives and later published the interviews in his book *The Underground Railroad*. It contained also letters, newspaper articles, and documents and remains an important source for those researching the story of the Underground Railroad. Still hoped the book would enhance the reputation of blacks. He said to an acquaintance: "We very much need works on various topics from the pens of colored men to represent the race intellectually."

In the 1850s Still wrote articles for two black Canadian abolitionist newspapers, the *Voice of the Fugitive* and *Provincial Freeman*. A report he wrote in 1855 after touring Canada indicated that former slaves were able to adjust to freedom and thus answered those who had claimed that blacks could never survive independently.

In 1859 Still advocated the desegregation of Philadelphia's street cars; the city finally passed a law to that effect several years later. Soon after the Civil War began he ended his work on the Underground Railroad, but he remained active in social reform when in 1862 he agreed to lead an employment office for freed persons, sponsored by the Pennsylvania Anti-Slavery Society. He relinquished the office less than a year later.

With the war raging, Still earned money by obtaining a government contract to supply provisions to Camp William Penn, near Philadelphia, which housed African-American soldiers. When the war ended he served on the Freedmen's Aid Commission and was appointed a member of the Philadelphia board of trade. In 1874 he raised a storm of controversy in Philadelphia's black community when he rejected the Republican candidate for mayor (most African Americans at the time voted Republican) and instead supported a reformer for the office. A Presbyterian, he founded in 1880 the first African-American Young Men's Christian Association. In addition he helped manage homes for elderly blacks and an orphan asylum for the children of black soldiers and sailors.

William Still died in Philadelphia on July 14, 1902. He has since been remembered as the "father of the Underground Railroad."

Further Reading

Khan, Lurey. *One Day, Levin . . . He Be Free: William Still and the Underground Railroad.* New York: E.P. Dutton, 1972.

Stone, I. F.
(Isidor Feinstein, Izzy Stone)
(1907–1989) *leftist activist*

An iconoclastic leftist journalist, Isidor "Izzy" Feinstein Stone was the founder of *I. F. Stone's Weekly.* He was born Isidor Feinstein on December 24, 1907, in Philadelphia, Pennsylvania, to Russian-Jewish immigrants Bernard Feinstein and Katy Novack Feinstein. In 1937 Isidor Feinstein legally changed his name from Feinstein to Stone so he would come across, as he said, "less Jewish," to readers.

Isidor Feinstein grew up in Haddonfield, New Jersey, and while still a child showed an attachment to progressive ideas. At age 14 he was publishing his own monthly newsletter, which contained editorials supporting Gandhi, Woodrow Wilson, and the League of Nations, and distributing it on his bicycle. Isidor quit the University of Pennsylvania at the end of his junior year in 1927 and worked as a reporter in New Jersey for the

Camden Courier-Post while briefly joining the Socialist Party. In 1929 he married Esther Roisman. They had three children and an extremely close and supportive relationship.

In 1931 Stone joined the *Philadelphia Record* as an editorial writer. Two years later he moved to New York City and worked in the same capacity for the *New York Post.* This was the era of the Great Depression, and Izzy Stone took a stand that angered Democrats and radicals alike. On the one hand, he supported President Franklin Roosevelt's New Deal as an effort, as he put it, "to save capitalism from itself." In so doing he antagonized those radicals who thought the New Deal a sellout to capitalists.

On the other hand, he criticized Roosevelt for failing to take reform far enough, and he supported a "Popular Front" alliance of leftist groups, including the communists. At that time Stone believed that the Soviet Union offered viable alternatives to capitalism, though he thought many of its policies misguided.

In 1938 Stone quite the *New York Post* in disagreement over its increasingly strident anticommunist position, and he joined the staff of the *Nation,* a leading left-wing weekly. He wrote columns for other leftist publications, too, most notably *PM,* a New York newspaper.

But the *Nation* fired him in 1946 in a dispute over articles he had written for *PM* about the attempt by Jews to build a state in Palestine. When Israel was formed in 1948, Stone strongly supported it, though he angered many Zionists by advocating a government that would include Arabs along with Jews.

With the emergence of the cold war after World War II, Stone criticized both Soviet expansionism and American interventionism. At the same time he opposed the Red Scare in the United States; the nationwide hunt for communist and other radicals and defended the right of communists to speak freely. His views caused the Federal Bureau of Investigation (FBI) to investigate him, as it did other prominent leftists and critics of American policy.

Stone began publishing *I.F. Stone's Weekly* in 1953, and it quickly developed a circulation in the thousands. With conformity gripping America in the 1950s and more and more newspapers and magazines placing a premium on entertainment, Stone offered intellectual analyses and articles that exposed inconsistencies in government policies and lies by political leaders.

In 1952 Stone wrote *The Hidden History of the Korean War,* in which he blamed the conflict not on aggression by Communist North Korea but on a conspiracy between South Korea and the United States. That radical departure from standard interpretations produced considerable criticism.

In the 1960s many young people liked Stone for his attacks on government secrecy and on the escalating arms race with the Soviet Union. They also liked his criticism of American cold war policy as a barrier to peaceful coexistence with the Soviet Union. Stone insisted that the United States could best work its influence and prevent nuclear war through cooperation rather than confrontation.

Stone's biographer Robert C. Cottrell believes that Stone's reputation as a dissident, along with some of his finest writing, rested primarily on his coverage of the Vietnam War. Unlike mainstream journalists, Stone questioned the American involvement in Vietnam from an early date. In *Izzy: A Biography of I. F. Stone* (1993) Cottrell says, "[Stone's] refusal to accept established 'truths,' whether articulated by the White House, the Pentagon, or the mass media, enabled him to view U.S. involvement in the war far more critically and incisively than did his journalistic colleagues or fellow intellectuals."

In 1962—long before America's large-scale commitment of troops—Stone used the pages of the *Weekly* to urge the peace movement to take note of what was happening in Vietnam and demand that the war be ended. He returned to that theme in 1964 when he told of reports that U.S. planes were killing more civilians in Vietnam than were the communist guerrillas. He said to peace groups, "Now's the time to speak up."

When President Lyndon Johnson asked Congress to pass the Gulf of Tonkin Resolution and give him a blank check to fight the war, Stone questioned whether the military and administration officials had lied about the details surrounding an attack by North Vietnamese gunboats on an American destroyer near the coast of North Vietnam. Years later those lies became public knowledge.

In 1966 Stone condemned what he called "a once flaming faith" that had "become a faith in napalm" in Vietnam. And he said, "It is the Machine, it is the prestige of the Machine, that is at stake. . . . It is Boeing and General Electric and Goodyear and General Dynamics. It is the electronic range-finder and the amphibious truck and the night-piercing radar. It is the defoliant and the herbicide, and the deodorant and the depilatory." Those material things had become more important than democracy.

Stone supported the rise of a New Left during the countercultural 1960s, and he tried to build a bridge between its young leaders and the leaders of the Old Left from his generation. But he refused to accept the New Left without criticism. For example, when radicals rioted outside the 1968 Democratic National Convention in Chicago, he said that getting involved in name calling and hate was something the right wing could do much better and that it only set precedents "which American Storm Troopers may some day apply to us."

Stone's criticism of the Vietnam War extended to imperialism in general. In 1969 he spoke out against the stationing by the United States of more than 1 million military personnel overseas, along with military missions in some 50 countries and the maintenance of some 2,300 military installations.

In 1971 ill health caused Stone to discontinue his *Weekly,* which had become a biweekly. That same year he published *The Killings at Kent State,* a book about the shooting of antiwar protesters at Kent State University in Ohio by members of the National Guard. Stone claimed that those who had fired the shots got away with murder. In 1972 he joined the *New York Review of Books,* where he worked until 1976. In the late 1970s and into the 1980s Stone published essays and reviews in various publications.

I. F. Stone died on June 18, 1989, in Boston of a heart attack. Activist Todd Gitlin recalled how Stone had influenced him and other leftists in the 1960s: "We applauded I. F. Stone when he came to [Harvard] to speak with . . . sympathy about Castro's Cuba, and I subscribed to his bea-con *Weekly,* which taught me, as it taught many of my contemporaries, that the government lied."

Further Reading

Cottrell, Robert C. *A Biography of I. F. Stone.* New Brunswick, N.J.: Rutgers University Press, 1993.

Stone, Lucy

(1818–1893) *abolitionist, women's rights activist*

An abolitionist and a crusader for black voting rights, Lucy Stone was primarily a strong advocate of women's rights. She was born on August 13, 1818, near West Brookfield, Massachusetts, to Francis Stone and Hannah Matthews Stone.

Lucy Stone developed her feminist views while still a child. Her father, a farmer, provided a comfortable environment for her and her brothers and sisters. "What an opulent home it was," Lucy recalled,

> barrels of meat, and my father used to drive to the Connecticut River and bring home a great wagon-load of shad, and have it salted down, and we ate it all through the year, freshened and cooked with cream; and such abundance of apples; and the very best butter. . . . We all worked hard, but we all worked together.

Beneath such harmony, though, discord appeared when Francis Stone insisted that God intended men to rule over women. Lucy disliked that idea and her father's insistence that it was supported by the Bible.

She subsequently decided that she would at-tend college so she could learn Greek and He-brew and determine whether the Bible had been mistranslated. Her father, however, opposed her pursuit of a higher education and refused to pay for it; Lucy's plan defied prevailing social beliefs about women's marrying and home making, and in any event, he said, it would cost too much money. Thus, temporarily thwarted, at age 16 Lucy began teaching school to raise funds for her college education.

Once again she felt the sting of oppression when she earned less than half the salary paid to male teachers. Religion also disappointed her. In one instance she was prohibited from casting a vote at her Congregational church in West Brook-field on an issue involving a deacon; the explana-tion was that only men could vote. In another the Congregational ministers of Massachusetts issued a pastoral letter in 1837 advising members to refrain from criticizing slavery and taking to task those women who took public stands on that and other issues. The ministers said only men should involve themselves in political debates—for women to do so would lead to "degeneracy and ruin." Lucy thought the letter a prime example of the male domination that kept women in their place.

She finally earned enough money to attend Oberlin College in 1843. Oberlin had been founded 10 years earlier in part to provide a col-lege education for women, and Lucy expected to find a liberated atmosphere. But her strong will and fearless attachment to principles again en-countered male rules. She was disappointed to find that the faculty had voted to exclude women from participation in classroom discussions and debates. "I hoped when I came to Oberlin that the course of study would permit such practice," she recalled, "but I was never in a place where women are so rigidly taught that they must not speak in public." Over the ensuring months she earned a reputation for radicalism as she spoke out in support of abo-litionism and women's rights.

Nevertheless, she worked hard and earned the respect of her fellow students and even her father, who finally agreed to support her financially in her last year in college. Lucy's classmates chose her to present the annual honorary graduation essay, but when she learned that her composition would have to be read by a male professor because college rules prohibited men and women from sharing the same speaker's platform, she refused to present her work; to do otherwise, she said, would amount to a "pub-lic acknowledgement of the rectitude of the princi-ple which takes away from women their rights."

Near the time of her graduation from Oberlin in 1847, she met the abolitionist WILLIAM LLOYD GARRISON, who said of Stone, "She is a very supe-rior young woman, and has a soul as free as the air, and is preparing to go forth as a lecturer, particularly in vindication of the rights of women."

Stone graduated from Oberlin the first Massachusetts woman ever to earn a college degree, and she then lectured on behalf of the Antislavery Society. Increasingly, she spoke about women's rights. On several occasions she was forced to face down hostile mobs, yet she was persuasive and often disarming. One of her opponents stated: "The moment that that woman spoke to me she had me at complete command. . . . She had the voice of an angel, and with that voice, she can't be anything but a good woman."

In 1850 Stone organized the first national Woman's Rights Convention at Worcester, Massachusetts. She was so dedicated to her cause that she thought she would never marry, but in 1855 she wed Henry Brown Blackwell, a prominent abolitionist. They made public their unusual pact:

> While acknowledging our mutual affection by . . . assuming the relationship of husband and wife . . . in justice to ourselves and a great principle, we deem it a duty to declare that this act on our part implies no sanction of, nor promise of voluntary obedience to, such of the present laws of marriage as refuse to recognize the wife as an independent rational being.

Stone continued to use her maiden name, insisting that the acceptance of her husband's name would imply her inferiority. Henry Brown Blackwell generally supported her crusade for women's rights, but their marriage proved rocky when his business interests and desire for attention conflicted with Stone's efforts.

After the Civil War Stone linked women's suffrage with black voting rights. She insisted that African Americans and women should vote as implied by the country's "theory of government," in which suffrage should be for everyone capable of making an "independent rational choice." She claimed that voting was important to democracy and that through the ballot box blacks and women could gain educational and employment opportunities.

Stone helped organize the New England Woman Suffrage Association in 1868 and served in the American Equal Rights Association (AERA). In 1869, however, a serious split occurred within that group, partly as a result of the personality clash between Stone and SUSAN BROWNELL ANTHONY. But policy differences were more important: Anthony opposed granting voting rights to blacks and thus fought against ratification of the Fifteenth Amendment on the basis that the former slaves were too ignorant to vote. She disagreed also with Stone's strategy to win women's suffrage by convincing the state legislatures to pass enabling statutes as opposed to focusing on action by the United States Congress.

The AERA fractured into the National Woman Suffrage Association (NWSA), led by Anthony, and the American Woman Suffrage Association (AWSA), in which Stone was an officer. In 1870 Stone founded *Woman's Journal*, an influential publication that combined short works of fiction with articles on women's suffrage. In 1890 the NWSA and AWSA joined forces to form the National American Woman Suffrage Association, and Stone served on its executive committee.

By that time Stone was tying the campaign for women's suffrage to corruption in politics. She blamed political evils on men, calling them weak, sexually debauched, and prone to graft. An infusion of women's morality, she insisted, would clean up the system.

Lucy Stone delivered her last lecture on women's rights at the World's Columbian Exposition in Chicago in the summer of 1893. She died at her home in Dorchester, Massachusetts, on October 18. Another women's rights advocate, ELIZABETH CADY STANTON, once said that Lucy Stone was "the first person by whom the heart of the American public was deeply stirred on the woman question."

Further Reading

Hays, Elinor Rice. *Morning Star*. New York: Harcourt, Brace & World, 1961.

Kerr, Andrea Moore. *Lucy Stone: Speaking Out for Equality*. New Brunswick, N.J.: Rutgers University Press, 1992.

Venet, Wendy Hamand. *Neither Ballots nor Bullets: Women Abolitionists and the Civil War*. Charlottesville: University Press of Virginia, 1991.

Strossen, Nadine
(1950–) *civil libertarian*

Since 1991 Nadine Strossen has served as president of the American Civil Liberties Union (ACLU), the first woman to head that organization. She was born on August 18, 1950, in Jersey City, New Jersey, to Woodrow John Strossen and Sylvia Simicich Strossen.

That Nadine Strossen's father had been interred in a Nazi concentration camp during World War II gave Strossen at an early age a deep concern for individual liberty. While a student at Radcliffe College in Massachusetts, she involved herself in women's rights and was especially drawn to the prochoice movement. She graduated from Radcliffe in 1972 and entered Harvard Law School, where she served as editor of the *Harvard Law Review.* Strossen earned a law degree in 1975 and clerked for one year with the Minnesota Supreme Court in Saint Paul. Beginning in 1976 she worked as an associate with the law firm Lindquist & Vennum in Minneapolis, then in 1978 she joined the firm Sullivan & Cromwell in New York City. Two years later she married Eli Michael Noam, a professor at Columbia University.

In 1983 Strossen was elected to the national board of the ACLU. While continuing in that position, the following year she became involved in civil rights law when she started working for the Civil Rights Clinic at the School of Law at New York University. In 1988 she left the clinic to become a professor of law at the college.

Meanwhile, Strossen had been elected to the ACLU's executive committee in 1985, and in 1986 she became the organization's general counsel. Then in 1991 she was elected the ACLU's first woman president. Writing in *Reason* magazine, Cathy Young says about that event:

> The 1991 election of Nadine Strossen . . . was widely interpreted as an attempt to return to the [ACLU's] traditional emphasis on civil liberties such as freedom of speech and of the press as opposed to its involvement with modish issues such as comparable worth and government aid to the homeless.

Strossen confirmed that view: "My priority is to be a prominent, visible spokesperson for civil liberties. Recent events have revealed that civil liberties are never going to be secure unless there is public understanding and support for them." One event quickly engaged her: the Persian Gulf War. While most Americans focused on the fighting, Strossen looked at what was happening to civil liberties. "We're violating our own citizens' liberties for the sake of a war for human rights," she said. She was especially concerned with protecting conscientious objectors and preventing the federal government from illegally questioning Arab-Americans about terrorism.

In 1995 Strossen published her book *Defending Pornography: Free Speech, Sex and the Fight for Women's Rights,* in which she took on feminists who wanted the government to restrict pornography. Strossen called them "pornophobic feminists," and she said that any restriction on such material would violate free speech. "Were we to ban words or images on that ground that they had incited some susceptible individuals to commit crimes," she said, "the first work to go would probably be the Bible."

In addition to her work with the ACLU, Strossen has served on the executive committees of Human Rights Watch and Middle East Watch and as a vice chair of Asia Watch. She has also served on the board of directors of the Coalition to Free Soviet Jews.

Further Reading
Strossen, Nadine. *Defending Pornography: Free Speech, Sex, and the Fight for Women's Rights.* New York: Scribner's, 1995.
Strossen, Nadine, and Philip D. Harvey. *The Government vs. Erotica: The Siege of Adam and Eve.* New York: Prometheus, 2001.

T

Tappan, Arthur (1786–1865) and Lewis Tappan (1788–1873)
abolitionists

Arthur Tappan and Lewis Tappan combined their success in business with a reformist zeal that promoted abolitionism. They were both born in Northampton, Massachusetts, to Benjamin Tappan, a goldsmith and merchant, and Sarah Homes Tappan.

Like many abolitionists, the Tappans were raised in in a religious family. Their mother was a devout Calvinist, and although Lewis ultimately strayed to the Unitarian faith, he returned to the fold and embraced a revivalist Congregationalism.

Arthur, more serious in appearance and more stern in personality than Lewis, earned considerable wealth selling silks in New York City. Lewis invested in a textile mill in 1823, but the economic recession of 1826 hurt him, and he struggled financially until in 1828 he joined Arthur in New York to form Arthur Tappan & Company, for which he worked as credit manager. That same year he took over Arthur's struggling newspaper, *Journal of Commerce,* which combined trade with religious news. Lewis sold the publication in 1831, after which it became a leading financial paper.

Arthur entered the abolitionist movement before Lewis and around 1830 began publishing the antislavery paper *Emancipator.* Lewis was influenced in his abolitionism by THEODORE DWIGHT WELD, whom he met in 1831 when he attended his son's commencement exercises at Oneida Academy in New York. Weld was then a student and one of several abolitionists who had graduated from the academy. In the course of two years of conversations with Weld, Lewis learned about immediatism, the belief that was promoted by WILLIAM LLOYD GARRISON: that slavery should be ended without delay. Both Lewis and Arthur saw slavery in moral terms and considered abolitionism a Christian crusade. Tappan biographer Bertram Wyatt-Brown in *Lewis Tappan and the Evangelical War Against Slavery* (1969), states that neither brother was a great thinker; rather, they adopted the ideas of others and applied them fervently. Lewis in particular was a do-gooder and a joiner who latched on to almost every liberal reform.

In 1833 Arthur Tappan took the lead in forming the New York Anti-Slavery Society, and Lewis offered encouragement and guidance whenever his brother's determination flagged. The society was formed under siege—when some New Yorkers learned about Arthur's plan to hold a meeting at Chatham Chapel in October to begin the organization, they stormed the meeting place with cries of "Garrison, Garrison, Tappan, Tappan, where are they, find them, find them!"

The attack only encouraged Lewis, who persuaded Arthur and other abolitionists to hold a meeting in Philadelphia that December, at which they began the American Anti-Slavery Society. Arthur was named president of the national organization, and Lewis was elected to the executive committee.

In July 1834 an antiabolitionist mob wrecked Lewis's house. He had stirred animosity by arranging for the publication of antislavery tracts, most notably *Human Rights*. Arthur Tappan suffered great financial losses in the economic depression of 1837 and never fully recovered from them. As a result Lewis took more of a lead in the abolitionist movement. From 1839 until 1841 he directed a committee that sought to secure the release of the African captives aboard the ship *Amistad*. During that period, in 1840, Arthur and Lewis broke with William Lloyd Garrison when Garrison advocated that women be given equal standing to men in the abolitionist movement and that abolitionists fight for women's rights.

Lewis Tappan subsequently founded the American and Foreign Anti-Slavery Society, which specifically forbade women from voting in the organization. Nevertheless, the society soon fell under Garrison's influence. According to Wyatt-Brown, "Throughout the 1840s, Lewis Tappan and William Lloyd Garrison shared the leadership of the antislavery crusade. Garrison retained his control of the radical elements . . . but Tappan served as the coordinator of the activities of a great number of abolitionists."

Lewis Tappan placed the American abolitionist movement in an international context and believed that if he could persuade the British to exert their influence on the United States, slavery would end. In 1843 he attended an international antislavery convention in London. When he found that established churches and missionary societies refused to join the abolitionist crusade, he founded the American Missionary Association in 1846, committed to fighting for black freedom and rights. That same year he began the Washington-based *National Era*, which became the leading journal of the Liberty Party and was an important influence in the antislavery movement.

In the meantime Lewis had also founded the Mercantile Agency, the first commercial-credit rating business in the United States. The agency, which later became Dun and Bradstreet, compiled information on merchants doing business in New York City. Lewis prospered, but he was uncomfortable with his success. He thought material pursuit harmful to Christian beliefs and in 1843 said to a friend: "How much wisdom there is in the advice

of the apostle Paul—'Owe no man anything—but to love one another.'" In 1849 he sold the business and applied all his time and a good part of his fortune to abolitionism.

The passage of the Fugitive Slave Act by Congress in 1850 caused Lewis to support the Underground Railroad and the assistance it gave to black slaves escaping from the South. He gradually modified his views toward women and allowed them a place in the male-dominated abolitionist organizations. He also came to believe that the federal government had the constitutional right to eliminate slavery in the states.

Whereas during the Civil War most Northerners fought to maintain the Union, Lewis Tappan saw the conflict as a way to end slavery. He worried that the war would either end too soon, and in the rapid Northern victory slavery would be left intact, or the North would surrender. When Abraham Lincoln issued the Emancipation Proclamation in 1863, Tappan called it a bold and revolutionary stroke.

Arthur Tappan died on July 21, 1865. When the Civil War ended, Lewis Tappan supported the American Missionary Association, which helped former slaves. In 1870 he published *The Life of Arthur Tappan*. He died on June 21, 1873, the victim of a paralytic stroke.

To the Tappans slavery was more than a system of human bondage—it was the source and symbol of American sin and selfishness. They believed abolitionism would begin a new moral era. Lewis Tappan wrote, "Our grandchildren will live in a more healthy political & moral atmosphere than we have done."

Further Reading

Wyatt-Brown, Bertram. *Lewis Tappan and the Evangelical War against Slavery*. Cleveland: The Press of Case Western Reserve University, 1969.

Tenayuca, Emma
(1916–1999) *Mexican-American activist, labor organizer*

Emma Tenayuca was an organizer for Mexican-American workers in Texas and a member of the Communist Party.

She was born on December 21, 1916, in San Antonio. Her mother was a descendant of one of the Spanish families who founded the city, and her father was an Indian.

Emma Tenayuca became a labor activist while still in high school; at age 16 she joined several hundred Mexican-American women in a strike at the Finck Cigar Company, and her protests landed her in jail.

Tenayuca's activism coincided with President Franklin Roosevelt's New Deal programs, which encouraged workers to organize, and it coincided with a deepening recognition of collective ethnic identity and class consciousness among Mexican Americans. In San Antonio's west side most Mexican Americans lived in a strong community setting, well aware of their mutual background and of their differences from the city's Anglos. Most of them also lived in poverty, in a four-square-mile zone dominated by shacks that housed, with the residents, disease, malnutrition, and infant deaths.

Many of these Mexican Americans held low-paying jobs—when they could find work at all—and women occupied most of them. According to historian Zaragosa Vargas, writing in the *Pacific Historical Review* in November 1997, women had 79 percent of the low-paid jobs in the garment, cigar, and pecan-shelling industries. Adding to their economic hardship, women not only made less money than Anglo men for similar jobs but also made less than Mexican-American men. They were, in short, forced to the bottom levels of the wage scale.

Hand in hand with economic deprivation was political oppression. An Anglo machine ran San Antonio by denying most Mexican Americans the right to vote. Anyone who challenged the power structure faced harassment and imprisonment.

Nevertheless, Tenayuca stood up to it. She joined the Unemployed Councils as a relief worker. Sponsored by the communist-led Trade Union Unity League, these councils were meant to help the unemployed by organizing them to march on relief agencies, defy eviction notices from landlords, and lobby for measures to relieve their plight. In *William Z. Foster and the Tragedy of American Radicalism* (1999), James R. Barrett writes: "The Communists' unemployed councils were not

the only unemployed organizations . . . but they were the most effective, leading hundreds of demonstrations and marches, fighting evictions, and counseling welfare recipients."

By 1935 Tenayuca had become secretary of the West Side Unemployed Council; it merged with the Workers' Alliance in 1936, and she set up chapters of that group, becoming secretary of 11 of them and executive secretary of the national organization. In 1937 Tenayuca joined the Communist Party and married an Anglo communist, Homer Brooks.

The San Antonio political bosses came crashing down on the Workers' Alliance by raiding a meeting, destroying literature, and arresting Tenayuca for unlawful assembly. Undaunted, she decided to help Mexican-American pecan shellers who made on average a paltry $192 a year. Tenayuca recalled:

> The Mexican workers . . . had no skills; there were people recruited [by the growers]; these were people who were peasants. . . . They worked here during the winter months, and they shelled pecans and this is the way they lived. They made a bit of money . . . and then about March or April—sometimes earlier—or May, they'd start getting on the trucks and going to the Valley. They'd start there, some of them would go to Colorado and wind up in Michigan beet fields. If they had a good year they would come back. They would buy a little piece of land and then start building little shacks.

As the depression worsened in 1937 and employers cut wages, Tenayuca urged the shellers to organize. Several thousand subsequently walked out in January 1938, and Tenayuca became their leader, working through the Workers' Alliance. The police promptly arrested her in a move that demonstrated how strongly the city bosses opposed her. Opposition arose as well from the small number of middle-class Mexican Americans in San Antonio, who disapproved of her communist links, and from the Catholic Church, which also disliked her ideology.

The Congress of Industrial Organization (CIO) opposed Tenayuca because it wanted to cleanse communists from the union movement. But after the CIO removed Tenayuca from the strike, the workers voted to take her back as an honorary leader. Tenayuca recalled: "I was removed because I was a communist. . . . I did not protest or anything, but I continued to write every circular."

As the strike wore on, the police tear-gassed picketers and arrested hundreds of workers on minor charges. The walkout failed, however, when the growers retaliated by mechanizing pecan shelling. In 1938 the Texas Communist Party chose Tenayuca to run for Congress from the San Antonio district. The party had little hope of winning, but its choice reaffirmed its commitment to Mexican Americans.

The following year the Communists stunned Tenayuca when they supported Soviet dictator Joseph Stalin's pact with Adolf Hitler, through which the Soviet Union obtained Poland's eastern lands. To Tenayuca, Stalin's act and the party's endorsement of it showed that the Communists cared only for what would benefit the Soviet Union and that they lacked any sincere attachment to Mexican Americans and other impoverished workers. So she quit the party, and soon afterward she and Homer Brooks divorced.

The Red Scare of the late 1940s (a reactionary, nationwide hunt of communists and other radicals) ruined Tenayuca financially when right-wingers blacklisted her and prevented her from obtaining employment. She recalled: "When I left here, about 1948 . . . I couldn't have gotten a job . . . I couldn't do anything. None of the unions would have me. . . . I went to San Francisco and stayed there for twenty years." In her new home she earned a bachelor's degree from San Francisco College. She returned to San Antonio in the 1960s and taught elementary school. Emma Tenayuca died on September 23, 1999. Although she had failed in the pecan strike, she had advanced Mexican-American solidarity.

Further Reading

Folsom, Franklin. *Impatient Armies of the Poor: The Story of Collective Action by the Unemployed, 1808–1942.* Niwot: University Press of Colorado, 1991.

Vargas, Zaragosa. "Tejana Radical: Emma Tenayuca and the San Antonio Labor Movement During the Great Depression." *Pacific Historical Review* 66 (November 1997): 553+.

Terry, Randall

(1959–) *antiabortion activist*

Randall Terry is the founder of Operation Rescue, a militant antiabortion group. He was born on April 25, 1959, in Rochester, New York, to Michael Terry and Doreen DiPasquale Terry, both of whom were public school teachers.

During his childhood Randall Terry showed nothing of the deep religious commitment that would characterize his adult life. Neither his mother nor his father adhered to a church life, but Doreen Terry taught in inner-city schools, and her sisters influenced Randall Terry at family gatherings with talk about their fight for civil rights and other social reforms. As a teenager Terry formed a rock band and wanted to make records.

In rebelling against his parents, he quit high school at age 16 despite a strong academic record. He then hitchhiked across the country, an event that changed his life. Seeing the world beyond Rochester and recognizing the evil in it drew him toward God, his one hope of salvation. Reading a Gideon Bible that he found in a motel room further stirred him. Finally, while working at an ice cream parlor near Rochester, he met a customer who was a lay minister at Elim Bible Institute, an evangelical missionary training school in Lima, New York. Through the friendship they established, in September 1976 he declared himself a Christian.

Two years later Terry enrolled at Elim. While a student he wrote, produced, and starred in a biblical rock opera. In class he studied the works of Francis August Schaffer, a conservative Presbyterian. Schaffer criticized secularized humanism and taught that the founding fathers had intended the United States to be a Judeo-Christian country. Schaffer advocated crusading for an issue that would reveal to society its waywardness and its need to return to Christianity. At first Schaffer thought prayer in public schools was the issue that should be pursued, but in 1981, in *A Christian Manifesto*, he advocated that Christians attack abortion.

Terry's reading of Schaffer coincided with his own expanding awareness of abortion. He began to think the practice wrong, though he as yet took no action to fight it.

In 1981 Terry graduated from Elim; he could have been ordained an Evangelical minister but chose to be a lay missionary. That same year he married Cindy Dean (they later raised three foster children) and prepared to do missionary work in Central America, but he never made the trip. Before he could leave he attended a prayer group in 1983 at the Church of Pierce Creek near Binghamton and listened to speakers who called abortion America's "Holocaust." That set him into action, and he soon began joining protesters in picketing a Binghamton abortion clinic. He engaged also in "sidewalk counseling," confronting women as they entered the clinic and advising them against ending their pregnancies. Terry later recounted how, over a two-week period, five women who listened to the counseling "turned away and chose life for their babies."

In 1984 he and his wife opened the Crisis Pregnancy Center in Binghamton, which counseled women and gave them advice about caring for their babies. At the same time he raised money for the House of Life, a residence he founded for unwed mothers.

Influenced by the civil disobedience tactics of the civil rights movement and by other antiabortion activists, in 1986 Terry intensified his protest. Along with his supporters, he invaded a Binghamton abortion clinic and sat down inside to impede all work. Refusing to move, he was arrested on charges of criminal trespass and was sentenced to 10 days in jail, the first of several jail terms he would serve as a result of his protests.

In November of the same year Terry founded Operation Rescue and called for other Christians to join him in blockading abortion clinics and risking arrest. "If you think abortion is murder," he said, "then act like it's murder." Terry, though, saw his movement as more than defeating abortion: It would reawaken America to its Christian roots and restore its moral values.

On November 28, 1987, he led nearly 300 protesters in a blockade of the Cherry Hill (New Jersey) Women's Clinic. In May 1988 Operation Rescue staged a massive blockade of abortion clinics in New York City and on Long Island. More than 1,500 protesters were arrested, including a Roman Catholic bishop, nuns, and rabbis.

During the Democratic National Convention in Atlanta, Georgia, in summer 1988, Terry led 24 blockades that resulted in more than 1,200 arrests. Early in 1989 more "rescues" were staged in New York City, Los Angeles, Washington, D.C., and elsewhere. One report claimed 683 blockades between May 1988 and August 1990 and 41,000 protesters arrested. Terry himself was arrested during the "Siege of Atlanta" and sentenced in 1989 to 24 months in prison for criminal assembly and unlawful trespassing. He was released in January 1990 after a donor paid his fine. Operation Rescue, meanwhile, attracted recruits by the thousands.

But prochoice groups struck back, and the federal government used existing laws to seize Operation Rescue's moneys and levy fines against Terry. In 1990 Kevin Tucci replaced Terry as leader of Operation Rescue, and Terry formed the Christian Defense Coalition to train protesters to resist "police brutality" and "political harassment." In 1992 he was again sentenced to jail, this time in Houston, Texas, for violating an order to protest no closer than 100 feet from abortion clinics in that city.

Although Terry never advocated killing abortion doctors, some observers blamed his militancy for encouraging others to do so. In 1994 Congress reacted to the blockades and the murder of a doctor outside a clinic in Pensacola, Florida, by passing a bill making it illegal to prevent access to abortion clinics.

In 1998 Terry ran for Congress as a Republican in New York's 26th District, but he lost. He owed millions of dollars in legal settlements from his protest activities, and to avoid paying them he filed for bankruptcy.

A dispute with Reverend Dan Little of the Pentecostal Landmark Church (formerly the Church at Pierce Creek), at which Terry served as an elder, as well as Terry's divorce from his wife, cost him nearly all of his support in the evangelical movement. In August 1999 he resigned as elder, and three months later Little censured him. The preacher claimed that Terry had abandoned his wife and engaged in "sinful relationships."

Terry joined a Long Island congregation of the Charismatic Episcopal Church, and other ministers rallied behind him and attacked Little for running a cult. But Operation Rescue, renamed Operation Save America, disowned Terry and posted Little's censure letter on its website, assuring that members of the movement knew about his fall from grace.

In January 2000 Terry married Andrea Kolimorgen. The following year found him selling used cars out of a trailer that he used as the office for his ministry. Speaking to a reporter for the *New York Times* in July 2001, Reverend Flip Benham said of Terry, "Now you see the unfortunate demise of one who was used so powerfully by God and is now on a back burner. And that's where he will forever stay." But Terry insisted, "Now I start building my comeback."

Further Reading

Blanchard, Dallas A. *The Anti-Abortion Movement and the Rise of the Religious Right: From Polite to Fiery Protest.* New York: Twayne Publishers, 1994.

Jacoby, Kerry N. *Souls, Bodies, Spirits: The Drive to Abolish Abortion Since 1973.* Westport, Conn.: Praeger, 1998.

Lawler, Philip F. *Operation Rescue: A Challenge to the Nation's Conscience.* Huntington, Ind.: Our Sunday Visitor, 1992.

Risen, Jim. *Wrath of Angels: The American Abortion War.* New York: Basic Books, 1998.

Terry, Randall A. *Accessory to Murder: The Enemies, Allies, and Accomplices to the Death of Our Culture.* Brentwood, Tenn.: Wolgemuth & Hyatt, 1990.

———. *Operation Rescue.* Binghamton, N.Y.: Self-published, 1988.

Thomas, Norman Mattoon

(1884–1968) *socialist leader, pacifist*

Norman Mattoon Thomas was a perennial candidate for president of the United States under the banner of the Socialist Party and was a committed pacifist. He was born on November 20, 1884, in Marion, Ohio, the son of Reverend Welling Evan Thomas and Emma Mattoon Thomas.

Norman Thomas graduated from Princeton University at the head of his class in 1905 and spent the next two years working in settlement houses to help the immigrant poor and traveling overseas. He then entered Union Theological Seminary where he received a divinity degree in 1911. That same year he was ordained in the Presbyterian Church and became a pastor in New York City's East Harlem Church. While enrolled at the seminary he married Frances Violet Stewart; they had six children.

As a college student Thomas had embraced the Progressive reform movement with its goal of ridding capitalism of its worst abuses. Now he was working in New York City's slums, and his experience there, along with the outbreak of World War I, convinced him that capitalism had to be replaced with socialism. In the slums Thomas saw the results of an economy rife with inequities; in the war he saw countries driven by greed for overseas markets and power.

Thomas believed that, unlike capitalism, socialism could provide for everyone. He said that "man has it in his power to use his scientific and technical skill for his own emancipation and not for his further enslavement to poverty, ugliness, drudgery, suspicion, and hate." He added: "The basic fact with which any indictment of our social order must start is the presence of bitter poverty in a nation equipped with machinery and resources to create plenty for all."

Thomas argued that unrestrained capitalism allowed the few to dominate resources and money. And he said that imperialism resulted from capitalists seeking raw materials from around the world and markets for the surpluses they had accumulated by depriving the workers of a fair reward for their labor.

Along with socialism, Thomas believed in pacifism. In 1916 he joined the Fellowship of Reconciliation, a Christian pacifist group, and from 1918 to 1921 edited its newspaper, *The World Tomorrow.* Thomas insisted that capitalism must be overthrown through a peaceful process and that in the course of change, civil liberties must be protected. Writing in *The World Tomorrow*, he said:

> I believe that the class struggle is one of the inescapable facts about human life in our present stage of capitalist organization. With all my heart and soul and mind and strength I desire a classless society in which there will be no more class struggle. . . . I wish to substitute other methods than the methods of war in carrying on this essential struggle to the end of the abolition of the class division in society. This is in line with my general opposition to the war method.

Thomas supported Morris Hillquit, the socialist candidate for mayor of New York City in 1917, and he joined ROGER NASH BALDWIN in founding the National Civil Liberties Bureau, which became the American Civil Liberties Union. Beginning in 1922 he served as codirector of the League for Industrial Democracy, the educational arm of the Socialist Party. He ran unsuccessfully as the socialist candidate for governor of New York in 1924, then for mayor of New York City in 1925 and 1929.

At first attracted to the Bolshevik Revolution in Russia, he rejected it after he visited the Soviet Union and saw firsthand how its totalitarian regime worked. With the death of EUGENE VICTOR DEBS, Thomas became leader of the Socialist Party and ran for president under its banner in every election from 1928 to 1948.

While the American people rejected Thomas's socialism, the two major political parties, most especially the Democrats, did what they have usually done when threatened by a radical reformer: They took over some of his proposals and grafted them onto capitalism. As a result Congress enacted a minimum wage; unemployment, accident, and health insurance; old-age pensions; and low-cost public housing.

In his later years Thomas advocated nuclear disarmament and cofounded the National Committee for a Sane Nuclear Policy. He opposed the Vietnam War. A prolific and articulate writer—in addition to being a brilliant orator—he wrote 20 books.

Norman Thomas died on December 19, 1968, and was memorialized as the "Conscience of America." He once said, "Socialism has the immense advantage of offering an ideal, a philosophy of . . . the dignity of labor."

Further Reading
Duram, James C. "Norman Thomas as a Presidential Conscience." *Presidential Studies Quarterly* 20 (Summer 1990): 581+.

Fleischman, Harry. *Norman Thomas: A Biography.* New York: Norton, 1964.

Gorham, Charles. *Leader at Large: The Long and Fighting Life of Norman Thomas.* New York: Farrar, Straus & Giroux, 1970.

Tijerina, Reies Lopez
(1926–) *Hispanic land rights activist*

Reies Lopez Tijerina rose above his dire migrant conditions to lead a violent attack against the Anglo theft of Hispanic-American land grants in New Mexico and elsewhere. "Our people had not a guide, no light, no knowledge," Tijerina later explained, "and God therefore has chosen me." He was born on September 21, 1926, near Falls City, Texas, a small town 40 miles southeast of San Antonio, to Antonio Tijerina and Herlinda Tijerina.

Tijerina's father worked as a sharecropper and later as a migrant farm laborer, following the seasonal harvests in Texas and Michigan. By age eight young Reies had joined his father in the beet fields, stooping alongside him in the hot sun, hours on end, so that his family could make enough money to survive. Reies attended school only sporadically and never received more than a sixth-grade education. But as he watched his father submit with meekness to the farm bosses, he determined to be strong and stand up to those who would rule him. At the same time, though his mother had died when he was still a child, her devout Catholicism and frequent visions bred in him a deep religious commitment.

At age 18 Reies Tijerina spurned his Catholic faith and entered the Assembly of God Bible Institute, a fundamentalist Pentecostal college, in Ysleta, Texas. Known for his sharp rhetoric and fervent commitment, he was expelled after three years for breaking the rules that governed dating.

In 1946 he married Mary Escobar; they had six children.

Tijerina then traveled through the Southwest as a circuit preacher for the Assemblies of God Church. At one point he lived for a year in a cave in California and claimed that his visions had convinced him that all religions were the same and that, irrespective of faith, the crucial conflict in the world was that between good and evil. In 1950 the Assemblies of God ousted him as preacher because he told impoverished church members in Victoria, Texas, that they should stop paying their tithe; the church, he said, should work for the poor rather than the poor for the church.

Tijerina continued preaching but as a nondenominational minister, and in the early 1950s he convinced 17 Spanish-American families to pool their finances and buy 160 acres of land in Pinal County, Arizona, where they could begin a utopian community dedicated to justice and harmony. Whereas he and his followers may have wanted togetherness, his neighbors wanted him to leave, and they destroyed the community by burning its buildings.

In July 1957 Tijerina was arrested for helping his brother break out of an Arizona jail. Before he went on trial he jumped bail—his life, he claimed, was in danger—and fled to California. There he experienced more visions, messianic ones in which three personages appeared on a cloud and told him that God wanted him to lead the fight in restoring Spanish and Mexican land grants to Hispanic Americans.

Tijerina had traveled to Mexico, where he studied hundreds of land grant records. He claimed that over the years Anglos had illegally taken millions of acres from the descendants of Spanish settlers in the Southwest. The Treaty of Guadalupe Hidalgo that had ended the Mexican War in 1848 had guaranteed land titles held under Spanish and Mexican rule, but through thievery and shady deals, and through confiscation by the U.S. Forest Service, Anglos had acquired the land.

Tijerina joined an effort already begun by Hispanic-American farmers in northern New Mexico to regain some 600,000 acres, called the Tierra Amarilla tract, one of more than 1,700 land grants they and other Hispanic-American settlers in the Southwest had received before U.S. control. While a fugitive from the law, Tijerina operated underground to build his movement and worked as a janitor in Albuquerque to earn money. He returned to the Catholic Church so he could develop a stronger appeal among Hispanic Americans.

When the statute of limitations in his bail-jumping case expired in 1962, he went public and the following year founded Alianza Federal de Mercedes (Federal Alliance of Land Grants). He declared that the group wanted the restoration of land grants to their Spanish descendants under the Treaty of Guadalupe Hidalgo. That same year he and his wife divorced, and soon afterward he married Patsy Romero, with whom he had two children.

Tijerina applied his talents as a preacher to his new mission and captivated audiences with a pounding, frenetic style filled with unbridled emotion. One observer at the time said, "Tijerina's sturdy physique and unusually mobile face framed by coal black hair, combined with a tremendous range of vocal pitch and intensity, enable him to hold audiences spellbound for hours. His hands and arms . . . move constantly, fisting, clapping, wringing, waving, flying into the air." Tijerina said, "This was and is my hardest task: to unclutter and awaken the mentality of my brothers, to redeem them from their inferiority complexes, to get rid of their fear."

At a time when protesters were challenging authority on an almost daily basis in the mid-1960s, Tijerina captivated national attention through his bold acts. In October 1966 he led a march from Albuquerque to Santa Fe to present the governor with demands relating to the land grants, and he led Alianza members in taking over the Echo Amphitheater campground in New Mexico's Kit Carson National Forest. The Alianzistas declared it a pueblo on the basis of a 19th-century land grant, elected a mayor and council, and held several rangers captive for trespassing on pueblo land. Several days later they released the rangers, and federal agents dispersed the occupiers while arresting Tijerina and other Alianzistas on assault charges.

In spring 1967 Anglo ranchers in northern New Mexico reported raids on their property.

Many held the Alianza responsible for them, and as tensions mounted, Tijerina disbanded his organization. But he soon founded Alianza Federal de los Pueblos Libres (Federal Alliance of Free City States), and in June 1967, after the district attorney, Alfonso Sanchez, tried to arrest several of the group's members in Coyote, New Mexico, about 20 Alianzistas retaliated by raiding Tierra Amarilla, a town in the tract of land claimed by Hispanic Americans and by attempting to make a citizen's arrest of Sanchez. They failed to find him, but they did take over the decaying Rio Arriba County courthouse and in a gun battle wounded a jailer and a state trooper.

Then they evacuated the town and retreated into the mountains with some 400 soldiers pursuing them along with police and state troopers supported by 200 military vehicles, including tanks. Tijerina was arrested in Albuquerque two weeks later with several other Alianzistas. When he appeared in court, supporters interrupted the legal proceedings with shouts of "Viva Tijerina!"

By now many activists in the radical New Left were calling Tijerina a hero, and he had established ties with two prominent Chicano leaders, the labor organizer CESAR CHAVEZ and the Colorado rights activist RODOLFO GONZALES. Young Chicanos rallied to Tijerina; despite his leadership on an issue they thought unimportant, they admired his courage and boldness in dealing with Anglos. Some Hispanic Americans, however, criticized his violent tactics.

In November 1967 Tijerina was found guilty of assault in the takeover at Echo Amphitheater. He had declared himself a candidate for governor under the banner of the People's Constitutional Party, but because of his felony conviction the state supreme court disqualified him. In 1968 Tijerina joined the Poor People's March on Washington, D.C., and spoke at several college campuses, where he condemned the Anglo power structure and the Vietnam War.

Also in 1968 Tijerina went on trial in Albuquerque for his role in the raid at Tierra Amarilla. Charged with two counts of assault to commit murder, kidnapping, possession of a deadly weapon, and destruction of state property, he fired his attorney and defended himself. Tijerina argued

that he had the right to attempt a citizen's arrest, and in December 1968, after only one person— Eulogio Salazar, the jailer at the Rio Arriba County courthouse—could positively identify Tijerina as among the 20 raiders, the jury acquitted him. Later Salazar was found beaten to death in his car.

Yet another showdown with Forest Service rangers, this one in the summer of 1969, caused Tijerina to be charged with assault and destruction of property. He was found guilty that October, and after an appeals court upheld his conviction in the Echo Amphitheater case, he began a two-year prison term at the federal penitentiary in La Tuna, Texas. In a letter that summer to his followers, Tijerina wrote: "What is my real crime? As I and the poor people see it, especially the Indo-Hispanos, my only crime is UPHOLDING OUR RIGHTS PROTECTED BY THE TREATY OF GUADALUPE HIDALGO." And he insisted: "We have the evidence to prove our claims to property as well as to the cultural rights of which we have been deprived."

Paroled in 1971, Tijerina was prohibited from holding any office in Alianza for five years. He subsequently pursued a more subdued approach and talked about building a brotherhood among people. At the same time he tried to persuade the Mexican government to pressure the United States into abiding by the land grant clauses in the Treaty of Guadalupe Hidalgo. Many young Chicanos who previously had admired him, however, now criticized him for having been tamed.

Tijerina resumed his presidency of Alianza in 1976, and in the mid-1980s he began blaming Jews for the loss of the land grants. He made several rambling and emotional statements to that effect while denying he was anti-Semitic.

In 1999 Tijerina met with Texas governor George W. Bush and tried to persuade the Republican to order an inventory of land grants in the state from the Spanish and Mexican eras, something he had obtained in 1971 from the state of New Mexico. Bush, then seeking his party's presidential nomination, apparently agreed to meet Tijerina as a way to court favor with Hispanic voters. That same year the once fiery activist turned over his personal archives to the Center for Southwest Research at the University of New Mexico. At a ceremony to honor Tijerina several persons praised him:

"You told us this was our country, our patria. You struggled for our independence and were willing to give your life for it," said Professor Charles Truxillo.

"[You] empowered us and taught us to be proud of being Chicanos," said a college administrator, Matthew Padilla.

"He was fighting for the rights of the people of this state. . . . He stood up for himself and made people believe in him," said state senator Shannon Robinson.

Earlier, former New Mexico governor David Cargo had said, "This whole thing—*Alianza*—it had little to do with grants. Their real fight was poverty. The *Alianza* was a historical aberration. It was about their social condition. They were poor, dirt poor, and they had no opportunity." Cargo's analysis accurately summarized the dominant condition that had sparked Tijerina's movement.

But to Tijerina his crusade meant more than economics. While the illegal taking of the land grants from Hispanic Americans had caused poverty, he believed, it had done much more—it had robbed his people of their culture and decimated their spirit.

Further Reading

Gardner, Richard. *Grito! Reies Tijerina and the New Mexico Land Grant War of 1967.* New York: Harper & Row, 1971.

Hammerback, John C., et al. *A War of Words: Chicano Protest in the 1960s and 1970s.* Westport, Conn.: Greenwood Press, 1985.

Jenkinson, Michael. *Tijerina.* Albuquerque, N.M.: Paisano Press, 1968.

Nabokov, Peter. *Tijerina and the Courthouse Raid.* Berkeley, Calif.: Ramparts Press, 1970.

Vigil, Ernesto B. *The Crusade for Justice: Chicano Militancy and the Government's War on Dissent.* Madison: University of Wisconsin Press, 1999.

Tourgée, Albion Winegar
(1838–1905) *civil rights activist*

Albion Tourgée served in the Union army during the Civil War, and as a politician and a writer he advocated black civil rights. He was born on May 2, 1838, in Williamsfield, Ohio, to Valentine Tourgée and Louisa Emma Winegar Tourgée.

Tourgée entered the University of Rochester in New York in 1859, but he withdrew in 1861 to teach school. A few weeks later he was wounded at the First Battle of Bull Run. While recovering he completed a bachelor of arts degree. Shortly afterward he returned to the Union army, but in 1863 he was captured by the Confederates at Murfreesboro, Tennessee. After his release he married Emma Lodoiska; they had one daughter.

Tourgée fought in the war a third time, but in December 1863 he resigned from the army and studied law. He moved to Greensboro, North Carolina, and for a brief period in 1867 published the *Union Register,* a newspaper dedicated to radical Reconstruction. The radicals wanted to purge the South of its Confederate influences and build the Republican Party with the support of African-American voters and those whites who supported black civil rights.

In 1868 Tourgée served in the state convention called by radicals to write a constitution. That same year he won election to the superior court. His outspoken criticism of former Confederates and of the Ku Klux Klan (KKK), along with his involvement in questionable business dealings, generated considerable opposition. In 1870 Tourgée expressed his views about the KKK in a letter to the *New York Tribune:*

> [Their] crimes have been of every character imaginable. Perhaps the most usual has been the dragging of men and women from their beds, and beating their naked bodies with hickory switches. . . . In this district I estimate their offenses as follows, in the past ten months: Twelve murders, 9 rapes, 11 arsons, 7 mutilations.

He went on to condemn the lack of governmental action: "I am ashamed of the nation that will let its citizens be slain by scores, and scourged by thousands, and offer no remedy or protection."

Physical violence threatened Tourgée. "I have very little doubt that I shall be one of the next victims," he said. "My steps have been dogged for months." Tourgée wrote his most notable novel, *A Fool's Errand,* in 1879, basing it on what he had seen of Reconstruction in the South. But because his race for Congress had ended in defeat a year earlier and more threats were made against him, he moved to New York, where he eventually settled in the town of Mayville in 1881.

In 1896 he represented Adolph Plessy, an African American, in the famous Supreme Court case *Plessy v. Ferguson.* "Justice is pictured blind and her daughter, the Law, ought at least to be colorblind," he argued. The court ruled against him, however, and declared separate but equal policies constitutional—a judgment that opened the door to more Jim Crow laws of racial segregation.

President William McKinley appointed Albion Tourgée American consul at Bordeaux, France, in 1897. There he died on May 21, 1905.

Further Reading

Curtis, Michael Kent. "Albion Tourgée: Remembering Plessy's Lawyer on the 100th Anniversary of Plessy v. Ferguson." *Constitutional Commentary* 13 (Summer 1996): 187–199.

Gross, Theodore L. *Albion W. Tourgée.* New York: Twayne Publishers, 1963.

Olsen, Otto H. *Carpetbagger's Crusade: The Life of Albion Winegar Tourgée.* Baltimore: Johns Hopkins University Press, 1965.

Townsend, Francis Everett

(1867–1960) *economic reformer*

Francis Everett Townsend was an advocate during the Great Depression of a pension plan for the elderly. He was born on January 13, 1867, near Fairbury, Illinois, the son of George Warren Townsend, a farmer, and Sara Ann Helper Townsend.

After the Townsend family moved to Franklin, Nebraska, Francis Townsend completed two years of classes at the Franklin Academy, a preparatory school. In 1887 he moved to California to make money in the land boom in Los Angeles, but he failed and returned nearly penniless to Franklin. He then tried farming his own homestead but failed at that, too. He drifted about and held odd jobs, saving enough money to enter Omaha Medical College in 1899. Townsend graduated in 1903 and started his practice in the Black Hills of South

Dakota, where he ministered to miners and ranchers. In 1906 he married Wilhelmina Mollie Brogue, a widow who had seven children; they had four children of their own.

Townsend served in the Army Medical Corps during World War I and then moved his family to Long Beach, California. But he struggled to make money from his medical practice, and when the Great Depression struck in 1929 he lost his meager savings. He was, however, able to find work with the Long Beach Health Office.

Townsend was already in his 60s when he devised what he called his Old Age Revolving Pension Plan. He wanted the federal government to provide $200 each month to retired Americans above age 60. He proposed that the program be financed by a 2 percent tax on all business transactions.

Townsend announced his pension plan in a letter he sent to the Long Beach newspaper in September 1933. In short order the public embraced what was called the "Townsend Plan" and his reasoning that it would not only help the elderly but also boost the economy because the elderly would use the money they received to buy consumer goods.

Townsend hired a real estate developer, Robert Earl Clements, to promote the plan, and by summer 1935 the doctor was claiming that 7,000 Townsend Clubs had been formed with more than 2 million members. Economists, though, ridiculed his plan and said it would add nothing to the economy because the tax would boost prices and take money away from consumers. Writing in *Freedom from Fear: The American People in Depression and War, 1929–1945* (1999), historian David M. Kennedy summarizes: "Fully funding the recommended monthly payments to the 9 percent of the American population over the age of sixty would soak up half the national income and double the national tax burden."

When Congress and President Franklin Roosevelt resisted the Townsend Plan, Townsend formed a political alliance with Huey Long and CHARLES EDWARD COUGHLIN, fellow advocates of unrealistic proposals to end the depression. Roosevelt then convinced Congress in 1935 to enact a social security program funded by a tax on employers and employees. He did so in part to defuse the Townsend movement. In 1936 the Union Party, which had been formed by Townsend, Long, and Coughlin, received only 10 percent of the presidential vote, and Townsend soon left it.

In 1937 Townsend was convicted of contempt of Congress when he refused to cooperate with a Senate committee investigating charges of corruption made against the Townsend Clubs. President Roosevelt, however, commuted his sentence.

Townsend continued to lecture, and he promoted a revised version of his plan into the year 1960. He died on September 1, 1960, in Los Angeles.

Further Reading

Bennett, David Harry. *Demagogues in the Depression: American Radicals and the Union Party, 1932–1936.* New Brunswick, N.J.: Rutgers University Press, 1969.

Gordon, John Steele. "Dr. Townsend's Crusade." *American Heritage,* October 2001, 49.

Holtzman, Abrahm. *The Townsend Movement: A Political Study.* New York: Bookman Associates, 1963.

Kennedy, David M. *Freedom from Fear: The American People in Depression and War, 1929–1945.* New York: Oxford University Press, 1999.

Trochmann, John
(1943–) *militia leader*

John Trochmann is a founder and the most prominent leader of the right-wing Militia of Montana (MOM). He was born in 1943 near Newfolden, Minnesota, and grew up a farm boy on the plains.

At age 17 Trochmann dropped out of high school and joined the Naval Air Force. He worked first as an engine mechanic and later as a flight engineer. His military service took him to Iceland and Puerto Rico, and during the 1962 Cuban missile crisis he flew in reconnaissance planes and took photographs of Soviet ships as part of an attempt to confirm that Russian missiles were being removed from Cuba. He later said that he believed that the missiles had remained and that American leaders had deceived the public by alleging that the Soviets had been forced to back down.

Trochmann left the military in the mid-1960s and opened an auto repair and race car business in Delano, Minnesota, which he later diversified to include snowmobiles.

Several years later he became attracted to Montana's wide-open spaces and moved there in 1988. He had a long-standing interest in politics and wanted, he later said, to warn the American people about threats to their freedom. So in 1990 he appeared at the national Aryan Nations Congress meeting in Idaho and spoke in support of that group's white-supremacist program. He subsequently denied any affinity for Aryan Nations, but the group's founder, Richard Girnt Butler, said a mutually supportive relationship existed with Trochmann.

As was the case for many activists in the 1990s militia movement, a shoot-out between white supremacist Randy Weaver and federal authorities at Ruby Ridge, Idaho, and an attack by federal agents on David Koresh and his Branch Davidian religious group at Waco, Texas, further convinced Trochmann that the federal government intended to destroy liberty. Frustrated that most Americans failed to recognize the threat, he moved to Alaska and planned to live there permanently. But when he saw more and more Americans criticizing the media and raising questions about their government, he returned to Montana to form a protest group. In January 1994 Trochmann, his wife Carolyn, his brother David, and his nephew Randy organized MOM. Trochmann claimed that MOM preferred education to violence and that the name *militia* simply signified strength. MOM, he claimed, would guard against a conspiracy by the United States government and foreign governments to establish a totalitarian state.

Many observers of radical organizations credited MOM with stimulating the formation of militias around the country through its literature and meetings. John Trochmann frequently traveled to other states and encouraged people to establish similar groups.

MOM created a storm of controversy with the books and videotapes it produced or sold, some of which advocated using violence against enemies. Both the Anti-Defamation League and the Montanan Human Rights Commission portrayed Trochmann as a white supremacist. He denied that charge and criticized both organizations for refusing to hear his side of the story.

Trochmann remained at the center of controversy in spring 1995, when sheriff's officers in Musselshell County, Montana, arrested him and charged him with conspiracy to interfere with justice. Trochmann apparently had sympathized with a prisoner being held in the county jail, a member of the radical right-wing Freemen, and may have been trying to help him escape. The state's attorney eventually concluded there was insufficient evidence to take Trochmann to trial, and the charges were dropped.

Later in 1995 Trochmann took part in a debate at Yale University on the militia movement and, by his own account, convinced many in the audience that a government conspiracy to limit individual liberty was at work. Trochmann was viewed by some of his critics as an opportunist intent on making money; by taking advantage of the surging militia movement and rampant extremist political rhetoric in the 1990s, they claimed, he was able to sell videotapes, audiotapes, books, and other items. Whatever the case surrounding these sales, and despite numerous instances in which he disagreed with other militia leaders, Trochmann wielded considerable clout in the militia movement. Even with the decline of militias after the year 2000, he remained in charge of MOM.

In 2001, when the Federal Bureau of Investigation (FBI) announced it had inadvertently withheld files from lawyers defending Timothy McVeigh, who had been convicted of bombing a federal building in Oklahoma City in 1995 and killing more than 100 people, Trochmann told the *San Francisco Chronicle*, "I know it would be a little arrogant of me to say I told you so, but." The "I told you so" referred to his long-held belief in government conspiracies. He added: "I know McVeigh had a part in [the bombing], but he had some kind of government help."

Further Reading

Stern, Kenneth S. *A Force upon the Plain: The American Militia Movement and the Politics of Hate.* New York: Simon & Schuster, 1996.

Voll, Daniel. "At Home with M.O.M." *Esquire*, July 1995, 46+.

Truth, Sojourner
(Isabella)
(ca. 1797–1883) *abolitionist, women's rights activist.*

After escaping from slavery Sojourner Truth advocated abolition and women's rights. She was born with the name Isabella in Ulster County, New York, 90 miles north of New York City, in about the year 1797 to John and Elizabeth, slaves owned by Colonel Johannis Hardenbergh, a Dutch immigrant.

In the part of the country where Isabella was born, Dutch immigrant farmers dominated the economy, and they used black slaves to work their large landholdings. About 10 percent of the total population in Ulster was black. Shortly after 1800 Isabella was sold to John Neely, an event that separated her from her parents and her brother. The Neely family treated her cruelly, often beating her. Shortly thereafter she was sold to a fisherman in Kingston, New York, and then to John J. Dumont, who owned a plantation nearby. Once again she suffered physical and even sexual abuse when she was assaulted by her mistress, Sally Dumont.

In 1827, about the same time the New York legislature passed a bill to emancipate all slaves, Isabella ran away from the Dumonts, who had indicated they would be slow to comply with the new law. She eventually made her way to New York City, where she worked as a domestic and began following a self-proclaimed prophet by the name of Matthias, formerly Robert Matthews. Matthias said that he had purged his soul of all sin and that the Holy Spirit had spoken to him and warned that the judgment day was near.

Isabella joined Matthias's commune, located at Sing Sing, New York, in the early 1830s and worshiped him as a messiah even after her friends had warned her that he was a fake. About 1835, however, Matthias and Isabella drifted apart. A few years later Isabella changed her name to Sojourner Truth. She claimed that God had told her to take the name "Sojourner" as part of her calling to preach and that she had decided to use the name "Truth" to indicate what she would be preaching.

Sojourner Truth began spreading the word of God in 1843, a time when evangelical movements were spreading in the North. She preached beneath the big tents at numerous Millerite camps. Although she never joined the Millerites, a group of adventists who were preparing for the end of the world, they received her warmly and directed her to the Northampton Association, a commune in western Massachusetts run by abolitionists. Truth later said that at the commune she enjoyed complete "liberty of thought and speech."

Truth lived at Northampton for several months, joined the ranks of antislavery supporters of women's rights, and in the late 1840s began traveling as an abolitionist speaker. That activity earned her some money, as did the publication of her *Narrative of Sojourner Truth* in 1850, written by abolitionist Olive Gilbert. In *Sojourner Truth: A Life, A Symbol* (1996), Nell Irvin Painter describes Truth at this stage of her life as "a singing evangelist whose religion is joyous, optimistic, and at times ecstatic."

In 1850 Truth spoke before the national women's rights meeting in Worcester, Massachusetts, where she expressed her faith in God and said that religious faith would end evil. She stated that women had "set the world wrong by eating the forbidden fruit" but that she would now set it right. At another meeting at Akron, Ohio, the following year, Truth asked permission to speak and, according to one reliable report, said:

> I am a woman's rights. I have as much muscle as any man. . . . I have plowed and reaped and husked and chopped and mowed, and can any man do more than that? . . . I have heard the Bible and have learned that Eve caused man to sin. Well if woman upset the world, do give her a chance to set it right side up again.

The legend is that she spoke these words before a hostile audience and used the phrase "Ain't I a woman?" But the true emphasis of her comments was her insistence that women could do the same work as men and that the Bible did not relegate women to a secondary status; consequently,

women should have equal rights. Truth expressed the link between women's rights and economics when, at another point, she said to a male audience, "When we get our rights, we shall not have to come to you for money, for then we shall have money enough in our own pockets and may be you will ask *us* for money."

Truth settled in Battle Creek, Michigan, in the mid-1850s and continued her reform campaign. During that decade she met the abolitionist author Harriet Beecher Stowe, and in 1863 Stowe wrote about Truth in an article for *Atlantic Monthly*, "Sojourner Truth, the Libyan Sibyl." Filled with as much myth as fact, the article paid tribute to Truth with a condescending tone and described her through fictional scenes, including

This photograph of Sojourner Truth, taken around 1864, bears the caption "I sell the shadow to support the substance." *(Library of Congress)*

her singing a hymn: "There is a holy city . . . [Truth] sang with the strong barbaric accent of the native African. . . . Sojourner, singing this hymn, seemed to impersonate the fervor of Ethiopia, wild savage, hunted of all nations, but burning after God in her tropic heart."

During the Civil War Truth collected food and clothing for black soldiers, and she met Abraham Lincoln at the White House. When the war ended she continued to advocate women's rights and urged the government to provide land out West for former slaves. She wanted the wording of the Fourteenth Amendment changed so that it would enable women to vote. Truth died in a sanatorium in Battle Creek on November 26, 1883.

Women's rights supporter Elizabeth Lukins described Truth in 1851: "Her heart is as soft and loving as a child's, her soul as strong and fixed as the everlasting rocks, and her moral sense has something like inspiration or divination." In her time Truth indeed inspired African Americans and women of both races; she continues to wield that influence today—a bold voice for equal rights.

Further Reading

Bernard, Jacqueline. *Journey toward Freedom: The Story of Sojourner Truth*. New York: Norton, 1967.

Painter, Nell Irvin, ed. *Narrative of Sojourner Truth*. New York: Penguin Books, 1998.

———. *Sojourner Truth: A Life, a Symbol*. New York: Norton, 1996.

Stetson, Erlene. *Glorying in Tribulation: The Lifework of Sojourner Truth*. East Lansing: Michigan State University Press, 1994.

Tubman, Harriet
(Araminta Ross)
(1820–1913) *abolitionist*

When the former slave Harriet Tubman eventually escaped to the North, she helped runaway slaves flee the South along the Underground Railroad. Her cry to the slaveholders, wrote Sarah H. Bradford in her eulogistic *Harriet, the Moses of Her People* (1886), "was ever like [Moses] to Pharaoh, 'Let my people go!'" Tubman was born in 1820 in Dorchester County on Maryland's Eastern Shore to slave parents Benjamin Ross and Harriet Green.

Harriet's first name at birth was Araminta, but at an early age she adopted her mother's name. One of 11 children, she grew up illiterate. During her teen years she endured hard physical labor on her master's plantation that included plowing the fields. Her hatred for slavery only increased over the years. According to Bradford:

> [At age 13 Harriet] had heard the shrieks and cries of women who were being flogged in the negro quarter; she had listened to the groaned out prayer, "Oh, Lord, have mercy!" She had already seen two older sisters taken away as part of a chain gang, and they had gone no one knew whither; she had seen the agonized expression on their faces as they turned to take a last look at their "Old Cabin Home"; and had watched them from the top of the fence, as they went off weeping and lamenting, till they were hidden from her sight forever. She saw the hopeless grief of the poor old mother and the silent despair of the aged father, and already she began to revolve in her mind the question, "Why should such things be?" "Is there no deliverance for my people?"

In 1844 Harriet married John Tubman, a free black. Little is known about him or their relationship, though some historians claim that her master forced her to marry him. Five years later Harriet Tubman took it upon herself to run away. She arrived in Pennsylvania "more alone than ever; but . . . no one could take her now, and she would never [again] call any man 'Master.'" On crossing into freedom she said, "I looked at my hands to see if I was the same person. . . . There was such a glory over everything; the sun came like gold through the trees and over the fields, and I felt like I was in heaven."

Yet she was alone and had to start her life anew. She did so by helping other slaves escape along the Underground Railroad, a network of private homes and shops whose owners provided runaways with money, food, and shelter. Some 40,000 to 100,000 slaves escaped through the Underground Railroad in the antebellum years, headed for the northern states and Canada. Tubman made about 19 trips to the South to help 200 to 300 slaves.

She began her bold action in 1850, when she returned to the South to retrieve her sister. In 1857 she rescued her elderly parents. Her tactic in all of her trips was to avoid entering any plantation; rather, she would position herself nearby and then let the word circulate among the slaves about her readiness to help them escape their masters. Her work required intelligence, boldness, and bravery, for she risked her life and the lives of the slaves. She had a deep religious faith and thought herself directed in her mission by God.

In one harrowing incident in Maryland, Tubman prepared to take a young slave, Tilly, with her on a ferry across Chesapeake Bay. She expected an accomplice to provide smooth passage, but when she arrived at the ferry the accomplice was nowhere to be found, and Tubman was forced to buy tickets from a white clerk. As she waited to purchase her fare, she worried that the clerk would suspect her and never let her proceed. Sarah H. Bradford graphically recounted the tense moment:

> Harriet led the young girl to the bow of the boat, where they were alone, and here, having no other help, she, as was her custom, addressed herself to the Lord. Kneeling on the seat, and supporting her head on her hands, and fixing her eyes on the waters of the bay, she groaned: "Oh, Lord! You've been wid me in six troubles, *don't desert me in the seventh!*"
>
> "Moses! Moses!" cried Tilly, pulling her by the sleeve. "Do go and see if you can't get tickets now."
>
> "Oh, Lord! You've been wid me in six troubles, *don't desert me in the seventh. . . .*"
>
> At length in terror Tilly exclaimed: "Oh, Moses! the man is coming. What shall we do?"
>
> "Oh, Lord, you've been wid me in six troubles!"
>
> Here the clerk touched her on the shoulder, and Tilly thought their time had come, but all he said was: "You can come now and get your tickets," and their troubles were over.
>
> What changed this man from his former suspicious and antagonistic aspect, Harriet never knew. Of course she said it was "de Lord," but as to the agency he used, she never troubled herself to inquire. She *expected* deliverance when she prayed, unless the Lord had ordered otherwise, and in that case she was perfectly willing to accept the Divine decree.

Harriet Tubman made about 19 trips to the South to help 200 to 300 slaves escape to freedom along the Underground Railroad. *(National Archives and Records Administration)*

Tubman knew that if, during a rescue, slaves changed their mind about escaping and returned to their plantation, they would be forced by their masters to reveal details about her activities. So she threatened to shoot recalcitrant slaves. In one instance she said about a slave: "I told the boys [with me] to get their guns ready and shoot him. They'd have done it in a minute; but when he heard that, he jumped up and went on as well as any body."

Tubman was assisted by several abolitionists in the North, among them WILLIAM STILL, an African American. Still said about her: "In point of courage, shrewdness, and disinterested exertions to rescue her fellowman, she was without equal." Thomas Garret, a Quaker who lived in Wilmington, Delaware, allowed Tubman to use his home as a way station and provided her with supplies.

Tubman earned money between trips to the South by working as a cook and by speaking to abolitionist groups. In 1857 she settled in Auburn, New York, a town noted for its support of abolitionist and feminist causes. She was a member of the New England Anti-Slavery Society and supported the radical JOHN BROWN in his plans to foment a slave uprising in Virginia.

In 1862, during the Civil War, she journeyed to South Carolina, where she worked behind Union lines nursing sick and wounded soldiers. She also helped organize a small cadre of blacks to scout the countryside and gather intelligence for the Union army.

At the end of the war she worked to establish schools in North Carolina for the former slaves. The account of her life, *Scenes in the Life of Harriet Tubman*, written by Sarah Hopkins in 1869, and later republished as *Harriet, the Moses of Her People*, earned her additional money. She used those funds to support destitute old people and children at her home in Auburn. That same year she married Nelson Davis, a former African-American soldier in the Union army and several years her junior.

In 1903 the Harriet Tubman Home for Aged and Indigent Colored People was founded on land she had bought adjacent to her house. Tubman died on March 10, 1913, of pneumonia. Reformer and writer THOMAS WENTWORTH HIGGINSON once said about Tubman: "Her tales of adventure are beyond anything in fiction and her ingenuity and generalship are extraordinary. . . . The slaves call her Moses."

Further Reading

Bennett, Lerone, Jr. "Free for Christmas." *Ebony*, December 1994, 52+.

Bradford, Sarah H. *Harriet, The Moses of Her People.* Reprint. Gloucester, Mass.: P. Smith, 1981.

Conrad, Earl. *Harriet Tubman.* Washington, D.C.: Associated Publishers, 1943.

V

Villard, Fanny Garrison
(Helen Francis Garrison)
(1844–1928) women's suffragist, pacifist

A women's suffrage leader and pacifist, Fanny Villard was raised by parents who taught her to reject society's view that women were second-class citizens. "We shall demand for her the rights of a human being, though she be a female," said her father. She was born Helen Frances Garrison on December 16, 1844, in Boston, the daughter of the abolitionist WILLIAM LLOYD GARRISON and Helen Eliza Benson Garrison, and throughout her life she was called Fanny.

Fanny Garrison attended the Winthrop School in Boston, taught piano, and in 1866 married Henry Villard, a German immigrant and a reporter for the *Chicago Tribune*. They had four children. Henry Villard became rich through several business ventures, including his presidency of the Northern Pacific Railroad, and the couple used his wealth to finance their philanthropic and social reform activities. Fanny Villard volunteered to work for the Diet Kitchen Association, which supplied food to the poor, and later served as its president. In addition she worked for the Consumers' League, the Working Women's Protective Association, and the National Association for the Advancement of Colored People (NAACP).

In the early 1900s Villard concluded that social reform could only be effective if women participated in politics. With the encouragement of her son, OSWALD GARRISON VILLARD, Fanny Villard joined the suffrage movement, serving on the executive board of the New York State Woman Suffrage Association and joining other similar organizations. She made numerous speeches to advocate women's right to vote and promoted the Nineteenth Amendment (which the states ratified in 1920).

Villard was also a pacifist and in 1914 organized and led a peace parade of 1,500 women down New York City's Fifth Avenue. When World War I began she appealed to President Woodrow Wilson to keep America out of it. In 1915 she and Progressive reformer JANE ADDAMS formed the Women's Peace Party.

But Villard left the party when it compromised its principles and said it would agree to the United State's entering the war if a belligerent act were committed against it. When America entered the war in 1917, Villard worked to help conscientious objectors, and in 1919 she founded the Woman's Peace League. She served as its president until her death on July 5, 1928, in Dobb's Ferry, New York.

Further Reading
Venet, Wendy Hamand. *Neither Ballots nor Bullets: Women Abolitionists and the Civil War.* Charlottesville: University Press of Virginia, 1991.

Villard, Oswald Garrison
(1872–1949) civil rights leader, pacifist

A founder of the National Association for the Advancement of Colored People (NAACP), Oswald

Garrison Villard was a strident opponent to America's entry into World War I and World War II. He was born on March 13, 1872, to Henry Villard, a businessman and philanthropist, and FANNY GARRISON VILLARD, a social reformer. Oswald Villard's birth occurred in Wiesbaden, Germany, where his parents were staying.

Villard graduated with a B.A. from Harvard in 1893 and then traveled with his father in Europe. He returned to Harvard for a master's degree, which he received in 1896, and worked as a research assistant to historian Albert Bushnell Hart. He wanted, however, a more active career, and since his father owned the *New York Evening Post* and *The Nation,* in 1897 he became an editorial writer for the *Evening Post.* When the elder Villard died in 1900 Oswald Villard took over both publications.

In 1909 Villard helped organize an interracial conference on African Americans, and from that meeting he and several other white reformers, along with black leader W. E. B. DU BOIS, organized the NAACP. The organization focused on legal challenges to racial segregation and took a less compromising stand on race relations than did another prominent black leader, BOOKER TALIAFERRO WASHINGTON.

A supporter of women's rights, Villard marched in a 1911 suffrage parade in New York City. Many men taunted him for his stand. On the issue of relations between blacks and whites, Villard, who had become chairman of the NAACP, hoped to influence President Woodrow Wilson on race policy and in 1913 proposed to the Democrat that he form a National Race Commission. Wilson eventually rejected the idea because it might antagonize southern congressmen. The difference in opinion between Villard and Wilson over the commission produced a sharp break between them as Villard traveled the country charging the president with acceding to racism.

When World War I erupted in Europe, Villard urged that the United States remain neutral, and in the 1916 presidential race he supported Republican candidate Charles Evans Hughes over Wilson, partly because of his earlier differences with the incumbent and partly because of his assessment that Hughes would be more likely to keep the United States out of the war. Wilson narrowly won reelection.

As Wilson pursued military preparedness, Villard objected that by building up its arsenal the United States would be pulled into combat. He wrote in the *Evening Post:*

> The preparedness policy signifies an entire change in our attitude towards the military. . . . A cardinal principle of our polity has always been the subordination of the military to the civil authority as a necessary safeguard for the republic, particularly in our national councils, and as to all matters affecting national policy. Today, in our sudden worship of the expert in uniform, we are told that what we need is a national council of defence comprising . . . fifteen military and naval officers with only seven civilians graciously given places at the council board.

He concluded:

> Against the god of might; against the god of force; against the policy of murder of millions by millions, there will be American citizens to protest as long as there are stars in their courses. Against every preparation for war men henceforth will rise to say no even with their backs to the wall and rifles in front of them.

Villard's continuing antiwar pronouncements after the United States entered the conflict in 1917 and his vociferous call to protect conscientious objectors caused readers to desert the *Evening Post,* and he sold the newspaper. He continued to publish the *Nation,* however, and as a voice of liberal America its circulation grew substantially over the next two decades.

Villard at first supported the Bolshevik Revolution in Russia, but he criticized its turn to totalitarianism. He had no liking for the Treaty of Versailles that ended World War I; he said that the result of retribution against Germany would be another major war.

In the 1920s Villard spoke out against corruption in politics, particularly the Teapot Dome Scandal under President Warren G. Harding, which involved fraud in the administering of government oil reserves. At the same time he supported prison reform, birth control, and the expansion of labor unions.

Villard retired as editor of the *Nation* in 1932 but worked as a contributing editor and writer. He supported most of President Franklin D. Roosevelt's New Deal, but when the *Nation* supported a military preparedness program he severed all ties with the magazine. Villard joined the isolationist America First Committee, despite its inclusion of conservatives who opposed his reform ideas.

The Japanese attack on Pearl Harbor in December 1941 caused Villard to retire to his country home and dedicate himself to his writing. He suffered a heart attack in 1944 and died on October 1, 1949.

Further Reading

Humes, Dollena Joy. *Oswald Garrison Villard, Liberal of the 1920's.* Syracuse, N.Y.: Syracuse University Press, 1960.

Wreszin, Michael. *Oswald Garrison Villard, Pacifist at War.* Bloomington: Indiana University Press, 1965.

Vorse, Mary Marvin Heaton

(1874–1966) *labor activist, writer*

Mary Marvin Heaton Vorse was a writer and activist for the labor movement. She was born Mary Marvin Heaton on October 11, 1874, in New York City to Hiram Heaton, a retired innkeeper, and Ellen Cordelia Blackman Heaton.

Raised amid her family's wealth in Amherst, Massachusetts, with frequent vacations overseas, Mary Heaton attended private schools and received much of her education in Europe, where she learned to speak French, Italian, and German. She studied art in Paris and New York City, and in 1898 she married Albert White Vorse, a journalist. They had two children.

In 1903 Mary and Albert moved their family to Europe in an attempt to spark Albert's writing career. Instead, the move sparked Mary's writing; she began submitting articles to American magazines and developed a wide readership. In time she would write more than 400 articles and 18 books. Her work appeared in such leading periodicals as *Woman's Home Companion*, *McCall's*, *New Republic*, *New Yorker*, *Atlantic*, and *Ladies' Home Journal*. She wrote also for newspaper wire services and for the *New York Post*, *New York World*, *Washington Post*, and many other papers.

Mary and her husband soon returned to the United States, and the family settled in an old house in Provincetown, Massachusetts, which became a gathering place for the American literati. Mary separated from her husband in 1909, and the following year he died. In 1912 she married Joseph O'Brien, also a journalist, but continued to use the name Mary Heaton Vorse. With him she had one child. Joseph O'Brien died in 1915.

Mary Heaton Vorse first engaged in labor activism shortly after 1900, when she was in Europe and participated in a strike. But her intense concern for the labor movement began in 1912, when she reported on a textile strike in Lawrence, Massachusetts. From then on most of her writing dealt with social causes, especially labor unions, and she often joined workers in their fight for improved wages and dignity.

Concerning the Lawrence strike she wrote:

> Something very good was being evolved here. People were thinking in unison. People were acting in unison. Marching together, singing together. Harmony, not disorder, was being established. . . .
>
> Both Joe O'Brien and I had come a long road to get to Lawrence. It was for us our point of intersection. Together we experienced the realization of the human cost of our industrial life. Something transforming had happened to both of us. We knew now where we belonged—on the side of the workers and not with the comfortable people among whom we were born.

Vorse's experience as a foreign correspondent in Europe during World War I bred in her a hatred for war. She said that seeing combat was "the difference between knowing academically that war exists and the emotional realization of it."

In 1919 she covered America's great steel strike, which spread to 10 states, and she wrote about it in her book *Men and Steel* (1920). In 1921 she traveled to Russia and reported on that country's famine.

Back in the United States, in 1926 she spoke to workers involved in a textile strike at Passaic, New Jersey, urging them to continue their protest. In 1929 she addressed a rally of the National Textile Workers Union in Gastonia, North Carolina, and in 1937 she suffered a bullet wound from vigilantes while she was reporting on a strike at the Republic Steel Corporation in Youngstown, Ohio.

She covered developments in Europe leading to the outbreak of World War II, and she later served in Italy with the United Nations Relief and Rehabilitation Administration. In 1962 she received the Social Justice Award from the United Auto Workers.

Mary Heaton Vorse died on June 14, 1966, at her home in Provincetown. Her close attachment to the labor movement was affirmed in a statement she had made at the time of the Lawrence strike: "Striving for light has appeared in many different forms. It has demanded religious freedom, freedom of scientific thought, political freedom. In our generation it is striving toward economic justice. It is this that sings our songs, makes the art and discoveries of a race and shakes off age-old tyrannies."

Further Reading

Garrison, Dee. *Mary Heaton Vorse: The Life of an American Insurgent.* Philadelphia: Temple University Press, 1989.

Tamplin, John C. "Mary Heaton Vorse, Journalist: Victim of Strike Violence?" *Labor History* 28 (Winter 1987): 84+.

Wald, Lillian

(1867–1940) *health reform activist, suffragist, pacifist*

A suffragist and pacifist, Lillian Wald is best remembered for inventing the practice of public health nursing. She was born on March 10, 1867, in Cincinnati, Ohio, to Max Wald, an optical goods dealer, and Minnie Schwarz Wald.

After Max Wald moved the family to Rochester, New York, in 1878, Lillian Wald attended Miss Cruttenden's English-French Boarding and Day School. Her learning, combined with her own innate intelligence and a family atmosphere that encouraged reading, enabled her to apply for admission to Vassar College at 16. She was rejected, though, because of her age.

Wald spent the next few years concerned more with the social scene than with education. In 1889, however, she enrolled in the nursing program at New York Hospital. On her graduation in 1891 she worked as a nurse at the New York Juvenile Asylum. The following year she quit that job and enrolled at the Women's Medical College in New York City with the intent of becoming a doctor.

She then underwent an experience that changed her direction. She had organized classes in home nursing for largely Jewish immigrant families on the Lower East Side when she was led by a child to a sick woman in a rundown tenement. The poverty that she saw shocked her and caused her to commit herself to providing affordable health care for the neighborhood.

At that time, Progressive reformers were trying to rid society of such abuses as child labor, political corruption, and slums. Some of the reformers had formed settlement houses to provide social services to poor immigrants. Wald fit into the Progressive movement and in 1895 established a new type of settlement house on Henry Street, the Nurses' Settlement, which concentrated on providing health care. Wald developed public health nursing, whereby nurses administered to the needy. By 1896 the settlement had nine trained nurses living in it, and just a few years later they were caring for 4,500 patients.

Wald soon expanded the Nurses' Settlement into a full-scale settlement house, the Henry Street Settlement, which provided classes for immigrants in English, homemaking, and drama, along with vocational training and social events. Unlike some other settlement house workers, Wald believed that the immigrants should maintain many of their cultural practices; to her, diversity was healthy to society.

Together with FLORENCE KELLEY and others, Wald founded the National Child Labor Committee in 1904 to campaign against child labor. In 1908 she joined several reformers in founding the National Association for the Advancement of Colored People (NAACP). That same year she worked on the New York Commission on Immigration, begun at her suggestion to investigate immigrant living and working conditions. In addition she supported the women's suffrage movement and campaigned for a suffrage law in New York.

About peace, Lillian Wald once said, "Women have a message to deliver, and because they are unfettered by custom and expediency, they can point out the hollowness of the appeals by which men have been stirred to battle." *(Library of Congress)*

A lifelong pacifist, Wald reacted to the outbreak of World War I in 1914 by joining Florence Kelley and JANE ADDAMS in founding the American Union Against Militarism, a group that sought to end the war through mediation. She thought women better able than men to effect peace in the world. "Women have a message to deliver," she said, "and because they are unfettered by custom and expediency, they can point out the hollowness of the appeals by which men have been stirred to battle." Nevertheless, the United States entered the war in 1917, and she headed a committee on home nursing formed by the Council of National Defense. In 1918 she coordinated several nursing agencies to counter an influenza epidemic.

Wald supported President Franklin Roosevelt's New Deal program during the Great Depression of the 1930s, but poor health limited her activities. In 1933 she resigned as head worker of the Henry Street Settlement and moved to Westport, Connecticut, where she wrote *Windows on Henry Street* to complement *The House on Henry Street,* which she had published in 1915.

Lillian Wald died on September 1, 1940, and was buried in Rochester, New York. In the year 2002 the Henry Street Settlement continued to help immigrants on New York City's Lower East Side. "Without claiming the gift of prophecy," Wald once said, "one can foresee that our sins, political and social, must recoil upon the heads of our descendants. We commit ourselves to any wrong or degradation or injury when we do not protest against it."

Further Reading

Buhler-Wilkerson, Karen. "Bringing Care to the People: Lillian Wald's Legacy to Public Health Nursing." *The American Journal of Public Health* 83 (December 1993): 1778 +.

Coss, Clare, ed. *Lillian D. Wald, Progressive Activist.* New York: Feminist Press, 1989.

Daniels, Doris. *Always a Sister: The Feminism of Lillian D. Wald.* New York: Feminist Press, 1989.

Walker, David
(1785–1830) *abolitionist, civil rights advocate*

David Walker was an abolitionist and civil rights advocate. He was born on September 28, 1785, in Wilmington, North Carolina, to a slave father and a free mother. Because of the status of his mother, he was legally free.

As Walker traveled extensively through the South in his youth, slavery and the racial prejudice exhibited by whites angered him. In the 1820s he moved to Boston, where he escaped the slave environment but found racial segregation firmly entrenched.

In that city Walker opened a secondhand clothing store and joined the fight to abolish slavery and win black civil rights when he became a member of the Massachusetts General Colored Association. In 1828 he made a speech to that group, and in 1829 he published a 76-page pamphlet, *Walker's Appeal.*

Walker held nothing back in his revolutionary demand. The *Appeal* boldly condemned slavery and called for slaves to rebel. Walker believed that slavery was so evil and oppressive that whatever violence it might take to end it was justified. Many whites and blacks criticized his radicalism, but he printed two more editions of his *Appeal* in 1830, the third more militant than the first.

When at one point friends suggested to Walker that for his own safety he should flee to Canada, he reportedly said, "I will stand my ground. *Somebody must die in this cause.* I may be doomed to the stake and to the fire, or to the scaffold tree, but it is not in me to falter if I can promote the work of emancipation."

Walker began his *Appeal* by declaring, "We (coloured people of these United States,) are the most degraded, wretched, and abject set of beings that ever lived since the world began." To slavery, he said, whites have added complete humiliation. Walker asked, "Have they not, after having reduced us to the deplorable condition of slaves under their feet, held us up as descending originally from the tribes of *Monkeys* or *Orang-Outangs* [sic]?"

The American Revolution, Walker insisted, had done nothing for blacks. "I must observe . . . that at the close of the first Revolution in this country with Great Britain, there were but thirteen States in the Union, now there are twenty-four, most of which are slave-holding States, and the whites are dragging us around in chains and in handcuffs to their new States and Territories to work their mines and farms."

Whites, he said, must awaken to the libertarian principles of the American Revolution and to their hypocrisy.

> See your Declaration Americans!!! Do you understand your own language? Hear your language, proclaimed to the world, July 4th, 1776—"We hold these truths to be self evident—that ALL MEN ARE CREATED EQUAL!! That they *are endowed by their Creator with certain unalienable rights;* that among these are life, *liberty,* and the pursuit of happiness!!" Compare your own language above . . . with your cruelties and murders inflicted by your cruel and unmerciful fathers and [by] yourselves on our fathers and on us.

Walker saw to it that his *Appeal* reached the South. He may have sewn copies of it into the lining of sailors' clothing that he distributed at his store with the intent that it be circulated below the Mason-Dixon line. Whatever the case, the *Appeal* was found in several southern states. The Georgia legislature quickly passed a law making it a capital offense to circulate material intended to incite slaves, and elsewhere in the South a price was put on Walker's head.

Walker, who had been married in 1828 (the couple had one child), died on June 28, 1830, in Boston. Some contemporaries said he was poisoned by his enemies, but no objective evidence has been found to support that charge.

Further Reading

Hinks, Peter P. *To Awaken My Afflicted Brethren: David Walker and the Problem of Antebellum Slave Resistance.* University Park: Pennsylvania State University Press, 1997.

Walling, William English
(1877–1936) *socialist*

A socialist, William English Walling was a founder of the National Association for the Advancement of Colored People (NAACP). He was born on March 14, 1877, in Louisville, Kentucky, to Willoughby Walling, a wealthy physician and diplomat, and Rosalind English Walling.

William English Walling earned a B.S. from the University of Chicago in 1897 and used his family's wealth to engage in reform. Influenced by Progressives, who sought to eliminate social ills, in the early 1900s he moved to New York City and lived on the Lower East Side at a settlement house, which had been founded to provide social services to poor immigrants. At the same time he became involved in the labor movement, and in 1903 he joined JANE ADDAMS and others in beginning the National Women's Trade Union League.

Walling witnessed a race riot in Springfield, Illinois, in 1908, whereupon he wrote two articles about relations between whites and blacks in the North. Published in the *Independent,* they were read by a social worker, Mary White Ovington, who as a result advocated forming an organization to fight for African-American rights. Walling responded to the idea by offering to gather several reformers together, and in 1910 they founded the NAACP, with Walling its first chair. Walling recruited black activist W. E. B. DU BOIS to edit the NAACP's publication, *The Crisis.*

Walling had earlier adopted socialism as his political philosophy, and in 1910 he joined the Socialist Party. He published *Socialism As It Is* in 1912 and *Larger Aspects of Socialism* in 1913. In those books he insisted that reform must do more than change immediate conditions: It must prepare people to embrace socialism.

But Walling broke with the Socialist Party when it opposed America's entry into World War I. He also disliked the turn taken by the Russian Revolution with the establishment of a totalitarian government.

In the 1920s Walling worked for the American Federation of Labor and wrote articles for its journal, the *American Federationist.* He ran for Congress from Connecticut in 1924 on the Democratic and Progressive tickets, but he lost.

During the 1930s he made several trips to Europe to organize workers there against fascism. On one such trip he died in Amsterdam on September 12, 1936.

Further Reading

Boylan, James R. *Revolutionary Lives: Anna Strunsky and William English Walling.* Amherst: University of Massachusetts Press, 1998.

Stuart, Jack. "A Note on William English Walling and His 'Cousin,' W.E.B. Du Bois." *The Journal of Negro History* 82 (Spring 1997): 270+.

Washington, Booker Taliaferro
(1856–1915) *civil rights activist*

The most powerful African-American leader of the early 1900s, Booker Taliaferro Washington advocated vocational training for blacks, but he compromised so extensively with whites that later generations, especially radicals in the 1960s, derided him as an "Uncle Tom." Washington was born into slavery on April 5, 1856, on a farm near Hale's Ford, Virginia. His mother was Jane Ferguson, a slave owned by James Burroughs; his father was a white man whose name is unknown.

The end of the Civil War in 1865 left Washington free but penniless. To make money he worked alongside his stepfather, Washington Ferguson, in the salt and coal mines in Malden, West Virginia. The long hours on the job left him with little opportunity to obtain an education, but for a brief period he was able to attend school part-time. Booker recalled in his autobiography, *The Story of My Life and Work* (1900), that he first took the surname Washington when he entered school and the teacher asked him who he was; like many former slaves he had no last name, so thinking quickly he adopted that of America's first president.

While still in his teens Washington served as a house servant for Lewis Ruffner. He later credited Ruffner and his wife, Viola, with teaching him to be clean and orderly. He thought those traits were essential to his advancement, and he embraced values that white middle-class society considered important. Washington always looked up to the Ruffners, and later historians claimed that he had the same attitude toward other wealthy whites.

In 1872 Washington entered Hampton Normal and Agricultural Institute in Hampton, Virginia, a school run by whites to educate former slaves largely in the vocational trades. The institute's principal, Samuel C. Armstrong, taught the pupils that since they were inferior to whites, they needed close supervision in learning tasks that would elevate them. He said that blacks should not agitate for civil rights; they would have such rights in time, he believed, when blacks had moved ahead economically and proved themselves worthy of full citizenship. Washington admired Armstrong and adopted his mentor's ideas.

Booker T. Washington graduated from Hampton Institute with honors in 1875 and for the next two years taught school in Malden. In 1878 he entered Wayland Seminary in Washington, D.C., with thoughts of becoming a minister, but he left after a few months to accept a teaching position at Hampton Institute. Although his stay in the nation's capital was brief, it was long enough to convince him that city life was sinful. Like whites in early America, he equated morality with an agricultural society of virtuous farmers who had small landholdings.

In 1881 Washington accepted the job as principal of a newly founded state school for blacks in Tuskegee, Alabama. He faced a considerable challenge: Many whites distrusted educating blacks; the school had no buildings; and it had little money. But he remembered what Armstrong had accomplished at Hampton Institute, and he set his sights on replicating the experience in Alabama, with one notable change: This would be a school for blacks run by blacks; it would be a school that had black, not white, administrators and teachers.

For money Washington turned primarily to the white community. And to allay fears that the school would teach blacks intellectual subjects, he reaffirmed his commitment to a largely vocational

Booker T. Washington was known as an "accommodationist" for his acceptance of racial segregation. *(Library of Congress)*

education. Boys would be taught manual labor so they could hold jobs as skilled carpenters, brick layers, and the like; they would also learn farming. Girls would learn cooking and sewing and other skills important to becoming good homemakers. Washington offered academic subjects—and trained some of his pupils to become teachers—but he always emphasized practical skills. Adopting what he had learned from the Ruffins, he also stressed cleanliness and orderly behavior.

In 1882 Washington married Fanny Norton Smith. They had one child, and Fanny died in 1884. One year later he married Olivia Davidson, and they had two sons. Three years after her death in 1889, he married Margaret James Murray. A graduate of all-black Fisk University in Nashville, Tennessee. She helped Washington at Tuskegee and assisted poor blacks in the surrounding community.

Booker T. Washington ran Tuskegee Institute with an iron hand; he allowed no dissent from his view about what was the proper education for blacks. Nor did he allow anyone to challenge his belief that blacks should forgo an immediate struggle for civil rights so they could obtain resources from whites that would allow them to advance economically.

He was, in short, an accommodationist, who wanted blacks to own their businesses and contribute to southern economic development but do nothing that would enflame racial relations with whites. Washington most eloquently expressed his view in his 1895 address to the Atlanta Exposition. Sometimes called the Atlanta Compromise for the concessions made to whites, the address certified his standing as the most prominent African-American leader. In support of vocational education, he said, "Our greatest danger is that in the great leap from slavery to freedom we may overlook the fact that the masses of us are to live by the productions of our hands, and fail to keep in mind that we shall prosper in proportion as we learn to dignify and glory common labour."

He asked whites to recognize the importance of black workers and to turn to them for southern economic development:

> To those of the white race who look to the in-coming of those of foreign birth . . . for the

prosperity of the South, were I permitted I would repeat what I say to my own race, "Cast down your bucket where you are." Cast it down among the eight millions of Negroes whose habits you know, whose fidelity and love you have tested in days when to have proved treacherous meant the ruin of your firesides.

And he assured whites that blacks would refrain from demanding their civil rights when he said in two famous statements:

> The wisest among my race understand that the agitation of questions of social equality is the extremist folly, and that progress in the enjoyment of all the privileges that will come to us must be the result of severe and constant struggle rather than artificial forcing.
>
> In all things that are purely social we can be as separate as the fingers, yet one as the hand in all things essential to mutual progress.

Washington developed the Tuskegee Machine, a powerful organization that wielded influence among whites to the point that it determined which black schools received charitable contributions. In keeping with Washington's desire for control, most moneys went to those who adhered to his ideas about vocational training. He wielded enormous influence in the White House, and through his close relations with presidents he determined which blacks would receive patronage appointments. In 1901 he dined at the executive mansion with President Theodore Roosevelt.

Several prominent blacks disagreed with Washington's ideas. W. E. B. DU BOIS, for one, accused him of behaving obsequiously with whites and of selling out to them. He demanded immediate equal rights for African Americans. Washington reacted by trying to destroy Du Bois's Niagara Movement and the biracial National Association for the Advancement of Colored People (NAACP), founded in 1909 to advance civil rights through legal action.

Washington's autobiographies, *The Story of My Life and Work* and *Up from Slavery* (1901), the first one largely ghost-written, extolled the self-made man and made it clear that blacks should work hard and get help from whites. Near the end of his life Washington began to change his unquestioning faith in such mainstream values and criticized the denial of voting rights to blacks. But by and large as the civil rights movement advanced, it left his ideas behind.

In October 1915 Booker T. Washington collapsed from overwork and nervous exhaustion. He had tried to control everything in his life and delegated little; now he had overexerted himself. He died on November 14, 1915, at Tuskegee.

Further Reading

Harlan, Louis R. *Booker T. Washington: The Making of a Black Leader, 1856–1901.* New York: Oxford University Press, 1972.

————. *Booker T. Washington: The Wizard of Tuskegee, 1901–1915.* New York: Oxford University Press, 1983.

Verney, Kevern. *The Art of the Possible: Booker T. Washington and Black Leadership in the United States, 1881–1925.* New York: Routledge, 2001.

Wattleton, Alyce Faye
(1943–) *women's rights activist*

Faye Wattleton was the first African-American president of the Planned Parenthood Federation of America (an organization made prominent by ALAN FRANK GUTTMACHER). She was born Alyce Faye Wattleton on July 8, 1943, in Saint Louis, Missouri, to George Wattleton and Ozie Garret Wattleton.

Because her mother was a preacher at the Church of God, Faye Wattleton was raised in an evangelical family. She attended Ohio State University in Columbus, where she studied nursing while earning money for school by working at a children's hospital. She graduated with a nursing degree in 1964 and in 1967 earned a master's degree in maternal and infant health care from Columbia University in New York City. She then became an instructor at the Miami School of Nursing in Dayton, Ohio, and until 1970 served as assistant director of nursing for the county public health district.

In her work Wattleton had contact with women and girls who suffered from unwanted pregnancies and illegal abortions. In 1970 she was named executive director of Dayton's Planned Parenthood Association and emerged as a leader in the fight to legalize abortion. Some fellow African Americans criticized her stand as one that would lower the birth rate among blacks and thus weaken the race. She refuted the charges, however, insisting that she was pro-choice, not proabortion, and that she was primarily concerned with the quality of life for children.

The Supreme Court supported women's right to abortion in the 1973 case *Roe v. Wade,* and Wattleton worked to prevent pro-life groups from overturning the decision. In 1978 she became president of the Planned Parenthood Federation of America, the first woman and the first black person to hold the office. She effectively solicited contributions and in the 1980s successfully lobbied the U.S. Senate to reject President Ronald Reagan's effort to turn family planning funding over to the states. When pro-life protesters picketed abortion clinics and even blocked the entranceways, Wattleton demanded that the federal government protect Planned Parenthood in its work at the facilities. The showdown with the pro-lifers became so intense that she began receiving hate mail and death threats.

Despite her courageous attachment to principles, some within Planned Parenthood thought that Wattleton had politicized the organization and had gone too far in her pro-choice crusade. They wanted Planned Parenthood to promote family planning by emphasizing contraceptive services and education.

Wattleton resigned as president of Planned Parenthood in 1992, saying the organization needed "fresh leadership." She then moved to Chicago and began hosting a syndicated television talk show. In 1996 she wrote a history of the Planned Parenthood Federation, *Life on the Line.* Married and divorced, she had one daughter.

Further Reading

"Faye Wattleton Preaches to the Choir." *Time* 148, no. 17 (1996): 99.

Wattleton, Faye. *Life on the Line.* New York: Ballantine, 1996.

Wayland, J. A.
(Julius Augustus Wayland)
(1854–1912) *publisher, socialist*

J. A. Wayland was a promoter of homespun socialism, or what he called "One-Hoss Philosophy." He was born Julius Augustus Wayland on April 26, 1854, in Versailles, Indiana, to John Wayland, a grocer, and Micha Wayland.

J. A. received less than two years of schooling and in his youth held several odd jobs. At age 16 he entered the publishing business as a printer's apprentice for the *Versailles Gazette.* Enamored of the newspaper world, he owned the *Versailles Index,* which he later renamed the *Ripley Index,* at age 19. Over the next decade he bought and sold several small-town newspapers, moving as he did so, and in the early 1880s he settled in Pueblo, Colorado.

Wayland had been conservative in outlook, but his proximity to the Rocky Mountain mining strikes of the 1880s and 1890s and his reading of radical pamphlets converted him first to Populism and then to socialism. Beginning with his publication of the Populist *Coming Crisis* in 1892, he applied money that he had made through real estate ventures to the printing of radical newspapers.

J. A. never developed a socialist philosophy; rather, he promoted his "One-Hoss Philosophy" through folk stories and homilies. His writing appealed to many laborers because it was clear and direct. His biographer, Elliot Shore, in *Talkin' Socialism: J. A. Wayland and the Radical Press* (1988), notes the following examples of Wayland's style:

> You can hire two men one day for two dollars now. Formerly you could hire but one man one day for two dollars. Are men depreciating? Socialism means social harmony—and perfect social harmony means the millennium. There are many who pray for the Millennium, for "on earth as it is in heaven"—who do all they can to prevent its being realized. They are not intentionally bad or hypocritical—they are simply ignorant of what it takes to have the prayer realized.

Wayland thought he knew what it took when he began a national newspaper, the *Coming Nation,* to popularize his views and in 1894 founded a "Co-operative Town," Ruskin, in Tennessee. "[It] will be the charter members," Wayland said, "who will proceed to organize the colony on such a basis of equality as in their judgment will produce justice." He dissociated himself from the town in 1895, however, and it soon failed, beleaguered by the country's economic depression and disputes between Wayland and the settlers.

In 1895 Wayland began the *Appeal to Reason,* called by Elliot Shore "the newspaper that would become the largest-circulation socialist publication in American history." Socialist leader EUGENE VICTOR DEBS worked for the *Appeal,* which serialized UPTON SINCLAIR's work *The Jungle.*

Three years after Wayland's first wife died in 1898, he married Pearl Hunt. They had no children. Her death in 1911 caused him to turn over daily supervision of the *Appeal* to Fred Warren, his editor in chief. Wayland supported Debs for president in 1912; on November 11 of that year, just days after Debs lost the election, Wayland committed suicide.

Further Reading
Brundage, W. Fitzhugh. *A Socialist Utopia in the New South: The Ruskin Colonies of Tennessee and Georgia, 1894–1901.* Urbana: University of Illinois Press, 1996.

Shore, Elliott. *Talkin' Socialism: J. A. Wayland and the Radical Press.* Lawrence: University Press of Kansas, 1988.

Welch, Robert Henry Winborne, Jr.
(1899–1985) *conservative reformer*

Robert Henry Winborne Welch, Jr., founded the radical right-wing John Birch Society. He was born on December 1, 1899, near Chowan, North Carolina, to Robert Welch, Sr., a cotton farmer, and Lina Welch, a former schoolteacher.

Early on, Robert Welch exhibited a precocious intellect: He learned to read when he was three years old, knew basic algebra at age six, and received his high school diploma at age 12. He entered the University of North Carolina at Chapel Hill in 1912 and graduated in the top third of his class in 1916. Then began a period of searching and dissatisfaction. He enrolled in the university's graduate school but stayed only a few months; he worked as a clerk and then in 1917 received an appointment to the U.S. Naval Academy, but he left there two years later; he tried writing a newspaper column, but that failed; and in 1921 he entered Harvard Law School, only to drop out, saying he was disillusioned with academia.

Welch then entered the candy business in 1921 by buying a fudge recipe from a candy store owner and beginning the Oxford Candy Company, which he operated from a loft in Cambridge, Massachusetts. The business was moderately successful until the Great Depression ruined it. Meanwhile, in 1922 he had married Marian Lucille Probert; they had two sons.

In 1932 Welch joined the staff of the country's largest candy manufacturer, E. J. Brach. Two years later he quit to become sales manager and vice president of his brother's candy business, the James O. Welch Company. Under his guidance the company's sales increased from $20,000 in 1935 to $20 million in 1956.

During that span of time Welch wrote *The Road to Salesmanship* (1941), and on a visit to England he studied and criticized socialism. With the advent of the cold war his conservatism hardened, and he made his only run for public office in 1950 when he campaigned in Massachusetts as a Republican for lieutenant governor. He attracted a sizable vote but was defeated.

In 1952 Welch joined the campaign of Ohio senator Robert A. Taft for president, but Taft lost the Republican nomination to Gen. Dwight D. Eisenhower. That year Welch wrote *May God Forgive Us,* a searing criticism of President Harry Truman's decision to dismiss General Douglas MacArthur from his command of United Nations forces in Korea.

Disheartened and angered by the Communist advances in China and Eastern Europe, Welch blamed the reverses on traitors operating within the United States. In 1954 he wrote *The Life of John Birch,* a patriotic story whose title referred to an American military intelligence officer who had been killed by the Chinese Communists just 10 days after World War II had ended. Welch portrayed him as "the first casualty of World War III."

To fight communism full-time Welch retired from the candy business in 1958, and at a meeting in Indianapolis, Indiana, he and 11 other men founded the John Birch Society, named after the intelligence officer and dedicated to "less government, more individual responsibility, and a better world." Welch once said that all Americans fell into one of four categories: "Communists, Communist dupes or sympathizers, the uniformed who have yet to be awakened to the Communist danger, and the ignorant."

The many accusations he made in the late 1950s and early 1960s fit his crimped view. He called President Dwight Eisenhower "a dedicated conscious agent of the Communist conspiracy," and said about the president's brother, Milton Eisenhower, that "the chances are very strong that [he] is actually Dwight Eisenhower's superior boss within the Communist Party." He called Secretary of State John Foster Dulles and Central Intelligence Agency (CIA) director Allen W. Dulles "tools of Communism."

Welch opposed civil rights programs, calling them a communist plot, and for the same reason he wanted the Supreme Court's decisions ending racial segregation in public schools to be overturned by a constitutional amendment. The John Birch Society paid for billboards that claimed to show the civil rights leader MARTIN LUTHER KING, JR., at a communist training school. Welch also wanted the United States to withdraw from the North Atlantic Treaty Organization and the United Nations. In 1960 he claimed in his monthly magazine *American Opinion* that 40 to 60 percent of the United States was under communist control.

The influence of the John Birch Society peaked in the mid-1960s. At that time the organization had upward of 85,000 to 100,000 members in some 4,000 chapters. It had 270 employees at its headquarters in Belmont, Massachusetts, and an annual budget in the range of $5 million to $8 million. It had also a publishing house, a radio program, and 400 bookstores. In 1964 it gained entry into the inner circles of the Republican Party with the nomination of the archconservative Barry Goldwater for president.

But a reaction against Welch and the Birch society set in as his views about Eisenhower and other people and events became more widely known. His ideas were called extreme, even lunatic; as a result he was deserted by most conservative Republicans—despite his right-wing views—partly out of fear that they, too, would come across as extremists and partly out of revulsion to his smear tactics.

Welch tried at one point to modify his assessment of Eisenhower, claiming that he never called him a communist, but only a dupe of the communists. Yet his conspiracy theories continued to run rampant; in the November 1966 issue of *American Opinion* he claimed that the communist conspiracy was part of a 200-year-old plot by a secret group, called the Illuminati, to rule the world.

Robert Welch died on January 6, 1985, in Winchester, Massachusetts. "It is my fervent hope," he once wrote, "that the John Birch Society will last for hundreds of years and exert an increasing influence for the temporal good and spiritual ennoblement of mankind throughout centuries."

Further Reading

Griffin, G. Edward. *The Life and Words of Robert Welch, Founder of the John Birch Society.* Thousand Oaks, Calif.: American Media, 1975.

Morganthau, Tom. "The Birchers After Welch." *Newsweek,* January 21, 1985, 38.

The Scribner Encyclopedia of American Lives. New York: Charles Scribner's Sons, 1998.

Weld, Theodore Dwight

(1803–1895) *abolitionist, women's rights activist*

Theodore Dwight Weld converted to revivalism in his 20s and became what one historian has described as the leading light of the evangelical wing of the antislavery movement. He was born in Hampton, Connecticut, on November 23, 1803, to Ludovicus Weld and Elizabeth Clark Weld.

Weld grew up in a religious family; his father, a Congregationalist minister, expected his son to enter the ministry. In attempting to meet that expectation, Weld enrolled at Andover Seminary in 1819, but suffering from exhaustion, he quit one year later. His serious and humorless manner bespoke an intensity that at times overwhelmed him and contributed to various physical ailments.

Over the next few years Weld honed his skill as an orator on a variety of topics and earned a reputation for his persuasive style. In 1825 he experienced a religious conversion after listening to the preaching of Charles G. Finney, a former lawyer committed to spreading the gospel. Weld rejected religious doctrine in favor of an emotional inner experience; he once advised an acquaintance "to direct communion with God" by aligning his spirit "with infinite purity and love." Soon after Weld converted he crusaded against alcohol as Finney's lay speaker, spreading the temperance message throughout western New York state. In that role he resembled many other future abolitionists, for the antislavery movement saw drunkenness as part of the immorality that allowed slavery to exist, demeaning individuals and promoting debauchery in the lives of both whites and blacks.

Weld studied for the ministry at Oneida Institute in Whitesboro, New York, while still involved in his temperance speech making, and as he delved deeper into the issue of moral values he began to question the practice of slavery. In 1831 supporters of WILLIAM LLOYD GARRISON, an immediatist who demanded that human bondage be ended without delay, drew Weld into the abolitionist movement.

Weld then obtained money from two wealthy merchants, ARTHUR TAPPAN and LEWIS TAPPAN, to support a seminary. The Tappans were known for their backing of numerous religious and reform causes and were allied with Finney. On Weld's recommendation, the Tappans funded the struggling Lane Seminary in Cincinnati, Ohio. Weld studied at the seminary and organized the Lane Debate, which over several days promoted the abolitionist crusade. The debate ended with the students supporting abolition, siding against those who said that once blacks were freed they must be colonized overseas, and forming an antislavery society along with programs to help Cincinnati's black community.

The trustees at Lane reacted negatively to Weld's efforts. In 1834 they formally declared that "education must be completed before the young are fitted to engage in the collisions of active life," and they ordered an end to the reform activities. Many of the students at Lane, however, were more than 26 years of age and unwilling to be prevented from participating in society at large. Weld subsequently convinced more than 40 students at the seminary to quit their studies. A number of them transferred to Oberlin College, located in Oberlin, Ohio, another school that had been founded in part by the Tappans.

Weld left Lane and became a speaker for the American Anti-Slavery Society. Through his powerful oratory he attracted a devout following, but he risked retribution for his abolitionist beliefs. His speeches often excited those Northerners who thought the antislavery crusaders nothing more than agitators bent on causing sectional warfare. Weld was attacked several times by angry mobs. One contemporary said that he "held increasing audiences at a fever pitch, with his flashing eye, his clarion tones and marvellous eloquence, without manuscript or note."

With such intense exertion Weld's voice gave out from strain in 1837, so he recruited antislavery speakers to pick up the torch and while doing so met SARAH MOORE GRIMKÉ and ANGELINA MOORE GRIMKÉ, sisters from a slaveholding family in South Carolina. They had become abolitionists and women's rights advocates. Weld married Angelina in 1838 and supported the women's rights movement, though he worried it might take energy away from abolitionism and divide abolitionists over the issue of women's status within reform organizations and society as a whole. (On the last point, at least, he was right: Abolitionists debated fiercely among themselves whether women should have a leadership role in their crusade.)

In 1839 Weld published *Slavery As It Is*, which presented contemporary descriptions of slave life in the South. It soon became the most popular of all the antislavery tracts and provided material for Harriet Beecher Stowe in the writing of her novel, *Uncle Tom's Cabin*. In the introduction to *Slavery As It Is*, Weld stated:

It is no marvel that slaveholders are always talking of their *kind treatment* of their slaves. The only marvel is, that men of sense can be gulled by such professions. Despots always insist that they are merciful.

He portrayed slavery starkly:

We will prove that the slaves in the United States are treated with barbarous inhumanity; that they are overworked, underfed, wretchedly clad and lodged, and have insufficient sleep; that they are often made to wear round their necks iron collars armed with prongs, to drag heavy chains and weights at their feet while working in the field, and to wear yokes, and bells, and iron horns; that they are often kept confined in the stocks day and night for weeks together, made to wear gags in their mouths for hours or days, have some of their front teeth torn out or broken off, that they may be easily detected when they run away; that they are frequently flogged with terrible severity, have red pepper rubbed in their lacerated flesh, and hot brine . . . poured over their gashes to increase the torture; that they are often stripped naked, their backs and limbs cut with knives, bruised and mangled by scores and hundreds of blows with the paddle . . . that they are often suspended by the arms and whipped and beaten till they faint, and when revived by restoratives, beaten again till they faint, and sometimes till they die; that their ears are often cut off, their eyes knocked out, their bones broken, their flesh branded with red hot irons, that they are maimed, mutilated and burned to death over slow fires.

One of the accounts presented by Weld told about the torture applied by the claws of cats:

The cat, which as a large gray tomcat, was then taken by [a] well-dressed gentleman, and placed upon the bare back of the prostrate black man, near the shoulders and forcibly dragged by the tail down the back, and along the bare thighs of the sufferer. The cat sunk his nails into the flesh, and tore off pieces of the skin with his teeth. The man roared with pain of the punishment, and would have rolled along the ground had he not have been held in his place by the force of four other slaves, each of whom confined a hand or a foot.

For Weld slavery was always more than an economic issue: It was a moral one. And it reached beyond the boundaries of slavery itself; it angered him and other abolitionists because it promoted the domination of one human being over another. He believed that such domination, in any guise, led to cruelty and abuse.

From 1841 to 1844 Weld helped those congressmen, among them John Quincy Adams, who were fighting against the gag rule, which prohibited the House of Representatives from considering any petitions dealing with slavery. In 1841 he wrote to a friend about his work: "[The congressmen] have little leisure for gathering materials, [and] request me to spend the winter here and aid them in the matter."

Before long, though, Weld retreated from the abolitionist movement; with his marriage to Angelina he had a family to care for; he also had tired of the public fight and was engaged in an inner religious and spiritual quest. William Lloyd Garrison lamented in 1842: "Where is Theodore D. Weld and his wife, and Sarah M. Grimké? All 'in the quiet' and far removed from all strife! . . . Once the land was shaken by their free spirits, but now they are neither seen nor felt."

Weld worked his farm in Belleville, New Jersey, and then became a director of a school there. From 1854 to 1862 he headed a racially integrated school at Perth Amboy, New Jersey. Many of the students were the children of his fellow abolitionists. He moved to Fairmont (later renamed Hyde Park) near Boston in 1862, where he taught English at a girls' school. During the Civil War he spoke in support of the Union. When the war ended he participated in women's suffrage protests, and in yet another reform campaign he defended full access for the public to controversial books.

Weld died on February 3, 1895, having outlived many of his comrades in reform, including his wife, Angelina Grimké; her sister, Sarah Grimké; and William Lloyd Garrison. His passion for the antislavery cause assured his place with them as a great abolitionist crusader.

Further Reading

Abzug, Robert H. *Passionate Liberator: Theodore Dwight Weld and the Dilemma of Reform.* New York: Oxford University Press, 1980.

Thomas, Benjamin Platt. *Theodore Weld: Crusader for Freedom.* New Brunswick, N.J.: Rutgers University Press, 1950.

Wells-Barnett, Ida Bell
(1862–1931) *civil rights activist*

An antilynching crusader and founder of the black women's club movement, Ida Bell Wells-Barnett was a militant in the fight for civil rights. She was born on July 16, 1862, a slave in Holly Springs, Mississippi, to James Wells and Elizabeth Bell Wells.

When Ida Wells was only three years old the Civil War ended and the Thirteenth Amendment abolished slavery (though Mississippi did not ratify it until more than a century later). She attended Rust College, a school started by northern Methodist missionaries in her hometown to provide former slaves with an education at all grade levels. Tragedy struck, however, in 1878, when a yellow fever epidemic killed her parents and her younger brother. At the age of 16 she was forced to take care of her remaining brothers and sisters, so she began teaching in a one-room schoolhouse in Holly Springs.

In 1884 Wells moved to Memphis, Tennessee, to be close to her relatives and to obtain a higher-paying teaching job. Her activism for black civil rights began later that year when she was forced to leave a car reserved for white passengers aboard the Chesapeake, Ohio, and Southwestern Railroad Company. She sued the company for its failure to provide her with the first-class accommodations she had paid for, and she won her case, only to have the decision overturned in 1887 by the Tennessee Supreme Court. The reversal disappointed and angered her, and she complained about the inability of blacks to obtain justice.

That same year Wells wrote an article about her experience with the railroad for *Living Way,* a weekly church publication. The favorable reaction to it caused her to write additional articles while continuing her teaching, She soon received the nickname "Princess of the Press" and became part owner and editor of the *Memphis Free Speech and Headlight,* a militant black newspaper.

In 1891 she reacted to the lynching of a black man in Georgetown, Kentucky, by writing that African Americans should retaliate with violence against such outrages. She also criticized the Memphis School Board for its meager funding of black schools, and the board reacted in 1891 by firing her from her teaching job.

Wells then devoted herself full-time to journalism. But in 1892 whites again acted to silence her. After three Memphis black men accused of rioting were hauled from their jail cell and killed, she wrote strongly worded editorials condemning the action, and lynchings in general, and ridiculing the notion that black men were prone to rape white women; consequently, while she was away in Philadelphia a mob destroyed the *Free Speech* press and offices on May 27, and she was warned to stay away from Memphis.

The violence caused Wells to move to New York City, where she became a columnist for *New York Age.* Her articles about lynching served as the basis for her booklet *Southern Horrors,* published in 1892, which was widely circulated and gained national attention.

In it she wrote that the example set by the South of lynching blacks was causing the practice to spread elsewhere. "The result is a growing disregard of human life," she said. "Lynch Law has spread its insidious influence till men in New York State, Pennsylvania and on the free Western plains feel they can take the law in their own hands with impunity, especially where an Afro-American is concerned." She called for blacks to stand up for themselves: "The Afro-American can do for himself what no one else can do for him," she said. "The world looks on with wonder that we have conceded so much, and remain law-abiding under such great outrage and provocation."

Where segregation existed, she wrote, blacks should stage boycotts against white businesses. And to protect themselves against lynch mobs blacks should go further:

Of the many inhuman outrages of this present year, the only case where the proposed lynch-

Ida B. Wells took the controversial stand that blacks should arm themselves with rifles for self-defense against white lynch mobs. *(Library of Congress)*

ing did *not* occur, was where the men armed themselves in Jacksonville, Florida, and Paducah, Kentucky, and prevented it. The only time an Afro-American who was assaulted got away has been when he had a gun, and used it in self-defence. The lesson this teaches, and which every Afro-American should ponder well, is that a Winchester rifle should have a place of honour in every black home, and that it should be used for that protection which the law refuses to give. When the white man, who is always the aggressor, knows he runs a great risk of biting the dust every time his Afro-American victim does, he will have greater respect for Afro-American life. The more the Afro-American yields and cringes and begs, the more he has to do so, the more he is insulted, outraged, and lynched.

Wells began lecturing against lynchings and helped found antilynching societies. In 1893 and again in 1894 she traveled to Britain and rallied public opinion there against racial segregation in the United States.

Wells was instrumental in forming black women's clubs so that women could become more involved in local and national issues. One that she organized in Chicago in 1893 was called the Ida B. Wells Club.

That year she moved to Chicago and began working for the city's first black newspaper, the *Chicago Conservator*. In 1895 she married the newspaper's founder, Ferdinand Lee Barnett, and although for the next several years she spent much of her time raising their four children, she continued to lecture and remained active with the Ida B. Wells Club as its president. Through the club she founded a kindergarten for African-American children.

In 1909 Wells-Barnett helped found the National Association for the Advancement of Colored People (NAACP) and served on its executive committee. In an ongoing dispute between BOOKER TALIAFERRO WASHINGTON, who sought accommodation and compromise with whites, and W. E. B. DU BOIS, who favored a militant stand toward whites and demanded equal rights immediately, Wells-Barnett sided with Du Bois. She backed the idea for *The Crisis*, a magazine to be published by the NAACP and edited by Du Bois.

Yet shortly afterward she split with the NAACP over what she considered to be its excessively conservative approach to civil rights. In 1910 she helped found the Negro Fellowship League, which established a settlement house in Chicago to provide shelter and guidance to blacks who had recently moved to the city from the South.

Also active in the women's suffrage movement, Wells founded the first black woman suffrage association, the Alpha Club of Chicago, in 1913. In 1924 she ran for president of the National Association of Colored Women but lost to MARY MCLEOD BETHUNE. Six years later she ran for the state senate but lost that race, too.

Ida Wells-Barnett died on March 25, 1931, in Chicago of kidney disease. In 1990 the United States Postal Service honored her with a stamp issued during Black History Month.

Further Reading

Duster, Alfreda M., ed. *Crusader for Justice: The Autobiography of Ida B. Wells.* Chicago: University of Chicago Press, 1970.

Royster, Jacqueline Jones, ed. *Southern Horrors and Other Writings: The Anti-Lynching Campaign of Ida B. Wells, 1892–1900.* Boston: Bedford Books, 1997.

Thompson, Mildred. *Ida B. Wells-Barnett: An Exploratory Story of an American Black Woman, 1893–1930.* Brooklyn, N.Y.: Carlson Publishing, 1990.

Wheeler, Wayne Bidwell
(1869–1927) *prohibitionist*

Wayne Bidwell Wheeler was instrumental in persuading the states to ratify a prohibition amendment. He was born on November 10, 1869, near Brookfield, Ohio, to Joseph Wheeler, a farmer and stockbroker, and Ursula Hutchinson Wheeler.

In his boyhood Wayne Wheeler worked long hours on his family's farm, but he also wanted to advance his education, so he earned money by teaching school and then entered Oberlin College in Ohio. He received a B.A. from that school in 1894.

It was at Oberlin that the spirit of reform attracted him, and during his junior year he spoke in favor of prohibition at the annual NEAL DOW celebration. Wheeler later recollected that Oberlin was a "hotbed of temperance people." While still a student he had come into contact with the recently organized Anti-Saloon League, and then he became a manager for its Dayton district.

Seeing that the league needed legal help, he studied law under an attorney in Cleveland, and from 1895 to 1898 he attended law school at Ohio's Western Reserve University. Degree in hand, he was named the league's legislative secretary. In 1901 he married Ella Belle Candy; they had three sons.

In 1904 Wheeler became the league's superintendent for all of Ohio. He was appointed general counsel for the national organization in 1915 and moved to Washington, D.C., to carry out his duties.

Wheeler had little patience for educating the public about the evils of drink. He instead favored moving quickly to enact legislation and punishing people for their transgressions. To many outside the movement he stood for the intolerance and self-righteousness that characterized prohibitionists.

He helped to write state and national prohibition legislation; defended prohibition laws before state and federal courts, including the U.S. Supreme Court; and prosecuted more than 2,000 cases involving the laws. He played a leading role in convincing the navy in 1914 to prohibit alcohol on all of its ships and at all naval yards and stations. When Congress passed the Eighteenth Amendment making illegal "the manufacture, sale, or transportation of intoxicating liquors," Wheeler lobbied the states to ratify it, and they did, thus causing it to be added to the Constitution in January 1919.

Wayne Wheeler did not live to see the repeal of the amendment in 1933, though he did witness the widespread violations of the act during the 1920s and the waning of the prohibition movement. He died on September 5, 1927, just weeks after his wife had died in a fire at their home.

Further Reading

Hamm, Richard F. *Shaping the Eighteenth Amendment: Temperance Reform, Legal Culture, and the Polity, 1880–1920.* Chapel Hill: University of North Carolina Press, 1995.

Kerr, K. Austin. *Organized for Prohibition: A New History of the Anti-Saloon League.* New Haven Conn.: Yale University Press, 1985.

Steuart, Justin. *Wayne Wheeler, Dry Boss: An Uncensored Biography of Wayne B. Wheeler.* New York: Fleming H. Revell, 1928.

White, Walter Francis

(1893–1955) *civil rights leader*

An outspoken proponent of antilynching laws, Walter Francis White was an indefatigable speaker, writer, and leader of the National Association for the Advancement of Colored People (NAACP). He was born on July 1, 1893, in Atlanta, Georgia, the son of George White, a letter carrier, and Madeleine Harrison White.

Although a mulatto, Walter White looked white. He had blue eyes, blond hair, and fair skin.

He could have "passed" into white society, much as other persons with that appearance had previously. But he identified with the black community, especially after the vicious race riots of 1906 in Atlanta, when a white mob threatened his family's home and he and his father protected it.

Walter White graduated from Atlanta University in 1916 and joined the Standard Life Insurance Company as a clerk. His civil rights activism began that year when the Atlanta Board of Education announced that in addition to eliminating the eighth grade for black students, as it had already done, it was going to eliminate the seventh grade so it could fund a new high school for whites. Incensed by the plan, Walter White helped organize a protest and took the lead in founding a local branch of the NAACP. The school board subsequently backed away from its plan, and in 1918 White joined the NAACP national staff in New York City as its assistant secretary.

The lynching of a black man in East Springs, Tennessee, caused White to investigate that brutal act and other hangings. When traveling in the South he often posed as a white man to gather information from whites about their prejudices. That ruse, however, sometimes got him into trouble with both races. When whites found out about him in Alabama, they nearly lynched him. And when blacks in Chicago took him to be white, they nearly shot him to death.

In the years immediately after World War I and into the 1920s, White lectured extensively, traveling thousands of miles each year. He gained a reputation as an expert on lynchings and tried but failed to convince Congress to pass a bill making lynching a federal crime.

In 1924 White wrote *The Fire in Flint*, a highly acclaimed novel about an African-American doctor burned at the stake after being falsely accused of the rape of a white woman. He followed that book with a second novel, *Flight* (1926), and in 1927 received a Guggenheim Fellowship in creative writing. He intended to write a third novel but instead wrote *Rope and Faggot: A Biography of Judge Lynch* (1929), which discussed the reasons for the proliferation of lynchings.

White became acting secretary of the NAACP in 1929, and with all of his energy he set an exhausting pace. Writing in *W. E. B. Du Bois: The Fight for Equality and The American Century, 1919–1963* (2000), David Levering Lewis says, "The acting secretary not only seemed to confound the axiom barring simultaneous appearance in two places, he seemed literally everywhere at once in New York or Washington, buttonholing, lobbying, nightclubbing, and name-dropping." White mobilized the NAACP to fight against the confirmation of John J. Parker, President Herbert Hoover's nominee for the Supreme Court, who opposed African-American participation in politics. The nomination went down to defeat by a one-vote margin.

In 1931 White took over as NAACP executive secretary and again tried but failed to convince Congress to pass antilynching legislation.

Walter White was an outspoken proponent of antilynching laws and leader of the National Association for the Advancement of Colored People. *(National Archives and Records Administration, courtesy of the Harmon Foundation)*

Amid the Great Depression the NAACP faced a financial crisis, and many members blamed White and the group's president, JOEL ELIAS SPINGARN, for the reduction in staff that followed. That crisis, added to White's autocratic personality, caused a clash between White and the equally headstrong W. E. B. DU BOIS, editor of the NAACP's magazine, *The Crisis*. The two men disagreed as well on the issue of segregation when in the 1930s Du Bois increasingly called for blacks to build their own economic institutions independent of white institutions. The dispute with White caused Du Bois to quit the NAACP in 1934, though he returned for a short period in the 1940s.

Under White the NAACP pursued court cases against white primaries, poll taxes, and segregation in housing and education. He exerted considerable influence with Democratic presidents, and in 1941 he convinced Franklin D. Roosevelt to prohibit racial discrimination in defense industries and to establish the Fair Employment Practices Commission. At White's urging Harry Truman formed the President's Committee on Civil Rights, whose report led the Democratic Party to include a statement on the subject in its platform in 1948.

That same year White published his autobiography, *A Man Called White*. But he soon encountered more trouble within the NAACP. Many branch leaders disliked his centralization of power and claimed that the time he spent lecturing and writing limited the attention he focused on leading the organization. David Levering Lewis states that White was known for his "micromanagement," so extensive in its reach that years earlier the office secretary had complained that he "insisted on opening and reading every piece of correspondence himself." Adding to the controversy, in 1949 he had divorced his black wife, Leah Gladys Powell, whom he had married in 1922 and with whom he had two children, and married a white woman, Poppy Cannon, a writer and advertising executive.

Walter White continued to hold his post as executive secretary in the early 1950s, but the NAACP board limited his powers. He died of a heart attack on March 21, 1955.

Further Reading

Lewis, David Levering. *W. E. B. Du Bois: The Fight for Equality and the American Century, 1919–1963.* New York: Henry Holt, 2000.

Waldron, Edward E. *Walter White and the Harlem Renaissance.* Port Washington, N.Y.: Kennikat Press, 1978

Wilson, Sondra Kathryn, ed. *In Search of Democracy: The NAACP Writings of James Weldon Johnson, Walter White, and Roy Wilkins (1920–1977).* New York: Oxford University Press, 1999.

Wilkins, Roy
(1901–1981) *civil rights leader*

Roy Wilkins served as executive director of the National Association for the Advancement of Colored People (NAACP). He was born on August 30, 1901, in Saint Louis, Missouri, the son of William D. Wilkins, a porter, and Mayfield Edmondson Wilkins. His mother died in 1905, and Wilkins was sent by his father to Saint Paul, Minnesota, where he was raised by a maternal aunt, Emma Williams, and her husband, Samuel.

Despite Wilkins's upbringing in the North, he traced his roots to the South. "I was not born in Mississippi," he wrote in his autobiography, *Standing Fast* (1982), "but my story begins there all the same, deep in the rolling hill country." There his grandparents worked as slaves, and their parents as slaves, and so on, to the distant traces of the Atlantic slave trade. He wrote, "My ancestors from the third generation back are now as lost as any missing tribe of Israel." That heritage left a deep mark on him and stimulated his commitment to civil rights.

Wilkins attended the overwhelmingly white George Weitbreit Mechanical Arts High School in Saint Paul with the intention of pursuing a career in engineering, but he found himself attracted to literature. He graduated in 1919 as class salutatorian and entered the University of Minnesota in Minneapolis. He joined the student newspaper as its first black reporter and during his senior year edited the *St. Paul Appeal,* a weekly African-American newspaper. At the same time, he earned money for his education by holding jobs in a munitions factory and a slaughterhouse and as a dining car waiter.

Wilkins experienced virulent racism for the first time during the summer of 1920 when a mob lynched three black circus roustabouts wrongly suspected of the rape of a white woman. Wilkins recalled:

> I read the stories [about the lynchings] in the newspapers and put them down feeling sick, scared, and angry all at the same time. This was Minnesota not Mississippi, but every Negro in the [circus] had been suspect in the eyes of the police and guilty in the eyes of the mob. . . . The mob was in touch with something—an awful hatred I had never seen or felt before. For the first time in my life I understood what [W. E. B.] DU BOIS had been writing about. I found myself thinking of black people as a very vulnerable *us*—and white people as an unpredictable, violent *them.*

In 1922 Wilkins joined the Saint Paul branch of the NAACP and soon afterward became its secretary. The following year he received a B.A. and became news editor for the *Kansas City* [Missouri] *Call,* a black weekly. Shortly thereafter he was promoted to managing editor. Wilkins changed the content of the *Call* to cover fewer crime stories and more stories about segregated schools, poor housing, and police brutality. He steered a middle course between the black nationalism espoused by MARCUS GARVEY and the accommodationism of groups who refused to pursue black civil rights.

During the 1920s Wilkins served as secretary of the Kansas City NAACP. In 1930 he earned the attention of the NAACP's national leadership when he led his local chapter's successful fight to defeat President Herbert Hoover's Supreme Court nominee, Judge John J. Parker. Several years earlier Parker, a North Carolinian, had said, "The participation of the Negro in politics is a source of evil and danger to both races and is not desired by the wise men in either race." WALTER FRANCIS WHITE, the newly selected NAACP national executive secretary, then convinced Wilkins to move to New York City in 1931 to become the organization's assistant secretary.

The following year White sent Wilkins and another NAACP member, George Schuyler, to Mississippi on an assignment to investigate working conditions among blacks building federally funded levees in the state. The two men posed as laborers themselves, well knowing that if they were ever found out they would be brutally beaten and perhaps killed. "I was a spy deep within enemy lines," Wilkins recalled, "and I was on my own." Wilkins's report helped convince the federal government to improve wages and working conditions for all unskilled laborers involved in the projects and to end the practice of paying blacks less than whites.

In 1934 W. E. B. Du Bois quit as editor of the NAACP's magazine, *The Crisis,* and Wilkins took his place. He made the publication more informal in style and more diverse with stories that covered black athletes and artists as well as legal and political reports.

Because white lynchings of blacks were an epidemic in the South, Wilkins lobbied President Franklin Roosevelt to support an antilynching law in Congress. Late in 1934 Wilkins participated in picketing a national crime conference in Washington, D.C., to protest Roosevelt's intransigence, and he was arrested for the first time. On his release he continued his fight for an antilynching law, but Roosevelt never supported the bill, and it failed to pass Congress. The experience caused Wilkins to distance himself from Roosevelt. Years later he wrote: "I have always felt that F.D.R. was overrated as a champion of the Negro. He was a New York patrician, distant, aloof, with no natural feel for the sensibilities of black people, no compelling inner commitment to their cause." And he added, "Roosevelt's refusal to support a federal antilynching law was extremely disappointing to me."

During World War II Wilkins protested against segregation in the military. "We argued that so long as segregation existed in the armed forces, the military would never be able to put black fighting men to good use; morale would always be rotten. Segregation wasn't just a factor; it was as deadly as nerve gas. Jim Crow had to go."

When Walter White took a one-year leave of absence from the NAACP in 1949, Wilkins became the acting executive secretary. A strong anticommunist, he convinced the organization in 1950 to pass a resolution rescinding the charters of any local chapters under communist control.

In April 1955, one month after White's death, Wilkins was promoted to executive secretary (renamed executive director in 1965). The NAACP had just scored a momentous victory in the case of *Brown v. Board of Education,* by which the Supreme Court ordered an end to school segregation. The decision encouraged Wilkins to pursue more legal challenges to topple racial discrimination.

Even as the civil rights movement took a new turn with MARTIN LUTHER KING, JR.,'s tactic of nonviolent protest in the 1950s, and even after young people staged a sit-in at a segregated lunch counter in Greensboro, North Carolina, in 1960, and sit-ins spread like wildfire across the South, Wilkins preferred court action. He feared that activist tactics would unleash violent protests by blacks and set back the civil rights movement. He was even reluctant to support the 1963 March on Washington organized by ASA PHILIP RANDOLPH. He did so only after its leaders agreed to cancel plans for civil disobedience and to remove BAYARD RUSTIN, a homosexual and former communist, as the march director.

Yet when nonviolent protest spread, Wilkins supported it in some instances. He even committed the NAACP to providing legal help to organization sponsoring the protests. In 1960 he led the NAACP in staging "wade-ins" at segregated public beaches, and in 1963 he was arrested during a protest in Jackson, Mississippi.

Nevertheless, he remained close to the Washington establishment, and President Lyndon Johnson called on him to rally support for the Civil Rights Act of 1964 and the Voting Rights Act of 1965, both of which passed Congress. Wilkins was the black leader whom Johnson relied on most for advice about civil rights.

In the late 1960s Wilkins served on the Kerner Commission, which investigated riots in America's urban ghettos. He endorsed the group's report that blamed the upheaval on white racism and criticized President Richard Nixon for his "indifference" to civil rights issues.

Many black radicals, however, claimed Wilkins was pandering to whites; militants called him an Uncle Tom, and he, in turn, condemned the black power movement and stuck by his commitment to a racially integrated society.

As the NAACP lost members in the early 1970s, pressure mounted on Wilkins to resign. But he continued as executive director until 1977, when he retired because of failing health. He spent his remaining years writing a syndicated newspaper column and his autobiography. Wilkins died of kidney failure on September 8, 1981, in New York City. He was survived by his wife, Aminda. The couple had no children.

Wilkins recalled in his autobiography: "History offers us a peculiar irony: the idea that the value of equality is probably nurtured most by the protests of the very people who do not have it. Without us, without our struggle, the country would have foundered in moral emptiness long ago."

Further Reading

"Roy Wilkins: July 31, 1977." *Jet*, August 4, 1997, 20.

Wilkins, Roy. *Standing Fast: The Autobiography of Roy Wilkins*. New York: Viking Press, 1982.

Willard, Frances Elizabeth Caroline

(1839–1898) *prohibitionist, women's suffragist*

President of the Women's Christian Temperance Union, Frances Elizabeth Caroline Willard was an advocate of reforms ranging from women's suffrage to socialism. She was born on September 28, 1839, in Churchville, New York, the daughter of Josiah Flint Willard and Mary Thompson Hill Willard.

While Frances Willard was still a child, her parents moved the family twice, the first time to Oberlin, Ohio, and the second time to Janesville, Wisconsin. In that wilderness setting Frances took advantage of her father's library and read avidly, while she also enjoyed outdoor activities such as hunting.

At age 17 she attended the Milwaukee Female College, founded by CATHARINE BEECHER, but the following year she transferred to the Northwestern Female College in Evanston, Illinois, from which she graduated in 1859. About that time she was briefly engaged to be married. An episode of typhoid fever preceded her decision to become a devout Christian by joining the Methodist Church.

Frances Willard was president of the Women's Christian Temperance Union and fought against publications that sexually exploited women. *(Library of Congress)*

Frances Willard taught in the country schools near Evanston before becoming a member of the faculty at the Pittsburgh (Pennsylvania) Female College in 1863 and in 1866 at the Genesee Wesleyan Seminary in Lima, New York. She continued to read extensively and was influenced by the writings of Charlotte Bronte and SARAH MARGARET FULLER and their insistence that women should live independently. She began to write, and several of her articles appeared in weekly papers and magazines. Her first book, *Nineteen Beautiful Years* (1864), recounted the life of her deceased younger sister.

In 1871 Willard was named president of the Northwestern Female College; when it merged with Northwestern University, she became the college's dean. She quit in 1874 over policy differences and joined the burgeoning temperance movement. Willard cast the fight against alcohol as one to protect Christianity and the family. That year she was elected president of the newly formed Chicago Women's Temperance Union.

Shortly afterward she became secretary of the Illinois Women's Christian Temperance Union.

There followed her elevation to secretary of the National Women's Christian Temperance Union (WCTU), but a dispute soon erupted when she challenged the group's more conservative members by advocating that the organization go well beyond temperance and pursue other social reforms. Her opponents criticized her attempt to promote a resolution supporting women's suffrage, and they forced her to resign as secretary. She spent her time lecturing, showing her persuasiveness, and continuing to receive backing from many within the WCTU.

In 1879 Willard rallied her supporters, defeated her conservative opponents, and won election to the presidency of the WCTU. She then broadened the organization's activities in accordance with her belief that women should express themselves in many endeavors and, as admonished in her slogan, "Do Everything." Over the next 10 years she created 39 departments, which handled matters such as women's suffrage, labor problems, pornography, peace, and immigrant settlement. On women's suffrage Willard's friend, Harriet A. Townsend, recalled in her memoirs the curious way in which Willard promoted the campaign, a story that today smacks of sexist overtones and stereotyping but back then was considered clever in its appeal. Townsend wrote that Willard would tell her audiences the following:

> I was in General Washington's kitchen at Mount Vernon last week and had a delightful visit with Aunt Dinah, the presiding genius of the place. . . . I asked her, "Aunt Dinah, do you want to vote?" The old woman stood up at the question and with arms akimbo, exclaimed, "Well, honey, you know that Uncle Sam's kitchen needs a cl'aring out once in a while, and when you are going to cl'ar out a kitchen you have got to have a woman to do it!"

In 1888 Willard helped found the International Council of Women, which sought to unite several women's organizations. She served also as the first president of the National Council of Women and in 1889 helped begin the General Federation of Women's Clubs, a vehicle for rallying middle-class women to reform.

In 1891 she told the National Council of Women that it should endorse many reforms, including the fight against publications and entertainment that sexually exploited females:

> An "Anatomical Museum" that I often pass on a Chicago street bears the words: "Gentlemen only admitted." Why do women passively accept these flaunting assumptions that men are expected to derive pleasures from objects that they would not for a moment permit their wives to see? Someday women will not accept them passively, and then these base exhibitions will cease, for women will purify every place they enter, and they will enter every place.

Beginning in 1892 Willard spent considerable time in England trying to persuade temperance leaders there to adopt her diverse approach to reform. She studied British socialism and began advocating its adoption. Her long absence from the United States nearly cost her the WCTU presidency, which she had to fight hard to retain in 1897.

The following year she contracted influenza, and she died on February 18, 1898, in New York City. "Miss Willard won instant attention," Harriet Townsend recalled, "her exquisite personality was so marked; her marvelous voice—like a silver trumpet sounding the note of a human right—thrilled every heart."

Further Reading

Bordin, Ruth Birgitta Anderson. *Frances Willard: A Biography.* Chapel Hill: University of North Carolina Press, 1986.

Leeman, Richard W. *"Do Everything" Reform: The Oratory of Frances E. Willard.* New York: Greenwood Press, 1992.

Woodhull, Victoria
(Victoria California Claflin)
(1838–1927) *women's rights activist, socialist*

Victoria Woodhull embraced some of the most radical doctrines of her time, among them women's rights, free love, and socialism. She was born Victoria California Claflin in Honer, Ohio, on September 23, 1838, to Reuben Buckman Claflin and Roxana Hummel Claflin, a couple universally described as "poor and eccentric."

While still a child Victoria, like her mother, claimed to possess clairvoyant powers. So her father, willing to do almost anything to earn money, put together a traveling spiritualist show in which she and her sister, Tennessee, told fortunes.

At age 15 Victoria married Canning Woodhull, a Cleveland doctor who was an alcoholic. She left her father's show but continued to tell fortunes. In 1864 she divorced Woodhull and in 1866 claimed she was married "by the spirits" to Colonel James Harvey Blood. She was divorced from him in 1868 and moved to New York City, where she ingratiated herself with the railroad and shipping magnate Cornelius Vanderbilt, himself an enthusiastic spiritualist. He bankrolled her and her sister in opening a stock brokerage office and gave them advice that made them rich.

In 1870 she and Tennessee began publishing *Woodhull and Claflin's Weekly,* in which she advocated socialism, equal rights for women, and free love. At that time she became the leader of the New York section of Karl Marx's Second International. As for free love, she said in 1871, "I am a free lover. I have an inalienable, constitutional and natural right to love whom I may."

That same year she testified on behalf of women's suffrage before the Judiciary Committee of the House of Representatives. In November she said in a lecture:

> Public opinion is against Equality, but it is simply from prejudice, which requires but to be informed to pass away. No greater prejudice exists against equality than there did against the proposition that the world was a globe. . . . I declare it as my candid belief that if women will do one-half their duty until Congress meets, that they will be compelled to pass such laws as are necessary to enforce the provisions of the XIV and XV Articles of Amendments to the Constitution, one of which is equal political rights for all citizens.

The then-hot topic of prostitution she called a "social evil," but at various times she said that it should be regulated and at other times that it

should be legalized. "Palliatives and curatives," she said, "will never remove a moral disorder whose causes lie deep in human instincts, and whose growth is festered by poverty and ignorance."

In 1872 the small Equal Rights Party nominated her for president of the United States, and she tried but failed to cast a vote in the election. Her candidacy highlighted the political and social oppression suffered by women, as did the numerous lectures she gave that year and in following years in advocating women's rights.

While Woodhull's ideas generated controversy, her charges against the renowned HENRY WARD BEECHER, pastor of Brooklyn's Plymouth Church, produced a sensation. She claimed that Beecher was having an affair with Elizabeth Tilton, the wife of Theodore Tilton, a member of the editorial board of the *Independent,* a religious publication. At the same time Woodhull revealed her own sexual relationship with Tilton. Beecher was put on trial for adultery but acquitted. Woodhull was tried for publishing an obscene work but was also acquitted.

Woodhull had previously remarried Blood, and in 1876 they divorced a second time; the following year she moved to England. In 1883 she married John Biddulph Martin, a wealthy English banker. She continued to lecture and in 1892 began publishing a magazine, the *Humanitarian.* She died on June 10, 1927.

Her extreme challenge to conventional ideas was evident in her "firsts"—the first woman to appear before a congressional committee and the first to be nominated for president of the United States—and her advocacy of socialism, free love, and women's rights. Woodhull's contemporaries and some historians have argued that her controversial background damaged the women's rights movement by discrediting it; others have concluded that her efforts added momentum to reform.

Further Reading

Gabriel, Mary. *Notorious Victoria: The Life of Victoria Woodhull, Uncensored.* Chapel Hill, N.C.: Algonquin Books, 1998.

Meade, Marion. *Free Woman: The Life and Times of Victoria Woodhull.* New York: Knopf, 1976.

Wright, Fanny
(Frances Wright)

(1795–1852) *abolitionist, utopian, women's rights activist*

Fanny Wright founded a commune dedicated to abolitionism and other radical ideas, and she lectured widely on women's rights, free education, and the oppression of workers. She was born Frances Wright on September 6, 1795, in Dundee, Scotland. Her father was James Wright and her mother was the daughter of an army officer.

Because both of her parents died when she was still a child, Wright was raised by relatives in London. In 1818 she visited the United States, and through *Views of Society and Manners in America,* a book she had written, which was published in 1821, she established a friendship with General Lafayette. When Lafayette toured America in 1824, Wright joined him. Convinced that slavery was evil, she took much of the considerable fortune she had inherited from her parents and in 1825 founded a commune, Nashoba, deep in the wilderness of southwestern Tennessee.

She intended Nashoba to be a place where she could implement several of her radical ideas; she wanted it to be free of what she called the "tyrannies" of marriage, religion, and capitalism. She intended also to buy slaves for Nashoba under a plan that would allow them within five years to work off their servitude and gain their freedom.

Wright believed that if her plan worked, other slaveowners would emulate her and slavery would soon end. She accompanied her antislavery views with support for miscegenation; if whites and blacks would interbreed, she said, then a bridge would be formed between the races, creating a hostile environment for slavery.

In her prospectus for Nashoba, she claimed:

> The Negro race is every where . . . held by a great majority of the population, in contempt and suspicion. Its very color is an object of disgust. And in the speeches and votes of congress, we find an evidence, that the most northern sections of the country harbour prejudices, equal in strength to those of the extreme south.

She wrote that slavery resulted from the education "stamped" on the "minds and hearts" of the slaveholders. Therefore, she insisted, "We must come to the slaveholder . . . not in anger, but in kindness, and when we ask him to change his whole mode of life, we must shew [*sic*] him the means by which he may do so, without the complete compromise of his ease and of his interests."

Trouble besieged Nashoba from the start. It was poorly financed and poorly led. Understandably, blacks at Nashoba distrusted Wright and the white settlers, who they believed would never set them free. Adding to Nashoba's problems, Wright spoke out on social issues at a time when women were supposed to maintain silence and remain at home to take care of their families. Thus, her appearances in front of mixed audiences of men and women generated enormous criticism. On top of that, she attacked religion for being oppressive and called for an end to marriage based on legal obligation. Couples, she said, should be united and remain united on their own terms.

Wright returned to Scotland in 1827 to regain her health, which had been weakened by malaria, whereupon the managers she left in charge at Nashoba mistreated the slaves. Scandal erupted when one manager admitted he was living with a female slave.

Wright returned to America, and with ROBERT Dale OWEN in 1828 she edited the *New Harmony Gazette,* a newspaper that circulated in the New Harmony commune in Indiana. The following year she bought the Ebenezer Baptist Church in New York City and directly assaulted religion by converting it into a Hall of Science. In 1830 she accompanied William Phiquepal, a Frenchman, in transporting slaves from the then-defunct Nashoba commune to Haiti, where they could live in freedom. During the voyage she conceived a child with him. In July 1831 she married Phiquepal, but they soon divorced. (Wright's daughter eventually became a conservative critic of the entire women's rights movement.)

Wright took another trip to Europe in 1835, during which she resumed her controversial lectures, advocating women's rights, birth control, and a more equitable distribution of property. She condemned banks and insisted that government should hold all capital and provide jobs for everyone.

Living near the East River in New York, she became a leader of the New York free thinkers, who promoted universal education to enlighten people about the gap between the theory of politics and the way government actually operates. She said, "By fostering the good, and repressing the evil tendencies, by developing every useful faculty and amiable feeling, and cultivating the peculiar talent or talents of every child . . . all human beings . . . might be rendered useful and happy." She proposed that children be taken from their parents at a young age and sent to boarding schools, where their minds could be liberated.

Wright joined the short-lived Workingmen's Party and in 1830 discussed class warfare in an article for the *Free Enquirer*. "What distinguishes the present from every other struggle in which the human race has been engaged," she wrote, in recognizing the spread of industry, "is, that the present is, evidently, openly and acknowlegedly, a war of class."

By the mid-1830s mainstream America considered Wright a dangerous person, and mobs assaulted her. Unlike other women who spoke out for women's rights, she wanted total change and condemned everything the middle class held sacred.

Many Americans applied the term *Fanny Wrightism* to discredit all reform, and even women's rights advocates criticized her, claiming that her extremism only gave credence to the conservative argument that women liberated would mean America corrupted. Women's rights advocate CATHARINE BEECHER said:

> Who can look without disgust and abhorrence upon such an one as Fanny Wright, with her great masculine person, her loud voice, her untasteful attire. . . . There she stands with brazen front and brawny arms, attacking . . . all that is venerable and sacred in religion. . . . I cannot perceive any thing in the shape of woman, more intolerably offensive and disgusting.

Fanny Wright died on December 13, 1852, in Cincinnati, Ohio. Near the end of her life she said that she felt like "a being fallen from a strange planet among a race whose senses and perceptions are all different from my own." She was placed in that position by her radicalism, which one historian has said challenged "every assumption about womanhood."

Further Reading

Eckardt, Celia Morris. *Fanny Wright: Rebel in America.* Cambridge, Mass.: Harvard University Press, 1984.

Travis, Molly Abel. "Frances Wright: The Other Woman of Early American Feminism." *Women's Studies* 22 (June 1993): 389+.

Yellin, Jean Fagan. *Women and Sisters: The Antislavery Feminists in American Culture.* New Haven, Conn.: Yale University Press, 1989.

X, Y

X, Malcolm See MALCOLM X.

Young, Whitney Moore, Jr.
(1921–1971) *civil rights leader*

While executive director of the National Urban League, Whitney Moore Young, Jr., was a moderate, at times even conservative, voice in the civil rights movement. He was born on July 31, 1921, in Lincoln Ridge, Kentucky, to Whitney Young, Sr., the president of Lincoln Institute, an all-black boarding school, and Laura Ray Young, a schoolteacher.

Raised in a family that valued education, Whitney Young, Jr., attended Lincoln Institute, graduated in 1937, and enrolled at Kentucky State College, an all-black school, in Frankfort. He received a B.A. in the spring of 1941 and then prepared to enter medical school. But after Japan attacked Pearl Harbor on December 7 he enlisted in the military. He at first worked for the War Department as a mechanic trainee in the Signal Service; he then became a junior repairman trainee and, in January 1943, an assistant radio mechanic technician.

A few months later he was assigned to the Army Specialized Training Program and hoped he would be placed in a medical school, but all the slots open to study at black colleges were taken. Instead, the army sent him to the Massachusetts Institute of Technology (MIT) to learn electrical engineering in preparation for serving in a combat

engineering unit. He arrived at MIT in October 1943, and in January 1944 he married Margaret Buckner, whom he had met while at Kentucky State. They had two children.

Later that year Young was sent to Europe as a private in an all-black engineer combat battalion. Most of the battalion's work involved building roads. As Young remembered it, the white officers, largely southern, imposed a discipline on the troops that reminded them of racism back home.

Discharged from the army, Young enrolled at the University of Minnesota, where he earned a master's degree in social work. As part of his field experience, he worked for the National Urban League of Saint Paul. The Urban League fought segregation by acting as a liaison with white employers to find jobs for blacks, rather than by initiating legal challenges.

Known for his articulate and gregarious manner, Young was so impressive that in 1950 the Urban League in Omaha, Nebraska, appointed him its executive director. His biographer, Nancy J. Weiss, writes in *Whitney M. Young, Jr. and the Struggle for Civil Rights* (1989) that Young "talked about the assets that blacks could offer to businesses in Omaha, and he argued that the economic consequences to the city as a whole of not hiring blacks were more harmful than the consequences of hiring them and taking advantage of their skills." Accordingly, the placement of blacks in unskilled, skilled, and professional positions increased.

Young left the Urban League in 1953 to become dean of the black Atlanta University School of Social Work in Georgia. In fall 1960 he took a leave from that post to attend Harvard University as a visiting scholar. In October 1961 he succeeded Lester B. Granger as executive director of the National Urban League.

Young immediately set his sights on improving the Urban League's finances by obtaining money from corporations. And he launched several new programs to improve employment opportunities for African Americans, including the National Skills Bank, which matched unemployed or underemployed workers with jobs suitable to their talents; On-the-Job Training, which placed unskilled workers in industries in which they could learn a trade; and the Secretarial Training Project, which prepared women to work as secretaries. Added to these, Young developed programs to improve black education, including tutoring for ghetto youths and street academies that prepared high school dropouts for college.

But his boldest effort was to remake the Urban League into a civil rights group. At a time when African Americans were engaging in legal challenges and street demonstrations to end racial segregation, he believed the Urban League needed to move beyond job placement. Young instructed the organization's affiliates to refrain from picketing and boycotting, but he advised them to encourage dialogue between protesters and white leaders.

When the civil rights activist ASA PHILIP RANDOLPH proposed a March on Washington for 1963, Young agreed that the Urban League should join it. He told a meeting of delegates: "It is becoming clear now, that if the impatience and heightened aspirations of the masses of Negro citizens are to be protected and to be channeled along constructive lines, then the Urban League must of necessity be involved in this feat of social engineering." The presence of the Urban League at the march helped ensure its success.

Some in the Urban League disagreed with Young's expanded role for the group and its alignment with those more attuned to activist protest. But Young insisted that the league's presence in the civil rights movement "says, and I hope loud and clear, that while intelligence, maturity, and strategy dictate that as Civil Rights agencies we use different methods, we are all united as never

before on the goal of securing first class citizenship for all Americans—NOW."

In 1965 Young joined MARTIN LUTHER KING, JR., in a bold march from Selma to Montgomery, Alabama, for black voting rights. "Now I would like to ask one question to the white citizens of Alabama," he said. "How long can you continue to afford the luxury of a political system and public officials who by their rigidity and vulgar racism have today been responsible for bringing in federally controlled troops?"

Yet whereas other civil rights groups stressed court action and public demonstrations, the Urban League pressed hardest in corporate boardrooms. Beyond the yelling and picketing, Young said, some group must act professionally to carry out the civil rights agenda, and that would be the Urban League. He told business leaders that the time had come for them to step forward and fight social injustice, that as they reaped the benefits from society, they must heal its wounds.

When John Kennedy was in the White House in the early 1960s, Young urged the president to move faster in inducing Congress to pass a civil rights bill, and he criticized Kennedy for delaying an executive order that would prohibit discrimination in housing. In all, he thought Kennedy too slow to act.

As President Lyndon Johnson expanded the Vietnam War, civil rights leaders found themselves in a predicament. To oppose the war might draw away energy and resources from the civil rights movement and might incur the wrath of Johnson, who had done so much for black America in the way of civil rights legislation. Martin Luther King, Jr., however, saw the war as an extension of racism at home, and in April 1967 he spoke out against it. Young disagreed with him. "I believe strongly that the urgent domestic problem of civil rights and the issue of the war in Vietnam should remain separate," he said. "The masses of Negro citizens . . . have as their first priority the immediate problem of survival in this country. . . . The limited resources and personnel available to civil rights agencies for work in their behalf should not be diverted into other channels."

Many blacks criticized Young for having limited vision or selling out to Johnson and the white power structure. If anything, though, Young showed an ability to reevaluate his position, and when protests against the war grew stronger and the fighting dragged on with yet more deaths, he decided to condemn it. In October 1968 he declared: "I am totally convinced that Vietnam is tragically diverting America's attention from its primary problem—the urban and racial crisis—at the very time that crisis is at a flash point." ROY INNIS, vice chairman of the Congress of Racial Equality (CORE), responded: "Welcome home, Baby."

Whitney Young died suddenly of a heart attack on March 11, 1971, while visiting Nigeria. From around the United States words of praise summed up his role in the civil rights movement:

> "A salesman for Negro rights," said NAACP leader ROY WILKINS.

> "One of those rare individuals who could communicate on almost all levels," said CORE leader Floyd McKissick.

> "So Whitney Young Jr. tried to build bridges. That was what he was all about," said the *Los Angeles Times*.

According to Young's biographer Nancy J. Weiss, the bridge was between the ghetto and the power structure; it was a bridge built "in ways no other black man of his generation was able to duplicate."

Further Reading

Dickerson, Dennis C. *Militant Mediator—Whitney M. Young, Jr.* Lexington: University Press of Kentucky, 1998.

Weiss, Nancy J. *Whitney M. Young, Jr., and the Struggle for Civil Rights.* Princeton, N.J.: Princeton University Press, 1989.

BIBLIOGRAPHY AND RECOMMENDED SOURCES

Abzug, Robert H. *American Reform and the Religious Imagination.* New York: Oxford University Press, 1994.

Aurand, Harold W. *From the Molly Maguires to the United Mine Workers: The Social Ecology of an Industrial Union, 1869–1897.* Philadelphia: Temple University Press, 1971.

Avrich, Paul. *Anarchist Voices: An Oral History of Anarchism in America.* Princeton, N.J.: Princeton University Press, 1995.

Bernstein, Irving. *The Lean Years: A History of the American Worker, 1920–1933.* New York: Da Capo, 1983.

———. *The Turbulent Years: A History of the American Worker, 1933–1941.* Boston: Houghton Mifflin, 1970.

Bordin, Ruth. *Woman and Temperance: The Quest for Power and Liberty, 1873–1900.* New Brunswick, N.J.: Rutgers University Press, 1990.

Branch, Taylor. *Parting the Waters: America in the King Years, 1954–63.* New York: Simon & Schuster, 1988.

Bristow, Nancy K. *Making Men Moral: Social Engineering During the Great War.* New York: New York University Press, 1996.

Buhle, Mary Jo. *Women and American Socialism, 1870–1920.* Urbana: University of Illinois Press, 1983.

Castro, Ginette. *American Feminism: A Contemporary History.* New York: New York University Press, 1990.

Chafe, William H. *Civilities and Civil Rights: Greensboro, North Carolina and the Black Struggle for Freedom.* New York: Oxford University Press, 1980.

———. *The Paradox of Change: American Women in the Twentieth Century.* New York: Oxford University Press, 1991.

Cott, Nancy F. *The Grounding of Modern Feminism.* New Haven, Conn.: Yale University Press, 1987.

Cremin, Lawrence A. *American Education: The Metropolitan Experience, 1876–1980.* New York: Harper & Row, 1988.

———. *The Transformation of the School: Progressivism in American Education, 1876–1957.* New York: Vintage, 1964.

Crocker, Ruth Hutchinson. *Social Work and Social Order: The Settlement Movement in Two Industrial Cities, 1889–1930.* Urbana: University of Illinois Press, 1992.

Crunden, Robert M. *Ministers of Reform: The Progressives' Achievements in American Civilization, 1889–1920.* Urbana: University of Illinois Press, 1984.

Davis, Allen F. *Spearheads for Reform: The Social Settlements and the Progressive Movement, 1890–1914.* New Brunswick, N.J.: Rutgers University Press, 1984.

Davis, Flora. *Moving the Mountain: The Woman's Movement Since 1960.* New York: Simon & Schuster, 1991.

Dubofsky, Melvyn. *Industrialism and the American Worker, 1865–1920.* 2nd ed. Arlington Heights, Ill.: Harlan Davidson, 1985.

Ebner, Michael H., and Eugene M. Tobin, eds. *The Age of Urban Reform: New Perspective on the*

Progressive Era. Port Washington, N.Y.: Kennikat, 1977.

Eichols, Alice. *Daring to Be Bad: Radical Feminism in America, 1967–1975*. Minneapolis: University of Minnesota Press, 1989.

Epstein, Barbara. *Political Protest and Cultural Revolution: Nonviolent Direct Action in the 1970s and 1980s*. Berkeley: University of California Press, 1991.

Farber, David R. *Chicago '68*. Chicago: University of Chicago Press, 1988.

Fixico, Donald L. *Termination and Relocation: Federal Indian Policy, 1945–1960*. Albuquerque: University of New Mexico Press, 1986.

Foner, Philip S. *History of the Labor Movement in the United States*. 8 vols. New York: International Publishers, 1972–1975.

Formisano, Ronald P. *Boston Against Busing: Race, Class and Ethnicity in the 1960s and 1970s*. Chapel Hill: University of North Carolina Press, 1991.

Franklin, John Hope, and Alfred A. Moss, Jr. *From Slavery to Freedom: A History of the Negro Americans*. 6th ed. New York: Knopf, 1988.

Garcia, Maro T. *Mexican Americans: Leadership, Ideology, and Identity, 1930–1960*. New Haven, Conn.: Yale University Press, 1989.

Ginzberg, Lori D. *Women and the Work of Benevolence: Morality, Politics, and Class in the Nineteenth-Century United States*. New Haven, Conn.: Yale University Press, 1990.

Goodwyn, Lawrence. *Democratic Promise: The Populist Movement in America*. New York: Oxford University Press, 1976.

Green, James R. *Grass-Roots Socialism: Radical Movements in the Southwest, 1895–1943*. Baton Rouge: Louisiana State University Press, 1972.

Griffin, Clifford Stephen. *Their Brothers' Keepers: Moral Stewardship in the United States, 1800–1865*. Westport, Conn.: Greenwood Press, 1983.

Gusfield, Joseph R. *Symbolic Crusade: Status Politics and the American Temperance Movement*. 2nd ed. Urbana: University of Illinois Press, 1986.

Hofstadter, Richard. *The Age of Reform: From Bryan to F. D. R.* New York: Knopf, 1955.

Howe, Irving, and Lewis Coser. *The American Communist Party: A Crucial History*. New York: Da Capo, 1974.

Isserman, Maurice. *If I Had a Hammer . . . The Death of the Old Left and the Birth of the New Left*. New York: Basic Books, 1987.

Jackson, Kenneth T. *The Ku Klux Klan in the City, 1915–1930*. New York: Oxford University Press, 1967.

Katz, Michael B. *Class, Bureaucracy, and Schools: The Illusion of Educational Change in America*. Rev. ed. New York: Praeger, 1975.

Klatch, Rebecca E. *Women of the New Right*. Philadelphia: Temple University Press, 1987.

Kraditor, Aileen S. *The Ideas of the Woman Suffrage Movement, 1890–1920*. New York: Norton, 1981.

Lasch, Christopher. *The New Radicalism in America, 1889–1963: The Intellectual as a Social Type*. New York: Norton, 1986.

Laslett, John H. M., and Seymour Martin Lipset, eds. *Failure of a Dream? Essays in the History of American Socialism*. Rev. ed. Berkeley: University of California Press, 1984.

Lawson, Stephen F. *Running for Freedom: Civil Rights and Black Politics in America Since 1941*. Philadelphia: Temple University Press, 1991.

Mandle, Jay R. *Not Slave, Not Free: The African American Economic Experience Since the Civil War*. Durham, N.C.: Duke University Press, 1992.

Marchand, C. Roland. *The American Peace Movement and Social Reform, 1898–1918*. Princeton, N.J.: Princeton University Press, 1973.

McKivigan, John R., ed. *Abolitionism and American Reform*. New York: Garland Publishers, 1999.

Miller, Jim. *"Democracy Is in the Streets": From Port Huron to the Siege of Chicago*. New York: Simon & Schuster, 1987.

Montgomery, David. *The Fall of the House of Labor: The Workplace, the State, and American Labor Activism, 1865–1925*. Cambridge: Cambridge University Press, 1987.

Muñoz, Carlos, Jr. *Youth, Identity, and Power: The Chicano Movement*. London: Verso, 1989.

Patterson, James T. *America's Struggle Against Poverty, 1900–1985*. Rev ed. Cambridge, Mass.: Harvard University Press, 1986.

Pease, William Henry, and Jane H. Pease. *Black Utopia: Negro Communal Experiments in America.* Madison: State Historical Society of Wisconsin, 1963.

———. *They Who Would Be Free: Blacks' Search for Freedom, 1830–1861.* Urbana: University of Illinois Press, 1990.

Perry, Lewis. *Radical Abolitionism: Anarchy and the Government of God in Antislavery Thought.* Ithaca, N.Y.: Cornell University Press, 1973.

Quarles, Benjamin. *Black Abolitionists.* New York: Da Capo, 1991.

———. *The Negro in the Making of America.* 2nd rev. ed. New York: Collier, 1987.

Reichert, William O. *Partisans of Freedom: A Study in American Anarchism.* Bowling Green, Ohio: Bowling Green University Popular Press, 1976.

Rosenberg, Rosalind. *Beyond Separate Sphere: Intellectual Roots of Modern Feminism.* New Haven, Conn.: Yale University Press, 1982.

Sale, Kirkpatrick. *SDS.* New York: Vintage, 1973.

Scharf, Lois, and Joan M. Jensen, eds. *Decades of Discontent: The Women's Movement, 1920–1940.* Boston: Northeastern University Press, 1987.

Scott, Anne Firor, and Andrew MacKay Scott. *One Half of the People: The Fight for Woman Suffrage.* Urbana: University of Illinois Press, 1982.

Sitkoff, Harvard. *The Struggle for Black Equality, 1954–1992.* Rev. ed. New York: Hill & Wang, 1993.

Tyler, Alice Felt. *Freedom's Ferment: Phases of American Social History to 1860.* Freeport, N.Y.: Books for Libraries Press, 1970.

Walters, Ronald G. *American Reformers, 1815–1860.* New York: Hill & Wang, 1978.

Ward, David. *Poverty, Ethnicity, and the American City, 1840–1925: Changing Conceptions of the Slum and the Ghetto.* Cambridge: Cambridge University Press, 1989.

Wolters, Raymond. *The Burden of Brown: Thirty Years of School Desegregation.* Knoxville: University of Tennessee Press, 1984.

Zieger, Robert. *American Workers, American Unions, 1920–1985.* Baltimore: Johns Hopkins University Press, 1986.

Entries by Area of Activity

CHILDREN'S REFORM
Abbot, Grace
Edelman, Marian Wright
Hine, Lewis Wickes
Lathrop, Julia Clifford

CIVIL LIBERTIES
Baldwin, Roger Nash
Penn, William
Strossen, Nadine

CIVIL RIGHTS
Abernathy, Ralph David
Ames, Jessie Daniel
Baker, Ella Josephine
Bethune, Mary McLeod
Bond, Julian
Carter, William Hodding, Jr.
Coffin, William Sloane, Jr.
Dees, Morris Seligman, Jr.
Du Bois, W. E. B.
Evers, Medgar Wiley
Evers-Williams, Myrlie
Farmer, James Leonard, Jr.
Grimké, Charlotte Forten
Grimké, Francis James
Hamer, Fannie Lou
Hernandez, Aileen Clarke
Hooks, Benjamin Lawson
Jackson, Jesse Louis
King, Coretta Scott
King, Martin Luther, Jr.
Lewis, John Robert
Meredith, James Howard
Mfume, Kweisi
Moses, Robert
Parks, Rosa
Randolph, Asa Philip
Robeson, Paul Leroy
Rustin, Bayard
Sharpton, Al
Spingarn, Joel Elias
Tourgée, Albion Winegar
Villard, Oswald Garrison
Walker, David
Washington, Booker
　　Taliaferro

Wells-Barnett, Ida Bell
White, Walter Francis
Wilkins, Roy
Young, Whitney Moore, Jr.

COMMUNE MOVEMENT
Noyes, John Humphrey
Owen, Robert

COMMUNISM
Davis, Angela Yvonne
Du Bois, W. E. B.
Flynn, Elizabeth Gurley
Foster, William Zebulon
Hall, Gus
Reed, John Silas
Robeson, Paul Leroy

COMMUNITY ACTIVISM
Alinsky, Saul

CONSERVATIVE ACTIVISM
Limbaugh, Rush Hudson
Schlafly, Phyllis Stewart
Welch, Robert Henry
　　Winborne, Jr.

CONSUMER RIGHTS
Nader, Ralph

ECONOMIC REFORM
Coughlin, Charles Edward
Townsend, Francis Everett

EDUCATION REFORM
Agassiz, Elizabeth Cary
Alcott, Amos Bronson
Alcott, William Andrus
Barnard, Henry
Beecher, Catharine
Butler, Nicholas Murray
Dewey, John
Eliot, Charles William
Mann, Horace

ENVIRONMENTAL MOVEMENT
Brower, David Ross

Brown, Lester Russell
Carson, Rachel Louise
Commoner, Barry
Fuller, Kathryn Scott
Muir, John
Nader, Ralph
Payne, Roger Searle
Scheffer, Victor Blanchard

ETHICAL REFORM
Adler, Felix

FEMINISM
Balch, Emily Greene
Brownmiller, Susan
Firestone, Shulamith
Friedan, Betty
Gilman, Charlotte Perkins
Ireland, Patricia
Millett, Kate
Morgan, Robin
Steinem, Gloria

FREE THOUGHT
Ingersoll, Robert Green

GAY RIGHTS
Kameny, Franklin
Milk, Harvey
O'Leary, Jean

HEALTH REFORM
Alcott, William Andrus
Barton, Clara
Blackwell, Elizabeth
Blackwell, Emily
Bowditch, Henry Ingersoll
Dix, Dorothea Lynde
Graham, Sylvester
Hamilton, Alice
Kellogg, John Harvey
McDowell, Mary Eliza
Reich, Wilhelm
Wald, Lillian

IMMIGRANT WELFARE
Abbott, Grace

Addams, Jane
McDowell, Mary Eliza

LABOR RIGHTS AND UNION MOVEMENT

Ameringer, Oscar
Andrews, John Bertram
Bridges, Harry
Chavez, Cesar
Darrow, Clarence Seward
Dubinsky, David
Flynn, Elizabeth Gurley
Foster, William Zebulon
Galarza, Ernesto
Gompers, Samuel
Green, William
Haywood, William Dudley
Hill, Joe
Hillman, Sidney
Hoffa, Jimmy
Huerta, Dolores Fernandez
Irons, Martin
Itliong, Larry Dulay
Jones, Mary Harris
Kelley, Florence
Lens, Sydney
Lewis, John Llewellyn
Meany, George
Murray, Philip
Powderly, Terence Vincent
Randolph, Asa Philip
Reuther, Walter Philip
Schneiderman, Rose
Stephens, Uriah Smith
Tenayuca, Emma
Vorse, Mary Marvin Heaton

MILITIA MOVEMENT

DePugh, Robert
Gale, William Potter
Trochmann, John

NEW LEFT/LEFTIST MOVEMENT

Hayden, Tom
Rudd, Mark
Savio, Mario
Stone, I. F.

PEACE MOVEMENT

Addams, Jane
Andrews, Fannie Fern
Baez, Joan
Balch, Emily Greene
Berrigan, Daniel
Berrigan, Philip
Boulding, Kenneth Ewart
Butler, Nicholas Murray
Catt, Carrie Chapman
Cox, Harvey Gallagher, Jr.
Day, Dorothy
Eastman, Crystal
Howe, Julia Ward
Ladd, William
Lens, Sydney
Lynd, Staughton
Merton, Thomas
Muste, A. J.
Pauling, Linus Carl
Rustin, Bayard
Spock, Benjamin
Thomas, Norman Mattoon
Villard, Fanny Garrison
Villard, Oswald Garrison
Wald, Lillian

POPULATION CONTROL

Guttmacher, Alan Frank
Sanger, Margaret Higgins

POPULIST MOVEMENT

Donnelly, Ignatius
Lease, Mary Elizabeth Clyens

PROGRESSIVISM

Addams, Jane
Croly, Herbert David
Ely, Richard Theodore
George, Henry
Kellogg, Paul Underwood
Kellor, Frances

PUERTO RICAN MOVEMENT

Hostos, Eugenio Maria de
Muñoz Rivera, Luis

PRO-LIFE MOVEMENT

Terry, Randall

RELIGIOUS REFORM

Cox, Harvey Gallagher, Jr.
Fox, Matthew

REVOLUTIONARY WAR MOVEMENT

Paine, Thomas
Shays, Daniel

SOCIAL REFORM

Coxey, Jacob Sechler
Day, Dorothy
Fuller, Richard Buckminister
Kellogg, Paul Underwood
Nearing, Scott
Riis, Jacob
Roosevelt, Eleanor
Rush, Benjamin

SOCIALISM

Ameringer, Oscar
Bellamy, Edward
De Leon, Daniel
Debs, Eugene Victor
Eastman, Max
Gilman, Charlotte Perkins
Harrington, Michael
Keller, Helen
Sinclair, Upton
Thomas, Norman Mattoon
Walling, William English
Wayland, J. A.
Woodhull, Victoria

TECHNOLOGICAL REFORM

Fuller, Richard Buckminster, Jr.

TEMPERANCE AND PROHIBITION

Dow, Neal
Livermore, Mary Ashton Rice
Nation, Carry

ENTRIES BY YEAR OF BIRTH

1600–1699
Penn, William

1700–1799
Alcott, Amos Bronson
Alcott, William Andrus
Allen, Richard
Graham, Sylvester
Grimké, Sarah Moore
Ladd, William
Lundy, Benjamin
Mann, Horace
Mott, Lucretia Coffin
Owen, Robert
Paine, Thomas
Ruffin, Edmund
Rush, Benjamin
Shays, Daniel
Tappan, Arthur
Tappan, Lewis
Truth, Sojourner
Walker, David
Wright, Fanny

1800–1809
Beecher, Catharine
Bowditch, Henry Ingersoll
Brown, John
Child, Lydia Maria Francis
Dix, Dorothea Lynde
Dow, Neal
Garrison, William Lloyd
Grimké, Angelina

Lovejoy, Elijah Parish
Weld, Theodore Dwight

1810–1819
Andrews, Stephen Pearl
Barnard, Henry
Beecher, Henry Ward
Bloomer, Amelia Jenks
Delany, Martin Robison
Douglass, Frederick
Fuller, Sarah Margaret
Garnet, Henry Highland
Howe, Julia Ward
Noyes, John Humphrey
Phillips, Wendell
Stanton, Elizabeth Cady
Stone, Lucy

1820–1829
Agassiz, Elizabeth Cary
Anthony, Susan Brownell
Barton, Clara
Blackwell, Antoinette
Blackwell, Elizabeth
Blackwell, Emily
Higginson, Thomas Wentworth
Irons, Martin
Livermore, Mary Ashton Rice
Stephens, Uriah Smith
Still, William
Tubman, Harriet

1830–1839
Donnelly, Ignatius

Eliot, Charles William
George, Henry
Grimké, Charlotte Forten
Hostos, Eugenio Maria De
Ingersoll, Robert Green
Jackson, Helen Hunt
Jones, Mary Harris
Muir, John
Tourgée, Albion W.
Willard, Frances Elizabeth
    Caroline
Woodhull, Victoria

1840–1849
Nation, Carry
Powderly, Terence Vincent
Riis, Jacob
Villard, Fanny Garrison

1850–1859
Adler, Felix
Avery, Rachel Foster
Bellamy, Edward
Blackwell, Alice Stone
Blatch, Harriot Stanton
Catt, Carrie Chapman
Coxey, Jacob Sechler
Darrow, Clarence Seward
De Leon, Daniel
Debs, Eugene Victor
Dewey, John
Eastman, Charles
Ely, Richard Theodore
Gompers, Samuel

King, Martin Luther, Jr.
Lynd, Staughton
Malcolm X
Schlafly, Phyllis Stewart
Tijerina, Reies Lopez
Young, Whitney Moore, Jr.

1930–1939
Banks, Dennis James
Brown, Lester Russell
Brownmiller, Susan
Cleaver, Eldridge
Dees, Morris Seligman, Jr.
Deloria, Vine, Jr.
Edelman, Marian Wright
Evers-Williams, Myrlie
Harris, LaDonna
Hoffman, Abbie
Huerta, Dolores Fernandez
Innis, Roy
Kramer, Larry
Means, Russell

Meredith, James Howard
Milk, Harvey
Millett, Kate
Moses, Robert
Nader, Ralph
Ortiz, Alfonso Alex
Payne, Roger Searle
Pierce, William Luther
Rubin, Jerry
Seale, Bobby
Steinem, Gloria

1940–1949
Aquash, Anna Mae Pictou
Baez, Joan
Bond, Julian
Carmichael, Stokely
Davis, Angela Yvonne
Echohawk, John
Firestone, Shulamith
Fox, Matthew
Fuller, Kathryn Scott

Gutiérrez, Jose Angel
Hayden, Tom
Ireland, Patricia
Jackson, Jesse Louis
Lewis, John Robert
Mfume, Kweisi
Morgan, Robin
Newton, Huey Percy
O'Leary, Jean
Peltier, Leonard
Rudd, Mark
Savio, Mario
Trochmann, John
Wattleton, Alyce Faye

1950–1959
Cervantes, Maggie
Duke, David Ernest
Limbaugh, Rush Hudson
Sharpton, Al
Strossen, Nadine
Terry, Randall

INDEX

Boldface locators indicate main entries. *Italic* locators indicate photographs.